Everyman, I will go with thee,
and be thy guide

THE EVERYMAN
LIBRARY

*The Everyman Library was founded by J. M. Dent
in 1906. He chose the name Everyman because he wanted
to make available the best books ever written in every
field to the greatest number of people at the cheapest possible
price. He began with Boswell's 'Life of Johnson';
his one-thousandth title was Aristotle's 'Metaphysics',
by which time sales exceeded forty million.*

*Today Everyman paperbacks remain true to
J. M. Dent's aims and high standards, with a wide range
of titles at affordable prices in editions which address
the needs of today's readers. Each new text is reset to give
a clear, elegant page and to incorporate the latest thinking
and scholarship. Each book carries the pilgrim logo,
the character in 'Everyman', a medieval morality play,
a proud link between Everyman
past and present.*

Geoffrey Chaucer

THE CANTERBURY TALES

Edited by
A. C. CAWLEY

Additions and Revisions by
MALCOLM ANDREW

EVERYMAN
J. M. DENT · LONDON
CHARLES E. TUTTLE
VERMONT

This edition was first published in Everyman's Library 1958
First published in paperback, with revisions, 1975
Reprinted 1975, 1979, 1982, 1984, 1986, 1989
Reissued 1990 with revisions
Reprinted twice 1992, 1993
Reprinted 1994, 1995

Reissued 1996 with revisions and amendments
Reprinted 1997

J. M. Dent
Orion Publishing Group
Orion House
5, Upper St Martin's Lane
London WC2H 9EA
and
Charles E. Tuttle Co., Inc.
28 South Main Street, Rutland, Vermont 05701, U.S.A.

Made in Great Britain by
The Guernsey Press Co. Ltd, Guernsey, C.I.

ISBN 0 460 87027 0

British Library Cataloguing-in-Publication Data
is available upon request.

CONTENTS

NOTE ON THE AUTHOR AND EDITORS

GEOFFREY CHAUCER, the son of a wine merchant in London, was born about 1343 or 1344. He was an omnivorous reader of Latin, French and Italian literature, and of works of science, philosophy and religion. Apart from the *Canterbury Tales* he wrote several long and distinguished poems – the *Book of the Duchess*, the *House of Fame*, the *Parliament of Fowls*, *Troilus and Criseyde* and the *Legend of Good Women*. He also made a prose translation of the *Consolation of Philosophy* by Boethius and of a treatise on the astrolabe. Yet the writing of poetry and prose was often a spare-time occupation for Chaucer, who was successively a member of the King's Household, a soldier, a diplomatic envoy to France and Italy, a high customs official, a justice of the peace, a member of parliament, and Clerk of the King's Works. From all these activities he gained the knowledge of men and women which made it possible for him to write the *Canterbury Tales*. Chaucer died at Westminster in 1400.

A. C. CAWLEY was Darnell Professor of English in the University of Queensland, 1959–65, and Professor of English Language and Medieval English Literature in the University of Leeds, 1965–79. His editions of *The Wakefield Pageants in the Towneley Cycle* and of *Everyman* were first published in 1958 and 1961, and *Chaucer's Mind and Art* in 1968.

MALCOLM ANDREW has been Professor of English Language and Literature at the Queen's University of Belfast since 1985. Among his publications on medieval and Renaissance literature are an edition of *The Poems of the Pearl Manuscript* (with Ronald Waldron, 1978), an annotated bibliography of writings on the *Gawain*-Poet (1979), and an edition of *Two Early Renaissance Bird Poems* (1984). More recently, his work on Chaucer has included a collection of essays on the *Canterbury Tales* (1981) and the Variorum edition of the *General Prologue* (with Charles Moorman and Daniel J. Ransom, 1983).

CHRONOLOGY OF CHAUCER'S LIFE

Year	Life
c.1312–13	Birth of Chaucer's father, John Chaucer
c.1343–4	Birth of Chaucer, son of John and Agnes Chaucer, in London
1357	In service as a page in the household of Elizabeth, Countess of Ulster (wife of Lionel, Earl of Ulster, second son of Edward III)
1359–60	Service in the retinue of Lionel on campaign in France; ransomed after being captured at the siege of Reims
c.1365–66	Marries Philippa Roet, eldest daughter of the Flemish knight Sir Paon de Roet, and sister of Katherine (later Katherine Swynford)
1366	Death of Chaucer's father; his mother shortly remarries. Philippa Chaucer mentioned as a 'domicelle' of Queen Philippa, wife of Edward III

CHRONOLOGY OF HIS TIMES

Year	Literary and Historical Events
1313	Birth of Boccaccio
1321	Death of Dante, soon after the completion of the *Divina Commedia*
1327	Accession of Edward III, aged 14
1337–1453	The Hundred Years' War between England and France
1338	Completion of Boccaccio's *Il Filostrato* (main source of Chaucer's *Troilus and Criseyde*)
1341	Completion of Boccaccio's *Teseide delle Nozze d'Emilia* (main source of the *Knight's Tale*)
1346	English victory at the battle of Crécy
1348–9	About one third of the population of England dies in the Black Death
1350s	Beginnings of the revival of alliterative poetry in the West and North-West of England
1356	English victory at the battle of Poitiers; capture of King John of France, who lives at the English court, 1357–60
1360	Treaty of Brétigny brings peace between England and France until 1369
1361–7	Jean Froissart, the French chronicler and poet, present in the household of Queen Philippa (wife of Edward III)
1364	Death of King John of France; accession of Charles V
mid 1360s	William Langland begins *Piers Plowman* (the 'A-text')

Year	Life
1367	In service as an esquire in the household of Edward III; granted an annuity for life by the King
c.1367	Birth of a son, Thomas
late 1360s	Translates part of the *Roman de la Rose*; possibly also writing poetry in French at this time
1368-9	Writes the *Book of the Duchess* on the death of Blanche, Duchess of Lancaster
1369	Serves in campaign of John of Gaunt in Northern France
1370	Travels to the Continent on the King's business
c.1372-7	Writes the poems later adapted as the *Second Nun's Tale* and the *Monk's Tale*
1372	Philippa Chaucer in service in the household of John of Gaunt
1372-3	Travels to Genoa (to establish an English port for Genoese trade) and to Florence (to negotiate a loan for the King)
1374	Granted a pitcher of wine daily by the King and an annuity of £10 by John of Gaunt. Appointed Controller of Customs for hides, skins, and wools in the port of London; leases a house above Aldgate
1377-81	Various journeys to France and Flanders in connection with matters including peace negotiations between England and France and a proposed marriage between King Richard and a French princess
1378	Travels to Lombardy on diplomatic business with Bernabò Visconti, Lord of Milan. Richard II confirms Edward III's annuity of 20 marks; Edward's grant of a pitcher of wine daily is commuted to a second annuity of 20 marks
c.1378-81	Writes the *House of Fame*, *Anelida and Arcite*, the *Parliament of Fowls*, and *Palamon and Arcite* (later adapted as the *Knight's Tale*). Translates the *De Consolatione Philosophiae* of Boethius as the *Boece*
1380	Accused, and acquitted, of the *raptus* (probably either rape or abduction) of Cecily Champain

Year	Literary and Historical Events
1367	January: birth of Richard of Bordeaux, later Richard II, second and only surviving son of Edward, the Black Prince (eldest son of Edward III) Battle of Najera, in which the Black Prince supports Pedro of Castile. The King addresses Parliament in English for the first time
1368	September: death of Blanche, Duchess of Lancaster, first wife of John of Gaunt (third son of Edward III)
1369	Assassination of Pedro of Castile. Renewal of war with France August: death of Queen Philippa
1370	Sack of Limoges in the final campaign of the Black Prince
c.1370	Katherine Swynford becomes the mistress of John of Gaunt
1371	September: John of Gaunt marries Costanza (Constance) of Castile, daughter of Pedro
1374	Death of Petrarch
1375	Death of Boccaccio
1376	June: death of the Black Prince
1377	June: Death of Edward III; accession of Richard II, aged 10
1378	Beginning of the Great Schism: popes in Avignon and Rome. First record of mystery plays in York
late 1370s	Langland revising *Piers Plowman* (the 'B-text')

Year	Life
1381	Birth of a son, Lewis, who was ten when Chaucer wrote the *Treatise of the Astrolabe* for him. Death of Chaucer's mother, Agnes
c.1382–86	Writes *Troilus and Criseyde* and the *Legend of Good Women*
1385–6	Serves as Justice of the Peace for Kent
1386	Elected Knight of the Shire for Kent; retires from Controllership of Customs and relinquishes lease on house in Aldgate
1387	Death of Chaucer's wife, Philippa
c.1387–1400	Writes the *Canterbury Tales*
1388	May: Chaucer's exchequer annuities transferred to John Scalby
1389	Appointed Clerk of the King's Works; responsibilities included construction at Westminster and the Tower of London
1390	Appointed Commissioner of Walls and Ditches, responsible for works on the Thames between Woolwich and Greenwich
1391	Retires from Clerkship of the King's Works. Appointed Deputy Forester of the Royal Forest of North Petherton, Somerset (a post later held by his son, Thomas). Writes the *Treatise of the Astrolabe*
1393	Awarded £10 by the King for services rendered
1394	Granted an annuity of £20 for life by the King
1395	Chaucer's son Thomas marries the heiress Maud Burghersh
1397	Granted a tun (252 gallons) of wine yearly by the King
1399	Confirmation by Henry IV of Richard's grant, with an additional annuity of 40 marks. Leases a residence in the garden of the Lady Chapel of Westminster Abbey
1400	Death; burial in Westminster Abbey (remains subsequently moved to 'Poets' Corner')

Year	Literary and Historical Events
1381	May: marriage of Richard II to Anne of Bohemia June: the Peasants' Revolt
early 1380s	Langland revising *Piers Plowman* (the 'C-text')
early 1382	Arrival of Queen Anne in England
1382	Official condemnation of the heretical views of John Wycliffe
1385	Death of Joan of Kent, mother of Richard II
1386	Richard II suffers a loss of power
c.1386	John Gower begins his English poem, *Confessio Amantis*, which contains a passage in praise of Chaucer
1388	The Lords Apellant remove some of the King's closest advisers
1389	Richard II regains power
1394	June: death of Queen Anne
1396	John of Gaunt marries Katherine Swynford
1399	February: death of John of Gaunt September: deposition of Richard II; accession of Henry IV

PREFACE

This edition of Chaucer's *Canterbury Tales* is published in the belief that there are many people who want to read and understand Chaucer's own words, even if it means glancing occasionally at a footnote or marginal gloss.

No maker of glosses is likely to agree with the friar of the Summoner's Tale that 'Glosynge is a glorious thyng.' On the contrary, it is a wearisome and difficult thing. Words like *hende*, *joly* and *gentillesse* often refuse to be translated; and how can anyone briefly and accurately gloss the Chaucerian variants for 'horse' – ambler, caple, courser, dexter, hackney, palfry, rouncy, stot, and the rest, all with their different shades of technical meaning?

The truth is that glosses and paraphrases of Chaucer's difficult words may be just as harmful as a modernized version of the whole, if they are allowed to take precedence over the original. Whenever they are not needed they should be ignored; and even when the reader finds it necessary to consult them, he should at once return to Chaucer's own words. Only by absorbing these in their context can the reader hope to savour the fullness of their meaning, and so come to know Chaucer as a laureate poet.

The Select Bibliography, which is limited to studies in book form, aims at giving the reader some idea of the critical and scholarly work done on the *Canterbury Tales* during the twentieth century. The reader is advised to deal with the secondary criticism as with the glosses: to seek enlightenment, and then hurry back to a pleasurable contemplation of Chaucer's own words.

Many distinguished authors have admired Chaucer and recorded their appreciation of his poetry – among them, in this century, Virginia Woolf, John Masefield, G. K. Chesterton, A. E. Housman, Aldous Huxley and Ezra Pound. The last, rather stern, word may be left to Ezra Pound who writes in *An A.B.C. of Reading*: 'Anyone who is too lazy to master the

comparatively small glossary to understand Chaucer deserves to
be shut out from the reading of good books for ever.'

Note: Acknowledgements are due to Houghton Mifflin Company and to Oxford University Press for permission to use the
critical text of the *Canterbury Tales* prepared by Professor F. N.
Robinson for his edition of *The Complete Works of Geoffrey
Chaucer*. The publishers and editor also wish to thank Houghton Mifflin Company and Oxford University Press for their
permission to incorporate in the Everyman edition a number
of amended readings which first appeared in *The Riverside
Chaucer* (3rd edition, 1987, 1988).

A. C. C.

INTRODUCTION

When Chaucer wrote the General Prologue to the *Canterbury Tales* in 1387 or thereabouts, he was a man of more than forty years of age who had held many offices in the King's service at home and abroad. He had served in the household of Prince Lionel and enjoyed the patronage of John of Gaunt, to whom he was related by marriage through his wife Philippa Chaucer; he had been an esquire of the Royal Household under Edward III; he had visited France several times both as soldier and diplomat, and taken part in embassies to Italy on at least two occasions (in 1372 and 1378); he had held the controllership of Customs in the port of London (1374–86); and he had been Justice of the Peace and Knight of the Shire for Kent (1386). This busy life of public service continued after he had started work on the *Canterbury Tales*. In 1389 he was appointed Clerk of the King's Works for the Palace of Westminster, the Tower of London and elsewhere, and in 1390 was given the task of supervising the repairs in St George's Chapel, Windsor, which Edward III had made the special chapel of the Knights of the Garter. In 1391 he became deputy forester of the royal forest of North Petherton in Somerset, and this appointment was renewed as late as 1398, two years before his death.

Chaucer's active career during all these years as soldier, courtier, diplomat, and civil servant gained him the knowledge of men and affairs which made it possible for him to write the *Canterbury Tales*. Further, his contacts with France and Italy introduced him to the works of the French and Italian poets – especially Deschamps, Dante, Petrarch, and Boccaccio – and greatly stimulated his development as a poet.

None of Chaucer's works has been preserved in his own hand-writing, unless we claim the late fourteenth-century Peterhouse manuscript, which contains a treatise in English on the planetary equatorium, as Chaucer's autograph.[1] Certainly no such claim

[1] See D. J. Price, ed., *The Equatorie of the Planetis*, Cambridge, England, 1955. (This work contains a linguistic analysis by R. M. Wilson.)

can be made for any of the eighty-odd surviving manuscripts of the *Canterbury Tales*. According to the best scholarly opinion, none of them is derived from a Chaucer autograph, or even from a single manuscript that Chaucer himself had finally arranged or revised. All the extant copies of the *Canterbury Tales* seem rather to be the result of attempts made by various fifteenth-century editors to assemble in an intelligible order the ten fragments of the *Tales* left unarranged by Chaucer at his death. Some modern editors, including Furnivall, Skeat, and Pollard, have changed the order of the fragments found in the Ellesmere manuscript: in particular, they have placed Fragment VII immediately after Fragment II, so that the reference to Rochester in the *Monk's Prologue*[2] precedes (as it apparently should) the reference to Sittingbourne in the *Wife of Bath's Prologue*.[3] These editors have labelled the different fragments A to I, with Fragments II and VII together forming Group B.[4] Other editors, Manly and Robinson among them, have preferred, in the absence of any definite knowledge of Chaucer's final intentions in the matter, to keep the imperfect order common to the Ellesmere manuscript and most of the best manuscripts of the *Canterbury Tales*. Robinson has numbered the Fragments I to X.[5]

As it stands, then, the text of the *Canterbury Tales* is incomplete and not finally arranged or corrected by Chaucer himself. This explains not only why the arrangement of the tales is unsatisfactory but why several of the thirty-odd pilgrims do not get their turn to tell a story, why the tales of the Cook and Squire are left unfinished, and why other tales are imperfectly adapted to the teller (e.g. the *Shipman's Tale*, which begins as though a woman were telling it, and the tale of the Second Nun,

[2] VII. 2723.
[3] III. 847.
[4] For arguments in support of placing Fragment VII after Fragment II see Robert A. Pratt, 'The Order of the *Canterbury Tales*,' in *Publications of the Modern Language Association of America*, lxvi (1951), 1141–67.
[5] The text of the present edition, which is based on that of the Ellesmere manuscript, preserves the Ellesmere order of the *Canterbury Tales*. This manuscript (now in the Huntington Library, California) contains an early fifteenth-century copy of the *Tales*. It is a beautifully decorated volume and is famous for its marginal pictures of the Canterbury pilgrims. In textual importance its only rival is the Hengwrt manuscript in the National Library of Wales; see editions of Hengwrt by Ruggiers and Blake in Suggestions for Further Reading.

who refers to herself as an 'unworthy sone of Eve').[6] Fortunately, however, there are certain constants. The text itself establishes that Chaucer intended the first tale to be told by the Knight and the last by the Parson. In other words, we know what Chaucer intended should be the beginning and the end of his great pilgrimage.

Students of Chaucer are still wondering how he came to hit upon the idea of a pilgrimage as a living framework for his collection of tales. He may have got it from the *Decameron*, from the *Novelle* of Giovanni Sercambi, or from some other literary source. But he had ample opportunities for observing the Canterbury pilgrimages for himself from his house in Greenwich, and he may even have taken part in such a pilgrimage during the illness or after the death of his wife in 1387. What is more important is that the pilgrimage device gave him an opportunity to bring together a band of pilgrims representing most of the occupations and social groups of his day. The diversity of the narrators in turn made possible an equally varied collection of tales. Chivalric romance (Knight), fabliau (Miller, Reeve), moral or spiritual allegory (Man of Law, Clerk, *Melibeus*), courtly lay (Franklin), miracle of the Virgin (Prioress), literary satire (*Sir Thopas*), beast fable (Nun's Priest), saint's life (Second Nun), and sermon (Parson) are all exemplified. Indeed, no important narrative *genre* practised in the fourteenth century is missing from the *Canterbury Tales*. And all the time, behind the tales, originating and interrupting them, interpenetrating and linking many of them together, is the great tale of the pilgrimage itself. For the pilgrims are no mere story-tellers: through lively monologue, dialogue, and action on the road to Canterbury, no less than through the tales themselves, they grow into human beings who have lost none of their vitality after five hundred years of social and linguistic change. They are Chaucer's primary audience; we are but readers of tales that have already been told and received with enthusiasm or distaste, according to the nature of each pilgrim and his motives for taking the way to Canterbury.

The *General Prologue* introduces all but two of the pilgrims to us (these are the Canon and his Yeoman, who join the company at 'Boghtoun under Blee').[7] We can read and enjoy the

[6] *Second Nun's Prologue*, VIII. 62.
[7] *Canon's Yeoman's Prologue*, VIII. 556.

Prologue for its own sake, marvelling at the lifelikeness of the pilgrims and, if we have the perception of William Blake, seeing them as visions of the 'eternal principles or characters of human life [which] appear to poets, in all ages.'[8] But the *Prologue* can perhaps be best appreciated if the series of portraits are viewed as 'a string of happy exordiums'[9] to the tales that follow. The more we read the tales, the more vividly we come to realize just how many details of the *Prologue* are echoed or repeated in them. The Reeve underlines the personal application of his scurrilous tale about a miller by using some details of the portrait of the Miller in the *Prologue*;[10] the Wife of Bath tells us how she came by her deafness, which we first hear of in the *Prologue*;[11] the Shipman's 'noble monk' is suspiciously reminiscent of the Canterbury Monk;[12] the description of 'hende Nicholas' in the *Miller's Tale*, by echoing the portrait of the Canterbury Clerk, emphasizes how vastly different two Oxford students can be.[13]

The *General Prologue* and the *Tales* complete each other in a yet more important sense. Some of the *Tales* add little to what we have already learned about their narrators from the *Prologue*. The Knight and the Parson, for example, are idealized types or 'essences,' and there is not much scope for character development in the tales they are given to tell. But in the case of two people like the Pardoner and the Wife of Bath the portrait bursts out of its frame, and the tale told by each of these pilgrims reveals depths of character of which there is little or no hint in the *Prologue*. The *Pardoner's Tale* is a mock-sermon against avarice deliberately designed to make simple folk part with their money to the Pardoner, whose own besetting sin is avarice. But the tale has implications of which the Pardoner himself is completely unaware. It is a tale about death – physical death and, still more, spiritual death. The idea of spiritual death is more than once referred to, but nowhere more memorably than in the episode of the old man:

---

[8] From a description of the Canterbury pilgrims in *A Descriptive Catalogue of Pictures . . . Painted by William Blake* (1809).
[9] These words are doubtfully attributed to Leigh Hunt (1823).
[10] *General Prologue*, I. 548, 558, 562; *Reeve's Tale*, I. 3928–30, 3939–40.
[11] *Gen. Prol.*, I. 446; *Wife of Bath's Prologue*, III. 636.
[12] *Gen. Prol.*, I. 166; *Shipman's Tale*, VII. 65.
[13] *Gen. Prol.*, I. 293 ff.; *Miller's Tale*, I. 3208 ff.

> Ne Deeth, allas! ne wol nat han my lyf.
> Thus walke I, lyke a restelees kaityf, . . .
> Allas! whan shul my bones been at reste?[14]

The significance of this episode becomes plain when we read in the *Parson's Tale* about the living death suffered by sinners in hell:

> For, as seith Seint Gregorie, 'To wrecche caytyves shal be deeth withoute deeth, and ende withouten ende, . . . And therfore seith Seint John the Evaungelist: 'They shullen folwe deeth, and they shul nat fynde hym; and they shul desiren to dye, and deeth shal flee fro hem.'[15]

The old man of the *Pardoner's Tale* is not only Death or the Messenger of Death; he is a symbol of that spiritual death which the three revellers – and the Pardoner himself – have already suffered. In fact, the *Pardoner's Tale* becomes a complete and entirely unselfconscious exposure of the Pardoner's inner self: he is led on to show himself not as he imagines himself to be but as he really is – the empty husk of a man, physically and spiritually.

The Wife of Bath, on the other hand, gains rather than loses by the self-revealing elements in her *Tale*. A woman who puts into the mouth of her 'loathly lady' a magnificent medieval discourse on the nature of true 'gentillesse'[16] is either merely voicing her maker's opinions or, as seems more likely, dramatically revealing a submerged aspect of her nature which has but little chance of finding expression in her aggressively amoral *Prologue*. Indeed, when Chaucer created the Wife of Bath and the Pardoner – and to these we might well add the Prioress – he got as near as he ever did to representing that 'interior nature of humanity' which Coleridge saw in Shakespeare's characters but not in Chaucer's.

As well as fulfilling the *General Prologue* the tales of the Canterbury pilgrims counterbalance and complete each other through parallelism and contrast. Although Chaucer's ultimate plan for the *Canterbury Tales* is not known, apart from the

[14] *Pardoner's Tale*, VI. 727–33.
[15] *Parson's Tale*, X, 428 ff.
[16] *Wife of Bath's Tale*, III. 1109 ff.

beginning and the end, it is generally agreed that Fragments III–V were meant by Chaucer to stand together as a group in the final sequence. Without doubt they are closely linked together, each tale naturally giving rise to the next. And most of them are concerned with one aspect or another of a common theme: this is the problem of whether sovereignty in marriage should rest with the husband (in accordance with medieval theory) or with the wife (in accordance with distressingly frequent medieval practice). In the discussion of this problem the domineering attitude of the Wife of Bath towers up against the equally domineering and sadistic behaviour of the husband of Griselda, and it is made clear that such extreme egoism, male or female, must inevitably lead to unhappiness in marriage. This group of tales fitly ends with the *Franklin's Tale*, which offers the ideal solution of a marriage made happy by the absence of sovereignty and by the presence of mutual love, trust, and forbearance.

It is evident that the discussion of marital relations is not confined to Fragments III–V, but brings in at least *Melibeus* and the *Nun's Priest's Tale*. Both these tales are concerned, among other things, with the value of wifely advice; both inquire whether a husband can accept his wife's advice without loss of face and, it may be, of life itself. *Melibeus* is an allegory, and its various personages are really symbols of man's spiritual condition. But its surface story, in which Melibeus and Prudence are represented as man and wife, shows that it is not only prudent but perfectly consistent with a husband's self-respect to accept his wife's advice, if he has reason to trust her wisdom and discretion. The *Nun's Priest's Tale* is a learned jest in humorous antithesis to *Melibeus*, for it shows just how disastrous a wife's advice can be in certain circumstances. Apart from its high entertainment value, it carries a warning to every husband, whether galline or human, not to be uxorious, but to use his own discretion (as Melibeus has done) before he submits to his wife's counsel.

Preoccupation with the 'Marriage Discussion' should not blind us to the fact that nearly all Chaucer's secular tales are concerned with one aspect or another of love and marriage: with courtly love and sensual love; with marriages made unhappy by disparity of age or by indifference or by the desire of one partner to dominate the other and finally, with the ideal marriage (as in *Melibeus* and the *Franklin's Tale*) based on mutual love and tolerance.

All this may seem to make the *Canterbury Tales* very solemn and serious. Serious they most certainly are, if viewed as a whole; seriousness, even high seriousness, is fundamental to high comedy. But solemnity is avoided by virtue of Chaucer's unfailing sense of proportion and unerring eye for the humorous incongruities of life. The serious outnumber the comic tales in the Canterbury collection; but balance is maintained by giving a serious tale a light-hearted prologue or epilogue, or even by getting the pilgrims themselves to interrupt a tale that has grown wearisome (both the Monk and Chaucer himself suffer this indignity). Again, a serious tale may be followed by a comic tale which parodies it. The *Knight's Tale* is followed by the *Miller's Tale*[17] which, on a low level, parallels some of the most striking features of the Knight's romance of chivalry. The courtly Palamon and impetuous Arcite turn up again in homespun guise in the persons of Absolon and Nicholas in the *Miller's Tale*; and Emily, whose ethereal beauty reminds the Palamons of this world of the lily and the rose, has her rustic counterpart in Alisoun, whose physical charms are sensuously conveyed with the help of the sights and sounds of the fruitful countryside in which she lives. The *Miller's Tale* is shot through with courtly sentiments and diction: Alisoun is 'gent and smal,' 'hende Nicholas' is an able exponent of 'deerne love,' Absolon suffers the harsh pangs of 'love-longynge.' It is rather like deliberately setting down a dish of caviare beside a platter of blood puddings; both are black, both come from a creature's inside, but there the resemblance ends.

In all this kaleidoscopic change from courtly to animal, from high seriousness to low comedy, there is one grand constant. This is the 'myrie' (i.e. pleasant) tale the Parson tells 'To knytte up al this feeste, and make an ende.'[18] The *Parson's Tale*, which is seldom read, is usually condemned as intolerably wearisome. Wearisome or not, the *Parson's Tale*, no less than *Melibeus* and the *Consolation of Philosophy*, gave Chaucer the rationale of his thinking about the nature and destiny of man. The *Parson's Tale*, in particular, provided him with the ecclesiastical norm of human behaviour, and in the *Canterbury Tales* he played all kinds of variations on it by showing some men and women conforming to it, others rebelling against it, and a few even

[17] We know from the text that the *Miller's Tale* was meant by Chaucer to follow immediately on the *Knight's Tale*; see the *Miller's Prologue*, I. 3109 ff.
[18] *Parson's Prologue*, X. 47.

rising above it. Thus the sins of Avarice, Wrath, and Gluttony, as described in the *Parson's Tale*, are all worked into the complicated pattern of the Pardoner's character; the Wife of Bath, by reversing the natural order of things, exemplifies the Parson's statement that 'ther as the womman hath the maistrie, she maketh to muche desray';[19] while Constance and Griselda both reach heights of constancy and patience which ordinary erring mortals can hardly hope to attain. It would be wrong to think of the *Canterbury Tales* as an entertaining handbook of the seven deadly sins, but there can be no doubt that Chaucer's serious study of the didactic literature of his day stimulated and also circumscribed his observation of human nature.

To any reader who accepts this groundwork of seriousness in the *Canterbury Tales* the *Retraction*[20] at the end will not come as an unpleasant surprise, nor seem any more conventional or insincere than the Christian ending of *Troilus and Criseyde*.[21] Nor will he find it necessary to suppose that the *Parson's Tale* and the *Retraction* were stuck on to the original design of the *Canterbury Tales* by a decrepit Chaucer in the throes of a deathbed repentance. From a Christian point of view, man's brief passage through life is a pilgrimage to the 'Jerusalem celestial,' as the Parson reminds his fellow pilgrims on the road to Canterbury.[22] The world of human love and of ordinary men and women engaged in their everyday pursuits is the world through which we must all pass on pilgrimage; and it is brilliantly described in Chaucer's secular tales. But, side by side with these secular tales, and often placed in contrast to them, are the tales of 'moralitee and hoolynesse,'[23] like those of the Man of Law, the Clerk, the Physician, the Pardoner, the Prioress, the Monk, the Second Nun, the Manciple, and of Chaucer himself. The *Retraction* is Chaucer's 'good ending' to a series of tales orientated by a medieval Christian view of life: it is the extreme but logical conclusion of Chaucer's grand scheme to show man as a pilgrim in this mortal life, in which worldly joys and sorrows are seen in perspective against a background of the 'endelees blisse of hevene.'[24]

[19] *Parson's Tale*, X. 2621–2.
[20] *Parson's Tale*, X. 3113–46.
[21] Everyman's Library, No. 992.
[22] *Parson's Prologue*, X. 49–51.
[23] *Miller's Prologue*. I. 3180.
[24] *Parson's Tale*, X. 3097.

Chaucer's language is wonderfully adequate to his lofty purpose. He is a master of natural idiom and rhetorical artifice alike. There is nothing he undertakes which he fails to do for want of words to express it, whether it is the echo of a drunken yawn, a transcript of the professional jargon of astrologer or alchemist, a philosophical discourse on the *primum mobile*, or a sigh for the sorrows of humanity:

> Infinite been the sorwes and the teeres
> Of olde folk, and folk of tendre yeeres.[25]

Sometimes an obsolete word, form, or meaning is in danger of obscuring for a modern reader the effect which Chaucer intended. But it is remarkable how often Chaucer's most completely satisfying verses are 'expressed in language pure and universally intelligible to this day.'[26] We need only recall the perfect line in the *Knight's Tale* which Dryden wisely left unchanged:

> Up roos the sonne, and up roos Emelye[27]

or the sinister glimpse of the smiling villain:

> The smylere with the knyf under the cloke[28]

or Griselda's pitiful plea:

> Lat me nat lyk a worm go by the weye[29]

or Alisoun's immortal giggle after the incident of the 'misdirected kiss':

> 'Tehee!' quod she, and clapte the wyndow to.[30]

[25] *Knight's Tale*, I. 2827-8.
[26] Wordsworth, *Preface to Lyrical Ballads* (1800).
[27] *Knight's Tale*, I. 2273.
[28] *Knight's Tale*, I. 1999.
[29] *Clerk's Tale*, IV. 880.
[30] *Miller's Tale*, I. 3740.

This is the stuff of poetry: words and rhythms holding fast a poet's vision of the world which is 'large, free, shrewd, benignant'[31] and exquisitely alive to sensuous beauty.

It need hardly be said that the sound and movement of Chaucer's words have an essential part to play in the making of his poetry.[32] While the music of this poetry cannot be fully recovered, there is no reason why anyone should not know the approximate rhythm and pronunciation of a line like

> That al the orient laugheth of the light[33]

or

> With knotty, knarry, bareyne trees olde[34]

or

> It tikleth me about myn herte roote.[35]

Ideally, Chaucer's verse should be read aloud; only in this way can a modern reader come to realize how sound and sense go together in Chaucer's best poetry 'With sownes full of hevenyssh melodie.'

[31] Matthew Arnold, Introduction to vol. i of *The English Poets* (ed. T. H. Ward) London, 1883, p. xlv.

[32] The reader's attention is drawn to the notes on Chaucer's pronunciation and versification in the Appendices.

[33] *Knight's Tale*, I. 1494.

[34] *Knight's Tale*, I. 1977.

[35] *Wife of Bath's Prologue*, III. 471.

POSTSCRIPT TO THE INTRODUCTION

The preceding introduction by Professor Cawley was written when the original version of the present edition was published, in 1958. It coincided with a period of rapid and exciting developments in the study and interpretation of Chaucer's work as a whole, and of the *Canterbury Tales* in particular. The publication in 1957 of a second, revised, edition of F. N. Robinson's enormously successful single-volume *Works of Geoffrey Chaucer* made a substantial contribution to textual studies. The Everyman edition of the *Canterbury Tales* was, from the outset, based on this text.[1] Critical interpretation of the *Canterbury Tales* was also developing apace, with the publication of several pioneering studies, especially those of E. Talbot Donaldson on 'Chaucer the Pilgrim' (1954), Ralph Baldwin on the pilgrimage structure (1955), and Charles Muscatine on the relationship between style and meaning (1957).[2] Donaldson contends that Chaucer establishes in the *General Prologue* the voice of a fictional *persona*, highly observant but prone to naïve opinions, whose voice thus creates a sense of the provisional and contingent nature of judgement. While Baldwin also considers Chaucer's treatment of the narrative voice, he focuses mainly on the significance of the beginning and end of the *Canterbury Tales*, arguing that the pilgrimage constitutes the essential motif and structural device of the work. Muscatine offers an elegant and sophisticated study of 'style and meaning', in which he considers Chaucer's treatment of inherited genres and conventions, and how, in the *Canterbury Tales*, this informs the interplay between the fictional tellers and the tales they tell. Perhaps the most striking feature of these and

[1] This is acknowledged in Professor Cawley's Preface, above.

[2] Donaldson's study was first published as an essay in *Publications of the Modern Language Association of America* (*PMLA*), vol. 69, and was reprinted in his collection of essays, *Speaking of Chaucer*. For full references to this and to the studies by Baldwin and Muscatine, see Suggestions for Further Reading, below.

other contemporary studies is the growing awareness they reflect of the significance of the subtle, complex, and controlled artifice of Chaucer's work. This shared tendency does not, however, lead to uniformity of opinion. The approaches summarized above (and others like them) can lead to strikingly varied perceptions of the *Canterbury Tales*, ranging from the assertion that it is a highly structured work with a clearly determined meaning to the conviction that its essential nature is to be artfully inconclusive.

Though the influence of such studies has continued and evolved over several decades, it will be apparent that Professor Cawley's introduction touches on most of the issues with which they engage. He does, however, begin his introduction by considering another topic: that of Chaucer's wide and varied experience of public life, both in England and abroad. Readers of Chaucer from the fifteenth century onwards have often been fascinated by potential connections between his work and his life, private as well as public. The chronological table which has been prepared for this revised edition is intended to facilitate consideration of the most significant known events of Chaucer's life with the most relevant contemporary social, political, and cultural events and developments. It happens that the surviving records of Chaucer's public life are remarkably full for a writer living in the Middle Ages. Nonetheless, the volume of *Chaucer Life Records*,[3] which extends to some 600 pages, gives little sense of his private life and does not contain a single reference to his work as a poet. This might tend to qualify any temptation to postulate simple connections between Chaucer's life and his work – a qualification which would accord both with critics' increasing awareness of the artifice of Chaucer's poetry, mentioned above, and with growing theoretical resistance to facile assumptions about connections between authors, the lives they lead, and the works they write. Thus, for instance, though it can be established both that Chaucer travelled to Italy on several occasions and that he was influenced by the work of several Italian poets – especially Boccaccio, but also Dante and Petrarch – the relationship between his journeys on diplomatic business and his interests as a poet would be largely a matter for speculation. Some of the most basic and intriguing questions to which this topic might give rise cannot, at least to date, be

---

[3] Edited by Martin M. Crow and Clair C. Olson: see Suggestions for Further Reading.

answered with any certainty. Did he ever meet Boccaccio? Did he own a copy of the *Teseida* or of *Il Filostrato*? Why is Boccaccio not mentioned by name in his work? Does a passage in the *Clerk's Prologue* (IV. 26ff.) suggest that he met Petrarch in Padua? How and when did he learn Italian?[4] The case regarding his relationship with John of Gaunt, third son of Edward III and Duke of Lancaster (to take but one of many possible examples), is broadly similar. Though the fact that the two men were virtual contemporaries and the existence of contact between them is a matter of record – and, as Professor Cawley observes in his introduction, they had a personal connection, in that Chaucer's wife and John of Gaunt's third wife were sisters[5] – it is difficult to know how close their relationship would have been. There can be no serious doubt that Chaucer's early poem, the *Book of the Duchess*, marks the death of Blanche, first wife of John of Gaunt, and represents the bereaved Duke as the 'man in black'. The characteristic indirection and elusiveness of Chaucer's narrative strategy and method in the poem do, however, make it extremely difficult to draw any firm conclusions about the events, relationships, and emotions which are represented.

Consideration of such topics will raise the issue of the audience for which the work was written. There was a tendency among scholars writing before the 1950s to think of Chaucer as a poet writing for 'the court', and to take the matter no further. In the case of the *Book of the Duchess*, the initial and primary audience could perhaps legitimately be described as 'the court', though this would be to ignore the nature of the subsequent and wider audience. With the *Canterbury Tales* – conspicuously varied in tone and content, and written in a piecemeal fashion over a substantial period – it will be obvious that simple generalizations about 'the audience' and 'the court' are inadequate. During the past few decades there have been substantial developments in the understanding of the nature and composition both of the court and royal administration in late medieval England and of what might be termed Chaucer's inner and

---

[4] Such questions are, of course, addressed by those who write about Chaucer's life: see, for instance, Howard (1987) and Pearsall (1992) in Suggestions for Further Reading.

[5] It is, however, at least potentially misleading to describe them as brothers-in-law, since Chaucer's wife, Philippa, had been dead for nearly ten years before her sister Katherine was married to John of Gaunt: see Chronology, above.

wider audiences. Such developments are based on research into and interpretation of history in its broadest sense: the study not just of important political events and prominent social trends, but also of prevailing and changing ideas, beliefs, attitudes, visual images, institutions, and social groupings and conditions. Work of this kind has generated some fine studies of Chaucer, including that of Paul Strohm (1989) on his audience and that of Lee Patterson (1991) on his historical awareness. The splendid critical biography by Derek Pearsall (1992) reflects the application of similar care and sophistication to the relationship between Chaucer's life and his works.

Other studies published during the past twenty years or so reflect such a variety of interests and approaches that it may be helpful here briefly to mention some of the dominant trends and some of the more significant contributions. Appreciation of Chaucer's language – the range and precision of which receives due praise at the end of Professor Cawley's introduction – is enhanced by the work of several scholars, especially Ralph W. V. Elliott (1974) and David Burnley (1984). While the best general book on the *Canterbury Tales* published during this period is, perhaps, that of Derek Pearsall (1985), a particularly interesting contribution is made by C. David Benson (1986), who argues that the tales represent an interchange between various genres and styles rather than between the psyches of their fictional tellers. V. A. Kolve's brilliant study (1984) of the key visual images in the first five tales brings added subtlety to the exploration of the relationship between Chaucer's narratives and iconography. New readings of Chaucer from a broadly Marxist perspective are offered by Stephen Knight and David Aers (both 1986). The development of feminism and the growing interest in the representation of women in literature has generated several challenging studies, including those of Carolyn Dinshaw (1989), Jill Mann (1991), and Susan Crane (1994). Otherwise, the influence of literary theory is most evident in Robert M. Jordan's account of 'Chaucer's Poetics' (1989), and in the studies by Carl Lindahl (1987) and John M. Ganim (1990), both of which draw on theoretical approaches to popular culture. Studies of Chaucer and the *Canterbury Tales* continue to reflect a variety and liveliness wholly appropriate to the poet and the work.

Today's readers can easily forget that they depend, for access to a text written in the Middle Ages, on the work of scholarly editors – the quality of which is, of course, various. The Everyman edition of the *Canterbury Tales* has provided work of exemplary quality, combining the excellent text prepared and revised by F. N. Robinson and the outstanding glosses of A. C. Cawley. By comparison, my own additions and revisions are modest indeed. Their purpose is, however, not insignificant: that of bringing up to date and thus extending the life of an exceptionally fine and useful edition.

MALCOLM ANDREW

edition. The qualities of which he is justly suspicious. The
everyman edition of the Prefaces... there are provided that
everthings really contain the excellent... it is... and
arged by F. N. Robinson's... annotation... masses of
Cantos. By comparison, the... addition and material are
modest, indeed, in comparison, however, not his admirable
... brought up to date, and this exceeding the... a
... and this and useful edition.

MALCOLM ANDREW

SUGGESTIONS FOR FURTHER READING

Modern Editions

Baugh, Albert C., ed., *Chaucer's Major Poetry* (New York, 1963; London, 1964).

Benson, Larry D., gen. ed., *The Riverside Chaucer* (Boston, 1987; Oxford, 1988).

Blake, N. F., ed., *The Canterbury Tales by Geoffrey Chaucer. Edited from the Hengwrt Manuscript*, York Medieval Texts, second series (London, 1980).

Donaldson, E. Talbot, ed. *Chaucer's Poetry: An Anthology for the Modern Reader* (New York, 1958; 2nd ed., 1975).

Kolve, V. A., and Glending Olson, eds., *Geoffrey Chaucer, The Canterbury Tales: Nine Tales and the General Prologue* (New York and London, 1989).

Manly, John Matthews, ed., *Canterbury Tales by Geoffrey Chaucer* (New York, 1928).

——, and Edith Rickert, ed., *The Text of the Canterbury Tales: Studied on the Basis of All Known Manuscripts*, 8 vols. (Chicago, 1940).

Pratt, Robert A., ed., *The Tales of Canterbury, Complete: Geoffrey Chaucer* (Boston, 1974).

Robinson, F. N., ed., *The Works of Geoffrey Chaucer* (1st ed., Boston, 1933; Boston and London, 1957).

Skeat, Rev. Walter W., ed., *The Complete Works of Geoffrey Chaucer*, vols. 4 and 5 (Oxford, 1894).

Variorum Chaucer:
  The Canterbury Tales: A Facsimile and Transcription of the Hengwrt Manuscript, with Variants from the Ellesmere Manuscript, ed. Paul G. Ruggiers (Norman, Okla., and Folkestone, 1979).
  The General Prologue, ed. Malcolm Andrew, Charles Moorman, and Daniel J. Ransom, 2 vols. (Norman, Okla. and London, 1993).
  The Miller's Tale, ed. Thomas W. Ross (1983).
  The Nun's Priest's Tale, ed. Derek Pearsall (1984).
  The Manciple's Tale, ed. Donald C. Baker (1984).
  The Squire's Tale, ed. Donald C. Baker (1990).

The Physician's Tale, ed. Helen Storm Corsa (1987).
The Prioress's Tale, ed. Beverly Boyd (1987).

Reference

Allen, Mark, and John H. Fisher, *The Essential Chaucer: an annotated bibliography of major modern studies* (Boston and London, 1987).

Baird, Lorrayne Y., *A Bibliography of Chaucer, 1964–1973* (Boston and London, 1977).

Baird-Lange, Lorrayne Y., and Hildegard Schnuttgen, *A Bibliography of Chaucer, 1974–1983* (Hamden, Conn. and Cambridge, 1988).

Boitani, Piero, and Jill Mann, eds., *The Cambridge Chaucer Companion* (Cambridge, 1986).

Brewer, Derek, ed., *Chaucer: The Critical Heritage*, 2 vols. (London, Henley, and Boston, 1978).

Bryan, W. F., and Germaine Dempster, eds., *Sources and Analogues of Chaucer's Canterbury Tales* (Chicago, 1941).

Crawford, William R., *Bibliography of Chaucer 1954–63* (Seattle and London, 1967).

Crow, Martin M., and Clair C. Olson, eds., *Chaucer Life-Records* (Oxford, 1966).

Davis, Norman, Douglas Gray, Patricia Ingham, and Anne Wallace-Hadrill, *A Chaucer Glossary* (Oxford, 1979).

Griffith, Dudley David, *Bibliography of Chaucer 1908–1953* (Seattle, 1955).

Hammond, Eleanor Prescott, *Chaucer: A Bibliographical Manual* (New York, 1908).

Leyerle, John, and Anne Quick, *Chaucer: A Bibliographical Introduction* (Toronto, Buffalo, and London, 1986).

Magoun, Francis P., Jr, *A Chaucer Gazeteer* (Chicago and Uppsala, 1961).

Miller, Robert P., ed., *Chaucer: Sources and Backgrounds* (New York, 1977).

Morris, Lynn King, *Chaucer Source and Analogue Criticism: A Cross-Referenced Guide* (New York and London, 1985).

Rowland, Beryl, ed., *Companion to Chaucer Studies* (New York, 1968; rev. ed., 1979).

Spurgeon, Caroline F. E., *Five Hundred Years of Chaucer Criticism and Allusion 1357–1900*, 3 vols. (Cambridge, 1925).

Studies in the Age of Chaucer. Annual annotated bibliographies (1979–   ).

Tatlock, John S. P., and Arthur G. Kennedy, *A Concordance to the*

Complete Works of Geoffrey Chaucer and to the Romaunt of the Rose (Washington, D.C., 1927).

Some Studies of Chaucer and of the Canterbury Tales

Aers, David, *Chaucer*, Harvester New Readings series (Brighton and Atlantic Highlands, N.J., 1986).

Anderson, J. J., ed., *Chaucer: The Canterbury Tales*, Casebook series (London, 1974).

Andrew, Malcolm, ed., *Critical Essays on Chaucer's Canterbury Tales* (Milton Keynes and Toronto, 1991).

Baldwin, Ralph, *The Unity of the Canterbury Tales*, Anglistica, 5 (Copenhagen, 1955).

Bennett, H. S., *Chaucer and the Fifteenth Century* (Oxford, 1947).

Bennett, J. A. W., *Chaucer at Oxford and at Cambridge* (Oxford and Toronto, 1974).

Benson, C. David, *Chaucer's Drama of Style: Poetic Variety and Contrast in the 'Canterbury Tales'* (Chapel Hill, N.C. and London, 1986).

—, and Elizabeth Robertson, eds., *Chaucer's Religious Tales*, Chaucer Studies, XV (Cambridge, 1990).

Bishop, Ian, *The Narrative Art of the Canterbury Tales: A Critical Study of the Major Poems* (London and Melbourne, 1987).

Bowden, Muriel, *A Commentary on the General Prologue to the Canterbury Tales*, (New York, 1948; rev. ed., 1967).

Brewer, Derek, *Chaucer* (London and New York, 1953; rev. ed., 1973).

—, *Chaucer in His Time* (London, 1963).

—, ed., *Geoffrey Chaucer*, Writers and their Background series (London, 1974; Athens, Ohio, 1975).

—, *An Introduction to Chaucer* (London and New York, 1984).

Brown, Peter, *Chaucer at Work: The Making of the Canterbury Tales* (London and New York, 1994).

Burlin, Robert B., *Chaucerian Fiction* (Princeton, 1977).

Burnley, David, *A Guide to Chaucer's Language* (London, 1983; Norman, Okla., 1984).

Burrow, J. A., ed., *Geoffrey Chaucer: A Critical Anthology* (Harmondsworth and Baltimore, 1969).

Cawley, A. C., ed., *Chaucer's Mind and Art* (London and New York, 1969).

Cooper, Helen, *The Structure of The Canterbury Tales* (London, 1983; Athens, Ga., 1984).

—, *The Canterbury Tales*, Oxford Guides to Chaucer (Oxford, 1989).

Crane, Susan, *Gender and Romance in Chaucer's 'Canterbury Tales'* (Princeton, 1994).

Curry, Walter Clyde, *Chaucer and the Mediaeval Sciences* (New York and London, 1926; rev. ed., 1960).

David, Alfred, *The Strumpet Muse: Art and Morals in Chaucer's Poetry* (Bloomington, Ind. and London, 1976).

Dillon, Janette, *Geoffrey Chaucer*, Writers in their Time series (Basingstoke and London, 1993).

Dinshaw, Carolyn, *Chaucer's Sexual Poetics* (Madison, Wis., 1989).

Donaldson, E. Talbot, *Speaking of Chaucer* (London, 1970).

Economou, George D., ed., *Geoffrey Chaucer: a collection of original articles* (New York, 1975).

Eliason, Norman E., *The Language of Chaucer's Poetry: An Appraisal of the Verse, Style and Structure*, Anglistica, 17 (Copenhagen, 1972).

Elliott, Ralph, W. V., *Chaucer's English* (London, 1974).

Fein, Susanna Greer, David Raybin, and Peter C. Braeger, eds., *Rebels and Rivals: The Contestive Spirit in 'The Canterbury Tales'* (Kalamazoo, Mich., 1991).

Ferster, Judith, *Chaucer on Interpretation* (Cambridge, 1985).

Fyler, John M., *Chaucer and Ovid* (New Haven and London, 1979).

Ganim, John M., *Chaucerian Theatricality* (Princeton, 1990).

Gardner, John, *The Life and Times of Chaucer* (New York and London, 1977).

——, *The Poetry of Chaucer* (Carbondale, Ill., 1977).

Hansen, Elaine Tuttle, *Chaucer and the Fictions of Gender* (Berkeley, Los Angeles, and Oxford, 1992).

Howard, Donald R., *The Idea of the Canterbury Tales* (Berkeley, Los Angeles, and London, 1976).

—— *Chaucer and the Medieval World* (London, 1987).

Hussey, Maurice, *Chaucer's World: A Pictorial Companion* (Cambridge, 1968).

Hussey, S. S., *Chaucer: An Introduction* (London and New York, 1981).

Jones, Terry, *Chaucer's Knight: The portrait of a medieval mercenary* (London and Baton Rouge, La., 1980).

Jordan, Robert M., *Chaucer and the Shape of Creation: The Aesthetic Possibilities of Inorganic Structure* (Cambridge, Mass. and London, 1967).

——, *Chaucer's Poetics and the Modern Reader* (Berkeley, Los Angeles, and London, 1987).

Kane, George, *Chaucer*, Past Masters series (Oxford and New York, 1984).

Kean, P. M., *Chaucer and the Making of English History*, 2 vols. (London and Boston, 1972).

Kittredge, George L., *Chaucer and His Poetry* (Cambridge, Mass., 1915).

Knapp, Peggy, *Chaucer and the Social Contest* (London and New York, 1990).

Knight, Stephen, *Geoffrey Chaucer*, Rereading Literature series (Oxford and New York, 1986).

Kolve, V. A., *Chaucer and the Imagery of Narrative: The First Five Canterbury Tales* (Stanford and London, 1984).

Lawler, Traugott, *The One and the Many in the Canterbury Tales* (Hamden, Conn., 1980).

Lawlor, John, *Chaucer* (London, 1968; New York, 1969).

Lawton, David, *Chaucer's Narrators*, Chaucer Studies, 13 (Cambridge, 1985).

Leicester, H. Marshall, Jr., *The Disenchanted Self: Representing the Subject in the 'Canterbury Tales'* (Berkeley, Los Angeles, and Oxford, 1990).

Lerer, Seth, *Chaucer and His Readers: Imagining the Author in Late Medieval England* (Princeton, 1993).

Lindahl, Carl, *Earnest Games: Folkloric Patterns in the Canterbury Tales*, (Bloomington and Indianapolis, 1987).

Manly, John Matthews, *Some New Light on Chaucer: Lectures delivered at the Lowell Institute* (New York and London, 1926).

Mann, Jill, *Chaucer and Medieval Estates Satire: The Literature of Social Classes and the 'General Prologue' to the 'Canterbury Tales'* (Cambridge, 1973).

—, *Geoffrey Chaucer*, Feminist Readings series (Hemel Hempstead, 1991).

Martin, Priscilla, *Chaucer's Women: Nuns, Wives, and Amazons* (Basingstoke, 1990).

Muscatine, Charles, *Chaucer and the French Tradition: A Study in Style and Meaning* (Berkeley and Los Angeles, 1957).

Owen, Charles A., Jr., *Pilgrimage and Storytelling in the Canterbury Tales: The Dialectic of 'Ernest' and 'Game'* (Norman, Okla., 1977).

—, *The Manuscripts of the Canterbury Tales*, Chaucer Studies, 17 (Cambridge, 1991).

Patterson, Lee, *Chaucer and the Subject of History* (Madison, Wis. and London, 1991).

Payne, Robert O., *The Key of Remembrance: A Study of Chaucer's Poetics* (New Haven and London, 1963).

Pearsall, Derek, *The Canterbury Tales* (London, Boston, and Sydney, 1985).

—, *The Life of Geoffrey Chaucer: A Critical Biography* (Oxford and Cambridge, Mass., 1992).

Robertson, D. W., Jr., *A Preface to Chaucer: Studies in Medieval Perspectives* (Princeton, 1962).

Ross, Thomas W., *Chaucer's Bawdy* (New York, Toronto, and Vancouver, 1972).

Ruggiers, Paul G., *The Art of the Canterbury Tales* (Madison, Wis., 1965).

—, ed., *Editing Chaucer: The Great Tradition* (Norman, Okla., 1984).

Salter, Elizabeth, *Chaucer: The Knight's Tale and the Clerk's Tale* (London, 1962).

Schoeck, Richard J., and Jerome Taylor, eds., *Chaucer Criticism*, vol. 1, *The Canterbury Tales* (Notre Dame and London, 1960).

Sklute, Larry, *Virtue of Necessity: Inconclusiveness and Narrative Form in Chaucer's Poetry* (Columbus, Ohio, 1984).

Strohm, Paul, *Social Chaucer* (Cambridge, Mass. and London, 1989).

Traversi, Derek, *The Canterbury Tales: A Reading* (London and Newark, N.J., 1983).

Wagenknecht, Edward, ed., *Chaucer: Modern Essays in Criticism* (New York, 1959).

Wetherbee, Winthrop, *Geoffrey Chaucer: The Canterbury Tales*, Landmarks of world literature series (Cambridge, 1989).

Whiting, Bartlett Jere, *Chaucer's Use of Proverbs* (Cambridge, Mass., 1934).

THE CANTERBURY TALES

THE CANTERBURY TALES

Fragment I (Group A)

GENERAL PROLOGUE

HERE BYGYNNETH THE BOOK OF THE TALES OF CAUNTERBURY

WHAN that Aprill with his shoures soote	*sweet*
The droghte of March hath perced to the roote,	
And bathed every veyne in swich licour	
Of which vertu engendred is the flour;	
5 Whan Zephirus eek with his sweete breeth	*also*
Inspired hath in every holt and heeth	*quickened; wood*
The tendre croppes, and the yonge sonne	*shoots*
Hath in the Ram his half cours yronne,	
And smale foweles maken melodye,	*birds*
10 That slepen al the nyght with open ye	
(So priketh hem nature in hir corages);	*incites; hearts*
Thanne longen folk to goon on pilgrimages,	
And palmeres for to seken straunge strondes,	
To ferne halwes, kowthe in sondry londes;	
15 And specially from every shires ende	
Of Engelond to Caunterbury they wende,	*go*
The hooly blisful martir for to seke,	*blessed; visit*
That hem hath holpen whan that they were	*helped*
seeke.	*sick*
Bifil that in that seson on a day,	
20 In Southwerk at the Tabard as I lay	*stayed*
Redy to wenden on my pilgrymage	
To Caunterbury with ful devout corage,	

3–4 And bathed every sap-vessel in moisture, by virtue of which the
flower is produced.
7–8 The young sun (i.e. the sun at the beginning of its annual journey) has
completed the second half of its course in the Ram. (In other words
the sun had left the zodiacal sign Aries, which it did in Chaucer's
time on 11th April. We know from the *Introduction to the Man of
Law's Tale*, II. 5, that the first or second day of the pilgrimage was
18th April.)
13 And palmers to visit foreign shores.
14 To distant shrines, well known in different lands.
17 i.e. St Thomas Becket.

1

At nyght was come into that hostelrye
Wel nyne and twenty in a compaignye,   *at least*
25 Of sondry folk, by aventure yfalle
In felaweshipe, and pilgrimes were they alle,
That toward Caunterbury wolden ryde.   *intended to*
The chambres and the stables weren wyde,
And wel we weren esed atte beste.
30 And shortly, whan the sonne was to reste,   *(gone) to rest*
So hadde I spoken with hem everichon   *each one*
That I was of hir felaweshipe anon,
And made forward erly for to ryse,   *agreement*
To take oure wey ther as I yow devyse.
35   But nathelees, whil I have tyme and   *nevertheless*
        space,   *opportunity*
Er that I ferther in this tale pace,   *before; proceed*
Me thynketh it acordaunt to resoun
To telle yow al the condicioun
Of ech of hem, so as it semed me,
40 And whiche they weren, and of what degree,
And eek in what array that they were inne;   *attire*
And at a knyght than wol I first bigynne.
   A KNYGHT ther was, and that a worthy man,
That fro the tyme that he first bigan
45 To riden out, he loved chivalrie,   *to go campaigning*
Trouthe and honour, fredom and curteisie.
Ful worthy was he in his lordes werre,   *war*
And therto hadde he riden, no man ferre,   *also; farther*
As wel in cristendom as in hethenesse,   *heathendom*
50 And evere honoured for his worthynesse.
At Alisaundre he was whan it was wonne.
Ful ofte tyme he hadde the bord bigonne
Aboven alle nacions in Pruce;   *Prussia*
In Lettow hadde he reysed and in Ruce,
55 No Cristen man so ofte of his degree.
In Gernade at the seege eek hadde he be
Of Algezir, and riden in Belmarye.

25 By chance met together.
29 And we were excellently entertained.
34 To where I tell you of.
37 It seems to me to be in order.
40 And what sort of men they were.
46 *Trouthe*, fidelity, loyalty; *fredom*, liberality; *curteisie*, gracious and
considerate conduct.
51 The Saracen stronghold of Alexandria was taken by Pierre de
Lusignan, King of Cyprus, in 1365.
52 He had very often sat in the seat of honour at table.
54 He had campaigned with the Teutonic knights against the bar-
barians of Lithuania and Russia.
56-7 He had taken part in the siege and capture of the Moorish
citadel of Algezir in Granada (1344); *Belmarye*, Benmarin, a Moorish
kingdom in North Africa.

At Lyeys was he and at Satalye,
Whan they were wonne; and in the Grete See   *Mediterranean*
60 At many a noble armee hadde he be.   *armed expedition*
At mortal batailles hadde he been fiftene,
And foughten for oure feith at Tramyssene
In lystes thries, and ay slayn his foo.   *lists; thrice*
This ilke worthy knyght hadde been also   *same*
65 Somtyme with the lord of Palatye   *once; Palatia*
Agayn another hethen in Turkye.
And everemoore he hadde a sovereyn prys;
And though that he were worthy, he was wys,   *eminent; wise*
And of his port as meeke as is a mayde.   *bearing*
70 He nevere yet no vileynye ne sayde
In all his lyf unto no maner wight.
He was a verray, parfit gentil knyght.
But, for to tellen yow of his array,   *outfit*
His hors were goode, but he was nat gay.   *horses*
75 Of fustian he wered a gypon
Al bismotered with his habergeon,
For he was late ycome from his viage,   *military expedition*
And wente for to doon his pilgrymage.
    With hym ther was his sone, a yong SQUIER,   *squire*
80 A lovyere and a lusty bacheler,
With lokkes crulle as they were leyd in presse.
Of twenty yeer of age he was, I gesse.
Of his stature he was of evene lengthe,   *medium height*
And wonderly delyvere, and of greet   *wonderfully active*
    strengthe.
85 And he hadde been somtyme in chyvachie   *on cavalry raids*
In Flaundres, in Artoys, and Pycardie,
And born hym weel, as of so litel space,
In hope to stonden in his lady grace.
Embrouded was he, as it were a meede   *meadow*
90 Al ful of fresshe floures, whyte and reede.
Synginge he was, or floytynge, al the day;   *fluting*
He was as fressh as is the month of May.
Short was his gowne, with sleves longe and wyde.
Wel koude he sitte on hors and faire ryde.   *excellently*

58 *Lyeys, Satalye,* Ayas (in Armenia) and Attalia (in Asia Minor),
  captured by de Lusignan in 1367 and 1361 respectively.
62 *Tramyssene,* Tlemcen in Algeria.
67 And always he had an outstanding reputation.
70–2 He had never in all his life spoken rudely to any sort of person.
  He was a true, complete, and noble knight.
75–6 He wore a surcoat of fustian (a course material of cotton and
  flax) all spotted with rust from his coat of mail.
80 A lover and a lusty young knight.
81 As curly as if they had been pressed by a curling-iron.
87 And conducted himself well, considering the short time of his
  service.

95 He koude songes make and wel endite,
    Juste and eek daunce, and weel purtreye   *joust; draw*
        and write.
    So hoote he lovede that by nyghtertale   *hotly; night*
    He sleep namoore than dooth a nyghtyngale.
    Curteis he was, lowely, and servysable,
100 And carf biforn his fader at the table.
        A YEMAN hadde he and servantz namo
    At that tyme, for hym liste ride so,   *he chose to*
    And he was clad in cote and hood of grene.
    A sheef of pecok arwes, bright and kene,
105 Under his belt he bar ful thriftily,   *carefully*
    (Wel koude he dresse his takel yemanly:
    His arwes drouped noght with fetheres lowe)
    And in his hand he baar a myghty bowe.
    A not heed hadde he, with a broun visage.   *close-cropped*
110 Of wodecraft wel koude he al the usage.   *knew*
    Upon his arm he baar a gay bracer,
    And by his syde a swerd and a bokeler,
    And on that oother syde a gay daggere
    Harneised wel and sharp as point of spere;   *mounted*
115 A Cristopher on his brest of silver sheene.
    An horn he bar, the bawdryk was of grene;   *baldric*
    A forster was he, soothly, as I gesse.   *forester; truly*
  ── Ther was also a Nonne, a PRIORESSE,
    That of hir smylyng was ful symple and   *unaffected*
        coy;   *modest*
120 Hire gretteste ooth was but by Seinte Loy;   *Eligius*
    And she was cleped madame Eglentyne.   *called*
    Ful weel she soong the service dyvyne,
    Entuned in hir nose ful semely,
    And Frenssh she spak ful faire and fetisly,   *elegantly*
125 After the scole of Stratford atte Bowe,
    For Frenssh of Parys was to hire unknowe.   *unknown*
    At mete wel ytaught was she with alle: *table; moreover*
    She leet no morsel from hir lippes falle,

    95 He was good at composing the music and words of songs.
    99 He was courteous, humble, and willing to be of service.
    101 *Yeman*, attendant; *he*, i.e. the Knight; *namo*, no other.
    104 *pecok arwes*, arrows with peacock feathers.
    106-7 He well knew how to prepare his tackle in yeoman-like
        fashion: there were no flattened feathers to make his arrows droop in
        flight.
    111 *bracer*, guard for the bow-arm.
    115 *Cristopher*, figure of St Christopher, the patron saint of foresters;
        sheene, bright.   + travellers
    123 Intoned in her nose in a very seemly manner.
    125 The Prioress spoke French with the accent she had learned in her
        convent (the Benedictine nunnery of St Leonard's, near Stratford-
        Bow in Middlesex).

Ne wette hir fyngres in hir sauce depe;   *nor; deeply*
130 Wel koude she carie a morsel and wel kepe   *take good care*
That no drope ne fille upon hire brest.
In curteisie was set ful muchel hir lest.
Hir over-lippe wyped she so clene
That in hir coppe ther was no ferthyng sene   *cup; spot*
135 Of grece, whan she dronken hadde hir draughte.
Ful semely after hir mete she raughte.   *food; reached*
And sikerly she was of greet desport,
And ful plesaunt, and amyable of port,
And peyned hire to countrefete cheere
140 Of court, and to been estatlich of manere,
And to ben holden digne of reverence.   *held worthy*
But, for to speken of hire conscience,   *tender feeling*
She was so charitable and so pitous   *compassionate*
She wolde wepe, if that she saugh a mous
145 Kaught in a trappe, if it were deed or bledde.   *if it bled*
Of smale houndes hadde she that she fedde
With rosted flessh, or milk and wastel-breed.
But soore wepte she if oon of hem were deed,
Or if men smoot it with a yerde smerte;
150 And al was conscience and tendre herte.
Ful semyly hir wympul pynched was,   *wimple; pleated*
Hir nose tretys, hir eyen greye as glas,   *well shaped; eyes*
Hir mouth ful smal, and therto softe and reed;
But sikerly she hadde a fair forheed;
155 It was almoost a spanne brood, I trowe;   *think*
For, hardily, she was nat undergrowe.
Ful fetys was hir cloke, as I was war.
Of smal coral aboute hire arm she bar   *carried*
A peire of bedes, gauded al with grene,
160 And theron heng a brooch of gold ful sheene,
On which ther was first write a crowned A,
And after *Amor vincit omnia.* ———— Love Conquers All
                                                                              Ovid
Another NONNE with hire hadde she,
That was hir chapeleyne, and preestes thre.
165   A MONK ther was, a fair for the maistrie,

132 She took great pleasure in polite manners.
137 And certainly she was a very cheerful person.
139-40 She took pains to imitate courtly behaviour, and to be dignified
    in her bearing.
147 *wastel-breed*, fine wheat bread.
149 Or if anyone struck it sharply with a stick.
156 For, certainly, she was not small in stature.
157 I noticed that her cloak was very elegant.
159 A rosary with 'gauds' (i.e. large beads for the Paternosters) of
    green.
161 *crowned A*, capital A with a crown above it.
164 One of the three priests later tells the *Nun's Priest's Tale*.
165 A most excellent one.

An outridere, that lovede venerie,
A manly man, to been an abbot able.   *fit*
Ful many a deyntee hors hadde he in stable,   *valuable*
And whan he rood, men myghte his brydel heere
170 Gynglen in a whistlynge wynd als cleere
And eek as loude as dooth the chapel belle.
Ther as this lord was kepere of the celle,
The reule of seint Maure or of seint Beneit,
By cause that it was old and somdel streit   *somewhat strict*
175 This ilke Monk leet olde thynges pace,   *slide*
And heeld after the newe world the space.
He yaf nat of that text a pulled hen,
That seith that hunters ben nat hooly men,
Ne that a monk, whan he is recchelees,
180 Is likned til a fissh that is waterlees,—   *to*
This is to seyn, a monk out of his cloystre.
But thilke text heeld he nat worth an oystre;   *that*
And I seyde his opinion was good.
What sholde he studie and make hymselven   *why*
                              wood,   *mad*
185 Upon a book in cloystre alwey to poure,
Or swynken with his handes, and laboure,   *toil*
As Austyn bit? How shal the world be served?
Lat Austyn have his swynk to hym reserved!   *himself*
Therfore he was a prikasour aright:
190 Grehoundes he hadde as swift as fowel in flight;
Of prikyng and of huntyng for the hare
Was al his lust, for no cost wolde he spare.   *pleasure*
I seigh his sleves purfiled at the hond
With grys, and that the fyneste of a lond;
195 And, for to festne his hood under his chyn,
He hadde of gold ywroght a ful curious pyn;
A love-knotte in the gretter ende ther was.
His heed was balled, that shoon as any glas,

166 *outridere*, monk who rode out to supervise the estates of a monas-
    tery; *venerie*, hunting.
172 *Ther as*, where; *celle*, subordinate monastery.
173 St Maurus was a disciple of St Benedict, who founded the
    Benedictine order in 529 and drew up the rule of life to be observed
    by it.
176 And followed the new order of things meanwhile.
177 He did not value that text at the price of a plucked hen.
179 *recchelees*, careless, i.e. neglectful of monastic discipline.
187 *Austyn*, St Augustine of Hippo (345–430); *How shal the world be
    served?*, i.e. who else is fitted to do all the valuable secular work now
    done by the clergy?
189 He was a real hard galloper.
191 *prikyng*, tracking of a hare by its footprints.
193–4 Trimmed at the cuff with costly grey fur.
196 He had a most elaborate brooch made of gold.
197 There was a true-love knot at the larger end.

And eek his face, as he hadde been enoynt. *anointed*
200 He was a lord ful fat and in good poynt; *condition*
His eyen stepe, and rollynge in his heed, *prominent*
That stemed as a forneys of a leed;
His bootes souple, his hors in greet estaat. *form*
Now certeinly he was a fair prelaat; *fine*
205 He was nat pale as a forpyned goost. *tormented*
A fat swan loved he best of any roost.
His palfrey was as broun as is a berye.

    A FRERE ther was, a wantowne and a merye, *jovial*
A lymytour, a ful solempne man.
210 In alle the ordres foure is noon that kan *knows*
So muchel of daliaunce and fair langage. *gossip; flattery*
He hadde maad ful many a mariage
Of yonge wommen at his owene cost.
Unto his ordre he was a noble post. *pillar*
215 Ful wel biloved and famulier was he
With frankeleyns over al in his contree,
And eek with worthy wommen of the toun;
For he hadde power of confessioun,
As seyde hymself, moore than a curat, *parish priest*
220 For of his ordre he was licenciat.
Ful swetely herde he confessioun,
And plesaunt was his absolucioun:
He was an esy man to yeve penaunce,
Ther as he wiste to have a good pitaunce.
225 For unto a povre ordre for to yive *poor*
Is signe that a man is wel yshryve; *shriven*
For if he yaf, he dorste make avaunt,
He wiste that a man was repentaunt; *knew*
For many a man so hard is of his herte,
230 He may nat wepe, althogh hym soore smerte.
Therfore in stede of wepynge and preyeres
Men moote yeve silver to the povre freres. *must give*

202 That (i.e. his eyes) glowed like the furnace under a cauldron.
209 A limiter (i.e. friar licensed to beg within a certain district), a very
    imposing man.
210 The four orders of friars were the Dominicans (Black Friars),
    Franciscans (Grey Friars), Carmelites (White Friars), and Augus-
    tinians. (Austin Friars).
212–13 These lines mean that the Friar found husbands or dowries for
    the many young women he had seduced.
216 With franklins everywhere in his district.
217 With women of standing in the towns.
218–20 i.e. he had a licence from his order to hear confessions and to
    grant absolution for serious offences which the parish priest had to
    refer to his bishop.
224 Where he knew he would receive generous alms.
227 For if a man gave freely, he (the Friar) dared to assert.
230 He cannot weep, although his sin hurts him grievously.

His typet was ay farsed ful of knyves   *tippet; stuffed*
And pynnes, for to yeven faire wyves.
235 And certeinly he hadde a murye note: *pleasant voice*
Wel koude he synge and pleyen on a rote;
Of yeddynges he baar outrely the pris.
His nekke whit was as the flour-de-lys;
Therto he strong was as a champioun.   *professional fighter*
240 He knew the tavernes wel in every toun
And everich hostiler and tappestere
Bet than a lazar or a beggestere;
For unto swich a worthy man as he
Acorded nat, as by his facultee,
245 To have with sike lazars aqueyntaunce.
It is nat honest, it may nat avaunce,
For to deelen with no swich poraille,
But al with riche and selleres of vitaille.
And over al, ther as profit sholde arise,
250 Curteis he was and lowely of servyse.   *courteous; humble*
Ther nas no man nowher so vertuous.
He was the beste beggere in his hous;
For thogh a wydwe hadde noght a sho,
So plesaunt was his 'In principio,'
255 Yet wolde he have a ferthyng, er he wente.   *small gift*
His purchas was wel bettre than his rente.
And rage he koude, as it were right a whelp.
In love-dayes ther koude he muchel help,
For ther he was nat lyk a cloysterer   *resident of a cloister*
260 With a thredbare cope, as is a povre scoler,   *out-door cloak*
But he was lyk a maister or a pope.   *master of arts*
Of double worstede was his semycope,   *short cloak*
That rounded as a belle out of the presse.
Somwhat he lipsed, for his wantownesse,

236 *rote*, stringed instrument.
237 In singing popular songs he excelled all others.
241–2 And every innkeeper and barmaid better than a leper or a beggar-woman.
244 It was not fitting, in view of his profession.
246–8 It is not respectable or profitable to have dealings with such poor people, but only with rich people and licensed victuallers.
249 And wherever profit was likely to arise.
251 Nowhere was there any man so capable.
254 *In principio*, the opening words of St John's Gospel, which were regarded in the Middle Ages as a charm against evil.
256 The proceeds of his begging were much better than his income. (That is to say, although he was a friar and so had no regular income, he managed to pick up quite a lot.)
257 He could play wantonly, just like a puppy.
258 He could give much help by acting as umpire on love-days (i.e. days appointed for settling disputes by arbitration).
263 That was as rounded as a bell out of the mould.
264 He lisped a little, by way of affectation.

265 To make his Englissh sweete upon his tonge;
And in his harpyng, whan that he hadde songe,
His eyen twynkled in his heed aryght   *just*
As doon the sterres in the frosty nyght.
This worthy lymytour was cleped Huberd.   *called Hubert*

270   A MARCHANT was ther with a forked berd,
In mottelee, and hye on horse he sat;   *motley*
Upon his heed a Flaundryssh bever hat,   *Flemish*
His bootes clasped faire and fetisly.   *elegantly*
His resons he spak ful solempnely,   *opinions*

275 Sownynge alwey th'encrees of his   *proclaiming*
      wynnyng.   *profits*
He wolde the see were kept for any thyng
Bitwixe Middelburgh and Orewelle.
Wel koude he in eschaunge sheeldes selle.
This worthy man ful wel his wit bisette:

280 Ther wiste no wight that he was in dette,   *knew; person*
So estatly was he of his governaunce
With his bargaynes and with his chevyssaunce.
For sothe he was a worthy man with alle,
But, sooth to seyn, I noot how men hym calle.

285   A CLERK ther was of Oxenford also,   *student*
That unto logyk hadde longe ygo.
As leene was his hors as is a rake,
And he nas nat right fat, I undertake,
But looked holwe, and therto sobrely.   *serious*

290 Ful thredbare was his overeste courtepy; *short outer coat*
For he hadde geten hym yet no benefice,
Ne was so worldly for to have office.   *secular employment*
For hym was levere have at his beddes heed *he would rather*
Twenty bookes, clad in blak or reed,   *bound*

295 Of Aristotle and his philosophie,
Than robes riche, or fithele, or gay sautrie. *fiddle; psaltery*
But al be that he was a philosophre,
Yet hadde he but litel gold in cofre;

276-7 He wished the sea to be guarded at all costs between Middelburg
(in Holland) and Orwell (near Harwich in Suffolk).
278 He well knew how to sell French crowns at a profit. (In doing so
the Merchant was breaking the law, since only royal money changers
were allowed to make a profit on exchange.)
279 Used his wits to the best advantage.
281-2 He conducted himself with such dignity in making his bargains
and loans.
284 But, to tell the truth, I don't know what he is called.
286 Who had long since proceeded to the study of logic. (The Clerk
was a university student who had taken the bachelor's degree and
was now studying for the master's degree.)
297 But although he was a philosopher. (There is a pun here on the
word 'philosopher,' which could also be used of an alchemist, who
spent his time trying to transmute baser metals into gold.)

But al that he myghte of his freendes hente,   *get*
300 On bookes and on lernynge he it spente,
And bisily gan for the soules preye   *did*
Of hem that yaf hym wherwith to scoleye.   *gave; study*
Of studie took he moost cure and moost heede. *care*
Noght o word spak he moore than was neede,
305 And that was seyd in forme and reverence,
And short and quyk and ful of hy sentence;
Sownynge in moral vertu was his speche,
And gladly wolde he lerne and gladly teche.
 A Sergeant of the Lawe, war and wys,
310 That often hadde been at the Parvys,
Ther was also, ful riche of excellence.
Discreet he was and of greet reverence—   *dignity*
He semed swich, his wordes weren so wise.
Justice he was ful often in assise,
315 By patente and by pleyn commissioun.
For his science and for his heigh renoun,   *knowledge*
Of fees and robes hadde he many oon.   *a one*
So greet a purchasour was nowher noon: *buyer of land*
Al was fee symple to hym in effect;
320 His purchasyng myghte nat been infect.
Nowher so bisy a man as he ther nas,
And yet he semed bisier than he was.
In termes hadde he caas and doomes alle
That from the tyme of kyng William were falle.
325 Therto he koude endite, and make a thyng,
Ther koude no wight pynche at his writyng; *find fault with*
And every statut koude he pleyn by rote.
He rood but hoomly in a medlee cote   *motley*
Girt with a ceint of silk, with barres smale;
330 Of his array telle I no lenger tale.

305 Formally and respectfully.
306 Lively and full of deep meaning.
307 i.e. his conversation was of an edifying nature.
309 The Sergeants-at-Law were high legal officers, from whom the judges of the King's courts were chosen; *war and wys*, cautious and prudent.
310 *Parvys*, the porch of St Paul's, where lawyers met their clients for consultation. (Another possible meaning is that he had often presided at the academic disputations of students in the inns of court.)
314–15 He had very often been a judge at the assizes, appointed by the King's letters patent and by a warrant giving him jurisdiction in all kinds of cases.
319–20 i.e. he always got absolute possession of any land he bought; his title to it could never be proved defective.
321 Nowhere was there so busy a man as he was.
323–4 He had an accurate knowledge of all the legal cases and judgments which had come about since the time of William the Conqueror.
325 Moreover he knew how to write and draw up a legal document.
327 He knew completely by heart.
329 A girdle of silk with narrow ornamental bars.

A FRANKELEYN was in his compaignye.
Whit was his berd as is the dayesye;
Of his complexioun he was sangwyn;   *temperament*
Wel loved he by the morwe a sop in wyn;
335 To lyven in delit was evere his wone,   *wont*
For he was Epicurus owene sone,   *son*
That heeld opinioun that pleyn delit   *pure delight*
Was verray felicitee parfit.
An housholdere, and that a greet, was he;
340 Seint Julian he was in his contree.
His breed, his ale, was alweys after oon;
A bettre envyned man was nowher noon.
Withoute bake mete was nevere his hous
Of fissh and flessh, and that so plentevous,
345 It snewed in his hous of mete and drynke,   *food*
Of alle deyntees that men koude thynke.   *delicacies*
After the sondry sesons of the yeer,
So chaunged he his mete and his soper.   *dinner*
Ful many a fat partrich hadde he in muwe,   *coop*
350 And many a breem and many a luce in stuwe.   *pike; fishpond*
Wo was his cook but if his sauce were
Poynaunt and sharp, and redy al his geere.
His table dormant in his halle alway
Stood redy covered al the longe day.
355 At sessiouns ther was he lord and sire;
Ful ofte tyme he was knyght of the shire.
An anlaas and a gipser al of silk   *dagger; pouch*
Heeng at his girdel, whit as morne milk.   *morning*
A shirreve hadde he been, and a countour.
360 Was nowher swich a worthy vavasour.   *landowner*
AN HABERDASSHERE and a CARPENTER,
A WEBBE, a DYERE, and a TAPYCER,—
And they were clothed alle in o lyveree
Of a solempne and a greet fraternitee.

331 A franklin was a substantial landowner of the gentry class.
334 Early in the morning a piece of bread dipped in wine.
340 *Seint Julian*, the patron saint of hospitality; *contree*, district.
341 Always of one standard, i.e. uniformly good.
342 No one anywhere had a wine cellar better stocked than his.
351-2 Woe to his cook if his sauce were not piquant and his utensils
    all ready.
353 *table dormant*, table fixed in its place, as distinct from one on
    trestles.
355 He presided at sessions of justices of the peace.
356 *knyght of the shire*, representative of the county in parliament.
359 *shirreve*, sheriff, a high administrative officer representing the royal
    authority in a shire; *countour*, auditor.
362 *Webbe*, weaver; *Tapycer*, tapestry-maker.
363-4 Since they belonged to different trades, the one livery they all
    wore must have been that of a religious guild or fraternity.

365 Ful fressh and newe hir geere apiked was;   *adorned*
　　Hir knyves were chaped noght with bras   *mounted*
　　But al with silver; wroght ful clene and weel   *neatly*
　　Hire girdles and hir pouches everydeel.   *in every detail*
　　Wel semed ech of hem a fair burgeys
370 To sitten in a yeldehalle on a deys.   *guildhall; dais*
　　Everich, for the wisdom that he kan,
　　Was shaply for to been an alderman.   *fit*
　　For catel hadde they ynogh and rente,   *property; revenue*
　　And eek hir wyves wolde it wel assente;
375 And elles certeyn were they to blame.
　　It is ful fair to been ycleped 'madame,'   *called*
　　And goon to vigilies al bifore,
　　And have a mantel roialliche ybore.   *borne*
　　　A Cook they hadde with hem for the nones   *on purpose*
380 To boille the chiknes with the marybones,
　　And poudre-marchant tart and galyngale.
　　Wel koude he knowe a draughte of Londoun ale.
　　He koude rooste, and sethe, and broille, and frye,
　　Maken mortreux, and wel bake a pye.   *thick soups*
385 But greet harm was it, as it thoughte me, *pity; seemed to me*
　　That on his shyne a mormal hadde he.   *sore*
　　For blankmanger, that made he with the beste.
　　　A Shipman was ther, wonynge fer by weste;
　　For aught I woot, he was of Dertemouthe.   *know*
390 He rood upon a rouncy, as he kouthe,
　　In a gowne of faldyng to the knee.   *coarse woollen cloth*
　　A daggere hangynge on a laas hadde he   *cord*
　　Aboute his nekke, under his arm adoun.
　　The hoote somer hadde maad his hewe al broun;
395 And certeinly he was a good felawe.
　　Ful many a draughte of wyn had he ydrawe
　　Fro Burdeux-ward, whil that the chapman sleep.
　　Of nyce conscience took he no keep.

371 Each one, for his wisdom (lit. for the wisdom that he knows).
377 *vigilies*, vigils, i.e. services held on the eve of a religious festival; *al bifore*, before everyone else.
381 *poudre-marchant tart*, tart flavouring powder; *galyngale*, spice prepared from the root of sweet cyperus.
382 He well knew how to recognize.
387 *blankmanger*, 'white food' made from minced fowl, cream, rice, almonds, etc.
388 Living far to the west.
390 He rode on a cob, as well as he knew how.
395 *good felawe*. This phrase often carries a suggestion of rascality, as here and in line 650 below. (Cf. III. 1385.)
396-7 Had he stolen on the voyage home from Bordeaux, while the merchant was sleeping.
398 He had no time for tender feelings.

If that he faught, and hadde the hyer hond,   *upper*
400 By water he sente hem hoom to every lond.
But of his craft to rekene wel his tydes,   *skill*
His stremes, and his daungers hym bisides,   *round about him*
His herberwe, and his moone, his lodemenage,
Ther nas noon swich from Hulle to Cartage.   *Cartagena*
405 Hardy he was and wys to undertake;
With many a tempest hadde his berd been shake.
He knew alle the havenes, as they were,
Fro Gootlond to the cape of Fynystere,
And every cryke in Britaigne and in Spayne.   *Brittany*
410 His barge ycleped was the Maudelayne.   *ship; Magdalen*
    With us ther was a DOCTOUR OF PHISIK;
In al this world ne was ther noon hym lik,
To speke of phisik and of surgerye,
For he was grounded in astronomye.   *astrology*
415 He kepte his pacient a ful greet deel
In houres by his magyk natureel.
Wel koude he fortunen the ascendent
Of his ymages for his pacient.
He knew the cause of everich maladye,
420 Were it of hoot, or coold, or moyste, or drye,
And where they engendred, and of what humour.
He was a verray, parfit praktisour:
The cause yknowe, and of his harm the roote,   *known; its*
Anon he yaf the sike man his boote.   *remedy*
425 Ful redy hadde he his apothecaries
To sende hym drogges and his letuaries,   *medicaments*
For ech of hem made oother for to wynne—
Hir frendshipe nas nat newe to bigynne.

400 i.e. he drowned his prisoners.

403 His harbours, phases of the moon, and pilotage.

405 He was bold and yet prudent in what he undertook.

408 *Gootlond*, Gotland, an island off the coast of Sweden; *Fynystere*, Finisterre, a cape in north-west Spain.

415–18 He watched his patient very carefully and chose by natural magic (as distinct from black magic) the right astrological hours for giving him treatment. He knew exactly how to find a favourable ascendant for making images in the interests of his patient. (The 'images' may have been either effigies of the patient or astrological emblems, made in this instance to benefit the sick person.)

420 These, according to medieval physiology, are the four chief elements of the body, which combine to produce the four humours or bodily moistures. It was believed that diseases are caused by an excess of one or more of the humours: *blood* in the sanguine, *phlegm* in the phlegmatic, *choler* or yellow-red bile in choleric persons, *melancholy* or black bile in the melancholic.

422 He was a true, complete practitioner.

427 Each put money into the other's pocket—the doctor by prescribing cheap drugs, the apothecary by overcharging for them.

Wel knew he the olde Esculapius,
430 And Deyscorides, and eek Rufus,
Olde Ypocras, Haly, and Galyen,   *Hippocrates; Galen*
Serapion, Razis, and Avycen,   *Avicenna*
Averrois, Damascien, and Constantyn,
Bernard, and Gatesden, and Gilbertyn.
435 Of his diete mesurable was he,   *temperate*
For it was of no superfluitee,
But of greet norissyng and digestible.
His studie was but litel on the Bible.
In sangwyn and in pers he clad was al,
440 Lyned with taffata and with sendal;   *fine silk*
And yet he was but esy of dispence;   *thrifty*
He kepte that he wan in pestilence.   *the plague*
For gold in phisik is a cordial,
Therefore he lovede gold in special.

445   A good WIF was ther of biside BATHE,   *from near Bath*
But she was somdel deef, and that was scathe.   *a pity*
Of clooth-makyng she hadde swich an haunt,   *skill*
She passed hem of Ypres and of Gaunt.   *surpassed; Ghent*
In al the parisshe wif ne was ther noon
450 That to the offrynge bifore hire sholde goon;
And if ther dide, certeyn so wrooth was she,   *certainly*
That she was out of alle charitee.
Hir coverchiefs ful fyne weren of ground;
I dorste swere they weyeden ten pound
455 That on a Sonday weren upon hir heed.
Hir hosen weren of fyn scarlet reed,   *stockings*
Ful streite yteyd, and shoes ful moyste and newe.
Boold was hir face, and fair, and reed of hewe.
She was a worthy womman al hir lyve:
460 Housbondes at chirche dore she hadde fyve,
Withouten oother compaignye in youthe,—   *besides*
But therof nedeth nat to speke as nowthe.   *at present*
And thries hadde she been at Jerusalem;

429–34 These are the names of some of the chief medical authorities
   of the Middle Ages. They are all Greeks and Arabs, except for
   Bernard Gordon (a fourteenth-century Scottish physician), John
   Gaddesden of Merton College, Oxford (*d.* 1361), and Gilbertus
   Anglicus.
443 Gold was held to be a sovereign remedy by medieval physicians.
   This, Chaucer ironically observes, is why the doctor loved gold so
   much.
449–50 No woman had to go to the offering before her. (The congregation went up in order of rank to make their offerings to
   the priest.)
453 Her head-dresses were of a very fine texture.
457 *streite yteyd*, tightly fastened; *moyste*, supple.
460 A medieval marriage was legalized in the church porch and followed
   by a nuptial mass at the altar.

She hadde passed many a straunge strem;   *foreign river*
465 At Rome she hadde been, and at Boloigne,
In Galice at Seint-Jame, and at Coloigne.
She koude muchel of wandrynge by the weye.   *knew a lot*
Gat-tothed was she, soothly for to seye.   *gap-toothed*
Upon an amblere esily she sat,   *ambling horse*
470 Ywympled wel, and on hir heed an hat
As brood as is a bokeler or a targe;   *buckler; shield*
A foot-mantel aboute hir hipes large,   *outer skirt*
And on hir feet a paire of spores sharpe.
In felaweshipe wel koude she laughe and carpe.   *talk*
475 Of remedies of love she knew per chaunce,
For she koude of that art the olde daunce.
   A good man was ther of religioun,
And was a povre PERSOUN OF A TOUN,   *village priest*
But riche he was of hooly thoght and werk.
480 He was also a lerned man, a clerk,
That Cristes gospel trewely wolde preche;
His parisshens devoutly wolde he teche.   *parishioners*
Benygne he was, and wonder diligent,   *wonderfully*
And in adversitee ful pacient,
485 And swich he was ypreved ofte sithes.   *oftentimes*
Ful looth were hym to cursen for his tithes,
But rather wolde he yeven, out of doute,   *without doubt*
Unto his povre parisshens aboute
Of his offryng and eek of his substaunce.
490 He koude in litel thyng have suffisaunce.   *sufficiency*
Wyd was his parisshe, and houses fer asonder,
But he ne lefte nat, for reyn ne thonder,
In siknesse nor in meschief to visite   *adversity*
The ferreste in his parisshe, muche   *farthest; great and small*
   and lite,
495 Upon his feet, and in his hand a staf.
This noble ensample to his sheep he yaf,
That first he wroghte, and afterward he taughte.
Out of the gospel he tho wordes caughte,
And this figure he added eek therto,   *figure of speech*
500 That if gold ruste, what shal iren do?

465–6 She had visited the image of the Virgin at Boulogne, the shrine
    of St James at Compostella (in Galicia, Spain), and the shrine of the
    Magi at Cologne.
470 Covered with a wimple.
475 She knew the cures for love without a doubt.   (The allusion is to
    Ovid's *Remedia Amoris*.)
476 i.e. she knew all the tricks of the trade.
486 He was most unwilling to have anyone excommunicated for not
    paying his tithes.
497 He first practised good works himself, and then taught others to do
    the same.
498 He took those words out of the Gospel (Matt. v. 19).

For if a preest be foul, on whom we truste,   *vicious*
No wonder is a lewed man to ruste;   *ignorant*
And shame it is, if a prest take keep,
A shiten shepherde and a clene sheep.   *dirty*
505 Wel oghte a preest ensample for to yive,
By his clennesse, how that his sheep sholde lyve.
He sette nat his benefice to hyre
And leet his sheep encombred in the myre   *nor left*
And ran to Londoun unto Seinte Poules   *nor ran*
510 To seken hym a chaunterie for soules,
Or with a bretherhed to been witholde;
But dwelt at hoom, and kepte wel his *took good care of*
  folde,
So that the wolf ne made it nat myscarie;
He was a shepherde and noght a mercenarie. *hireling*
515 And though he hooly were and vertuous,
He was to synful men nat despitous,   *scornful*
Ne of his speche daungerous ne digne, *arrogant; disdainful*
But in his techyng discreet and benygne. *courteous; kind*
To drawen folk to hevene by fairnesse, *goodness of life*
520 By good ensample, this was his bisynesse.
But it were any persone obstinat,   *if there was*
What so he were, of heigh or lough estat, *whatever*
Hym wolde he snybben sharply for the nonys.
A bettre preest I trowe that nowher noon ys.
525 He waited after no pompe and reverence, *looked for*
Ne maked him a spiced conscience,
But Cristes loore and his apostles twelve
He taughte, but first he folwed it hymselve.
  With hym ther was a PLOWMAN, was his *(who) was*
   brother,
530 That hadde ylad of dong ful many a fother; *carted; load*
A trewe swynkere and a good was he,   *labourer*
Lyvynge in pees and parfit charitee.
God loved he best with al his hoole herte
At alle tymes, thogh him gamed or smerte,
535 And thanne his neighebor right as hymselve.
He wolde thresshe, and therto dyke and delve, *ditch; dig*
For Cristes sake, for every povre wight,
Withouten hire, if it lay in his myght.   *wages*

503 If a priest will but take heed.
507 He did not hire out his benefice.
510 To try to get a chantry, i.e. an endowment for a priest to sing masses
  for the soul of a dead person.
511 Or to be retained as chaplain by a guild.
523 He would rebuke him very sharply.
526 Nor was he too fastidious (in his dealings with his flock).
527 But the doctrine of Christ and his twelve apostles.
529 *brother*, i.e. fellow Christian.
534 Whether it gave him pleasure or pain.

His tithes payde he ful faire and wel,
540 Bothe of his propre swynk and his catel.
    In a tabard he rood upon a mere.   *labourer's smock; mare*
       Ther was also a REVE, and a MILLERE,
    A SOMNOUR, and a PARDONER also,
    A MAUNCIPLE, and myself—ther were namo.   *no others*
545   The MILLERE was a stout carl for the nones;
    Ful byg he was of brawn, and eek of bones.   *muscle*
    That proved wel, for over al ther he cam,
    At wrastlynge he wolde have alwey the ram.
    He was short-sholdred, brood, a thikke knarre;
550 Ther was no dore that he nolde heve of harre,
    Or breke it at a rennyng with his heed.
    His berd as any sowe or fox was reed,
    And therto brood, as though it were a spade.
    Upon the cop right of his nose he hade   *right on the tip*
555 A werte, and theron stood a toft of herys,
    Reed as the brustles of a sowes erys;
    His nosethirles blake were and wyde.   *nostrils*
    A swerd and a bokeler bar he by his syde.
    His mouth as greet was as a greet forneys.
560 He was a janglere and a goliardeys,
    And that was moost of synne and harlotries.   *scurrility*
    Wel koude he stelen corn and tollen thries;
    And yet he hadde a thombe of gold, pardee.   *indeed*
    A whit cote and a blew hood wered he.
565 A baggepipe wel koude he blowe and sowne,   *play*
    And therwithal he broghte us out of towne.
       A gentil MAUNCIPLE was ther of a temple,
    Of which achatours myghte take exemple   *buyers*
    For to be wise in byynge of vitaille;   *shrewd; food*
570 For wheither that he payde or took by taille,   *on credit*
    Algate he wayted so in his achaat
    That he was ay biforn and in good staat.

539–40 Honestly and in full, both on the wages he earned and on the
    increase of his flock.
545 An exceedingly strong fellow.
547 That was evident enough, for wherever he came.
548 A ram was the usual reward given to the winner of a wrestling match.
549 A thickset, sturdy fellow.
550 There was no door he was unwilling to heave off its hinges.
560 A loud talker and a coarse buffoon.
562 And take three times the legal toll on the corn he ground.
563 i.e. he was neither more nor less honest than other millers. (There
    is an allusion here to the old proverb 'An honest miller has a golden
    thumb,' which apparently means 'There are no honest millers.')
567 *gentil*, worthy; *Maunciple*, servant who bought provisions for an
    inn of court (*temple*).
571–2 At all times he was so cautious in his buying that he was always
    ahead of others and in an advantageous position.

Now is nat that of God a ful fair grace
That swich a lewed mannes wit shal pace   *ignorant; surpass*
575 The wisdom of an heep of lerned men?
Of maistres hadde he mo than thries ten,
That weren of lawe expert and curious,   *skilful*
Of which ther were a duszeyne in that hous
Worthy to been stywardes of rente and lond   *revenue*
580 Of any lord that is in Engelond,
To make hym lyve by his propre good   *on his own income*
In honour dettelees (but if he were   *unless he was mad*
    wood),
Or lyve as scarsly as hym list desire;
And able for to helpen al a shire
585 In any caas that myghte falle or happe;
And yet this Manciple sette hir aller cappe.
   The REVE was a sclendre colerik man.
His berd was shave as ny as ever he kan;   *shaven; close*
His heer was by his erys ful round yshorn;
590 His top was dokked lyk a preest biforn.
Ful longe were his legges and ful lene,
Ylyk a staf, ther was no calf ysene.   *like; visible*
Wel koude he kepe a gerner and a bynne;
Ther was noon auditour koude on him wynne.
595 Wel wiste he by the droghte and by the reyn   *knew*
The yeldynge of his seed and of his greyn.
His lordes sheep, his neet, his dayerye,   *cattle; dairy cows*
His swyn, his hors, his stoor, and his pultrye   *live-stock*
Was hoolly in this Reves governynge,   *charge*
600 And by his covenant yaf the rekenynge,
Syn that his lord was twenty yeer of age.
Ther koude no man brynge hym in arrerage.
Ther nas baillif, ne hierde, nor oother   *herdsman*
    hyne,   *labourer*
That he ne knew his sleighte and his covyne;
605 They were adrad of hym as of the deeth.
His wonyng was ful faire upon an heeth;   *dwelling*
With grene trees yshadwed was his place.

576 i.e. he had more than thirty lawyers to provide for.
583 As economically as he pleases.
585 In any emergency that might arise
586 Made fools of them all.
589-90 His hair was shorn all round above his ears; on top it was docked
   in front, like a priest's.
593 He could take good care of a granary or corn bin.
594 Who could get the better of him.
600 By the agreement he had with his lord he always rendered an
   account of the property entrusted to his charge.
602 No one could prove him to be in arrears.
604-5 Whose cunning and deceit were unknown to him; they were
   afraid of him as of death itself.

He koude bettre than his lord purchace.
Ful riche he was astored pryvely:
610 His lord wel koude he plesen subtilly,   *cunningly*
To yeve and lene hym of his owene good,
And have a thank, and yet a cote and hood.   *thanks*
In youthe he hadde lerned a good myster;   *trade*
He was a wel good wrighte, a carpenter.   *workman*
615 This Reve sat upon a ful good stot,   *stallion*
That was al pomely grey and highte Scot.
A long surcote of pers upon he hade,
And by his syde he baar a rusty blade.
Of Northfolk was this Reve of which I telle,
620 Biside a toun men clepen Baldeswelle.
Tukked he was as is a frere aboute,
And evere he rood the hyndreste of oure   *hindmost*
    route.   *company*
  A SOMONOUR was ther with us in that place,
That hadde a fyr-reed cherubynnes face.
625 For saucefleem he was, with eyen narwe,   *pimply*
As hoot he was and lecherous as a sparwe,
With scalled browes blake and piled berd.   *scabby; scraggy*
Of his visage children were aferd.
Ther nas quyk-silver, lytarge, ne brymstoon,   *litharge*
630 Boras, ceruce, ne oille of tartre noon,   *borax; ceruse*
Ne oynement that wolde clense and byte,   *burn*
That hym myghte helpen of his whelkes white,   *pimples*
Nor of the knobbes sittynge on his chekes.
Wel loved he garleek, oynons, and eek lekes,
635 And for to drynken strong wyn, reed as blood;
Thanne wolde he speke and crie as he were wood.   *mad*
And whan that he wel dronken hadde the wyn,
Thanne wolde he speke no word but Latyn.
A fewe termes hadde he, two or thre,
640 That he had lerned out of som decree—
No wonder is, he herde it al the day;
And eek ye knowen wel how that a jay

609 He had secretly amassed a rich store of goods.
611 By giving and lending him his (i.e. the lord's) own goods.
616 That was all dapple-grey and called Scot.
617 He had on a long outer coat of blue-grey cloth.
620 Near a village called Bawdeswell (in Norfolk).
621 i.e. he shortened his coat by tucking it under his girdle in the manner of a friar.
623 The Summoner was a minor official employed to summon offenders before an ecclesiastical court, especially one presided over by an archdeacon.
624 Cherubim were usually painted with red faces by the medieval artist.
626 The sparrow was traditionally associated with lechery.
639–40 i.e. he had picked up two or three Latin tags in the court where he served.

Kan clepen 'Watte' as wel as kan the pope.   *Walter*
But whoso koude in oother thyng hym grope,
645 Thanne hadde he spent al his philosophie;
Ay '*Questio quid iuris*' wolde he crie.
He was a gentil harlot and a kynde;   *charming rascal*
A bettre felawe sholde men noght fynde.
He wolde suffre for a quart of wyn
650 A good felawe to have his concubyn
A twelf month, and excuse hym atte fulle;   *fully*
Ful prively a fynch eek koude he pulle.
And if he foond owher a good felawe,   *anywhere*
He wolde techen him to have noon awe   *fear*
655 In swich caas of the ercedekenes curs,
But if a mannes soule were in his purs;
For in his purs he sholde ypunysshed be.
'Purs is the ercedekenes helle,' seyde he.
But wel I woot he lyed right in dede;   *know*
660 Of cursyng oghte ech gilty man him drede,
For curs wol slee right as assoillyng savith,   *absolution*
And also war hym of a *Significavit*.
In daunger hadde he at his owene gise
The yonge girles of the diocise,
665 And knew hir conseil, and was al hir reed.
A gerland hadde he set upon his heed
As greet as it were for an ale-stake.
A bokeleer hadde he maad hym of a cake.   *loaf of bread*
With hym ther rood a gentil PARDONER   *noble*
670 Of Rouncivale, his freend and his compeer,   *companion*
That streight was comen from the court of Rome.
Ful loude he soong 'Com hider, love, to me!'

644 But if anyone knew how to test him further.
646 'The question is, what is the law on this point?'
652 i.e. on the quiet he indulged in illicit intercourse himself.
655 *In swich caas*, i.e. if he were caught in incontinence.
658 In other words, when the archdeacon threatens a sinner with hell,
   the real place of punishment for the victim will be his own purse.
660 Every guilty man ought to be afraid of excommunication.
662 *Significavit*, the first word of a writ for the imprisonment of an
   excommunicated person.
663-4 He had the young people of the diocese at his mercy, to do with
   as he pleased.
665 And knew their secrets, and was their adviser in everything.
667 *ale-stake*, support for the garland or bush which was the sign of a
   tavern.
669 *Pardoner*, an official whose true function was to convey papal
   indulgences (i.e. remissions of temporal punishment) to those who
   had received the sacrament of penance. According to canon law,
   he had no right to sell indulgences to all and sundry, as Chaucer's
   Pardoner is guilty of doing.
670 *Rouncivale*, the hospital and chapel of St Mary Roncevall, near
   Charing Cross in London.
672 Possibly a verse from some popular song of the time.

This Somonour bar to hym a stif burdoun;
Was nevere trompe of half so greet a soun.   *trumpet; sound*
675 This Pardoner hadde heer as yelow as wex,   *wax*
But smothe it heeng as dooth a strike of flex;
By ounces henge his lokkes that he hadde,   *in thin clusters*
And therwith he his shuldres overspradde;   *covered*
But thynne it lay, by colpons oon and oon.   *in single shreds*
680 But hood, for jolitee, wered he noon,   *fun; wore*
For it was trussed up in his walet.
Hym thoughte he rood al of the newe jet;
Dischevelee, save his cappe, he rood al bare.
Swiche glarynge eyen hadde he as an hare.
685 A vernycle hadde he sowed upon his cappe.
His walet, biforn hym in his lappe,
Bretful of pardoun, comen from Rome al hoot.
A voys he hadde as smal as hath a goot.
No berd hadde he, ne nevere sholde have;
690 As smothe it was as it were late shave.   *lately shaven*
I trowe he were a geldying or a mare.
But of his craft, from Berwyk into Ware,   *at his trade*
Ne was ther swich another pardoner.
For in his male he hadde a pilwe-beer,   *bag; pillow-case*
695 Which that he seyde was Oure Lady veyl:
He seyde he hadde a gobet of the seyl   *piece*
That Seint Peter hadde, whan that he wente
Upon the see, til Jhesu Crist hym hente.   *caught hold of*
He hadde a croys of latoun ful of stones,
700 And in a glas he hadde pigges bones.
But with thise relikes, whan that he fond   *found*
A povre person dwellynge upon lond,
Upon a day he gat hym moore moneye
Than that the person gat in monthes tweye;   *two*
705 And thus, with feyned flaterye and japes,   *tricks*
He made the person and the peple his apes.   *dupes*
But trewely to tellen atte laste,
He was in chirche a noble ecclesiaste.

673 Accompanied him with a powerful bass.
676 It hung down smoothly like a hank of flax.
682 He imagined he rode in the very latest fashion.
683 With his hair hanging loose, he rode bareheaded except for his cap.
685 *vernycle*, miniature copy of St Veronica's sacred handkerchief,
    upon which Christ's features were miraculously imprinted. This was
    the usual token brought back by pilgrims to Rome, and the Pardoner
    no doubt wore one in order to give the impression that he had lately
    come from Rome.
687 Brimful of indulgences.
692 From Berwick to Ware (in Hertfordshire), i.e. from the north to
    the south of England.
699 A cross of brass, studded with false gems.
702 A poor parson living in the country.

 Wel koude he rede a lessoun or a storie,
710 But alderbest he song an offertorie;
 For wel he wiste, whan that song was songe,   *knew*
 He moste preche and wel affile his tonge
 To wynne silver, as he ful wel koude;   *knew how*
 Therefore he song the murierly and loude.   *more pleasantly*
715 Now have I toold you soothly, in a clause,   *few words*
 Th'estaat, th'array, the nombre, and eek   *rank; attire*
  the cause
 Why that assembled was this compaignye
 In Southwerk at this gentil hostelrye   *noble*
 That highte the Tabard, faste by the Belle.
720 But now is tyme to yow for to telle
 How that we baren us that ilke nyght,
 Whan we were in that hostelrie alyght;
 And after wol I telle of our viage   *journey*
 And al the remenaunt of oure pilgrimage.   *rest*
725 But first I pray yow, of youre curteisye,
 That ye n'arette it nat my vileynye,
 Thogh that I pleynly speke in this mateere,
 To telle yow hir wordes and hir cheere,   *behaviour*
 Ne thogh I speke hir wordes proprely.   *exactly*
730 For this ye knowen al so wel as I,
 Whoso shal telle a tale after a man,
 He moot reherce as ny as evere he kan
 Everich a word, if it be in his charge,
 Al speke he never so rudeliche and large,
735 Or ellis he moot telle his tale untrewe,   *untruly*
 Or feyne thyng, or fynde wordes newe.
 He may nat spare, althogh he were his brother;
 He moot as wel seye o word as another.
 Crist spak hymself ful brode in hooly writ,   *plainly*
740 And wel ye woot no vileynye is it.
 Eek Plato seith, whoso kan hym rede,
 The wordes moote be cosyn to the dede.   *cousin*

709 *lessoun*, passage from Scripture read at divine service; *storie*, series
 of lessons from Scripture or from the life of a saint.
710 But best of all he sang an offertory. (This is the anthem usually
 sung while the people are making their offerings; but the Pardoner
 had found that he could persuade his congregation to give more
 generously by preaching them an eloquent sermon between the anthem
 and the collection.)
712 He had to preach and polish up his words.
719 That is called the Tabard, hard by the Bell (both Southwark inns).
721 What we did that same night.
726 That you do not attribute it to my bad manners.
731-4 Whoever tells a tale as someone else has told it must, if he has
 undertaken to do so, repeat every word as near as he can, however
 rudely and broadly he speaks.
738 He is bound to treat every word alike.
740 And you well know there is nothing coarse in what he says.

Also I prey yow to foryeve it me,

Al have I nat set folk in hir degree   *although*

745 Heere in this tale, as that they sholde stonde.

My wit is short, ye may wel understonde.

    Greet chiere made oure Hoost us everichon,   *good cheer*

And to the soper sette he us anon.

He served us with vitaille at the beste;

750 Strong was the wyn, and wel to drynke us leste.

A semely man OURE HOOSTE was withalle

For to been a marchal in an halle.

A large man he was with eyen stepe—   *prominent*

A fairer burgeys was ther noon in Chepe—

755 Boold of his speche, and wys, and wel ytaught,

And of manhod hym lakkede right naught.

Eek therto he was right a myrie man,

And after soper pleyen he bigan,   *to jest*

And spak of myrthe amonges othere thynges,

760 Whan that we hadde maad our rekenynges,   *paid*

And seyde thus: 'Now, lordynges, trewely,   *sirs*

Ye been to me right welcome, hertely;   *really*

For by my trouthe, if that I shal nat lye,

I saugh nat this yeer so myrie a compaignye   *saw*

765 Atones in this herberwe as is now.   *at one time; inn*

Fayn wolde I doon yow myrthe, wiste I how.

And of a myrthe I am right now bythoght,

To doon yow ese, and it shal coste noght.

    Ye goon to Caunterbury—God yow speede,

770 The blisful martir quite yow youre meede!   *reward you*

And wel I woot, as ye goon by the weye,

Ye shapen yow to talen and to pleye;

For trewely, confort ne myrthe is noon

To ride by the weye doumb as a stoon;

775 And therfore wol I maken yow disport,   *entertainment*

As I seyde erst, and doon yow som confort.   *before*

And if yow liketh alle by oon assent

For to stonden at my juggement,   *abide by*

And for to werken as I shal yow seye,   *do*

780 To-morwe, whan ye riden by the weye,

Now, by my fader soule that is deed,

But ye be myrie, I wol yeve yow myn heed!   *unless*

Hoold up youre hondes, withouten moore speche.'

750 It pleased us well to drink.

752 *marchal*, marshal, an official in a noble household who was responsible for the arrangement of banquets and ceremonies.

754 There is no better burgess in Cheapside.

766 I would gladly amuse you, if I knew how.

768 To give you pleasure, and it shall cost you nothing.

772 You intend to tell tales.

777 If you all with one accord find it agreeable.

783 *Hoold up youre hondes*, i.e. to signify assent.

Oure conseil was nat longe for to seche.   *opinion; seek*
785 Us thoughte it was noght worth to make it wys,
And graunted hym withouten moore avys,
And bad him seye his voirdit as hym leste.
'Lordynges,' quod he, 'now herkneth for the beste;
But taak it nought, I prey yow, in desdeyn.
790 This is the poynt, to speken short and pleyn,
That ech of yow, to shorte with oure weye,
In this viage shal telle tales tweye   *two*
To Caunterbury-ward, I mene it so,   *towards Canterbury*
And homward he shal tellen othere two,
795 Of aventures that whilom han bifalle.
And which of yow that bereth hym best of   *acquits himself*
alle,
That is to seyn, that telleth in this caas
Tales of best sentence and moost solaas,
Shal have a soper at oure aller cost
800 Heere in this place, sittynge by this post,
Whan that we come agayn fro Caunterbury.
And for to make yow the moore mury,
I wol myselven goodly with yow ryde,   *gladly*
Right at myn owene cost, and be youre gyde;
805 And whoso wole my juggement withseye   *gainsay*
Shal paye al that we spenden by the weye.
And if ye vouche sauf that it be so,
Tel me anon, withouten wordes mo,   *more*
And I wol erly shape me therfore.'
810   This thyng was graunted, and oure othes swore   *sworn*
With ful glad herte, and preyden hym also   *(we) begged*
That he wolde vouche sauf for to do so,
And that he wolde been oure governour,   *ruler*
And of our tales juge and reportour,   *umpire*
815 And sette a soper at a certeyn pris,
And we wol reuled been at his devys   *will*
In heigh and lough; and thus by oon assent
We been acorded to his juggement.
And therupon the wyn was fet anon;
820 We dronken, and to reste wente echon,
Withouten any lenger taryynge.
Amorwe, whan that day bigan to sprynge,   *next morning*

785 It seemed to us it was not worth deliberating about.
787 Give whatever verdict he liked.
791 To shorten our journey with.
795 That have happened in the past.
797 *in this caas*, i.e. in the event of your doing this.
798 The most instructive and entertaining tales.
799 At the expense of us all.
809 And I will prepare for it without delay.
817 *In heigh and lough*, in high and low, i.e. in all things.

Up roos oure Hoost, and was oure aller cok,
And gadrede us togidre alle in a flok,
825 And forth we riden a litel moore than paas   *footpace*
Unto the wateryng of Seint Thomas;
And there oure Hoost bigan his hors areste   *stop*
And seyde, 'Lordynges, herkneth, if yow leste.   *please*
Ye woot youre foreward, and I it yow recorde.
830 If even-song and morwe-song accorde,
Lat se now who shal telle the firste tale.
As evere mote I drynke wyn or ale,
Whoso be rebel to my juggement
Shal paye for al that by the wey is spent.
835 Now draweth cut, er that we ferrer twynne;
He which that hath the shorteste shal bigynne.
Sire Knyght,' quod he, 'my mayster and my lord,
Now draweth cut, for that is myn accord.   *agreement*
Cometh neer,' quod he, 'my lady Prioresse.
840 And ye, sire Clerk, lat be youre shamefastnesse,
Ne studieth noght; ley hond to, every man!'
Anon to drawen every wight bigan,   *person*
And shortly for to tellen as it was,
Were it by aventure, or sort, or cas,
845 The sothe is this, the cut fil to the Knyght,   *truth; fell*
Of which ful blithe and glad was every wyght,
And telle he moste his tale, as was resoun,   *right*
By foreward and by composicioun,   *agreement; compact*
As ye han herd; what nedeth wordes mo?   *more*
850 And whan this goode man saugh that it was so,
As he that wys was and obedient
To kepe his foreward by his free assent,
He seyde, 'Syn I shal bigynne the game,   *since*
What, welcome be the cut, a Goddes name!
855 Now lat us ryde, and herkneth what I seye.'
And with that word we ryden forth oure weye,
And he bigan with right a myrie cheere   *cheerfully*
His tale anon, and seyde as ye may heere.

823 Was cock for all of us, i.e. awoke us all.
826 A place for watering horses two miles from London on the pilgrims'
    way to Canterbury.
829 You know your agreement, and I remind you of it.
830 If evensong and matins agree, i.e. if you are still of the same mind
    this morning.
832 As I hope never to drink anything but wine or ale.
835 Now draw lots before we go any farther.
841 And stop your musing.
844 Whether it was by luck, or fate, or chance.
854 Why, let the draw be welcome, in God's name.

THE KNIGHT'S TALE

HEERE BIGYNNETH THE KNYGHTES TALE

WHILOM, as olde stories tellen us,   *once*
860 Ther was a duc that highte Theseus;   *was called*
     Of Atthenes he was lord and governour,
     And in his tyme swich a conquerour,
     That gretter was ther noon under the sonne.
     Ful many a rich contree hadde he wonne;
865 What with his wysdom and his chivalrie,   *knightly deeds*
     He conquered al the regne of Femenye,   *kingdom; Amazons*
     That whilom was ycleped Scithia,   *called*
     And weddede the queen Ypolita,   *Hippolyta*
     And broghte hire hoom with hym in his contree
870 With muchel glorie and greet solempnytee,   *much*
     And eek hir yonge suster Emelye.   *also*
     And thus with victorie and with melodye
     Lete I this noble duc to Atthenes ryde,   *leave*
     And al his hoost in armes hym bisyde.
875   And certes, if it nere to long to heere,   *certainly*
     I wolde have toold yow fully the manere
     How wonnen was the regne of Femenye
     By Theseus and by his chivalrye;   *knights*
     And of the grete bataille for the nones
880 Bitwixen Atthenes and Amazones;   *Athenians*
     And how asseged was Ypolita,   *besieged*
     The faire, hardy queene of Scithia;   *brave*
     And of the feste that was at hir weddynge,
     And of the tempest at hir hoom-comynge;
885 But al that thyng I moot as now forbere.
     I have, God woot, a large feeld to ere,   *knows; plough*
     And wayke been the oxen in my plough.   *weak*
     The remenant of the tale is long ynough.   *remainder*
     I wol nat letten eek noon of this route;
890 Lat every felawe telle his tale aboute,
     And lat se now who shal the soper wynne;   *let's*
     And ther I lefte, I wol ayeyn bigynne.
     This duc, of whom I make mencioun,
     Whan he was come almoost unto the toun,
895 In al his wele and in his mooste pride,   *success*
     He was war, as he caste his eye aside,   *aware*

879 And of the exceedingly great battle.
885 I must now forbear to mention.
889 Also I don't wish to delay anyone else in this company.
890 Let every one of my fellow pilgrims tell his tale in turn.
892 Where I left off, I will again begin.
894 *toun*, i.e. Athens.

Where that ther kneled in the heighe weye
A compaignye of ladyes, tweye and tweye,   *two by two*
Ech after oother, clad in clothes blake;
900 But swich a cry and swich a wo they make   *such; lament*
That in this world nys creature lyvynge   *is not*
That herde swich another waymentynge;   *lamentation*
And of this cry they nolde nevere stenten
Til they the reynes of his brydel henten.   *caught hold of*
905 'What folk been ye, that at myn homcomynge
Perturben so my feste with criynge?'   *festival*
Quod Theseus. 'Have ye so greet envye
Of myn honour, that thus compleyne and crye?
Or who hath yow mysboden or offended?   *insulted; injured*
910 And telleth me if it may been amended,   *put right*
And why that ye been clothed thus in blak.'
    The eldeste lady of hem alle spak,
Whan she hadde swowned with a deedly cheere,
That it was routhe for to seen and heere.   *a pity*
915 She seyde, 'Lord, to whom Fortune hath yiven
Victorie, and as a conqueror to lyven,
Nat greveth us youre glorie and youre honour,
But we biseken mercy and socour.   *beseech*
Have mercy on oure wo and oure distresse!
920 Som drope of pitee, thurgh thy gentillesse,   *nobleness*
Upon us wrecched wommen lat thou falle.
For, certes, lord, ther is noon of us alle,
That she ne hath been a duchesse or a queene.
Now be we caytyves, as it is wel seene,
925 Thanked be Fortune and hire false wheel,
That noon estaat assureth to be weel.
And certes, lord, to abyden youre presence,
Heere in this temple of the goddesse Clemence   *Clemency*
We han ben waitynge al this fourtenyght.   *watching*
930 Now help us, lord, sith it is in thy myght.
    I, wrecche, which that wepe and wayle thus,
Was whilom wyf to kyng Cappaneus,
That starf at Thebes—cursed be that day!—   *died*
And alle we that been in this array   *condition*
935 And maken al this lamentacioun,
We losten alle oure housbondes at that toun,

903 Nor would they stop their crying.
913 Swooned with a deathly look.
917 Your glory and honour do not grieve us.
924 Now we are wretched creatures, it is plain to see.
925-6 Thanks to Fortune and her treacherous wheel, that allows no
    prosperity to be permanent. (In medieval literature Fortune is
    commonly represented as a goddess turning a wheel, on which men
    rise to prosperity and afterwards fall to misery.)
930 Since it is in your power to do so.

Whil that the seege theraboute lay.
And yet now the olde Creon, weylaway!   *alas*
That lord is now of Thebes the citee,
940 Fulfild of ire and of iniquitee,   *filled with*
He, for despit and for his tirannye,
To do the dede bodyes vileynye
Of alle oure lordes whiche that been yslawe,
Hath alle the bodyes on an heep ydrawe,
945 And wol nat suffren hem, by noon assent,
Neither to been yburyed nor ybrent,   *burnt*
But maketh houndes ete hem in despit.'
And with that word, withouten moore respit   *delay*
They fillen gruf and criden pitously,
950 'Have on us wrecched wommen som mercy,
And lat oure sorwe synken in thyn herte.'
This gentil duc doun from his courser sterte   *noble; leapt*
With herte pitous, whan he herde hem speke.   *pitiful*
Hym thoughte that his herte wolde breke,   *it seemed to him*
955 Whan he saugh hem so pitous and so maat,   *pitiable; dejected*
That whilom weren of so greet estaat;
And in his armes he hem alle up hente,   *took*
And hem conforteth in ful good entente,
And swoor his ooth, as he was trewe knyght,
960 He wolde doon so ferforthly his myght   *all in his power*
Upon the tiraunt Creon hem to wreke,
That al the peple of Grece sholde speke
How Creon was of Thesus yserved
As he that hadde his deeth ful wel deserved.
965 And right anoon, withouten moore abood,   *delay*
His baner he desplayeth, and forth rood   *displays; rode*
To Thebes-ward, and al his hoost biside.
No neer Atthenes wolde he go ne ride,
Ne take his ese fully half a day,   *nor*
970 But onward on his wey that nyght he lay,
And sente anon Ypolita the queene,
And Emelye, hir yonge suster sheene,   *beautiful*
Unto the toun of Atthenes to dwelle,
And forth he rit; ther is namoore to telle.   *rides*
975   The rede statue of Mars, with spere and targe,
So shyneth in his white baner large,   *on*

941-4 He (i.e. Creon), moved by spite and tyranny to do outrage on
    the bodies of our slaughtered husbands, dragged them all into a heap.
945 And will on no account allow them.
949 They fell prostrate and cried piteously.
958 Comforts them with all good will.
963-4 Served by Theseus as one who had.
967 Towards Thebes, and all his host with him.
968 No nearer Athens would he march or ride.
970 But encamped that night on his way to Thebes.
975 The red image of Mars, with spear and shield.

That alle the feeldes glyteren up and doun;
And by his baner born is his penoun   *pennon*
Of gold ful riche, in which ther was ybete   *embroidered*
980 The Mynotaur, which that he wan in Crete.   *conquered*
Thus rit this duc, thus rit this conquerour,
And in his hoost of chivalrie the flour,
Til that he cam to Thebes and alighte
Faire in a feeld, ther as he thoughte to fighte.
985 But shortly for to speken of this thyng,
With Creon, which that was of Thebes kyng,
He faught, and slough hym manly as a knyght
In pleyn bataille, and putte the folk to flyght;
And by assaut he wan the citee after,   *assault*
990 And rente adoun bothe wall and sparre and   *tore; beam*
    rafter;
And to the ladyes he restored agayn
The bones of hir freendes that were slayn,   *husbands*
To doon obsequies, as was tho the gyse.   *then; custom*
But it were al to longe for to devyse   *describe*
995 The grete clamour and the waymentynge
That the ladyes made at the brennynge   *burning*
Of the bodies, and the grete honour
That Theseus, the noble conquerour,
Dooth to the ladyes, whan they from hym wente;
1000 But shortly for to telle is myn entente.
    Whan that this worthy duc, this Theseus,
Hath Creon slayn, and wonne Thebes thus,
Stille in that feeld he took al nyght his reste,
And dide with al the contree as hym leste.
1005 To ransake in the taas of bodyes dede,   *heap*
Hem for to strepe of harneys and of wede,
The pilours diden bisynesse and cure
After the bataille and disconfiture.   *rout*
And so bifel that in the taas they founde,
1010 Thurgh-girt with many a grevous blody   *pierced through*
    wounde,
Two yonge knyghtes liggynge by and by,
Bothe in oon armes, wroght ful richely,
Of whiche two Arcita highte that oon,
And that oother knyght highte Palamon.

977 The fields glitter on all sides (with the light reflected from the banner).
983-4 Alighted in splendour on a field, where he planned to fight.
987-8 Slew him manfully, as a knight should, in open fight.
1004 And did what he liked with all the country.
1006-7 To strip them of their armour and clothing, the pillagers worked busily.
1011-12 Lying side by side, both bearing the same heraldic device most richly emblazoned.
1013 One of which two knights was called Arcita.

1015 Nat fully quyke, ne fully dede they were,   *alive*
     But by hir cote-armures and by hir gere
     The heraudes knewe hem best in special
     As they that weren of the blood roial
     Of Thebes, and of sustren two yborn.
1020 Out of the taas the pilours han hem torn,
     And han hem caried softe unto the tente   *gently*
     Of Theseus; and he ful soone hem sente
     To Atthenes, to dwellen in prisoun
     Perpetuelly,—he nolde no raunsoun.
1025 And whan this worthy duc hath thys ydon,
     He took his hoost, and hoom he rit anon
     With laurer crowned as a conquerour;
     And ther he lyveth in joye and in honour
     Terme of his lyf; what nedeth wordes mo?   *more*
1030 And in a tour, in angwissh and in wo,
     This Palamon and his felawe Arcite   *comrade*
     For everemoore; ther may no gold hem quite.   *ransom*
       This passeth yeer by yeer and day by day,
     Till it fil ones, in a morwe of May,
1035 That Emelye, that fairer was to sene   *behold*
     Than is the lylie upon his stalke grene,   *its*
     And fressher than the May with floures newe—
     For with the rose colour stroof hire hewe,
     I noot which was the fyner of hem two—   *do not know*
1040 Er it were day, as was hir wone to do,   *wont*
     She was arisen and al redy dight;   *dressed*
     For May wole have no slogardie a-nyght.
     The sesoun priketh every gentil herte,   *incites; noble*
     And maketh it out of his slep to sterte,
1045 And seith 'Arys, and do thyn observaunce.'
     This maked Emelye have remembraunce
     To doon honour to May, and for to ryse.
     Yclothed was she fressh, for to devyse;
     Hir yelow heer was broyded in a tresse
1050 Bihynde hir bak, a yerde long, I gesse.
     And in the gardyn, at the sonne upriste,   *sun's uprising*
     She walketh up and doun, and as hire liste   *she pleased*
     She gadereth floures, party white and rede,   *mixed*
     To make a subtil gerland for hire hede;   *intricate*

1016 A *cote-armure* was a sleeveless coat embroidered with a heraldic
     device and worn over the armour.
1024 He would not accept any ransom.
1034 Till once it happened, on a May morning.
1038 For her complexion vied in colour with the rose.
1042 May will have no slothfulness at night.
1045 Do homage. (May Day ceremonies were observed by all classes
     of people in the Middle Ages.)
1048 Now to describe her: she was brightly clad.

1055 And as an aungel hevenysshly she soong.   *divinely*
  The grete tour, that was so thikke and stroong,
  Which of the castel was the chief dongeoun,
  (Ther as the knyghtes weren in prisoun   *where*
  Of which I tolde yow and tellen shal)   *whom*
1060 Was evene joynant to the gardyn wal   *close-adjoining*
  Ther as this Emelye hadde hir pleyynge.   *amused herself*
  Bright was the sonne and cleer that morwenynge,
  And Palamoun, this woful prisoner,
  As was his wone, by leve of his gayler,   *jailer*
1065 Was risen and romed in a chambre an heigh,
  In which he al the noble citee seigh,   *saw*
  And eek the gardyn, ful of braunches grene,
  Ther as this fresshe Emelye the shene
  Was in hire walk, and romed up and doun.   *wandered*
1070 This sorweful prisoner, this Palamoun,
  Goth in the chambre romynge to and fro,
  And to hymself compleynynge of his wo.
  That he was born, ful ofte he seyde, 'allas!'
  And so bifel, by aventure or cas,   *luck; chance*
1075 That thurgh a wyndow, thikke of many a barre   *full of bars*
  Of iren greet and square as any sparre,   *beam*
  He cast his eye upon Emelya,
  And therwithal he bleynte and cride, 'A!'   *turned pale*
  As though he stongen were unto the herte.   *pierced*
1080 And with that cry Arcite anon up sterte,
  And seyde, 'Cosyn myn, what eyleth thee,   *ails*
  That art so pale and deedly on to see?   *deathly to behold*
  Why cridestow? Who hath thee doon offence?   *injury*
  For Goddes love, taak al in pacience
1085 Oure prisoun, for it may noon oother be,   *cannot be otherwise*
  Fortune hath yeven us this adversitee.
  Som wikke aspect or disposicioun
  Of Saturne, by som constellacioun,
  Hath yeven us this, although we hadde it sworn;
1090 So stood the hevene whan that we were born.
  We moste endure it; this is the short and playn.'
   This Palamon answerde and seyde agayn:
  'Cosyn, for sothe, of this opinioun
  Thow hast a veyn ymaginacioun.
1095 This prison caused me nat for to crye,
  But I was hurt right now thurghout myn ye   *through; eye*

1065 Had risen, and was pacing about in a room on high.
1087-9 Some evil position of Saturn in relation to the other heavenly
  bodies has brought us to this, although we had sworn the contrary.
  (For Saturn as a planet of malign influence see 2453 ff.).
1091 We must endure it; this is the long and short of it.
1093-4 In truth, this opinion of yours is an idle fancy.

Into myn herte, that wol my bane be.   *death*
The fairnesse of that lady that I see
Yond in the gardyn romen to and fro   *yonder; wandering*
1100 Is cause of al my criyng and my wo.
I noot wher she be womman or goddesse,   *whether*
But Venus is it soothly, as I gesse.'   *truly*
And therwithal on knees doun he fil,
And seyde: 'Venus, if it be thy wil
1105 Yow in this gardyn thus to transfigure
Bifore me, sorweful, wrecched creature,
Out of this prisoun help that we may scapen.   *escape*
And if so be my destynee be shapen
By eterne word to dyen in prisoun,
1110 Of oure lynage have som compassioun,   *lineage*
That is so lowe ybroght by tirannye.'
And with that word Arcite gan espye   *saw*
Wher as this lady romed to and fro,   *where*
And with that sighte hir beautee hurte hym so,
1115 That, if that Palamon was wounded sore,
Arcite is hurt as muche as he, or moore.
And with a sigh he seyde pitously:
'The fresshe beautee sleeth me sodeynly
Of hire that rometh in the yonder place,
1120 And but I have hir mercy and hir grace,   *unless*
That I may seen hire atte leeste weye,
I nam but deed; ther nis namoore to seye.'
     This Palamon, whan he tho wordes herde,   *those*
Dispitously he looked and answerde,   *angrily*
1125 'Wheither seistow this in ernest or in pley?'
     'Nay,' quod Arcite, 'in ernest, by my fey!   *faith*
God helpe me so, me list ful yvele pleye.'
     This Palamon gan knytte his browes tweye.   *knitted; two*
'It nere,' quod he, 'to thee no greet honour   *would not be*
1130 For to be fals, ne for to be traitour
To me, that am thy cosyn and thy brother
Ysworn ful depe, and ech of us til oother,
That nevere, for to dyen in the peyne,
Til that the deeth departe shal us tweyne,   *part*
1135 Neither of us in love to hyndre oother,
Ne in noon oother cas, my leeve brother;

1105 In this garden thus to transfigure yourself.
1108-9 And if my destiny, as determined by eternal ordinance, is to die
     in prison.
1121-2 That I may at least see her, I shall surely die.
1125 Do you say this seriously or jokingly?
1127 I am in no mood for joking.
1132 Deeply sworn, and each of us pledged to the other.
1133 Though we should die by torture for it.
1135-6 Should either of us cross the other in love, or in any other matter,
     my dear brother.

But that thou sholdest trewely forthren me   *help*
In every cas, as I shal forthren thee,—
This was thyn ooth, and myn also, certeyn;
1140 I woot right wel, thou darst it nat withseyn.
Thus artow of my conseil, out of doute,
And now thow woldest falsly been aboute
To love my lady, whom I love and serve,
And evere shal til that myn herte sterve.   *die*
1145 Nay, certes, false Arcite, thow shalt nat so!
I loved hire first, and tolde thee my wo
As to my conseil and my brother sworn   *confidant*
To forthre me, as I have toold biforn.
For which thou art ybounden as a knyght
1150 To helpen me, if it lay in thy myght,
Or elles artow fals, I dar wel seyn.'
    This Arcite ful proudly spak ageyn:
'Thow shalt,' quod he, 'be rather fals than I;   *sooner*
And thou art fals, I telle thee outrely,   *plainly*
1155 For paramour I loved hire first er thow.
What wiltow seyen? Thou woost nat yet now   *know*
Wheither she be a womman or goddesse!
Thyn is affeccioun of hoolynesse,   *a holy kind*
And myn is love, as to a creature;
1160 For which I tolde thee myn aventure
As to my cosyn and my brother sworn.
I pose that thow lovedest hire biforn;
Wostow nat wel the olde clerkes sawe,   *author's words*
That 'who shal yeve a lovere any lawe?'   *give*
1165 Love is a gretter lawe, by my pan,   *head*
Than may be yeve to any erthely man;   *given*
And therfore positif lawe and swich decree
Is broken al day for love in ech degree.
A man moot nedes love, maugree his heed.
1170 He may nat fleen it, thogh he sholde be deed,
Al be she mayde, or wydwe, or elles wyf.   *whether she be*
And eek it is nat likly al thy lyf
To stonden in hir grace; namoore shal I;
For wel thou woost thyselven, verraily,   *know; truly*
1175 That thou and I be dampned to prisoun
Perpetuelly; us gayneth no raunsoun.   *helps*

1140 I know very well you dare not deny it.
1141 You enjoy my confidence, without doubt.
1142-3 You would falsely set about loving.
1155 I loved her as a woman before you did.
1162 I grant for the sake of argument that you were the first to love her.
1167 *positif lawe*, law of decree, as distinct from natural law.
1168 Is continually being broken for love in every walk of life.
1169 A man must love, in spite of himself.
1170 He cannot escape it, though he should die (for it).
1172-3 And further, you are not likely to enjoy her favour all your life.

We stryve as dide the houndes for the boon;   *bone*
They foughte al day, and yet hir part was noon.   *share*
Ther cam a kyte, whil that they were so wrothe,
1180 And baar awey the boon bitwixe hem bothe. *carried; between*
And therfore, at the kynges court, my brother,
Ech man for hymself, ther is noon oother.   *no other* (way)
Love, if thee list, for I love and ay shal;   *you like*
And soothly, leeve brother, this is al.
1185 Heere in this prisoun moote we endure,
And everich of us take his aventure.'   *each; chance*
     Greet was the strif and long bitwix hem tweye,   *strife*
If that I hadde leyser for to seye,
But to th'effect. It happed on a day,
1190 To telle it yow as shortly as I may,
A worthy duc that highte Perotheus,   *was called*
That felawe was unto duc Theseus   *friend*
Syn thilke day that they were children lite,
Was come to Atthenes his felawe to visite,
1195 And for to pleye as he was wont to do;   *enjoy himself*
For in this world he loved no man so,
And he loved hym als tendrely agayn.
So wel they lovede, as olde bookes sayn,
That whan that oon was deed, soothly to telle,
1200 His felawe wente and soughte hym doun in helle,—
But of that storie list me nat to write.   *I do not wish*
Duc Perotheus loved wel Arcite,
And hadde hym knowe at Thebes yeer by yere,
And finally at requeste and preyere
1205 Of Perotheus, withouten any raunsoun,
Duc Theseus hym leet out of prisoun
Frely to goon wher that hym liste over al,
In swich a gyse as I you tellen shal.
     This was the forward, pleynly for t'endite, *agreement; tell*
1210 Bitwixen Theseus and hym Arcite:
That if so were that Arcite were yfounde
Evere in his lif, by day or nyght, oo stounde   *a single hour*
In any contree of this Theseus,
And he were caught, it was acorded thus,
1215 That with a swerd he sholde lese his heed.   *lose*
Ther nas noon oother remedie ne reed;
But taketh his leve, and homward he him spedde.
Lat hym be war ! his nekke lith to wedde.   *lies in pawn*

1189 But to the point. It happened one day.
1193 Since the day they were little children together.
1197 Just as tenderly in return.
1207 To go freely anywhere he liked.
1208 But on one condition, which I shall tell you.
1216 Nothing more could be done for him.
1217 (Arcite) took his leave, and hurried home.

How greet a sorwe suffreth now Arcite!
1220 The deeth he feeleth thurgh his herte smyte;
He wepeth, wayleth, crieth pitously;
To sleen hymself he waiteth prively.
He seyde, 'Allas that day that I was born!
Now is my prisoun worse than biforn;   *before*
1225 Now is me shape eternally to dwelle,   *am I destined*
Noght in purgatorie, but in helle.
Allas, that evere knew I Perotheus!
For elles hadde I dwelled with Theseus,
Yfetered in his prisoun everemo.
1230 Thanne hadde I been in blisse, and nat in wo.
Oonly the sighte of hire whom that I serve,
Though that I nevere hir grace may deserve,
Wolde han suffised right ynough for me.
O deere cosyn Palamon,' quod he,
1235 'Thyn is the victorie of this aventure.   *turn of fortune*
Ful blisfully in prison maistow dure,—   *you may stay*
In prison? certes nay, but in paradys!
Wel hath Fortune yturned thee the dys, —
That hast the sighte of hire, and I th'absence.
1240 For possible is, syn thou hast hire presence,   *since*
And art a knyght, a worthy and an able,
That by som cas, syn Fortune is chaungeable, —
Thow maist to thy desir somtyme atteyne.
But I, that am exiled and bareyne   *devoid*
1245 Of alle grace, and in so greet dispeir,
That ther nys erthe, water, fir, ne eir,
Ne creature that of hem maked is,
That may me helpe or doon confort in this,
Wel oughte I sterve in wanhope and distresse.
1250 Farwel my lif, my lust, and my gladnesse!   *joy*
Allas, why pleynen folk so in commune
On purveiaunce of God, or of Fortune,
That yeveth hem ful ofte in many a gyse   *gives; guise*
Wel bettre than they kan hemself devyse?
1255 Som man desireth for to han richesse,
That cause is of his mordre or greet siknesse;
And som man wolde out of his prisoun fayn,
That in his hous is of his meynee slayn.   *servants*

1222 He watches secretly for a chance to kill himself.
1231 The mere sight of her whom I serve (as a lover).
1238 Fortune has turned up the dice well for you.
1247 Nor creature that is made of them. (Cf. 420.)
1249 I have good reason to die of despair.
1251-2 Why do people so commonly complain of God's providence.
1254 Something far better than they can devise for themselves.
1255 One man desires to have wealth.
1257 Another man would gladly get out of prison.

Infinite harmes been in this mateere.

1260 We witen nat what thing we preyen heere: *know; pray for*
We faren as he that dronke is as a mous.
A dronke man woot wel he hath an hous,   *drunken; knows*
But he noot which the righte wey is thider,   *knows not*
And to a dronke man the wey is slider.   *slippery*

1265 And certes, in this world so faren we;
We seken faste after felicitee,   *eagerly*
But we goon wrong ful often, trewely.
Thus may we seyen alle, and namely I,   *say; especially*
That wende and hadde a greet opinioun

1270 That if I myghte escapen from prisoun,
Thanne hadde I been in joye and perfit heele,   *health*
Ther now I am exiled from my wele.
Syn that I may nat seen you, Emelye,
I nam but deed; ther nys no remedye.'

1275   Upon that oother syde Palamon,   *on the other hand*
Whan that he wiste Arcite was agon,   *knew; gone*
Swich sorwe he maketh that the grete tour
Resouneth of his youlyng and clamour.   *wailing*
The pure fettres on his shynes grete

1280 Weren of his bittre, salte teeres wete.
'Allas,' quod he, 'Arcita, cosyn myn,
Of al oure strif, God woot, the fruyt is thyn.   *benefit*
Thow walkest now in Thebes at thy large,   *at large*
And of my wo thow yevest litel charge.

1285 Thou mayst, syn thou hast wisdom and manhede,   *manliness*
Assemblen alle the folk of oure kynrede,   *kindred*
And make a werre so sharp on this citee,   *fierce*
That by som aventure or som tretee   *chance; treaty*
Thow mayst have hire to lady and to wyf

1290 For whom that I moste nedes lese my lyf.   *lose*
For, as by wey of possibilitee,   *it is possible*
Sith thou art at thy large, of prisoun free,
And art a lord, greet is thyn avauntage
Moore than is myn, that sterve here in a cage.   *die*

1295 For I moot wepe and wayle, whil I lyve,   *must*
With al the wo that prison may me yive,
And eek with peyne that love me yeveth also,
That doubleth al my torment and my wo.'
Therwith the fyr of jalousie up sterte   *leapt*

1300 Withinne his brest, and hente him by the herte   *seized*
So woodly that he lyk was to biholde   *madly*
The boxtree or the asshen dede and colde.   *ashes*

1261 We behave like someone as drunk as a mouse.
1269 Who imagined and arrogantly believed.
1272 Whereas now I am exiled from my happiness.
1279–80 The very fetters on his shins were heavy with his . . . tears.
1284 You give little thought to my sorrow.

Thanne seyde he, 'O crueel goddes that governe
This world with byndyng of youre word eterne,
1305 And writen in the table of atthamaunt   *adamant*
Youre parlement and youre eterne graunt,   *decree award*
What is mankynde moore unto you holde
Than is the sheep that rouketh in the folde?   *huddles*
For slayn is man right as another beest,
1310 And dwelleth eek in prison and arreest,
And hath siknesse and greet adversitee,
And ofte tymes giltelees, pardee.
   What governance is in this prescience,
That giltelees tormenteth innocence?
1315 And yet encresseth this al my penaunce,
That man is bounden to his observaunce,
For Goddes sake, to letten of his wille,
Ther as a beest may al his lust fulfille.   *desire*
And whan a beest is deed he hath no peyne;
1320 But man after his deeth moot wepe and pleyne,   *wail*
Though in this world he have care and wo;
Withouten doute it may stonden so.
The answere of this lete I to dyvynys,   *leave; divines*
But wel I woot that in this world greet pyne ys.   *suffering*
1325 Allas, I se a serpent or a theef,   *criminal*
That many a trewe man hath doon mescheef,   *harm*
Goon at his large, and where hym list may turne.
But I moot been in prisoun thurgh Saturne,
And eek thurgh Juno, jalous and eek wood,   *mad*
1330 That hath destroyed wel ny al the blood
Of Thebes with his waste walles wyde;
And Venus sleeth me on that oother syde   *slays*
For jalousie and fere of hym Arcite.'   *fear of Arcite*
   Now wol I stynte of Palamon a lite,
1335 And lete hym in his prisoun stille dwelle,   *leave*
And of Arcita forth I wol yow telle.
   The somer passeth, and the nyghtes longe
Encressen double wise and peynes stronge   *doubly*
Bothe of the lovere and the prisoner.
1340 I noot which hath the wofuller mester.
For, shortly for to seyn, this Palamoun
Perpetuelly is dampned to prisoun,

1307 How is mankind of greater concern to you.
1313–14 What controlling mind is there in such prescience, that tor-
    ments guiltless innocence?
1315–17 And my penance is still more increased by this—that man is
    duty-bound, for God's sake, to curb his will.
1327 Remain at large, and go where he will.
1331 With its wide walls laid waste.
1334 I will say no more about Palamon for a while.
1336 I will go on and tell you about Arcita.
1340 I don't know which is in the sadder plight.

In cheynes and in fettres to been deed;   *die*
And Arcite is exiled upon his heed
1345 For everemo, as out of that contree,
Ne nevere mo ne shal his lady see.
    Yow loveres axe I now this questioun,
Who hath the worse, Arcite or Palamoun?
That oon may seen his lady day by day,   *the one*
1350 But in prison he moot dwelle alway;   *for ever*
That oother wher hym list may ride or go,   *he pleases*
But seen his lady shal he nevere mo.
Now demeth as yow liste, ye that kan,
For I wol telle forth as I bigan.

EXPLICIT PRIMA PARS

SEQUITUR PARS SECUNDA

1355   Whan that Arcite to Thebes comen was,
Ful ofte a day he swelte and seyde 'Allas!'   *swooned*
For seen his lady shal he nevere mo.
And shortly to concluden al his wo,
So muche sorwe hadde nevere creature
1360 That is, or shal, whil that the world may dure.   *last*
His slep, his mete, his drynke, is hym biraft,
That lene he wex and drye as is a shaft;
His eyen holwe, and grisly to biholde,   *hollow; awful*
His hewe falow and pale as asshen colde,   *colour; sallow*
1365 And solitarie he was and evere allone,
And waillynge al the nyght, makynge his mone;   *lament*
And if he herde song or instrument,
Thanne wolde he wepe, he myghte nat be stent.   *stopped*
So feble eek were his spiritz, and so lowe,
1370 And chaunged so, that no man koude knowe
His speche nor his voys, though men it herde.
And in his geere for al the world he ferde,
Nat oonly lik the loveris maladye
Of Hereos, but rather lyk manye,
1375 Engendred of humour malencolik,
Biforen, in his celle fantastik.

1344 On pain of losing his head.
1353 Judge as you think fit.
1358 And briefly to give you the sum of his misery.
1361-2 He was robbed of all desire for sleep or food and drink, so that
he grew as thin and dry as an arrow-shaft.
1372-6 And with his changes of mood he behaved for all the world
like someone afflicted not merely with the lover's malady of Eros,
but rather with a mania engendered by the melancholic humour in
the front of his brain, in the cell where fancy dwells.

And shortly, turned was al up so doun   *upside*
Bothe habit and eek disposicioun
Of hym, this woful lovere daun Arcite.   *lord*
1380   What sholde I al day of his wo endite?
Whan he endured hadde a yeer or two
This crueel torment and this peyne and wo,
At Thebes, in his contree, as I seyde,
Upon a nyght in sleep as he hym leyde,
1385 Hym thoughte how that the wynged god   *it seemed to him*
     Mercurie
Biforn hym stood and bad hym to be murie.
His slepy yerde in hond he bar uprighte;
An hat he werede upon his heris brighte.   *wore; hair*
Arrayed was this god, as he took keep,
1390 As he was whan that Argus took his sleep;
And seyde hym thus: 'To Atthenes shaltou wende,   *go*
Ther is thee shapen of thy wo an ende.'   *destined*
And with that word Arcite wook and sterte.   *woke with a start*
'Now trewely, hou soore that me smerte,'
1395 Quod he, 'to Atthenes right now wol I fare,
Ne for the drede of deeth shal I nat spare
To se my lady, that I love and serve.
In hire presence I recche nat to sterve.'
    And with that word he caughte a greet mirour,   *took hold of*
1400 And saugh that chaunged was al his colour,
And saugh his visage al in another kynde.
And right anon it ran hym in his mynde,
That, sith his face was so disfigured
Of maladye the which he hadde endured,
1405 He myghte wel, if that he bar hym lowe,
Lyve in Atthenes everemoore unknowe,
And seen his lady wel ny day by day.
And right anon he chaunged his array,   *clothes*
And cladde hym as a povre laborer,
1410 And al allone, save oonly a squier
That knew his privetee and al his cas,   *private affairs*
Which was disgised povrely as he was,
To Atthenes is he goon the nexte way.
And to the court he wente upon a day,

1380 Why should I keep on telling of his misery?
1384 One night as he lay asleep.
1387 He carried his wand of sleep upright in his hand.
1389 As he (Arcite) noticed.
1394 However much I suffer for it.
1396–7 Nor shall fear of death prevent me from seeing my lady.
1398 I don't care if I die.
1401 And saw that his face was quite altered.
1402 Immediately it occurred to him.
1405 If he was humble in his bearing.
1413 He took the shortest way to Athens.

1415	And at the gate he profreth his servyse	*offers*
	To drugge and drawe, what so men wol devyse.	
	And shortly of this matere for to seyn,	
	He fil in office with a chamberleyn	*got employment*
	The which that dwellynge was with Emelye;	*who was*
1420	For he was wys and koude soone espye	
	Of every servaunt which that serveth here.	
	Wel koude he hewen wode, and water bere,	
	For he was yong and myghty for the nones,	*very strong*
	And therto he was long and big of bones	
1425	To doon that any wight kan hym devyse.	
	A yeer or two he was in this servyse,	
	Page of the chambre of Emelye the brighte;	
	And Philostrate he seyde that he highte.	*was called*
	But half so wel biloved a man as he	
1430	Ne was ther nevere in court of his degree;	
	He was so gentil of condicioun	*noble; nature*
	That thurghout al the court was his renoun.	
	They seyden that it were a charitee	*would be*
	That Theseus wolde enhauncen his degree,	
1435	And putten hym in worshipful servyse,	*honourable*
	Ther as he myghte his vertu excercise.	*where; virtues*
	And thus withinne a while his name is spronge,	
	Bothe of his dedes and his goode tonge,	
	That Theseus hath taken hym so neer,	
1440	That of his chambre he made hym a squier,	
	And gaf hym gold to mayntene his degree.	
	And eek men broghte hym out of his contree,	
	From yeer to yeer, ful pryvely his rente;	*secretly; revenue*
	But honestly and slyly he it spente,	
1445	That no man wondred how that he it hadde.	
	And thre yeer in this wise his lif he ladde,	
	And bar hym so, in pees and eek in werre,	*conducted himself*
	Ther was no man that Theseus hath derre.	*holds more dearly*
	And in this blisse lete I now Arcite,	*leave*
1450	And speke I wole of Palamon a lite.	*little*
	In derknesse and horrible and strong prisoun	
	Thise seven yeer hath seten Palamoun	*dwelt*
	Forpyned, what for wo and for distresse.	*in torment*
	Who feeleth double soor and hevynesse	*pain; sorrow*
1455	But Palamon, that love destreyneth so	*afflicts*

1416 To drudge and carry, or do anything he was told.
1420–1 For he (the chamberlain) was an astute man who kept a sharp eye on everyone who served her.
1425 To do what anyone told him to do.
1437–40 In a short time he became so famous both for his deeds and courteous speech that Theseus gave him a position close to himself as a squire of his chamber.
1444 Suitably (i.e. in accordance with his modest rank) and prudently.

That wood out of his wit he goth for wo?
And eek therto he is a prisoner
Perpetuelly, noght oonly for a yer.
   Who koude ryme in Englyssh proprely   *fitly*
1460 His martirdom? for sothe it am nat I;
Therfore I passe as lightly as I may.   *quickly*
   It fel that in the seventhe yer, of May
The thridde nyght, (as olde bookes seyn,
That al this storie tellen moore pleyn)   *fully*
1465 Were it by aventure or destynee—   *chance*
As, whan a thyng is shapen, it shal be—
That soone after the mydnyght Palamoun,
By helpyng of a freend, brak his prisoun
And fleeth the citee faste as he may go.
1470 For he hadde yeve his gayler drynke so
Of a clarree maad of a certeyn wyn,
With nercotikes and opie of Thebes fyn,
That al that nyght, thogh that men wolde him shake,
The gayler sleep, he myghte nat awake;   *slept*
1475 And thus he fleeth as faste as evere he may.
The nyght was short and faste by the day,   *near to*
That nedes cost he moot hymselven hyde;
And til a grove faste ther bisyde
With dredeful foot thanne stalketh Palamon.
1480 For, shortly, this was his opinion,
That in that grove he wolde hym hyde al day,
And in the nyght thanne wolde he take his way
To Thebes-ward, his freendes for to preye   *towards Thebes*
On Theseus to helpe him to werreye;   *make war*
1485 And shortly, outher he wolde lese his lif,
Or wynnen Emelye unto his wyf.
This is th'effect and his entente pleyn.
   Now wol I turne to Arcite ageyn,
That litel wiste how ny that was his care,
1490 Til that Fortune had broght him in the snare.
   The bisy larke, messager of day,   *messenger*
Salueth in hir song the morwe gray,   *salutes; morning*
And firy Phebus riseth up so bright
That al the orient laugheth of the light,   *with*
1495 And with his stremes dryeth in the greves   *beams; thickets*
The silver dropes hangynge on the leves.

1456 That his misery nearly drives him mad.
1466 For, when a thing is fated, it has to be.
1470–1 He had given his jailer so much to drink of a sweet liquor.
1472 Fine opiate of Thebes.
1477 That of necessity he must hide himself.
1478–9 To a grove that grew close by Palamon then stole with fearful tread.
1485 He was determined either to lose his life.
1487 This, in effect, was his plain intention.
1489 Who little knew how near he was to trouble.

And Arcita, that in the court roial
With Theseus is squier principal,
Is risen and looketh on the myrie day.   *pleasant*
1500 And for to doon his observaunce to May.
Remembrynge on the poynt of his desir,   *object*
He on a courser, startlynge as the fir,
Is riden into the feeldes hym to pleye,   *to amuse himself*
Out of the court, were it a myle or tweye.   *about a mile or two*
1505 And to the grove of which that I yow tolde
By aventure his wey he gan to holde,
To maken hym a gerland of the greves,   *sprays*
Were it of wodebynde or hawethorn leves,
And loude he song ayeyn the sonne shene:
1510 'May, with alle thy floures and thy grene,
Welcome be thou, faire, fresshe May,
In hope that I som grene gete may.'   *greenery*
And from his courser, with a lusty herte,   *joyful*
Into the grove ful hastily he sterte,   *sprang*
1515 And in a path he rometh up and doun,
Ther as by aventure this Palamoun
Was in a bussh, that no man myghte hym se,
For soore afered of his deeth was he.   *afraid*
No thyng ne knew he that it was Arcite:
1520 God woot he wolde have trowed it ful lite.
But sooth is seyd, go sithen many yeres,
That 'feeld hath eyen and the wode hath eres.'
It is ful fair a man to bere hym evene,
For al day meeteth men at unset stevene.
1525 Ful litel woot Arcite of his felawe,
That was so ny to herknen al his sawe,
For in the bussh he sitteth now ful stille.
      Whan that Arcite hadde romed al his fille,
And songen al the roundel lustily,
1530 Into a studie he fil sodeynly,   *reverie*
As doon thise loveres in hir queynte geres,
Now in the crope, now doun in the beres,
Now up, now doun, as boket in a welle.
Right as the Friday, soothly for to telle,

1502 On a swift steed, shying like a (flickering) flame.
1506 By chance he made his way.
1508 Either of woodbine or hawthorn leaves.
1509 Loudly he sang to greet the bright sun.
1519 He had no idea it was Arcite.
1520 God knows he would have thought it possible.
1521 But it has long been truly said.
1523-4 i.e. it is good for a man to be constantly prepared for the
  unexpected meeting, which may come at any time.
1526 Who was near enough to hear all he said.
1531 As lovers do in their strange caprices.
1532 Now on the heights, now down among the briars.

1535 Now it shyneth, now it reyneth faste,   *hard*
     Right so kan geery Venus overcaste   *changeful*
     The hertes of hir folk; right as hir day
     Is gereful, right so chaungeth she array.   *changeable*
     Selde is the Friday al the wowke ylike.
1540   Whan that Arcite had songe, he gan to sike,   *sigh*
     And sette hym doun withouten any moore.
     'Allas,' quod he, 'that day that I was bore!   *born*
     How longe, Juno, thurgh thy crueltee,
     Woltow werreyen Thebes the citee?   *make war on*
1545 Allas, ybroght is to confusioun
     The blood roial of Cadme and Amphioun,—
     Of Cadmus, which that was the firste man
     That Thebes bulte, or first the toun bigan,   *built*
     And of the citee first was crouned kyng.
1550 Of his lynage am I and his ofspryng   *lineage*
     By verray ligne, as of the stok roial,
     And now I am so caytyf and so thral,   *wretched; servile*
     That he that is my mortal enemy,
     I serve hym as his squier povrely.   *poorly*
1555 And yet dooth Juno me wel moore shame,   *much*
     For I dar noght biknowe myn owene name;   *confess*
     But ther as I was wont to highte Arcite,   *be called*
     Now highte I Philostrate, noght worth a myte.
     Allas, thou felle Mars! allas, Juno!   *cruel*
1560 Thus hath youre ire oure lynage al fordo,   *destroyed*
     Save oonly me and wrecched Palamoun,
     That Theseus martireth in prisoun.
     And over al this, to sleen me outrely,   *slay; utterly*
     Love hath his firy dart so brennyngly   *burningly*
1565 Ystiked thurgh my trewe, careful herte,   *thrust; sorrowful*
     That shapen was my deeth erst than my sherte.
     Ye sleen me with youre eyen, Emelye!   *kill*
     Ye been the cause wherfore that I dye.
     Of al the remenant of myn oother care
1570 Ne sette I nat the montance of a tare,
     So that I koude doon aught to youre plesaunce.'
     And with that word he fil doun in a traunce
     A longe tyme, and after he up sterte.
        This Palamoun, that thoughte that thurgh his herte

1539 Seldom is Friday like the rest of the week. (A proverbial saying.)
1541 And straightway sat down.
1551 Descended in true line from royal stock.
1566 (So) that my death was fashioned before my shirt, i.e. the manner
     of his death was fixed by destiny even before his first garment was
     made for him.
1569–71 All the rest of my misery I'd count as nothing (lit. as worth no
     more than a weed), if I could do anything to please you.
1573 And then he rose up suddenly.

1575 He felt a coold swerd sodeynliche glyde,   *sword; suddenly*
     For ire he quook, no lenger wolde he byde.
     And whan that he had herd Arcites tale,
     As he were wood, with face deed and pale,
     He stirte hym up out of the buskes thikke,   *jumped; bushes*
1580 And seide: 'Arcite, false traytour wikke,   *wicked*
     Now artow hent, that lovest my lady so,   *caught*
     For whom that I have al this peyne and wo,
     And art my blood, and to my conseil sworn,
     As I ful ofte have told thee heerbiforn,   *before now*
1585 And hast byjaped heere duc Theseus,   *tricked*
     And falsly chaunged hast thy name thus!
     I wol be deed, or elles thou shalt dye.   *will die*
     Thou shalt nat love my lady Emelye,
     But I wol love hire oonly and namo;   *no other*
1590 For I am Palamon, thy mortal foo.
     And though that I no wepene have in this place,
     But out of prison am astert by grace,   *escaped*
     I drede noght that outher thow shalt dye,   *doubt; either*
     Or thow ne shalt nat loven Emelye.
1595 Chees which thou wolt, or thou shalt nat asterte!'
       This Arcite, with ful despitous herte,   *angry*
     Whan he hym knew, and hadde his tale herd,
     As fiers as leon pulled out his swerd.
     And seyde thus: 'By God that sit above,   *dwells*
1600 Nere it that thou art sik and wood for love,
     And eek that thow no wepne hast in this place,
     Thou sholdest nevere out of this grove pace,   *go*
     That thou ne sholdest dyen of myn hond.
     For I defye the seurete and the bond   *renounce; surety*
1605 Which that thou seist that I have maad to thee.
     What, verray fool, thynk wel that love is free,
     And I wol love hire maugree al thy myght!
     But for as muche thou art a worthy knyght,
     And wilnest to darreyne hire by bataille,
1610 Have heer my trouthe, tomorwe I wol nat faille,
     Withoute wityng of any oother wight,
     That heere I wol be founden as a knyght,
     And bryngen harneys right ynough for thee;   *armour*
     And ches the beste, and leef the worste for me.   *choose; leave*

1576 He trembled with anger, and would not stay hidden any longer.
1578 As if he were mad, i.e. like a madman.
1583 My kinsman and sworn confidant.
1603 But should die by my hand.
1606 Fool that you are, remember love is free.
1607 In spite of all you can do.
1609 And wish to decide your right to her by battle.
1610 You have my word of honour that to-morrow.
1611 Without anyone else knowing.

1615 And mete and drynke this nyght wol I brynge   *food*
     Ynough for thee, and clothes for thy beddynge.
     And if so be that thou my lady wynne,
     And sle me in this wode ther I am inne,
     Thow mayst wel have thy lady as for me.'
1620   This Palamon answerde, 'I graunte it thee.'
     And thus they been departed til amorwe,
     Whan ech of hem had leyd his feith to borwe.
     O Cupide, out of alle charitee!
     O regne, that wolt no felawe have with thee!   *ruler; partner*
1625 Ful sooth is seyd that love ne lordshipe   *truly it is said*
     Wol noght, his thankes, have no felaweshipe.
     Wel fynden that Arcite and Palamoun.
     Arcite is riden anon unto the toun,
     And on the morwe, er it were dayes light,
1630 Ful prively two harneys hath he dight,   *prepared*
     Bothe suffisaunt and mete to darreyne   *suitable; settle*
     The bataille in the feeld bitwix hem tweyne;   *between*
     And on his hors, allone as he was born,
     He carieth al the harneys hym biforn.
1635 And in the grove, at tyme and place yset,
     This Arcite and this Palamon ben met.
     To chaungen gan the colour in hir face;
     Right as the hunters in the regne of Trace,   *realm*
     That stondeth at the gappe with a spere,   *gap*
1640 Whan hunted is the leon or the bere,   *bear*
     And hereth hym come russhyng in the greves,
     And breketh bothe bowes and the leves,   *boughs*
     And thynketh, 'Heere cometh my mortal enemy!
     Withoute faille, he moot be deed, or I;   *must die*
1645 For outher I moot sleen hym at the gappe,
     Or he moot sleen me, if that me myshappe,'—   *I am unfortunate*
     So ferden they in chaungyng of hir hewe,
     As fer as everich of hem oother knewe.
        Ther nas no good day, ne no saluyng,   *greeting*
1650 But streight, withouten word or rehersyng,   *parley*
     Everich of hem heelp for to armen oother
     As freendly as he were his owene brother;
     And after that, with sharpe speres stronge
     They foynen ech at oother wonder longe.   *thrust; amazingly*
1655 Thou myghtest wene that this Palamon   *think*
     In his fightyng were a wood leon,   *mad*

     1621–2 They parted till next morning, after each of them had pledged
        his word.
     1626 Will not willingly brook a rival.
     1627 Palamon and Arcite find that out well enough.
     1647–8 Just so they behaved, the change of colour in their faces reflecting
        the knowledge that each of them had of the other, i.e. that each had of
        his opponent's quality.
     1651 Each of them helped to arm the other.

And as a crueel tigre was Arcite;
As wilde bores gonne they to smyte,   *began*
That frothen whit as foom for ire wood.
1660 Up to the ancle foghte they in hir blood.
And in this wise I lete hem fightyng dwelle,
And forth I wole of Theseus yow telle.
⟶   The destinee, ministre general,
That executeth in the world over al
1665 The purveiaunce that God hath seyn biforn,
So strong it is that, though the world had sworn
The contrarie of a thyng by ye or nay,
Yet somtyme it shal fallen on a day
That falleth nat eft withinne a thousand yeer.
1670 For certeinly, oure appetites heer,
Be it of werre, or pees, or hate, or love,   *whether for war*
Al is this reuled by the sighte above.   *foresight*
    This mene I now by myghty Theseus,
That for to hunten is so desirus,
1675 And namely at the grete hert in May,
That in his bed ther daweth hym no day
That he nys clad, and redy for to ryde
With hunte and horn and houndes hym bisyde.   *huntsman*
For in his huntyng hath he swich delit
1680 That it is al his joye and appetit
To been hymself the grete hertes bane,   *slayer*
⟶   For after Mars he serveth now Dyane.
    Cleer was the day, as I have toold er this,
And Theseus with alle joye and blis,
1685 With his Ypolita, the faire queene,
And Emelye, clothed al in grene,
On huntyng be they riden roially.   *ridden*
And to the grove that stood ful faste by,   *close*
In which ther was an hert, as men hym tolde,
1690 Duc Theseus the streight wey hath holde.
And to the launde he rideth hym ful right,   *clearing*
For thider was the hert wont have his flight,
And over a brook, and so forth on his weye.
This duc wol han a cours at hym or tweye   *course*
1695 With houndes swiche as that hym list comaunde.

1659 That foam with white froth in their mad rage.
1661 I will leave them still fighting.
1664-5 That carries out all over the world the providence which God
    has foreseen.
1666-9 Though the whole world had solemnly sworn the contrary of a
    thing, yet will that thing happen on a certain day and not again for
    a thousand years.
1673 This I mean with reference to mighty Theseus.
1675 Especially after the great hart in May.
1676 So that for him in bed there dawns no day.
1695 With such hounds as it pleased him to command.

And whan this duc was come unto the launde,
Under the sonne he looketh, and anon
He was war of Arcite and Palamon, *aware*
That foughten breme, as it were bores two. *fiercely; boars*
1700 The brighte swerdes wenten to and fro
So hidously that with the leeste strook
It semed as it wolde felle an ook.
But what they were, no thyng he ne woot.
This duc his courser with his spores smoot, *struck*
1705 And at a stert he was bitwix hem two, *bound*
And pulled out a swerd, and cride, 'Hoo!
Namoore, up peyne of lesynge of youre heed! *losing*
By myghty Mars, he shal anon be deed
That smyteth any strook that I may seen.
1710 But telleth me what myster men ye been, *kind of*
That been so hardy for to fighten heere *rash*
Withouten juge or oother officere,
As it were in a lystes roially.'
This Palamon answerde hastily, *promptly*
1715 And seyde, 'Sire, what nedeth wordes mo?
We have the deeth disserved bothe two.
Two woful wrecches been we, two caytyves,
That been encombred of oure owene lyves; *encumbered by*
And as thou art a rightful lord and juge,
1720 Ne yif us neither mercy ne refuge, *do not give*
But sle me first, for seinte charitee!
But sle my felawe eek as wel as me;
Or sle hym first, for though thow knowest it lite, *little*
This is thy mortal foo, this is Arcite,
1725 That fro thy lond is banysshed on his heed,
For which he hath deserved to be deed.
For this is he that cam unto thy gate
And seyde that he highte Philostrate. *was called*
Thus hath he japed thee ful many a yer, *tricked*
1730 And thou hast maked hym thy chief squier;
And this is he that loveth Emelye.
For sith the day is come that I shal dye,
I make pleynly my confessioun
That I am thilke woful Palamoun *that (same)*
1735 That hath thy prisoun broken wikkedly.
I am thy mortal foo, and it am I *is*
That loveth so hoote Emelye the brighte *passionately*
That I wol dye present in hir sighte. *now*

1697 i.e. the sun was still low in the sky.
1703 But he had no idea who they were.
1708 He shall straightway die.
1713 Yet as if fighting royally in the lists.
1721 In the name of holy charity.
1725 On pain of losing his head.

Wherfore I axe deeth and my juwise;   *ask for; sentence*
1740 But sle my felawe in the same wise,
For bothe han we deserved to be slayn.'
    This worthy duc answerde anon agayn,
And seyde, 'This is a short conclusioun.
Youre owene mouth, by youre confessioun,
1745 Hath dampned yow, and I wol it recorde;   *witness*
It nedeth noght to pyne yow with the corde.   *torture*
Ye shal be deed, by myghty Mars the rede!'   *red*
    The queene anon, for verray wommanhede,
Gan for to wepe, and so dide Emelye,
1750 And alle the ladyes in the compaignye.
    Greet pitee was it, as it thoughte hem alle,   *seemed to them*
That evere swich a chaunce sholde falle;   *misfortune; occur*
For gentil men they were of greet estaat,   *noble*
And no thyng but for love was this debaat;
1755 And saugh hir blody woundes wyde and soore,   *saw*
And alle crieden, bothe lasse and moore,
'Have mercy, Lord, upon us wommen alle!'
And on hir bare knees adoun they falle,
And wolde have kist his feet ther as he stood;   *where*
1760 Til at the laste aslaked was his mood,   *softened*
For pitee renneth soone in gentil herte.   *flows swiftly*
And though he first for ire quook and sterte,
He hath considered shortly, in a clause,   *briefly*
The trespas of hem bothe, and eek the cause,
1765 And although that his ire hir gilt accused,
Yet in his resoun he hem bothe excused,
As thus: he thoghte wel that every man
Wol helpe hymself in love, if that he kan,
And eek delivere hymself out of prisoun.
1770 And eek his herte hadde compassioun
Of wommen, for they wepen evere in oon;
And in his gentil herte he thoughte anon,
And softe unto hymself he seyde, 'Fy   *softly*
Upon a lord that wol have no mercy,
1775 But been a leon, bothe in word and dede,   *lion*
To hem that been in repentaunce and drede,
As wel as to a proud despitous man
That wole mayntene that he first bigan.

1743 This is quickly decided.
1748 At once the queen, with true womanly feeling.
1754 And this quarrel was for love alone.
1761 Cf. IV. 1986; V. 479.
1762 At first he trembled and started violently with rage.
1765 Accused them of guilt.
1771 On the women, for they wept incessantly.
1776-7 To those who are repentant and afraid, as much as to a proud and scornful man.

That lord hath litel of discrecioun,
1780 That in swich cas kan no divisioun,   *knows; distinction*
But weyeth pride and humblesse after oon.'
And shortly, whan his ire is thus agoon,
He gan to looken up with eyen lighte,   *joyful*
And spak thise same wordes al on highte: *aloud*
1785 'The god of love, a, *benedicite!*   *bless us*
How myghty and how greet a lord is he!
Ayeyns his myght ther gayneth none obstacles.   *prevail*
He may be cleped a god for his myracles;   *called*
For he kan maken, at his owene gyse,
1790 Of everich herte as that hym list divyse.
Lo heere this Arcite and this Palamoun,
That quitly weren out of my prisoun,
And myghte han lyved in Thebes roially,
And witen I am hir mortal enemy,   *know*
1795 And that hir deth lith in my myght also;   *lies*
And yet hath love, maugree hir eyen two,
Broght hem hyder bothe for to dye.
Now looketh, is nat that an heigh folye?   *the height of folly*
Who may been a fool, but if he love?   *unless*
1800 Bihoold, for Goddes sake that sit above,   *dwells*
Se how they blede! be they noght wel arrayed?   *placed*
Thus hath hir lord, the god of love, ypayed
Hir wages and hir fees for hir servyse!
And yet they wenen for to been ful wyse   *think*
1805 That serven love, for aught that may bifalle. *whatever happens*
But this is yet the beste game of alle,
That she for whom they han this jolitee   *sport*
Kan hem therfore as muche thank as me.
She woot namoore of al this hoote fare,
1810 By God, than woot a cokkow or an hare!   *cuckoo*
But all moot ben assayed, hoot and coold;
A man moot ben a fool, or yong or oold,—   *either*
I woot it by myself ful yore agon,
For in my tyme a servant was I oon.   *a lover*
1815 And therfore, syn I knowe of loves peyne,
And woot hou soore it kan a man distreyne,   *afflict*
As he that hath ben caught ofte in his laas,
I yow foryeve al hoolly this trespaas,

1781 Counts pride and humility as one.
1789–90 For he can, in his own fashion, do what he likes with every
    heart.
1792 Who had escaped scot-free from my prison.
1796 In spite of their two eyes, i.e. in spite of themselves.
1808 Is no more grateful to them for it than she is to me.
1809 She knows no more about these passionate goings-on.
1811 But we must try everything once, come what may.
1813 I've known this myself a long, long time.
1817 As one who has often been caught in its snare.

At requeste of the queene, that kneleth heere,
1820 And eek of Emelye, my suster deere.
And ye shul bothe anon unto me swere
That nevere mo ye shal my contree dere,　　　　　*harm*
Ne make werre upon me nyght ne day,
But been my freendes in al that ye may.
1825 I yow foryeve this trespas every deel.'　　　　*altogether*
And they hym sworen his axyng faire and weel,
And hym of lordshipe and of mercy preyde,
And he hem graunteth grace, and thus he seyde:
　'To speke of roial lynage and richesse,　　　　*wealth*
1830 Though that she were a queene or a princesse,
Ech of you bothe is worthy, doutelees,
To wedden whan tyme is, but nathelees　　*the time comes*
I speke as for my suster Emelye,
For whom ye have this strif and jalousye.
1835 Ye woot yourself she may nat wedden two
Atones, though ye fighten everemo.　　　　　*at once*
That oon of you, al be hym looth or lief,
He moot go pipen in an yvy leef;
This is to seyn, she may nat now han bothe,
1840 Al be ye never so jalouse ne so wrothe.
And forthy I yow putte in this degree,
That ech of yow shal have his destynee
As hym is shape, and herkneth in what wyse;　　*ordained*
Lo heere youre ende of that I shal devyse.
1845　My wyl is this, for plat conclusioun,
Withouten any repplicacioun,—
If that you liketh, take it for the beste:
That everich of you shal goon where hym leste　*each; he likes*
Frely, withouten raunson or daunger;
1850 And this day fifty wykes, fer ne ner,
Everich of you shal brynge an hundred knyghtes
Armed for lystes up at alle rightes,
Al redy to darreyne hire by bataille.
And this bihote I yow withouten faille,　　　　*promise*
1855 Upon my trouthe, and as I am a knyght,　　　*word*
That wheither of yow bothe that hath myght,—　*whichever*
This is to seyn, that wheither he or thow　　　*whether*
May with his hundred, as I spak of now,

1826 They readily swore to do as he asked.
1827 They begged him to be their merciful lord.
1837–8 One of you, whether he likes it or not, must go whistle.
1841 And so I will do this much for you.
1844 Listen to what I have in mind for you.
1845–6 To make a plain decision, which admits of no reply.
1850 And exactly a year from to-day.
1852 Armed at all points for fighting in the lists.
1853 To decide by battle who has the better claim to her.

Sleen his contrarie, or out of lystes dryve,   *opponent*
1860 Thanne shal I yeve Emelya to wyve   *for wife*
To whom that Fortune yeveth so fair a grace.
The lystes shal I maken in this place,
And God so wisly on my soule rewe,
As I shal evene juge been and trewe.   *impartial*
1865 Ye shul noon oother ende with me maken,
That oon of yow ne shal be deed or taken.
And if yow thynketh this is weel ysayd,   *it seems to you*
Seyeth youre avys, and holdeth you apayd.
This is youre ende and youre conclusioun.'
1870   Who looketh lightly now but Palamoun?   *cheerful*
Who spryngeth up for joye but Arcite?
Who kouthe telle, or who kouthe it endite,   *could; write*
The joye that is maked in the place
Whan Theseus hath doon so fair a grace?
1875 But doun on knees wente every maner wight,
And thonked hym with al hir herte and myght,
And namely the Thebans often sithe.
And thus with good hope and with herte blithe   *glad*
They taken hir leve, and homward gonne they ride   *rode*
1880 To Thebes, with his olde walles wyde.   *its*

EXPLICIT SECUNDA PARS

SEQUITUR PARS TERCIA

I trowe men wolde deme it necligence
If I foryete to tellen the dispence   *expenditure*
Of Theseus, that gooth so bisily   *goes about*
To maken up the lystes roially,   *build*
1885 That swich a noble theatre as it was,   *amphitheatre*
I dar wel seyen in this world ther nas.
The circuit a myle was aboute,   *circumference*
Walled of stoon, and dyched al withoute.   *on the outside*
Round was the shap, in manere of compas,   *circle*
1890 Ful of degrees, the heighte of sixty pas,   *tiers; feet*
That whan a man was set on o degree,
He letted nat his felawe for to see.

1863-4 And may God have pity on my soul even as.
1865-6 No conclusion will satisfy me but that one of you shall die or
be taken prisoner.
1868 Say so (lit. say your opinion), and be satisfied.
1874 Has granted so great a favour.
1875 Every sort of person (i.e. whatever his rank).
1877 And especially the Thebans, time and again.
1892 He did not prevent the spectators behind from seeing.

   Estward ther stood a gate of marbul whit,
   Westward right swich another in the opposit.
1895 And shortly to conclude, swich a place
   Was noon in erthe, as in so litel space;
   For in the lond ther was no crafty man   *craftsman*
   That geometrie or ars-metrike kan,   *arithmetic; knows*
   Ne portreyour, ne kervere of ymages,   *painter*
1900 That Thesus ne yaf him mete and wages,   *gave; food*
   The theatre for to maken and devyse.
   And for to doon his ryte and sacrifise,   *rites*
   He estward hath, upon the gate above,
   In worshipe of Venus, goddesse of love,
1905 Doon make an auter and an oratorie;   *had made; altar*
   And on the gate westward, in memorie
   Of Mars, he maked hath right swich another,
   That coste largely of gold a fother.
   And northward, in a touret on the wal,   *turret*
1910 Of alabastre whit and reed coral,
   An oratorie, riche for to see,
   In worshipe of Dyane of chastitee,
   Hath Theseus doon wroght in noble wyse.
   But yet hadde I foryeten to devyse   *describe*
1915 The noble kervyng and the portreitures,   *pictures*
   The shap, the contenaunce, and the figures,
   That weren in thise oratories thre.
   First in the temple of Venus maystow se
   Wroght on the wal, ful pitous to biholde,   *piteous*
1920 The broken slepes, and the sikes colde,   *sighs*
   The sacred teeris, and the waymentynge, *lamentation*
   The firy strokes of the desirynge   *lashes; desire*
   That loves servantz in this lyf enduren;
   The othes that hir covenantz assuren;   *confirm*
1925 Plesaunce and Hope, Desir, Foolhardynesse, *pleasure*
   Beautee and Youthe, Bauderie, Richesse,   *gaiety*
   Charmes and Force, Lesynges, Flaterye,   *lies*
   Despense, Bisynesse, and Jalousye, *extravagance; intrigue*
   That wered of yelewe gooldes a gerland,
1930 And a cokkow sittynge on hir hand;
   Festes, instrumentz, caroles, daunces,
   Lust and array, and alle the circumstaunces *joy; display*
   Of love, which that I rekned and rekne shal,
   By ordre weren peynted on the wal,   *in due order*

1894 Westwards, opposite, another just like it.
1895–6 There was no other place like it on earth, considering it was built
  in so short a time.
1908 That cost him fully one load of gold.
1929 Who wore a garland of yellow marigolds.
1931 *caroles*, ring-dances, accompanied by song.
1933 Which I have mentioned and shall mention again.

1935 And mo than I kan make of mencioun.
     For soothly al the mount of Citheroun,
     Ther Venus hath hir principal dwellynge,   *where*
     Was shewed on the wal in portreyynge,
     With al the gardyn and the lustynesse.   *delight*
1940 Nat was foryeten the porter, Ydelnesse,
     Ne Narcisus the faire of yore agon,   *long ago*
     Ne yet the folye of kyng Salomon,
     Ne yet the grete strengthe of Ercules—
     Th'enchauntementz of Medea and Circes—
1945 Ne of Turnus, with the hardy fiers corage,   *bold*
     The riche Cresus, kaytyf in servage.   *wretched; captivity*
     Thus may ye seen that wysdom ne richesse,
     Beautee ne sleighte, strengthe ne hardynesse, *cunning; boldness*
     Ne may with Venus holde champartie,
1950 For as hir list the world than may she gye.
     Lo, alle thise folk so caught were in hir las,   *snare*
     Til they for wo ful ofte seyde 'allas!'
     Suffiseth heere ensamples oon or two,
     And though I koude rekene a thousand mo.
1955   The statue of Venus, glorious for to se,
     Was naked, fletynge in the large see,   *floating on; broad*
     And fro the navele doun al covered was
     With wawes grene, and brighte as any glas.   *waves*
     A citole in hir right hand hadde she,
1960 And on hir heed, ful semely for to se,   *most lovely*
     A rose gerland, fressh and wel smellynge;
     Above hir heed hir dowves flikerynge.   *fluttering*
     Biforn hire stood hir sone Cupido;   *son*
     Upon his shuldres wynges hadde he two,
1965 And blynd he was, as it is often seene;
     A bowe he bar and arwes brighte and kene.   *carried*
        Why sholde I noght as wel eek telle yow al
     The portreiture that was upon the wal
     Withinne the temple of myghty Mars the rede?
1970 Al peynted was the wal, in lengthe and brede,
     Lyk to the estres of the grisly place   *interior*
     That highte the grete temple of Mars in Trace,   *is called*
     In thilke colde, frosty regioun   *that*
     Ther as Mars hath his sovereyn mansioun.   *where*
1975   First on the wal was peynted a forest,
     In which ther dwelleth neither man ne best,
     With knotty, knarry, bareyne trees olde   *gnarled*
     Of stubbes sharpe and hidouse to biholde,   *stumps; hideous*

     1949 Cannot share authority with Venus.
     1950 For she can govern the world as she likes.
     1959 *citole*, a stringed instrument.
     1966 Cf. III. 1381.

In which ther ran a rumbel in a swough,
1980 As though a storm sholde bresten every bough. *would break*
And dounward from an hille, under a bente,
Ther stood the temple of Mars armypotente, *mighty in arms*
Wroght al of burned steel, of which the *burnished*
 entree *entrance*
Was long and streit, and gastly for to see. *narrow; horrible*
1985 And therout came a rage and swich a veze
That it made al the gate for to rese. *shake*
The northren lyght in at the dores shoon, *shone*
For wyndowe on the wal ne was ther noon,
Thurgh which men myghten any light discerne.
1990 The dore was al of adamant eterne, *eternal*
Yclenched overthwart and endelong
With iren tough; and for to make it strong,
Every pyler, the temple to sustene,
Was tonne-greet, of iren bright and shene.
1995 Ther saugh I first the derke ymaginyng *saw*
Of Felonye, and al the compassyng;
The crueel Ire, reed as any gleede; *Wrath; ember*
The pykepurs, and eek the pale Drede; *Fear*
The smylere with the knyf under the cloke;
2000 The shepne brennynge with the blake smoke; *shippen*
The tresoun of the mordrynge in the bedde; *murdering*
The open werre, with woundes al bibledde; *covered with blood*
Contek, with blody knyf and sharp manace. *strife; threat*
Al ful of chirkyng was that sory place. *grating noises*
2005 The sleere of hymself yet saugh I ther,— *slayer*
His herte-blood hath bathed al his heer; *hair*
The nayl ydryven in the shode a-nyght; *temple; at night*
The colde deeth, with mouth gapyng upright.
Amyddes of the temple sat Meschaunce, *Mischance*
2010 With disconfort and sory contenaunce.
Yet saugh I Woodnesse, laughynge in his rage, *Madness*
Armed Compleint, Outhees, and fiers Outrage;
The careyne in the busk, with throte ycorve;
A thousand slayn, and nat of qualm ystorve;
2015 The tiraunt, with the pray by force yraft; *seized*
The toun destroyed, ther was no thyng laft.

1979 Through which there ran a rumbling and a soughing.
1981 At the foot of a grassy slope.
1985 Came such a raging blast.
1991 Riveted across and along.
1994 As big as a barrel, and made of iron shining bright.
1996 And every detail of its execution.
2008 Lying on his back with gaping mouth.
2010 With sad and miserable countenance.
2012 Armed Grievance, Hue and Cry, and fierce Excess.
2013 The corpse in the bush, with throat all slit.
2014 Who had not died of plague.

Yet saugh I brent the shippes hoppesteres;
The hunte strangled with the wilde beres;   *hunter; by*
The sowe freten the child right in the cradel;   *devouring*
2020 The cook yscalded, for al his longe ladel.
Noght was foryeten by the infortune of Marte:
The cartere overryden with his carte,   *by*
Under the wheel ful lowe he lay adoun.
Ther were also, of Martes divisioun,   *Mars' following*
2025 The barbour, and the bocher, and the smyth,   *butcher*
That forgeth sharpe swerdes on his styth.   *anvil*
And al above, depeynted in a tour,   *painted*
Saugh I Conquest, sittynge in greet honour,
With the sharpe swerd over his heed
2030 Hangynge by a soutil twynes threed.   *a fine thread*
Depeynted was the slaughtre of Julius,
Of grete Nero, and of Antonius;
Al be that thilke tyme they were unborn,   *although at that*
Yet was hir deth depeynted ther-biforn
2035 By manasynge of Mars, right by figure.
So was it shewed in that portreiture,
As is depeynted in the sterres above   *depicted*
Who shal be slayn or elles deed for love.   *die*
Suffiseth oon ensample in stories olde;   *one example*
2040 I may nat rekene hem alle though I wolde.
      The statue of Mars upon a carte stood   *chariot*
Armed, and looked grym as he were wood;   *mad*
And over his heed ther shynen two figures
Of sterres, that been cleped in scriptures,
2045 That oon Puella, that oother Rubeus—
This god of armes was arrayed thus.
A wolf ther stood biforn hym at his feet
With eyen rede, and of a man he eet;   *ate*
With soutil pencel was depeynted this storie   *brush*
2050 In redoutynge of Mars and of his glorie.   *reverence*
      Now to the temple of Dyane the chaste,
As shortly as I kan, I wol me haste,
To telle yow al the descripsioun.
Depeynted been the walles up and doun
2055 Of huntyng and of shamefast chastitee.
Ther saugh I how woful Calistopee,   *Callisto*

2017 And then I saw the dancing ships burnt up.
2021 No aspect of the malign influence of Mars was forgotten.
(Chaucer is here less concerned with Mars the pagan deity than with
Mars the planet, and with the evil attributes assigned to it by medieval
astrologers.)
2022 The charioteer run over by his chariot.
2034-6 Yet their death, brought about by the threatening of Mars, was
portrayed in advance, exact in every detail.
2044-5 Stars which are called Puella and Rubeus in occult writings.
2055 With scenes of hunting and of modest chastity.

Whan that Diane agreved was with here,   *displeased with her*
Was turned from a womman til a bere,   *bear*
And after was she maad the loode-sterre;   *polar star*
2060 Thus was it peynted, I kan sey yow no ferre.   *more*
Hir sone is eek a sterre, as men may see.
Ther saugh I Dane, yturned til a tree,—   *Daphne*
I mene nat the goddesse Diane,.
But Penneus doghter, which that highte Dane.   *was called*
2065 Ther saugh I Attheon an hert ymaked,   *Actaeon; hart*
For vengeaunce that he saugh Diane al naked;
I saugh how that his houndes have hym caught
And freeten hym, for that they knewe hym naught.   *devoured*
Yet peynted was a litel forther moor   *farther on*
2070 How Atthalante hunted the wilde boor,   *Atalanta*
And Meleagre, and many another mo,   *as well*
For which Dyane wroghte hym care and wo.
Ther saugh I many another wonder storie,   *wonderful*
The which me list nat drawen to memorie.
2075   This goddesse on an hert ful hye seet,   *sat*
With smale houndes al aboute hir feet;
And undernethe hir feet she hadde a moone,—
Wexynge it was and sholde wanye soone.
In gaude grene hir statue clothed was,   *bright green*
2080 With bowe in honde, and arwes in a cas.
Hir eyen caste she ful lowe adoun,
Ther Pluto hath his derke regioun.
A womman travaillynge was hire biforn;   *in labour*
But for hir child so longe was unborn,   *because*
2085 Ful pitously Lucyna gan she calle,
And seyde, 'Help, for thou mayst best of alle!'
Wel koude he peynten lifly that it wroghte;
With many a floryn he the hewes boghte.
   Now been thise lystes maad, and Theseus,   *made*
2090 That at his grete cost arrayed thus   *adorned*
The temples and the theatre every deel,   *part*
Whan it was doon, hym lyked wonder weel.
But stynte I wole of Theseus a lite,
And speke of Palamon and of Arcite.
2095   The day approcheth of hir retournynge,
That everich sholde an hundred knyghtes brynge   *each*

2066 As a punishment for seeing.
2074 Which I don't wish to recall now.
2078 It was waxing, and would be waning soon.
2085 She cried piteously to Lucina (i.e. Diana).
2087 The man who did it could paint a lively picture.
2088 i.e. the colours cost him dear.
2092 It pleased him exceedingly.
2093 I will say no more about Theseus for a while.

The bataille to darreyne, as I yow tolde. *decide*
And til Atthenes, hir covenant for to holde,
Hath everich of hem broght an hundred knyghtes,
2100 Wel armed for the werre at alle rightes. *at all points*
And sikerly ther trowed many a man
That nevere, sithen that the world bigan, *since*
As for to speke of knyghthod of hir hond,
As fer as God hath maked see or lond,
Nas of so fewe so noble a compaignye.
̄or every wight that lovede chivalrye,
nd wolde, his thankes, han a passant name,
iath preyed that he myghte been of that game;
nd wel was hym that therto chosen was.
2110 ̄or if ther fille tomorwe swich a cas,
Ye knowen wel that every lusty knyght
That loveth paramours and hath his myght, *passionately*
Were it in Engelond or elleswhere,
They wolde, hir thankes, wilnen to be there,—
2115 To fighte for a lady, *benedicitee!*
It were a lusty sighte for to see.
    And right so ferden they with Palamon.
With hym ther wenten knyghtes many on; *a one*
Som wol ben armed in an haubergeoun,
2120 And in a brestplate and a light gypoun;
And som wol have a paire plates large;
And som wol have a Pruce sheeld or a targe; *Prussian*
Som wol ben armed on his legges weel, *well*
And have an ax, and som a mace of steel—
2125 Ther is no newe gyse that it nas old.
Armed were they, as I have yow told,
Everych after his opinioun.
    Ther maistow seen, comynge with Palamoun,
Lygurge hymself, the grete kyng of Trace. *Lycurgus*
2̄ Blak was his berd, and manly was his face;
The cercles of his eyen in his heed,
They gloweden bitwixen yelow and reed,

2101 And certainly many a man believed.
2103–5 When it comes to prowess in war, was there in all God's creation
    so noble and select a company.
2107 And would gladly win a glorious name.
2109 Happy the man who was chosen for it.
2110 If such a thing were to happen to-morrow.
2114 They would gladly like to be there.
2116 It would be a joyful sight.
2117 And just so they came with Palamon.
2119 One is armed in a coat of mail.
2120 *gypoun*, surcoat worn over the armour.
2121 Another has a suit of plate armour.
2125 There is no new fashion that is not old, i.e. there is nothing new
    under the sun. (Chaucer is humorously justifying the up-to-date
    armour worn by Palamon's knights.)

And lik a grifphon looked he aboute,   *gryphon*
With kempe heeris on his browes stoute;   *shaggy; beetling*
2135 His lymes grete, his brawnes harde and stronge,   *muscles*
His shuldres brode, his armes rounde and longe;
And as the gyse was in his contree,   *custom*
Ful hye upon a chaar of gold stood he,   *chariot*
With foure white boles in the trays.   *traces*
2140 In stede of cote-armure over his harnays,
With nayles yelewe and brighte as any gold,
He hadde a beres skyn, col-blak for old.
His longe heer was kembd bihynde his bak;
As any ravenes fethere it shoon for blak;   *shone jet-black*
2145 A wrethe of gold, arm-greet, of huge wighte,
Upon his heed, set ful of stones brighte,
Of fyne rubyes and of dyamauntz.
Aboute his chaar ther wenten white alauntz,   *wolf-hounds*
Twenty and mo, as grete as any steer,
2150 To hunten at the leoun or the deer,
And folwed hym with mosel faste ybounde,   *muzzle; tightly*
Colered of gold, and tourettes fyled rounde.
An hundred lordes hadde he in his route,   *company*
Armed ful wel, with hertes stierne and stoute.
2155   With Arcita, in stories as men fynde,
The grete Emetreus, the kyng of Inde,
Upon a steede bay trapped in steel,
Covered in clooth of gold, dyapred weel,
Cam ridynge lyk the god of armes, Mars.
2160 His cote-armure was of clooth of Tars   *Tartary*
Couched with perles white and rounde and grete;   *set*
His sadel was of brend gold newe ybete;
A mantelet upon his shulder hangynge,   *short mantle*
Bret-ful of rubyes rede as fyr sparklynge;   *brimful*
2165 His crispe heer lyk rynges was yronne,   *curly; clustered*
And that was yelow, and glytered as the sonne.
His nose was heigh, his eyen bright citryn,   *aquiline; citron*
His lippes rounde, his colour was sangwyn;   *ruddy*
A fewe frakenes in his face yspreynd,   *freckles; sprinkled*
2170 Bitwixen yelow and somdel blak ymeynd;
And as a leon he his lookyng caste.
Of fyve and twenty yeer his age I caste.   *reckon*

2140-2 Instead of a coat-armour over his mail, he had a bearskin coal-
    black with age, with claws as yellow and bright as gold.
2145 A wreath of gold, arm-thick, of huge weight.
2152 Wearing collars of gold, with collar-rings filed round.   (A *tourette*
    is a ring by which the leash was attached to the collar.)
2157 On a bay steed with trappings of steel.
2158 Decorated with small diamond-shaped patterns.
2162 Forged gold, newly hammered.
2170 Yellow in colour, shading into black.
2171 He glared like a lion.

His berd was wel bigonne for to sprynge;
His voys was as a trompe thonderynge.   *trumpet*
2175 Upon his heed he wered of laurer grene   *wore; laurel*
A gerland, fressh and lusty for to sene.   *delightful*
Upon his hand he bar for his deduyt   *pleasure*
An egle tame, as any lilye whyt.
An hundred lordes hadde he with hym there,
2180 Al armed, save hir heddes, in al hir gere,
Ful richely in alle maner thynges.
For trusteth wel that dukes, erles, kynges
Were gadered in this noble compaignye,
For love and for encrees of chivalrye.   *increase; martial glory*
2185 Aboute this kyng ther ran on every part   *side*
Ful many a tame leon and leopart.
And in this wise thise lordes, alle and some,   *one and all*
Been on the Sonday to the citee come
About pryme, and in the toun alight.   *alighted*
2190   This Theseus, this duc, this worthy knyght,
Whan he had broght hem into his citee,
And inned hem, everich at his degree,   *housed; each*
He festeth hem, and dooth so greet labour
To esen hem and doon hem al honour,   *entertain*
2195 That yet men wenen that no mannes wit
Of noon estaat ne koude amenden it.
  The mynstralcye, the service at the feeste,
The grete yiftes to the meeste and leeste,   *highest; lowest*
The riche array of Theseus paleys,
2200 Ne who sat first ne last upon the deys,   *dais*
What ladyes fairest been or best daunsynge,
Or which of hem kan dauncen best and synge,
Ne who moost felyngly speketh of love;
What haukes sitten on the perche above,
2205 What houndes liggen on the floor adoun,—   *lie; down*
Of al this make I now no mencioun,
But al th'effect, that thynketh me the beste.
Now cometh the point, and herkneth if yow leste.   *please*
  The Sonday nyght, er day bigan to sprynge,   *dawn*
2210 Whan Palamon the larke herde synge,
(Although it nere nat day by houres two,   *was not*
Yet song the larke) and Palamon right tho   *just then*
With hooly herte and with an heigh corage,
He roos to wenden on his pilgrymage   *go*

2180-1 But for their heads, they were fully equipped in richly wrought
armour.
2189 *pryme*, 9 a.m.
2193 He feasts them, and takes such great pains.
2195-6 The belief still persists that no man's wit, however good, could
improve on it (i.e. on Theseus' hospitality).
2207 But only what is significant, for that seems best to me.

2215 Unto the blisful Citherea benigne,—
    I mene Venus, honurable and digne.   *worthy*
    And in hir houre he walketh forth a pas
    Unto the lystes ther hire temple was,   *where*
    And doun he kneleth, and with humble cheere   *mien*
2220 And herte soor, he seyde as ye shal heere: *aching*
    'Faireste of faire, o lady myn, Venus,
    Doughter to Jove, and spouse of Vulcanus,
    Thow gladere of the mount of Citheron,   *gladdener*
    For thilke love thow haddest to Adoon,   *that; Adonis*
2225 Have pitee of my bittre teeris smerte,   *painful*
    And taak myn humble preyere at thyn herte.   *to*
    Allas! I ne have no langage to telle
    Th'effectes ne the tormentz of myn helle;
    Myn herte may myne harmes nat biwreye;   *sufferings; reveal*
2230 I am so confus that I kan noght seye   *confused*
    But, "Mercy, lady bright, that knowest weele
    My thought, and seest what harmes that I feele!"
    Considere al this and rewe upon my soore,
    As wisly as I shal for everemoore,
2235 Emforth my myght, thy trewe servant be,
    And holden werre alwey with chastitee.
    That make I myn avow, so ye me helpe!   *vow*
    I kepe noght of armes for to yelpe,
    Ne I ne axe nat tomorwe to have victorie,   *ask*
2240 Ne renoun in this cas, ne veyne glorie
    Of pris of armes blowen up and doun;
    But I wolde have fully possessioun
    Of Emelye, and dye in thy servyse.
    Fynd thow the manere hou, and in what wyse:
2245 I recche nat but it may bettre be
    To have victorie of hem, or they of me,
    So that I have my lady in myne armes.
    For though so be that Mars is god of armes,
    Youre vertu is so greet in hevene above   *influence*
2250 That if yow list, I shal wel have my love.
    Thy temple wol I worshipe everemo,
    And on thyn auter, where I ride or go,

2217 In her hour (i.e. the second hour before sunrise, dedicated to
    Venus) he made his way.
2233 Have pity on my pain.
2234–6 Even as I shall ever, to the limit of my strength, be your true
    servant, and wage perpetual war on chastity.
2238 I don't care to boast of deeds of arms.
2240–1 Nor the empty glory of honour won in battle trumpeted up
    and down.
2244 Find the method and means of doing this.
2245 I don't care whether it is better.
2252 Whether I ride or walk, i.e. whatever happens to me.

I wol doon sacrifice and fires beete.   *kindle*
And if ye wol nat so, my lady sweete,
2255 Thanne preye I thee, tomorwe with a spere   *spear*
That Arcita me thurgh the herte bere.   *pierce*
Thanne rekke I noght, whan I have lost my lyf,   *care*
Though that Arcita wynne hire to his wyf.   *for*
This is th'effect and ende of my preyere: *point; purpose*
2260 Yif me my love, thow blisful lady deere.'   *give*
    Whan the orison was doon of Palamon,   *prayer*
His sacrifice he dide, and that anon,
Ful pitously, with alle circumstaunces,   *formalities*
Al telle I noght as now his observaunces;   *although*
2265 But atte laste the statue of Venus shook,
And made a signe, wherby that he took   *understood*
That his preyere accepted was that day.
For thogh the signe shewed a delay,
Yet wiste he wel that graunted was his boone;   *prayer*
2270 And with glad herte he wente hym hoom   *went home*
        ful soone.
    The thridde houre inequal that Palamon
Bigan to Venus temple for to gon,
Up roos the sonne, and up roos Emelye,
And to the temple of Dyane gan hye.   *hastened*
2275 Hir maydens, that she thider with hire ladde,   *took*
Ful redily with hem the fyr they hadde,
Th'encens, the clothes, and the remenant al   *rest*
That to the sacrifice longen shal;   *belong*
The hornes fulle of meeth, as was the gyse: *mead; custom*
2280 Ther lakked noght to doon hir sacrifise.
Smokynge the temple, ful of clothes faire,
This Emelye, with herte debonaire,   *gentle*
Hir body wessh with water of a welle.   *washed*
But hou she dide hir ryte I dar nat telle,   *rite*
2285 But it be any thing in general;
And yet it were a game to heeren al.
To hym that meneth wel it were no charge;
But it is good a man been at his large.
Hir brighte heer was kembd, untressed al;   *hanging loose*
2290 A coroune of a grene ook cerial

2271-2 The third unequal hour since Palamon first went to the temple
    of Venus. (An astrological hour, which was a twelfth of the period
    from sunrise to sunset and from sunset to sunrise, was unequal in
    that the daylight hours were longer or shorter than the night hours,
    except at the equinoxes.)
2280 Nothing was lacking that was needed for her sacrifice.
2281 Burning incense in the temple, which was draped with beautiful
    hangings.
2285-6 Except in general terms; and yet it would be pleasant to hear
    all of it.

Upon hir heed was set ful fair and meete.   *becomingly*
Two fyres on the auter gan she beete,   *altar; kindled*
And dide hir thynges, as men may biholde   *performed; rites*
In Stace of Thebes and thise bookes olde.
2295 Whan kyndled was the fyr, with pitous cheere
Unto Dyane she spak as ye may heere:
    'Oh chaste goddesse of the wodes grene,
To whom bothe hevene and erthe and see is sene,   *visible*
Queene of the regne of Pluto derk and lowe,   *kingdom*
2300 Goddesse of maydens, that myn herte hast knowe
Ful many a yeer, and woost what I desire,   *know*
As keepe me fro thy vengeaunce and thyn ire,   *please protect*
That Attheon aboughte cruelly.   *Actaeon; suffered*
Chaste goddesse, wel wostow that I   *do you know*
2305 Desire to ben a mayden al my lyf,
Ne nevere wol I be no love ne wyf.   *lover*
I am, thow woost, yet of thy compaignye,   *still*
A mayde, and love huntynge and venerye,   *the chase*
And for to walken in the wodes wilde.
2310 And noght to ben a wyf and be with childe.
Noght wol I knowe compaignye of man.
Now help me, lady, sith ye may and kan,
For tho thre formes that thou hast in thee.
And Palamon, that hath swich love to me,
2315 And eek Arcite, that loveth me so soore,   *ardently*
(This grace I preye thee withoute moore)   *delay*
As sende love and pees bitwixe hem two,
And fro me turne awey hir hertes so
That al hire hoote love and hir desir,
2320 And al hir bisy torment, and hir fir   *restless*
Be queynt, or turned in another place.   *quenched*
And if so be thou wolt nat do me grace,
Of if my destynee be shapen so   *ordained*
That I shal nedes have oon of hem two,   *must needs*
2325 As sende me hym that moost desireth me.
Bihoold, goddesse of clene chastitee,
The bittre teeris that on my chekes falle.
Syn thou art mayde and kepere of us alle,   *since*
My maydenhede thou kepe and wel conserve,   *preserve*
2330 And whil I lyve, a mayde I wol thee serve.'
    The fires brenne upon the auter cleere,
Whil Emelye was thus in hir preyere.

2287 There would be no harm in it for a well-meaning person.
2288 It is good for a man to be free (to speak or not, as he thinks fit).
2290 A crown of evergreen oak.
2294 In the *Thebaid* of Statius and in other old books.
2313 By virtue of those three forms. (The goddess was Luna in
     heaven, Diana on earth, and Proserpina in Hades.)

But sodeynly she saugh a sighte queynte,   *strange*
For right anon oon of the fyres queynte,
2335 And quyked agayn, and after that anon   *revived*
That oother fyr was queynt and al agon;
And as it queynte it made a whistelynge,
As doon thise wete brondes in hir brennynge,
And at the brondes ende out ran anon
2340 As it were blody dropes many oon;   *a one*
For which so soore agast was Emelye   *terrified*
That she was wel ny mad, and gan to crye,   *cried out*
For she ne wiste what it signyfied;   *did not know*
But oonly for the feere thus hath she cried,
2345 And weep that it was pitee for to heere.   *wept*
And therwithal Dyane gan appeere,   *appeared*
With bowe in honde, right as an hunteresse,
And seyde, 'Doghter, stynt thyn hevynesse.   *stop; grieving*
Among the goddes hye it is affermed,
2350 And by eterne word writen and confermed,   *eternal*
Thou shalt ben wedded unto oon of tho   *those*
That han for thee so muchel care and wo;
But unto which of hem I may nat telle.
Farwel, for I ne may no lenger dwelle.
2355 The fires which that on myn auter brenne   *burn*
Shulle thee declaren, er that thou go henne,   *hence*
Thyn aventure of love, as in this cas.'
And with that word, the arwes in the caas   *arrows; quiver*
Of the goddesse clateren faste and rynge,   *clatter*
2360 And forth she wente, and made a vanysshynge;
For which this Emelye astoned was,   *amazed*
And seyde, 'What amounteth this, allas?   *means*
I putte me in thy proteccioun,
Dyane, and in thy disposicioun.'   *disposal*
2365 And hoom she goth anon the nexte weye.   *nearest*
This is th'effect; ther is namoore to seye.
     The nexte houre of Mars folwynge this,
Arcite unto the temple walked is   *has walked*
Of fierse Mars, to doon his sacrifise,
2370 With alle the rytes of his payen wyse.
With pitous herte and heigh devocioun,
Right thus to Mars he seyde his orisoun:
'O stronge god, that in the regnes colde   *realms*
Of Trace honoured art and lord yholde,   *held as*

2334 For all at once one of the fires went out.
2338 As wet brands do while burning.
2344 It was for fear alone that she cried out as she did.
2357 Your fortune in love in this instance.
2366 This is the gist of what happened.
2367 In the hour of Mars immediately following this.
2370 With all the rites required by pagan custom.

2375 And hast in every regne and every lond
     Of armes al the brydel in thyn hond,
     And hem fortunest as thee lyst devyse,
     Accepte of me my pitous sacrifise.
     If so be that my youthe may deserve,
2380 And that my myght be worthy for to serve
     Thy godhede, that I may been oon of thyne,
     Thanne preye I thee to rewe upon my pyne.
     For thilke peyne, and thilke hoote fir   *once; burned*
     In which thow whilom brendest for desir,
2385 Whan that thow usedest the beautee   *enjoyed*
     Of faire, yonge, fresshe Venus free,   *noble*
     And haddest hire in armes at thy wille—
     Although thee ones on a tyme mysfille,
     Whan Vulcanus hadde caught thee in his las,   *net*
2390 And foond thee liggynge by his wyf, allas!—   *found; lying*
     For thilke sorwe that was in thyn herte,
     Have routhe as wel upon my peynes smerte.   *pity; grievous*
     I am yong and unkonnynge, as thow woost,   *ignorant; know*
     And, as I trowe, with love offended moost
2395 That evere was any lyves creature;
     For she that dooth me al this wo endure   *makes*
     Ne reccheth nevere wher I synke or fleete.
     And wel I woot, er she me mercy heete,   *will promise*
     I moot with strengthe wynne hire in the place;
2400 And, wel I woot, withouten help or grace
     Of thee, ne may my strengthe noght availle.
     Thanne help me, lord, tomorwe in my bataille,
     For thilke fyr that whilom brente thee,
     As wel as thilke fyr now brenneth me,
2405 And do that I tomorwe have victorie.   *bring it about*
     Myn be the travaille, and thyn be the glorie!   *labour*
     Thy sovereyn temple wol I moost honouren   *most*
     Of any place, and alwey moost labouren
     In thy plesaunce and in thy craftes stronge,
2410 And in thy temple I wol my baner honge
     And alle the armes of my compaignye;
     And everemo, unto that day I dye,
     Eterne fir I wol bifore thee fynde.   *provide*
     And eek to this avow I wol me bynde: *vow*

2376 The bridles of great armies in your hand.
2377 And give them whatever fortune you please.
2382 To have pity on my suffering.
2383 For the sake of that torture and that scorching fire.
2388 Although misfortune once befell you.
2394-5 The most injured by love of any living creature.
2397 Does not care whether I sink or swim.
2399 I must win her by strength in the lists.
2409 To give you pleasure and practise your strong crafts.

2415 My beerd, myn heer, that hongeth long adoun,
    That nevere yet ne felte offensioun   *injury*
    Of rasour nor of shere, I wol thee yive,   *shears*
    And ben thy trewe servant whil I lyve.
    Now, lord, have routhe upon my sorwes soore;   *pity*
2420 Yif me victorie, I aske thee namoore.'
        The preyere stynt of Arcita the stronge,
    The rynges on the temple dore that honge,
    And eek the dores, clatereden ful faste,
    Of which Arcita somwhat hym agaste.
2425 The fyres brenden upon the auter brighte,   *burned*
    That it gan al the temple for to lighte;
    A sweete smel the ground anon up yaf,
    And Arcita anon his hand up haf,   *raised*
    And moore encens into the fyr he caste,
2430 With othere rytes mo; and atte laste
    The statue of Mars bigan his hauberk rynge;
    And with that soun he herde a murmurynge
    Ful lowe and dym, and seyde thus, 'Victorie!'   *(it) said*
    For which he yaf to Mars honour and glorie.
2435 And thus with joye and hope wel to fare
    Arcite anon unto his in is fare,
    As fayn as fowel is of the brighte sonne.   *glad; bird*
        And right anon swich strif ther is bigonne,
    For thilke grauntyng, in the hevene above,
2440 Bitwixe Venus, the goddesse of love,
    And Mars, the stierne god armypotente,   *powerful in arms*
    That Juppiter was bisy it to stente;   *stop*
    Til that the pale Saturnus the colde,
    That knew so manye of aventures olde,   *ancient happenings*
2445 Foond in his olde experience an art
    That he ful soone hath plesed every part.
    As sooth is seyd, elde hath greet avantage;
    In elde is bothe wysdom and usage;   *experience*
    Men may the olde atrenne, and noght atrede.   *outrun; outwit*
2450 Saturne anon, to stynten strif and drede,   *doubt*
    Al be it that it is agayn his kynde,   *against; nature*
    Of al this strif he gan remedie fynde.

    2421 The prayer of Arcita . . . being finished.
    2424 At which Arcita took fright a little.
    2426 So that it lit up all the temple.
    2427 The ground at once gave off a sweet smell.
    2431 The hauberk on the statue of Mars began to resound.
    2435 And in the hope of doing well.
    2436 Arcite at once went to his dwelling.
    2438-9 Immediately such strife broke out in heaven over what had been
        granted.
    2445-6 A skilful device by which he soon pleased both sides.
    2447 As it is truly said, age has a great advantage.
    2452 Found a remedy for all this strife.

'My deere doghter Venus,' quod Saturne,
'My cours, that hath so wyde for to turne,
2455 Hath moore power than woot any man.   *knows*
Myn is the drenchyng in the see so wan;   *drowning*
Myn is the prison in the derke cote;   *dungeon*
Myn is the stranglyng and hangyng by the throte,
The murmure and the cherles rebellyng,   *murmuring*
2460 The groynynge, and the pryvee empoysonyng;
I do vengeance and pleyn correccioun,
Whil I dwelle in the signe of the leoun.   *Leo*
Myn is the ruyne of the hye halles,   *ruin*
The fallynge of the toures and of the walles
2465 Upon the mynour or the carpenter.   *sapper*
I slow Sampsoun, shakynge the piler;   *slew*
And myne be the maladyes colde,
The derke tresons, and the castes olde;   *long-laid plots*
My lookyng is the fader of pestilence.   *aspect*
2470 Now weep namoore, I shal doon diligence
That Palamon, that is thyn owene knyght,
Shal have his lady, as thou hast him hight.   *promised*
Though Mars shal helpe his knyght, yet nathelees *nevertheless*
Bitwixe yow ther moot be som tyme pees,   *must*
2475 Al be ye noght of o compleccioun,
That causeth al day swich divisioun.
I am thyn aiel, redy at thy wille;   *grandfather*
Weep now namoore, I wol thy lust fulfille.'   *desire*
  Now wol I stynten of the goddes above,
2480 Of Mars, and of Venus, goddesse of love,
And telle yow as pleynly as I kan
The grete effect, for which that I bygan.

EXPLICIT TERCIA PARS

SEQUITUR PARS QUARTA

  Greet was the feeste in Atthenes that day,
And eek the lusty seson of that May   *joyful*
2485 Made every wight to been in swich   *everyone*
  plesaunce   *pleasure*
That al that Monday justen they and daunce,   *joust*

2454 My heavenly orbit, which covers so vast a space.
2459 Probably an allusion to the Peasants' Revolt of 1381. (Cf. VII. 3394.)
2460 The groaning, and the secret poisoning.
2461 I exact vengeance and demand full punishment.
2470 I shall do my utmost to see.
2475 Although you are not of the same temperament.
2482 The grand conclusion for the sake of which I began this tale.

And spenden it in Venus heigh servyse.
But by the cause that they sholde ryse   *had to*
Eerly, for to seen the grete fight,
2490 Unto hir reste wenten they at nyght.
And on the morwe, whan that day gan sprynge,   *dawned*
Of hors and harneys noyse and claterynge   *armour*
Ther was in hostelryes al aboute;   *inns*
And to the paleys rood ther many a route   *company*
2495 Of lordes upon steedes and palfreys.
Ther maystow seen devisynge of harneys   *preparing*
So unkouth and so riche, and wroght so weel   *rare*
Of goldsmythrye, of browdynge, and of steel;
The sheeldes brighte, testeres, and   *headpieces*
     trappures,   *trappings*
2500 Gold-hewen helmes, hauberkes, cote-armures;   *gold-forged*
Lordes in parementz on hir courseres,   *rich array*
Knyghtes of retenue, and eek squieres
Nailynge the speres, and helmes bokelynge;
Giggynge of sheeldes, with layneres lacynge
2505 (There as nede is they weren no thyng ydel);
The fomy steedes on the golden brydel
Gnawynge, and faste the armurers also   *quickly*
With fyle and hamer prikynge to and fro;   *file; riding*
Yemen on foote, and communes   *attendants; commoners*
     many oon
2510 With shorte staves, thikke as they may goon;
Pypes, trompes, nakers, clariounes,   *kettle-drums*
That in the bataille blowen blody sounes;   *bloodthirsty*
The paleys ful of peple up and doun,
Heere thre, ther ten, holdynge hir questioun,
2515 Dyvynynge of thise Thebane knyghtes two.
Somme seyden thus, somme seyde 'it shal be so';
Somme helden with hym with the blake berd,   *sided*
Somme with the balled, somme with the   *bald*
     thikke herd;   *thick-haired*
Somme seyde he looked grymme, and he wolde fighte;
2520 'He hath a sparth of twenty pound of   *battle-axe*
     wighte.'   *weight*
Thus was the halle ful of divynynge,
Longe after that the sonne gan to sprynge.   *rose*

2498 With goldsmiths' work, embroidery, and steel.
2502 *Knyghtes of retenue*, knights in attendance on their lords.
2503 Fastening the heads of spears to shafts, and buckling on helms.
2504 Fitting straps to shields, and lacing thongs.
2505 Where there was need of them they were by no means idle.
2510 Crowding as thick as they could go.
2514–15 Arguing and prophesying about these two Theban knights.
2519 Some said this fellow looked fierce, and that one would fight hard.

The grete Theseus, that of his sleep awaked
With mynstralcie and noyse that was maked,
2525 Heeld yet the chambre of his paleys riche,
Til that the Thebane knyghtes, bothe yliche   *alike*
Honured, were into the paleys fet.   *fetched*
Duc Theseus was at a wyndow set,   *seated*
Arrayed right as he were a god in trone.   *throne*
2530 The peple preesseth thiderward ful soone   *throng*
Hym for to seen, and doon heigh reverence,
And eek to herkne his heste and his sentence.   *command*
An heraud on a scaffold made an 'Oo!'   *herald; oyez*
Til al the noyse of peple was ydo,
2535 And whan he saugh the peple of noyse al stille,
Tho shewed he the myghty dukes wille.
'The lord hath of his heigh discrecioun
Considered that it were destruccioun
To gentil blood to fighten in the gyse   *noble; way*
2540 Of mortal bataille now in this emprise.   *enterprise*
Wherfore, to shapen that they shal nat dye,   *contrive*
He wol his firste purpos modifye.
No man therfore, up peyne of los of lyf,   *on pain*
No maner shot, ne polax, ne short knyf
2545 Into the lystes sende, or thider brynge;   *may send*
Ne short swerd, for to stoke with poynt bitynge,
No man ne drawe, ne bere it by his syde.
Ne no man shal unto his felawe ryde
But o cours, with a sharpe ygrounde spere;
2550 Foyne, if hym list, on foote, hymself to were.
And he that is at meschief shal be take
And noght slayn, but be broght unto the stake
That shal ben ordeyned on either syde;   *set up*
But thider he shal by force, and there abyde.   *be forced to go*
2555 And if so falle the chieftayn be take   *happen*
On outher syde, or elles sleen his make,   *equal*
No lenger shal the turneiynge laste.   *tourney*
God spede you! gooth forth, and ley on faste!
With long swerd and with mace fighteth youre fille.
2560 Gooth now youre wey, this is the lordes wille.'
The voys of peple touchede the hevene,
So loude cride they with murie stevene,   *voice*
'God save swich a lord, that is so good,
He wilneth no destruccion of blood!'   *desires*
2565 Up goon the trompes and the melodye,

2525 Stayed in his own room in his splendid palace.
2531 And pay him their profound respects.
2544 No kind of dart, or pole-axe.
2546 With sharpened point for stabbing with.
2550 But, if he wishes, he may thrust on foot, to defend himself.
2551 Anyone in trouble shall be taken prisoner.

And to the lystes rit the compaignye,   *rides*
By ordinance, thurghout the citee large,
Hanged with clooth of gold, and nat with sarge.   *serge*
   Ful lik a lord this noble duc gan ryde,
2570 Thise two Thebans upon either syde;
And after rood the queene, and Emelye,
And after that another compaignye
Of oon and oother, after hir degree.   *according to*
And thus they passen thurghout the citee,
2575 And to the lystes come they by tyme.   *in good time*
It nas nat of the day yet fully pryme
Whan set was Theseus ful riche and hye,
Ypolita the queene, and Emelye,
And othere ladys in degrees aboute.
2580 Unto the seetes preesseth al the route.   *crowd*
And westward, thurgh the gates under Marte,   *Mars*
Arcite, and eek the hondred of his parte,   *party*
With baner reed is entred right anon;   *red*
And in that selve moment Palamon
2585 Is under Venus, estward in the place,   *lists*
With baner whyt, and hardy chiere and face.   *valiant mien*
In al the world, to seken up and doun,
So evene, withouten variacioun,
Ther nere swiche compaignyes tweye;
2590 For ther was noon so wys that koude seye
That any hadde of oother avauntage
Of worthynesse, ne of estaat, ne age,   *valour; rank*
So evene were they chosen, for to gesse.
And in two renges faire they hem dresse.
2595 Whan that hir names rad were everichon,
That in hir nombre gyle were ther noon,
Tho were the gates shet, and cried was loude: *then; shut*
'Do now youre devoir, yonge knyghtes proude!'   *duty*
   The heraudes lefte hir prikyng up and doun;   *stopped riding*
2600 Now ryngen trompes loude and clarioun.   *trumpets; clarion*
Ther is namoore to seyn, but west and est
In goon the speres ful sadly in arrest;
In gooth the sharpe spore into the syde.
Ther seen men who kan juste and who kan ryde;   *joust*

2567 *By ordinance*, in due order of precedence; *large*, at large, freely.
2569 The noble duke rode in a most lordly fashion.
2576–7 It was not quite nine o'clock when Theseus was magnificently
   seated on high.
2587–9 Nowhere in all the world, however hard you looked, would you
   find two such companies so evenly matched, without anything to
   choose between them.
2594 And they form themselves in two splendid ranks.
2595–6 When all their names had been read out, so that there should be
   no cheating over numbers.
2602 In go the spears, fixed firmly in their rest.

2605 Ther shyveren shaftes upon sheeldes thikke;   *splinter*
    He feeleth thurgh the herte-spoon the prikke.
    Up spryngen speres twenty foot on highte;   *on high*
    Out goon the swerdes as the silver brighte;
    The helmes they tohewen and toshrede;
2610 Out brest the blood with stierne stremes rede;   *burst*
    With myghty maces the bones they tobreste.   *break in pieces*
    He thurgh the thikkeste of the throng gan threste;   *thrust*
    Ther stomblen steedes stronge, and doun gooth al;
    He rolleth under foot as dooth a bal;
2615 He foyneth on his feet with his tronchoun,   *broken spear-shaft*
    And he hym hurtleth with his hors adoun;
    He thurgh the body is hurt and sithen take,   *afterwards*
    Maugree his heed, and broght unto the stake:
    As forward was, right there he moste abyde.   *agreement*
2620 Another lad is on that oother syde.   *taken*
    And som tyme dooth hem Theseus to reste,
    Hem to refresshe and drynken, if hem leste.
    Ful ofte a day han thise Thebanes two   *that day*
    Togydre ymet, and wroght his felawe wo;
2625 Unhorsed hath ech oother of hem tweye.
    Ther nas no tygre in the vale of Galgopheye,
    Whan that hir whelp is stole whan it is lite,   *little*
    So crueel on the hunte as is Arcite   *to the hunter*
    For jelous herte upon this Palamon.
2630 Ne in Belmarye ther nys so fel leon,
    That hunted is, or for his hunger wood,
    Ne of his praye desireth so the blood,
    As Palamon to sleen his foo Arcite,   *slay*
    The jelous strokes on hir helmes byte;
2635 Out renneth blood on bothe hir sydes rede.
    Som tyme an ende ther is of every dede.   *deed*
    For er the sonne unto the reste wente,
    The stronge kyng Emetreus gan hente   *caught*
    This Palamon, as he faught with Arcite,
2640 And made his swerd depe in his flessh to byte;
    And by the force of twenty is he take   *strength*
    Unyolden, and ydrawen to the stake.

2606 One rider feels the prick of a spear through his midriff.
2609 They hew and cut the helms to pieces.
2614–15 *He . . . He*, one man . . . another.
2618 In spite of his head, i.e. in spite of all his efforts.
2621–2 Sometimes Theseus makes them rest, to refresh themselves and
    drink, if they wish.
2624 Met together, and done each other harm.
2630–1 There is no lion in Benmarin so fierce when hunted or when
    mad with hunger.
2635 From their gory sides.
2642 Without surrendering, and dragged off to the stake.

And in the rescus of this Palamoun
The stronge kyng Lygurge is born adoun,
2645 And kyng Emetreus, for al his strengthe,
Is born out of his sadel a swerdes lengthe,   *flung*
So hitte him Palamoun er he were take;
But al for noght, he was broght to the stake.
His hardy herte myghte hym helpe naught: *valiant*
2650 He moste abyde, whan that he was caught,   *had to*
By force and eek by composicioun.   *agreement*
    Who sorweth now but woful Palamoun,   *grieves*
That moot namoore goon agayn to fighte?   *may*
And whan that Theseus hadde seyn this sighte,
2655 Unto the folk that foghten thus echon
He cryde, 'Hoo! namoore, for it is doon!
I wol be trewe juge, and no partie.   *partisan*
Arcite of Thebes shal have Emelie,
That by his fortune hath hire faire ywonne.'   *fairly*
2660 Anon ther is a noyse of peple bigonne
For joye of this, so loude and heighe withalle,
It semed that the lystes sholde falle.
    What kan now faire Venus doon above?
What seith she now?   What dooth this queene of love,
2665 But wepeth so, for wantynge of hir wille,
Til that hir teeres in the lystes fille?   *fell*
She seyde, 'I am ashamed, doutelees.'
    Saturnus seyde, 'Doghter, hoold thy pees!
Mars hath his wille, his knyght hath al his boone,
2670 And, by myn heed, thow shalt been esed soone.'
    The trompours, with the loude mynstralcie,   *trumpeters*
The heraudes, that ful loude yelle and crie,
Been in hire wele for joye of daun Arcite.
But herkneth me, and stynteth noyse a lite,
2675 Which a myracle ther bifel anon.   *how great*
    This fierse Arcite hath of his helm ydon,   *taken off*
And on a courser, for to shewe his face,
He priketh endelong the large place   *rides all along*
Lokynge upward upon this Emelye;
2680 And she agayn hym caste a freendlich ye   *friendly eye*
(For wommen, as to speken in comune,   *generally speaking*
Thei folwen alle the favour of Fortune)
And was al his chiere, as in his herte.

2643 In his attempt to rescue Palamon.
2647 So hard did Palamon strike him before he was captured.
2655 To all the people who were fighting thus.
2665 But weeps so hard because she cannot have her own way.
2670 *by myn heed*, an asseveration; *esed*, comforted.
2673 Are cock-a-hoop with joy on Lord Arcite's account.
2674 Keep quiet for a little while.
2683 And was all the delight of his heart.

      Out of the ground a furie infernal sterte,   *started*
2685 From Pluto sent at requeste of Saturne,
      For which his hors for fere gan to turne,   *fear; swerved*
      And leep aside, and foundred as he leep;   *leapt; stumbled*
      And er that Arcite may taken keep,   *care*
      He pighte hym on the pomel of his heed,
2690 That in the place he lay as he were deed,   *as if*
      His brest tobrosten with his sadel-bowe.
      As blak he lay as any cole or crowe,   *coal*
      So was the blood yronnen in his face.
      Anon he was yborn out of the place,   *carried*
2695 With herte soor, to Theseus paleys.
      Tho was he korven out of his harneys,   *cut; armour*
      And in a bed ybrought ful faire and blyve;   *quickly*
      For he was yet in memorie and alyve,
      And alwey criynge after Emelye.   *for*
2700   Duc Theseus, with al his compaignye,
      Is comen hoom to Atthenes his citee,
      With alle blisse and greet solempnitee.   *pomp*
      Al be it that this aventure was falle,
      He nolde noght disconforten hem alle.   *dishearten*
2705 Men seyde eek that Arcite shal nat dye;
      He shal been heeled of his maladye.
      And of another thyng they weren as fayn,   *glad*
      That of hem alle was ther noon yslayn,
      Al were they soore yhurt, and namely oon,   *although; especially*
2710 That with a spere was thirled his brest boon.
      To othere woundes and to broken armes   *for*
      Somme hadden salves, and somme hadden charmes;
      Fermacies of herbes, and eek save
      They dronken, for they wolde hir lymes have.   *drank*
2715 For which this noble duc, as he wel kan,
      Conforteth and honoureth every man,
      And made revel al the longe nyght
      Unto the straunge lordes, as was right.   *foreign*
      Ne ther was holden no disconfitynge,
2720 But as a justes, or a tourneiynge;
      For soothly ther was no disconfiture.   *in truth; defeat*
      For fallyng nys nat but an aventure,

2689 He pitched him on top of his head.
2691 His breast shattered by his saddle-bow.
2693 For all the blood had rushed to his face.
2698 For he was still alive and conscious.
2703 Although this misfortune had happened.
2710 Whose breast-bone was pierced by a spear.
2713 *Fermacies*, medicines; *save*, sage.
2719–20 Nor was there any question of defeat, except according to the
    strict rules of joust or tournament.
2722 For falling is only a matter of chance, i.e. something which can
    happen to the best of knights.

Ne to be lad by force unto the stake   *led*
Unyolden, and with twenty knyghtes take,   *unyielding; by*
2725 O persone allone, withouten mo,   *others (to help him)*
And haryed forth by arme, foot, and too,   *dragged along*
And eke his steede dryven forth with staves
With footmen, bothe yemen and eek knaves,—   *servants*
It nas arretted hym no vileynye;
2730 Ther may no man clepen it cowardye.   *call; cowardice*
For which anon duc Theseus leet crye,   *made proclamation*
To stynten alle rancour and envye,   *stop*
The gree as wel of o syde as of oother,
And eyther syde ylik as ootheres brother;
2735 And yaf hem yiftes after hir degree,
And fully heeld a feeste dayes three,
And conveyed the kynges worthily
Out of his toun a journee largely.   *a good day's journey*
And hoom wente every man the righte way.   *shortest*
2740 Ther was namoore but 'Fare wel, have good day!'
Of this bataille I wol namoore endite,   *tell*
But speke of Palamon and of Arcite.
    Swelleth the brest of Arcite, and the soore   *pain*
Encreesseth at his herte moore and moore.
2745 The clothered blood, for any lechecraft,
Corrupteth, and is in his bouk ylâft,
That neither veyne-blood, ne ventusynge,
Ne drynke of herbes may ben his helpynge.
The vertu expulsif, or animal,
2750 Fro thilke vertu cleped natural
Ne may the venym voyden ne expelle.
The pipes of his longes gonne to swelle,   *lungs*
And every lacerte in his brest adoun
Is shent with venym and corrupcioun.   *injured*
2755 Hym gayneth neither, for to gete his lif,
Vomyt upward, ne dounward laxatif.
Al is tobrosten thilke regioun;
Nature hath now no dominacioun.
And certeinly, ther Nature wol nat wirche,   *where; work*
2760 Fare wel phisik! go ber the man to chirche!   *carry*

2729 It was not counted a disgrace to him.
2733 That both sides were equally outstanding.
2737 *the kynges*, i.e. Lycurgus and Emetreus.
2745-7 The clotted blood, despite the leech's skill, putrefies and stays in his body, so that neither the letting nor cupping of blood.
2749-51 The expulsive or 'animal' power cannot expel the poison from his liver (where the 'natural' power of the body was held to reside).
2753 Every muscle deep down in his breast.
2755-6 Neither emetic nor purgative helps him in his struggle for life.
2757 That part (of his body) is all shattered.

This al and som, that Arcita moot dye;
For which he sendeth after Emelye,
And Palamon, that was his cosyn deere.
Thanne seyde he thus, as ye shal after heere:
2765 'Naught may the woful spirit in myn herte
Declare o point of alle my sorwes smerte
To yow, my lady, that I love moost;
But I biquethe the servyce of my goost   *spirit*
To yow aboven every creature,
2770 Syn that my lyf may no lenger dure.   *last*
Allas, the wo! allas, the peynes stronge,
That I for yow have suffred, and so longe!
Allas, the deeth! allas, myn Emelye!
Allas, departynge of oure compaignye!   *parting*
2775 Allas, myn hertes queene! allas, my wyf!
Myn hertes lady, endere of my lyf!
What is this world? what asketh men to have?
Now with his love, now in his colde grave
Allone, withouten any compaignye.
2780 Fare wel, my sweete foo, myn Emelye!
And softe taak me in youre armes tweye,   *gently*
For love of God, and herkneth what I seye.
    I have heer with my cosyn Palamon
Had strif and rancour many a day agon   *passed*
2785 For love of yow, and for my jalousye.
And Juppiter so wys my soule gye,
To speken of a servaunt proprely,   *lover*
With alle circumstances trewely—
That is to seyen, trouthe, honour, knyghthede,
2790 Wysdom, humblesse, estaat, and heigh kynrede,
Fredom, and al that longeth to that art—
So Juppiter have of my soule part,
As in this world right now ne knowe I non
So worthy to ben loved as Palamon,
2795 That serveth yow, and wol doon al his lyf.
And if that evere ye shul ben a wyf,
Foryet nat Palamon, the gentil man.'   *noble*
And with that word his speche faille gan,   *failed*
For from his feet up to his brest was come

2761 This is the long and short of it, that Arcita must die.
2766 The least one of my grievous sorrows.
2775 *my wyf.* In Boccaccio's *Teseide*, on which Chaucer's poem is
  based, Arcita is actually married to Emily.
2777 What is it man wants?
2786 And may Jupiter surely guide my soul.
2788 With a true regard for all the (courtly) attributes.
2790-1 Humility, rank, and noble kindred, liberality, and all that is
  essential to the lover's art.
2792-3 Even as Jupiter may have part in my soul's salvation, I swear I
  know of no one in this world.

2800 The coold of deeth, that hadde hym overcome,
And yet mooreover, for in his armes two   *because*
The vital strengthe is lost and al ago.
Oonly the intellect, withouten moore,   *delay*
That dwelled in his herte syk and soore,
2805 Gan faillen whan the herte felte deeth.
Dusked his eyen two, and failled breeth,   *darkened*
But on his lady yet caste he his ye;
His laste word was, 'Mercy, Emelye!'
His spirit chaunged hous and wente ther,
2810 As I cam nevere, I kan nat tellen wher.
Therfore I stynte, I nam no divinistre;
Of soules fynde I nat in this registre,
Ne me ne list thilke opinions to telle
Of hem, though that they writen wher they dwelle.
2815 Arcite is coold, ther Mars his soule gye!
Now wol I speken forth of Emelye.
      Shrighte Emelye, and howleth Palamon,   *shrieked*
And Theseus his suster took anon
Swownynge, and baar hire fro the corps away.   *carried*
2820 What helpeth it to tarien forth the day   *waste*
To tellen how she weep bothe eve and morwe?   *wept*
For in swich cas wommen have swich sorwe,
Whan that hir housbondes ben from hem ago,
That for the moore part they sorwen so,   *grieve so much*
2825 Or ellis fallen in swich maladye,
That at the laste certeinly they dye.
      Infinite been the sorwes and the teeres
Of olde folk, and folk of tendre yeeres,
In al the toun for deeth of this Theban.
2830 For hym ther wepeth bothe child and man;
So greet wepyng was ther noon, certayn,
Whan Ector was ybroght, al fressh yslayn,
To Troye.   Allas, the pitee that was ther,
Cracchynge of chekes, rentynge eek of   *scratching; tearing*
      heer.
2835 'Why woldestow be deed,' thise wommen crye,
'And haddest gold ynough, and Emelye?'
      No man myghte gladen Theseus,   *comfort*
Savynge his olde fader Egeus,

2809-10 Went where I cannot tell of, since I was never there.
2811 And so I'll hold my tongue; I'm no divine.
2812 I don't find any mention of souls in the list of contents of this
      book.
2813-14 Nor do I want to give the opinions of those who have written
      about the dwelling-place of souls.
2815 May Mars guide his soul!
2831 Certainly, there was not so much weeping.
2835 Why did you have to die.

That knew this worldes transmutacioun,   *mutability*
2840 As he hadde seyn it chaunge bothe up and doun,
Joye after wo, and wo after gladnesse,
And shewed hem ensamples and liknesse.
    'Right as ther dyed nevere man,' quod he,
'That he ne lyvede in erthe in som degree,
2845 Right so ther lyvede never man,' he seyde,
'In al this world, that som tyme he ne deyde.
This world nys but a thurghfare ful of wo,   *thoroughfare*
And we been pilgrymes, passynge to and fro.
Deeth is an ende of every worldly soore.'   *pain*
2850 And over al this yet seyde he muchel   *over and above*
    moore
To this effect, ful wisely to enhorte   *exhort*
The peple that they sholde hem reconforte.   *take heart*
    Duc Theseus, with al his bisy cure,   *care*
Caste now wher that the sepulture   *considered; sepulchre*
2855 Of good Arcite may best ymaked be,
And eek moost honurable in his degree.
And at the laste he took conclusioun
That ther as first Arcite and Palamoun   *where*
Hadden for love the bataille hem bitwene,
2860 That in that selve grove, swoote and grene,   *selfsame; sweet*
Ther as he hadde his amorouse desires,
His compleynte, and for love his hoote fires,
He wolde make a fyr in which the office   *rites*
Funeral he myghte al accomplice.   *carry out*
2865 And leet comande anon to hakke and hewe
The okes olde, and leye hem on a rewe   *in a row*
In colpons wel arrayed for to brenne.
His officers with swifte feet they renne   *run*
And ryde anon at his comandement.
2870 And after this, Theseus hath ysent
After a beere, and it al over spradde   *bier*
With clooth of gold, the richeste that he hadde.
And of the same suyte he cladde Arcite;
Upon his hondes hadde he gloves white,
2875 Eek on his heed a coroune of laurer grene,   *laurel*
And in his hond a swerd ful bright and kene.
He leyde hym, bare the visage, on the beere;   *with face bare*
Therwith he weep that pitee was to heere.   *wept*
And for the peple sholde seen hym alle,

2842 And told them stories of similar happenings.
2844 Who has not lived on earth in some walk of life.
2856 And do most honour to his rank.
2862 Where he made his lament.   (See 1540 ff.)
2865 And at once commanded men.
2867 In bundles well arranged for burning.
2873 And he clad Arcite in a cloth to match.

2880 Whan it was day, he broghte hym to the halle,
That roreth of the criyng and the soun.
Tho cam this woful Theban Palamoun, *then*
With flotery berd and ruggy, asshy heeres,
In clothes blake, ydropped al with teeres; *bedewed*
2885 And, passynge othere of wepynge, Emelye,
The rewefulleste of al the compaignye. *most sorrowful*
In as muche as the servyce sholde be
The moore noble and riche in his degree, *in degree*
Duc Theseus leet forth thre steedes brynge,
2890 That trapped were in steel al gliterynge,
And covered with the armes of daun Arcite.
Upon thise steedes, that weren grete and white,
Ther seten folk, of whiche oon baar his sheeld, *were seated*
Another his spere up on his hondes heeld,
2895 The thridde baar with hym his bowe Turkeys *Turkish*
(Of brend gold was the caas and eek the harneys);
And riden forth a paas with sorweful cheere
Toward the grove, as ye shul after heere.
The nobleste of the Grekes that ther were
2900 Upon hir shuldres caryeden the beere,
With slakke paas, and eyen rede and wete, *slow*
Thurghout the citee by the maister *along the main street*
strete,
That sprad was al with blak, and wonder hye
Right of the same is the strete ywrye.
2905 Upon the right hond wente olde Egeus,
And on that oother syde duc Theseus,
With vessels in hir hand of gold ful fyn,
Al ful of hony, milk, and blood, and wyn;
Eek Palamon, with ful greet compaignye;
2910 And after that cam woful Emelye,
With fyr in honde, as was that tyme the gyse, *custom*
To do the office of funeral servyse.
Heigh labour and ful greet apparaillynge
Was at the service and the fyr-makynge,
2915 That with his grene top the hevene raughte; *its; reached*
And twenty fadme of brede the armes straughte—

2881 That resounds with cries of lamentation.
2883 With fluttering beard and shaggy, ash-strewn hair.
2885 Weeping more than any other.
2889–90 Had three steeds brought forth, with trappings all of glittering steel.
2894 Another held up his spear in his hands.
2896 The quiver and also the fittings were of forged gold.
2897 They rode forth at a walking pace, with sorrowful mien.
2903–4 And the street is covered to a wondrous height with hangings of exactly the same colour.
2913–14 Great was the labour and the preparation.
2916 And its arms stretched out twenty fathoms in breadth.

This is to seyn, the bowes weren so brode.   *boughs; broad*
Of stree first ther was leyd ful many a lode.   *straw*
But how the fyr was maked upon highte,   *on high*
2920 Ne eek the names that the trees highte,
As ook, firre, birch, aspe, alder, holm, popler,   *aspen*
Wylugh, elm, plane, assh, box, chasteyn,   *chestnut*
    lynde, laurer,   *lime*
Mapul, thorn, bech, hasel, ew, whippeltree,—   *cornel-tree*
How they weren feld, shal nat be toold for me;
2925 Ne hou the goddes ronnen up and doun,   *ran*
Disherited of hire habitacioun,
In which they woneden in reste and pees,   *lived; quiet*
Nymphes, fawnes and amadrides,   *hamadryads*
Ne hou the beestes and the briddes alle
2930 Fledden for fere, whan the wode was falle;   *had fallen*
Ne how the ground agast was of the light,   *terrified*
That was nat wont to seen the sonne bright;
Ne how the fyr was couched first with stree,   *laid*
And thanne with drye stikkes cloven a thre,   *split in*
2935 And thanne with grene wode and spicerye,   *spices*
And thanne with clooth of gold and with
    perrye,   *precious stones*
And gerlandes, hangynge with ful many a flour;   *hung*
The mirre, th'encens, with al so greet odour;
Ne how Arcite lay among al this,
2940 Ne what richesse aboute his body is;   *rich splendour*
Ne how that Emelye, as was the gyse,
Putte in the fyr of funeral servyse;
Ne how she swowned whan men made the fyr,
Ne what she spak, ne what was hir desir;
2945 Ne what jeweles men in the fyre caste,
Whan that the fyr was greet and brente faste;   *strongly*
Ne how somme caste hir sheeld, and somme hir spere,
And of hire vestimentz, whiche that they were,
And coppes fulle of wyn, and milk, and blood,   *cups*
2950 Into the fyr, that brente as it were wood;   *burned; mad*
Ne how the Grekes, with an huge route,   *gathering*
Thries riden al the fyr aboute   *thrice*
Upon the left hand, with a loud shoutynge,   *to the left*
And thries with hir speres claterynge;
2955 And thries how the ladyes gonne crye;   *cried out*
And how that lad was homward Emelye;   *led*
Ne how Arcite is brent to asshen colde;
Ne how that lyche-wake was yholde   *vigil over the body*

2920 Or the names by which the trees were called.
2924 How they were felled, shall not be told, for my part.
2938 The myrrh, the incense, so heavy with fragrance.
2942 i.e. applied the torch to the funeral pyre.
2948 And some the very clothes they were wearing.

Al thilke nyght; ne how the Grekes pleye
2960 The wake-pleyes, ne kepe I nat to seye;   *funeral games; care*
Who wrastleth best naked with oille enoynt,   *anointed*
Ne who that baar hym best, in no disjoynt.
I wol nat tellen eek how that they goon
Hoom til Atthenes, whan the pley is doon;   *games*
2965 But shortly to the point thanne wol I wende,
And maken of my longe tale an ende.
By processe and by lengthe of certeyn yeres,
Al stynted is the moornynge and the teres   *ended*
Of Grekes, by oon general assent.
2970 Thanne semed me ther was a parlement   *I think*
At Atthenes, upon certein pointz and caas;
Among the whiche pointz yspoken was,
To have with certein contrees alliaunce,
And have fully of Thebans obeisaunce.
2975 For which this noble Theseus anon
Leet senden after gentil Palamon,
Unwist of hym what was the cause and why;
But in his blake clothes sorwefully
He cam at his comandement in hye.   *haste*
2980 Tho sente Theseus for Emelye.   *then*
Whan they were set, and hust was al the place,   *seated; hushed*
And Theseus abiden hadde a space   *waited; for a while*
Er any word cam fram his wise brest,
His eyen sette he ther as was his lest,
2985 And with a sad visage he siked stille,   *sighed; softly*
And after that right thus he seyde his wille:
'The Firste Moevere of the cause above,
Whan he first made the faire cheyne of love,
Greet was th'effect, and heigh was his entente.
2990 Wel wiste he why, and what therof he mente;
For with that faire cheyne of love he bond   *bound*
The fyr, the eyr, the water, and the lond   *air*
In certeyn boundes, that they may nat flee.
That same Prince and that Moevere,' quod he,
2995 'Hath stablissed in this wrecched world   *established*
adoun   *below*
Certeyne dayes and duracioun

2962 Or who proved himself the best man in a fix.
2967 In course of time and after certain years.
2971 To discuss certain points and matters of moment.
2974 And get complete obedience from the Thebans.
2976–7 Had noble Palamon sent for, without his knowing why or
wherefore.
2984 He gazed about him where he pleased.
2987 i.e. the prime mover and first cause of things.
2990 He well knew why he did it, and what he meant by it.
2996 A certain length of days.

To al that is engendred in this place,
Over the whiche day they may nat pace, *beyond; go*
Al mowe they yet tho dayes wel abregge.
3000 Ther nedeth noght noon auctoritee t'allegge,
For it is preeved by experience,
But that me list declaren my sentence.
Thanne may men by this ordre wel discerne
That thilke Moevere stable is and eterne.
3005 Wel may men knowe, but it be a fool,
That every part dirryveth from his hool; *its whole*
For nature hath nat taken his bigynnyng
Of no partie or cantel of a thyng, *from; portion*
But of a thyng that parfit is and stable, *perfect*
3010 Descendynge so til it be corrumpable.
And therfore, of his wise purveiaunce,
He hath so wel biset his ordinaunce,
That speces of thynges and progressiouns
Shullen enduren by successiouns,
3015 And nat eterne, withouten any lye.
This maystow understonde and seen at ye. *at a glance*
 Loo the ook, that hath so long a norisshynge *growth*
From tyme that it first bigynneth to sprynge,
And hath so long a lif, as we may see,
3020 Yet at the laste wasted is the tree.
 Considereth eek how that the harde stoon
Under oure feet, on which we trede and goon,
Yet wasteth it as it lyth by the weye.
The brode ryver somtyme wexeth dreye;
3025 The grete tounes se we wane and wende. *pass away*
Thanne may ye se that al this thyng hath ende.
 Of man and womman seen we wel also
That nedes, in oon of thise termes two,
This is to seyn, in youthe or elles age,
3030 He moot be deed, the kyng as shal a page;
Som in his bed, som in the depe see,
Som in the large feeld, as men may see;
Ther helpeth noght, al goth that ilke weye.
Thanne may I seyn that al this thyng moot deye. *must die*

2999 Although they may easily shorten their days.
3000 There is no need to cite authority.
3002 Except that I want to make my meaning clear.
3005 Any but a fool will know.
3010 Descending by degrees till it becomes corruptible.
3011-15 Therefore in his wise providence he has established his decree
 that things and processes of every kind shall renew themselves by
 continual succession, and not be eternal—this is certainly true.
3028 That of necessity, in one of these two periods.
3030 Everyone must die, the king no less than a page.
3031 *Som . . . som*, one . . . another.
3033 There is no help for it, all go the same way.

3035   What maketh this but Juppiter, the kyng,   *causes*
        That is prince and cause of alle thyng,
        Convertynge al unto his propre welle
        From which it is dirryved, sooth to telle?
        And heer-agayns no creature on lyve,
3040   Of no degree, availleth for to stryve.
        Thanne is it wysdom, as it thynketh me,   *seems to*
        To maken vertu of necessitee,
        And take it weel that we may nat eschue,
        And namely that to us alle is due.
3045   And whoso gruccheth ought, he dooth folye,
        And rebel is to hym that al may gye.   *guide*
        And certeinly a man hath moost honour
        To dyen in his excellence and flour,
        Whan he is siker of his goode name;   *certain*
3050   Thanne hath he doon his freend, ne hym, no shame.
        And gladder oghte his freend been of his deeth,   *should*
        Whan with honour up yolden is his breeth,   *yielded*
        Than whan his name apalled is for age,   *enfeebled*
        For al forgeten is his vassellage.   *prowess*
3055   Thanne is it best, as for a worthy fame,
        To dyen whan that he is best of name.
        The contrarie of al this is wilfulnesse.
        Why grucchen we, why have we hevynesse,   *sorrow*
        That goode Arcite, of chivalrie flour,
3060   Departed is with duetee and honour   *respect*
        Out of this foule prisoun of this lyf?
        Why grucchen heere his cosyn and his wyf
        Of his welfare, that loved hem so weel?
        Kan he hem thank? Nay, God woot, never   *not a bit*
           a deel,
3065   That both his soule and eek hemself offende,
        And yet they mowe hir lustes nat amende.
        What may I conclude of this longe serye,   *argument*
        But after wo I rede us to be merye,   *advise*
        And thanken Juppiter of al his grace?
3070   And er that we departen from this place

3037–8 Turning all things back to the source from which, in truth, they
    are derived.
3039–40 Against this fate no living creature, whatever his degree, can
    hope to strive successfully.
3043 Take in good part what we cannot avoid.
3044 Especially those things that are due to all of us.
3045 Anyone who complains at all commits a folly.
3055–6 Then it is best for nobleness of fame that a man should die
    when his reputation is at its height.
3064–6 Does he owe them any thanks? No, God knows, none at all,
    for they harm both his spirit and themselves, and yet do nothing to
    make themselves happier.

I rede that we make of sorwes two
O parfit joye, lastynge everemo.   *one*
And looketh now, wher moost sorwe is herinne,
Ther wol we first amenden and bigynne.   *remedy*
3075   'Suster,' quod he, 'this is my fulle assent,
With al th'avys heere of my parlement,
That gentil Palamon, youre owene knyght,
That serveth yow with wille, herte, and myght,
And ever hath doon syn ye first hym knewe,
3080 That ye shul of youre grace upon hym rewe,   *have pity*
And taken hym for housbonde and for lord.
Lene me youre hond, for this is oure accord.   *give*
Lat se now of youre wommanly pitee.   *now show*
He is a kynges brother sone, pardee;   *brother's*
3085 And though he were a povre bacheler,   *young knight*
Syn he hath served yow so many a yeer,
And had for yow so greet adversitee,
It moste been considered, leeveth me;
For gentil mercy oghte to passen right.'
3090   Thanne seyde he thus to Palamon the knight:
'I trowe ther nedeth litel sermonyng
To make yow assente to this thyng.
Com neer, and taak youre lady by the hond.'
Bitwixen hem was maad anon the bond
3095 That highte matrimoigne or mariage,
By al the conseil and the baronage.
And thus with alle blisse and melodye
Hath Palamon ywedded Emelye.
And God, that al this wyde world hath wroght,
3100 Sende hym his love that hath it deere aboght;
For now is Palamon in alle wele,   *prosperity*
Lyvynge in blisse, in richesse, and in heele,   *health*
And Emelye hym loveth so tendrely,
And he hire serveth so gentilly,   *honourably*
3105 That nevere was ther no word hem bitwene
Of jalousie or any oother teene.   *trouble*
Thus endeth Palamon and Emelye;
And God save al this faire compaignye!   Amen.

HEERE IS ENDED THE KNYGHTES TALE

3088 This should be taken into consideration, believe me.
3089 For noble mercy ought to prevail over strict justice.
3096 By all the council and nobility.
3100 Who has paid dearly for it.
3107 So ends the story of Palamon and Emily.

THE MILLER'S PROLOGUE

HEERE FOLWEN THE WORDES BITWENE THE HOOST AND THE MILLERE

WHAN that the Knyght had thus his tale ytoold,
3110 In al the route nas ther yong ne oold
That he ne seyde it was a noble storie,
And worthy for to drawen to memorie;   *be remembered*
And namely the gentils everichon.
Oure Hooste lough and swoor, 'So moot I gon,
3115 This gooth aright; unbokeled is the male.
Lat se now who shal telle another tale;   *let's see*
For trewely the game is wel bigonne.
Now telleth ye, sir Monk, if that ye konne,
Somwhat to quite with the Knyghtes tale.'   *repay*
3120 The Millere, that for dronken was al pale,
So that unnethe upon his hors he sat,   *with difficulty*
He nolde avalen neither hood ne hat,   *take off*
Ne abyde no man for his curteisie,
But in Pilates voys he gan to crie,
3125 And swoor, 'By armes, and by blood and   *Christ's arms*
bones,
I kan a noble tale for the nones,   *occasion*
With which I wol now quite the Knyghtes tale.'
Oure Hooste saugh that he was dronke of ale,
And seyde, 'Abyd, Robyn, my leeve brother;   *dear*
3130 Som bettre man shal telle us first another.
Abyd, and lat us werken thriftily.'   *profitably*
'By Goddes soule,' quod he, 'that wol nat I;
For I wol speke, or elles go my wey.'
Oure Hoost answerde, 'Tel on, a devel wey! *in the devil's name*

3110–11 In all the company there was no one, young or old, who did
    not say.
3113 And especially all the gentlefolk.
3114–15 Our Host laughed and exclaimed, 'Upon my life, this is going
    well; the pack is opened (i.e. we have now sampled our wares).'
3120 Who was quite pale with drink.
3123 Nor had he the manners to wait for anyone else.
3124 A reference to the ranting Pilate of the Corpus Christi plays.

83

3135 Thou art a fool; thy wit is overcome.'
           'Now herkneth,' quod the Millere, 'alle and   *one and all*
                 some!
           But first I make a protestacioun
           That I am dronke, I knowe it by my soun;
           And therfore if that I mysspeke or seye,   *speak wrongly*
3140 Wyte it the ale of Southwerk, I you preye.   *blame it on*
           For I wol telle a legende and a lyf   *story*
           Bothe of a carpenter and of his wyf,
           How that a clerk hath set the wrightes cappe.'
                 The Reve answerde and seyde, 'Stynt thy   *shut your row*
                 clappe!
3145 Lat be thy lewed dronken harlotrye.
           It is a synne and eek a greet folye
           To apeyren any man, or hym defame,   *injure*
           And eek to bryngen wyves in swich fame.
           Thou mayst ynogh of othere thynges seyn.'
3150   This dronke Millere spak ful soone ageyn   *in reply*
           And seyde, 'Leve brother Osewold,   *dear; Oswald*
           Who hath no wyf, he is no cokewold.   *cuckold*
           But I sey nat therfore that thou art oon;
           Ther been ful goode wyves many oon,
3155 And evere a thousand goode ayeyns oon   *for every bad one*
                 badde.
           That knowestow wel thyself, but if thou   *unless you're mad*
                 madde.
           Why artow angry with my tale now?
           I have a wyf, pardee, as wel as thow;   *indeed*
           Yet nolde I, for the oxen in my plogh,
3160 Take upon me moore than ynogh,
           As demen of myself that I were oon;
           I wol bileve wel that I am noon.
           An housbonde shal nat been inquisityf
           Of Goddes pryvetee, nor of his wyf.   *secret purpose*
3165 So he may fynde Goddes foyson there,
           Of the remenant nedeth nat enquere.'
                 What sholde I moore seyn, but this Millere
           He nolde his wordes for no man forbere,   *spare*
           But told his cherles tale in his manere.   *churl's*

3138 By the sound of my own voice.
3143 How a student made a fool of the carpenter.
3145 Have done with your ignorant drunken ribaldry.   (The Reeve's
     annoyance is explained by the fact that he is a carpenter himself by
     trade; see 614.)
3148 And also to bring wives into disrepute.
3149 There are lots of other things for you to talk about.
3160–1 Presume to consider myself one (i.e. a cuckold).
3165 Provided he finds God's plenty there, i.e. provided his wife gives
     him all he wants.

3170 M'athynketh that I shal reherce it heere.
      And therfore every gentil wight I preye,   *person*
      For Goddes love, demeth nat that I seye
      Of yvel entente, but for I moot reherce
      Hir tales alle, be they bettre or werse,
3175 Or elles falsen som of my mateere.   *falsify*
      And therfore, whoso list it nat yheere,
      Turne over the leef and chese another tale;   *leaf; choose*
      For he shal fynde ynowe, grete and smale,   *enough*
      Of storial thyng that toucheth gentillesse,
3180 And eek moralitee and hoolynesse.   *also*
      Blameth nat me if that ye chese amys.   *wrongly*
      The Millere is a cherl, ye knowe wel this;
      So was the Reve eek and othere mo,
      And harlotrie they tolden bothe two.   *ribaldry*
3185 Avyseth yow, and put me out of blame;   *think well*
      And eek men shal nat maken ernest of game.

THE MILLER'S TALE

HEERE BIGYNNETH THE MILLERE HIS TALE

      WHILOM ther was dwellynge at Oxenford   *once*
      A riche gnof, that gestes heeld to bord,
      And of his craft he was a carpenter.
3190 With hym ther was dwellynge a poure scoler,
      Hadde lerned art, but al his fantasye   *fancy*
      Was turned for to lerne astrologye,

      3170 I'm sorry to have to repeat it here.
      3172–4 For the love of God, don't imagine I speak with any evil
      intention, but because I'm bound to tell all their tales.
      3176–7 Anyone who doesn't wish to hear it.
      3179 Of historical matter concerned with noble conduct.
      3186 i.e. take a joke seriously.
      3188 A well-off churl, who took in lodgers.
      3190–1 A poor scholar who had studied the arts.

And koude a certeyn of conclusiouns,
To demen by interrogaciouns,
3195 If that men asked hym in certein houres
Whan that men sholde have droghte or elles shoures,
Or if men asked hym what sholde bifalle
Of every thyng; I may nat rekene hem alle.
     This clerk was cleped hende Nicholas.
3200 Of deerne love he koude and of solas;
And therto he was sleigh and ful privee,   *sly; secretive*
And lyk a mayden meke for to see.
A chambre hadde he in that hostelrye   *lodging-house*
Allone, withouten any compaignye,
3205 Ful fetisly ydight with herbes swoote;
And he hymself as sweete as is the roote
Of lycorys, or any cetewale.   *liquorice; ginger*
His Almageste, and bookes grete and smale,
His astrelabie, longynge for his art,
3210 His augrym stones layen faire apart,
On shelves couched at his beddes heed;   *placed*
His presse ycovered with a faldyng reed;
And al above ther lay a gay sautrie,   *psaltery*
On which he made a-nyghtes melodie
3215 So swetely that all the chambre rong;
And *Angelus ad virginem* he song;
And after that he song the Kynges Noote.
Ful often blessed was his myrie throte.
And thus this sweete clerk his tyme spente
3220 After his freendes fyndyng and his rente.
     This carpenter hadde wedded newe a wyf,   *newly*
Which that he lovede moore than his lyf;
Of eighteteene yeer she was of age.
Jalous he was, and heeld hire narwe in cage,   *closely*
3225 For she was wylde and yong, and he was old,

3193 ff. He knew a certain number of astrological operations for obtain-
ing answers to questions concerning the future, including the state of
the weather.
3199 This student was called gentle (pleasant, courteous) Nicholas.
3200 He knew all about secret love and consolation.
3202 As meek as a maiden to look at.
3205 Most handsomely decked with sweet-smelling herbs.
3208 *Almageste*, an astronomical treatise by Ptolemy, who lived at
Alexandria in the second century A.D.
3209 His astrolabe, relating to his special skill.
3210 His counters (counting-stones) lay neatly apart.
3212 His cupboard covered with a red woollen cloth.
3216 *Angelus ad virginem*, the Angel to the virgin (a hymn on the
Annunciation).
3217 *the Kynges Noote*, possibly the same as a medieval song called
'King William's Note.'
3220 On his friends' charity and his own income.

And demed hymself been lik a cokewold.
He knew nat Catoun, for his wit was rude,
That bad man sholde wedde his simylitude.
Men sholde wedden after hire estaat,
3230 For youthe and elde is often at debaat.   *variance*
But sith that he was fallen in the snare,   *since*
He moste endure, as oother folk, his care.   *sorrow*
   Fair was this yonge wyf, and therwithal
As any wezele hir body gent and smal.
3235 A ceynt she werede, barred al of silk,
A barmclooth as whit as morne milk
Upon hir lendes, ful of many a goore.
Whit was hir smok, and broyden al bifoore   *embroidered*
And eek bihynde, on hir coler aboute,
3240 Of col-blak silk, withinne and eek withoute.
The tapes of hir white voluper   *cap*
Were of the same suyte of hir coler;   *matched her collar*
Hir filet brood of silk, and set ful hye.
And sikerly she hadde a likerous ye;   *certainly; wanton eye*
3245 Ful smale ypulled were hire browes two,
And tho were bent and blake as any sloo.   *they; sloe*
She was ful moore blisful on to see
Than is the newe pere-jonette tree,
And softer than the wolle is of a wether.   *wool*
3250 And by hir girdel heeng a purs of lether,
Tasseled with silk, and perled with latoun.
In al this world, to seken up and doun,
There nys no man so wys that koude thenche   *imagine*
So gay a popelote or swich a wenche.   *poppet; such*
3255 Ful brighter was the shynyng of hir hewe
Than in the Tour the noble yforged newe.
But of hir song, it was as loude and yerne   *as for; eager*
As any swalwe sittynge on a berne.   *swallow; barn*

3226 And thought himself no better than a cuckold.
3227 He did not know Cato (the supposed author of a collection of
    Latin maxims studied in the grammar schools), for his mind was
    untutored.
3228 Who bade a man marry someone like himself.
3229 In keeping with their condition.
3234 Her body was as graceful and slender as a weasel's.
3235 She wore a girdle decorated with bars of silk.
3236-7 A gored apron, as white as morning milk, over her loins.
3239-40 All round her collar, with coal-black silk, inside and out.
3243 Her fillet was a broad band of silk, set high on her head.
3245 Her eyebrows were plucked to a narrow line.
3248 Than is the early pear-tree in new leaf.
3251 Studded with pearl-shaped knobs of brass.
3252 If you search high and low.
3255-6 She was brighter of complexion than a gold noble freshly minted
    in the Tower of London.

Therto she koude skippe and make game,   *frolic*
3260 As any kyde or calf folwynge his dame.   *its*
Hir mouth was sweete as bragot or the meeth,
Or hoord of apples leyd in hey or heeth.   *store; heather*
Wynsynge she was, as is a joly colt,
Long as a mast, and upright as a bolt.
3265 A brooch she baar upon hir lowe coler,
As brood as is the boos of a bokeler.   *boss; shield*
Hir shoes were laced on hir legges hye.
She was a prymerole, a piggesnye,
For any lord to leggen in his bedde,   *lay*
3270 Or yet for any good yeman to wedde.
     Now, sire, and eft, sire, so bifel the cas,
That on a day this hende Nicholas
Fil with this yonge wyf to rage and pleye,   *began; wanton*
Whil that hir housbonde was at Oseneye,
3275 As clerkes ben ful subtile and ful queynte;   *artful; sly*
And prively he caughte hire by the queynte,   *stealthily*
And seyde, 'Ywis, but if ich have my wille,   *unless I*
For deerne love of thee, lemman, I spille.'   *perish*
And heeld hire harde by the haunchebones,
3280 And seyde, 'Lemman, love me al atones, *sweetheart; at once*
Or I wol dyen, also God me save!'   *so*
And she sproong as a colt dooth in the trave,
And with hir heed she wryed faste awey,   *turned*
And seyde, 'I wol nat kisse thee, by my fey!   *faith*
3285 Why, lat be,' quod she, 'lat be, Nicholas,   *stop it*
Or I wol crie "out, harrow" and "allas!"
Do wey youre handes, for youre curteisye!'
     This Nicholas gan mercy for to crye,
And spak so faire, and profred him so faste,
3290 That she hir love hym graunted atte laste,
And swoor hir ooth, by seint Thomas of Kent,
That she wol been at his comandement,
Whan that she may hir leyser wel espie.   *opportunity*
'Myn housbonde is so ful of jalousie

3261 As bragget (a drink made of ale and honey) or mead.
3263 She was as frisky and skittish as a colt.
3264 Straight as a crossbow-bolt.
3268 She was a primrose, a pigsney (a term of endearment).
3270 *yeman*, yeoman, a servant of a superior grade, ranking between a
    squire and a page.
3274 *Oseneye*, Osney, near Oxford.
3282 *trave*, wooden frame for holding unruly horses while they are
    being shod.
3286 *out, harrow*, a cry for help.
3287 Be good enough to take your hands away.
3289 Spoke so civilly, and offered his services so eagerly.
3291 i.e. St Thomas Becket.

3295 That but ye wayte wel and been privee,   *watch; stealthy*
I woot right wel I nam but deed,' quod she.
'Ye moste been ful deerne, as in this cas.'   *discreet*
    'Nay, therof care thee noght,' quod Nicholas.   *worry*
'A clerk hadde litherly biset his whyle,
3300 But if he koude a carpenter bigyle.'
And thus they been accorded and ysworn
To wayte a tyme, as I have told biforn.
    Whan Nicholas had doon thus everideel,   *done all this*
And thakked hire aboute the lendes weel,   *smacked*
3305 He kiste hire sweete and taketh his sawtrie,
And pleyeth faste, and maketh melodie.
    Thanne fil it thus, that to the paryssh chirche,   *happened*
Cristes owene werkes for to wirche,   *do*
This goode wyf went on an haliday.   *religious festival*
3310 Hir forheed shoon as bright as any day,
So was it wasshen whan she leet hir werk.   *left off*
Now was ther of that chirche a parissh clerk,
The which that was ycleped Absolon.   *called*
Crul was his heer, and as the gold it shoon,   *curly*
3315 And strouted as a fanne large and brode;
Ful streight and evene lay his joly shode.   *parting*
His rode was reed, his eyen greye as goos.   *complexion; goose*
With Poules wyndow corven on his shoos,
In hoses rede he wente fetisly.   *elegantly*
3320 Yclad he was ful smal and propraly   *finely; handsomely*
Al in a kirtel of a lyght waget;   *jacket; blue*
Ful faire and thikke been the poyntes set.
And therupon he hadde a gay surplys
As whit as is the blosme upon the rys.   *bough*
3325 A myrie child he was, so God me save.   *gay lad*
Wel koude he laten blood and clippe and shave,
And maken a chartre of lond or acquitaunce.   *deed of release*
In twenty manere koude he trippe and daunce   *different ways*
After the scole of Oxenforde tho,   *at that time*
3330 And with his legges casten to and fro,   *fling*
And pleyen songes on a smal rubible;   *fiddle*
Therto he song som tyme a loud quynyble;   *falsetto*

3296 I know for certain it will be the death of me.
3299–3300 A student has made bad use of his time if he can't deceive a carpenter.
3312 *parissh clerk*, an official in minor orders who assisted the parish priest to perform the church services.
3315 And spread out as wide and broad as a fan (i.e. a basket used in winnowing grain).
3318 i.e. the leather uppers of his shoes were cut with designs resembling the tracery of a window in St Paul's.
3322 i.e. he had laces in profusion for fastening his jacket.
3326 He knew all about letting blood, cutting hair, and shaving.

And as wel koude he pleye on a giterne. *guitar*
In al the toun nas brewhous ne taverne
3335 That he ne visited with his solas, *entertainment*
Ther any gaylard tappestere was. *lively barmaid*
But sooth to seyn, he was somdeel *somewhat*
    squaymous *squeamish*
Of fartyng, and of speche daungerous. *fastidious*
    This Absolon, that jolif was and gay, *sprightly*
3340 Gooth with a sencer on the haliday, *censer*
Sensynge the wyves of the parisshe faste; *vigorously*
And many a lovely look on hem he caste,
And namely on this carpenteris wyf. *especially*
To looke on hire hym thoughte a myrie lyf, *seemed to him*
3345 She was so propre and sweete and likerous. *comely; wanton*
I dar wel seyn, if she hadde been a mous,
And he a cat, he wolde hire hente anon. *catch*
This parissh clerk, this joly Absolon,
Hath in his herte swich a love-longynge *passionate longing*
3350 That of no wyf took he noon offrynge; *offering*
For curteisie, he seyde, he wolde noon. *wanted none*
    The moone, whan it was nyght, ful
      brighte shoon, *brightly shone*
And Absolon his gyterne hath ytake,
For paramours he thoghte for to wake.
3355 And forth he gooth, jolif and amorous,
Til he cam to the carpenteres hous
A litel after cokkes hadde ycrowe,
And dressed hym up by a shot-wyndowe
That was upon the carpenteris wal.
3360 He syngeth in his voys gentil and smal, *thin*
'Now, deere lady, if thy wille be, *if it please you*
I praye yow that ye wole rewe on me,' *take pity*
Ful wel acordaunt to his gyternynge.
This carpenter awook, and herde him synge,
3365 And spak unto his wyf, and seyde anon,
'What! Alison! herestow nat Absolon,
That chaunteth thus under oure boures wal?' *bedroom*
And she answerde hir housbonde therwithal,
'Yis, God woot, John, I heere it every deel.' *knows; all*
3370   This passeth forth; what wol ye bet than weel?
Fro day to day this joly Absolon
So woweth hire that hym is wo bigon.
He waketh al the nyght and al the day;
He kembeth his lokkes brode, and made hym gay; *combs*

3354 For love's sake he resolved to stay awake.
3358 And took his stand near a casement window.
3363 To the tuneful accompaniment of his guitar.
3370 And so it went; what more do you want?
3372 Woos her so hard that he feels utterly miserable.

3375 He woweth hire by meenes and brocage,
     And swoor he wolde been hir owene page;
     He syngeth, brokkynge as a nyghtyngale;   *quavering*
     He sente hire pyment, meeth, and spiced ale,
     And wafres, pipyng hoot out of the   *wafer-cakes*
          gleede;   *embers*
3380 And, for she was of towne, he profred meede.
     For som folk wol ben wonnen for richesse,
     And somme for strokes, and somme for gentillesse.
          Somtyme, to shewe his lightnesse and   *agility*
               maistrye,   *great skill*
     He pleyeth Herodes upon a scaffold hye.
3385 But what availleth hym as in this cas?
     She loveth so this hende Nicholas
     That Absolon may blowe the bukkes horn;
     He ne hadde for his labour but a scorn.
     And thus she maketh Absolon hire ape,   *dupe*
3390 And al his ernest turneth til a jape.
     Ful sooth is this proverbe, it is no lye,   *very true; lie*
     Men seyn right thus, 'Alwey the nye slye
     Maketh the ferre leeve to be looth.'
     For though that Absolon be wood or wrooth,
3395 By cause that he fer was from hire sight,
     This nye Nicholas stood in his light.
          Now ber thee wel, thou hende Nicholas,   *do your best*
     For Absolon may waille and synge 'allas.'
     And so bifel it on a Saterday,
3400 This carpenter was goon til Osenay;
     And hende Nicholas and Alisoun
     Acorded been to this conclusioun,
     That Nicholas shal shapen hym a wyle   *hatch a plot*
     This sely jalous housbonde to bigyle;   *foolish*
3405 And if so be the game wente aright,
     She sholde slepen in his arm al nyght,
     For this was his desir and hire also.   *hers*
     And right anon, withouten wordes mo,   *more*

3375 With the help of go-betweens and agents.
3378 He sent her sweetened wine, mead.
3380 i.e. he offered her money because she lived in a town and so would
     have opportunities for spending it.
3381-2 Some people will be won by money, some by blows, and some
     by courtesy.
3384 He plays the part of Herod in a miracle play on a stage high above
     the ground.
3387 'To blow the buck's horn' means 'to work without reward.'
3390 And makes a joke of all his earnest efforts.
3392-3 'The sly one near at hand always makes the distant lover
     hateful.' (Cf. 'out of sight, out of mind.')
3394-6 Mad though he was about it, Absalom was out of her sight, and
     so the handy Nicholas stood in his light.

This Nicholas no lenger wolde tarie,
3410 But dooth ful softe unto his chambre carie   *softly*
Bothe mete and drynke for a day or tweye,
And to hire housbonde bad hire for to seye,
If that he axed after Nicholas,
She sholde seye she nyste where he was,   *did not know*
3415 Of al that day she saugh hym nat with ye;   *during*
She trowed that he was in maladye,
For for no cry hir mayde koude hym calle,
He nolde answere for thyng that myghte falle.

      This passeth forth al thilke Saterday,   *goes on; that*
3420 That Nicholas stille in his chambre lay,   *quietly*
And eet and sleep, or dide what hym leste,   *he pleased*
Til Sonday, that the sonne gooth to reste.
This sely carpenter hath greet merveyle
Of Nicholas, or what thyng myghte hym eyle,   *ail*
3425 And seyde, 'I am adrad, by Seint Thomas,   *afraid*
It stondeth nat aright with Nicholas.
God shilde that he deyde sodeynly!
This world is now ful tikel, sikerly.   *unreliable; certainly*
I saugh to-day a cors yborn to chirche   *corpse; carried*
3430 That now, on Monday last, I saugh hym wirche.
      'Go up,' quod he unto his knave anoon,   *servant*
'Clepe at his dore, or knokke with a stoon.   *call*
Looke how it is, and tel me boldely.'
      This knave gooth hym up ful sturdily,
3435 And at the chambre dore whil that he stood,
He cride and knokked as that he were wood,   *mad*
'What! how! what do ye, maister Nicholay?
How may ye slepen al the longe day?'
But al for noghte, he herde nat a word.   *nothing*
3440 An hole he foond, ful lowe upon a bord,
Ther as the cat was wont in for to crepe,   *where*
And at that hole he looked in ful depe,
And at the laste he hadde of hym a sight.
This Nicholas sat evere capyng upright,
3445 As he had kiked on the newe moone.   *as if he had gazed*
Adoun he gooth, and tolde his maister soone   *down*
In what array he saugh this ilke man.
      This carpenter to blessen hym bigan,   *cross himself*

3416 She thought he must be ill.
3417-18 Her maid couldn't attract his attention for all her shouting;
      he just wouldn't answer at all.
3423-4 Wondered a great deal about Nicholas.
3426 All is not well with Nicholas.
3427 God forbid he should die suddenly.
3430 Of someone I saw working on Monday last.
3444 Sat staring straight up all the time.
3447 In what condition he had seen the man.

And seyde, 'Help us, seinte Frydeswyde!
3450 A man woot litel what hym shal bityde.   *knows; happen*
This man is falle, with his astromye,   *astrology*
In som woodnesse or in som agonye.   *madness*
I thoghte ay wel how that it sholde be!
Men sholde nat knowe of Goddes pryvetee.
3455 Ye, blessed be alwey a lewed man   *ignorant*
That noght but oonly his bileve kan!
So ferde another clerk with astromye;   *fared*
He walked in the feeldes, for to prye   *peer*
Upon the sterres, what ther sholde bifalle,
3460 Til he was in a marle-pit yfalle;   *fallen*
He saugh nat that.   But yet, by seint Thomas,
Me reweth soore of hende Nicholas.
He shal be rated of his studiyng,   *scolded for*
If that I may, by Jhesus, hevene kyng!
3465 Get me a staf, that I may underspore,
Whil that thou, Robyn, hevest up the dore.
He shal out of his studiyng, as I gesse'—   *leave off*
And to the chambre dore he gan hym dresse.   *went up*
His knave was a strong carl for the nones,
3470 And by the haspe he haaf it of atones;   *heaved*
Into the floor the dore fil anon.   *onto; fell*
This Nicholas sat ay as stille as stoon,
And evere caped upward into the eir.
This carpenter wende he were in despeir,   *supposed*
3475 And hente hym by the sholdres myghtily,   *seized*
And shook hym harde, and cride spitously,   *angrily*
'What! Nicholay! what, how! what, looke adoun!
Awak, and thenk on Cristes passioun!
I crouche thee from elves and fro wightes.
3480 Therwith the nyght-spel seyde he anon-rightes
On foure halves of the hous aboute,   *sides*
And on the thresshfold of the dore withoute: *outside*
'Jhesu Crist and seinte Benedight,   *Benedict*
Blesse this hous from every wikked wight,   *creature*
3485 For nyghtes verye, the white *pater-noster!*
Where wentestow, seinte Petres soster?'
     And atte laste this hende Nicholas
Gan for to sike soore, and seyde, 'Allas!   *sigh*

3456 Who knows nothing but his creed.
3459 To find out from them what was going to happen.
3462 I am very sorry for gentle Nicholas.
3465 So that I can push it under.
3469 Cf. 545.
3479 I will protect you with the sign of the cross from elves and other
     creatures.
3480 *nyght-spel*, charm recited at night to ward off evil spirits;
     anon-rightes, straightway.
3485–6 The meaning of these lines is obscure.

Shal al the world be lost eftsoones now?'   *very soon*
3490 This carpenter answerde, 'What seystow?
What! thynk on God, as we doon, men that swynke.'   *labour*
This Nicholas answerde, 'Fecche me drynke,
And after wol I speke in pryvetee   *private*
Of certeyn thyng that toucheth me and thee.   *concerns*
3495 I wol telle it noon oother man, certeyn.'
This carpenter goth doun, and comth ageyn,   *back*
And broghte of myghty ale a large quart;
And whan that ech of hem had dronke his part,   *share*
This Nicholas his dore faste shette,   *shut*
3500 And doun the carpenter by hym he sette.
He seyde 'John, myn hooste, lief and deere,   *beloved*
Thou shalt upon thy trouthe swere me heere   *honour*
That to no wight thou shalt this conseil wreye;
For it is Cristes conseil that I seye,
3505 And if thou telle it man, thou art forlore;   *damned*
For this vengeaunce thou shalt han therfore,   *for it*
That if thou wreye me, thou shalt be wood.'   *betray; mad*
'Nay, Crist forbede it, for his hooly blood!'   *forbid*
Quod tho this sely man, 'I nam no labbe;
3510 Ne, though I seye, I nam nat lief to gabbe.
Sey what thou wolt, I shal it nevere telle
To child ne wyf, by hym that harwed helle!'
'Now John,' quod Nicholas, 'I wol nat lye;
I have yfounde in myn astrologye,
3515 As I have looked in the moone bright,   *gazed at*
That now a Monday next, at quarter nyght,
Shal falle a reyn, and that so wilde and wood,
That half so greet was nevere Noes flood.   *Noah's*
This world,' he seyde, 'in lasse than an hour
3520 Shal al be dreynt, so hidous is the   *overwhelmed; hideous*
shour.
Thus shal mankynde drenche, and lese hir lyf.'   *drown; lose*
This carpenter answerde, 'Allas, my wyf!
And shal she drenche? allas, myn Alisoun!'
For sorwe of this he fil almoost adoun,   *almost collapsed*
3525 And seyde, 'Is ther no remedie in this cas?'
'Why, yis, for Gode,' quod hende Nicholas,   *by God*
'If thou wolt werken after loore and reed.

3500 And sat the carpenter down beside him.
3503 That you won't reveal this secret to a living soul.
3509–10 This simple man then said, 'I am no tell-tale; nor, though I
say it myself, am I fond of idle gossip.'
3512 By Him who harrowed hell, i.e. Christ.
3516 On Monday next, when a quarter of the night is gone, i.e. at about
9 p.m.
3517 A deluge of rain shall fall, so wild and violent.
3527 If you will act on my instruction and advice.

Thou mayst nat werken after thyn   *on your own account*
  owene heed;
For thus seith Salomon, that was ful trewe,
3530 "Werk al by conseil, and thou shalt nat rewe."
And if thou werken wolt by good conseil,
I undertake, withouten mast and seyl,
Yet shal I saven hire and thee and me.
Hastow nat herd hou saved was Noe,
3535 Whan that oure Lord hadde warned hym biforn   *beforehand*
That al the world with water sholde be lorn?'   *destroyed by*
 'Yis,' quod this Carpenter, 'ful yoore ago.' *long, long ago*
 'Hastou nat herd,' quod Nicholas, 'also
The sorwe of Noe with his felaweshipe,
3540 Er that he myghte gete his wyf to shipe?   *on board*
Hym hadde be levere, I dar wel undertake,
At thilke tyme, than alle his wetheres blake
That she hadde had a ship hirself allone.
And therfore, woostou what is best to doone?
3545 This asketh haste, and of an hastif thyng   *urgent*
Men may nat preche or maken tariyng.   *delay*
 Anon go gete us faste into this in
A knedyng-trogh, or ellis a kymelyn,
For ech of us, but looke that they be large,   *see*
3550 In which we mowe swymme as in a barge,
And han therinne vitaille suffisant   *food*
But for a day,—fy on the remenant!
The water shal aslake and goon away   *grow less*
Aboute pryme upon the nexte day.
3555 But Robyn may nat wite of this, thy knave,   *know; servant*
Ne eek thy mayde Gille I may nat save;
Axe nat why, for though thou aske me,
I wol nat tellen Goddes pryvetee.   *secret purpose*
Suffiseth thee, but if thy wittes madde,
3560 To han as greet a grace as Noe hadde.   *have*

3530 'Do all things by advice, and you shall not regret it.'   (Cf. Ecclus. xxxii. 19.)

3539 ff. The trouble Noah had to persuade his wife to go on board the Ark is one of the main comic episodes of the play of Noah in most of the English cycles of miracle plays.

3541-3 I dare say he would have given all his black wethers for her to have had a ship to herself on that occasion.

3544 Do you know what is the best thing to do?

3547 Go and quickly fetch into the house.

3548 A kneading-trough, or else a shallow tub (used for brewing).

3550 In which we can float as in a ship.

3552 Never mind the rest (i.e. don't worry about food for the following days).

3554 *pryme*, 9 a.m.

3559 You should be satisfied, unless you're mad.

Thy wyf shal I wel saven, out of doute.
Go now thy wey, and speed thee heer-aboute. *hurry up about it*
  But whan thou hast, for hire and thee and me,
Ygeten us thise knedyng-tubbes thre, *got*
3565 Thanne shaltow hange hem in the roof ful hye,
That no man of oure purveiaunce espye.
And whan thou thus hast doon, as I have seyd,
And hast oure vitaille faire in hem yleyd, *properly; laid*
And eek an ax, to smyte the corde atwo.'
3570 Whan that the water comth, that we may go,
And breke an hole an heigh, upon the gable,
Unto the gardyn-ward, over the stable,
That we may frely passen forth oure way,
Whan that the grete shour is goon away,
3575 Thanne shaltou swymme as myrie, I undertake, *merrily*
As dooth the white doke after hire drake. *duck*
Thanne wol I clepe, 'How, Alison! how, John!
Be myrie, for the flood wol passe anon.'
And thou wolt seyn, 'Hayl, maister Nicholay!
3580 Good morwe, I se thee wel, for it is day.'
And thanne shul we be lordes al oure lyf
Of al the world, as Noe and his wyf.
  But of o thyng I warne thee ful right: *straight*
Be wel avysed on that ilke nyght *very careful*
3585 That we ben entred into shippes bord,
That noon of us ne speke nat a word,
Ne clepe, ne crie, but be in his preyere;
For it is Goddes owene heeste deere. *command*
  Thy wyf and thou moote hange fer atwynne; *far apart*
3590 For that bitwixe yow shal be no synne,
Namoore in lookyng than ther shal in deede,
This ordinance is seyd. Go, God thee speede! *rule is made*
Tomorwe at nyght, whan men ben alle aslepe,
Into oure knedyng-tubbes wol we crepe,
3595 And sitten there, abidyng Goddes grace.
Go now thy wey, I have no lenger space *time*
To make of this no lenger sermonyng.
Men seyn thus, 'sende the wise, and sey no thyng:'
Thou art so wys, it needeth thee nat teche.
3600 Go, save oure lyf, and that I the biseche.'

3561 Your wife I shall certainly save, never fear.
3566 So that no one can see what provision we have made for
    ourselves.
3571 And break a hole high up in the gable.
3572 Facing the garden, above the stable.
3587 Call or cry out, or do anything but pray.
3590 So that there shall be no sinful conduct between you.
3597 To speak of this at greater length.
3598 i.e. 'a word to the wise.'

This sely carpenter goth forth his wey.   *simple*
Ful ofte he seide 'allas' and 'weylawey,'
And to his wyf he tolde his pryvetee,   *secret*
And she was war, and knew it bet than he,   *aware; better*
3605 What al this queynte cast was for to seye.
But nathelees she ferde as she wolde deye,
And seyde, 'Allas! go forth thy wey anon,
Help us to scape, or we been dede echon!   *escape*
I am thy trewe, verray wedded wyf;   *faithful*
3610 Go, deere spouse, and help to save oure lyf.'
Lo, which a greet thyng is affeccioun!
Men may dyen of ymaginacioun,
So depe may impressioun be take.
This sely carpenter bigynneth quake;   *tremble*
3615 Hym thynketh verraily that he may see
Noees flood come walwynge as the see   *rolling*
To drenchen Alisoun, his hony deere.
He wepeth, weyleth, maketh sory cheere;
He siketh with ful many a sory swogh;
3620 He gooth and geteth hym a knedyng-trogh,
And after that a tubbe and a kymelyn,
And pryvely he sente hem to his in,
And heng hem in the roof in pryvetee.   *hung*
His owene hand he made laddres thre,   *with his own hand*
3625 To clymben by the ronges and the stalkes   *rungs; uprights*
Unto the tubbes hangynge in the balkes,   *beams*
And hem vitailled, bothe trogh and tubbe,   *provisioned*
With breed and chese, and good ale in a jubbe,   *jug*
Suffisynge right ynogh as for a day.
3630 But er that he hadde maad al this array,   *preparation*
He sente his knave, and eek his wenche also,   *maid*
Upon his nede to London for to go.
And on the Monday, whan it drow to nyght,   *drew near*
He shette his dore withoute candel-lyght,
3635 And dressed alle thyng as it sholde be.   *made ready*
And shortly, up they clomben alle thre;   *climbed*
They seten stille wel a furlong way.
'Now, *Pater-noster*, clom!' seyde Nicholay,
And 'clom,' quod John, and 'clom,' seyde Alisoun.
3640 This carpenter seyde his devocioun,

3605 What all this curious scheming meant.
3606 Nevertheless she behaved like someone in danger of death.
3611 What a strong thing feeling is!
3613 So deep an impression may be made by it.
3615 It seems to him he can really see.
3618–19 He weeps, wails, and glooms; he heaves many a sad sigh.
3632 To London to attend to some business for him.
3637 They sat still for a short while.
3638 *clom*, mum, be quiet.

And stille he sit, and biddeth his preyere,   *sits; says*
Awaitynge on the reyn, if he it heere.
   The dede sleep, for wery bisynesse,
Fil on this carpenter right, as I gesse,   *fell*
3645 Aboute corfew-tyme, or litel moore;
For travaille of his goost he groneth soore
And eft he routeth, for his heed myslay.
Doun of the laddre stalketh Nicholay,   *from; creeps*
And Alisoun ful softe adoun she spedde;   *hurried down*
3650 Withouten wordes mo they goon to bedde,
Ther as the carpenter is wont to lye.   *where*
Ther was the revel and the melodye;   *revelry*
And thus lith Alison and Nicholas,   *lie*
In bisynesse of myrthe and of solas,
3655 Til that the belle of laudes gan to rynge,
And freres in the chauncel gonne synge.
   This parissh clerk, this amorous Absolon,
That is for love alwey so wo bigon,
Upon the Monday was at Oseneye
3660 With compaignye, hym to disporte and pleye,   *amuse himself*
And axed upon cas a cloisterer
Ful prively after John the carpenter;   *in strict confidence*
And he drough hym apart out of the chirche,   *drew; aside*
And seyde, 'I noot, I saugh hym heere nat wirche
3665 Syn Saterday; I trowe that he be went
For tymber, ther oure abbot hath hym sent;   *to where*
For he is wont for tymber for to go,
And dwellen at the grange a day or two;
Or elles he is at his hous, certeyn.
3670 Where that he be, I kan nat soothly seyn.'   *truly*
   This Absolon ful joly was and light,   *light-hearted*
And thoghte, 'Now is tyme to wake al nyght;   *stay awake*
For sikirly I saugh hym nat stirynge   *certainly*
Aboute his dore, syn day bigan to sprynge.
3675 So moot I thryve, I shal, at cokkes crowe,
Ful pryvely knokken at his wyndowe   *stealthily*

3642 Watching and listening for the rain.
3643 Brought on by his exhausting work.
3645 *corfew-tyme*, about 8 p.m.
3646-7 Disturbed in spirit, he groans loudly, and then he snores, for
   his head lay askew.
3654 Engaged in pleasant, entertaining work.
3655 *laudes*, lauds, the service following matins and usually sung at
   daybreak.
3661 Asked by chance a cloisterer (i.e. monk).
3664-5 I don't know, I haven't seen him working here since Saturday;
   I think he has gone.
3668 *grange*, granary (one belonging to a religious house is meant here).
3673-4 For certainly I haven't seen him stir outside his house since day
   began.
3675 As I hope to prosper.

That stant ful lowe upon his boures wal.
To Alison now wol I tellen al
My love-longynge, for yet I shal nat mysse   *fail*
3680 That at the leeste wey I shal hire kisse.
Som maner confort shal I have, parfay.   *upon my word*
My mouth hath icched al this longe day;   *itched*
That is a signe of kissyng atte leeste.
Al nyght me mette eek I was at a feeste.   *I dreamt also*
3685 Therfore I wol go slepe an houre or tweye,
And al the nyght thanne wol I wake and pleye.'
      Whan that the firste cok hath crowe, anon
Up rist this joly lovere Absolon,   *gets*
And hym arraieth gay, at poynt-devys.
3690 But first he cheweth greyn and   *cardamom*
      lycorys,   *liquorice*
To smellen sweete, er he hadde kembd his heer.   *combed; hair*
Under his tonge a trewe-love he beer,
For therby wende he to ben gracious.
He rometh to the carpenteres hous,   *makes his way*
3695 And stille he stant under the shot-wyndowe—
Unto his brest it raughte, it was so lowe—   *reached*
And softe he cougheth with a semy soun: *gentle sound*
'What do ye, hony-comb, sweete Alisoun,
My faire bryd, my sweete cynamome?   *bird; cinnamon*
3700 Awaketh, lemman myn, and speketh to me!   *beloved*
Wel litel thynken ye upon my wo,
That for youre love I swete ther I go.
No wonder is thogh that I swelte and swete;   *swoon*
I moorne as dooth a lamb after the tete.   *mourn; teat*
3705 Ywis, lemman, I have swich love-longynge,
That lik a turtel trewe is my moornynge.   *turtle-dove*
I may nat ete na moore than a mayde.'   *eat*
      'Go fro the wyndow, Jakke fool,' she sayde;
'As help me God, it wol nat be "com pa me."
3710 I love another—and elles I were to blame—
Wel bet than thee, by Jhesu, Absolon.
Go forth thy wey, or I wol caste a ston,
And lat me slepe, a twenty devel wey!'   *in the devil's name*
      'Allas,' quod Absolon, 'and weylawey,
3715 That trewe love was evere so yvel biset!'   *badly used*

3677 That is set low in the wall of his bedroom.
3689 And dresses himself in gay clothes, with every care.
3692–3 He carried a leaf of herb paris under his tongue, for he thought
in this way to make himself agreeable.
3701–2 You give little thought to my sorrow, and how I sweat for love
of you where'er I walk.
3708 *Jakke*, Jack (here used derisively).
3709 It won't be a case of 'come kiss me,' i.e. you won't get a kiss
from me. (The words *com pa me* may be from a popular song of the
time.)

Thanne kysse me, syn it may be no bet,
For Jhesus love, and for the love of me.'
  'Wiltow thanne go thy wey therwith?' quod she.
'Ye, certes, lemman,' quod this Absolon.
3720 'Thanne make thee redy,' quod she, 'I come anon.'
And unto Nicholas she seyde stille,   *softly*
'Now hust, and thou shalt laughen al thy fille.'   *hush*
  This Absolon doun sette hym on his knees   *knelt down*
And seyde, 'I am a lord at alle degrees;
3725 For after this I hope ther cometh moore.
Lemman, thy grace, and sweete bryd, thyn oore!'
  The wyndow she undoth, and that in haste.
'Have do,' quod she, 'com of, and speed the faste,
Lest that oure neighebores thee espie.'
3730   This Absolon gan wype his mouth ful drie.
Derk was the nyght as pich, or as the cole,   *pitch; coal*
And at the wyndow out she putte hir hole,
And Absolon, hym fil no bet ne wers,
But with his mouth he kiste hir naked ers
3735 Ful savourly, er he were war of this.   *enjoyably*
Abak he stirte, and thoughte it was amys,
For wel he wiste a womman hath no berd.
He felte a thyng al rough and long yherd,   *haired*
And seyde, 'Fy! allas! what have I do?'   *done*
3740 'Tehee!' quod she, and clapte the wyndow to,
And Absolon gooth forth a sory pas.   *miserably*
  'A berd! a berd!' quod hende Nicholas,
'By Goddes corpus, this goth faire and weel.'
  This sely Absolon herde every deel,   *wretched; everything*
3745 And on his lippe he gan for anger byte,
And to hymself he seyde, 'I shal thee quyte.'   *pay you back*
  Who rubbeth now, who froteth now his lippes   *chafes*
With dust, with sond, with straw, with clooth,
    with chippes,   *shavings*
But Absolon, that seith ful ofte, 'Allas!
3750 My soule bitake I unto Sathanas,   *commend*
But me were levere than al this toun,' quod he,
'Of this despit awroken for to be.
Allas,' quod he, 'allas, I ne hadde ybleynt!'
His hoote love was coold and al yqueynt;   *quenched*

3716 Since there's no hope of anything better.
3718 Will you go away when you've had it?
3724 I'm happy as a lord of high degree.
3726 Thy grace, beloved, and favour, my sweet bird.
3728 Have done . . . come along and be quick about it.
3733 Nothing better nor worse happened to him.
3736 He started back, and thought something was wrong.
3751-2 I would rather be revenged for this insult than own all this town.
3753 Alas, that I didn't turn aside.

3755 For fro that tyme that he hadde kist hir ers,   *from*
     Of paramours he sette nat a kers;
     For he was heeled of his maladie.   *cured*
     Ful ofte paramours he gan deffie,
     And weep as dooth a child that is ybete.   *wept; beaten*
3760 A softe paas he wente over the strete
     Until a smyth men cleped daun Gerveys,
     That in his forge smythed plough harneys;   *made; fittings*
     He sharpeth shaar and kultour bisily.   *share; coulter*
     This Absolon knokketh al esily,   *gently*
3765 And seyde, 'Undo, Gerveys, and that anon.'
         'What, who artow?'   'It am I, Absolon.'
     'What, Absolon! for Cristes sweete tree,   *cross*
     Why rise ye so rathe? ey, *benedicitee!*   *early; bless me*
     What eyleth yow? Som gay gerl, God it woot,   *ails; knows*
3770 Hath broght yow thus upon the viritoot.
     By seinte Note, ye woot wel what I mene.'   *Neot*
         This Absolon ne roghte nat a bene
     Of all his pley; no word agayn he yaf;
     He hadde moore tow on his distaf
3775 Than Gerveys knew, and seyde, 'Freend so deere,
     That hoote kultour in the chymenee heere,
     As lene it me, I have therwith to doone,
     And I wol brynge it thee agayn ful soone.'
         Gerveys answerde, 'Certes, were it gold,
3780 Or in a poke nobles alle untold,
     Thou sholdest have, as I am trewe smyth.
     Ey, Cristes foo! what wol ye do therwith?'   *foe*
         'Therof,' quod Absolon, 'be as be may.
     I shal wel telle it thee to-morwe day'—
3785 And caughte the kultour by the colde stele.   *handle*
     Ful softe out at the dore he gan to stele,   *softly; stole*
     And wente unto the carpenteris wal.
     He cogheth first, and knokketh therwithal   *coughs*
     Upon the wyndowe, right as he dide er.   *before*
3790   This Alison answerde, 'Who is ther
     That knokketh so?   I warante it a theef.'
         'Why, nay,' quod he, 'God woot, my sweete leef,   *beloved*

3756 He didn't care a damn (lit. cress) for wenches.
3758 Many a time he renounced all earthly love.
3760-1 He crept quietly across the street to a blacksmith called master
     Gervais.
3770 *upon the viritoot,* astir, on the trot.
3772-3 Didn't think much of (lit. care a bean for) his joke; he said
     nothing in reply.
3774 i.e. he had other business on hand.
3777 Please lend it me; there's something I have to do with it.
3780 Or an untold number of gold nobles in a bag.
3784 I shall tell you all about it to-morrow.

I am thyn Absolon, my deerelyng.
Of gold,' quod he, 'I have thee broght a ryng.
3795 My mooder yaf it me, so God me save;
Ful fyn it is, and therto wel ygrave.   *engraved*
This wol I yeve thee, if thou me kisse.'
    This Nicholas was risen for to pisse,
And thoughte he wolde amenden al the jape;
3800 He sholde kisse his ers er that he scape.   *got away*
And up the wyndowe dide he hastily,
And out his ers he putteth pryvely   *stealthily*
Over the buttok, to the haunche-bon;
And therwith spak this clerk, this Absolon,
3805 'Spek, sweete bryd, I noot nat where thou art.'
    This Nicholas anon leet fle a fart,   *let fly*
As greet as it had been a thonder-dent,   *clap of thunder*
That with the strook he was almoost yblent;
And he was redy with his iren hoot,
3810 And Nicholas amydde the ers he smoot,   *in the middle of*
Of gooth the skyn an hande-brede aboute,
The hoote kultour brende so his toute,   *backside*
And for the smert he wende for to dye.
As he were wood, for wo he gan to crye,
3815 'Help! water! water! help, for Goddes herte!'
    This carpenter out of his slomber sterte,   *started*
And herde oon crien 'water' as he were wood,   *someone*
And thoughte, 'Allas, now comth Nowelis flood!'
He sit hym up withouten wordes mo,
3820 And with his ax he smoot the corde atwo,
And doun gooth al; he foond neither to selle,
Ne breed ne ale, til he cam to the celle
Upon the floor, and ther aswowne he lay.   *in a swoon*
    Up stirte hire Alison and Nicholay,   *jumped*
3825 And criden 'out' and 'harrow' in the strete.
The neighebores, bothe smale and grete,
In ronnen for to gauren on this man,   *ran; stare at*
That yet aswowne lay, bothe pale and wan,
For with the fal he brosten hadde his arm.   *broken*

3799 Improve on the joke.
3800 *He*, i.e. Absalom.
3803 Past the buttocks.
3808 So that he (i.e. Absalom) was almost blinded by the blast.
3811 A handsbreadth all round.
3813 He thought he would die with the pain of it.
3818 *Nowelis*, Noah's. (The illiterate carpenter has confused *Noe*
'Noah' and *Nowel* 'Christmas.')
3819-20 He sits up and without more ado he cuts the rope in two
with his axe.
3821-3 He found neither bread nor ale for sale (i.e. he found nothing to
stop him) till he reached the floor-boards.
3825 *out, harrow*, cries for help.

3830 But stonde he moste unto his owene harm;
      For whan he spak, he was anon bore doun   *talked down*
      With hende Nicholas and Alisoun.   *by*
      They tolden every man that he was wood,   *mad*
      He was agast so of Nowelis flood   *terrified*
3835 Thurgh fantasie, that of his vanytee
      He hadde yboght hym knedyng-tubbes thre,
      And hadde hem hanged in the roof above;
      And that he preyed hem, for Goddes love,
      To sitten in the roof, *par compaignye*.   *for company*
3840   The folk gan laughen at his fantasye;   *laughed*
      Into the roof they kiken and they cape,   *peep; gape*
      And turned al his harm unto a jape.
      For what so that this carpenter answerde,   *whatever*
      It was for noght, no man his reson herde.
3845 With othes grete he was so sworn adoun
      That he was holde wood in al the toun;   *considered mad*
      For every clerk anonright heeld with oother.
      They seyde, 'The man is wood, my leeve brother';
      And every wight gan laughen at this stryf.   *commotion*
3850 Thus swyved was this carpenteris wyf,   *copulated with*
      For al his kepyng and his jalousye;
      And Absolon hath kist hir nether ye;   *eye*
      And Nicholas is scalded in the towte.
      This tale is doon, and God save al the rowte!   *company*

HEERE ENDETH THE MILLERE HIS TALE

      3830 He had to put up with his injury.
      3835-6 In his imagination, that he had been foolish enough to buy
          himself three kneading-tubs.
      3842 And made a joke of all his suffering.
      3844 It was in vain, for no one listened to what he said.
      3847 i.e. every student immediately took Nicholas's part.

THE REEVE'S PROLOGUE

THE PROLOGE OF THE REVES TALE

3855   WHAN folk hadde laughen at this nyce cas   *ludicrous affair*
    Of Absolon and hende Nicholas,
    Diverse folk diversely they seyde,
    But for the moore part they loughe and pleyde.
    Ne at this tale I saugh no man hym greve,   *get angry*
3860 But it were oonly Osewold the Reve.   *except*
    By cause he was of carpenteris craft,
    A litel ire is in his herte ylaft;   *left*
    He gan to grucche, and blamed it a lite.   *grumble; little*
    'So theek,' quod he, 'ful wel koude I thee quite
3865 With bleryng of a proud milleres ye,
    If that me liste speke of ribaudye.
    But ik am oold, me list not pley for age;
    Gras tyme is doon, my fodder is now forage;
    This white top writeth myne olde yeris;
3870 Myn herte is also mowled as myne heris,
    But if I fare as dooth an open-ers,—
    That ilke fruyt is ever lenger the wers,
    Til it be roten in mullok or in stree.
    We olde men, I drede, so fare we: *I'm afraid*
3875 Til we be roten, kan we nat be rype;
    We hoppen alwey whil that the world wol pype.
    For in ouer wyl ther stiketh evere a nayl,
    To have an hoor heed and a grene tayl,   *hoary; tail*
    As hath a leek; for thogh oure myght be goon,   *strength*
3880 Oure wyl desireth folie evere in oon.

3857 Different people expressed different opinions of the tale.
3858 But for the most part they laughed and joked about it.
3864–6 As I hope to prosper . . . I could pay you back in full with a
    story of the hoodwinking of a proud miller, if I chose to tell a ribald
    tale.
3867 But I am old; I'm past the age for fun.
3868 My grazing time is over, I now feed on hay (as horses do in winter).
3869 These white hairs announce my age.
3870 My heart is grown as mouldy as my hair.
3871–3 Unless I'm like a medlar, which goes from bad to worse, until
    at last it rots in straw or on a rubbish-heap. (The fruit of the medlar-
    tree is eaten when it has decayed.)
3876 We dance as long as the world will pipe for us. (Cf. Matt. xi. 17.)
3877 For there is always this hindrance to our desire.
3880 We go on hankering after folly.

For whan we may nat doon, than wol we speke;
Yet in oure asshen olde is fyr yreke.
    Foure gleedes han we, which I shal   *embers*
       devyse,—   *mention*
Avauntyng, liyng, anger, coveitise;   *boasting; covetousness*
3885 Thise foure sparkles longen unto eelde,
Oure olde lemes mowe wel been unweelde,
But wyl ne shal nat faillen, that is sooth.   *desire; truth*
And yet ik have alwey a coltes tooth,
As many a yeer as it is passed henne
3890 Syn that my tappe of lif bigan to renne.   *since; run*
For sikerly, whan I was bore, anon
Deeth drough the tappe of lyf and leet it gon;
And ever sithe hath so the tappe yronne
Til that almoost al empty is the tonne.   *cask*
3895 The streem of lyf now droppeth on the chymbe.
The sely tonge may wel rynge and chymbe   *foolish; chime*
Of wrecchednesse that passed is ful yoore.   *long ago*
With olde folk, save dotage, is namoore!'
    What that oure Hoost hadde herd this sermonyng,
3900 He gan to speke as lordly as a kyng.
He seide, 'What amounteth al this wit?
What shul we speke alday of hooly writ?
The devel made a reve for to preche,
Or of a soutere a shipman or a leche.   *cobbler; physician*
3905 Sey forth thy tale, and tarie nat the tyme;   *waste*
Lo Depeford! and it is half-wey pryme.
Lo Grenewych, ther many a shrewe is inne!
It were al tyme thy tale to bigynne.'   *quite*
    'Now, sires,' quod this Osewold the Reve,
3910 'I pray yow alle that ye nat yow greve,
Thogh I answere, and somdeel sette his howve;
For leveful is with force force of-showve.

3882 Still, in our old ashes, there is fire raked together.
3885 These four small sparks belong to old age.
3886 Our old limbs may well be feeble.
3888 *a coltes tooth*, one of the first set of teeth of a horse, and hence 'youthful or wanton desires.'
3889 In spite of the many years that have passed.
3891–2 For certainly, when I was born, death at once turned on the tap of life and let it run.
3895 Now drips on to the rim (of the cask), i.e. no longer flows out in a steady stream.
3898 There is nothing left for old folk but their dotage.
3901 What does all this wisdom amount to?
3902 Why must we always speak of holy writ?
3906 *half-wey pryme*, midway between 6 and 9 a.m.
3907 There's Greenwich, where many a rascal lives.
3911 And make a bit of a fool of him (i.e. the Miller).
3912 For it is allowable to repel force by force.

This dronke Millere hath ytoold us heer
How that bigyled was a carpenteer,
3915 Peraventure in scorn, for I am oon.   *perhaps*
And, by youre leve, I shal hym quite anoon;   *pay him back*
Right in his cherles termes wol I speke.
I pray to God his nekke mote to-breke;   *may break*
He kan wel in myn eye seen a stalke,   *piece of straw*
3920 But in his owene he kan nat seen a balke.'   *beam*

THE REEVE'S TALE

Heere bigynneth the Reves Tale

At trumpyngtoun, nat fer fro Cantebrigge,   *Cambridge*
Ther gooth a brook, and over that a brigge,   *runs*
Upon the whiche brook ther stant a melle;   *stands; mill*
And this is verray sooth that I yow telle.   *exact truth*
3925 A millere was ther dwellynge many a day;
As any pecok he was proud and gay.
Pipen he koude and fisshe, and nettes beete,
And turne coppes, and wel wrastle and sheete;
Ay by his belt he baar a long panade.
3930 And of a swerd ful trenchant was the blade.   *sword; sharp*
A joly poppere baar he in his pouche;   *handsome dagger*
Ther was no man, for peril, dorste hym touche.
A Sheffeld thwitel baar he in his hose.   *Sheffield knife*
Round was his face, and camus was his nose;   *flat*

3917 I shall use just the same low language as he has done.
3919–20 Cf. Matt. vii. 3–5.
3927 He could play the bagpipes . . . and mend nets.
3928 Turn wooden cups, and wrestle and shoot well (with a bow).
3929 He always carried a large knife at his belt.
3932 No one dared touch him; it was too dangerous.

3935 As piled as an ape was his skulle.   *bald*
      He was a market-betere atte fulle.
      Ther dorste no wight hand upon hym legge,
      That he ne swoor he sholde anon abegge.
      A theef he was for sothe of corn and mele,   *in truth*
3940 And that a sly, and usaunt for to stele.   *accustomed*
      His name was hoote deynous Symkyn.
      A wyf he hadde, ycomen of noble kyn;   *family*
      The person of the toun hir fader was.
      With hire he yaf ful many a panne of bras,
3945 For that Symkyn sholde in his blood allye.
      She was yfostred in a nonnerye;   *brought up*
      For Symkyn wolde no wyf, as he sayde,
      But she were wel ynorissed and a mayde,   *well bred*
      To saven his estaat of yomanrye.
3950 And she was proud, and peert as is a pye.   *saucy; magpie*
      A ful fair sighte was it upon hem two;
      On halydayes biforn hire wolde he go   *religious festivals*
      With his typet wound aboute his heed,   *tippet*
      And she cam after in a gyte of reed;   *gown*
3955 And Symkyn hadde hosen of the same.
      Ther dorste no wight clepen hire but 'dame';
      Was noon so hardy that wente by the weye   *bold*
      That with hire dorste rage or ones pleye,
      But if he wolde be slayn of Symkyn   *unless*
3960 With panade, or with knyf, or boidekyn.   *dagger*
      For jalous folk ben perilous everemo;   *dangerous*
      Algate they wolde hire wyves wenden so.
      And eek, for she was somdel smoterlich,
      She was as digne as water in a dich,
3965 And ful of hoker and of bisemare.   *scorn; contempt*
      Hir thoughte that a lady sholde hire spare,
      What for hire kynrede and hir nortelrie
      That she hadde lerned in the nonnerie.

3936 *market-betere*, a swaggering nuisance at markets.
3937–8 No one dared lay a finger on him without his swearing to make him pay for it directly.
3941 He was known as scornful Simkin (a diminutive of Simon).
3943 Her father was the village priest (i.e. she was illegitimate).
3944–5 He gave away with her a dowry of valuable brass pans, so that Simkin should marry into his family.
3949 To keep up his yeoman's rank.
3951 They made a handsome pair.
3956 No one dared call her anything but 'madam.'
3958 Romp or even dally with her.
3962 At any rate they'd like their wives to think them so.
3963–4 Also, because she was somewhat sullied in reputation (by reason of her illegitimacy), she was as dignified as ditch-water (i.e. stinking with pride).
3966–7 It seemed to her that a lady should hold herself aloof, on account of her family background and her education.

A doghter hadde they bitwixe hem two   *between*
3970 Of twenty yeer, withouten any mo,   *other (children)*
Savynge a child that was of half yeer age;
In cradel it lay and was a propre page.   *fine-looking lad*
This wenche thikke and wel ygrowen was,   *plump*
With kamus nose, and eyen greye as glas,
3975 With buttokes brode, and brestes rounde and hye;
But right fair was hire heer, I wol nat lye.   *very pretty*
This person of the toun, for she was feir,
In purpos was to maken hire his heir,
Bothe of his catel and his mesuage,   *goods; house*
3980 And straunge he made it of hir mariage.
His purpos was for to bistowe hire hye
Into som worthy blood of auncetrye;
For hooly chirches good moot been despended
On hooly chirches blood, that is descended.
3985 Therfore he wolde his hooly blood honoure,
Though that he hooly chirche sholde devoure.
Greet sokene hath this millere, out of doute,   *toll*
With whete and malt of al the land aboute;
And nameliche ther was a greet collegge   *in particular*
3990 Men clepen the Soler Halle at Cantebregge;   *call*
Ther was hir whete and eek hir malt ygrounde.
And on a day it happed in a stounde,   *happened suddenly*
Sik lay the maunciple on a maladye;
Men wenden wisly that he sholde dye.
3995 For which this millere stal bothe mele and corn   *stole*
An hundred tyme moore than biforn;
For therbiforn he stal but curteisly,   *politely*
But now he was a theef outrageously,
For which the wardeyn chidde and made fare.
4000 But therof sette the millere nat a tare;
He craketh boost, and swoor it was nat so.   *boasts loudly*
Thanne were ther yonge povre scolers two,   *poor*
That dwelten in this halle, of which I seye.
Testif they were, and lusty for to pleye,
4005 And, oonly for hire myrthe and revelrye,
Upon the wardeyn bisily they crye   *eagerly; beg*

3977 *This person of the toun*, the village priest (her grandfather).
3980 And he made difficulties about her marriage.
3983–4 For holy church's goods (i.e. the priest's *catel* and *mesuage*)
    must be spent on those descended from the blood of holy church
    (i.e. on his grand-daughter).
3986 Though he devoured holy church to do it.
3991 *Ther*, i.e. at Simkin's mill.
3993 *maunciple.* See 567.
3994 They were quite sure he was going to die.
3999 The warden (of the college) complained and made a to-do.
4000 But the miller didn't give a bean (lit. tare).
4004 They were headstrong and eager for a lark.

To yeve hem leve, but a litel stounde,   *while*
To goon to mille and seen hir corn ygrounde;
And hardily they dorste leye hir nekke
4010 The millere sholde not stele hem half a pekke
Of corn by sleighte, ne by force hem reve;   *trickery; rob*
And at the laste the wardeyn yaf hem leve.
John highte that oon, and Aleyn highte   *was called; Alan*
  that oother;
Of o toun were they born, that highte   *in the same village*
  Strother,
4015 Fer in the north, I kan nat telle where.
  This Aleyn maketh redy al his gere,
And on an hors the sak he caste anon.
Forth goth Aleyn the clerk, and also John,   *student*
With good swerd and with bokeler by hir syde.
4020 John knew the wey,—hem nedede no gyde,—   *they needed*
And at the mille the sak adoun he layth.
Aleyn spak first, 'Al hayl, Symond, y-fayth!   *welcome*
Hou fares thy faire doghter and thy wyf?'
  'Aleyn, welcome,' quod Symkyn, 'by my lyf!
4025 And John also, how now, what do ye heer?'
  'Symond,' quod John, 'by God, nede   *necessity; equal*
  has na peer.
Hym boes serve hymself that has na swayn,
Or elles he is a fool, as clerkes sayn.
Oure manciple, I hope he wil be deed,
4030 Swa werkes ay the wanges in his heed;
And forthy is I come, and eek Alayn,
To grynde oure corn and carie it ham agayn;   *home*
I pray yow spede us heythen that ye may.'
  'It shal be doon,' quod Symkyn, 'by my fay!   *faith*
4035 What wol ye doon whil that it is in hande?'
  'By God, right by the hopur wil I stande,'
Quod John, 'and se howgates the corn gas in.   *in what way*
Yet saugh I nevere, by my fader kyn,   *saw; father's*
How that the hopur wagges til and fra.'
4040   Aleyn answerde, 'John, and wiltow swa?   *so*
Thanne wil I be bynethe, by my croun,
And se how that the mele falles doun

4009 They were ready to wager their head.
4014–15 Chaucer mimics the Northern speech of the students in this
  tale, and does so with remarkable accuracy.
4027 A man who has no servant must serve himself.
4029–30 I expect he will die, his molar teeth are aching so much.
4031 And that's why I have come.
4033 Please help us to get away as quickly as you can.
4036 *hopur*, hopper, through which the grain passed into the mill.
4039 Waggles to and fro.
4041 *by my croun*, by my crown (an asseveration).

Into the trough; that sal be my disport.
For John, y-faith, I may been of youre sort;
4045 I is as ille a millere as ar ye.'   *poor*
      This millere smyled of hir nycetee,   *at; simplicity*
And thoghte, 'Al this nys doon but for a wyle.   *trick*
They wene that no man may hem bigyle,
But by my thrift, yet shal I blere hir ye,
4050 For al the sleighte in hir philosophye.   *cunning*
The moore queynte crekes that they make,   *artful tricks*
The moore wol I stele whan I take.
In stide of flour yet wol I yeve hem bren.   *instead; bran*
"The gretteste clerkes been noght wisest men,"
4055 As whilom to the wolf thus spak the mare.   *once*
Of al hir art ne counte I noght a tare.'
      Out at the dore he gooth ful pryvely,   *stealthily*
Whan that he saugh his tyme, softely.
He looketh up and doun til he hath founde
4060 The clerkes hors, ther as it stood ybounde
Bihynde the mille, under a levesel;   *leafy arbour*
And to the hors he goth hym faire and wel;
He strepeth of the brydel right anon.   *strips off*
And whan the hors was laus, he gynneth gon   *loose; raced*
4065 Toward the fen, ther wilde mares renne,
And forth with 'wehee,' thurgh thikke and thurgh
      thenne.   *thin*
      This millere gooth agayn, no word he seyde,
But dooth his note, and with the clerkes pleyde,   *job; joked*
Til that hir corn was faire and weel ygrounde.
4070 And whan the mele is sakked and ybounde,
This John goth out and fynt his hors away,
And gan to crie 'Harrow!' and 'Weylaway!
Oure hors is lorn, Alayn, for Goddes banes,   *lost; bones*
Step on thy feet!   Com of, man, al atanes!
4075 Allas, our wardeyn has his palfrey lorn.'
This Aleyn al forgat, bothe mele and corn;
Al was out of his mynde his housbondrie.
'What, whilk way is he geen?' he gan to crie.   *which; gone*
      The wyf cam lepynge inward with a ren.
4080 She seyde, 'Allas! youre hors goth to the fen
With wilde mares, as faste as he may go.

4043 That'll be fun for me.
4044 I'm rather like you.
4049 But, as I live, I'll hoodwink them.
4055 An allusion to the Aesop fable of the Wolf and the Mare.
4062 And he goes up to the horse in a friendly manner.
4066 *wehee*, an imitation of the whinnying of a horse.
4072 *Harrow*, a cry for help; *Weylaway*, alas.
4074 Step lively!   Come on, man, be quick!
4077 All thoughts of economy had fled from his mind.
4079 Came running in quickly.

Unthank come on his hand that boond hym so,
And he that bettre sholde han knyt the reyne!'   *fastened*
  'Allas,' quod John, 'Aleyn, for Cristes peyne,
4085 Lay doun thy swerd, and I wil myn alswa.   *also*
I is ful wight, God waat, as is a raa;
By Goddes herte, he sal nat scape us bathe!   *escape; both*
Why ne had thow pit the capul in the lathe?
Ilhayl! by God, Alayn, thou is a fonne!'   *bad luck; fool*
4090   Thise sely clerkes han ful faste yronne   *wretched*
Toward the fen, bothe Aleyn and eek John.
  And whan the millere saugh that they were gon,
He half a busshel of hir flour hath take,   *taken*
And bad his wyf go knede it in a cake.
4095 He seyde, 'I trowe the clerkes were aferd.
Yet kan a millere make a clerkes berd,
For al his art; now lat hem goon hir weye!
Lo, wher he gooth! ye, lat the children pleye.
They gete hym nat so lightly, by my croun.'   *easily*
4100   Thise sely clerkes rennen up and doun
With 'Keep! keep! stand! stand! jossa, warderere,
Ga whistle thou, and I shal kepe hym heere!'   *go*
But shortly, til that it was verray nyght,   *briefly*
They koude nat, though they dide al hir myght,
4105 Hir capul cacche, he ran alwey so faste,   *always*
Til in a dych they caughte hym atte laste.
  Wery and weet, as beest is in the reyn,   *wet*
Comth sely John, and with him comth Aleyn.
'Allas,' quod John, 'the day that I was born!
4110 Now are we dryve til hethyng and til scorn.
Oure corn is stoln, men wil us fooles calle,
Bathe the wardeyn and oure felawes alle,   *friends*
And namely the millere, weylaway!'   *especially*
  Thus pleyneth John as he gooth by the way   *complains*
4115 Toward the mille, and Bayard in his hond.
The millere sittynge by the fyr he fond,   *found*
For it was nyght, and forther myghte they noght;
But for the love of God they hym bisoght
Of herberwe and of ese, as for hir peny.
4120   The millere seyde agayn, 'If ther be eny,

4082 Bad luck to the hand that tied him so carelessly.
4086 I'm as nimble, God knows, as a roe.
4088 Why didn't you put the nag in the barn?
4095 I think those students have had a fright.
4096 A miller can still deceive a student.
4101 Come up! stand! down here! look out behind!
4110 Now we're brought into contempt.
4115 Leading Bayard (a common name for a horse).
4117 And they could go no further.
4118–19 For the love of God, and for a penny, they begged him for shelter and hospitality.

Swich as it is, yet shal ye have youre part.   *such; share*
Myn hous is streit, but ye han lerned art;
Ye konne by argumentes make a place
A myle brood of twenty foot of space.   *broad; from*
4125 Lat se now if this place may suffise,   *let's see*
Or make it rowm with speche, as is youre gise.'
      'Now, Symond,' seyde John, 'by seint Cutberd,   *Cuthbert*
Ay is thou myrie, and this is faire answerd.
I have herd seyd, "man sal taa of twa thynges
4130 Slyk as he fyndes, or taa slyk as he brynges."
But specially I pray thee, hooste deere,
Get us som mete and drynke, and make us
        cheere,   *good cheer*
And we wil payen trewely atte fulle.   *in full*
With empty hand men may na haukes tulle;   *no; lure*
4135 Loo, heere oure silver, redy for to spende.'
      This millere into toun his doghter sende
For ale and breed, and rosted hem a goos,
And boond hire hors, it sholde namoore go loos;
And in his owene chambre hem made a bed,
4140 With sheetes and with chalons faire yspred,   *blankets*
Noght from his owene bed ten foot or twelve.
His doghter hadde a bed, al by hirselve,
Right in the same chambre by and by.
It myghte be no bet, and cause why?
4145 Ther was no roumer herberwe in the place.
They soupen and they speke, hem to   *to cheer themselves up*
        solace,
And drynken evere strong ale atte beste.
Aboute mydnyght wente they to reste.
      Wel hath this millere vernysshed his heed;   *oiled*
4150 Ful pale he was for dronken, and nat reed.
He yexeth, and he speketh thurgh the nose   *hiccoughs*
As he were on the quakke, or on the pose.
To bedde he goth, and with hym goth his wyf.
As any jay she light was and jolyf,   *spry; saucy*
4155 So was hir joly whistle wel ywet.
The cradel at hir beddes feet is set,

4122 My house is small, but you have studied the arts.
4126 Or talk it into being larger, in your usual fashion.
4128 You will have your little joke, and that's a fair answer.
4129-30 'A man must take one of two things—such as he finds or such
        as he brings,' i.e. a man must take things as he finds them.
4143 *by and by,* close by (her parents' bed).
4144 There was nothing else for it, and why?
4145 There was no larger room in the place.
4147 Drink strong ale with unflagging zeal.
4150 He looked quite pale with drink.
4152 As though he had asthma or a cold in the head.

To rokken, and to yeve the child to sowke.   *suck*
And whan that dronken al was in the crowke,   *jug*
To bedde wente the doghter right anon;
4160 To bedde goth Aleyn and also John;
Ther nas na moore,—hem nedede no dwale.
This millere hath so wisely bibbed ale
That as an hors he fnorteth in his sleep,   *snorts*
Ne of his tayl bihynde he took no keep.   *heed*
4165 His wyf bar hym a burdon, a ful strong;
Men myghte hir rowtyng heere two furlong;   *snoring*
The wenche rowteth eek, *par compaignye.*   *for company*
    Aleyn the clerk, that herde this melodye,
He poked John, and seyde, 'Slepestow?
4170 Herdestow evere slyk a sang er now?   *such; before*
Lo, swilk a complyn is ymel hem alle,
A wilde fyr upon thair bodyes falle!   *erysipelas*
Wha herkned evere slyk a ferly thyng?
Ye, they sal have the flour of il endyng.
4175 This lange nyght ther tydes me na reste;
But yet, nafors, al sal be for the beste.   *no matter*
For, John,' seyde he, 'als evere moot I thryve,
If that I may, yon wenche wil I swyve.
Som esement has lawe yshapen us;
4180 For, John, ther is a lawe that says thus,
That gif a man in a point be agreved,
That in another he sal be releved.
Oure corn is stoln, sothly, it is na nay,
And we han had an il fit al this day;   *bad turn*
4185 And syn I sal have neen amendement   *no compensation*
Agayn my los, I will have esement.
By Goddes sale, it sal neen other bee!'
    This John answerde, 'Alayn, avyse thee!   *have a care*
The millere is a perilous man,' he seyde,
4190 'And gif that he out of his sleep abreyde,   *wakes up*
He myghte doon us bathe a vileynye.'   *great harm*
    Aleyn answerde, 'I counte hym nat a flye.'
And up he rist, and by the wenche he crepte.   *gets*
This wenche lay uprighte, and faste slepte,   *on her back*

4161 After that came silence—they needed no sleeping-draught.
4165 Accompanied him with a powerful bass. (Cf. 673.)
4171 They're singing compline (i.e. evening service) so well between
    them.
4173 Whoever heard such a weird noise?
4174 Yes, they'll have the worst of it in the end.
4175 I shan't sleep a wink the whole night.
4179 The law provides us some redress.
4183 It's true, there's no denying it.
4187 By God's soul, it shall not be otherwise!
4192 He's no more nuisance than a fly.

4195 Til he so ny was, er she myghte espie,
That it had been to late for to crie,
And shortly for to seyn, they were aton.   *united*
Now pley, Aleyn, for I wol speke of John.
     This John lith stille a furlong wey or two,
4200 And to hymself he maketh routhe and wo.
'Allas!' quod he, 'this is a wikked jape;   *bad joke*
Now may I seyn that I is but an ape.
Yet has my felawe somwhat for his harm;
He has the milleris doghter in his arm.
4205 He auntred hym, and has his nedes sped,
And I lye as a draf-sak in my bed;   *sack of chaff*
And when this jape is tald another day,
I sal been halde a daf, a cokenay!
I wil arise and auntre it, by my fayth!
4210 "Unhardy is unseely," thus men sayth.'
And up he roos, and softely he wente
Unto the cradel, and in his hand it hente,   *took*
And baar it softe unto his beddes feet.
     Soone after this the wyf hir rowtyng leet,   *left off*
4215 And gan awake, and wente hire out to pisse,   *woke up*
And cam agayn, and gan hir cradel mysse,   *missed*
And groped heer and ther, but she foond noon.
'Allas!' quod she, 'I hadde almoost mysgoon;
I hadde almoost goon to the clerkes bed.
4220 Ey, *benedicite!* thanne hadde I foule ysped.'
And forth she gooth til she the cradel fond.
She gropeth alwey forther with hir hond,
And foond the bed, and thoghte noght but good, *all was well*
By cause that the cradel by it stood.
4225 And nyste wher she was, for it was derk;   *did not know*
But faire and wel she creep in to the clerk,   *crept*
And lith ful stille, and wolde han caught a sleep. *gone to sleep*
Withinne a while this John the clerk up leep,   *leapt*
And on this goode wyf he leith on soore.   *lays on hard*
4230 So myrie a fit ne hadde she nat ful yoore;
He priketh harde and depe as he were mad.
This joly lyf han thise two clerkes lad
Til that the thridde cok bigan to synge.

4195 He was so close to her before she noticed him.
4199 John lies still for a few minutes.
4200 He moans and grumbles to himself.
4205 He took a chance, and has done well for himself.
4208 I shall be held a sissy and a fool.
4210 'A coward has no luck.'
4213 Carried it gently to the foot of his bed.
4218 I nearly went astray.
4220 Eh, bless us, then I'd have had a bad time of it.
4230 She hadn't had such a merry bout for ages.
4233 *thridde cok*, i.e. near dawn.

Aleyn wax wery in the dawenynge,
4235 For he had swonken al the longe nyght,   *toiled*
And seyde, 'Fare weel, Malyne, sweete   *Molly*
wight!   *creature*
The day is come, I may no lenger byde;
But everemo, wher so I go or ryde,
I is thyn awen clerk, swa have I seel!'
4240 'Now, deere lemman,' quod she, 'go, far weel!   *sweetheart*
But er thow go, o thyng I wol thee telle:
Whan that thou wendest homward by the melle,   *mill*
Right at the entree of the dore bihynde
Thou shalt a cake of half a busshel fynde   *loaf*
4245 That was ymaked of thyn owene mele,
Which that I heelp my sire for to stele.   *helped; father*
And, goode lemman, God thee save and kepe!'
And with that word almoost she gan to wepe.

Aleyn up rist, and thoughte, 'Er that it dawe,   *dawns*
4250 I wol go crepen in by my felawe';
And fond the cradel with his hand anon.
'By God,' thoughte he, 'al wrang I have mysgon.
Myn heed is toty of my swynk to-nyght,
That makes me that I ga nat aright.
4255 I woot wel by the cradel I have mysgo;
Heere lith the millere and his wyf also.'
And forth he goth, a twenty devel way,
Unto the bed ther as the millere lay.
He wende have cropen by his felawe John,
4260 And by the millere in he creep anon,
And caughte hym by the nekke, and softe he
spak.
He seyde, 'Thou John, thou swynes-heed, awak,   *hogshead*
For Cristes saule, and heer a noble game.   *hear*
For by that lord that called is seint Jame,
4265 As I have thries in this shorte nyght
Swyved the milleres doghter bolt upright,   *flat on her back*
Whil thow hast, as a coward, been agast.'   *scared*
'Ye, false harlot,' quod the millere, 'hast?   *rogue*
A, false traitour! false clerk!' quod he,
4270 Thow shalt be deed, by Goddes dignitee!   *die*
Who dorste be so boold to disparage
My doghter, that is come of swich lynage?'

4238 Evermore, wherever I walk or ride (i.e. through thick and thin).
4239 I am your own true student, as I hope for happiness.
4243 Just near the back door.
4253 My head is dizzy with my toil this night.
4254 That's why I'm not going the right way.
4257 *a twenty devel way,* i.e. with devilish bad luck.
4259 He thought he was creeping in with his companion John.
4271 How dare you be so bold as to dishonour.

And by the throte-bolle he caughte Alayn,   *Adam's apple*
And he hente hym despitously agayn,
4275 And on the nose he smoot hym with his fest.   *fist*
Doun ran the blody streem upon his brest;
And in the floor, with nose and mouth tobroke,   *broken*
They walwe as doon two pigges in a poke;   *roll about; bag*
And up they goon, and doun agayn anon,
4280 Til that the millere sporned at a stoon,   *tripped over*
And doun he fil bakward upon his wyf,
That wiste no thyng of this nyce stryf;   *knew; foolish*
For she was falle aslepe a lite wight
With John the clerk, that waked hadde al nyght,
4285 And with the fal out of hir sleep she breyde.   *started*
'Help! hooly croys of Bromeholm,' she seyde,
'*In manus tuas!* Lord, to thee I calle!
Awak, Symond! the feend is on me falle.   *fallen*
Myn herte is broken; help! I nam but deed!
4290 Ther lyth oon upon my wombe and on myn heed.   *someone*
Help, Symkyn, for the false clerkes fighte!'
    This John stirte up as faste as ever he myghte,
And graspeth by the walles to and fro,   *gropes*
To fynde a staf; and she stirte up also,
4295 And knew the estres bet than dide this John,   *interior*
And by the wal a staf she foond anon,
And saugh a litel shymeryng of a light,   *glimmer*
For at an hole in shoon the moone bright;
And by that light she saugh hem bothe two,
4300 But sikerly she nyste who was who,   *certainly*
But as she saugh a whit thyng in hir ye.
And whan she gan this white thyng espye,
She wende the clerk hadde wered a volupeer,
And with the staf she drow ay neer and neer,   *drew; nearer*
4305 And wende han hit this Aleyn at the fulle,
And smoot the millere on the pyled skulle,   *bald*
That doun he gooth, and cride, 'Harrow! I dye!'   *so that*
Thise clerkes beete hym weel and lete hym lye;
And greythen hem, and tooke hir hors anon,   *get ready*
4310 And eek hire mele, and on hir wey they gon.
And at the mille yet they tooke hir cake
Of half a busshel flour, ful wel ybake.   *baked*

4274 And he (Alan) furiously grabbed back at him.
4283 For she had just fallen asleep.
4287 *In manus tuas*, into thy hands (I commend my spirit); Luke
      xxiii. 46.
4289 I'm as good as dead.
4301 Except that she saw a white thing.
4303 She thought the student had been wearing a nightcap.
4305 With the idea of hitting Alan a great wallop.

Thus is the proude millere wel ybete,   *beaten*
And hath ylost the gryndynge of the whete,
4315 And payed for the soper everideel
Of Aleyn and of John, that bette hym weel.   *beat*
His wyf is swyved, and his doghter als.   *also*
Lo, swich it is a millere to be fals!
And therfore this proverbe is seyd ful sooth,   *truly*
4320 'Hym thar nat wene wel that yvele dooth';
A gylour shal hymself bigyled be.   *trickster*
And God, that sitteth heighe in magestee,
Save al this compaignye, grete and smale!
Thus have I quyt the Millere in my tale.   *paid back*

Heere is ended the Reves Tale

4314 *ylost*, got no payment for.
4315 Paid in full for the supper.
4318 See what comes of being a dishonest miller.
4320 'He must not expect good who does evil.'

THE COOK'S PROLOGUE

The Prologe of the Cokes Tale

4325　THE COOK of Londoun, whil the Reve spak,
　　　For joye him thoughte he clawed him on the bak.
　　　'Ha! ha!' quod he, 'for Cristes passion,
　　　This millere hadde a sharp conclusion
　　　Upon his argument of herbergage!
4330　Wel seyde Salomon in his langage,
　　　'Ne bryng nat every man into thyn hous';
　　　For herberwynge by nyghte is perilous.
　　　Wel oghte a man avysed for to be
　　　Whom that he broghte into his pryvetee.
4335　I pray to God, so yeve me sorwe and care　　　　　　　*give*
　　　If evere, sitthe I highte Hogge of Ware,
　　　Herde I a millere bettre yset a-werk.
　　　He hadde a jape of malice in the derk.
　　　But God forbede that we stynte heere;　　　　　　　　*stop*
4340　And therfore, if ye vouche-sauf to heere
　　　A tale of me, that am a povre man,　　　　　　　　　*poor*
　　　I wol yow telle, as wel as evere I kan,
　　　A litel jape that fil in oure citee.'　　　*joke; happened*
　　　　Oure Hoost answerde and seide, 'I graunte it thee.
4345　Now telle on, Roger, looke that it be good;
　　　For many a pastee hastow laten blood,
　　　And many a Jakke of Dovere hastow soold
　　　That hath been twies hoot and twies coold.
　　　Of many a pilgrym hastow Cristes curs,
4350　For of thy percely yet they fare the wors,
　　　That they han eten with thy stubbel goos;
　　　For in thy shoppe is many a flye loos.　　　　　　　*loose*

4326 In his joy it seemed to him that the Reeve was scratching his back,
　　i.e. he had the sort of pleasure he would have felt if the Reeve had been
　　scratching an itch on his back.
4329 To his argument about a lodging for the night. (See 4122 ff.)
4331 Ecclus. xi. 29.
4333-4 A man certainly ought to be careful about whom he welcomes
　　into the privacy of his own home.
4336 Since I was called Hodge of Ware.
4337 I heard of a miller scored off more neatly.
4338 He had a spiteful trick played on him in the dark.
4346 Many a pasty have you let blood, i.e. drained of its gravy.
4347 *Jakke of Dovere*, a warmed-up pie.
4350 For they're still feeling the effects of that parsley of yours.
4351 *stubbel goos*, an old goose fed on stubble.

118

Now telle on, gentil Roger by thy name.   *worthy*
But yet I pray thee, be nat wroth for game;
4355 A man may seye ful sooth in game and pley.'
    'Thou seist ful sooth,' quod Roger, 'by my fey!
But "sooth pley, quaad pley," as the Flemyng seith.
And therfore, Herry Bailly, by thy feith,   *Harry*
Be thou nat wrooth, er we departen heer,
4360 Though that my tale be of an hostileer.   *innkeeper*
But nathelees I wol nat telle it yit;
But er we parte, ywis, thou shalt be quit.'   *certainly; paid back*
And therwithal he lough and made cheere,
And seyde his tale, as ye shul after heere.

THE COOK'S TALE

HEERE BIGYNNETH THE COOKES TALE

4365 A PRENTYS whilom dwelled in oure citee,   *apprentice; once*
And of a craft of vitailliers was hee.   *victuallers*
Gaillard he was as goldfynch in the shawe,   *gay; wood*
Broun as a berye, a propre short felawe,
With lokkes blake, ykembd ful fetisly.   *combed; neatly*
4370 Dauncen he koude so wel and jolily   *merrily*
That he was cleped Perkyn Revelour.   *called; the Reveller*
He was as ful of love and paramour   *love-making*
As is the hyve ful of hony sweete:
Wel was the wenche with hym myghte meete.

    4354 Don't be angry at a little fun.
    4355 i.e. there's many a true word spoken in jest.
    4356 You're quite right . . . upon my word.
    4357 'A true jest is a bad jest.'
    4363 And with that he laughed and made merry.
    4368 A short, good-looking fellow.
    4374 Happy the wench that chanced to meet him.

4375 At every bridale wolde he synge and hoppe;
He loved bet the taverne than the shoppe.   *better*
For whan ther any ridyng was in Chepe,
Out of the shoppe thider wolde he lepe—
Til that he hadde al the sighte yseyn,   *seen*
4380 And daunced wel, he wolde nat come ayeyn—   *back*
And gadered hym a meynee of his sort
To hoppe and synge and maken swich disport;
And ther they setten stevene for to meete,
To pleyen at the dys in swich a streete.   *such and such*
4385 For in the toune nas ther no prentys   *was not*
That fairer koude caste a paire of dys   *better*
Than Perkyn koude, and therto he was free   *besides*
Of his dispense, in place of pryvetee.
That fond his maister wel in his chaffare;
4390 For often tyme he foond his box ful bare.
For sikerly a prentys revelour   *certainly*
That haunteth dys, riot, or paramour,
His maister shal it in his shoppe abye,   *pay dearly for*
Al have he no part of the mynstralcye.
4395 For thefte and riot, they been convertible
Al konne he pleye on gyterne or ribible.
Revel and trouthe, as in a lowe degree,
They been ful wrothe al day, as men may see.
This joly prentys with his maister bood,   *stayed*
4400 Til he were ny out of his prentishood,   *nearly*
Al were he snybbed bothe erly and late,
And somtyme lad with revel to Newegate.
But atte laste his maister hym bithoghte,
Upon a day, whan he his papir soughte,

4377 Any procession in Cheapside.
4378 He would dash towards it.
4381-2 Gathered round him a crowd of people of his own sort to dance,
    sing, and have fun.
4383 They made a date to meet.
4388 In his spending, on the quiet.
4389 His master found good evidence of this in his daily business.
4392 Who makes a practice of dicing, wenching, and riotous living.
4394-6 Although he (the master) has no share in the musical entertain-
    ment, and his apprentice enjoys himself playing on a guitar or fiddle;
    for theft and riotous living are interchangeable. (The meaning is
    that the master pays the piper, while his dishonest servant calls the
    tune.)
4397-8 Revelry and honesty, in a man of low degree, are always at
    odds with each other.
4401 Although he was continually being reprimanded.
4402 Sometimes led off with minstrelsy to jail. (In Chaucer's day
    disorderly persons were marched off to prison to the sound of music,
    which was meant to advertise their disgrace.)
4403-4 At last his master called to mind, when he was examining his
    accounts one day.

4405 Of a proverbe that seith this same word,
      'Wel bet is roten appul out of hoord
      Than that it rotie al the remenaunt.'
      So fareth it by a riotous servaunt;
      It is ful lasse harm to lete hym pace,   *much less; go*
4410 Than he shende alle the servantz in the place   *ruin*
      Therfore his maister yaf hym acquitance,   *release*
      And bad hym go, with sorwe and with meschance!
      And thus this joly prentys hadde his leve.
      Now lat hym riote al the nyghte or leve.
4415 And for ther is no theef withoute a lowke,   *since; accomplice*
      That helpeth hym to wasten and to sowke   *embezzle*
      Of that he brybe kan or borwe may,   *steal*
      Anon he sente his bed and his array   *clothing*
      Unto a compeer of his owene sort,   *comrade*
4420 That lovede dys, and revel, and disport,   *pleasure*
      And hadde a wyf that heeld for contenance
      A shoppe, and swyved for hir sustenance.   *living*

                                              prostitute

4406–7 'Better remove a rotten apple from the store than let it rot the
       rest.'
4408 So it is with a dissolute servant.
4412 *with sorwe and with meschance*, and bad luck go with him.
4414 Now let him revel or not all night, as he likes.
4421–2 Who kept a shop for the sake of appearances.

Fragment II (Group B¹)

INTRODUCTION TO THE MAN OF LAW'S TALE

The Wordes of the Hoost to the Compaignye

OURE HOOSTE saugh wel that the brighte sonne
The ark of his artificial day hath ronne
The ferthe part, and half an houre and moore,
And though he were nat depe ystert in loore,
5 He wiste it was the eightetethe day   *knew; eighteenth*
Of Aprill, that is messager to May;   *messenger*
And saugh wel that the shadwe of every tree
Was as in lengthe the same quantitee
That was the body erect that caused it.
10 And therfore by the shadwe he took his wit   *calculated*
That Phebus, which that shoon so clere and brighte,   *shone*
Degrees was fyve and fourty clombe on highte;
And for that day, as in that latitude,
It was ten of the clokke, he gan conclude,   *concluded*
15 And sodeynly he plighte his hors aboute.   *pulled; round*
'Lordynges,' quod he, 'I warne yow, al   *gentlemen*
    this route,   *company*
The fourthe party of this day is gon.   *part*
Now, for the love of God and of Seint John,
Leseth no tyme, as ferforth as ye may.
20 Lordynges, the tyme wasteth nyght and day,
And steleth from us, what pryvely slepynge,
And what thurgh necligence in oure wakynge,
As dooth the streem that turneth nevere agayn,   *back*
Descendynge fro the montaigne into playn.

1-3 The Host saw that the sun had traversed a fourth part of the horizon-
arc between the points of sunrise and sunset. This it would do in
April by about 9.20 a.m. Add *half an houre and moore* (3), and the
Host's *ten of the clokke* (14) is found to be correct.
4 Not deeply versed in astronomical lore.
12 Had climbed forty-five degrees in height.
19 Lose no more time than you can help.
20-2 Time passes both by night and day, and steals away from us, now
stealthily in our sleep, now through our own negligence in our waking
hours.

122

25 Wel kan Senec and many a philosophre   *Seneca*
   Biwaillen tyme moore than gold in cofre;   *bewail; coffer*
   For "los of catel may recovered be,
   But los of tyme shendeth us," quod he.   *ruins*
   It wol nat come agayn, withouten drede,   *doubt*
30 Namoore than wole Malkynes maydenhede,
   Whan she hath lost it in hir wantownesse.
   Lat us nat mowlen thus in ydelnesse.   *grow mouldy*
    'Sire Man of Lawe,' quod he, 'so have ye blis,
   Telle us a tale anon, as forward is.   *at once; agreement*
35 Ye been submytted, thurgh youre free assent,
   To stonden in this cas at my juggement.
   Acquiteth yow now of youre biheeste;
   Thanne have ye do youre devoir atte leeste.'   *duty; at least*
    'Hooste,' quod he, '*depardieux*, ich assente; *in God's name*
40 To breke forward is nat myn entente.   *intention*
   Biheste is dette, and I wole holde fayn
   Al my biheste, I kan no bettre sayn.
   For swich lawe as a man yeveth another wight,
   He sholde hymselven usen it, by right;   *observe*
45 Thus wole oure text.   But nathelees, certeyn,
   I kan right now no thrifty tale seyn
   That Chaucer, thogh he kan but lewedly
   On metres and on rymyng craftily,
   Hath seyd hem in swich Englissh as he kan
50 Of olde tyme, as knoweth many a man;
   And if he have noght seyd hem, leve brother,
   In o book, he hath seyd hem in another.   *one*
   For he hath toold of loveris up and doun
   Mo than Ovide made of mencioun
55 In his Episteles, that been ful olde.   *very*
   What sholde I tellen hem, syn they been tolde?   *why*

27 Loss of property may be made good.
30 *Malkyn*, diminutive of Mary; a proverbial name for a wanton woman.
33 As you hope for happiness.
35-6 You have freely agreed to submit to my judgment in this matter.
37 Now do your duty by keeping your promise.
41 Promise is debt (proverbial).
41-2 And I will gladly keep my promise.
45 So our maxim demands. (The Man of Law may be referring to his legal maxim in 43-4.)
46-50 Just now I can't tell any tale worth listening to that Chaucer, though he knows little enough about metre and the niceties of rhyming, has not already told long since in such English as he has at his command.
51 *leve brother*, dear brother. (The Man of Law is politely addressing the Host.)
53-4 For in one place or another he has told stories about more lovers than Ovid made mention of.

In youthe he made of Ceys and Alcione,
And sitthen hath he spoken of everichone,   *since; every one*
Thise noble wyves and thise loveris eke.
60 Whoso that wole his large volume seke,   *look through*
Cleped the Seintes Legende of Cupide,
Ther may he seen the large woundes wyde
Of Lucresse, and of Babilan Tesbee;
The swerd of Dido for the false Enee;
65 The tree of Phillis for hire Demophon;
The pleinte of Dianire and of Hermyon,   *lament*
Of Adriane, and of Isiphilee;
The bareyne yle stondynge in the see;
The dreynte Leandre for his Erro;
70 The teeris of Eleyne, and eek the wo   *Helen*
Of Brixseyde, and of the, Ladomya;   *thee*
The crueltee of the, queene Medea,
Thy litel children hangynge by the hals,   *neck*
For thy Jason, that was of love so fals!
75 O Ypermystra, Penelopee, Alceste,
Youre wifhod he comendeth with the beste!
     But certeinly no word ne writeth he
Of thilke wikke ensample of Canacee,
That loved hir owene brother synfully;
80 (Of swiche cursed stories I sey fy!)   *fie*
Or ellis of Tyro Appollonius,   *of Tyre*
How that the cursed kyng Antiochus
Birafte his doghter of hir maydenhede,   *bereft*
That is so horrible a tale for to rede,
85 Whan he hir threw upon the pavement.
And therfore he, of ful avysement,   *with due deliberation*
Nolde nevere write in none of his sermons   *writings*
Of swiche unkynde abhomynacions,   *unnatural*
Ne I wol noon reherce, if that I may.
90   But of my tale how shal I doon this day?
Me were looth be likned, doutelees,
To Muses that men clepe Pierides—   *call*

---

57 In his youth he wrote the story of Ceyx and Alcyone (in the *Book of the Duchess*).
59 Of noble women and of lovers too.
61 Called the Legend of Cupid's Saints, i.e. the *Legend of Good Women.*
63 Of Lucretia and Babylonian Thisbe.
64 Dido's death by the sword because of false Aeneas.
69 Of Leander drowned for Hero's sake.
71 *Brixseyde,* Briseida, the beloved of Troilus whose name becomes Criseyde in Chaucer's great poem.
76 He (i.e. Chaucer) commends your womanhood as highly as possible.
78 Of that wicked story of Canace.
89 Nor will I repeat any of them, if I can help it.
90 What shall I do about my tale to-day?
91 I should certainly hate to be compared.

Methamorphosios woot what I mene;
But nathelees, I recche noght a bene
95 Though I come after hym with hawebake.
I speke in prose, and lat him rymes make.'
And with that word he, with a sobre cheere,   *sober mien*
Bigan his tale, as ye shal after heere.

The Prologe of the Mannes Tale of Lawe

O hateful harm, condicion of poverte!
100 With thurst, with coold, with hunger so confoundid!   *by*
To asken help thee shameth in thyn herte;   *ask for*
If thou noon aske, with nede artow so woundid
That verray nede unwrappeth al thy wounde hid!
Maugree thyn heed, thou most for indigence
105 Or stele, or begge, or borwe thy despence!

Thow blamest Crist, and seist ful bitterly,
He mysdeparteth richesse temporal;
Thy neighebor thou wytest synfully,   *blame*
And seist thou hast to lite, and he hath al.   *little*
110 'Parfay,' seistow, 'somtyme he rekene shal,
Whan that his tayl shal brennen in the gleede,   *burn; fire*
For he noght helpeth needfulle in hir neede.'

Herkne what is the sentence of the wise: *opinion*
'Bet is to dyen than have indigence';   *better*
115 'Thy selve neighebor wol thee despise.'   *very*
If thou be povre, farwel thy reverence!   *poor; dignity*
Yet of the wise man take this sentence:
'Alle the dayes of povre men been wikke.'   *are evil*
Be war, therfore, er thou come to that prikke!   *critical pass*

120 If thou be povre, thy brother hateth thee,
And alle thy freendes fleen from thee, allas!
O riche marchauntz, ful of wele been yee,   *success*
O noble, o prudent folk, as in this cas!   *in this respect*

93 A reader of the *Metamorphoses* will know what I mean.
94-5 I don't care a bean if I tag behind him (i.e. Chaucer) with my
    plain fare (lit. baked haw).
96 *I speke in prose*, I shall speak in prose. (When Chaucer wrote this
    Introduction he evidently intended the Man of Law to tell a prose
    tale.)
103 Sheer necessity lays bare your hidden wound.
104 In spite of all you can do.
105 Either . . . or borrow your keep.
107 He shares out temporal wealth unfairly.
110 Upon my word . . . one day he will have to account for it.
112 Because he doesn't help the needy in their need.

Youre bagges been nat fild with ambes as,
125 But with sys cynk, that renneth for youre chaunce;
At Cristemasse myrie may ye daunce!   *merrily*

Ye seken lond and see for yowre wynnynges;   *scour; profits*
As wise folk ye knowen al th'estaat
Of regnes; ye been fadres of tidynges
130 And tales, bothe of pees and of debaat.   *war*
I were right now of tales desolaat,
Nere that a marchant, goon is many a yeere,
Me taughte a tale, which that ye shal heere.

THE MAN OF LAW'S TALE

Heere begynneth the Man of Lawe his Tale

In Surrye whilom dwelte a compaignye   *Syria*
135 Of chapmen riche, and therto sadde and trewe,
That wyde-where senten hir spicerye,
Clothes of gold, and satyns riche of hewe.   *hue*
Hir chaffare was so thrifty and so newe
That every wight hath deyntee to chaffare
140 With hem, and eek to sellen hem hire ware.

124-5 Not filled with double aces (a losing throw at dice), but with a six and a five (a winning throw).
128-9 You know all about the state that kingdoms are in; you are the fathers of tidings.
131-2 I should now be barren of tales, if it weren't that a merchant, many years ago.
135 Rich merchants, sober and honest.
136 Who sent out their spices far and wide.
138-9 Their merchandise was so profitable (to the buyer) that everyone was very pleased to trade.

Now fil it that the maistres of that sort
Han shapen hem to Rome for to wende,
Were it for chapmanhod or for disport;
Noon oother message wolde they thider sende,   *messenger*
145 But comen hemself to Rome, this is the ende;
And in swich place as thoughte hem avantage
For hire entente, they take hir herbergage.

Sojourned han thise marchantz in that toun
A certein tyme, as fil to hire plesance.
150 And so bifel that th'excellent renoun
Of the Emperoures doghter, dame Custance,   *Lady Constance*
Reported was, with every circumstance,
Unto thise Surryen marchantz in swich wyse,
Fro day to day, as I shal yow devyse.   *tell*

155 This was the commune voys of every man:
'Oure Emperour of Rome—God hym see!—   *protect*
A doghter hath that, syn the world bigan,   *since*
To rekene as wel hir goodnesse as beautee,
Nas nevere swich another as is shee.
160 I prey to God in honour hire susteene,   *maintain*
And wolde she were of al Europe the queene.

'In hire is heigh beautee, withoute pride,   *great*
Yowthe, withoute grenehede or folye;   *wantonness*
To alle hire werkes vertu is hir gyde;
165 Humblesse hath slayn in hire al tirannye.   *humility*
She is mirour of alle curteisye;
Hir herte is verray chambre of hoolynesse,   *the very*
Hir hand, ministre of fredam for almesse.'

And al this voys was sooth, as God is trewe.
170 But now to purpos lat us turne agayn.   *our purpose*
Thise marchantz han doon fraught hir shippes newe,
And whan they han this blisful mayden sayn,   *seen*
Hoom to Surrye been they went ful fayn,
And doon hir nedes as they han doon yoore,
175 And lyven in wele; I kan sey yow namoore.   *prosperity*

141-3 It happened that some leading merchants of this sort planned to
     go to Rome, either for business or for pleasure.
145 But in the event they came to Rome themselves.
146-7 They took lodgings in a place that seemed to suit their purpose
     best.
149 For such time as they pleased.
158 Taking into account both her goodness and her beauty.
168 Her hand the minister of generous almsgiving.
171 Had their ships loaded up again.
173 Home to Syria have they gladly gone.
174 And go about their business as they did before.

    Now fil it that thise marchantz stode in grace   *happened*
Of hym that was the Sowdan of Surrye;   *Sultan*
For whan they cam from any strange place,
He wolde, of his benigne curteisye,
180 Make hem good chiere, and bisily espye
Tidynges of sondry regnes, for to leere   *various; learn*
The wondres that they myghte seen or heere.

    Amonges othere thynges, specially,
Thise marchantz han hym toold of dame Custance
185 So greet noblesse in ernest, ceriously,
That this Sowdan hath caught so greet plesance
To han hir figure in his remembrance,
That al his lust and al his bisy cure   *desire; endeavour*
Was for to love hire while his lyf may dure.   *last*

190 Paraventure in thilke large book   *perhaps; that*
Which that men clepe the heven ywriten was   *call*
With sterres, whan that he his birthe took,
That he for love sholde han his deeth, allas!
For in the sterres, clerer than is glas,
195 Is writen, God woot, whoso koude it rede,
The deeth of every man, withouten drede.   *doubt*

    In sterres, many a wynter therbiforn,   *before the event*
Was writen the deeth of Ector, Achilles,
Of Pompei, Julius, er they were born;   *Pompey*
200 The strif of Thebes; and of Ercules,   *strife*
Of Sampson, Turnus, and of Socrates
The deeth; but mennes wittes ben so dulle
That no wight kan wel rede it atte fulle.   *no one; fully*

    This Sowdan for his privee conseil sente,   *privy council*
205 And, shortly of this matiere for to pace,
He hath to hem declared his entente,
And seyde hem, certein, but he myghte have grace
To han Custance withinne a litel space,
He nas but deed; and charged hem in hye
210 To shapen for his lyf som remedye.

180 Entertain them well, and eagerly inquire after.
184–5 Told him in such earnest detail about the nobility of Lady
    Constance.
186–7 The Sultan got so much pleasure out of thinking about her.
195 God knows, for anyone who can read it.
205 And to pass quickly over this matter.
207–8 Unless he had the good fortune to win Constance very soon.
209–10 He would surely die; and charged them quickly to devise some
    way of saving his life.

Diverse men diverse thynges seyden;
They argumenten, casten up and doun;
Many a subtil resoun forth they leyden;
They speken of magyk and abusioun.   *witchcraft*
215 But finally, as in conclusioun,
They kan nat seen in that noon avantage,
Ne in noon oother wey, save mariage.

Thanne sawe they therinne swich difficultee
By wey of reson, for to speke al playn,
220 By cause that ther was swich diversitee
Bitwene hir bothe lawes, that they sayn
They trowe, 'that no Cristen prince wolde fayn   *willingly*
Wedden his child under oure lawe sweete
That us was taught by Mahoun, oure prophete.'   *Mahomet*

225   And he answerde, 'Rather than I lese   *should lose*
Custance, I wol be cristned, doutelees.
I moot been hires, I may noon oother chese.
I prey yow hoold youre argumentz in pees;
Saveth my lyf, and beth noght recchelees   *negligent*
230 To geten hire that hath my lyf in cure;
For in this wo I may nat longe endure.'

What nedeth gretter dilatacioun?   *elaboration*
I seye, by tretys and embassadrie,   *treaty; negotiation*
And by the popes mediacioun,
235 And al the chirche, and al the chivalrie,   *nobility*
That in destruccioun of mawmettrie,
And in encrees of Cristes lawe deere,
They been acorded, so as ye shal heere: *agreed*

How that the Sowdan and his baronage   *nobles*
240 And alle his liges sholde ycristned be,
And he shal han Custance in mariage,
And certein gold, I noot what quantitee;   *know not*
And heer-to founden sufficient suretee.
This same accord was sworn on eyther syde;
245 Now, faire Custance, almyghty God thee gyde!

212–13 They argue, propose this and that, and offer many clever opinions.
216–17 Any advantage in such methods, or any way out of it all, except
    marriage.
219 On rational grounds, to speak quite plainly.
227 I must be hers, I can make no other choice.
228 I beg you to keep your arguments to yourselves (lit. in peace, in
    silence).
230 To win her who has my life in her power.
236–7 That for the destruction of idolatry and for the increase.
243 Sufficient security was provided to ensure that this would be done.

Now wolde som men waiten, as I gesse,   *expect*
That I sholde tellen al the purveiance   *preparation*
That th'Emperour, of his grete noblesse,
Hath shapen for his doghter, dame Custance.   *made*
250 Wel may men knowen that so greet ordinance
May no man tellen in a litel clause
As was arrayed for so heigh a cause.

Bisshopes been shapen with hire for to wende,   *prepared*
Lordes, ladies, knyghtes of renoun,
255 And oother folk ynowe, this is th'ende;
And notified is thurghout the toun
That every wight, with greet devocioun,   *person*
Sholde preyen Crist that he this mariage
Receyve in gree, and spede this viage.

260   The day is comen of hir departynge,   *departure*
I seye, the woful day fatal is come,
That ther may be no lenger tariynge,   *further delay*
But forthward they hem dressen, alle and some.
Custance, that was with sorwe al overcome,
265 Ful pale arist, and dresseth hire to wende;
For wel she seeth ther is noon oother ende.

Allas! what wonder is it thogh she wepte,
That shal be sent to strange nacioun
Fro freendes that so tendrely hire kepte,
270 And to be bounden under subjeccioun
Of oon, she knoweth nat his condicioun?
Housbondes been alle goode, and han ben yoore;
That knowen wyves; I dar sey yow na moore.

'Fader,' she seyde, 'thy wrecched child Custance,
275 Thy yonge doghter fostred up so softe,
And ye, my mooder, my soverayn plesance   *pleasure*
Over alle thyng, out-taken Crist on-lofte,
Custance youre child hire recomandeth ofte   *commends herself*
Unto youre grace, for I shal to Surrye,
280 Ne shal I nevere seen yow moore with ye.

250–3 But it will be realized that no one can briefly describe all the
great preparations that were made for so important an occasion.
255 And many other people, in a word.
258–9 To look with favour on this marriage, and make this voyage a
success.
263 They prepare to set forth, one and all.
265 Arises, her face very pale, and prepares to go.
271 Of one whose character she does not know.
272 All husbands are good men, and so they were of old.
275 Brought up so tenderly.
277 Except for Christ on high.
279–80 For I must go to Syria, and never see you again.

'Allas! unto the Barbre nacioun   *Barbary*
I moste anoon, syn that it is youre wille;
But Crist, that starf for our redempcioun   *died*
So yeve me grace his heestes to fulfille!
285 I, wrecche womman, no fors though I spille!
Wommen are born to thraldom and penance,
And to been under mannes governance.'

      I trowe at Troye, whan Pirrus brak the wal,   *Pyrrhus*
Or Ilion brende, at Thebes the citee,
290 N'at Rome, for the harm thurgh Hanybal
That Romayns hath venquysshed tymes thre,
Nas herd swich tendre wepyng for pitee
As in the chambre was for hire departynge;
But forth she moot, wher-so she wepe or synge.

295   O firste moevyng! crueel firmament,
With thy diurnal sweigh that crowdest ay
And hurlest al from est til occident
That naturelly wolde holde another way,
Thy crowdyng set the hevene in swich array
300 At the bigynnyng of this fiers viage,
That crueel Mars hath slayn this mariage.

Infortunat ascendent tortuous,
Of which the lord is helplees falle, allas,
Out of his angle into the derkeste hous!
305 O Mars, o atazir, as in this cas!   *influence*
O fieble moone, unhappy been thy paas!
Thou knyttest thee ther thou art nat receyved;
Ther thou were weel, fro thennes artow weyved.

---

284 Give me the grace to obey His commands.
285 No matter though I die.
289 Before Ilion burned.
290 Because of the harm done by Hannibal.
294 But, weep or sing, she has to go.
295 *firste moevyng*, primum mobile (the outermost sphere which,
    according to Ptolemaic astronomy, revolves round the earth from
    east to west, carrying with it the inner spheres of the planets and fixed
    stars).
296–8 That, with thy diurnal motion, dost ever push and hurl from
    east to west all that naturally would take another way.
299 ff. i.e. the movement of the primum mobile placed the planets in
    unfavourable positions at the beginning of Constance's voyage, and
    so wrecked her marriage.   For the evil influence of the planet Mars
    cf. I. 1995 ff.   The moon (supposed to have a special influence on
    voyages) was not in conjunction with any beneficent planet, and was
    therefore too feeble to help.

Imprudent emperour of Rome, allas!
310 Was ther no philosophre in al thy toun?   *astrologer*
Is no tyme bet than oother in swich cas?   *better*
Of viage is ther noon eleccioun,
Namely to folk of heigh condicioun?   *especially for*
Noght whan a roote is of a burthe yknowe?
315 Allas, we been to lewed or to slowe!   *too ignorant; slothful*

To shippe is brought this woful faire mayde
Solempnely, with every circumstance.
'Now Jhesu Crist be with yow alle!' she sayde;
Ther nys namoore, but 'Farewel, faire Custance!'
320 She peyneth hire to make good contenance;
And forth I lete hire saille in this manere,
And turne I wol agayn to my matere.

The mooder of the Sowdan, welle of vices,   *mother*
Espied hath hir sones pleyn entente,
325 How he wol lete his olde sacrifices;   *give up*
And right anon she for hir conseil sente,   *council*
And they been come to knowe what she mente.   *had in mind*
And whan assembled was this folk in-feere,   *together*
She sette hire doun, and seyde as ye shal heere.   *sat*

330   'Lordes,' quod she, 'ye knowen everichon,   *each one*
How that my sone in point is for to lete
The hooly lawes of oure Alkaron,   *Koran*
Yeven by Goddes message Makomete.   *messenger*
But oon avow to grete God I heete,
335 The lyf shal rather out of my body sterte
Or Makometes lawe out of myn herte!

'What sholde us tyden of this newe lawe
But thraldom to oure bodies and penance,
And afterward in helle to be drawe,   *dragged*
340 For we reneyed Mahoun oure creance?   *denied; belief*
But, lordes, wol ye maken assurance,
As I shal seyn, assentynge to my loore,
And I shal make us sauf for everemoore?'   *safe*

312 Are there no astrological means of choosing a favourable time for
   a voyage?
314 Not even when the exact moment of the traveller's birth is known?
317 With pomp and circumstance.
320 She does her best to look composed.
324 Saw what her son was plainly intent on doing.
334 A vow I make to mighty God.
335-6 Sooner shall life leave my body than Mahomet's law my heart.
337 What would this new religion bring us.
341-2 Will you give me your assurance that you will do as I say, and
   agree to obey my instructions.

They sworen and assenten, every man,
345 To lyve with hire and dye, and by hire stonde,
And everich, in the beste wise he kan,   *each*
To strengthen hire shal alle his frendes   *support*
    fonde;   *persuade*
And she hath this emprise ytake on honde,
Which ye shal heren that I shal devyse,
350 And to hem alle she spak right in this wyse:

'We shul first feyne us cristendom to take,—
Coold water shal nat greve us but a lite!
And I shal swich a feeste and revel make
That, as I trowe, I shal the Sowdan quite.   *pay out*
355 For thogh his wyf be cristned never so white,
She shal have nede to wasshe awey the rede,   *red (blood)*
Thogh she a font-ful water with hire lede.'   *bring*

O Sowdanesse, roote of iniquitee!
Virago, thou Semyrame the secounde!   *Semiramis*
360 O serpent under femynynytee,
Lik to the serpent depe in helle ybounde!
O feyned womman, al that may confounde   *deceitful*
Vertu and innocence, thurgh thy malice,
Is bred in thee, as nest of every vice!

365 O Sathan, envious syn thilke day   *since the*
That thou were chaced from oure heritage,
Wel knowestow to wommen the olde way!
Thou madest Eva brynge us in servage;   *bondage*
Thou wolt fordoon this Cristen mariage.   *destroy*
370 Thyn instrument so, weylawey the while!
Makestow of wommen, whan thou wolt bigile.

This Sowdanesse, whom I thus blame and warye,   *curse*
Leet prively hire conseil goon hire way.
What sholde I in this tale lenger tarye?   *why*
375 She rydeth to the Sowdan on a day,
And seyde hym that she wolde reneye hir lay,   *renounce; faith*
And cristendom of preestes handes fonge,   *receive*
Repentynge hire she hethen was so longe;

348-9 She embarked on this business, which you shall hear me describe.
352 Cold water can't hurt us very much.
360 In the form of a woman.   (An allusion to the medieval legend that
    the serpent which tempted Eve had a woman's head.)
366 i.e. driven from heaven.
367 You know of old how to get your way with women.
370-1 Thus when you mean to deceive, you make women, alas, your
    instrument.
373 Dismissed her counsellors secretly.

Bisechynge hym to doon hire that honour,
380 That she moste han the Cristen folk to feeste,—   *might have*
'To plesen hem I wol do my labour.'   *take pains*
The Sowdan seith, 'I wol doon at youre heeste';
And knelynge thanketh hire of that requeste.   *for*
So glad he was, he nyste what to seye.   *knew not*
385 She kiste hir sone, and hoom she gooth hir weye.

EXPLICIT PRIMA PARS

SEQUITUR PARS SECUNDA

Arryved been this Cristen folk to londe
In Surrye, with a greet solempne route,   *imposing company*
And hastifliche this Sowdan sente his   *quickly*
     sonde,   *messenger*
First to his mooder, and al the regne aboute,   *mother; realm*
390 And seyde his wyf was comen, out of doute,
And preyde hire for to ryde agayn the queene,   *to meet*
The honour of his regne to susteene.   *maintain*

Greet was the prees, and riche was th'array   *throng*
Of Surryens and Romayns met yfeere;   *together*
395 The mooder of the Sowdan, riche and gay,
Receyveth hire with also glad a cheere   *as; welcome*
As any mooder myghte hir doghter deere,
And to the nexte citee ther bisyde
A softe paas solemnpnely they ryde.

400   Noght trowe I the triumphe of Julius,   *believe*
Of which that Lucan maketh swich a boost,
Was roialler ne moore curius   *fine*
Than was th'assemblee of this blisful hoost.
But this scorpioun, this wikked goost,   *evil spirit*
405 The Sowdanesse, for al hire flaterynge,
Caste under this ful mortally to stynge.

The Sowdan comth hymself soone after this
So roially, that wonder is to telle,
And welcometh hire with alle joye and blis.
410 And thus in murthe and joye I lete hem dwelle;

382 I will do as you command.
398 To the nearest city, which was close by.
399 They ride slowly and in solemn state.
403 Than was the coming together of this joyful host.
406 Planned under cover of this to plant a deadly sting.

The fruyt of this matiere is that I telle.
Whan tyme cam, men thoughte it for the beste
That revel stynte, and men goon to hir reste.   *should end*

    The tyme cam, this olde Sowdanesse
415 Ordeyned hath this feeste of which I tolde,
And to the feeste Cristen folk hem dresse   *make their way*
In general, ye, bothe yonge and olde.
Heere may men feeste and roialtee biholde,
And deyntees mo than I kan yow devyse;   *describe*
420 But al to deere they boghte it er they ryse.

    O sodeyn wo, that evere art successour
To worldly blisse, spreynd with bitternesse!   *mingled*
The ende of the joye of oure worldly labour!
Wo occupieth the fyn of oure gladnesse.
425 Herke this conseil for thy sikernesse: *safety*
Upon thy glade day have in thy mynde
The unwar wo or harm that comth bihynde.

    For shortly for to tellen, at o word,   *in*
The Sowdan and the Cristen everichone
430 Been al tohewe and stiked at the bord,
But it were oonly dame Custance allone.
This olde Sowdanesse, cursed krone,
Hath with hir freendes doon this cursed dede,
For she hirself wolde al the contree lede.   *rule*

435 Ne ther was Surryen noon that was converted,
That of the conseil of the Sowdan woot,
That he nas al tohewe er he asterted.
And Custance han they take anon, foot-hoot,
And in a ship al steereless, God woot,   *rudderless*
440 They han hir set, and bidde hire lerne saille
Out of Surrye agaynward to Ytaille.   *back again*

    A certein tresor that she thider ladde,
And, sooth to seyn, vitaille greet plentee
They han hire yeven, and clothes eek she hadde,
445 And forth she sailleth in the salte see.

411 It's the gist of this matter I'm giving you.
420 But they paid all too dearly for it before they rose from their seats.
424 Sorrow lives in the confines of our happiness.
429–31 The Sultan and the Christians are all stabbed and hacked to
    pieces while sitting at table, all but the Lady Constance.
435–7 There was no Syrian convert in the confidence of the Sultan who
    was not hacked to pieces before he could escape.
438 *foot-hoot*, hot-foot, instantly.
442 A certain amount of treasure she had brought with her.
443 And, to tell the truth, a great store of food.

O my Custance, ful of benignytee,
O Emperoures yonge doghter deere,
He that is lord of Fortune be thy steere!   *guide*

She blesseth hire, and with ful pitous voys
450 Unto the croys of Crist thus seyde she:
'O cleere, o welful auter, hooly croys,   *bright; happy altar*
Reed of the Lambes blood ful of pitee,
That wessh the world fro the olde iniquitee,   *washed*
Me fro the feend and fro his clawes kepe,
455 That day that I shal drenchen in the depe.   *drown*

Victorious tree, proteccioun of trewe,   *cross; the faithful*
That oonly worthy were for to bere   *alone*
The Kyng of Hevene with his woundes newe,
The white Lamb, that hurt was with a spere,
460 Flemere of feendes out of hym and here
On which thy lymes feithfully extenden,
Me kepe, and yif me myght my lyf t'amenden.'

Yeres and dayes fleet this creature   *floated*
Thurghout the See of Grece unto the Strayte
465 Of Marrok, as it was hire aventure.
On many a sory meel now may she bayte;
After hir deeth ful often may she wayte,
Er that the wilde wawes wol hire dryve   *waves*
Unto the place ther she shal arryve.

470   Men myghten asken why she was nat slayn
Eek at the feeste? who myghte hir body save?
And I answere to that demande agayn,
Who saved Danyel in the horrible cave
Ther every wight save he, maister and knave,
475 Was with the leon frete er he asterte?
No wight but God, that he bar in his herte.

God liste to shewe his wonderful myracle   *was pleased*
In hire, for we sholde seen his myghty werkis;
Crist, which that is to every harm triacle,   *remedy*
480 By certeine meenes ofte, as knowen clerkis,   *scholars*

449 She crosses herself, and with a piteous voice.
452 Red with the Lamb's compassionate blood.
460–1 Banisher of fiends from the man or woman over whom your
  arms faithfully extend (i.e. from everyone marked with the sign of
  the cross).
464–5 Right through the Mediterranean Sea to the Straits of Gibraltar,
  as chance decreed.
466–7 She will have to eat many a wretched meal, and very often live
  in expectation of death.
474–5 Where everyone but he, master and slave alike, was eaten by the
  lion before he could escape.

Dooth thyng for certein ende that ful derk is   *dark*
To mannes wit, that for oure ignorance
Ne konne noght knowe his prudent purveiance.   *providence*

   Now sith she was nat at the feeste yslawe,   *since; slain*
485 Who kepte hire fro the drenchyng in the see?   *drowning*
Who kepte Jonas in the fisshes mawe
Til he was spouted up at Nynyvee?   *Nineveh*
Wel may men knowe it was no wight but he
That kepte peple Ebrayk from hir drenchynge,   *Hebrew*
490 With drye feet thurghout the see passynge.

   Who bad the foure spirites of tempest
That power han t'anoyen lond and see,   *trouble*
Bothe north and south, and also west and est,
'Anoyeth neither see, ne land, ne tree'?
495 Soothly, the comandour of that was he
That fro the tempest ay this womman kepte
As wel whan she wook as whan she slepte.   *was awake*

   Where myghte this womman mete and drynke have   *food*
Thre yeer and moore? how lasteth hire vitaille?
500 Who fedde the Egipcien Marie in the cave,
Or in desert?   No wight but Crist, sanz faille.   *without*
Fyve thousand folk it was as greet mervaille
With loves fyve and fisshes two to feede.
God sente his foyson at hir grete neede.   *plenty*

   She dryveth forth into oure occian   *is driven along*
Thurghout oure wilde see, til atte laste
Under an hoold that nempnen I ne kan,
Fer in Northumberlond the wawe hire caste,
And in the sond hir ship stiked so faste   *sand; stuck*
510 That thennes wolde it noght of al a tyde;
The wyl of Crist was that she sholde abyde.

   The constable of the castel doun is fare   *gone*
To seen this wrak, and al the ship he soghte,   *wreck; searched*
And foond this wery womman ful of care;
515 He foond also the tresor that she broghte.
In hir langage mercy she bisoghte,
The lyf out of hir body for to twynne,
Hire to delivere of wo that she was inne.

494 Rev. vii. 3.
502–3 It was just as great a miracle to feed five thousand folk.
507 Beneath a castle I do not know the name of.
510 It would not budge from there during one whole tide.
517 To sever her life from her body, i.e. kill her.

A maner Latyn corrupt was hir speche,
520 But algates therby was she understonde.   *all the same*
The constable, whan hym lyst no lenger seche,
This woful womman broghte he to the londe.
She kneleth doun and thanketh Goddes sonde;
But what she was she wolde no man seye,
525 For foul ne fair, thogh that she sholde deye.

She seyde she was so mazed in the see
That she forgat hir mynde, by hir trouthe.
The constable hath of hire so greet pitee,
And eek his wyf, that they wepen for routhe.
530 She was so diligent, withouten slouthe,   *sloth*
To serve and plesen everich in that place,   *everyone*
That alle hir loven that looken in hir face.   *at*

This constable and dame Hermengyld, his wyf,
Were payens, and that contree everywhere;
535 But Hermengyld loved hire right as hir lyf,
And Custance hath so longe sojourned there,
In orisons, with many a bitter teere,   *prayers*
Til Jhesu hath converted thurgh his grace
Dame Hermengyld, constablesse of that place.

540 In al that lond no Cristen dorste route;   *meet together*
Alle Cristen folk been fled fro that contree
Thurgh payens, that conquereden al aboute   *because of*
The plages of the north, by land and see.   *regions*
To Walys fledde the Cristyanytee
545 Of olde Britons dwellynge in this ile;
Ther was hir refut for the meene while.   *refuge*

But yet nere Cristene Britons so exiled
That ther nere somme that in hir privetee   *in secret*
Honoured Crist and hethen folk bigiled,   *deceived*
550 And ny the castel swiche ther dwelten three.
That oon of hem was blynd and myghte nat see,
But it were with thilke eyen of his mynde
With whiche men seen, after that they ben blynde.

519 A corrupt kind of Latin.
521 i.e. when he was satisfied that there was nothing more to find in
    the ship.
525 On any account, though she should die for it.
526–7 So dazed by her experience at sea that, in truth, she had lost her
    memory.
529 They wept with compassion.
534 Were pagans, and everyone else in those parts.
547 Yet the Christian Britons were not so completely driven into exile.
550 Near the castle there dwelt three such (Christians).
552 Except with the eyes of his mind.

Bright was the sonne as in that someres day,
555 For which the constable and his wyf also
And Custance han ytake the righte way
Toward the see a furlong wey or two,
To pleyen and to romen to and fro;   *wander*
And in hir walk this blynde man they mette.
560 Croked and oold, with eyen faste yshette.   *shut*

'In name of Crist,' cride this blinde Britoun,
'Dame Hermengyld, yif me my sighte agayn!'   *give*
This lady weex affrayed of the soun,
Lest that hir housbonde, shortly for to sayn,
565 Wolde hire for Ihesu Cristes love han slayn,
Til Custance made hire boold, and bad hire wirche   *do*
The wyl of Crist, as doghter of his chirche.

The constable weex abasshed of that sight,
And seyde, 'What amounteth al this fare?'
570 Custance answerde, 'Sire, it is Cristes myght,
That helpeth folk out of the feendes snare.'
And so forferth she gan oure lay declare
That she the constable, er that it was eve
Converteth, and on Crist made hym bileve.   *in*

575 This constable was nothyng lord of this place   *not at all*
Of which I speke, ther he Custance fond,   *where*
But kepte it strongly many a wyntres space
Under Alla, kyng of al Northhumbrelond,   *Aella*
That was ful wys, and worthy of his hond
580 Agayn the Scottes, as men may wel heere;
But turne I wole agayn to my mateere.

Sathan, that evere us waiteth to bigile,
Saugh of Custance al hire perfeccioun,   *saw*
And caste anon how he myghte quite hir while,
585 And made a yong knyght that dwelte in that toun
Love hire so hoote, of foul affeccioun,
That verraily hym thoughte he sholde spille,
But he of hire myghte ones have his wille.   *unless*

556–7 Took the shortest path to the sea, a few minutes away.
563 This lady was frightened by his words. (The constable's wife had
   not told him of her conversion to Christianity.)
565 Would kill her for her love of Jesus.
568 Was upset by what he saw.
569 What's all this about?
572 And she explained our faith so well.
579–80 And fought with great valour against the Scots.
582 Who is always on the look-out to deceive us.
584 At once considered how he could pay her out.
586 So violently, and with a lust so foul.
587 He thought he would surely die.

He woweth hire, but it availleth noght;
590 She wolde do no synne, by no weye.   *in any way*
And for despit he compassed in his thoght
To maken hire on shameful deeth to deye.   *die*
He wayteth whan the constable was aweye,
And pryvely upon a nyght he crepte
595 In Hermengyldes chambre, whil she slepte.

Wery, forwaked in hire orisouns,
Slepeth Custance, and Hermengyld also.
This knyght, thurgh Sathanas temptaciouns,
Al softely is to the bed ygo,   *gone*
600 And kitte the throte of Hermengyld atwo,   *cut*
And leyde the blody knyf by dame Custance,
And wente his wey, ther God yeve hym
        meschance!   *misfortune*

Soone after cometh this constable hoom agayn,
And eek Alla, that kyng was of that lond,   *also*
605 And saugh his wyf despitously yslayn,   *cruelly*
For which ful ofte he weep and wroong his hond, *wept; wrung*
And in the bed the blody knyf he fond
By Dame Custance.   Allas! what myghte she seye?
For verray wo hir wit was al aweye.

610   To kyng Alla was toold al this meschance,   *calamity*
And eek the tyme, and where, and in what wise
That in a ship was founden this Custance,
As heer-biforn that ye han herd devyse.
The kynges herte of pitee gan agryse,
615 Whan he saugh so benigne a creature   *gracious*
Falle in disese and in mysaventure.   *misery; misfortune*

For as the lomb toward his deeth is broght,   *lamb*
So stant this innocent bifore the kyng.   *stands*
This false knyght, that hath this tresoun wroght,
620 Berth hire on hond that she hath doon thys thyng.
But nathelees, ther was greet moornyng
Among the peple, and seyn they kan nat gesse   *imagine*
That she had doon so greet a wikkednesse;

591 And spitefully he planned in his mind.
593 He watches out for the moment.
596 Exhausted with watching and praying.
609 She was distracted with sheer grief.
614 Was moved to pity.
620 Falsely accuses her of having done this thing.

For they han seyn hire evere so vertuous,
625 And lovynge Hermengyld right as hir lyf.
Of this baar witnesse everich in that hous,
Save he that Hermengyld slow with his knyf.   *slew*
This gentil kyng hath caught a greet motyf
Of this witnesse, and thoghte he wolde enquere
630 Depper in this, a trouthe for to lere.   *more deeply; learn*

Allas! Custance, thou hast no champioun,
Ne fighte kanstow noght, so weylaway!
But he that starf for our redempcioun,   *died*
And boond Sathan (and yet lith ther he lay),
635 So be thy stronge champion this day!
For, but if Crist open myracle kithe,
Withouten gilt thou shalt be slayn as swithe.

She sette hire doun on knees, and thus she sayde:
'Immortal God, that savedest Susanne
640 Fro false blame, and thou, merciful mayde,
Marie I meene, doghter to Seint Anne,
Bifore whos child angeles synge Osanne,   *Hosanna*
If I be giltlees of this felonye,
My socour be, for ellis shal I dye!'

645 Have ye nat seyn somtyme a pale face,
Among a prees, of hym that hath be lad   *crowd; led*
Toward his deeth, wher as hym gat no grace,
And swich a colour in his face hath had,
Men myghte knowe his face that was bistad,
650 Amonges alle the faces in that route?
So stant Custance, and looketh hire aboute.   *stands*

O queenes, lyvynge in prosperitee,
Duchesses, and ye ladyes everichone,
Haveth som routhe on hire adversitee!   *pity*
655 An Emperoures doghter stant allone;
She hath no wight to whom to make hir mone.   *complaint*
O blood roial, that stondest in this drede,   *deadly fear*
Fer been thy freendes at thy grete nede!   *far away*

626 Everyone in the house bore witness to this.
628-9 The noble king was strongly impressed by this witness.
632 Nor can you fight to defend yourself, alas! (There is an allusion
in this and the preceding line to trial by battle.)
634 Who still lies where first he lay.
636-7 Unless Christ performs an obvious miracle, you shall swiftly be
killed, guiltless though you are.
647 Since he could get no pardon for himself.
649-50 You could tell it from all the other faces in the crowd as the
face of a man in mortal peril.

This Alla kyng hath swich compassioun,
660 As gentil herte is fulfild of pitee,
That from his eyen ran the water doun.
'Now hastily do fecche a book,' quod he,   *go and fetch*
'And if this knyght wol sweren how that she
This womman slow, yet wol we us avyse
665 Whom that we wole that shal been oure justise.'

A Britoun book, written with Evaungiles,
Was fet, and on this book he swoor anoon   *fetched*
She gilty was, and in the meene whiles
An hand hym smoot upon the nekke-boon,
670 That doun he fil atones as a stoon,   *fell at once*
And bothe his eyen broste out of his face   *burst*
In sighte of every body in that place.

A voys was herd in general audience,
And seyde, 'Thou hast desclaundred, giltelees,   *defamed*
675 The doghter of hooly chirche in heigh presence;
Thus hastou doon, and yet holde I my pees!'
Of this mervaille agast was al the prees;   *terrified*
As mazed folk they stoden everichone,   *dazed*
For drede of wreche, save Custance allone.   *vengeance*

680   Greet was the drede and eek the repentance
Of hem that hadden wrong suspecioun
Upon this sely innocent, Custance;
And for this miracle, in conclusioun,
And by Custances mediacioun,
685 The kyng—and many another in that place—
Converted was, thanked be Cristes grace!

This false knyght was slayn for his untrouthe
By juggement of Alla hastifly;   *promptly*
And yet Custance hadde of his deeth greet routhe.
690 And after this Jhesus, of his mercy,
Made Alla wedden ful solempnely
This hooly mayden, that is so bright and sheene;   *beautiful*
And thus hath Crist ymaad Custance a queene.   *made*

But who was woful, if I shal nat lye,
695 Of this weddyng but Donegild, and namo,
The kynges mooder, ful of tirannye?
Hir thoughte hir cursed herte brast atwo.

660 For a noble heart is full of pity.
664–5 We shall then consider whom we wish to act as judge.
666 i.e. a gospel book written in the British language.
675 In the royal presence.
682 Of this blameless and innocent woman.
694–6 But who, to tell the truth, was grieved at this wedding—who but
    Donegild alone, the king's tyrant of a mother?
697 She felt her wicked heart would break in two.

She wolde noght hir sone had do so;
Hir thoughte a despit that he sholde take
700 So strange a creature unto his make.   *alien; wife*

    Me list nat of the chaf, ne of the stree,
    Maken so long a tale as of the corn.
    What sholde I tellen of the roialtee   *why; majesty*
    At mariage, or which cours goth biforn;
705 Who bloweth in a trumpe or in an horn?
    The fruyt of every tale is for to seye:
    They ete, and drynke, and daunce, and synge, and pleye.

    They goon to bedde, as it was skile and right;   *reasonable*
    For thogh that wyves be ful hooly thynges,
710 They moste take in pacience at nyght
    Swiche manere necessaries as been plesynges
    To folk that han ywedded hem with rynges,
    And leye a lite hir hoolynesse aside,   *little*
    As for the tyme,—it may no bet bitide.

715 On hire he gat a knave child anon,   *begot; male*
    And to a bisshop, and his constable eke,
    He took his wyf to kepe, whan he is gon
    To Scotlond-ward, his foomen for to seke.
    Now faire Custance, that is so humble and meke,
720 So longe is goon with childe, til that stille
    She halt hire chambre, abidyng Cristes wille.

    The tyme is come a knave child she beer;   *bore*
    Mauricius at the fontstoon they hym calle.   *font*
    This constable dooth forth come a messageer,
725 And wroot unto his kyng, that cleped was Alle,   *called*
    How that this blisful tidyng is bifalle,   *event; come to pass*
    And othere tidynges spedeful for to seye.
    He taketh the lettre, and forth he gooth his weye.

698 She had not wanted her son to do this.
699 She thought it a dishonour.
701–2 I don't want to say as much about the chaff and straw (i.e. the
    unimportant things) as about the corn.
704 Or which course (of the feast) came first.
706 The essence of every story must be given.
711 Such things as are necessary to please.
714 For the time being—this is the best thing to do.
717 He gave his wife to be taken care of.
718 To Scotland, to seek out his enemies.
720–1 Is now so far gone with child that she stays quietly in her own
    room.
724 Summons a messenger.
727 Other news he thought expedient to report.

    This messager, to doon his avantage,
730 Unto the kynges mooder rideth swithe,   *quickly*
    And salueth hire ful faire in his langage: *greets*
    'Madame,' quod he, 'ye may be glad and blithe,
    And thanketh God an hundred thousand sithe!   *times*
    My lady queene hath child, withouten doute,   *a doubt*
735 To joye and blisse to al this regne aboute.

    Lo, heere the lettres seled of this thyng,
    That I moot bere with al the haste I may.   *must*
    If ye wol aught unto youre sone the kyng,
    I am youre servant, bothe nyght and day.'
740 Donegild answerde, 'As now at this tyme, nay;
    But heere al nyght I wol thou take thy reste.
    To-morwe wol I seye thee what me leste.'   *I desire*

    This messager drank sadly ale and wyn,   *deep*
    And stolen were his lettres pryvely   *secretly*
745 Out of his box, whil he sleep as a swyn;   *was sleeping*
    And countrefeted was ful subtilly   *forged; skilfully*
    Another lettre, wroght ful synfully,
    Unto the kyng direct of this mateere
    Fro his constable, as ye shal after heere.

750 The lettre spak the queene delivered was
    Of so horrible a feendly creature   *fiendish*
    That in the castel noon so hardy was
    That any while dorste ther endure.
    The mooder was an elf, by aventure
755 Ycomen, by charmes or by sorcerie,
    And every wight hateth hir compaignye.

    Wo was this kyng whan he this lettre had sayn,   *sad; seen*
    But to no wight he tolde his sorwes soore,   *grievous*
    But of his owene hand he wroot agayn,   *in reply*
760 'Welcome the sonde of Crist for everemoore
    To me that am now lerned in his loore!
    Lord, welcome be thy lust and thy plesaunce;   *will*
    My lust I putte al in thyn ordinaunce.   *at thy command*

729 To advance his own interests.
735 To the joy and bliss of every part of this realm.
736 See, here is a sealed letter about this thing.
738 If you want me to take anything to your son.
747–8 Wickedly purporting to be addressed to the king by his constable
    on this subject (of the royal birth).
752–3 None was bold enough to stay for any length of time in the castle.
754–5 Perhaps sent by charms or sorcery.
760–1 May Christ's dispensation be always welcome to me, who am
    now well instructed in His teaching.

Kepeth this child, al be it foul or feir,   *ugly; beautiful*
765 And eek my wyf, unto myn hoom-comynge.
Crist, whan hym list, may sende me an heir   *it pleases Him*
Moore agreable than this to my likynge.'
This lettre he seleth, pryvely wepynge,   *secretly*
Which to the messager was take soone,   *taken*
770 And forth he gooth; ther is na moore to doone.   *be done*

O messager, fulfild of dronkenesse,   *sodden in*
Strong is thy breeth, thy lymes faltren ay,   *keep faltering*
And thou biwreyest alle secreenesse.   *betray; secrecy*
Thy mynde is lorn, thou janglest as a jay,
775 Thy face is turned in a newe array.
Ther dronkenesse regneth in any route,
Ther is no conseil hyd, withouten doute.   *secret*

O Donegild, I ne have noon Englissh digne   *worthy*
Unto thy malice and thy tirannye!
780 And therfore to the feend I thee resigne;   *devil*
Lat hym enditen of thy traitorie!
Fy, mannysh, fy!—o nay, by God, I lye—   *unwomanly*
Fy, feendlych spirit, for I dar wel telle,   *fiendish*
Thogh thou heere walke, thy spirit is in helle!

785 This messager comth fro the kyng agayn,
And at the kynges moodres court he lighte,   *alighted*
And she was of this messager ful fayn,
And plesed hym in al that ever she myghte.
He drank, and wel his girdel underpighte;   *underpinned*
790 He slepeth, and he fnorteth in his gyse
Al nyght, til the sonne gan aryse.   *arose*

Eft were his lettres stolen everychon,   *again*
And countrefeted lettres in this wyse:
'The king comandeth his constable anon,
795 Up peyne of hangyng, and on heigh juyse,
That he ne sholde suffren in no wyse   *on no account*
Custance in-with his reawme for t'abyde   *within; realm*
Thre dayes and o quarter of a tyde;   *tide*

774 Your wits are gone, you chatter like a jay.
775 Your features are completely changed.
776 Where drunkenness rules the roost.
781 Let him write about your treachery.
787 She was very glad to see this messenger.
790 He snorts in his own swinish manner.
793 And a letter forged to this effect.
795 On pain of hanging and of sternest justice.

'But in the same ship as he hire fond,   *found*
800 Hire, and hir yonge sone, and al hir geere,
He sholde putte, and croude hire fro the lond,   *shove*
And charge hire that she never eft coome theere.'   *again*
O my Custance, wel may thy goost have feere,   *spirit; fear*
And, slepynge, in thy dreem been in penance,
805 Whan Donegild cast al this ordinance.

This messager on morwe, whan he wook,   *awoke*
Unto the castel halt the nexte way,   *takes; nearest*
And to the constable he the lettre took;
And whan that he this pitous lettre say,   *sad; saw*
810 Ful ofte he seyde, 'Allas! and weylaway!'
'Lord Crist,' quod he, 'how may this world endure,
So ful of synne is many a creature?

'O myghty God, if that it be thy wille,
Sith thou art rightful juge, how may it be   *since; righteous*
815 That thou wolt suffren innocentz to spille,   *perish*
And wikked folk regne in prosperitee?
O goode Custance, allas! so wo is me
That I moot be thy tormentour, or deye
On shames deeth; ther is noon oother weye.'

820   Wepen bothe yonge and olde in al that place,
Whan that the kyng this cursed lettre sente,
And Custance, with a deedly pale face,
The ferthe day toward hir ship she wente.   *fourth*
But nathelees she taketh in good entente
825 The wyl of Crist, and knelynge on the stronde,   *strand*
She seyde, 'Lord, ay welcome be thy sonde!   *dispensation*

'He that me kepte fro the false blame
While I was on the lond amonges yow,
He kan me kepe from harm and eek fro shame
830 In salte see, althogh I se noght how.
As strong as evere he was, he is yet now.
In hym triste I, and in his mooder deere,   *trust*
That is to me my seyl and eek my steere.'   *sail; rudder*

Hir litel child lay wepyng in hir arm,
835 And knelynge, pitously to hym she seyde,
'Pees, litel sone, I wol do thee noon harm.'
With that hir coverchief of hir heed she   *kerchief; snatched*
     breyde,

804 And suffer torment as you sleep and dream.
805 When Donegild hatched all this plot.
818-19 I must either be your executioner or die a shameful death.
824 Nevertheless she gladly accepts.

And over his litel eyen she it leyde,   *eyes*
And in hir arm she lulleth it ful faste,
840 And into hevene hire eyen up she caste.

'Mooder,' quod she, 'and mayde bright, Marie,
Sooth is that thurgh wommanes eggement   *instigation*
Mankynde was lorn, and damned ay to dye,
For which thy child was on a croys yrent.   *cross; torn*
845 Thy blisful eyen sawe al his torment;   *blessed*
Thanne is ther no comparison bitwene
Thy wo and any wo man may sustene.   *endure*

'Thow sawe thy child yslayn bifore thyne yen,
And yet now lyveth my litel child, parfay!
850 Now, lady bright, to whom alle woful cryen,
Thow glorie of wommanhede, thow faire may,   *maiden*
Thow haven of refut, brighte sterre of day,   *refuge*
Rewe on my child, that of thy gentillesse,
Rewest on every reweful in distresse.

855   'O litel child, allas! what is thy gilt,
That nevere wroghtest synne as yet, pardee?
Why wil thyn harde fader han thee spilt?   *killed*
O mercy, deere constable,' quod she,
'As lat my litel child dwelle heer with thee;   *please let*
860 And if thou darst nat saven hym, for blame,   *for fear of*
So kys hym ones in his fadres name!'

Therwith she looked bakward to the londe,
And seyde, 'Farewel, housbonde routhelees!'   *pitiless*
And up she rist, and walketh doun the stronde
865 Toward the ship,—hir folweth al the prees,—   *crowd*
And evere she preyeth hire child to holde his pees; *be quiet*
And taketh hir leve, and with an hooly entente   *holy heart*
She blisseth hire, and into ship she wente.   *crosses herself*

Vitailled was the ship, it is no drede,
870 Habundantly for hire ful longe space,
And othere necessaries that sholde nede   *be needed*
She hadde ynogh, heryed be Goddes grace!   *praised*

843 Mankind was lost, and condemned to everlasting death.
853-4 Have pity on my child, thou who dost graciously have pity on
   every sad creature in distress.
856 Who never yet sinned, indeed (lit. by God).
864 And up she rose (from her kneeling position).
869-70 The ship was stored with food enough, no doubt, to last her
   for a very long time.

For wynd and weder almyghty God purchace,   *provide*
And brynge hire hoom! I kan no bettre seye,
875 But in the see she dryveth forth hir weye.   *is driven on*

EXPLICIT SECUNDA PARS

SEQUITUR PARS TERCIA

Alla the kyng comth hoom soone after this
Unto his castel, of the which I tolde,
And asketh where his wyf and his child is.
The constable gan aboute his herte colde,
880 And pleynly al the manere he hym tolde
As ye han herd—I kan telle it no bettre—
And sheweth the kyng his seel and eek his lettre,   *seal*

And seyde, 'Lord, as ye comanded me
Up peyne of deeth, so have I doon, certein.'   *certainly*
885 This messager tormented was til he   *tortured*
Moste biknowe and tellen, plat and pleyn,
Fro nyght to nyght, in what place he had leyn;   *stayed*
And thus, by wit and sotil enquerynge,
Ymagined was by whom this harm gan sprynge.

890 The hand was knowe that the lettre wroot,
And al the venym of this cursed dede,
But in what wise, certeinly, I noot.
Th'effect is this, that Alla, out of drede,
His mooder slow—that may men pleynly rede—   *slew*
895 For that she traitour was to hire ligeance.   *allegiance*
Thus endeth olde Donegild, with meschance!   *curse her*

The sorwe that this Alla nyght and day
Maketh for his wyf, and for his child also,
Ther is no tonge that it telle may.
900 But now wol I unto Custance go,
That fleteth in the see, in peyne and wo,   *floats on*
Fyve yeer and moore, as liked Cristes sonde,
Er that hir ship approched unto londe.

879 Felt his heart grow cold.
886 Was forced to confess and tell plainly and fully.
888-9 By quick thinking and skilful questioning they were able to guess
     who was responsible for this evil deed.
890-2 They recognized the hand that wrote the letter and venomously
     plotted this accursed deed; but how they worked it out, I don't know
     at all.
893 The upshot, without doubt, was this, that Aella.
902 As it pleased Christ to ordain.

Under an hethen castel, atte laste,
905 Of which the name in my text noght I fynde,
Custance, and eek hir child, the see up caste.
Almyghty God, that saveth al mankynde,
Have on Custance and on hir child som mynde,
That fallen is in hethen hand eft soone,
910 In point to spille, as I shal telle yow soone.

Doun fro the castel comth ther many a wight   *person*
To gauren on this ship and on Custance.   *stare*
But shortly, from the castel, on a nyght,
The lordes styward—God yeve hym meschance!—
915 A theef, that hadde reneyed oure creance,
Cam into ship allone, and seyde he sholde   *would*
Hir lemman be, wher-so she wolde or nolde.

Wo was this wrecched womman tho bigon;
Hir child cride, and she cride pitously.
920 But blisful Marie heelp hire right anon;   *helped*
For with hir struglyng wel and myghtily
The theef fil over bord al sodeynly,
And in the see he dreynte for vengeance;   *punishment*
And thus hath Crist unwemmed kept Custance.   *unspotted*

925 O foule lust of luxurie, lo, thyn ende!   *lechery*
Nat oonly that thou feyntest mannes mynde,   *weaken*
But verraily thou wolt his body shende.   *ruin*
Th'ende of thy werk, or of thy lustes blynde,
Is compleynyng. Hou many oon may men   *lamentation*
        fynde
930 That noght for werk somtyme, but for th'entente
To doon this synne, been outher slayn or shente!

How may this wayke womman han this strengthe   *feeble*
Hire to defende agayn this renegat?   *renegade*
O Golias, unmesurable of lengthe,
935 Hou myghte David make thee so maat,

905 *my text.* The main source of this tale is the Anglo-Norman
    Chronicle of Nicholas Trivet (first half of fourteenth century).
908–10 Spare some thought for Constance and her child, who once
    again has fallen into heathen hands, and is in danger of her life.
915 A scoundrel who had renounced our faith.
917 Be her lover, whether she liked it or not.
918 *Wo . . . bigon*, overcome with grief.
929–31 How many people you will find who are killed or ruined for
    their sinful intention and not for the sin itself!
934 Goliath, immeasurably tall.
935 How could David bring you so low.

So yong and of armure so desolaat?
Hou dorste he looke upon thy dredful face?
Wel may men seen, it nas but Goddes grace.

Who yaf Judith corage or hardynesse   *boldness*
940 To sleen hym Olofernus in his tente,   *slay; Holofernes*
And to deliveren out of wrecchednesse
The peple of God?   I seye, for this entente,
That right as God spirit of vigour sente
To hem, and saved hem out of meschance,
945 So sente he myght and vigour to Custance.

    Forth gooth hir ship thurghout the narwe mouth
Of Jubaltare and Septe, dryvynge ay
Somtyme west, and somtyme north and south,
And somtyme est, ful many a wery day,
950 Til Cristes mooder—blessed be she ay!—
Hath shapen, thurgh hir endelees goodnesse,   *planned*
To make an ende of al hir hevynesse.   *sorrow*

    Now lat us stynte of Custance but a throwe,
And speke we of the Romayn Emperour,
955 That out of Surrye hath by lettres knowe
The slaughtre of cristen folk, and dishonour
Doon to his doghter by a fals traytour,
I mene the cursed wikked Sowdanesse
That at the feeste leet sleen bothe moore and lesse.

960 For which this Emperour hath sent anon
His senatour, with roial ordinance,   *array*
And othere lordes, God woot, many oon,   *knows*
On Surryens to taken heigh vengeance.
They brennen, sleen, and brynge hem to meschance
965 Ful many a day; but shortly, this is th'ende,
Homward to Rome they shapen hem to wende.

    936 And so completely unarmed.
    938 It could only have been God's grace.
    942–4 I say all this in order to show that just as God sent these people
      a vigorous spirit and saved them from disaster.
    947 Gibraltar and Ceuta (opposite Gibraltar, on the coast of Morocco).
    953 Now let us say no more about Constance for a while.
    955 Who has learned by means of a letter sent to him from Syria.
    959 Had everyone murdered.
    964 They burn, kill, and heap disaster on them.
    965–6 But briefly, at the end of it all, they prepare to return home to
      Rome.

This senatour repaireth with victorie
To Rome-ward, saillynge ful roially,
And mette the ship dryvynge, as seith the storie,
970 In which Custance sit ful pitously.   *sits; sadly*
Nothyng ne knew he what she was, ne why
She was in swich array, ne she nyl seye
Of hire estaat, althogh she sholde deye.

He bryngeth hire to Rome, and to his wyf
975 He yaf hire, and hir yonge sone also;
And with the senatour she ladde hir lyf.   *lived*
Thus kan Oure Lady bryngen out of wo
Woful Custance, and many another mo.
And longe tyme dwelled she in that place,
980 In hooly werkes evere, as was hir grace.

The senatoures wyf hir aunte was,
But for al that she knew hire never the moore.
I wol no lenger tarien in this cas,
But to kyng Alla, which I spak of yoore,
985 That for his wyf wepeth and siketh soore,   *sighs*
I wol retourne, and lete I wol Custance   *leave*
Under the senatoures governance.   *care*

Kyng Alla, which that hadde his mooder slayn,
Upon a day fil in swich repentance
990 That, if I shortly tellen shal and playn,   *briefly; plainly*
To Rome he comth to receyven his penance;
And putte hym in the popes ordinance
In heigh and logh, and Jhesu Crist bisoghte
Foryeve his wikked werkes that he wroghte.   *to forgive*

995 The fame anon thurgh Rome toun is born,
How Alla kyng shal comen in pilgrymage,
By herbergeours that wenten hym biforn;
For which the senatour, as was usage,
Rood hym agayns, and many of his lynage,
1000 As wel to shewen his heighe magnificence
As to doon any kyng a reverence.

971-3 He had no idea who she was, or why she was reduced to such a
   plight, nor would she speak of her condition, though her life depended
   on it.
982 But for all that she (i.e. the senator's wife) did not recognize her.
984 Of whom I spoke some time ago.
989 One day he was seized with such great remorse.
992 And placed himself at the Pope's command in all things.
995 The report quickly spreads through Rome.
997 *herbergeours*, harbingers, providers of lodgings.
998-1001 The senator and many of his kinsfolk rode out to meet him,
   as the custom was, both to show his own magnificence and to pay
   reverence to the king.

Greet cheere dooth this noble senatour   *entertainment*
To kynge Alla, and he to hym also;
Everich of hem dooth oother greet honour.   *each*
1005 And so bifel that in a day or two
This senatour is to kyng Alla go   *gone*
To feste, and shortly, if I shal nat lye,
Custances sone wente in his compaignye.

Som men wolde seyn at requeste of Custance
1010 This senatour hath lad this child to feeste;
I may nat tellen every circumstance,—
Be as be may, ther was he at the leeste.
But sooth is this, that at his moodres heeste   *request*
Biforn Alla, durynge the metes space,   *meal-time*
1015 The child stood, lookynge in the kynges face.

This Alla kyng hath of this child greet wonder,
And to the senatour he seyde anon,
'Whos is that faire child that stondeth yonder?'
'I noot,' quod he, 'by God, and by seint John!   *don't know*
1020 A mooder he hath, but fader hath he noon
That I of woot'—and shortly, in a stounde,   *moment*
He tolde Alla how that this child was founde.

'But God woot,' quod this senatour also,
'So vertuous a lyvere in my lyf
1025 Ne saugh I nevere as she, ne herde of mo,
Of worldly wommen, mayde, ne of wyf.
I dar wel seyn hir hadde levere a knyf
Thurghout hir brest, than ben a womman wikke;
There is no man koude brynge hire to that prikke.'   *pass*

1030 Now was this child as lyk unto Custance
As possible is a creature to be.
This Alla hath the face in remembrance
Of dame Custance, and ther on mused he
If that the childes mooder were aught she
1035 That is his wyf, and pryvely he sighte,   *secretly; sighed*
And spedde hym fro the table that he myghte.

1012 Be that as it may, there he certainly was.
1025-6 Nor heard of any other like her, maid or wife, among the women of this world.
1027 I'm quite sure she would rather have a knife.
1031 As it is possible for a living thing to be.
1034-5 If there were any chance of the child's mother being his own wife.
1036 And hurried away from the table as soon as he could.

'Parfay,' thoghte he, 'fantome is in myn heed!   *illusion*
I oghte deme, of skilful juggement,
That in the salte see my wyf is deed.'
1040 And afterward he made his argument:
'What woot I if that Crist have hyder ysent
My wyf by see, as wel as he hire sente
To my contree fro thennes that she wente?'

And after noon, hoom with the senatour
1045 Goth Alla, for to seen this wonder chaunce.
This senatour dooth Alla greet honour,
And hastifly he sente after Custaunce.   *quickly*
But trusteth weel, hire liste nat to daunce,
Whan that she wiste wherfore was that sonde;
1050 Unnethe upon hir feet she myghte stonde.   *hardly*

Whan Alla saugh his wyf, faire he hire grette,   *greeted*
And weep, that it was routhe for to see;   *wept; pitiful*
For at the firste look he on hire sette,
He knew wel verraily that it was she.   *beyond doubt*
1055 And she, for sorwe, as doumb stant as a tree,   *stands*
So was hir herte shet in hir distresse,
Whan she remembred his unkyndenesse.

Twyes she swowned in his owene sighte;
He weep, and hym excuseth pitously.
1060 'Now God,' quod he, 'and his halwes brighte
So wisly on my soule as have mercy,
That of youre harm as giltelees am I
As is Maurice my sone, so lyk youre face;
Elles the feend me fecche out of this place!'

1065   Long was the sobbyng and the bitter peyne,
Er that hir woful hertes myghte cesse;
Greet was the pitee for to heere hem pleyne,   *lament*
Thurgh whiche pleintes gan hir wo encresse.
I pray yow alle my labour to relesse;

1038 I ought to believe, if my judgment is at all rational.
1041-3 How do I know that Christ has not sent my wife here by sea,
    just as He sent her to my country from wherever she came?
1045 i.e. in the hope of seeing this marvellous chance come true.
1048-9 But you can be sure she felt no desire to dance with joy when
    she knew the reason for this summons.
1056 Her heart was shut so firmly in distress.
1060-2 Now God and all his shining saints have mercy on my soul, I
    swear I am as innocent of hurting you.
1063 Who is so like you to look at.
1068 And with their lamenting their sorrow increased.
1069 To release me from my labour (i.e. the labour of describing their
    distress in detail).

1070 I may nat telle hir wo until to-morwe,
     I am so wery for to speke of sorwe.

     But finally, whan that the sothe is wist   *known*
     That Alla giltelees was of hir wo,
     I trowe an hundred tymes been they kist,   *kissed*
1075 And swich a blisse is ther bitwix hem two
     That, save the joye that lasteth everemo,
     Ther is noon lyk that any creature   *none like it*
     Hath seyn or shal, whil that the world may dure.

     Tho preyde she hir housbonde mekely,   *humbly*
1080 In relief of hir longe, pitous pyne,
     That he wolde preye hir fader specially
     That of his magestee he wolde enclyne
     To vouche sauf som day with hym to dyne.
     She preyde hym eek he sholde by no weye   *on no account*
1085 Unto hir fader no word of hire seye.

     Som men wolde seyn how that the child Maurice
     Dooth this message unto this Emperour;
     But, as I gesse, Alla was nat so nyce
     To hym that was of so sovereyn honour
1090 As he that is of Cristen folk the flour,
     Sente any child, but it is bet to deeme   *suppose*
     He wente hymself, and so it may wel seeme.

     This Emperour hath graunted gentilly   *agreed; graciously*
     To come to dyner, as he hym bisoughte;
1095 And wel rede I he looked bisily   *curiously*
     Upon this child, and on his doghter thoghte.
     Alla goth to his in, and as hym oghte,
     Arrayed for this feste in every wise
     As ferforth as his konnyng may suffise.

1100   The morwe cam, and Alla gan hym dresse,
     And eek his wyf, this emperour to meete;
     And forth they ryde in joye and in gladnesse.
     And whan she saugh hir fader in the strete,

1080 To ease her long and pitiable suffering.
1081-3 He would specially ask her father to condescend, of his majesty,
   to dine with him one day.
1088-91 So foolish in his conduct towards one who was of outstanding
   honour, and the very flower of Christian folk, as to send any child
   to him.
1097-9 Aella went back to his lodging and, as he was bound to do,
   made every kind of preparation he possibly could.
1100-1 Aella, and his wife as well, got ready to meet the emperor.

She lighte doun, and falleth hym to feete.
1105 'Fader,' quod she, 'youre yonge child Custance
Is now ful clene out of youre remembrance.

I am youre doghter Custance,' quod she,
'That whilom ye han sent unto Surrye.
It am I, fader, that in the salte see
1110 Was put allone and dampned for to dye.
Now, goode fader, mercy I yow crye!
Sende me namoore unto noon hethenesse,   *heathen land*
But thonketh my lord heere of his kyndenesse.'   *for*

Who kan the pitous joye tellen al
1115 Bitwixe hem thre, syn they been thus ymette?
But of my tale make an ende I shal;
The day goth faste, I wol no lenger lette.   *delay*
This glade folk to dyner they hem sette;   *sat down*
In joye and blisse at mete I lete hem dwelle
1120 A thousand fool wel moore than I kan telle.   *greater*

This child Maurice was sithen Emperour   *afterwards*
Maad by the pope, and lyved cristenly;   *as a Christian*
To Cristes chirche he dide greet honour.
But I lete al his storie passen by;
1125 Of Custance is my tale specially.
In the olde Romayn geestes may men fynde   *stories*
Maurices lyf; I bere it noght in mynde.

This kyng Alla, whan he his tyme say,   *saw*
With his Custance, his hooly wyf so sweete,
1130 To Engelond been they come the righte way,
Wher as they lyve in joye and in quiete.
But litel while it lasteth, I yow heete,   *promise*
Joye of this world, for tyme wol nat abyde;
Fro day to nyght it changeth as the tyde.

1135 Who lyved euere in swich delit o day   *a single*
That hym ne moeved outher conscience,
Or ire, or talent, or som kynnes affray,
Envye, or pride, or passion, or offence?   *resentment*
I ne seye but for this ende this sentence,
1140 That litel while in joye or in plesance
Lasteth the blisse of Alla with Custance.

1104 She alighted, and fell down at his feet.
1124 But I will leave all his story be.
1127 I do not remember it.
1130 They went straight to England.
1136-7 As to be unmoved by conscience or anger, or desire, or fear
of some kind.
1139 I only say this in order to bring home to you.

For deeth, that taketh of heigh and logh his rente,
Whan passed was a yeer, evene as I gesse,
Out of this world this kyng Alla he hente,   *took*
1145 For whom Custance hath ful greet hevynesse.   *sorrow*
Now lat us prayen God his soule blesse!
And dame Custance, finally to seye,
Toward the toun of Rome goth hir weye.

To Rome is come this hooly creature,
1150 And fyndeth hire freendes hoole and sounde;   *safe*
Now is she scaped al hire aventure.
And whan that she hir fader hath yfounde,
Doun on hir knees falleth she to grounde;
Wepynge for tendrenesse in herte blithe,
1155 She heryeth God an hundred thousand sithe.   *praises; times*

In vertu and in hooly almus-dede   *deeds of charity*
They lyven alle, and nevere asonder wende;
Til deeth departeth hem, this lyf they lede.
And fareth now weel! my tale is at an ende.
1160 Now Jhesu Crist, that of his myght may sende
Joye after wo, governe us in his grace,
And kepe us alle that been in this place!   Amen.

HEERE ENDETH THE TALE OF THE MAN OF LAWE

THE EPILOGUE OF THE MAN OF LAW'S TALE

OWRE HOOST upon his stiropes stood anon,
And seyde, 'Goode men, herkeneth everych on!   *every one*
1165 This was a thrifty tale for the nones!
Sir Parisshe Prest,' quod he, 'for Goddes bones,

1143 When exactly a year had passed, I think.
1151 Now she is safely through all her adventures.
1157 And never leave each other.
1165 A profitable tale for this occasion.

Telle us a tale, as was thi forward yore.
I se wel that ye lerned men in lore
Can moche good, by Goddes dignitee!'
1170   The Parson him answerde, '*Benedicite!*   *bless us*
What eyleth the man, so synfully to swere?'
Oure Host answerde, 'O Jankin, be ye there?
I smelle a Lollere in the wynd,' quod he.
'Now! goode men,' quod oure Hoste, 'herkeneth me;
1175 Abydeth, for Goddes digne passioun,   *noble*
For we schal han a predicacioun;   *sermon*
This Lollere heer wil prechen us somwhat.'
      'Nay, by my fader soule, that schal he nat!'   *father's*
Seyde the Shipman; 'heer schal he nat preche;
1180 He schal no gospel glosen here ne teche.
We leven alle in the grete God,' quod he;   *believe*
'He wolde sowen som difficulte,
Or springen cokkel in our clene corn.   *spread tares*
And therfore, Hoost, I warne thee biforn,   *in advance*
1185 My joly body schal a tale telle,   *self*
And I schal clynken you so mery a belle,
That I schal waken al this compaignie.
But it schal not ben of philosophie,
Ne phislyas, ne termes queinte of lawe.   *curious*
1190 Ther is but litel Latyn in my mawe!'

1167 As you agreed to do some time ago.
1168–9 You learned men know many good things.
1172 *Jankin*, Johnny. (Priests were often nicknamed *Sir John*; cf.
      VII. 2810.)
1173 *Lollere*, Lollard, a contemptuous name for the followers of Wyclif,
      who strongly objected to the use of profane oaths.
1180 He shan't expound any gospel text or start teaching here.
1186 i.e. I'll make it such a lively one.
1189 *phislyas* possibly means '(legal) files or cases.'

Fragment III (Group D)

THE WIFE OF BATH'S PROLOGUE

The Prologe of the Wyves Tale of Bathe

'EXPERIENCE, though noon auctoritee   *authoritative text*
Were in this world, is right ynogh for me   *quite*
To speke of wo that is in mariage;
For, lordynges, sith I twelve yeer was of age,   *since*
5 Thonked be God that is eterne on lyve,
Housbondes at chirche dore I have had fyve,—
If I so ofte myghte have ywedded bee,—
And alle were worthy men in hir degree.
But me was toold, certeyn, nat longe agoon is,
10 That sith that Crist ne wente nevere but onis   *once*
To weddyng, in the Cane of Galilee,   *Cana*
That by the same ensample taughte he me   *example*
That I ne sholde wedded be but ones.
Herkne eek, lo, which a sharp word for the nones,
15 Biside a welle, Jhesus, God and man,
Spak in repreeve of the Samaritan: *reproof*
"Thou hast yhad fyve housbondes," quod he,
"And that ilke man that now hath thee   *same*
Is noght thyn housbonde," thus seyde he certeyn.
20 What that he mente therby, I kan nat seyn;   *say*
But that I axe, why that the fifthe man   *this I ask*
Was noon housbonde to the Samaritan?   *no*
How manye myghte she have in mariage?
Yet herde I nevere tellen in myn age   *life*
25 Upon this nombre diffinicioun.
Men may devyne and glosen, up and doun,
But wel I woot, expres, withoute lye,
God bad us for to wexe and multiplye;

5 Who lives eternally.
6 *at chirche dore.* See I. 460.
7 i.e. if so many marriages could be valid.
8 In their own walk of life.
9 But it was certainly told me not so long ago.
14 Consider, too, how very sharply.
25 A precise statement of the number.
26 Men may guess and expound in various ways.
27 But I know quite positively, and I'm not telling lies

158

That gentil text kan I wel understonde.   *noble*
30 Eek wel I woot, he seyde myn housbonde
Sholde lete fader and mooder, and take to me.   *leave*
But of no nombre mencion made he,
Of bigamye, or of octogamye;
Why sholde men thanne speke of it vileynye?   *evil*
35   Lo, heere the wise kyng, daun Salomon;
I trowe he hadde wyves mo than oon.   *believe; more*
As wolde God it leveful were unto me
To be refresshed half so ofte as he!
Which yifte of God hadde he for alle his wyvys!
40 No man hath swich that in this world alyve is.
God woot, this noble kyng, as to my wit,   *mind*
The firste nyght had many a myrie fit   *bout*
With ech of hem, so wel was hym on lyve.
Yblessed be God that I have wedded fyve!
45 Welcome the sixte, whan that evere he shal.
For sothe, I wol nat kepe me chaast in al.
Whan myn housbonde is fro the world ygon,   *from*
Som Cristen man shal wedde me anon,   *at once*
For thanne, th'apostle seith that I am free
50 To wedde, a Goddes half, where it liketh me.
He seith that to be wedded is no synne;
Bet is to be wedded than to brynne.   *better; burn*
What rekketh me, thogh folk seye vileynye   *do I care*
Of shrewed Lameth and his bigamye?   *wicked Lamech*
55 I woot wel Abraham was an hooly man,
And Jacob eek, as ferforth as I kan;   *far as I know*
And ech of hem hadde wyves mo than two,
And many another holy man also.
Wher can ye seye, in any manere age,
60 That hye God defended mariage
By expres word?   I pray yow, telleth me.
Or where comanded he virginitee?
I woot as wel as ye, it is no drede,   *without doubt*
Th'apostel, whan he speketh of maydenhede,
65 He seyde that precept therof hadde he noon.
Men may conseille a womman to been oon,   *remain single*

33 *bigamye, octogamye*, marrying two (eight) husbands in succession.
35 Take that wise king, Lord Solomon.
37 Now would to God it were lawful for me.
39 What a gift from God.
43 So glad was he to be alive.
45 Welcome the sixth, whenever he comes.
46 In truth, I won't keep myself completely chaste.
49 *th'apostle*, i.e. St. Paul (1 Cor. vii).
50 In God's name, where I like.
59–61 Can you say that God, at any time, expressly forbade marriage?
65 He said that he had no precept concerning it (1 Cor. vii. 25).

But conseillyng is no comandement.
He putte it in oure owene juggement;   *left it to*
For hadde God comanded maydenhede,
70 Thanne hadde he dampned weddyng with the dede.
And certes, if ther were no seed ysowe,   *certainly; sown*
Virginitee, thanne wherof sholde it growe?
Poul dorste nat comanden, atte leeste,   *in any case*
A thyng of which his maister yaf noon heeste.   *commandment*
75 The dart is set up for virginitee:
Cacche whoso may, who renneth best lat see.
   But this word is nat taken of every wight,
But ther as God lust gyve it of his myght.
I woot wel that th'apostel was a mayde;   *virgin*
80 But nathelees, thogh that he wroot and sayde   *wrote*
He wolde that every wight were swich as he,   *wished; such*
Al nys but conseil to virginitee.
And for to been a wyf he yaf me leve
Of indulgence; so nys it no repreve
85 To wedde me, if that my make dye,
Withouten excepcion of bigamye.
Al were it good no womman for to touche,—
He mente as in his bed or in his couche;
For peril is bothe fyr and tow t'assemble: *bring together*
90 Ye knowe what this ensample may resemble.
This is al and som, he heeld virginitee
Moore parfit than weddyng in freletee.   *perfect; frailty*
Freletee clepe I, but if that he and she
Wolde leden al hir lyf in chastitee.
95   I graunte it wel, I have noon envie,
Thogh maydenhede preferre bigamye.
It liketh hem to be clene, body and goost;
Of myn estaat I nyl nat make no boost.

70 Then in doing so he would have condemned marriage.
72 What would virginity grow from then?
75 *dart*, prize in a running contest.
76 Catch as catch can; let's see who runs the best.
77–8 This counsel of perfection is not for everyone, but only for those
    whom God is pleased to make strong enough.
82 It's all mere counsel to stay a virgin.
83–6 He was indulgent enough to give me leave to be a wife; so there's no
    sin in marrying me, if my husband dies, not excepting that of bigamy.
87 Although it would be a good thing.
88 *He*, i.e. St. Paul, in 1 Cor. vii. 1.
90 You know what this metaphor is meant to suggest.
91 This is the long and short of it.
93 I call it frailty, unless a man and wife are resolved to live chastely
    all their lives.
95–6 I freely admit I'm not envious, even though maidenhood is pre-
    ferable to marrying more than once.
97 It pleases them (i.e. virgins) to be pure in body and soul.
98 I don't want to boast at all about my own condition.

For wel ye knowe, a lord in his housholde,
100 He nath nat every vessel al of gold;
    Somme been of tree, and doon hir lord servyse.   *wood*
    God clepeth folk to hym in sondry wyse,   *calls; ways*
    And everich hath of God a propre yifte,
    Som this, som that, as hym liketh shifte.
105   Virginitee is greet perfeccion,
    And continence eek with devocion,
    But Crist, that of perfeccion is welle,
    Bad nat every wight he sholde go selle
    Al that he hadde, and gyve it to the poore,
110 And in swich wise folwe hym and his foore.   *footsteps*
    He spak to hem that wolde lyve parfitly;   *perfectly*
    And lordynges, by youre leve, that am nat I.
    I wol bistowe the flour of al myn age   *flower*
    In the actes and in fruyt of mariage.
115   Telle me also, to what conclusion   *end*
    Were membres maad of generacion,
    And of so parfit wys a wright ywroght?
    Trusteth right wel, they were nat maad for noght.
    Glose whoso wole, and seye bothe up and doun,
120 That they were maked for purgacioun   *discharge*
    Of uryne, and oure bothe thynges smale
    Were eek to knowe a femele from a male,
    And for noon oother cause,—sey ye no?
    The experience woot wel it is noght so.   *knows*
125 So that the clerkes be nat with me wrothe,
    I sey this, that they maked ben for bothe,
    That is to seye, for office, and for ese   *use; pleasure*
    Of engendrure, ther we nat God displese.
    Why sholde men elles in hir bookes sette   *set down*
130 That man shal yelde to his wyf hire dette?   *pay; debt*
    Now wherwith sholde he make his paiement,
    If he ne used his sely instrument?   *blessed*
    Thanne were they maad upon a creature
    To purge uryne, and eek for engendrure.
135   But I seye noght that every wight is holde,   *obliged*
    That hath swich harneys as I to yow tolde,   *equipment*
    To goon and usen hem in engendrure.
    Thanne sholde men take of chastitee no cure.   *heed*

103 Everyone has from God his own special gift.
104 As it pleases Him to provide.
106 And so is continence if devoutly meant.
116 Were the generative organs made.
117 And fashioned by so perfectly wise a maker.
119 Explain things away, if you like, and say.
123 Did someone say no?
125 If the learned won't be angry with me.
128 Providing we do not displease God.

Crist was a mayde, and shapen as a man,
140 And many a seint, sith that the world bigan;
Yet lyved they evere in parfit chastitee.
I nyl envye no virginitee.
Lat hem be breed of pured whete-seed,   *fine*
And lat us wyves hoten barly-breed;   *be called*
145 And yet with barly-breed, Mark telle kan,
Oure Lord Jhesu refresshed many a man.
In swich estaat as God hath cleped us
I wol persevere; I nam nat precius.   *continue; particular*
In wyfhod I wol use myn instrument   *as a wife*
150 As frely as my Makere hath it sent.
If I be daungerous, God yeve me sorwe!   *hard to please*
Myn housbonde shal it have bothe eve and morwe,
Whan that hym list come forth and paye his dette. *it pleases*
An housbonde I wol have, I wol nat lette,   *won't delay*
155 Which shal be bothe my dettour and my thral,   *debtor*
And have his tribulacion withal
Upon his flessh, whil that I am his wyf.
I have the power durynge al my lyf
Upon his propre body, and noght he.   *own*
160 Right thus the Apostel tolde it unto me;
And bad oure housbondes for to love us weel.
Al this sentence me liketh every deel'—
  Up stirte the Pardoner, and that anon: *started*
'Now, dame,' quod he, 'by God and by seint John!
165 Ye been a noble prechour in this cas.
I was aboute to wedde a wyf; allas!
What sholde I bye it on my flessh so deere?
Yet hadde I levere wedde no wyf to-yeere!'
  'Abyde!' quod she, 'my tale is nat bigonne.
170 Nay, thou shalt drynken of another tonne,   *cask*
Er that I go, shal savoure wors than ale.
And whan that I have toold thee forth my tale
Of tribulacion in mariage,
Of which I am expert in al myn age,
175 This is to seyn, myself have been the whippe,—
Than maystow chese wheither thou wolt sippe   *choose*
Of thilke tonne that I shal abroche.
Be war of it, er thou to ny approche;   *near*
For I shal telle ensamples mo than ten.

147 In that way of life to which God has called me.
160 This is exactly what the Apostle told me to do.
162 I find this pronouncement very gratifying.
165 *in this cas*, i.e. on the text you've chosen.
167 Why should my flesh pay so dearly for it?
168 I'd rather never have a wife.
170–1 i.e. before I've done, you'll have a nasty taste in your mouth.
174 On which I've been an expert all my life.
177 Of the contents of the cask I shall broach.

180 "Whoso that nyl be war by othere men,   *take warning*
     By hym shul othere men corrected be."
     The same wordes writeth Ptholomee;
     Rede in his Almageste, and take it there.'   *find*
        'Dame, I wolde praye yow, if youre wyl it were,'
185 Seyde this Pardoner, 'as ye bigan,
     Telle forth youre tale, spareth for no man,
     And teche us yonge men of youre praktike.'
        'Gladly,' quod she, 'sith it may yow like;   *please*
     But yet I praye to al this compaignye,
190 If that I speke after my fantasye,   *fancy*
     As taketh not agrief of that I seye;
     For myn entente nys nat but for to pleye.
        Now, sire, now wol I telle forth my tale.—
     As evere moote I drynken wyn or ale,
195 I shal seye sooth, tho housbondes that I hadde,   *truth; those*
     As thre of hem were goode, and two were badde.
     The thre were goode men, and riche, and olde;
     Unnethe myghte they the statut holde
     In which that they were bounden unto me.
200 Ye woot wel what I meene of this, pardee!   *(by God), indeed*
     As help me God, I laughe whan I thynke
     How pitously a-nyght I made hem swynke!   *toil*
     And, by my fey, I tolde of it no stoor.
     They had me yeven hir lond and hir tresoor;
205 Me neded nat do lenger diligence
     To wynne hir love, or doon hem reverence.
     They loved me so wel, by God above,
     That I ne tolde no deyntee of hir love!
     A wys womman wol bisye hire evere in oon
210 To gete hire love, ye, ther as she hath noon.
     But sith I hadde hem hoolly in myn hond,   *wholly*
     And sith they hadde me yeven al hir lond,
     What sholde I taken keep hem for to plese,
     But it were for my profit and myn ese?   *unless; pleasure*
215 I sette hem so a-werke, by my fey,
     That many a nyght they songen "weilawey!"   *alas*

183 *Almageste.* See I. 3208.
187 Something of your technique.
191-2 Please don't be offended by anything I say; for my aim is only
     to amuse.
194 As I hope to go on drinking wine or ale.
198 They could hardly obey the statute.
203 By my faith, I made little account of it.
205 I had no need to try any longer.
208 I set no store by their love.
209-10 A prudent woman will continually make an effort to get herself
     a lover if, indeed, she hasn't one.
213 Why should I bother to please them.
215 I made them work so hard, to be sure.

The bacon was nat fet for hem, I trowe,	*fetched*
That som men han in Essex at Dunmowe.	*get*
I governed hem so wel, after my lawe,	*by my own law*

220 That ech of hem ful blisful was and fawe   *glad*
    To brynge me gaye thynges fro the fayre.   *fair*
    They were ful glad whan I spak to hem faire;   *kindly*
    For, God it woot, I chidde hem spitously.   *spitefully*
      Now herkneth hou I baar me proprely,   *behaved*
225 Ye wise wyves, that kan understonde.
    Thus shulde ye speke and bere hem   *falsely accuse them*
      wrong on honde;
    For half so boldely kan ther no man
    Swere and lyen, as a womman kan.
    I sey nat this by wyves that been wyse,
230 But if it be whan they hem mysavyse.
    A wys wyf, if that she kan hir good,
    Shal beren hym on honde the cow is wood,
    And take witnesse of hir owene mayde
    Of hir assent; but herkneth how I sayde:
235   "Sire olde kaynard, is this thyn array?
    Why is my neighebores wyf so gay?
    She is honoured over al ther she gooth;   *everywhere*
    I sitte at hoom, I have no thrifty clooth.   *decent clothes*
    What dostow at my neighebores hous?   *are you doing*
240 Is she so fair? artow so amorous?
    What rowne ye with oure mayde? *Benedicite!*   *whisper*
    Sire olde lecchour, lat thy japes be!   *antics*
    And if I have a gossib or a freend,   *boon companion*
    Withouten gilt, thou chidest as a feend,
245 If that I walke or pleye unto his hous!
    Thou comest hoom as dronken as a mous,
    And prechest on thy bench, with yvel preef!   *bad luck to you*
    Thou seist to me it is a greet meschief   *misfortune*
    To wedde a povre womman, for costage;   *because of the cost*
250 And if that she be riche, of heigh parage,   *noble birth*
    Thanne seistow that it is a tormentrie   *torture*
    To soffre hire pride and hire malencolie.

218 An allusion to the flitch of bacon offered at Dunmow (in Essex) to any couple who, after a year of marriage, could swear they had lived together in perfect harmony.
229 I don't say this for the benefit of knowing wives, except when their plans go wrong.
231 If she knows what is good for her.
232 Convince him that the chough is mad. (A reference to the story of the jealous husband who employs a talking bird to report on his wife's behaviour. See the *Manciple's Tale*.)
233–4 And get her maid, who's in league with her, to act as a witness.
235 Old Sir dotard, is this the way you do things?
244 In spite of my innocence, you scold like the devil.
245 If I walk to his house or amuse myself there.

And if that she be fair, thou verray knave,   *arrant*
Thou seyst that every holour wol hire have;   *lecher*
255 She may no while in chastitee abyde,
That is assailled upon ech a syde.   *every*
    Thou seyst som folk desiren us for richesse,   *wealth*
Somme for oure shap, and somme for oure fairnesse, *beauty*
And som for she kan outher synge or daunce,
260 And som for gentillesse and daliaunce;
Som for hir handes and hir armes smale: *slender*
Thus goth al to the devel, by thy tale.
Thou seyst men may nat kepe a castel wal,   *defend*
It may so longe assailled been over al.   *on all sides*
265   And if that she be foul, thou seist that she   *ugly*
Coveiteth every man that she may se,   *lusts after*
For as a spaynel she wol on hym lepe,
Til that she fynde som man hire to chepe.
Ne noon so grey goos gooth ther in the lake
270 As, sëistow, wol been withoute make.
And seyst it is an hard thyng for to welde
A thyng that no man wole, his thankes, helde.
Thus seistow, lorel, whan thow goost to bedde;   *wretch*
And that no wys man nedeth for to wedde,   *sensible*
275 Ne no man that entendeth unto hevene.   *hopes for*
With wilde thonder-dynt and firy levene
Moote thy welked nekke be tobroke!
    Thow seyst that droppyng houses, and eek smoke,   *leaky*
And chidyng wyves maken men to flee
280 Out of hir owene houses; a! *benedicitee!*
What eyleth swich an old man for to chide?   *ails*
    Thow seyst we wyves wol oure vices hide
Til we be fast, and thanne we wol hem shewe,—
Wel may that be a proverbe of a shrewe!
285   Thou seist that oxen, asses, hors, and houndes,   *horses*
They been assayed at diverse stoundes;
Bacyns, lavours, er that men hem bye,
Spoones and stooles and al swich
            housbondrye,   *household things*

260 For our good breeding and playfulness.
268 To do business with her.
269–70 You say there's no goose on the lake too grey to give up
    thoughts of mating.
271–2 You say it's a hard thing for a man to control what he is not
    willing to keep.
276 By wild thunderbolts and fiery lightning.
277 May your withered neck be broken in two!
282 *fast*, safe, i.e. safely married.
284 There's a wicked saying for you!
286 Are tested out at different times.
287 Basins, ewers, before we buy them.

And so been pottes, clothes, and array;   *furnishings*
290 But folk of wyves maken noon assay,   *trial*
Til they be wedded; olde dotard shrewe!   *wicked old dotard*
And thanne, seistow, we wol oure vices shewe.
    Thou seist also that it displeseth me
But if that thou wolt preyse my beautee,   *unless*
295 And but thou poure alwey upon my face,   *gaze*
And clepe me 'faire dame' in every place;   *call; lady*
And but thou make a feeste on thilke day   *that*
That I was born, and make me fressh and gay;
And but thou do to my norice honour,
300 And to my chamberere withinne my bour,
And to my fadres folk and his allyes,—   *relations*
Thus seistow, olde barel-ful of lyes!
    And yet of oure apprentice Janekyn,   *Johnny*
For his crispe heer, shynynge as gold so fyn, *curly*
305 And for he squiereth me bothe up and doun,
Yet hastow caught a fals suspecioun.
I wol hym noght, thogh thou were deed   *don't want him*
    tomorwe!
    But tel me this: why hydestow, with sorwe, *bad luck to you*
The keyes of thy cheste awey fro me?
310 It is my good as wel as thyn, pardee!   *property*
What, wenestow make an ydiot of oure dame?
Now by that lord that called is Seint Jame, *James*
Thou shalt nat bothe, thogh that thou were wood,
Be maister of my body and of my good;
315 That oon thou shalt forgo, maugree thyne yen.
What helpith it of me to enquere or spyen?
I trowe thou woldest loke me in thy chiste! *lock; chest*
Thou sholdest seye, 'Wyf, go wher thee liste; *you like*
Taak youre disport, I wol nat leve no talys.
320 I knowe yow for a trewe wyf, dame Alys.' *mistress*
We love no man that taketh kep or charge
Wher that we goon; we wol ben at oure large.
    Of alle men yblessed moot he be,   *may*
The wise astrologien, Daun Ptholome,   *astrologer*
325 That seith this proverbe in his Almageste:
'Of alle men his wysdom is the hyeste   *highest*

298 And buy me bright, gay clothes.
300 To my maid who waits on me in my bower (i.e. private apartment).
311 Do you intend to make an idiot of your wife?
313–14 You can be as mad as you like, but you shan't be master of both
    my body and my property.
315 You must give up one of them, in spite of everything (lit. in spite
    of your eyes).
316 What good does it do to inquire into my affairs or spy on me?
319 Enjoy yourself; I won't believe any tales about you.
321 Who takes particular note.
322 We want to be free to go anywhere.

That rekketh nevere who hath the world in honde.'
By this proverbe thou shalt understonde,
Have thou ynogh, what thar thee recche or care
330 How myrily that othere folkes fare?
For, certeyn, olde dotard, by youre leve,
Ye shul have queynte right ynogh at eve.   *pudendum*
He is to greet a nygard that wolde werne   *refuse*
A man to lighte a candle at his lanterne;
335 He shal have never the lasse light, pardee.
Have thou ynogh, thee thar nat pleyne thee.
    Thou seyst also, that if we make us gay
With clothyng, and with precious array,
That it is peril of oure chastitee;
340 And yet, with sorwe! thou most enforce thee,
And seye thise wordes in the Apostles name:
'In habit maad with chastitee and shame   *garments*
Ye wommen shul apparaille yow,' quod he,   *yourselves*
'And noght in tressed heer and gay perree,
345 As perles, ne with gold, ne clothes riche.'
After thy text, ne after thy rubriche,
I wol nat wirche as muchel as a gnat.
    Thou seydest this, that I was lyk a cat;
For whoso wolde senge a cattes skyn,
350 Thanne wolde the cat wel dwellen in his in;
And if the cattes skyn be slyk and gay,   *sleek*
She wol nat dwelle in house half a day,
But forth she wole, er any day be dawed,
To shewe hir skyn, and goon a-caterwawed.   *a-caterwauling*
355 This is to seye, if I be gay, sire shrewe,
I wol renne out, my borel for to shewe.   *clothes*
    Sire olde fool, what helpeth thee to spyen?
Thogh thou preye Argus with his hundred yen
To be my warde-cors, as he kan best,   *bodyguard*
360 In feith, he shal nat kepe me but me lest;   *unless I wish*
Yet koude I make his berd, so moot I thee.
    Thou seydest eek that ther been thynges thre,
The whiche thynges troublen al this erthe,
And that no wight may endure the ferthe.   *no one; fourth*

327 Who doesn't care what man holds the world in fee.
329–30 If you have enough, why need you worry or care how well-off
    other people are?
336 You need not complain.
340 And then, confound you, you feel obliged to strengthen your hand.
343–4 1 Tim. ii. 9.
344 And not with braided hair and fine jewellery.
346–7 I won't work as hard as a gnat to follow your text and rubric.
349–50 For if anyone singes a cat's fur, the cat will certainly stay at
    home.
353 But out she'll go, before day has dawned.
361 I could still deceive him, as I hope to prosper!

365 O leeve sire shrewe, Jhesu shorte thy lyf!
　　Yet prechestow and seyst an hateful wyf　　　　*you preach*
　　Yrekened is for oon of thise meschances.
　　Been ther none othere maner resemblances
　　That ye may likne youre parables to,
370 But if a sely wyf be oon of tho?
　　　Thou liknest eek wommenes love to helle,　　　*liken*
　　To bareyne lond, ther water may nat dwelle.　　*barren*
　　Thou liknest it also to wilde fyr;
　　The moore it brenneth, the moore it hath desir　*burns*
375 To consume every thyng that brent wole be.　　*burnt*
　　Thou seyest, right as wormes shende a tree,　　*destroy*
　　Right so a wyf destroyeth hire housbonde;
　　This knowe they that been to wyves bonde."　　*subservient*
　　　Lordynges, right thus, as ye have understonde,
380 Baar I stifly myne olde housbondes on honde
　　That thus they seyden in hir dronkenesse;
　　And al was fals, but that I took witnesse
　　On Janekyn, and on my nece also.
　　O Lord! the peyne I dide hem and the wo,
385 Ful giltelees, by Goddes sweete pyne!
　　For as an hors I koude byte and whyne.　　　　*whinny*
　　I koude pleyne, and yit was in the gilt,　　*complain; wrong*
　　Or elles often tyme hadde I been spilt.　　*undone*
　　Whoso that first to mille comth, first grynt;　　*grinds*
390 I pleyned first, so was oure werre ystynt.　　*war; ended*
　　They were ful glade to excuse hem blyve　*themselves; quickly*
　　Of thyng of which they nevere agilte hir lyve.
　　Of wenches wolde I beren hem on honde,
　　Whan that for syk unnethes myghte they stonde.
395 　Yet tikled I his herte, for that he
　　Wende that I hadde of hym so greet chiertee!
　　I swoor that al my walkynge out by nyghte　　*swore*
　　Was for t'espye wenches that he dighte;　*spy on; lay with*
　　Under that colour hadde I many a myrthe.　*pretext; lark*
400 For al swich wit is yeven us in oure byrthe;
　　Deceite, wepyng, spynnyng God hath yive　　　*given*
　　To wommen kyndely, whil that they may lyve.　*naturally*

365 My dear rascally sir, Jesus shorten your life.
368-70 Are there no other things you can use for the purpose of com-
　　parison without making an innocent wife one of them?
373 *wilde fyr*, an inflammable substance, used in warfare, which could
　　not be quenched by water.
380 I boldly accused my old husbands.
382-3 Only I got Johnny and my niece as well to witness it was true.
385 Although they were completely innocent, by God's sweet passion!
392 Of things they were never guilty of in all their lives.
393-4 I would accuse them of wenching when they were so ill that they
　　could hardly stand.
395-6 Yet I pleased him because he thought I was so fond of him.

And thus of o thyng I avaunte me,   *boast*
Atte ende I hadde the bettre in ech degree,
405 By sleighte, or force, or by som maner thyng,
As by continueel murmur or grucchyng.   *grumbling*
Namely abedde hadden they meschaunce:
Ther wolde I chide, and do hem no plesaunce;
I wolde no lenger in the bed abyde,   *stay*
410 If that I felte his arm over my syde,
Til he had maad his raunson unto me;   *ransom*
Thanne wolde I suffre hym do his nycetee.
And therfore every man this tale I telle,
Wynne whoso may, for al is for to selle;
415 With empty hand men may none haukes lure.
For wynnyng wolde I al his lust endure,   *for my own profit*
And make me a feyned appetit;
And yet in bacon hadde I nevere delit;
That made me that evere I wolde hem chide.
420 For thogh the pope hadde seten hem biside,   *sat beside them*
I wolde nat spare hem at hir owene bord;   *table*
For, by my trouthe, I quitte hem word for   *paid them back*
   word.
As helpe me verray God omnipotent,
Though I right now sholde make my testament,
425 I ne owe hem nat a word that it nys quit.   *is not*
I broghte it so aboute by my wit
That they moste yeve it up, as for the beste,
Or elles hadde we nevere been in reste.   *at*
For thogh he looked as a wood leon,   *raging lion*
430 Yet sholde he faille of his conclusion.
   Thanne wolde I seye, "Goode lief, taak keep
How mekely looketh Wilkyn, oure sheep!   *meekly*
Com neer, my spouse, lat me ba thy cheke!   *nearer; kiss*
Ye sholde been al pacient and meke,
435 And han a sweete spiced conscience,
Sith ye so preche of Jobes pacience.
Suffreth alwey, syn ye so wel kan preche;   *be patient*
And but ye do, certein we shal yow teche   *unless*

404 In the end I got the better (of my first three husbands) in every way.
405 By trickery, or force, or somehow or other.
407 In bed they were especially unlucky.
412 Allow him to indulge his lust.
413–14 And so to every man I say: let him get it who can, for it's all
   for sale.
417 Assume a fictitious appetite.
418 *bacon*, old meat (with reference to her old husbands).
419 That's why I was always chiding them.
427 They had to surrender, as the best thing they could do.
430 Yet he was bound to fail in his purpose.
431 My dear good husband, take note.
435 And have a sweet and tender conscience.

That it is fair to have a wyf in pees.   *good; at peace*
440 Oon of us two moste bowen, doutelees;   *give way*
And sith a man is moore resonable
Than womman is, ye moste been suffrable.   *patient*
What eyleth yow to grucche thus and grone?
Is it for ye wolde have my queynte allone?   *all to yourself*
445 Wy, taak it al! lo, have it every deel!   *bit*
Peter! I shrewe yow, but ye love it weel;   *curse*
For if I wolde selle my *bele chose*,
I koude walke as fressh as is a rose;
But I wol kepe it for youre owene tooth.
450 Ye be to blame, by God! I sey yow sooth."   *truth*
  Swiche manere wordes hadde we on honda
Now wol I speken of my fourthe housbonde.
  My fourthe housbonde was a revelour;   *rake*
This is to seyn, he hadde a paramour;   *mistress*
455 And I was yong and ful of ragerye,   *wantonness*
Stibourn and strong, and joly as a pye.
How koude I daunce to an harpe smale,
And synge, ywis, as any nyghtyngale,   *to be sure*
Whan I had dronke a draughte of sweete wyn!
460 Metellius, the foule cherl, the swyn,   *filthy lout*
That with a staf birafte his wyf hir lyf,
For she drank wyn, thogh I hadde been his wyf,   *because*
He sholde nat han daunted me fro drynke!
And after wyn on Venus moste I thynke,
465 For al so siker as cold engendreth hayl,
A likerous mouth moste han a likerous tayl.   *lecherous*
In wommen vinolent is no defence,—
This knowen lecchours by experience.
  But, Lord Crist! whan that it remembreth me   *I remember*
470 Upon my yowthe, and on my jolitee,
It tikleth me aboute myn herte roote.
Unto this day it dooth myn herte boote   *good*
That I have had my world as in my tyme.
But age, allas! that al wole envenyme,   *poison*
475 Hath me biraft my beautee and my pith.   *robbed*
Lat go, farewel! the devel go therwith!
The flour is goon, ther is namoore to telle;
The bren, as I best kan, now moste I selle;   *bran*
But yet to be right myrie wol I fonde.   *try*
480 Now wol I tellen of my fourthe housbonde.

451 Such words as these we had between us.
456 Stubborn and strong, and merry as a magpie.
461 i.e. who beat his wife to death.
463 He wouldn't have frightened me off drinking.
465 For just as surely as cold produces hail.
467 A woman full of wine has no defence.
470 And the fun I've had.
471 It warms the cockles of my heart.
473 To remember that I've had my fling.

I seye, I hadde in herte greet despit   *resentment*
That he of any oother had delit.
But he was quit, by God and by Seint Joce!   *paid back*
I made hym of the same wode a croce;   *cross*
485 Nat of my body, in no foul manere,
But certeinly, I made folk swich cheere
That in his owene grece I made hym frye   *fat*
For angre, and for verray jalousye.
By God! in erthe I was his purgatorie,   *on*
490 For which I hope his soule be in glorie.
For, God it woot, he sat ful ofte and song,
Whan that his shoo ful bitterly hym wrong.
Ther was no wight, save God and he, that wiste,
In many wise, how soore I hym twiste.
495 He deyde whan I cam fro Jerusalem,
And lith ygrave under the roode beem,
Al is his tombe noght so curyus   *although; elaborate*
As was the sepulcre of hym Daryus,
Which that Appelles wroghte subtilly;   *skilfully*
500 It nys but wast to burye hym preciously.
Lat hym fare wel, God yeve his soule reste!
He is now in his grave and in his cheste.   *coffin*
    Now of my fifthe housbonde wol I telle.
God lete his soule nevere come in helle!
505 And yet was he to me the mooste shrewe;
That feele I on my ribbes al by rewe,
And evere shal unto myn endyng day.
But in oure bed he was so fressh and gay,
And therwithal so wel koude he me glose,   *flatter*
510 Whan that he wolde han my *bele chose*,
That thogh he hadde me bete on every bon,   *beaten*
He koude wynne agayn my love anon.
I trowe I loved hym best, for that he
Was of his love daungerous to me.   *niggardly*
515 We wommen han, if that I shal nat lye,
In this matere a queynte fantasye;   *curious fancy*
Wayte what thyng we may nat lightly have,
Therafter wol we crie al day and crave.   *continually*

486 I offered folk such generous hospitality.
491 *song*, sang a sorry tune, complained miserably.
492 When his shoe pinched him hard.
493–4 No one knew, but God and he, how painfully I tortured him in
    many ways.
496 Lies buried under the rood-beem (in church, between the chancel
    and the nave).
500 A costly burial would have been a waste of money.
505 The worst-tempered of them all.
506 *al by rewe*, one after another, i.e. one and all.
517 Whatever we cannot easily get.

Forbede us thyng, and that desiren we;
520 Preesse on us faste, and thanne wol we fle.
With daunger oute we al oure chaffare;
Greet prees at market maketh deere ware,
And to greet cheep is holde at litel prys:
This knoweth every womman that is wys.
525   My fifthe housbonde, God his soule blesse!
Which that I took for love, and no richesse,   *not for money*
He som tyme was a clerk of Oxenford,   *once; student*
And hadde left scole, and wente at hom to bord
With my gossib, dwellyne in oure toun;   *friend*
530 God have hir soule! hir name was Alisoun.
She knew myn herte, and eek my privetee,   *secrets*
Bet than oure parisshe preest, so moot I thee!
To hire biwreyed I my conseil al.   *revealed*
For hadde myn housbonde pissed on a wal,
535 Or doon a thyng that sholde han cost his lyf,   *done*
To hire, and to another worthy wyf,
And to my nece, which that I loved weel,   *whom*
I wolde han toold his conseil every deel.
And so I dide ful often, God it woot,
540 That made his face often reed and hoot   *hot*
For verray shame, and blamed hymself for he
Had toold to me so greet a pryvetee.
    And so bifel that ones in a Lente—   *once*
So often tymes I to my gossyb wente,
545 For evere yet I loved to be gay,
And for to walke in March, Averill, and May,
Fro hous to hous, to heere sondry talys—
That Jankyn clerk, and my gossyb dame Alys,
And I myself, into the feeldes wente.
550 Myn housbonde was at Londoun al that Lente;
I hadde the bettre leyser for to pleye,   *opportunity*
And for to se, and eek for to be seye   *seen*
Of lusty folk.   What wiste I wher my grace
Was shapen for to be, or in what place?
555 Therfore I made my visitaciouns
To vigilies and to processiouns,
To prechyng eek, and to thise pilgrimages,

521 We offer our wares with caution, for a great crowd of buyers in the
    market makes things dear, and too great a bargain is held to be of
    little value.
528 Had left the university, and gone to lodge.
532 Better . . . as I hope to prosper!
538 Every one of his secrets.
544 As I so often did, I went to my friend.
550 *Myn housbonde,* i.e. her fourth husband.
553-4 By lusty lads.   How was I to know the person or the place where
    my favour was destined to be granted?
556 *vigilies.* See I. 377.

To pleyes of myracles, and to mariages,
And wered upon my gaye scarlet gytes.
560 Thise wormes, ne thise motthes, ne thise mytes,
Upon my peril, frete hem never a deel;
And wostow why? for they were used weel.
   Now wol I tellen forth what happed me.   *happened to*
I seye that in the feeldes walked we,
565 Til trewely we hadde swich daliance,   *flirtation*
This clerk and I, that of my purveiance   *with foresight*
I spak to hym and seyde hym how that he,
If I were wydwe, sholde wedde me.
For certeinly, I sey for no bobance,   *boast*
570 Yet was I nevere withouten purveiance
Of mariage, n'of othere thynges eek.
I holde a mouses herte nat worth a leek
That hath but oon hole for to sterte to,   *run*
And if that faille, thanne is al ydo.   *over*
575   I bar hym on honde he hadde enchanted me,—   *assured him*
My dame taughte me that soutiltee.   *mother; trick*
And eek I seyde I mette of hym al nyght,   *dreamt*
He wolde han slayn me as I lay upright,   *on my back*
And al my bed was ful of verray blood;   *real*
580 But yet I hope that ye shal do me good,
For blood bitokeneth gold, as me was taught.
And al was fals; I dremed of it right naught,   *not at all*
But as I folwed ay my dames loore,
As wel of this as of othere thynges moore.
585   But now, sire, lat me se, what I shal seyn?
A ha! by God, I have my tale ageyn.
   Whan that my fourthe housbonde was on beere,   *bier*
I weep algate, and made sory cheere,
As wyves mooten, for it is usage,   *must; custom*
590 And with my coverchief covered my visage,   *kerchief*
But for that I was purveyed of a make,
I wepte but smal, and that I undertake.
   To chirche was myn housbonde born
      a-morwe   *on the morrow*
With neighebores, that for hym maden sorwe;   *by*
595 And Jankyn, oure clerk, was oon of tho.   *those*
As help me God! whan that I saugh hym go

558 *pleyes of myracles*, miracle plays, i.e. vernacular religious plays
performed outside the church.
559 And wore my gay scarlet gowns.
560-1 Worms, moths, and mites—I say it at my peril—never ate a
single thread of them.
572 I don't think much of a mouse.
583 But all along I followed my mother's advice.
585 *sire*, i.e. the Host.
588 I wept all the time and looked miserable.
591 But since I was provided with a husband.

After the beere, me thoughte he hadde a paire
Of legges and of feet so clene and faire   *handsome*
That al myn herte I yaf unto his hoold.
600 He was, I trowe, twenty wynter oold,
And I was fourty, if I shal seye sooth;
But yet I hadde alwey a coltes tooth.
Gat-tothed I was, and that bicam me weel;   *gap-toothed*
I hadde the prente of seinte Venus seel.
605 As help me God! I was a lusty oon,
And faire, and riche, and yong, and wel bigon;   *happy*
And trewely, as myne housbondes tolde me,
I hadde the beste *quoniam* myghte be.
For certes, I am al Venerien
610 In feelynge, and myn herte is Marcien.
Venus me yaf my lust, my likerousnesse,   *wantonness*
And Mars yaf me my sturdy hardynesse;   *boldness*
Myn ascendent was Taur, and Mars therinne.
Allas! allas! that evere love was synne!
615 I folwed ay myn inclinacioun
By vertu of my constellacioun;
That made me I koude noght withdrawe
My chambre of Venus from a good felawe.
Yet have I Martes mark upon my face,   *Mars'*
620 And also in another privee place.
For God so wys be my savacioun,   *God save me*
I ne loved nevere by no discrecioun,   *with any*
But evere folwede myn appetit,
Al were he short, or long, or blak or whit;   *whether he was*
625 I took no kep, so that he liked me,
How poore he was, ne eek of what degree.
    What sholde I seye? but, at the monthes ende,
This joly clerk, Jankyn, that was so hende,   *gay; gracious*
Hath wedded me with greet solempnytee;
630 And to hym yaf I al the lond and fee   *property*
That evere was me yeven therbifoore.
But afterward repented me ful soore;
He nolde suffre nothyng of my list.
By God! he smoot me ones on the lyst,   *ear*
635 For that I rente out of his book a leef,   *because*

599 I gave him my heart to have and hold.
602 *coltes tooth.* See I. 3888.
604 I had the imprint of St Venus' birthmark.
609–10 *Venerien, Marcien,* influenced by the planets Venus and Mars.
613 Taurus (one of the 'mansions' of Venus) was in the ascendant at
   the time of my birth, and Mars was in it.
616 By virtue of the position of the planets when I was born.
625 I didn't care, so long as he pleased me.
632 I bitterly regretted it.
633 He wouldn't let me have anything I wanted.

That of the strook myn ere wax al deef.
Stibourn I was as is a leonesse,   *fierce*
And of my tonge a verray jangleresse,   *real chatterbox*
And walke I wolde, as I had doon biforn,
640 From hous to hous, although he had it sworn;
For which he often tymes wolde preche,
And me of olde Romayn geestes teche;   *stories*
How he Symplicius Gallus lefte his wyf,
And hire forsook for terme of al his lyf,
645 Noght but for open-heveded he hir say
Lookynge out at his dore upon a day.
     Another Romayn tolde he me by name,
That, for his wyf was at a someres game,
Withouten his wityng, he forsook hire eke.   *knowledge*
650 And thanne wolde he upon his Bible seke
That ilke proverbe of Ecclesiaste   *same*
Where he comandeth, and forbedeth faste,   *firmly*
Man shal nat suffre his wyf go roule aboute.   *gad*
Thanne wolde he seye right thus, withouten doute:
655 "Whoso that buyldeth his hous al of salwes,   *willow-twigs*
And priketh his blynde hors over the   *spurs*
     falwes,   *fallow fields*
And suffreth his wyf to go seken halwes,   *visit; shrines*
Is worthy to been hanged on the galwes!"
But al for noght, I sette noght an hawe
660 Of his proverbes n'of his olde sawe,
Ne I wolde nat of hym corrected be.   *by*
I hate hym that my vices telleth me,
And so doo mo, God woot, of us than I.
This made hym with me wood al outrely;   *flaming mad*
665 I nolde noght forbere hym in no cas.
     Now wol I seye yow sooth, by seint Thomas,   *truly*
Why that I rente out of his book a leef,
For which he smoot me so that I was deef.
     He hadde a book that gladly, nyght and day,
670 For his desport he wolde rede alway;   *amusement*
He cleped it Valerie and Theofraste,   *Valerius; Theophrastus*
At which book he lough alwey ful faste.

636 So that my ear went quite deaf from the blow. (Cf. I. 446.)
640 Although he'd sworn I shouldn't.
645 Just because he saw her bareheaded.
648 Because his wife was at a summer-game (a reference to revels on
    Midsummer Eve).
651 Ecclus. xxv. 25.
659–60 But it was all in vain; I didn't care a jot for (lit. set the value
    of a haw on) his . . . old sayings.
665 I wouldn't give him a moment's peace.
669ff. This book is a compendious anthology of the most famous
    medieval satires on women.
672 He always laughed uproariously.

And eek ther was somtyme a clerk at Rome, *once*
A cardinal, that highte Seint Jerome, *was called*
675 That made a book agayn Jovinian;
In which book eek ther was Tertulan, *Tertullian*
Crisippus, Trotula, and Helowys, *Heloïse*
That was abbesse nat fer fro Parys;
And eek the Parables of Salomon,
680 Ovides Art, and bookes many on, *a one*
And alle thise were bounden in o volume.
And every nyght and day was his custume,
Whan he hadde leyser and vacacioun *time to spare*
From oother worldy occupacioun,
685 To reden on this book of wikked wyves. *from*
He knew of hem mo legendes and lyves
Than been of goode wyves in the Bible.
For trusteth wel, it is an impossible *impossibility*
That any clerk wol speke good of wyves, *cleric*
690 But if it be of hooly seintes lyves, *unless*
Ne of noon oother womman never the mo.
Who peyntede the leon, tel me who?
By God! if wommen hadde writen stories,
As clerkes han withinne hire oratories,
695 They wolde han writen of men moore wikkednesse
Than al the mark of Adam may redresse. *race*
The children of Mercurie and of Venus
Been in hir wirkyng ful contrarius;
Mercurie loveth wysdam and science,
700 And Venus loveth ryot and dispence. *revelry; extravagance*
And, for hire diverse disposicioun,
Ech falleth in otheres exaltacioun.
And thus, God woot, Mercurie is desolat
In Pisces, wher Venus is exaltat;
705 And Venus falleth ther Mercurie is reysed. *where*
Therfore no womman of no clerk is preysed. *by*
The clerk, whan he is oold, and may noght do
Of Venus werkes worth his olde sho,

679 i.e. the Book of Proverbs.
680 Ovid's *Ars Amandi*.
686 He knew more stories and biographies of them.
691 And never of a single other woman.
692 An allusion to the fable of Aesop in which a sculptor represents a man conquering a lion. The lion observes that if he and his kind were sculptors they would have their own ideas about the identity of the victor.
697–8 Men (i.e. *clerkes*) and women, who are born under the dominant influence of Mercury and Venus respectively, are totally opposed in all they do.
701–2 Because of their different natures, each of these planets has its fall in the sign in which the other has its exaltation (and therefore its greatest influence).
708 Any work for Venus that's worth his old shoe.

Thanne sit he doun, and writ in his dotage	*sits; writes*
710 That wommen kan nat kepe hir mariage!	*be faithful in*

But now to purpos, why I tolde thee
That I was beten for a book, pardee!
Upon a nyght Jankyn, that was oure sire,   *husband*
Redde on his book, as he sat by the fire,
715 Of Eva first, that for hir wikkednesse
Was al mankynde broght to wrecchednesse,
For which that Jhesu Crist hymself was slayn,
That boghte us with his herte blood agayn.   *redeemed*
Lo, heere expres of womman may ye fynde,
720 That womman was the los of al mankynde.   *ruin*
  Tho redde he me how Sampson loste his heres: *then; hair*
  Slepynge, his lemman kitte it with hir   *sweetheart; cut*
    sheres;
  Thurgh which treson loste he bothe his yen.   *eyes*
  Tho redde he me, if that I shal nat lyen,
725 Of Hercules and of his Dianyre,   *Deianira*
  That caused hym to sette hymself afyre.   *on fire*
    No thyng forgat he the care and the wo
  That Socrates hadde with his wyves two;
  How Xantippa caste pisse upon his heed.
730 This sely man sat stille as he were deed;   *poor; dead*
  He wiped his heed, namoore dorste he seyn,
  But "Er that thonder stynte, comth a reyn!"   *stops*
    Of Phasipha, that was the queene of Crete,   *Pasiphaë*
  For shrewednesse, hym thoughte the tale swete;
735 Fy! spek namoore—it is a grisly thyng—   *terrible*
  Of hire horrible lust and hir likyng.   *infatuation*
    Of Clitermystra, for hire lecherye,   *Clytemnestra*
  That falsly made hire housbonde for to dye,
  He redde it with ful good devocioun.
740   He tolde me eek for what occasioun   *reason*
  Amphiorax at Thebes loste his lyf.   *Amphiaraus*
  Myn housbonde hadde a legende of his wyf,
  Eriphilem, that for an ouche of gold   *Eriphyle; brooch*
  Hath prively unto the Grekes told
745 Wher that hir housbonde hidde hym in a place,
  For which he hadde at Thebes sory grace.
    Of Lyvia tolde he me, and of Lucye: *Lucia*
  They bothe made hir housbondes for to dye;

711–12 But now to come back to my subject—why I got beaten, as I
  told you, for the sake of a book.
715–16 For whose wickedness all mankind was brought to misery.
719 In this story you can find it explicitly stated.
727 He by no means forgot.
734 He wickedly thought the tale was sweet.
745–6 Where her husband had his hiding-place, and in consequence he
  suffered a miserable fate at Thebes.

That oon for love, that oother was for hate.
750 Lyvia hir housbonde, on an even late,   *late one evening*
Empoysoned hath, for that she was his fo;   *foe*
Lucia, likerous, loved hire housbonde so   *wanton*
That, for he sholde alwey upon hire thynke,
She yaf hym swich a manere love-drynke
755 That he was deed er it were by the morwe;   *before morning*
And thus algates housbondes han sorwe.   *in every way*
    Thanne tolde he me how oon Latumyus
Compleyned unto his felawe Arrius
That in his gardyn growed swich a tree
760 On which he seyde how that his wyves thre
Hanged hemself for herte despitus.   *for spite*
"O leeve brother," quod this Arrius,   *dear*
"Yif me a plante of thilke blissed tree,   *cutting*
And in my gardyn planted shal it bee."
765   Of latter date, of wyves hath he red
That somme han slayn hir housbondes in hir bed,
And lete hir lecchour dighte hire al the   *lecher; lie with*
    nyght,
Whan that the corps lay in the floor upright.
And somme han dryve nayles in hir brayn,
770 Whil that they slepte, and thus they han hem slayn.
Somme han hem yeve poysoun in hire drynke.   *given*
He spak moore harm than herte may bithynke;   *think of*
And therwithal he knew of mo proverbes   *more*
Than in this world ther growen gras or herbes.
775 "Bet is," quod he, "thyn habitacioun   *better*
Be with a leon or a foul dragoun,
Than with a womman usynge for to chyde."   *accustomed*
"Bet is," quod he, "hye in the roof abyde,
Than with an angry wyf doun in the hous;
780 They been so wikked and contrarious,   *contrary*
They haten that hir housbondes loven ay."
He seyde, "a womman cast hir shame away,   *throws*
Whan she cast of hir smok;" and forthermo,   *off*
"A fair womman, but she be chaast also,   *chaste*
785 Is lyk a gold ryng in a sowes nose."
Who wolde wene, or who wolde suppose,   *believe; imagine*
The wo that in myn herte was, and pyne?   *torment*
    And whan I saugh he wolde never fyne   *finish*
To reden on this cursed book al nyght,
790 Al sodeynly thre leves have I plyght   *plucked*
Out of his book, right as he radde, and eke
I with my fest so took hym on the cheke   *fist*

754 Such a powerful love-potion.
768 While the dead man lay on his back on the floor.
781 They always hate what their husbands love.
791 Even as he was reading.

That in oure fyr he fil bakward adoun.
And he up stirte as dooth a wood leoun,   *started; lion*
795 And with his fest he smoot me on the heed,
That in the floor I lay as I were deed.
And whan he saugh how stille that I lay,
He was agast, and wolde han fled his way,   *terrified*
Til atte laste out of my swogh I breyde.
800 "O! hastow slayn me, false theef?" I seyde,   *wretch*
"And for my land thus hastow mordred me?
Er I be deed, yet wol I kisse thee."   *die*
    And neer he cam, and kneled faire adoun,   *closer; gently*
And seyde, "Deere suster Alisoun,
805 As help me God! I shal thee nevere smyte.
That I have doon, it is thyself to wyte.
Foryeve it me, and that I thee biseke!"   *beseech*
And yet eftsoones I hitte hym on the cheke,   *once again*
And seyde, "Theef, thus muchel am I wreke;   *much; avenged*
810 Now wol I dye, I may no lenger speke."
But atte laste, with muchel care and wo,
We fille acorded by us selven two.
He yaf me al the bridel in myn hond,
To han the governance of hous and lond,   *management*
815 And of his tonge, and of his hond also;
And made hym brenne his book anon right tho.
And whan that I hadde geten unto me,   *got for myself*
By maistrie, al the soveraynetee,   *masterful behaviour*
And that he seyde, "Myn owene trewe wyf,
820 Do as thee lust the terme of al thy lyf;   *you please*
Keep thyn honour, and keep eek myn estaat"—
After that day we hadden never debaat.   *quarrel*
God helpe me so, I was to hym as kynde
As any wyf from Denmark unto Ynde,
825 And also trewe, and so was he to me.
I prey to God, that sit in magestee,   *dwells*
So blesse his soule for his mercy deere.
Now wol I seye my tale, if ye wol heere.'

BIHOLDE THE WORDES BITWENE THE SOMONOUR
AND THE FRERE

    The Frere lough, whan he hadde herd al this;   *laughed*
830 'Now dame,' quod he, 'so have I joye or blis,   *madam*

799 Till at last I recovered from my faint.
804 *suster* is used here, as *brother* sometimes is, as a friendly mode of address to a fellow Christian.
806 You are yourself to blame for what I've done.
812 We made it up together.
816 I made him burn his book there and then.
821 Protect your honour and my standing, too.
827 To bless his soul for His dear mercy's sake.

This is a long preamble of a tale!'
And whan the Somonour herde the Frere gale,   *cry out*
'Lo,' quod the Somonour, 'Goddes armes two!
A frere wol entremette hym everemo.
835 Lo, goode men, a flye and eek a frere
Wol falle in every dyssh and eek mateere.
What spekestow of preambulacioun?   *preambling*
What! amble, or trotte, or pees, or go sit doun!   *keep still*
Thou lettest oure disport in this manere.'   *spoil; sport*
840   'Ye, woltow so, sire Somonour?' quod the Frere;
'Now, by my feith, I shal, er that I go,
Telle of a somonour swich a tale or two,
That alle the folk shal laughen in this place.'
        'Now elles, Frere, I bishrewe thy face,'   *curse*
845 Quod this Somonour, 'and I bishrewe me,
But if I telle tales two or thre   *if I don't*
Of freres, er I come to Sidyngborne,   *Sittingbourne*
That I shal make thyn herte for to morne,   *grieve*
For wel I woot thy pacience is gon.'
850   Oure Hooste cride 'Pees! and that anon!'   *peace*
And seyde, 'Lat the womman telle hire tale.
Ye fare as folk that dronken ben of ale.
Do, dame, telle forth youre tale, and that is best.'
        'Al redy, sire,' quod she, 'right as yow lest,   *wish*
855 If I have licence of this worthy Frere.'   *permission*
        'Yis, dame,' quod he, 'tel forth, and I wol heere.'   *on*

HEERE ENDETH THE WYF OF BATHE HIR PROLOGE

—————

THE WIFE OF BATH'S TALE

HEERE BIGYNNETH THE TALE OF THE WYF OF BATHE

IN TH'OLDE dayes of the Kyng Arthour,
Of which that Britons speken greet honour,   *of whom*
Al was this land fulfild of fayerye.

834 A friar will always be meddling.
859 Full of fairy folk.

860 The elf-queene, with hir joly compaignye,
Daunced ful ofte in many a grene mede. *meadow*
This was the olde opinion, as I rede;
I speke of manye hundred yeres ago.
But now kan no man se none elves mo,
865 For now the grete charitee and prayeres
Of lymytours and othere hooly freres,
That serchen every lond and every streem,
As thikke as motes in the sonne-beem,
Blessynge halles, chambres, kichenes, boures, *bowers*
870 Citees, burghes, castels, hye toures, *boroughs*
Thropes, bernes, shipnes, dayeryes—
This maketh that ther ben no fayeryes. *fairies*
For ther as wont to walken was an elf, *where*
Ther walketh now the lymytour hymself
875 In undermeles and in morwenynges, *afternoons*
And seyth his matyns and his hooly thynges *says*
As he gooth in his lymytacioun.
Wommen may go saufly up and doun. *safely*
In every bussh or under every tree
880 Ther is noon oother incubus but he,
And he ne wol doon hem but dishonour.
      And so bifel that this kyng Arthour
Hadde in his hous a lusty bacheler, *young knight*
That on a day cam ridynge fro ryver;
885 And happed that, allone as he was born,
He saugh a mayde walkynge hym biforn,
Of which mayde anon, maugree hir heed,
By verray force, he rafte hire maydenhed; *brute; ravished*
For which oppressioun was swich clamour *act of violence*
890 And swich pursute unto the kyng Arthour, *petitioning*
That dampned was this knyght for to be *condemned; die*
      deed,
By cours of lawe, and sholde han lost his heed— *would have*
Paraventure swich was the statut tho—
But that the queene and othere ladyes mo
895 So longe preyeden the kyng of grace, *for mercy*
Til he his lyf hym graunted in the place,

864 Now no one can see elves any more.
866 *lymytours*, begging friars. (See I. 209.)
871 Villages, barns, shippens, dairies.
877 As he walks about his district.
880 *incubus*, an evil spirit that assaults women in their sleep.
881 He will do nothing but dishonour them.
884 Came from hawking by the river.
887 *maugree hir heed*, in spite of all her struggles (lit. despite her head).
893 Perhaps the statute in force then was of such severity.

And yaf hym to the queene, al at hir wille,
To chese wheither she wolde hym save or   *choose*
   spille.   *destroy*
   The queene thanketh the kyng with al hir myght,
900 And after this thus spak she to the knyght,
Whan that she saugh hir tyme, upon a day: *opportunity*
'Thou standest yet,' quod she, 'in swich array   *plight*
That of thy lyf yet hastow no suretee.
I grante thee lyf, if thou kanst tellen me
905 What thyng is it that wommen moost desiren.
Be war, and keep thy nekke-boon from iren!   *the sword*
And if thou kanst nat tellen it anon,   *immediately*
Yet wol I yeve thee leve for to gon   *leave*
A twelf-month and a day, to seche and leere   *seek; learn*
910 An answere suffisant in this mateere;
And suretee wol I han, er that thou pace,   *depart*
Thy body for to yelden in this place.'
   Wo was this knyght, and sorwefully he siketh;   *sad; sighs*
But what! he may nat do al as hym liketh.
915 And at the laste he chees hym for to wende,   *chose; go*
And come agayn, right at the yeres ende,
With swich answere as God wolde hym purveye;   *provide*
And taketh his leve, and wendeth forth his weye.
   He seketh every hous and every place   *visits*
920 Where as he hopeth for to fynde grace,
To lerne what thyng wommen loven moost;
But he ne koude arryven in no coost
Wher as he myghte fynde in this mateere
Two creatures accordynge in-feere.   *together*
925 Somme seyde wommen loven best richesse,   *wealth*
Somme seyde honour, somme seyde jolynesse,   *jollity*
Somme riche array, somme seyden lust abedde,   *clothes; in bed*
And oftetyme to be wydwe and wedde.
Somme seyde that oure hertes been moost esed   *comforted*
930 Whan that we been yflatered and yplesed.
He gooth ful ny the sothe, I wol nat lye.   *near; truth*
A man shal wynne us best with flaterye;
And with attendance, and with bisynesse,   *attentiveness; fuss*
Been we ylymed, bothe moore and lesse.
935   And somme seyen that we loven best
For to be free, and do right as us lest,   *we please*
And that no man repreve us of oure vice,   *should reprove*

897 And placed him entirely at the queen's disposal.
903 You have no guarantee you will keep your life.
912 That you will surrender yourself in this place.
914 But there! he cannot do just as he likes.
922 He came to no part of the world.
928 To be widowed often, and re-wed.
934 Are we caught (as birds with bird-lime), all of us.

But seye that we be wise, and no thyng   *by no means*
    nyce.   *foolish*
For trewely ther is noon of us alle,
940 If any wight wol clawe us on the galle,
That we nel kike, for he seith us sooth.
Assay, and he shal fynde it that so dooth;
For, be we never so vicious withinne,
We wol been holden wise and clene of synne.
945   And somme seyn that greet delit han we
For to been holden stable, and eek secree,
And in o purpos stedefastly to dwelle,
And nat biwreye thyng that men us telle.   *reveal*
But that tale is nat worth a rake-stele.
950 Pardee, we wommen konne no thyng hele;
Witnesse on Myda,—wol ye heere the tale?   *Midas*
    Ovyde, amonges othere thynges smale,   *little*
Seyde Myda hadde, under his longe heres,
Growynge upon his heed two asses eres,
955 The whiche vice he hydde, as he best myghte,   *deformity*
Ful subtilly from every mannes sighte,   *artfully*
That, save his wyf, ther wiste of it namo.
He loved hire moost, and trusted hire also;
He preyede hire that to no creature
960 She sholde tellen of his disfigure.   *disfigurement*
    She swoor him, 'Nay,' for al this world to wynne,
She nolde do that vileynye or synne,
To make hir housbonde han so foul a name.
She nolde nat telle it for hir owene shame.
965 But nathelees, hir thoughte that she dyde,
That she so longe sholde a conseil hyde;   *secret*
Hir thoughte it swal so soore aboute hir herte
That nedely som word hire moste asterte;
And sith she dorste telle it to no man,   *since*
970 Doun to a mareys faste by she ran—   *marsh; near*
Til she cam there, hir herte was a-fyre—   *on fire*
And as a bitore bombleth in the myre,

939–41 Truly there's none of us who will not kick if someone scratches
    us on a sore spot, just because he tells us the truth.
942 Try it, and you'll find it's true.
946–7 To be thought reliable, as well as discreet, and unshakeably firm
    of purpose.
949 That sort of talk is not worth a rake-handle.
950 Goodness (lit. by God), we women can't keep anything secret.
957 No one else knew of it.
962 She wouldn't do such a mean or sinful thing.
965 She thought (lit. it seemed to her) she would die.
967–8 It swelled so painfully in her heart that some word of it just had
    to burst out.
972 And like a bittern booming in the marsh.

She leyde hir mouth unto the water doun:
'Biwreye me nat, thou water, with thy soun,'　　*betray*
975 Quod she; 'to thee I telle it and namo;
Myn housbonde hath longe asses erys two!
Now is myn herte al hool, now is it oute.
I myghte no lenger kepe it, out of doute.'　　*doubtless*
Heere may ye se, thogh we a tyme abyde,
980 Yet out it moot; we kan no conseil hyde.　　*must*
The remenant of the tale if ye wol heere,　　*rest*
Redeth Ovyde, and ther ye may it leere.　　*find out*
　　This knyght, of which my tale is specially,
Whan that he saugh he myghte nat come therby,　　*by it*
985 This is to seye, what wommen love moost,
Withinne his brest ful sorweful was the goost.　　*spirit*
But hoom he gooth, he myghte nat sojourne;　　*home*
The day was come that homward moste he tourne.
And in his wey it happed hym to ryde,　　*he chanced*
990 In al this care, under a forest syde,
Wher as he saugh upon a daunce go
Of ladyes foure and twenty, and yet mo;　　*more*
Toward the whiche daunce he drow ful yerne,　　*drew; eagerly*
In hope that som wysdom sholde he lerne.
995 But certeinly, er that he cam fully there,
Vanysshed was this daunce, he nyste where.　　*knew not*
No creature saugh he that bar lyf,
Save on the grene he saugh sittynge a wyf—
A fouler wight ther may no man devyse.
1000 Agayn the knyght this olde wyf gan ryse,
And seyde, 'Sire knyght, heer forth ne lith no wey.
Tel me what that ye seken, by youre fey!　　*faith*
Paraventure it may the bettre be;
Thise olde folk kan muchel thyng,' quod she.
1005 　'My leeve mooder,' quod this knyght, 'certeyn
I nam but deed, but if that I kan seyn
What thyng it is that wommen moost desire.
Koude ye me wisse, I wolde wel quite youre hire.'
　-　'Plight me thy trouthe heere in myn hand,'
　　quod she,
1010 'The nexte thyng that I requere thee,　　*ask*

979 Though we endure it for a time.
990 In all this sorrow, at the edge of a forest.
997 He saw no living creature.
998 Except that he saw a woman sitting on the grass.
999 No one could imagine an uglier creature.
1000 This old woman rose to meet the knight.
1001 There's no way on from here.
1003 Perhaps you'll be the better for it.
1004 Old people know many things.
1006 I'm as good as dead, unless I can say.
1008 If you could tell me, I would pay you well for your trouble.

Thou shalt it do, if it lye in thy myght,   *lies*
And I wol telle it yow er it be nyght.'
  'Have heer my trouthe,' quod the knyght, 'I grante.'
  'Thanne,' quod she, 'I dare me wel avante
1015 Thy lyf is sauf; for I wol stonde therby,
Upon my lyf, the queene wol seye as I.
Lat se which is the proudeste of hem alle,
That wereth on a coverchief or a calle,
That dar seye nay of that I shal thee teche.
1020 Lat us go forth, withouten lenger speche.'
  Tho rowned she a pistel in his ere,   *whispered; message*
And bad hym to be glad, and have no fere.   *fear*
  Whan they be comen to the court, this knyght
Seyde he had holde his day, as he hadde hight,   *kept; promised*
1025 And redy was his answere, as he sayde.
Ful many a noble wyf, and many a mayde,
And many a wydwe, for that they been wise,
The queene hirself sittynge as a justise,   *judge*
Assembled been, his answere for to heere;
1030 And afterward this knyght was bode appeere.   *summoned to*
    To every wight comanded was silence,
And that the knyght sholde telle in audience
What thyng that worldly wommen loven best.
This knyght ne stood nat stille as doth a best,   *dumb; beast*
1035 But to his questioun anon answerde   *immediately*
With manly voys, that al the court it herde:
  'My lige lady, generally,' quod he,   *liege*
'Wommen desiren to have sovereynetee
As wel over hir housbond as hir love,
1040 And for to been in maistrie hym above.
This is youre mooste desir, thogh ye me kille.   *greatest*
Dooth as yow list; I am heer at youre wille.'   *please*
  In al the court ne was ther wyf, ne mayde,
Ne wydwe, that contraried that he sayde,   *contradicted*
1045 But seyden he was worthy han his lyf.   *to have*
  And with that word up stirte the olde wyf,   *started*
Which that the knyght saugh sittynge on the grene: *whom*
'Mercy,' quod she, 'my sovereyn lady queene!
Er that youre court departe, do me right.
1050 I taughte this answere unto the knyght;
For which he plighte me his trouthe there,
The firste thyng that I wolde hym requere,

1013 You have my promise . . . I agree.
1014 I don't mind boasting.
1015 Your life is safe; for I'll guarantee.
1017 Show me the proudest of them all, who wears a kerchief or a
    head-dress.
1032 In the hearing of them all.
1039 Over their husband no less than their lover.
1040 To have mastery over him.

He wolde it do, if it lay in his myght.
Bifore the court thanne preye I thee, sir knyght,'
1055 Quod she, 'that thou me take unto thy wyf;
For wel thou woost that I have kept thy lyf.   *know; saved*
If I seye fals, sey nay, upon thy fey!'
This knyght answerde, 'Allas! and weylawey!
I woot right wel that swich was my biheste.   *promise*
1060 For Goddes love, as chees a newe requeste!
Taak al my good, and lat my body go.'   *goods*
'Nay, thanne,' quod she, 'I shrewe us bothe two!   *curse*
For thogh that I be foul, and oold, and poore,   *ugly*
I nolde for al the metal, ne for oore,
1065 That under erthe is grave, or lith above,
But if thy wyf I were, and eek thy love.'
'My love?' quod he, 'nay, my dampnacioun!
Allas! that any of my nacioun   *noble birth*
Sholde evere so foule disparaged be!'
1070 But al for noght; the ende is this, that he
Constreyned was, he nedes moste hire wedde;
And taketh his olde wyf, and gooth to bedde.
Now wolden som men seye, paraventure,
That for my necligence I do no cure   *take no trouble*
1075 To tellen yow the joye and al th'array   *preparations*
That at the feeste was that ilke day.   *same*
To which thyng shortly answeren I shal:
I seye ther nas no joye ne feeste at al;   *was (not)*
Ther nas but hevynesse and muche sorwe.   *heaviness of heart*
1080 For prively he wedded hire on morwe,
And al day after hidde hym as an owle,   *himself*
So wo was hym, his wyf looked so foule.
Greet was the wo the knyght hadde in his thoght,
Whan he was with his wyf abedde ybroght;   *to bed*
1085 He walweth and he turneth to and fro.   *tosses*
His olde wyf lay smylynge everemo,   *all the time*
And seyde, 'O deere housbonde, *benedicitee!*   *bless us*
Fareth every knyght thus with his wyf as ye?
Is this the lawe of kyng Arthures hous?
1090 Is every knyght of his so dangerous?   *hard to please*
I am youre owene love and youre wyf;
I am she which that saved hath youre lyf,
And, certes, yet ne dide I yow nevere unright; *certainly; wrong*
Why fare ye thus with me this firste nyght?

1057 If I speak falsely, deny it on your honour.
1060 For the love of God, please make a new request.
1064–6 I'd rather be your wife and your beloved than have all the
    metal and ore that's buried in the earth or lies above it.
1069–70 Should ever be disgraced by such an unequal match! But it
    was all in vain.
1080 For he married her secretly next day.
1082 He was so miserable.

1095 Ye faren lyk a man had lost his wit.
      What is my gilt? For Goddes love, tel it,   *offence*
      And it shal been amended, if I may.'   *put right*
        'Amended?' quod this knyght, 'allas! nay, nay!
      It wol nat been amended nevere mo.
1100 Thou art so loothly, and so oold also,   *hideous*
      And therto comen of so lough a kynde,
      That litel wonder is thogh I walwe and wynde.   *toss; turn*
      So wolde God myn herte wolde breste!'
        'Is this,' quod she, 'the cause of youre unreste?'
1105   'Ye, certeinly,' quod he, 'no wonder is.'
        'Now, sire,' quod she, 'I koude amende al this,
      If that me liste, er it were dayes thre,
      So wel ye myghte bere yow unto me.
        But, for ye speken of swich gentillesse
1110 As is descended out of old richesse,
      That therfore sholden ye be gentil men,
      Swich arrogance is nat worth an hen.
      Looke who that is moost vertuous alway,
      Pryvee and apert, and moost entendeth ay
1115 To do the gentil dedes that he kan;
      Taak hym for the grettest gentil man.
      Crist wole we clayme of hym oure gentillesse,   *Him*
      Nat of oure eldres for hire old richesse.   *ancestors*
      For thogh they yeve us al hir heritage,   *give*
1120 For which we clayme to been of heigh parage,   *rank*
      Yet may they nat biquethe, for no thyng,   *by any means*
      To noon of us hir vertuous lyvyng,   *mode of living*
      That made hem gentil men ycalled be,
      And bad us folwen hem in swich degree.
1125   Wel kan the wise poete of Florence,
      That highte Dant, speken in this sentence.
      Lo, in swich maner rym is Dantes tale:
      "Ful selde up riseth by his branches smale
      Prowesse of man, for God, of his goodnesse,
1130 Wole that of hym we clayme oure gentillesse";

      1101 And, moreover, so low-born.
      1103 Would to God my heart would break!
      1107–8 If I wished, in a day or two, if only you behaved more
        courteously to me.
      1109–12 But to say that people like yourself should be gentlemen
        because you have the sort of gentility that comes from ancient,
        inherited wealth—such arrogance is not worth a straw (lit. hen).
      1113–15 Whoever is the most virtuous all the time, in public and in
        private, and who strives the hardest to do all the noble deeds he can.
      1124 And encouraged us to follow in their footsteps.
      1126 Who was called Dante, speak on this subject.
      1127 This is what he has to say in rhyme.
      1128–9 Man very seldom climbs to excellence along his own slender
        branches.

For of oure eldres may we no thyng clayme
But temporel thyng, that man may hurte and mayme.
   Eek every wight woot this as wel as I,
If gentillesse were planted natureely
1135 Unto a certeyn lynage doun the lyne,
Pryvee and apert, thanne wolde they nevere fyne   *cease*
To doon of gentillesse the faire office;
They myghte do no vileynye or vice.   *base or vicious deed*
   Taak fyr, and ber it in the derkeste hous
1140 Bitwix this and the mount of Kaukasous,   *Caucasus*
And lat men shette the dores and go thenne;   *thence*
Yet wole the fyr as faire lye and brenne   *blaze; burn*
As twenty thousand men myghte it biholde;   *as it would if*
His office natureel ay wol it holde,   *its*
1145 Up peril of my lyf, til that it dye.
   Heere may ye se wel how that genterye
Is nat annexed to possessioun,
Sith folk ne doon hir operacioun
Alwey, as dooth the fyr, lo, in his kynde.
1150 For, God it woot, men may wel often fynde
A lordes sone do shame and vileynye;
And he that wole han pris of his gentrye,
For he was boren of a gentil hous,   *because*
And hadde his eldres noble and vertuous,
1155 And nel hymselven do no gentil dedis,   *will not*
Ne folwen his gentil auncestre that deed is,
He nys nat gentil, be he duc or erl;
For vileyns synful dedes make a cherl.
For gentillesse nys but renomee
1160 Of thyne auncestres, for hire heigh bountee,
Which is a strange thyng to thy persone.
Thy gentillesse cometh fro God allone.
Thanne comth oure verray gentillesse of grace;
It was no thyng biquethe us with oure place.
1165   Thenketh hou noble, as seith Valerius,
Was thilke Tullius Hostillius,

1134–6 If gentility were implanted naturally in a family, and showed
   itself in each succeeding generation, in public and in private.
1145 Upon my life, till it dies out.
1146–9 From this you may see that gentility is not annexed to possessions, since people do not always behave as fire naturally does, i.e.
   their qualities do not always burn brightly in their descendants.
1152 A man who wants to be esteemed for his gentility.
1156 Nor follow the noble example of his dead ancestor.
1158 For base and sinful actions make a man a churl.
1159–61 Gentility is neither more nor less than the renown your
   ancestors won for their outstanding goodness, which is something
   alien to your person.
1163 From Him, by grace, comes true gentility.
1164 It is by no means bequeathed to us with rank.

That out of poverte roos to heigh noblesse. *nobility*
Reedeth Senek, and redeth eek Boece; *Seneca; Boethius*
Ther shul ye seen expres that it no drede is
1170 That he is gentil that dooth gentil dedis.
And therfore, leeve housbonde, I thus conclude: *dear*
Al were it that myne auncestres were rude, *although; humble*
Yet may the hye God, and so hope I,
Grante me grace to lyven vertuously.
1175 Thanne am I gentil, whan that I bigynne
To lyven vertuously and weyve synne. *put aside*
    And ther as ye of poverte me repreeve,
The hye God, on whom that we bileeve,
In wilful poverte chees to lyve his lyf. *willing*
1180 And certes every man, mayden, or wyf,
May understonde that Jhesus, hevene kyng,
Ne wolde nat chese a vicious lyvyng.
Glad poverte is an honest thyng, certeyn;
This wole Senec and othere clerkes seyn. *learned men*
1185 Whoso that halt hym payd of his poverte,
I holde hym riche, al hadde he nat a sherte.
He that coveiteth is a povre wight,
For he wolde han that is nat in his myght;
But he that noght hath, ne coveiteth have,
1190 Is riche, although ye holde hym but a knave. *low-born person*
Verray poverte, it syngeth proprely;
Juvenal seith of poverte myrily: *pleasantly*
"The povre man, whan he goth by the weye,
Bifore the theves he may synge and pleye."
1195 Poverte is hateful good and, as I gesse,
A ful greet bryngere out of bisynesse;
A greet amendere eek of sapience *improver; sagacity*
To hym that taketh it in pacience.
Poverte is this, although it seme alenge, *miserable*
1200 Possessioun that no wight wol chalenge.
Poverte ful ofte, whan a man is lowe, *lowly*
Maketh his God and eek hymself to knowe.
Poverte a spectacle is, as thynketh me, *glass*
Thurgh which he may his verray freendes see.
1205 And therfore, sire, syn that I noght yow greve, *harm*
Of my poverte namoore ye me repreve.

1169–70 There you will see it made clear, beyond all doubt, that a
   gentleman is one who is gentle in deed.
1177 Whereas you reproach me for my poverty.
1185 Anyone who is content to live in poverty.
1187 A covetous man is a poor man.
1191 True poverty has a song of its own.
1195 *hateful good*, i.e. hard to endure and yet good for us.
1196 A very great producer of work.
1202 Makes him know his God and also himself.

Now, sire, of elde ye repreve me;   *old age*
And certes, sire, thogh noon auctoritee   *authoritative text*
Were in no book, ye gentils of honour
1210 Seyn that men sholde an oold wight doon favour,
And clepe hym fader, for youre gentillesse;   *call*
And auctours shal I fynden, as I gesse.
    Now ther ye seye that I am foul and old,
Than drede you noght to been a cokewold;
1215 For filthe and eelde, also moot I thee,
Been grete wardeyns upon chastitee.
But nathelees, syn I knowe youre delit,
I shal fulfille youre worldly appetit.
    Chese now,' quod she, 'oon of thise thynges tweye:
1220 To han me foul and old til that I deye,
And be to yow a trewe, humble wyf,
And nevere yow displese in al my lyf;
Or elles ye wol han me yong and fair,
And take youre aventure of the repair
1225 That shal be to youre hous by cause of me,
Or in som oother place, may wel be.
Now chese yourselven, wheither that yow   *whichever you like*
        liketh.'
    This knyght avyseth hym and sore siketh,
But atte laste he seyde in this manere:
1230 'My lady and my love, and wyf so deere,
I put me in youre wise governance;   *rule*
Cheseth youreself which may be moost plesance,   *pleasure*
And moost honour to yow and me also.
I do no fors the wheither of the two;
1235 For as yow liketh, it suffiseth me.'
    'Thanne have I gete of yow maistrie,' quod she,
'Syn I may chese and governe as me lest?'   *I please*
'Ye, certes, wyf,' quod he, 'I holde it best.'   *think*
'Kys me,' quod she, 'we be no lenger wrothe;
1240 For, by my trouthe, I wol be to yow bothe,
This is to seyn, ye, bothe fair and good.   *yea*
I prey to God that I moote sterven wood,
But I to yow be also good and trewe   *unless; as*
As evere was wyf, syn that the world was newe.
1245 And but I be to-morn as fair to seene   *behold*

1209–10 You gentlefolk say that men should treat an old person kindly.
1212 i.e. authors who write the same thing.
1214 Then you have no fear of being a cuckold.
1215 As I hope to prosper.
1224–5 And take your chance how many visit your house because of me.
1228 The knight thinks hard and sighs deeply.
1234–5 I don't care which of the two it is; for anything that pleases
    you is good enough for me.
1242 I may die in madness.

As any lady, emperice, or queene,   *empress*
That is bitwixe the est and eke the west,
Dooth with my lyf and deth right as yow lest.
Cast up the curtyn, looke how that it is.'   *lift*
1250   And whan the knyght saugh verraily al this,
That she so fair was, and so yong therto,   *as well*
For joye he hente hire in his armes two,   *took*
His herte bathed in a bath of blisse.
A thousand tyme a-rewe he gan hire kisse,
1255 And she obeyed hym in every thyng
That myghte doon hym plesance or likyng.   *delight*
    And thus they lyve unto hir lyves ende
In parfit joye; and Jhesu Crist us sende
Housbondes meeke, yonge, and fressh abedde,
1260 And grace t'overbyde hem that we wedde;   *outlive*
And eek I praye Jhesu shorte hir lyves   *shorten*
That noght wol be governed by hir wyves;
And olde and angry nygardes of dispence,
God sende hem soone verray pestilence!   *a very*

HEERE ENDETH THE WYVES TALE OF BATHE

1248 i.e. you can kill me if you like.
1254 He kissed her a thousand times in quick succession.
1263 Old and angry misers, chary of expense.

THE FRIAR'S PROLOGUE

The Prologe of the Freres Tale

1265   This worthy lymytour, this noble Frere,
       He made alwey a maner louryng chiere
       Upon the Somonour, but for honestee   *good manners*
       No vileyns word as yet to hym spak he.   *rude*
       But atte laste he seyde unto the wyf,
1270   'Dame,' quod he, 'God yeve yow right good lyf!   *give*
       Ye han heer touched, also moot I thee,
       In scole-matere greet difficultee.
       Ye han seyd muche thyng right wel, I seye;
       But, dame, heere as we ryde by the weye,
1275   Us nedeth nat to speken but of game,
       And lete auctoritees, on Goddes name,
       To prechyng and to scoles of clergye.
       But if it lyke to this compaignye,
       I wol yow of a somonour telle a game.
1280   Pardee, ye may wel knowe by the name   *joke*
       That of a somonour may no good be sayd;
       I praye that noon of you be yvele apayd.   *displeased*
       A somonour is a rennere up and doun
       With mandementz for fornicacioun,   *summonses*
1285   And is ybet at every townes ende.'   *beaten*
           Oure Hoost tho spak, 'A! sire, ye sholde be hende   *polite*
       And curteys, as a man of youre estaat;   *rank*
       In compaignye we wol have no debaat.   *quarrelling*
       Telleth youre tale, and lat the Somonour be.'
1290   'Nay,' quod the Somonour, 'lat hym seye to me
       What so hym list; whan it comth to my lot,
       By God! I shal hym quiten every grot.
       I shal hym tellen which a greet honour   *what a*
       It is to be a flaterynge lymytour;

1265 *lymytour.* See I. 209.
1266 A sort of louring look.
1271 As I hope to prosper.
1272 A scholastic question of great difficulty.
1275 We needn't speak of anything that's not amusing.
1276 And leave quotations from the authorities. (Cf. 1208.)
1277 And to schools of higher learning.
1291–2 Whatever he likes; when it comes to my turn, by God! I'll pay him back in full.

192

1295 And of many another manere cryme
Which nedeth nat rehercen at this tyme;   *recount*
And his office I shal hym telle, ywis.'
Oure Hoost answerde, 'Pees, namoore of this!'
And after this he seyde unto the Frere,
1300 'Tel forth youre tale, leeve maister deere.'   *beloved*

THE FRIAR'S TALE

HEERE BIGYNNETH THE FRERES TALE

WHILOM ther was dwellynge in my contree   *once; district*
An erchedeken, a man of heigh degree,
That boldely dide execucioun
In punysshynge of fornicacioun,
1305 Of wicchecraft, and eek of bawderye,   *pandering*
Of diffamacioun, and avowtrye,
Of chirche reves, and of testamentz,
Of contractes and of lakke of sacramentz,
Of usure, and of symonye also.   *usury*
1310 But certes, lecchours dide he grettest wo;
They sholde syngen if that they were hent;
And smale tytheres weren foule yshent,
If any persoun wolde upon hem   *parish priest*
pleyne   *complain*
Ther myghte asterte hym no pecunyal peyne.

1297 I'll certainly tell him how he carries out his duties.
1304 ff. These are some of the sins for which offenders could be cited
by a summoner to appear before the archdeacon's court, and for
which they could be excommunicated.
1306 *diffamacioun*, defamation of character; *avowtrye*, adultery.
1307 *chirche reves*, robbing of churches; *testamentz*, forging of wills or
interference with the proper execution of them.
1312 And people who failed to pay their tithes in full were grievously
punished.
1314 No fine could escape him (i.e. the archdeacon).

1315 For smale tithes and for smal offrynge
     He made the peple pitously to synge.
     For er the bisshop caughte hem with his hook,
     They weren in the erchedeknes book.
     Thanne hadde he, thurgh his jurisdiccioun,
1320 Power to doon on hem correccioun.
     He hadde a somonour redy to his hond;
     A slyer boye nas noon in Engelond;   *rascal*
     For subtilly he hadde his espiaille,   *craftily; spies*
     That taughte hym wel wher that hym myghte availle.   *profit*
1325 He koude spare of lecchours oon or two,
     To techen hym to foure and twenty mo.   *lead; more*
     For thogh this Somonour wood were as an hare,   *mad*
     To telle his harlotrye I wol nat spare;   *villainy*
     For we been out of his correccioun.
1330 They han of us no jurisdiccioun,
     Ne nevere shullen, terme of alle hir lyves.—
        'Peter! so been wommen of the styves,'   *brothels*
     Quod the Somonour, 'yput out of oure cure!'   *charge*
        'Pees! with myschance and with mysaventure!'
1335 Thus seyde oure Hoost, 'and lat hym telle his tale.
     Now telleth forth, thogh that the Somonour gale;   *cry out*
     Ne spareth nat, myn owene maister deere.'—
        This false theef, this somonour, quod the Frere,
     Hadde alwey bawdes redy to his hond,
1340 As any hauk to lure in Engelond,
     That tolde hym al the secree that they knewe;
     For hire acqueyntance was nat come of newe.
     They weren his approwours prively.   *agents; secretly*
     He took hymself a greet profit thereby;
1345 His maister knew nat alwey what he wan.
     Withouten mandement a lewed man
     He koude somne, on peyne of Cristes curs,
     And they were glade for to fille his purs,
     And make hym grete feestes atte nale.   *at the ale-house*
1350 And right as Judas hadde purses smale,
     And was a theef, right swich a theef was he;
     His maister hadde but half his duetee.   *due*
     He was, if I shal yeven hym his laude,   *praise*

1320 Power to punish them.
1329 For we are outside his corrective authority. (The friars were not
     subject to the authority of a bishop or his disciplinary officers, but
     were answerable only to the general of their order.)
1331 As long as they live.
1334 *with . . . mysaventure*, bad luck to you!
1346-7 He knew how to trump up a summons against an ignorant man
     and threaten him with sentence of excommunication.
1350-1 i.e. like Judas he had charge of his master's purse, and helped
     himself to its contents. (See John xii. 6.)

A theef, and eek a somnour, and a baude.
1355 He hadde eek wenches at his retenue,
That, wheither that sir Robert or sir Huwe,
Or Jakke, or Rauf, or whoso that it were
That lay by hem, they tolde it in his ere.
Thus was the wenche and he of oon assent;
1360 And he wolde fecche a feyned mandement,   *faked*
And somne hem to chapitre bothe two,
And pile the man, and lete the wenche go.
Thanne wolde he seye, 'Freend, I shal for thy sake
Do striken hire out of oure lettres blake;
1365 Thee thar namoore as in this cas travaille.
I am thy freend, ther I thee may availle.'
Certeyn he knew of briberyes mo
Than possible is to telle in yeres two.
For in this world nys dogge for the bowe
1370 That kan an hurt deer from an hool yknowe   *unwounded*
Bet than this somnour knew a sly lecchour,
Or an avowtier, or a paramour.   *adulterer; concubine*
And for that was the fruyt of al his rente,
Therfore on it he sette al this entente.
1375   And so bifel that ones on a day
This somnour, evere waityng on his pray,
Rood for to somne an old wydwe, a ribibe,   *old woman*
Feynynge a cause, for he wolde brybe.
And happed that he saugh bifore hym ryde   *it happened*
1380 A gay yeman, under a forest syde.
A bowe he bar, and arwes brighte and kene;   *carried*
He hadde upon a courtepy of grene,   *short coat*
An hat upon his heed with frenges blake.
'Sire,' quod this somnour, 'hayl, and wel atake!' *well met*
1385 'Welcome,' quod he, 'and every good felawe!
Wher rydestow, under this grene-wode shawe?'
Seyde this yeman, 'wiltow fer to day?'
This somnour hym answerde and seyde, 'Nay;

1359 *of oon assent*, in collusion.
1361 *chapitre*, chapter, i.e. ecclesiastical court.
1364-5 Have her struck from our black books; you needn't trouble
    yourself any more about it.
1366 Wherever I can be of service to you.
1367 Certainly he knew more methods of stealing money.
1369 *dogge for the bowe*, a dog trained to accompany an archer and
    follow up a wounded deer.
1373-4 And since that was the main part of his income he gave all his
    attention to it.
1376 Always on the look-out for prey.
1378 Inventing a charge, because he wanted to rob her.
1380 A gay yeoman, on the edge of a forest.
1387 Are you going far to-day?

Heere faste by,' quod he, 'is myn entente
1390 To ryden, for to reysen up a rente   *collect*
That longeth to my lordes duetee.'
      'Artow thanne a bailly?'   'Ye,' quod he.   *bailiff*
He dorste nat, for verray filthe and shame
Seye that he was a somonour, for the name.
1395 'Depardieux,' quod this yeman, 'deere broother,
Thou art a bailly, and I am another.
I am unknowen as in this contree;   *district*
Of thyn aqueyntance I wolde praye thee,
And eek of bretherhede, if that yow leste.
1400 I have gold and silver in my cheste;
If that thee happe to comen in oure shire,
Al shal be thyn, right as thou wolt desire.'
      'Grantmercy,' quod this somonour, 'by my feith!'
Everych in ootheres hand his trouthe leith,
1405 For to be sworne bretheren til they deye.
In daliance they ryden forth and pleye.
      This somonour, which that was as ful of jangles,   *chatter*
As ful of venym been thise waryangles,
And evere enqueryng upon every thyng,
1410 'Brother,' quod he, 'where is now youre dwellyng,
Another day if that I sholde yow seche?'   *seek*
This yeman hym answerde in softe speche,
      'Brother,' quod he, 'fer in the north contree,
Where-as I hope som tyme I shal thee see.
1415 Er we departe, I shal thee so wel wisse   *direct*
That of myn hous ne shaltow nevere mysse.'
      'Now, brother,' quod this somonour, 'I yow preye,
Teche me, whil that we ryden by the weye,
Syn that ye been a baillif as am I,
1420 Som subtiltee, and tel me feithfully   *trick*
In myn office how that I may moost wynne;
And spareth nat for conscience ne synne,
But as my brother tel me, how do ye.'
      'Now, by my trouthe, brother deere,' seyde he,
1425 'As I shal tellen thee a feithful tale,
My wages been ful streite and ful smale.   *stingy*
My lord is hard to me and daungerous,   *niggardly*
And myn office is ful laborous,
And therfore by extorcions I lyve.
1430 For sothe, I take al that men wol me yive.   *in truth*
Algate, by sleyghte or by violence,   *at any rate*

1391 That is due to my lord.
1404 Each grasps the other's hand and pledges his word.
1406 Chatting pleasantly together, they ride on their way.
1408 *waryangles*, butcher-birds or shrikes, which stock their larders by
     impaling live beetles, moths and fledglings on thorns. Such thorns
     are afterwards poisonous, it was once believed.

Fro yeer to yeer I wynne al my dispence.   *expenses*
I kan no bettre telle, feithfully.'
    'Now certes,' quod this Somonour, 'so fare I.
1435 I spare nat to taken, God it woot,
But if it be to hevy or to hoot.
What I may gete in conseil prively,   *secret*
No maner conscience of that have I.
Nere myn extorcioun, I myghte nat lyven,
1440 Ne of swiche japes wol I nat be shryven.
Stomak ne conscience ne knowe I noon;
I shrewe thise shrifte-fadres everychoon.
Wel be we met, by God and by Seint Jame!
But, leeve brother, tel me thanne thy name,'
1445 Quod this somonour.   In this meene while
This yeman gan a litel for to smyle.
    'Brother,' quod he, 'wiltow that I thee telle?
I am a feend; my dwellyng is in helle,   *devil*
And heere I ryde aboute my purchasyng,
1450 To wite wher men wol yeve me any thyng.   *find out*
My purchas is th'effect of al my rente.
Looke how thou rydest for the same entente,
To wynne good, thou rekkest nevere how;   *care*
Right so fare I, for ryde wolde I now
1455 Unto the worldes ende for a preye.'
    'A!' quod this somonour, '*benedicite!* what   *bless us!*
        sey ye?
I wende ye were a yeman trewely.
Ye han a mannes shap as wel as I;
Han ye thanne determinat   *definite*
1460 In helle, ther ye been in youre estat?'
    'Nay, certeinly,' quod he, 'ther have we noon;
But whan us liketh, we kan take us oon,   *we like*
Or elles make yow seme we been shape
Somtyme lyk a man, or lyk an ape,
1465 Or lyk an angel kan I ryde or go.
It is no wonder thyng thogh it be so;
A lowsy jogelour kan deceyve thee,
And pardee, yet kan I moore craft than he.'

1435-6 I'm ready to take anything, God knows, if it's not too heavy
    or too hot to hold. (A proverbial expression.)
1439-40 If it weren't for my extortion I couldn't make a living, and my
    confessor is not going to hear about these tricks.
1441 I know no pity or remorse.
1442 I curse all father-confessors.
1449 *purchasyng*, illegal acquisition of property.
1451 My illegal gains are the main part of my income. (Cf. I. 256.)
1454 I behave in just the same way.
1460 Where you are in your normal condition.
1463 Or else make it seem to you we are shaped.
1468 I have more skill than he has.

'Why,' quod this somonour, 'ryde ye thanne or goon
1470 In sondry shap, and nat alwey in oon?'   *various shapes*
'For we,' quod he, 'wol us swiche formes make
As moost able is oure preyes for to take.'   *suitable*
'What maketh yow to han al this labour?'
'Ful many a cause, leeve sire somonour,'
1475 Seyde this feend, 'but alle thyng hath tyme.
The day is short, and it is passed pryme,
And yet ne wan I nothyng in this day.   *won*
I wol entende to wynnyng, if I may,   *attend*
And nat entende oure wittes to declare.
1480 For, brother myn, thy wit is al to bare
To understonde, althogh I tolde hem thee.
But, for thou axest why labouren we—
For somtyme we been Goddes instrumentz,
And meenes to doon his comandementz,
1485 Whan that hym list, upon his creatures,   *it pleases Him*
In divers art and in diverse figures.
Withouten hym we have no myght, certayn,
If that hym list to stonden ther-agayn.   *to be opposed*
And somtyme, at oure prayere, han we leve   *permission*
1490 Oonly the body and nat the soule greve;
Witnesse on Job, whom that we diden wo.
And somtyme han we myght of bothe two,
This is to seyn, of soule and body eke.   *also*
And somtyme be we suffred for to seke
1495 Upon a man, and doon his soule unreste,
And nat his body, and al is for the beste.
Whan he withstandeth oure temptacioun,
It is a cause of his savacioun,   *salvation*
Al be it that it was nat oure entente   *although*
1500 He sholde be sauf, but that we wolde hym hente.   *safe; seize*
And somtyme be we servant unto man,
As to the erchebisshop Seint Dunstan,
And to the apostles servant eek was I.'
'Yet tel me,' quod the somonour, 'feithfully,
1505 Make ye yow newe bodies thus alway
Of elementz?'   The feend answerde, 'Nay.
Somtyme we feyne, and somtyme we aryse   *dissemble*
With dede bodyes, in ful sondry wyse,
And speke as renably and faire and wel   *fluently*
1510 As to the Phitonissa dide Samuel.

1475 But there is a time for everything.
1476 *pryme,* 9 a.m.
1479 And not to telling you all we know.
1486 In different employments and in different shapes.
1494-5 We are allowed to harass a man.
1506 *elementz.*   See I. 420.
1510 *Phitonissa,* Pythoness, i.e. the witch of Endor (1 Sam. xxviii. 8-25).

(And yet wol som men seye it was nat he;
I do no fors of youre dyvynytee.)   *care nothing for*
But o thyng warne I thee, I wol nat jape,—   *joke*
Thou wolt algates wite how we been shape;
1515 Thou shalt herafterward, my brother deere,
Come there the nedeth nat of me to leere.   *learn*
For thou shalt, by thyn owene experience,
Konne in a chayer rede of this sentence
Bet than Virgile, while he was on lyve,
1520 Or Dant also.   Now lat us ryde blyve,   *quickly*
For I wole holde compaignye with thee
Til it be so that thou forsake me.'
     'Nay,' quod this somonour, 'that shal nat bityde!   *happen*
I am a yeman, knowen is ful wyde;
1525 My trouthe wol I holde, as in this cas.   *promise*
For though thou were the devel Sathanas,
My trouthe wol I holde to my brother,
As I am sworn, and ech of us til oother,   *to*
For to be trewe brother in this cas;
1530 And bothe we goon abouten oure purchas.
Taak thou thy part, what that men wol thee yive,   *share*
And I shal myn; thus may we bothe lyve.
And if that any of us have moore than oother,
Lat hym be trewe, and parte it with his brother.'   *share*
1535   'I graunte,' quod the devel, 'by my fey.'   *agree; faith*
And with that word they ryden forth hir wey.
And right at the entryng of the townes ende,
To which this somonour shoop hym for to   *intended to*
     wende,   *go*
They saugh a cart that charged was with hey,   *saw*
1540 Which that a cartere droof forth in his wey.
Deep was the wey, for which the carte stood.
The cartere smoot, and cryde as he were wood,
'Hayt, Brok! hayt, Scot! what spare ye for the stones?
The feend,' quod he, 'yow fecche, body and bones,
1545 As ferforthly as evere were ye foled,
So muche wo as I have with yow tholed!   *suffered*
The devel have al, bothe hors and cart and hey!'
     This somonour seyde, 'Heere shal we have a pley.'

1514 You will in any case find out how we are made.
1518 Be able to lecture like a professor on this subject.
1519-20 The allusion is to Virgil's *Aeneid*, vi, and to Dante's *Inferno*.
1537 And just as they were entering the outskirts of the town.
1541 The road was deep in mud (or grit), for which reason the cart
     stuck fast.
1542 The carter lashed his horses, and shouted at them like a madman.
1543 *Hayt*, gee up; *what spare ye for the stones.* why do you let the
     stones stop you?
1545 As sure as ever you were foaled.

And neer the feend he drough, as noght ne were,
1550 Ful prively, and rowned in his ere: *whispered*
'Herkne, my brother, herkne, by thy feith!
Herestow nat how that the cartere seith?
Hent it anon, for he hath yeve it thee,   *seize; given*
Bothe hey and cart, and eek his caples thre.'   *horses*
1555 'Nay,' quod the devel, 'God woot, never a deel! *not at all*
It is nat his entente, trust me weel.
Axe hym thyself, if thou nat trowest me;   *ask*
Or elles stynt a while, and thou shalt see.'   *stop*
    This cartere thakketh his hors upon the   *smacks*
        croupe,   *croup*
1560 And they bigonne to drawen and to stoupe.   *bend*
'Heyt! now,' quod he, 'ther Jhesu Crist yow blesse,
And al his handwerk, bothe moore and lesse!
That was wel twight, myn owene lyard boy.
I pray God save thee, and Seinte Loy!
1565 Now is my cart out of the slow, pardee!'   *slough*
    'Lo, brother,' quod the feend, 'what tolde I thee?
Heere may ye se, myn owene deere brother,
The carl spak oo thing, but he thoghte another.   *fellow*
Lat us go forth abouten oure viage;   *journey*
1570 Heere wynne I nothyng upon cariage.'
    Whan that they coomen somwhat out of towne,
This somonour to his brother gan to rowne:
'Brother,' quod he, 'heere woneth an old   *lives*
        rebekke,   *woman*
That hadde almoost as lief to lese hire nekke
1575 As for to yeve a peny of hir good.
I wole han twelf pens, though that she be wood,   *mad*
Or I wol sompne hire unto oure office;   *summon*
And yet, God woot, of hire knowe I no vice.
But for thou kanst nat, as in this contree,
1580 Wynne thy cost, taak heer ensample of me.' *expenses; example*
    This somonour clappeth at the wydwes gate.   *knocks*
'Com out,' quod he, 'thou olde virytrate!   *hag*
I trowe thou hast som frere or preest with thee.'   *friar*
    'Who clappeth?' seyde this wyf, '*benedicitee!*
1585 God save you, sire, what is youre sweete wille?'
    'I have,' quod he, 'of somonce here a bille;

1549 He drew closer to the devil, as if nothing were the matter.
1561–2 Now may Jesu Christ bless you and all His creatures, great
    and small.
1563 That was well pulled, my own grey rascal.
1564 *Seinte Loy,* St Eligius, invoked here as the patron of carters.
1570 I've gained nothing here by giving up my claim to the cart and
    team. (Cf. X. 2047–8.)
1574 Who would almost as soon lose her head (lit. neck).

Up peyne of cursyng, looke that thou be
To-morn bifore the erchedeknes knee,
T'answere to the court of certeyn thynges.'
1590 'Now, Lord,' quod she, 'Crist Jhesu, kyng of kynges,
So wisely helpe me, as I ne may.
I have been syk, and that ful many a day.   *ill*
I may nat go so fer,' quod she, 'ne ryde,
But I be deed, so priketh it in my syde.
1595 May I nat axe a libel, sire somonour,
And answere there by my procuratour   *attorney*
To swich thyng as men wole opposen me?'   *lay to my charge*
      'Yis,' quod this somonour, 'pay anon, lat se,
Twelf pens to me, and I wol thee acquite.
1600 I shal no profit han therby but lite;   *have; little*
My maister hath the profit, and nat I.
Com of, and lat me ryden hastily;   *come along*
Yif me twelf pens, I may no lenger tarye.'   *give*
      'Twelf pens!' quod she, 'now, lady Seinte Marie
1605 So wisly help me out of care and synne,
This wyde world thogh that I sholde wynne,
Ne have I nat twelf pens withinne myn hoold.
Ye knowen wel that I am povre and oold;   *poor*
Kithe youre almesse on me povre wrecche.'
1610 'Nay thanne,' quod he, 'the foule feend me fecche
If I th'excuse, though thou shul be spilt!'   *ruined*
      'Allas!' quod she, 'God woot, I have no gilt.'
      'Pay me,' quod he, 'or by the sweete seinte Anne,
As I wol bere awey thy newe panne
1615 For dette which thou owest me of old.
Whan that thou madest thyn housbonde cokewold,   *cuckold*
I payde at hoom for thy correccioun.'
      'Thou lixt!' quod she, 'by my savacioun,   *lie*
Ne was I nevere er now, wydwe ne wyf,   *before*
1620 Somoned unto youre court in al my lyf;
Ne nevere I nas but of my body trewe!
Unto the devel blak and rough of hewe
Yeve I thy body and my panne also!'
      And whan the devel herde hire cursen so
1625 Upon hir knees, he seyde in this manere,
'Now, Mabely, myn owene mooder deere,
Is this youre wyl in ernest that ye seye?'

1590-1 So help me Jesus Christ . . . I swear I cannot come.
1594 Without dying, my side hurts me so.
1595 May I not ask for a copy of the indictment.
1604-7 Even as I hope St Mary will rescue me from sorrow and sin, I
    swear I haven't got twelve pennies in my possession, not even to win
    this wide world.
1609 Show me your charity, poor wretch that I am.
1617 I paid your fine for you.

'The devel,' quod she, 'so fecche hym er he deye,
And panne and al, but he wol hym repente!'   *unless*
1630 'Nay, olde stot, that is nat myn entente,'   *cow*
Quod this somonour, 'for to repente me
For any thyng that I have had of thee.
I wolde I hadde thy smok and every clooth!'
'Now, brother,' quod the devel, 'be nat wrooth;
1635 Thy body and this panne been myne by right.   *are*
Thou shalt with me to helle yet to-nyght,
Where thou shalt knowen of oure privetee   *private affairs*
Moore than a maister of dyvynytee.'
And with that word this foule feend hym hente;
1640 Body and soule he with the devel wente
Where as that somonours han hir heritage.
And God, that maked after his ymage
Mankynde, save and gyde us, alle and some,
And leve thise somonours goode men bicome!   *grant*
1645   Lordynges, I koude han toold yow, quod this Frere,
Hadde I had leyser for this Somnour heere,
After the text of Crist, Poul, and John,
And of oure othere doctours many oon,
Swiche peynes that youre hertes myghte agryse,   *tremble*
1650 Al be it so no tonge may it devyse,
Thogh that I myghte a thousand wynter telle
The peynes of thilke cursed hous of helle.
But for to kepe us fro that cursed place,   *protect ourselves*
Waketh, and preyeth Jhesu for his grace   *be watchful*
1655 So kepe us fro the temptour Sathanas.
Herketh this word! beth war, as in this cas: *beware*
'The leoun sit in his awayt alway
To sle the innocent, if that he may.'
Disposeth ay youre hertes to withstonde
1660 The feend, that yow wolde make thral and bonde.
He may nat tempte yow over youre myght,   *beyond*
For Crist wol be youre champion and knyght.
And prayeth that thise somonours hem repente
Of hir mysdedes, er that the feend hem hente!   *seize*

HEERE ENDETH THE FRERES TALE

1646 If this Summoner here had given me the chance.
1650 Although no tongue can describe it properly.
1657 The lion always sits in wait (Ps. x. 8–9).

THE SUMMONER'S PROLOGUE

THE PROLOGE OF THE SOMONOURS TALE

1665 THIS Somonour in his styropes hye stood;
Upon this Frere his herte was so wood   *furious*
That lyk an aspen leef he quook for ire.   *trembled*
  'Lordynges,' quod he, 'but o thyng I desire;   *sirs; one*
I yow biseke that, of youre curteisye,   *beseech*
1670 Syn ye han herd this false Frere lye,   *since*
As suffreth me I may my tale telle.
This Frere bosteth that he knoweth helle,
And God it woot, that it is litel wonder;   *knows*
Freres and feendes been but lyte asonder.
1675 For, pardee, ye han ofte tyme herd telle   *indeed*
How that a frere ravysshed was to helle
In spirit ones by a visioun;
And as an angel ladde hym up and doun,   *led*
To shewen hym the peynes that ther were,   *torments*
1680 In al the place saugh he nat a frere;   *saw*
Of oother folk he saugh ynowe in wo.
Unto this angel spak the frere tho: *then*
  "Now, sire," quod he, "han freres swich a grace   *have*
That noon of hem shal come to this place?"
1685   "Yis," quod this angel, "many a millioun!"
And unto Sathanas he ladde hym doun.
"And now hath Sathanas," seith he, "a tayl
Brodder than of a carryk is the sayl.   *barge*
Hold up thy tayl, thou Sathanas!" quod he;
1690 "Shewe forth thyn ers, and lat the frere se   *arse*
Where is the nest of freres in this place!"
And er that half a furlong wey of space,
Right so as bees out swarmen from an hyve,
Out of the develes ers ther gonne dryve   *rushed*
1695 Twenty thousand freres on a route,   *mob*
And thurghout helle swarmed al aboute,
And comen agayn as faste as they may gon,   *go*
And in his ers they crepten everychon.   *each one*

1671 You will allow me to tell my tale.
1674 Friars and devils are not so far apart.
1676–7 How once in a vision a friar was carried off in spirit to hell.
1681 He saw lots of other people living in misery.
1692 And in a few seconds.

He clapte his tayl agayn and lay ful stille.   *clapped to*
1700 This frere, whan he looked hadde his fille
Upon the tormentz of this sory place,
His spirit God restored, of his grace,
Unto his body agayn, and he awook.
But natheles, for fere yet he quook,
1705 So was the develes ers ay in his mynde,
That is his heritage of verray kynde.
God save yow alle, save this cursed Frere!
My prologe wol I ende in this manere.'

THE SUMMONER'S TALE

HEERE BIGYNNETH THE SOMONOUR HIS TALE

LORDYNGES, ther is in Yorkshire, as I gesse,
1710 A mersshy contree called Holdernesse,   *district*
In which ther wente a lymytour aboute,
To preche, and eek to begge, it is no doute.   *without doubt*
And so bifel that on a day this frere
Hadde preched at a chirche in his manere,   *usual manner*
1715 And specially, aboven every thyng,
Excited he the peple in his prechyng
To trentals, and to yeve, for Goddes sake,
Wherwith men myghte hooly houses make,
Ther as divine servyce is honoured,   *where*
1720 Nat ther as it is wasted and devoured,
Ne ther it nedeth nat for to be yive,
As to possessioners, that mowen lyve,   *can*

1706 As being the natural heritage of his kind.
1711 *lymytour.* See l. 209.
1717 To pay for trentals (i.e. offices of thirty masses sung for the benefit
of souls in purgatory).
1718 Money with which friars could build their holy houses.
1721 Nor where there is no need for giving.
1722 *possessioners,* the monastic orders and beneficed clergy, as distinct
from the friars, who were supposed to have no endowments.

Thanked be God, in wele and habundaunce.   *prosperity*
'Trentals,' seyde he, 'deliveren fro penaunce
1725 Hir freendes soules, as wel olde as   *both old and young*
    yonge,—
Ye, whan that they been hastily ysonge,
Nat for to holde a preest joly and gay—
He syngeth nat but o masse in a day.
Delivereth out,' quod he, 'anon the soules!
1730 Ful hard it is with flesshook or with oules   *awls*
To been yclawed, or to brenne or bake.   *burn*
Now spede yow hastily, for Cristes sake!'
And whan this frere had seyd al his entente,
With *qui cum patre* forth his wey he wente.
1735   Whan folk in chirche had yeve him what
    hem leste,   *they would*
He wente his wey, no lenger wolde he reste.
With scrippe and tipped staf, ytukked hye,
In every hous he gan to poure and prye,   *peer*
And beggeth mele and chese, or elles corn.   *cheese*
1740 His felawe hadde a staf tipped with horn,   *companion*
A peyre of tables al of yvory,
And a poyntel polysshed fetisly,
And wroot the names alwey, as he stood,
Of alle folk that yaf hym any good,   *goods*
1745 Ascaunces that he wolde for hem preye.   *as if*
'Yif us a busshel whete, malt, or reye,   *rye*
A Goddes kechyl or, a trype of chese,
Or elles what yow lyst, we may nat chese;   *please; choose*
A Goddes halfpeny, or a masse peny,
1750 Or yif us of youre brawn, if ye have eny;
A dagon of youre blanket, leeve dame,   *piece; dear lady*
Oure suster deere,—lo! heere I write youre
    name,—
Bacon or beef, or swich thyng as ye fynde.   *such*
A sturdy harlot wente ay hem bihynde,   *fellow*

1726 Yes, when they're quickly sung (i.e. when all thirty masses are sung in one day by a friar), and not at the rate of one a day by some easy-going priest.
1729 Release those souls without delay! (The friar is still exhorting his congregation to buy trentals for their friends.)
1734 *qui cum patre*, a part of the formula used for ending prayers and sermons: 'who with the Father and the Holy Spirit lives and reigns for ever and ever.'
1737 *scrippe*, a bag for alms; *ytukked hye*, i.e. with his gown tucked up high under his girdle.
1741-2 A set of ivory writing tablets, and an exquisitely polished stylus. (The ivory was covered with wax, and the writing done with a sharp-pointed instrument.)
1747 A little cake of God, or a small piece of cheese.
1749 *masse peny*, an offering for a mass.

1755 That was hir hostes man, and bar a sak,
     And what men yaf hem, leyde it on his bak.   *whatever*
     And whan that he was out at dore, anon
     He planed awey the names everichon   *smoothed*
     That he biforn had writen in his tables;
1760 He served hem with nyfles and with fables.   *silly stories*
        'Nay, ther thou lixt, thou Somonour!' quod the Frere. *lie*
        'Pees,' quod oure Hoost, 'for Cristes mooder deere! *peace*
     Tel forth thy tale, and spare it nat at al.'
        'So thryve I,' quod this Somonour, 'so I shal!'
1765   So longe he wente, hous by hous, til he   *on he went*
     Cam til an hous ther he was wont to be   *to*
     Refresshed moore than in an hundred placis.
     Syk lay the goode man whos that the place is;
     Bedrede upon a couche lowe he lay.   *bedridden*
1770 '*Deus hic!*' quod he, 'o Thomas, freend,   *God be here*
        good day!'
     Seyde this frere, curteisly and softe.   *softly*
     'Thomas,' quod he, 'God yelde yow! ful ofte   *repay*
     Have I upon this bench faren ful weel;   *fared*
     Heere have I eten many a myrie meel.'
1775 And fro the bench he droof awey the cat,   *drove*
     And leyde adoun his potente and his hat,   *staff*
     And eek his scrippe, and sette hym softe adoun.
     His felawe was go walked into toun
     Forth with his knave, into that hostelrye   *servant; inn*
1780 Where as he shoop hym thilke nyght to lye.
        'O deere maister,' quod this sike man,
     'How han ye fare sith that March bigan?   *since*
     I saugh yow noght this fourtenyght or moore.'
     'God woot,' quod he, 'laboured I have full soore,   *hard*
1785 And specially, for thy savacion
     Have I seyd many a precious orison,
     And for oure othere freendes, God hem blesse!
     I have to day been at youre chirche at messe,   *mass*
     And seyd a sermon after my symple wit,   *according to*
1790 Nat al after the text of hooly writ;
     For it is hard to yow, as I suppose,
     And therfore wol I teche yow al the glose.
     Glosynge is a glorious thyng, certeyn,   *certainly*
     For lettre sleeth, so as we clerkes seyn.   *clerics*
1795 There have I taught hem to be charitable,

1755 *hostes man*, servant to the guests at the friars' convent.
1764 As I hope to prosper.
1777 And snugly settled down.
1778 His companion had gone walking.
1780 Where he planned to spend the night.
1792 *glose*, gloss, interpretation (of the words of the Bible).
1794 2 Cor. iii. 6.

And spende hir good ther it is resonable; *goods; where*
And there I saugh oure dame,—a! where is she?'
 'Yond in the yerd I trowe that she be,'
Seyde this man, 'and she wol come anon.'
1800 'Ey, maister, welcome be ye, by Seint John!'
Seyde this wyf, 'how fare ye, hertely?'
 The frere ariseth up ful curteisly,
And hire embraceth in his armes narwe, *closely*
And kiste hire sweete, and chirketh as a sparwe *chirps*
1805 With his lyppes: 'Dame,' quod he, 'right weel,
As he that is youre servant every deel,
Thanked be God, that yow yaf soule and lyf!
Yet saugh I nat this day so fair a wyf
In al the chirche, God so save me!'
1810 'Ye, God amende defautes, sire,' quod *correct my faults*
  she.
'Algates, welcome be ye, by my fey!'
'Graunt mercy, dame, this have I founde alwey.
But of youre grete goodnesse, by youre leve,
I wolde prey yow that ye nat yow greve,
1815 I wole with Thomas speke a litel throwe. *while*
Thise curatz been ful necligent and slowe *parish priests*
To grope tendrely a conscience *examine*
In shrift; in prechyng is my diligence, *confession*
And studie in Petres wordes and in Poules.
1820 I walke, and fisshe Cristen mennes soules,
To yelden Jhesu Crist his propre rente;
To sprede his word is set al myn entente.'
 'Now, by youre leve, o deere sire,' quod she,
'Chideth him weel, for seinte Trinitee! *by the holy*
1825 He is as angry as a pissemyre, *ant*
Though that he have al that he kan desire,
Though I hym wrye a-nyght and make hym *cover; at night*
  warm,
And over hym leye my leg outher myn arm, *or*
He groneth lyk oure boor, lith in oure sty.
1830 Oother desport right noon of hym have I; *sport*
I may nat plese hym in no maner cas.' *in any way*
 'O Thomas, *je vous dy*, Thomas! Thomas!

1797 *oure dame*, i.e. the mistress of the house.
1801 How are you now, really?
1806 As one who is your servant in all things.
1811 At any rate you're welcome, upon my word.
1814 I beg you not to be offended.
1819–20 Preaching is my main care, and studying the words of Peter
 and Paul.
1821 In order to give Christ His proper due.
1822 My whole mind is devoted to the task of spreading His word.
1829 He grunts like our boar, lying in its sty.
1832 I tell you (a French phrase in familiar use, like that in 1838).

208 THE CANTERBURY TALES

This maketh the feend; this moste ben amended.
Ire is a thyng that hye God defended,   *anger; forbade*
1835 And therof wol I speke a word or two.'
      'Now, maister,' quod the wyf, 'er that I go,
What wol ye dyne?   I wol go theraboute.'
      'Now, dame,' quod he, 'now *je vous dy sanz doute*,
Have I nat of a capon but the lyvere,
1840 And of youre softe breed nat but a shyvere,   *sliver*
And after that a rosted pigges heed—
But that I nolde no beest for me were deed—
Thanne hadde I with yow hoomly suffisaunce.
I am a man of litel sustenaunce;
1845 My spirit hath his fostryng in the Bible.
The body is ay so redy and penyble
To wake, that my stomak is destroyed.
I prey yow, dame, ye be nat anoyed,
Though I so freendly yow my conseil shewe.
1850 By God! I wolde nat telle it but a fewe.'
      'Now, sire,' quod she, 'but o word er I go.
My child is deed withinne thise wykes two,
Soone after that ye wente out of this toun.'
      'His deeth saugh I by revelacioun,'
1855 Seide this frere, 'at hoom in oure dortour.   *dormitory*
I dar wel seyn that, er that half an hour   *less than*
After his deeth, I saugh hym born to blisse
In myn avision, so God me wisse!   *vision; guide*
So dide oure sexteyn and oure fermerer,
1860 That han been trewe freres fifty yeer;   *years*
They may now—God be thanked of his loone!—   *grace*
Maken hir jubilee and walke allone.
And up I roos, and al oure covent eke,   *arose; convent*
With many a teere trillyng on my cheke,   *flowing*
1865 Withouten noyse or claterynge or belles;
Te Deum was oure song, and nothyng elles,
Save that to Crist I seyde an orison,
Thankynge hym of his revelacion.   *for*

1833 This is the devil's work; this must be corrected.
1837 I will go and see about it.
1838 I tell you without doubt.
1839 If I could have just a capon's liver.
1842 Though I shouldn't like a beast to die for me.
1843 Then I'd have sufficient homely fare.
1844 I'm a man who needs but little food.
1845 My spirit gets its nourishment from the Bible.
1846 My body is so inured to keeping vigil.
1849 Though I tell you these intimate details in such a friendly fashion.
1859 *sexteyn*, sacristan; *fermerer*, friar in charge of the infirmary.
1862 Celebrate their jubilee and walk alone. (After serving fifty years in the convent, friars obtained the privilege of going about alone, instead of with a companion.)

For, sire and dame, trusteth me right weel,
1870 Oure orisons been moore effectueel,
And moore we seen of Cristes secree thynges,   *secret*
Than burel folk, although they weren kynges.   *lay*
We lyve in poverte and in abstinence,
And burell folk in richesse and despence   *riches; expense*
1875 Of mete and drynke, and in hir foul delit.   *food; delight*
We han this worldes lust al in despit.
Lazar and Dives lyveden diversly,   *in different ways*
And divers gerdon hadden they therby.   *reward*
Whoso wol preye, he moot faste and be clene,
1880 And fatte his soule, and make his body lene.   *fatten*
We fare as seith th'apostle; clooth and foode
Suffisen us, though they be nat ful goode.   *very*
The clennesse and the fastynge of us freres
Maketh that Crist accepteth oure preyeres.

1885   Lo, Moyses fourty dayes and fourty nyght
Fasted, er that the heighe God of myght
Spak with hym in the mountayne of Synay.
With empty wombe, fastynge many a day,
Receyved he the lawe that was writen
1890 With Goddes fynger; and Elye, wel ye witen,   *Elijah; know*
In mount Oreb, er he hadde any speche
With hye God, that is oure lyves leche,
He fasted longe, and was in contemplaunce.

   Aaron, that hadde the temple in governaunce,   *charge*
1895 And eek the othere preestes everichon,
Into the temple whan they sholde gon   *had to go*
To preye for the peple, and do servyse,   *hold a service*
They nolden drynken in no maner wyse
No drynke which that myghte hem dronke make,
1900 But there in abstinence preye and wake,   *keep vigil*
Lest that they deyden.   Taak heede what I seye!   *should die*
But they be sobre that for the peple preye,   *unless*
War that I seye—namoore, for it suffiseth.
Oure Lord Jhesu, as hooly writ devyseth,   *relates*
1905 Yaf us ensample of fastynge and preyeres.
Therfore we mendynantz, we sely freres,   *mendicants; simple*
Been wedded to poverte and continence,
To charite, humblesse, and abstinence,
To persecucioun for rightwisnesse,   *righteousness*
1910 To wepynge, misericorde, and clennesse.   *mercy; purity*

1876 We have nothing but contempt for worldly pleasures.
1879 Whoever would pray must fast and be pure.
1881 1 Tim. vi. 8.
1892 The physician of our souls.
1893 And dwelt in contemplation.
1898 They would on no account drink.
1903 Take note of what I say—but no more, for this will do.

And therfore may ye se that oure preyeres—
I speke of us, we mendynantz, we freres—
Been to the hye God moore acceptable
Than youres, with youre feestes at the table.
1915 Fro Paradys first, if I shal nat lye,
Was man out chaced for his glotonye;   *driven*
And chaast was man in Paradys, certeyn.   *chaste*
  But herkne now, Thomas, what I shal seyn.
I ne have no text of it, as I suppose,
1920 But I shal fynde it in a maner glose,
That specially oure sweete Lord Jhesus
Spak this by freres, whan he seyde thus: *about*
  "Blessed be they that povere in spirit been."
And so forth al the gospel may ye seen,
1925 Wher it be likker oure professioun,
Or hirs that swymmen in possessioun.
Fy on hire pompe and on hire glotonye!
And for hir lewednesse I hem diffye.   *ignorance; despise*
  Me thynketh they been lyk Jovinyan,
1930 Fat as a whale, and walkynge as a swan,
Al vinolent as botel in the spence.
Hir preyere is of ful greet reverence,
Whan they for soules seye the psalm of Davit;   *David*
Lo, "buf!" they seye, "*cor meum eructavit!*"
1935 Who folweth Cristes gospel and his foore,   *footsteps*
But we that humble been, and chaast, and poore,
Werkeris of Goddes word, nat auditours?   *doers*
Therfore, right as an hauk up at a sours
Up springeth into th'eir, right so prayeres   *the air*
1940 Of charitable and chaste bisy freres
Maken hir sours to Goddes eres two.   *soar up*
Thomas! Thomas! so moote I ryde or go,
And by that lord that clepid is Seint Yve,   *called*
Nere thou oure brother, sholdestou nat thryve.

1920 In a kind of gloss (on Matt. v. 3).
1924–5 And similarly with the rest of the gospel you can see whether it
  is closer to our profession.
1926 Or to theirs that swim in possessions. (An allusion to 'possessioners'; see 1722.)
1929 This refers to the treatise of St Jerome against the heretic
  Jovinian.
1931 As full of wine as a bottle in the buttery.
1934 *buf*, imitating a belch; *cor meum eructavit* (*verbum bonum*) are the
  opening words of Ps. xliv in the Vulgate, where the corresponding
  psalm (xlv) in A.V. has 'My heart is inditing a good matter.' The
  Summoner's friar is playing on the literal and figurative meanings of
  eructavit.
1938 With soaring flight.
1942 Upon my life (lit. so may I ride or walk).
1944 If you weren't our brother, you would not prosper.

1945 In our chapitre praye we day and nyght
     To Crist, that he thee sende heele and myght   *health; strength*
     Thy body for to weelden hastily.'
         'God woot,' quod he, 'no thyng therof feele I!
     As help me Crist, as I in fewe yeres,
1950 Have spent upon diverse manere freres
     Ful many a pound; yet fare I never the bet.   *better*
     Certeyn, my good have I almoost biset.   *used up*
     Farwel, my gold, for it is al ago!'   *gone*
         The frere answerde, 'O Thomas, dostow so?
1955 What nedeth yow diverse freres seche?
     What nedeth hym that hath a parfit leche   *physician*
     To sechen othere leches in the toun?
     Youre inconstance is youre confusioun.   *ruin*
     Holde ye thanne me, or elles oure covent,   *consider*
1960 To praye for yow been insufficient?
     Thomas, that jape nys nat worth a myte.
     Youre maladye is for we han to lyte.
     A! yif that covent half a quarter otes!   *oats*
     A! yif that covent foure and twenty grotes!
1965 A! yif that frere a peny, and lat hym go!
     Nay, nay, Thomas, it may no thyng be so!
     What is a ferthyng worth parted in twelve?
     Lo, ech thyng that is oned in himselve   *united*
     Is moore strong than whan it is toscatered.   *scattered abroad*
1970 Thomas, of me thou shalt nat been yflatered;   *by*
     Thou woldest han oure labour al for noght.
     The hye God, that al this world hath wroght,
     Seith that the werkman worthy is his hyre.
     Thomas, noght of youre tresor I desire
1975 As for myself, but that al oure covent
     To preye for yow is ay so diligent,   *always*
     And for to buylden Cristes owene chirche.   *build*
     Thomas, if ye wol lernen for to wirche,
     Of buyldynge up of chirches may ye fynde,
1980 If it be good, in Thomas lyf of Inde.
     Ye lye heere ful of anger and of ire,
     With which the devel set youre herte afyre,   *sets; on fire*
     And chiden heere the sely innocent,   *simple*
     Youre wyf, that is so meke and pacient.

1947 Quickly to have the full use of your body.
1950 On various kinds of friars.
1961 Such deceitful behaviour is not worth a mite.
1962 You're ill because we get too little.
1966 It's not nearly good enough.
1975 But because all our convent.
1978 If you want to learn to do (what is good).
1979–80 You can find out in the life of St Thomas of India whether the
       building of churches is a good thing.

1985 And therfore, Thomas, trowe me if thee leste,   *you like*
    Ne stryve nat with thy wyf, as for thy beste;
    And ber this word awey now, by the feith,
    Touchynge swich thyng, lo, what the wise seith:
    "Withinne thyn hous ne be thou no leon;   *lion*
1990 To thy subgitz do noon oppression,   *servants*
    Ne make thyne aqueyntances nat to flee."
    And, Thomas, yet eft-soones I charge thee,   *once again*
    Be war from Ire that in thy bosom slepeth;   *of*
    War fro the serpent that so slily crepeth
1995 Under the gras, and styngeth subtilly.   *craftily*
    Be war, my sone, and herkne paciently,
    That twenty thousand men han lost hir lyves
    For stryvyng with hir lemmans and hir wyves.   *sweethearts*
    Now sith ye han so hooly meke a wyf,   *wholly*
2000 What nedeth yow, Thomas, to maken stryf?
    Ther nys, ywys, no serpent so cruel,   *truly*
    Whan man tret on his tayl, ne half so fel,   *treads; deadly*
    As womman is, whan she hath caught an ire;
    Vengeance is thanne al that they desire.
2005 Ire is a synne, oon of the grete of sevene,
    Abhomynable unto the God of hevene;
    And to hymself it is destruccion.
    This every lewed viker or person
    Kan seye, how ire engendreth homycide.
2010 Ire is, in sooth, executour of pryde.   *truth*
    I koude of ire seye so muche sorwe,
    My tale sholde laste til to-morwe.
    And therfore preye I God, bothe day and nyght,
    An irous man, God sende hym litel myght!   *angry; power*
2015 It is greet harm and certes greet pitee
    To sette an irous man in heigh degree.
      Whilom ther was an irous potestat,   *potentate*
    As seith Senek, that, durynge his estaat,
    Upon a day out ryden knyghtes two,
2020 And as Fortune wolde that it were so,   *willed it*
    That oon of hem cam hoom, that oother noght.
    Anon the knyght bifore the juge is broght,
    That seyde thus, "Thou hast thy felawe slayn,   *companion*
    For which I deme thee to the deeth, certayn."   *condemn*

1986 If you know what's good for you.
1987–8 Bear in mind what the wise man has said on this subject.
1989–91 Ecclus. iv. 30.
2003 When anger gets the better of her.
2005 One of the chief of the seven deadly sins.
2007 And to the angry man himself.
2008 Every ignorant vicar or parson.
2018 As Seneca says, during whose term of office.
2021 One of them came home, the other not.

2025 And to another knyght comanded he,
　　　"Go lede hym to the deeth, I charge thee."
　　　And happed, as they wente by the weye   *it happened*
　　　Toward the place ther he sholde deye,   *was to die*
　　　The knyght cam which men wenden had be deed.   *supposed*
2030 Thanne thoughte they it were the beste reed   *plan*
　　　To lede hem bothe to the juge agayn.
　　　They seiden, "Lord, the knyght ne hath nat slayn
　　　His felawe; heere he standeth hool alyve."   *alive and well*
　　　"Ye shul be deed," quod he, "so moot I thryve!
2035 That is to seyn, bothe oon, and two, and thre!"
　　　And to the firste knyght right thus spak he,
　　　"I dampned thee; thou most algate be deed.
　　　And thou also most nedes lese thyn heed,   *lose*
　　　For thou art cause why thy felawe deyth."   *dies*
2040 And to the thridde knyght right thus he seith,
　　　"Thou hast nat doon that I comanded thee."   *what*
　　　And thus he dide doon sleen hem alle thre.
　　　　　Irous Cambises was eek dronkelewe,
　　　And ay delited hym to been a shrewe.
2045 And so bifel, a lord of his meynee,   *retinue*
　　　That loved vertuous moralitee,
　　　Seyde on a day bitwix hem two right thus:
　　　"A lord is lost, if he be vicius;
　　　And dronkenesse is eek a foul record
2050 Of any man, and namely in a lord.   *especially*
　　　Ther is ful many an eye and many an ere
　　　Awaityng on a lord, and he noot where.   *spying; knows not*
　　　For Goddes love, drynk moore attemprely!   *moderately*
　　　Wyn maketh man to lesen wrecchedly   *lose*
2055 His mynde and eek his lymes everichon."
　　　　　"The revers shaltou se," quod he, "anon,
　　　And preve it by thyn owene experience,
　　　That wyn ne dooth to folk no swich offence.   *harm*
　　　Ther is no wyn bireveth me my myght   *robs me of*
2060 Of hand ne foot, ne of myne eyen sight."
　　　And for despit he drank ful muchel moore,
　　　An hondred part, than he hadde don bifoore;   *hundredfold*

2034-5 You shall die . . . as I hope to prosper! All three of you, I
　　　mean.
2037 I condemned you; so you must die in any case.
2042 He had all three of them killed.
2043-4 Wrathful Cambyses was also a drunkard, and always took
　　　delight in being wicked.
2047 One day in private said to him as follows.
2049 A foul thing to report.
2055 His reason and the use of all his limbs.
2056 You'll soon find the opposite is true.
2061 And scornfully he drank a great deal more.

And right anon this irous, cursed wrecche
Leet this knyghtes sone bifore hym fecche,
2065 Comandynge hym he sholde bifore hym stonde.
And sodeynly he took his bowe in honde,
And up the streng he pulled to his ere,
And with an arwe he slow the child right there.
"Now wheither have I a siker hand or noon?"
2070 Quod he; "is al my myght and mynde agon?
Hath wyn bireved me myn eyen sight?"
What sholde I telle th'answere of the knyght?   *why*
His sone was slayn, ther is namoore to seye.
Beth war, therfore, with lordes how ye pleye.
2075 Syngeth *Placebo*, and "I shal, if I kan,"
But if it be unto a povre man.
To a povre man men sholde his vices telle,
But nat to a lord, thogh he sholde go to helle.
    Lo irous Cirus, thilke Percien,
2080 How he destroyed the ryver of Gysen,
For that an hors of his was dreynt   *because; drowned*
          therinne,
Whan that he wente Babiloigne to wynne.   *Babylon*
He made that the ryver was so smal
That wommen myghte wade it over al.
2085 Lo, what seyde he that so wel teche kan?
"Ne be no felawe to an irous man,
Ne with no wood man walke by the weye,   *furious*
Lest thee repente;" I wol no ferther seye.
    Now, Thomas, leeve brother, lef thyn ire;   *dear; leave*
2090 Thou shalt me fynde as just as is a squyre.
Hoold nat the develes knyf ay at thyn herte—
Thyn angre dooth thee al to soore smerte—
But shewe to me al thy confessioun.'
    'Nay,' quod the sike man, 'by Seint Symoun!   *Simon*
2095 I have be shryven this day at my curat.   *by my priest*
I have hym toold hoolly al myn estat;
Nedeth namoore to speken of it,' seith he,
'But if me list, of myn humylitee.'   *unless I wish*

2064 Had this knight's son brought before him.
2068 Slew the noble youth then and there.
2069 Now have I a steady hand or not?
2075 *Placebo*, I will please, taken from Ps. cxiv. 9 in the Vulgate, is
    the first word of an anthem in the office for the dead. 'To sing
    placebo' came to mean 'to flatter' or 'be servile.'
2077 It's all right to tell a poor man of his vices.
2078 Though he is bound for hell.
2085 *he*, i.e. Solomon. (See Prov. xxii. 24–5.)
2090 As exact as a carpenter's square. (He means that he will be
    strictly just to Thomas and impose full penance on him for his sins.)
2092 Your anger makes you suffer all too painfully.
2096 I've told him all about my condition.

'Yif me thanne of thy gold, to make oure cloystre,'
2100 Quod he, 'for many a muscle and many an oystre,
      Whan othere men han ben ful wel at eyse,
      Hath been oure foode, our cloystre for to reyse.
      And yet, God woot, unnethe the   *hardly*
         fundement   *foundation*
      Parfourned is, ne of our pavement   *finished*
2105 Nys nat a tyle yet withinne oure wones.   *dwelling*
      By God! we owen fourty pound for stones.
        Now help, Thomas, for hym that harwed helle!
      For elles moste we oure bookes selle.
      And if yow lakke oure predicacioun,   *preaching*
2110 Thanne goth the world al to destruccioun.
      For whoso wolde us fro this world bireve,   *remove*
      So God me save, Thomas, by youre leve,
      He wolde bireve out of this world the sonne.   *sun*
      For who kan teche and werchen as we konne?   *work*
2115 And that is nat of litel tyme,' quod he,
      'But syn Elye was, or Elise,   *Elijah; Elisha*
      Han freres been, that fynde I of record,   *on*
      In charitee, ythanked be oure Lord!
      Now Thomas, help, for seinte charitee!'
2120 And doun anon he sette hym on his knee.
        This sike man wax wel ny wood for ire;
      He wolde that the frere had been on-fire,
      With his false dissymulacioun.
      'Swich thyng as is in my possessioun,'
2125 Quod he, 'that may I yeve, and noon oother.   *give*
      Ye sey me thus, how that I am youre brother'?'
        'Ye, certes,' quod the frere, 'trusteth weel.
      I took oure dame oure lettre with oure seel.'
        'Now wel,' quod he, 'and somwhat shal I yive
2130 Unto youre hooly covent whil I lyve;
      And in thyn hand thou shalt it have anon,
      On this condicion, and oother noon,
      That thou departe it so, my deere brother,   *divide*
      That every frere have also muche as oother.   *as*
2135 This shaltou swere on thy professioun,   *by*
      Withouten fraude or cavillacioun.'   *cavilling*

2101 Have lived in comfort.
2102 So that we should have money to build our cloister.
2107 By Him who harrowed hell, i.e. Christ.
2115 And this is not a recent thing.
2118 Devoted to works of charity.
2119 In the name of holy charity.
2121 Went nearly mad with rage.
2122 He wanted to consign the friar to the flames.
2128 i.e. the letter of fraternity granted by the friar's convent to Thomas
     and his wife, conferring certain spiritual benefits on them in return
     for gifts of money or property.

216   THE CANTERBURY TALES

'I swere it,' quod this frere, 'by my feith!'
And therwithal his hand in his he leith,   *thereupon; lays*
'Lo, heer my feith; in me shal be no lak.'
2140   'Now thanne, put in thyn hand doun by my bak,'
Seyde this man, 'and grope wel bihynde.
Bynethe my buttok there shaltow fynde
A thyng that I have hyd in pryvetee.'   *for secrecy*
'A!' thoghte this frere, 'that shal go with me!'
2145   And doun his hand he launcheth to the   *pushes*
        clifte,   *(anal) cleft*
In hope for to fynde there a yifte.
And whan this sike man felte this frere
Aboute his tuwel grope there and heere,   *hole*
Amydde his hand he leet the frere a fart.
2150   Ther nys no capul, drawynge in a cart,   *cart-horse*
That myghte have lete a fart of swich a soun.   *sound*
        The frere up stirte as dooth a wood leoun,—   *mad lion*
'A! false cherl,' quod he, 'for Goddes bones!
This hastow for despit doon for the nones.
2155   Thou shalt abye this fart, if that I may!'   *pay dearly*
His meynee, whiche that herden this   *servants*
        affray,   *commotion*
Cam lepynge in and chaced out the frere;
And forth he gooth, with a ful angry cheere,   *look*
And fette his felawe, ther as lay his stoor.
2160   He looked as it were a wilde boor;
He grynte with his teeth, so was he wrooth.
A sturdy paas doun to the court he gooth,
Wher as ther woned a man of greet honour,   *where lived*
To whom that he was alwey confessour.   *always*
2165   This worthy man was lord of that village.
This frere cam as he were in a rage,
Where as this lord sat etyng at his bord;   *table*
Unnethes myghte the frere speke a word,   *hardly*
Til atte laste he seyde, 'God yow see!'   *keep you*
2170   This lord gan looke, and seide,   *looked*
        ' Benedicitee !   *bless us*
What, frere John, what maner world is this?
I se wel that som thyng ther is amys;
Ye looken as the wode were ful of thevys.   *as if; wood*

2139 I give you my word.
2149 Into the friar's hand he released.
2154 You've done this on purpose to insult me.
2159 And fetched his companion, who was looking after their possessions.
2161 He gnashed his teeth, he was so furious.
2162 He strode down to the manor-house.
2166 The friar came raging in.
2171 What sort of world is this, i.e. what's the matter?

Sit doun anon, and tel me what youre grief is,   *grievance*
2175 And it shal been amended, if I may.'
    'I have,' quod he, 'had a despit this day,   *insult*
God yelde yow, adoun in youre village,   *reward*
That in this world is noon so povre a page
That he nolde have abhomynacioun
2180 Of that I have receyved in youre toun.
And yet ne greveth me nothyng so soore,
As that this olde cherl with lokkes hoore   *hoary*
Blasphemed hath oure hooly covent eke.'   *too*
    'Now, maister,' quod this lord, 'I yow biseke,—'
2185   'No maister, sire,' quod he, 'but servitour,   *servant*
Thogh I have had in scole that honour.
God liketh nat that "Raby" men us calle,   *Rabbi*
Neither in market ne in youre large halle.'
    'No fors,' quod he, 'but tel me al youre grief.'   *never mind*
2190   'Sire,' quod this frere, 'an odious meschief   *calamity*
This day bityd is to myn ordre and me,   *befallen*
And so, *per consequens*, to ech degree
Of hooly chirche, God amende it soone!'
    'Sire,' quod the lord, 'ye woot what is   *know*
      to doone.   *be done*
2195 Distempre yow noght, ye be my confessour;   *don't be vexed*
Ye been the salt of the erthe and the savour.
For Goddes love, youre pacience ye holde!   *be patient*
Tel me youre grief'; and he anon hym tolde,
As ye han herd biforn, ye woot wel what.
2200   The lady of the hous ay stille sat
Til she had herd what the frere sayde.
'Ey, Goddes mooder,' quod she, 'Blisful mayde!   *blessed*
Is ther oght elles? telle me feithfully.'
    'Madame,' quod he, 'how thynke ye herby?'
2205   'How that me thynketh?' quod she, 'so God me
      speede,   *help*
I seye, a cherl hath doon a cherles dede.
What shold I seye? God lat hym nevere thee!
His sike heed is ful of vanytee;   *folly*
I holde hym in a manere frenesye.'
2210   'Madame,' quod he, 'by God, I shal nat lye,
But I on oother wyse may be wreke,
I shal disclaundre hym over al ther I speke,

2178–9 No serving-lad so poor that he would have anything but loathing.
2181 Yet nothing grieves me so much.
2186 i.e. he had received the degree of Master of Divinity at the university (*in scole*).
2204 What do you think of this?
2207 What else can I say? God let him never prosper!
2209 I think he's in a kind of frenzy.
2211 If I can't be revenged in some other way.
2212 I shall slander him everywhere I preach.

This false blasphemour, that charged me
To parte that wol nat departed be,   *divide*
2215 To every man yliche, with meschaunce!'
    The lord sat stille as he were in a traunce,   *trance*
And in his herte he rolled up and doun,
'How hadde this cherl ymaginacioun
To shewe swich a probleme to the frere?   *pose*
2220 Nevere erst er now herde I of swich mateere.   *before now*
I trowe the devel putte it in his mynde.
In ars-metrike shal ther no man fynde,
Biforn this day, of swich a question.
Who sholde make a demonstracion
2225 That every man sholde have yliche his part
As of the soun or savour of a fart?
O nyce, proude cherl, I shrewe his face!
Lo, sires,' quod the lord, 'with harde grace!   *bad luck to him!*
Who evere herde of swich a thyng er now?
2230 To every man ylike, tel me how?
It is an inpossible, it may nat be.   *impossibility*
Ey, nyce cherl, God lete him nevere thee!
The rumblynge of a fart, and every soun,
Nis but of eir reverberacioun,
2235 And evere it wasteth litel and litel awey.
Ther is no man kan deemen, by my fey,   *judge*
If that it were departed equally.
What, lo, my cherl, lo, yet how shrewedly   *maliciously*
Unto my confessour to-day he spak!
2240 I holde hym certeyn a demonyak!   *madman*
Now ete youre mete, and lat the cherl go pleye;
Lat hym go honge hymself a devel weye!'

    The wordes of the lordes squier and
his kervere for departynge of the fart   *carver; dividing*
on twelve.

    Now stood the lordes squier at the bord,
That karf his mete, and herde word by word   *carved*
2245 Of alle thynges whiche I have yow sayd.
'My lord,' quod he, 'be ye nat yvele apayd,   *displeased*

2215 Among us all equally—the devil take him!
2217 And turned this question over and over in his mind.
2222-3 In all arithmetic you couldn't find a problem like this one before
    to-day.
2224-5 Who would be willing to demonstrate a way of giving everyone
    an equal share of such a thing.
2227 The proud and foolish fellow, curse him!
2234 Is only reverberation of the air.
2235 And it gradually gets less and less.
2242 The devil take him!

I koude telle, for a gowne-clooth,
To yow, sire frere, so ye be nat wrooth,   *angry*
How that this fart sholde evene deled be
2250 Among youre covent, if it lyked me.'   *I liked*
'Tel,' quod the lord, 'and thou shalt have anon
A gowne-clooth, by God and by Seint John!'
'My lord,' quod he, 'whan that the weder is fair,
Withouten wynd or perturbynge of air,
2255 Lat brynge a cartwheel heere into this halle;
But looke that it have his spokes alle,—   *its*
Twelve spokes hath a cartwheel comunly.
And bryng me thanne twelve freres, woot ye why?   *know*
For thrittene is a covent, as I gesse.
2260 Youre confessour heere, for his worthynesse,
Shal parfourne up the nombre of his covent.   *complete*
Thanne shal they knele doun, by oon assent,   *with one accord*
And to every spokes ende, in this manere,
Ful sadly leye his nose shal a frere.
2265 Youre noble confessour—there God hym save!—
Shal holde his nose upright under the nave.   *right up; hub*
Thanne shal this cherl, with bely stif and toght
As any tabour, hyder been ybroght;   *drum*
And sette hym on the wheel right of this cart,
2270 Upon the nave, and make hym lete a fart.
And ye shul seen, up peril of my lyf,
By preeve which that is demonstratif,   *proof; demonstrable*
That equally the soun of it wol wende,   *travel*
And eke the stynk, unto the spokes ende,
2275 Save that this worthy man, youre confessour,
By cause he is a man of greet honour,
Shal have the firste fruyt, as resoun is.
The noble usage of freres yet is this,   *custom*
The worthy men of hem shul first be served;
2280 And certeinly he hath it weel disserved.   *well deserved*
He hath to-day taught us so muche good
With prechyng in the pulpit ther he stood,   *where*
That I may vouche sauf, I sey for me,
He hadde the firste smel of fartes thre;
2285 And so wolde al his covent hardily,
He bereth hym so faire and hoolily.'

2247 *gowne-clooth*, cloth to make a gown.
2249 Would be evenly divided.
2255 Have a cartwheel brought.
2259 Thirteen make a convent, I believe.
2264 A friar shall lay his nose very firmly.
2267 *this cherl*, i.e. Thomas; *toght*, taut.
2271 I'll stake my life on it.
2283–4 That, for my own part, I'm willing to let him have.
2285–6 And so would all his convent, I am sure, his conduct is so
     excellent, so holy.

The lord, the lady, and ech man, save the frere,
Seyde that Jankyn spak, in this matere, *Johnny*
As wel as Euclide dide or Ptholomee.
2290 Touchynge the cherl, they seyde, subtiltee
And heigh wit made hym speken as he spak;
He nys no fool, ne no demonyak.
And Jankyn hath ywonne a newe gowne.—
My tale is doon; we been almoost at towne.

HEERE ENDETH THE SOMONOURS TALE

2289 *Ptholomee*, Ptolemy. (See I. 3208.)
2290-1 As for the churl, they said, a subtle and profound wit.

Fragment IV (Group E)

THE CLERK'S PROLOGUE

Heere folweth the Prologe of the Clerkes Tale of Oxenford

'Sire Clerk of Oxenford,' oure Hooste sayde,
'Ye ryde as coy and stille as dooth a mayde   *shy; silent*
Were newe spoused, sittynge at the bord;
This day ne herde I of youre tonge a word.
5 I trowe ye studie aboute som sophyme;
But Salomon seith "every thyng hath tyme."
   For Goddes sake, as beth of bettre cheere!
It is no tyme for to studien heere.
Telle us som myrie tale, by youre fey!   *faith*
10 For what man that is entred in a pley,
He nedes moot unto the pley assente.
But precheth nat, as freres doon in Lente,   *friars*
To make us for oure olde synnes wepe,
Ne that thy tale make us nat to slepe.
15   Telle us som murie thyng of aventures.
Youre termes, youre colours, and youre figures,
Keepe hem in stoor til so be ye endite   *reserve; write*
Heigh style, as whan that men to kynges write.   *elevated*
Speketh so pleyn at this tyme, we yow preye,   *plainly*
20 That we may understonde what ye seye.'
   This worthy clerk benignely answerde: *gently*
'Hooste,' quod he, 'I am under youre yerde;   *authority*
Ye han of us as now the governance,
And therfore wol I do yow obeisance,   *obey you*
25 As fer as resoun axeth, hardily.
I wol yow telle a tale which that I

---

3 Who happens to be newly married, sitting at table.
5 I believe you're pondering some subtle argument.
6 'To every thing there is a season' (Eccles. iii. 1).
7 Please be more cheerful.
10–11 Anyone who has joined in a game must keep to the rules.
14 And don't let your tale send us to sleep.
16 Your technical expressions, your rhetorical ornaments, and your figures of speech.
23 You have charge of us for the time being.
25 As far as reason allows, certainly.

221

Lerned at Padowe of a worthy clerk,
As preved by his wordes and his werk.   *as he is proved*
He is now deed and nayled in his cheste,   *coffin*
30 I prey to God so yeve his soule reste!
   Frounceys Petrak, the lauriat poete,
Highte this clerk, whos rethorike sweete   *was called; rhetoric*
Enlumyned al Ytaille of poetrie,
As Lynyan dide of philosophie
35 Or lawe, or oother art particuler;
But deeth, that wol nat suffre us dwellen heer,
But as it were a twynklyng of an ye,
Hem bothe hath slayn, and alle shul we dye.   *must*
   But forth to tellen of this worthy man
40 That taught me this tale, as I bigan,
I seye that first with heigh stile he enditeth,
Er he the body of his tale writeth,   *before*
A prohemye, in the which discryveth he   *preface; describes*
Pemond, and of Saluces the contree,
45 And speketh of Apennyn, the hilles hye,   *Apennines*
That been the boundes of West Lumbardye,
And of Mount Vesulus in special,   *Monte Viso*
Where as the Poo out of a welle smal   *river Po; spring*
Taketh his firste spryngyng and his sours, *beginning; source*
50 That estward ay encresseth in his cours
To Emele-ward, to Ferrare, and Venyse;
The which a long thyng were to devyse.
And trewely, as to my juggement,
Me thynketh it a thyng impertinent,
55 Save that he wole conveyen his mateere;
But this his tale, which that ye may heere.'   *this (is)*

27 Learned at Padua from a distinguished scholar.
30 I pray God rest his soul.
31 Francesco Petrarca (1304–74), archdeacon of Padua.
33 Illumined all Italy with his poetry.
34 Giovanni da Lignaco (*d.* 1383), professor of Canon Law at Bologna.
35 Or any other special branch of learning.
44 Piedmont and the district of Saluzzo.
50–1 That continually increases on its course as it flows eastwards
    towards Emilia, Ferrara, and Venice.
54–5 It seems to me to be irrelevant, except in so far as he is intent on
    introducing his main subject.

THE CLERK'S TALE

HEERE BIGYNNETH THE TALE OF THE
CLERK OF OXENFORD

THER IS, at the west syde of Ytaille,
Doun at the roote of Vesulus the colde,   *foot*
A lusty playn, habundant of vitaille,
60 Where many a tour and toun thou mayst biholde,
That founded were in tyme of fadres olde,   *remote ancestors*
And many another delitable sighte,   *delightful*
And Saluces this noble contree highte.

A markys whilom lord was of that lond,   *marquis; once*
65 As were his worthy eldres hym bifore;
And obeisant, ay redy to his hond,   *obedient*
Were alle his liges, bothe lasse and moore.   *lieges*
Thus in delit he lyveth, and hath doon yoore,   *for long*
Biloved and drad, thurgh favour of Fortune,   *feared*
70 Bothe of his lordes and of his commune.   *commons*

Therwith he was, to speke as of lynage,   *besides; lineage*
The gentilleste yborn of Lumbardye,   *noblest*
A fair persone, and strong, and yong of age,   *handsome*
And ful of honour and of curteisye;
75 Discreet ynogh his contree for to gye,   *enough; govern*
Save in somme thynges that he was to blame;
And Walter was this yonge lordes name.

I blame hym thus, that he considered noght
In tyme comynge what myghte hym bityde,
80 But on his lust present was al his thoght,   *pleasure*
As for to hauke and hunte on every syde.   *hawk*
Wel ny alle othere cures leet he slyde,
And eek he nolde—and that was worst of alle—   *would not*
Wedde no wyf, for noght that may bifalle.   *whatever happened*

85   Oonly that point his peple bar so soore
That flokmeele on a day they to hym wente,   *in a flock*

59 A pleasant and fertile plain.
78-9 I blame him for this, that he did not consider what might happen
to him in the future.
82 He neglected almost all other pursuits.
85 That one point (i.e. his unwillingness to marry) his people took so
hard.

And oon of hem, that wisest was of loore—
Or elles that the lord best wolde assente
That he sholde telle hym what his peple mente,
90 Or elles koude he shewe wel swich mateere—
He to the markys seyde as ye shul heere:

    'O noble markys, youre humanitee   *graciousness*
Asseureth us and yeveth us hardinesse,   *boldness*
As ofte as tyme is of necessitee,
95 That we to yow mowe telle oure hevynesse.   *may; sorrow*
Accepteth, lord, now of youre gentillesse   *courtesy*
That we with pitous herte unto yow pleyne,
And lat youre eres nat my voys desdeyne.   *ears*

    'Al have I noght to doone in this mateere
100 Moore than another man hath in this place,
Yet for as muche as ye, my lord so deere,
Han alwey shewed me favour and grace
I dar the bettre aske of yow a space
Of audience, to shewen oure requeste,
105 And ye, my lord, to doon right as yow leste.

    'For certes, lord, so wel us liketh yow
And al youre werk, and evere han doon, that we
Ne koude nat us self devysen how   *imagine*
We myghte lyven in moore felicitee,
110 Save o thyng, lord, if it youre wille be,
That for to been a wedded man yow leste,
Thanne were youre peple in sovereyn hertes reste.

    'Boweth youre nekke under that blisful yok   *yoke*
Of soveraynetee, noght of servyse,
115 Which that men clepe spousaille or wedlok;
And thenketh, lord, among youre thoghtes wyse
How that oure dayes passe in sondry wyse;   *various ways*
For thogh we slepe, or wake, or rome, or ryde,
Ay fleeth the tyme; it nyl no man abyde.   *will not*

87 One of them, who was the wisest and best informed.
88–9 Or else the man most acceptable to his lord as the one who should
    tell him what the people had in mind.
90 Or else the man best able to explain such a matter.
97 What we with heavy hearts complain to you about.
99–100 Although I have no more to do with this matter than anyone
    else present.
103–5 I dare all the more to ask you for the opportunity of an audience,
    to make known our request, and you, my lord, must do exactly as you
    wish.
106–7 For certainly, lord, you and all your actions please us so much,
    and always have done.
110–11 If it were your will and pleasure to be a married man.
112 In supreme peace of mind.

120   'And thogh youre grene youthe floure as yit,   *flourishes*
     In crepeth age alwey, as stille as stoon,
     And deeth manaceth every age, and smyt   *threatens; strikes*
     In ech estaat, for ther escapeth noon;   *rank*
     And al so certein as we knowe echoon   *just as certainly*
125 That we shul deye, as uncerteyn we alle
     Been of that day whan deeth shal on us falle.

     'Accepteth thanne of us the trewe entente,
     That nevere yet refuseden youre heeste,   *command*
     And we wol, lord, if that ye wole assente,
130 Chese yow a wyf, in short tyme atte leeste,
     Born of the gentilleste and of the meeste   *noblest; greatest*
     Of al this land, so that it oghte seme
     Honour to God and yow, as we kan deeme.   *judge*

     'Delivere us out of al this bisy drede,   *anxious fear*
135 And taak a wyf, for hye Goddes sake!
     For if it so bifelle, as God forbede,
     That thurgh youre deeth youre lyne sholde slake,   *cease*
     And that a straunge successour sholde take
     Youre heritage, O, wo were us alyve!
140 Wherfore we pray you hastily to wyve.'   *marry*

     Hir meeke preyere and hir pitous cheere
     Made the markys herte han pitee.
     'Ye wol,' quod he, 'myn owene peple deere,
     To that I nevere erst thoughte streyne me.
145 I me rejoysed of my liberte,
     That seelde tyme is founde in mariage;   *seldom*
     Ther I was free, I moot been in servage.

     'But nathelees I se youre trewe entente,   *nevertheless*
     And truste upon youre wit, and have doon ay;   *wisdom*
150 Wherfore of my free wyl I wole assente
     To wedde me, as soone as evere I may.
     But ther as ye han profred me to-day   *where*
     To chese me a wyf, I yow relesse
     That choys, and prey yow of that profre cesse.

121 As silent as a stone, i.e. in perfect silence.
130 Choose you a wife with as little delay as possible.
139 Life would be miserable for us.
141 Their humble petition and sad demeanour.
144 Constrain me to do something I never thought of before.
147 Where I was free, I must be in servitude.
153-4 I relieve you of the task of making that choice, and pray you to withdraw the offer.

155   'For God it woot, that children ofte been   *knows*
      Unlyk hir worthy eldres hem bifore;
      Bountee comth al of God, nat of the streen   *goodness; stock*
      Of which they been engendred and ybore.   *born*
      I truste in Goddes bountee, and therfore
160 My mariage and myn estaat and reste
      I hym bitake; he may doon as hym leste.   *entrust; he pleases*

      'Lat me allone in chesynge of my wyf,—   *(the) choosing*
      That charge upon my bak I wole endure.   *burden*
      But I yow preye, and charge upon youre lyf,
165 What wyf that I take, ye me assure   *whatever*
      To worshipe hire, whil that hir lyf may dure,   *honour; last*
      In word and werk, bothe heere and everywheere,   *deed*
      As she an emperoures doghter weere.   *as if*

      'And forthermoore, this shal ye swere, that ye
170 Agayn my choys shul neither grucche ne stryve;   *grumble*
      For sith I shal forgoon my libertee   *since; forgo*
      At youre requeste, as evere moot I thryve,
      Ther as myn herte is set, ther wol I wyve;   *where*
      And but ye wole assente in swich manere,
175 I prey yow, speketh namoore of this matere.'

      With hertely wyl they sworen and assenten *sincere goodwill*
      To al this thyng, ther seyde no wight nay;   *no one refused*
      Bisekynge hym of grace, er that they wenten,
      That he wolde graunten hem a certein day
180 Of his spousaille, as soone as evere he may;
      For yet alwey the peple somwhat dredde,   *still; were afraid*
      Lest that the markys no wyf wolde wedde.

      He graunted hem a day, swich as hym leste,
      On which he wolde be wedded sikerly,   *without fail*
185 And seyde he dide al this at hir requeste.
      And they, with humble entente, buxomly,   *hearts; obediently*
      Knelynge upon hir knees ful reverently,
      Hym thonken alle; and thus they han an ende
      Of hire entente, and hoom agayn they wende.

160 My state of life and peace of mind.
172 As I hope to prosper.
174 And unless you will agree to these conditions.
178–80 Beseeching him to be gracious enough, before they went, to
    grant them a definite day for his marriage, which they hoped would be
    as soon as possible.
183 A day that suited him best.
188–9 And so they have achieved their aim, and they go home again.

190   And heerupon he to his officeres
     Comaundeth for the feste to purveye,   *prepare*
     And to his privee knyghtes and squieres   *personal*
     Swich charge yaf as hym liste on hem leye;
     And they to his comandement obeye,
195 And ech of hem dooth al his diligence   *utmost*
     To doon unto the feeste reverence.   *honour*

EXPLICIT PRIMA PARS

INCIPIT SECUNDA PARS

     Noght fer fro thilke paleys honurable,
     Wher as this markys shoop his mariage,
     There stood a throop, of site delitable,   *village; delightful*
200 In which that povre folk of that village   *poor*
     Hadden hir beestes and hir herbergage,   *dwellings*
     And of hire labour tooke hir sustenance,   *from*
     After that the erthe yaf hem habundance.   *according as*

     Amonges thise povre folk ther dwelte a man
205 Which that was holden povrest of hem alle;   *regarded as*
     But hye God somtyme senden kan
     His grace into a litel oxes stalle;
     Janicula men of that throop hym calle.
     A doghter hadde he, fair ynogh to sighte,
210 And Grisildis this yonge mayden highte.   *was called*

     But for to speke of vertuous beautee,
     Thanne was she oon the faireste under sonne;   *one (of)*
     For povreliche yfostred up was she,   *poorly; bred*
     No likerous lust was thurgh hire herte yronne.
215 Wel ofter of the welle than of the tonne
     She drank, and for she wolde vertu plese,
     She knew wel labour, but noon ydel ese.

     But thogh this mayde tendre were of age,
     Yet in the brest of hire virginitee   *in her virgin breast*
220 Ther was enclosed rype and sad corage;
     And in greet reverence and charitee

193 Gave such duties as he wished them to perform.
198 Where the marquis made preparations for his marriage.
207 An allusion to the Nativity.
209 Most beautiful to behold.
214 No wanton desire had tainted her heart.
215–16 She drank more often from the spring than from the wine-cask,
    and because she made virtue a pleasure.
220 A mature and constant heart.

Hir olde povre fader fostred shee.   *cherished*
A fewe sheep, spynnynge, on feeld she kepte;
She wolde noght been ydel til she slepte.

225   And whan she homward cam, she wolde brynge
Wortes or othere herbes tymes ofte,   *roots*
The whiche she shredde and seeth for hir lyvynge,
And made hir bed ful hard and nothyng softe;   *not at all*
And ay she kepte hir fadres lyf on-lofte
230 With everich obeisaunce and diligence
That child may doon to fadres reverence.

Upon Grisilde, this povre creature,
Ful ofte sithe this markys sette his ye   *very often; eye*
As he on huntyng rood paraventure;   *rode; by chance*
235 And whan it fil that he myghte hire espye,   *happened*
He noght with wantown lookyng of folye
His eyen caste on hire, but in sad wyse
Upon hir chiere he wolde hym ofte avyse,

Commendynge in his herte hir wommanhede,
240 And eek hir vertu, passynge any wight
Of so yong age, as wel in chiere as dede.
For thogh the peple have no greet insight
In vertu, he considered ful right
Hir bountee, and disposed that he wolde   *determined*
245 Wedde hire oonly, if evere he wedde sholde.

The day of weddyng cam, but no wight kan   *no one*
Telle what womman that it sholde be;   *would*
For which merveille wondred many a man,   *marvel*
And seyden, whan they were in privetee,   *private*
250 'Wol nat oure lord yet leve his vanytee?   *folly*
Wol he nat wedde? allas, allas, the while!
Why wole he thus hymself and us bigile?'   *deceive*

But nathelees this markys hath doon make   *had made*
Of gemmes, set in gold and in asure,
255 Brooches and rynges, for Grisildis sake;
And of hir clothyng took he the mesure

223 While spinning, she minded a few sheep in the field.
227 Which she shredded and boiled for their food.
229–31 And always she cared for her father with all the obedience and
attention that a child can show in a father's honour.
236 With a wanton, wicked look.
237–8 But often he gave serious thought to her appearance.
240–1 Outstanding for anyone of her tender years, both in looks and
actions.
242–4 Though the common people have no great insight into virtue,
he (the noble marquis) fully appreciated her goodness.

By a mayde lyk to hire stature,
And eek of othere aornementes alle   *ornaments*
That unto swich a weddyng sholde falle.   *befit*

260 The time of undren of the same day   *mid morning*
Approcheth, that this weddyng sholde be;
And al the paleys put was in array,   *order*
Bothe halle and chambres, ech in his degree;   *its*
Houses of office stuffed with plentee
265 Ther maystow seen, of deyntevous vitaille
That may be founde as fer as last Ytaille.

This roial markys, richely arrayed,
Lordes and ladyes in his compaignye,
The whiche that to the feeste weren yprayed,   *invited*
270 And of his retenue the bachelrye,   *young knights*
With many a soun of sondry melodye,   *varied*
Unto the village of the which I tolde,
In this array the righte wey han holde.

Grisilde of this, God woot, ful innocent,
275 That for hire shapen was al this array,   *prepared; pomp*
To fecchen water at a welle is went,   *gone*
And cometh hoom as soone as ever she may;
For wel she hadde herd seyd that thilke day   *that (same)*
The markys sholde wedde, and if she myghte,   *was to*
280 She wolde fayn han seyn som of that sighte.

She thoghte, 'I wole with othere maydens stonde,
That been my felawes, in oure dore and se   *companions*
The markysesse, and therfore wol I fonde,   *marchioness; try*
To doon at hoom, as soone as it may be,
285 The labour which that longeth unto me;
And thanne I may at leyser hire biholde,
If she this wey unto the castel holde.'   *takes*

And as she wolde over hir thresshfold gon,
The markys cam, and gan hire for to calle;   *called her*
290 And she set doun hir water pot anon,
Biside the thresshfold, in an oxes stalle,
And doun upon hir knes she gan to falle,
And with sad contenance kneleth stille,   *serious; silently*
Til she had herd what was the lordes wille.

264–6 There you could see store-rooms filled with an abundance of the
    choicest food to be found throughout the length and breadth of Italy.
273 Took the shortest way.
280 She would gladly see something of the sight.
285 The work I have to do.
288 As she was about to cross her threshold.

295   This thoghtful markys spak unto this mayde
       Ful sobrely, and seyde in this manere:
       'Where is youre fader, O Grisildis?' he sayde.
       And she with reverence, in humble cheere,   *frame of mind*
       Answerde, 'Lord, he is al redy heere.'
300 And in she gooth withouten lenger lette,   *longer delay*
       And to the markys she hir fader fette.   *fetched*

       He by the hand thanne took this olde man,
       And seyde thus, whan he hym hadde asyde:
       'Janicula, I neither may ne kan   *cannot possibly*
305 Lenger the plesance of myn herte hyde.   *pleasure*
       If that thou vouche sauf, what so bityde,
       Thy doghter wol I take, er that I wende,   *before; go*
       As for my wyf, unto hir lyves ende.

       'Thou lovest me, I woot it wel certeyn,   *know for certain*
310 And art my feithful lige man ybore;   *born*
       And al that liketh me, I dar wel seyn   *pleases*
       It liketh thee, and specially therfore
       Tel me that poynt that I have seyd bifore,
       If that thou wolt unto that purpos drawe,
315 To take me as for thy sone-in-lawe.'

       This sodeyn cas this man astonyed   *happening; astounded*
         so
       That reed he wax; abayst and al quakynge
       He stood; unnethes seyde he wordes mo,   *hardly; more*
       But oonly thus: 'Lord,' quod he, 'my willynge   *wish*
320 Is as ye wole, ne ayeynes youre likynge
       I wol no thyng, ye be my lord so deere;
       Right as yow lust, governeth this mateere.'

       'Yet wol I,' quod this markys softely,
       'That in thy chambre I and thou and she
325 Have a collacioun, and wostow   *conference; do you know*
         why?
       For I wol axe if it hire wille be   *ask*
       To be my wyf, and reule hire after me.
       And al this shal be doon in thy presence;
       I wol noght speke out of thyn audience.'   *hearing*

306 If you allow it, whatever the consequences.
313–15 Tell me what you feel about the thing I have just mentioned—
    whether you will agree to my proposal and take me as your son-in-law.
317 He turned red; abashed and all trembling.
320–1 Nor do I want anything that is not to your liking.
322 Arrange this matter as you think best.
327 And be ruled by me.

330 And in the chambre, whil they were aboute
 Hir tretys, which as ye shal after heere,
 The peple cam unto the hous withoute,   *outside*
 And wondred hem in how honest manere
 And tentifly she kepte hir fader deere.
335 But outrely Grisildis wondre myghte,
 For nevere erst ne saugh she swich a sighte. *before; saw*

 No wonder is thogh that she were astoned
 To seen so greet a gest come in that place;   *guest*
 She nevere was to swiche gestes woned,   *used*
340 For which she looked with ful pale face.
 But shortly forth this matere for to chace, *briefly; go on with*
 Thise arn the wordes that the markys sayde *are*
 To this benigne, verray, feithful mayde.   *gentle; true*

 'Grisilde,' he seyde, 'ye shal wel understonde
345 It liketh to youre fader and to me   *pleases*
 That I yow wedde, and eek it may so stonde,
 As I suppose, ye wol that it so be.
 But thise demandes axe I first,' quod he,
 'That, sith it shal be doon in hastif wyse, *hasty fashion*
350 Wol ye assente, or elles yow avyse?

 'I seye this, be ye redy with good herte
 To al my lust, and that I frely may,
 As me best thynketh, do yow laughe or smerte,
 And nevere ye to grucche it, nyght ne day? *resent*
355 And eek whan I sey "ye," ne sey nat "nay," *yea*
 Neither by word ne frownyng contenance?
 Swere this, and heere I swere oure alliance.' *swear to*

 Wondrynge upon this word, quakynge *trembling with fear*
  for drede,
 She seyde, 'Lord, undigne and unworthy *undeserving*
360 Am I to thilke honour that ye me beede; *offer*
 But as ye wole youreself, right so wol I.
 And heere I swere that nevere willyngly,
 In werk ne thoght, I nyl yow disobeye,   *deed*
 For to be deed, though me were looth to deye.'

331 Their marriage treaty, which you shall hear more of later.
333-4 They wondered at the decent and attentive way she looked after
 her dear father.
335 But Griselda herself might well be wondering most of all.
340 For which reason she looked very pale.
346 And it is also possible.
350 Or would you like to think it over?
352-3 To do all I wish, and may I freely, as I think best, make you
 laugh or suffer pain.
364 Even though I should die for it (i.e. for my obedience), and yet be
 lo..th to die.

365   'This is ynogh, Grisilde myn,' quod he.
        And forth he gooth, with a ful sobre cheere,
        Out at the dore, and after that cam she,
        And to the peple he seyde in this manere:
        'This is my wyf,' quod he, 'that standeth heere.
370   Honoureth hire and loveth hire, I preye,
        Whoso me loveth; ther is namoore to seye.'

        And for that no thyng of hir olde geere   *clothing*
        She sholde brynge into his hous, he bad
        That wommen sholde dispoillen hire right theere;   *undress*
375   Of which thise ladyes were nat right glad
        To handle hir clothes, wherinne she was clad.
        But nathelees, this mayde bright of hewe
        Fro foot to heed they clothed han al newe.

        Hir heris han they kembd, that lay   *hair*
            untressed   *unplaited*
380   Ful rudely, and with hir fyngres smale
        A corone on hire heed they han ydressed,
        And sette hire ful of nowches grete and smale.
        Of hire array what sholde I make a tale?   *long story*
        Unnethe the peple hir knew for hire fairnesse,   *hardly*
385   Whan she translated was in swich richesse.

        This markys hath hire spoused with a ryng   *married*
        Broght for the same cause, and thanne hire sette
        Upon an hors, snow-whit and wel amblyng,   *easy-paced*
        And to his paleys, er he lenger lette,
390   With joyful peple that hire ladde and mette,
        Conveyed hire, and thus the day they spende
        In revel, til the sonne gan descende.   *revelry*

        And shortly forth this tale for to chace,
        I seye that to this newe markysesse
395   God hath swich favour sent hire of his grace,
        That it ne semed nat by liklynesse   *probable*
        That she was born and fed in rudenesse,   *rustic surroundings*
        As in a cote or in an oxe-stalle,   *cottage*
        But norissed in an emperoures halle.   *brought up*

        375 i.e. the ladies of the court.
        380–1 With their slender fingers they placed a nuptial garland on her
            head.
        382 And adorned her dress with jewelled clasps.
        385 When she stood transfigured in such rich array.
        389 To his palace, without more delay.
        390 Who met and escorted her.

400   To every wight she woxen is so deere
    And worshipful that folk ther she was bore,
    And from hire birthe knewe hire yeer by yeere,
    Unnethe trowed they,—but dorste han swore—
    That to Janicle, of which I spak bifore,
405 She doghter were, for, as by conjecture,
    Hem thoughte she was another creature.

    For though that evere vertuous was she,
    She was encressed in swich excellence
    Of thewes goode, yset in heigh bountee,
410 And so discreet and fair of eloquence,
    So benigne and so digne of reverence,
    And koude so the peples herte embrace,
    That ech hire lovede that looked on hir face.

    Noght oonly of Saluces in the toun
415 Publiced was the bountee of hir name,
    But eek biside in many a regioun,   *round about*
    If oon seide wel, another seyde the same;
    So spradde of hire heighe bountee the fame
    That men and wommen, as wel yonge as olde,   *both . . . and*
420 Goon to Saluce, upon hire to biholde.   *go*

    Thus Walter lowely—nay, but roially—   *humbly*
    Wedded with fortunat honestetee,
    In Goddes pees lyveth ful esily   *quietly*
    At hoom, and outward grace ynogh had he;
425 And for he saugh that under low degree
    Was ofte vertu hid, the peple hym heelde
    A prudent man, and that is seyn ful seelde.   *seen*

    Nat oonly this Grisildis thurgh hir wit
    Koude al the feet of wyfly hoomlinesse,
430 But eek, whan that the cas required it,
    The commune profit koude she redresse.

400–1 To everyone she grew so dear and so deserving of honour that the people who lived where she was born.
403 They hardly believed—and would even have sworn it was impossible.
405–6 For, if they had not known her, they would have guessed her to be some other person.
407–9 For though she was no more virtuous than she had always been, her excellent qualities of character, grounded on noble goodness, had increased.
412 She had such power over people's hearts.
422 With honour and good fortune.
424 And outside his home (i.e. among his people) he found great favour.
429 Could carry out all a wife's domestic duties.
431 She could promote the public good.

Ther nas discord, rancour, ne hevynesse   *sorrow*
In al that land, that she ne koude apese,   *appease*
And wisely brynge hem alle in reste and ese.

435 Though that hire housbonde absent were anon,   *for a while*
If gentil men or othere of hire contree
Were wrothe, she wolde bryngen hem aton;   *reconcile them*
So wise and rype wordes hadde she,   *such; mature*
And juggementz of so greet equitee,
440 That she from hevene sent was, as men wende,   *thought*
Peple to save and every wrong t'amende.

Nat longe tyme after that this Grisild
Was wedded, she a doghter hath ybore.   *given birth to*
Al had hire levere have born a knave child,
445 Glad was this markys and the folk therfore;
For though a mayde child coome al bifore,   *girl; first*
She may unto a knave child atteyne
By liklihede, syn she nys nat bareyne.

EXPLICIT SECUNDA PARS

INCIPIT TERCIA PARS

Ther fil, as it bifalleth tymes mo,
450 Whan that this child had souked but a   *sucked*
          throwe,   *little while*
This markys in his herte longeth so
To tempte his wyf, hir sadnesse for to knowe,   *test; constancy*
That he ne myghte out of his herte throwe
This merveillous desir his wyf t'assaye;   *to make trial of*
455 Nedelees, God woot, he thoghte hire for t'affraye.

He hadde assayed hire ynogh bifore,
And foond hire evere good; what neded it   *always*
Hire for to tempte, and alwey moore and moore,   *test*
Though som men preise it for a subtil wit?
460 But as for me, I seye that yvele it sit
To assaye a wyf whan that it is no nede,
And putten hire in angwyssh and in drede.

444 Although she would rather have had a boy.
447–8 She may very likely succeed in having a boy, since she is not
     barren.
449 It happened, as it sometimes does.
453 That he could not drive from his heart.
455 Needlessly, God knows, he meant to frighten her.
459 Praise it as a subtle proof of intelligence.
460 It ill becomes (a husband).

For which this markys wroghte in this manere:
He cam allone a-nyght, ther as she lay,
465 With stierne face and with ful trouble   *troubled*
    cheere,   *features*
And seyde thus: 'Grisilde,' quod he, 'that day
That I yow took out of youre povere array,   *condition*
And putte yow in estaat of heigh noblesse,—   *high honour*
Ye have nat that forgeten, as I gesse?

470 'I seye, Grisilde, this present dignitee,
In which that I have put yow, as I trowe,
Maketh yow nat foryetful for to be
That I yow took in povre estaat ful lowe,   *humble*
For any wele ye moot youreselven knowe.
475 Taak heede of every word that y yow seye;
Ther is no wight that hereth it but we tweye.   *hears; two*

'Ye woot youreself wel how that ye cam heere
Into this hous, it is nat longe ago;
And though to me that ye be lief and deere,   *beloved*
480 Unto my gentils ye be no thyng so.
They seyn, to hem it is greet shame and wo   *say*
For to be subgetz and been in servage   *subjects; servitude*
To thee, that born art of a smal village.

'And namely sith thy doghter was ybore.   *especially*
485 Thise wordes han they spoken, doutelees.
But I desire, as I have doon bifore,
To lyve my lyf with hem in reste and pees.   *peace and quiet*
I may nat in this caas be recchelees;   *negligent*
I moot doon with thy doghter for the beste,
490 Nat as I wolde, but as my peple leste.   *wish*

'And yet, God woot, this is ful looth to me;
But nathelees withoute youre wityng   *knowledge*
I wol nat doon; but this wol I,' quod he,   *act*
'That ye to me assente as in this thyng.
495 Shewe now youre pacience in youre werkying,   *actions*
That ye me highte and swore in youre village   *promised*
That day that maked was oure mariage.'

463 For which reason the marquis did as follows.
471-2 To which I have raised you does not, I believe, make you forgetful.
474 And gave you any happiness you have known since.
480 To my nobles you are not so by any means.
489 I must do what is best for your daughter.

Whan she had herd al this, she noght   *was not disturbed*
          ameved
Neither in word, or chiere, or contenaunce;   *mien*
500 For, as it semed, she was nat agreved.
She seyde, 'Lord, al lyth in youre plesaunce.
My child and I, with hertely obeisaunce,   *sincere obedience*
Been youres al, and ye mowe save or spille   *may; destroy*
Youre owene thyng; werketh after youre wille.

505   'Ther may no thyng, God so my soule save,
Liken to yow that may displese me;
Ne I desire no thyng for to have,
Ne drede for to leese, save oonly yee.   *lose*
This wyl is in myn herte, and ay shal be;
510 No lengthe of tyme or deeth may this deface,
Ne chaunge my corage to another place.'   *heart*

Glad was this markys of hire answeryng
But yet he feyned as he were nat so;   *pretended*
Al drery was his cheere and his lookyng,   *gloomy*
515 Whan that he sholde out of the chambre go.
Soone after this, a furlong wey or two,   *in a little while*
He prively hath toold al his entente   *secretly; intention*
Unto a man, and to his wyf hym sente.

A maner sergeant was this privee man,   *sort of attendant*
520 The which that feithful ofte he founden hadde
In thynges grete, and eek swich folk wel kan
Doon execucioun in thynges badde.
The lord knew wel that he hym loved and dradde;   *feared*
And whan this sergeant wiste his lordes wille,   *knew*
525 Into the chambre he stalked hym ful stille.   *stole; softly*

'Madame,' he seyde, 'ye moote foryeve it   *must forgive*
          me,
Though I do thyng to which I am constreyned.
Ye been so wys that ful wel knowe ye
That lordes heestes mowe nat been yfeyned;
530 They mowe wel been biwailled or compleyned,
But men moote nede unto hire lust obeye,   *will*
And so wol I; ther is namoore to seye.

504 Your own possessions; do as you will.
505-6 God save my soul, but there's nothing pleasing to you that can
     displease me.
529 A lord's commands cannot be evaded.

'This child I am comanded for to take,'—
And spak namoore, but out the child he hente
535 Despitously, and gan a cheere make
As thogh he wolde han slayn it er he wente.
Grisildis moot al suffre and al consente;
And as a lamb she sitteth meke and stille,
And leet this crueel sergeant doon his wille.   *let*

540 Suspecious was the diffame of this man,   *ill fame*
Suspect his face, suspect his word also;
Suspect the tyme in which he this bigan.
Allas! hir doghter that she loved so,
She wende he wolde han slawen it right tho.
545 But nathelees she neither weep ne syked,   *sighed*
Conformynge hire to that the markys lyked.

But atte laste to speken she bigan,
And mekely she to the sergeant preyde,
So as he was a worthy gentil man,
550 That she moste kisse hire child er that it deyde.   *might*
And in hir barm this litel child she leyde   *bosom*
With ful sad face, and gan the child to blisse,
And lulled it, and after gan it kisse.

And thus she seyde in hire benigne voys,   *gentle*
555 'Fareweel my child! I shal thee nevere see.
But sith I thee have marked with the croys   *cross*
Of thilke Fader—blessed moote he be!—   *that (same)*
That for us deyde upon a croys of tree,   *wood*
Thy soule, litel child, I hym bitake,   *commend*
560 For this nyght shaltow dyen for my sake.'

I trowe that to a norice in this cas   *nurse*
It had been hard this reuthe for to se;   *pitiful sight*
Wel myghte a mooder thanne han cryd 'allas!'
But nathelees so sad stidefast was she   *firmly*
565 That she endured al adversitee,
And to the sergeant mekely she sayde,
'Have heer agayn youre litel yonge mayde.

534–6 But cruelly snatched the child away, and looked as if he meant
to kill it.
542 *Suspect the tyme.* The time was night (see 464).
544 She thought he meant to kill it then and there.
552 With a very grave face, and blessed the child (i.e. marked it with
the sign of the cross).

'Gooth now,' quod she, 'and dooth my lordes heeste;
But o thyng wol I prey yow of youre grace,
570 That, but my lord forbad yow, atte leeste   *unless; at least*
Burieth this litel body in som place
That beestes ne no briddes it torace.'   *birds; tear to pieces*
But he no word wol to that purpos seye,   *effect*
But took the child and wente upon his weye.

575   This sergeant cam unto his lord ageyn,
And of Grisildis wordes and hire cheere   *demeanour*
He tolde hym point for point, in short and pleyn,
And hym presenteth with his doghter deere.
Somwhat this lord hadde routhe in his manere,
580 But nathelees his purpos heeld he stille,
As lordes doon, whan they wol han hir wille;

And bad this sergeant that he pryvely   *secretly*
Sholde this child ful softe wynde and wrappe,
With alle circumstances tendrely,
585 And carie it in a cofre or in a lappe;   *chest; piece of cloth*
But, upon peyne his heed of for to swappe,
That no man sholde knowe of his entente,
Ne whenne he cam, ne whider that he wente;   *whence*

But at Boloigne to his suster deere,   *Bologna*
590 That thilke tyme of Panik was countesse,
He sholde it take, and shewe hire this mateere,   *explain*
Bisekynge hire to doon hire bisynesse
This child to fostre in alle gentillesse;
And whos child that it was he bad hire hyde
595 From every wight, for oght that may   *whatever happened*
          bityde.

The sergeant gooth, and hath fulfild this thyng;
But to this markys now retourne we.
For now gooth he ful faste ymaginyng
If by his wyves cheere he myghte se,
600 Or by hire word aperceyve, that she
Were chaunged; but he nevere hire koude fynde
But evere in oon ylike sad and kynde.

577 In brief, plain words.
579 The lord showed some signs of pity.
584 With all possible tenderness.
586 On pain of having his head cut off.
592-3 Beseeching her to do her utmost to bring up the child in a manner
     befitting its noble birth.
598-602 For now he's busy wondering whether he can tell from his
     wife's words or looks if she is changed; but he could never find her
     anything but constant and kind.

As glad, as humble, as bisy in servyse,
And eek in love, as she was wont to be,
605 Was she to hym in every maner wyse;   *kind of way*
Ne of hir doghter noght a word spak she.
Noon accident, for noon adversitee,
Was seyn in hire, ne nevere hir doghter name   *daughter's*
Ne nempned she, in ernest nor in game.

EXPLICIT TERCIA PARS

SEQUITUR PARS QUARTA

610   In this estaat ther passed been foure yeer   *are*
Er she with childe was, but, as God wolde,
A knave child she bar by this Walter,   *boy*
Ful gracious and fair for to biholde.
And whan that folk it to his fader tolde,
615 Nat oonly he, but al his contree merye
Was for this child, and God they thanke and herye. *praise*

When it was two yeer old, and fro the brest
Departed of his norice, on a day   *one day*
This markys caughte yet another lest
620 To tempte his wyf yet ofter, if he may.   *test; oftener*
O nedelees was she tempted in assay!
But wedded men ne knowe no mesure,   *moderation*
Whan that they fynde a pacient creature.

'Wyf,' quod this markys, 'ye han herd er this,
625 My peple sikly berth oure mariage;   *dislike*
And namely sith my sone yboren is,   *especially*
Now is it worse than evere in al oure age.   *life*
The murmur sleeth myn herte and my corage,
For to myne eres comth the voys so smerte
630 That it wel ny destroyed hath myn herte.

'Now sey they thus: "Whan Walter is agon,   *gone*
Thanne shal the blood of Janicle succede   *offspring*
And been oure lord, for oother have we noon."
Swiche wordes seith my peple, out of drede.   *without doubt*
635 Wel oughte I of swich murmur taken heede;
For certeinly I drede swich sentence,   *opinions*
Though they nat pleyn speke in myn audience.   *hearing*

607 No outward sign of any adversity.
609 i.e. on any account.
619 Again felt a desire.
621 Needlessly was she subjected to these trials.
628 The murmuring afflicts my mind and heart.
629 For the voice of complaint strikes my ear so sharply.

'I wolde lyve in pees, if that I myghte;
Wherfore I am disposed outrely,   *absolutely determined*
640 As I his suster servede by nyghte,
Right so thenke I to serve hym pryvely.
This warne I yow, that ye nat sodeynly
Out of youreself for no wo sholde outreye;
Beth pacient, and therof I yow preye.'

645 'I have,' quod she, 'seyd thus, and evere shal:
I wol no thyng, ne nyl no thyng, certayn,
But as yow list.   Naught greveth me at al,
Though that my doughter and my sone be slayn,—
At youre comandement, this is to sayn.   *say*
650 I have noght had no part of children tweyne   *share; two*
But first siknesse, and after, wo and peyne.   *pain*

'Ye been oure lord, dooth with youre owene thyng
Right as yow list; axeth no reed at me.   *ask no advice of*
For as I lefte at hoom al my clothyng,
655 Whan I first cam to yow, right so,' quod she,
'Lefte I my wyl and al my libertee,
And took youre clothyng; wherfore I yow preye,
Dooth youre plesaunce, I wol youre lust obeye.

'And certes, if I hadde prescience
660 Youre wyl to knowe, er ye youre lust me tolde,
I wolde it doon withouten necligence;
But now I woot youre lust, and what ye wolde,
Al youre plesance ferme and stable I holde;
For wiste I that my deeth wolde do yow ese,   *if I knew*
665 Right gladly wolde I dyen, yow to plese.

'Deth may noght make no comparisoun
Unto youre love.'   And whan this markys say   *saw*
The constance of his wyf, he caste adoun   *constancy*
His eyen two, and wondreth that she may
670 In pacience suffre al this array;   *plight*
And forth he goth with drery contenance,   *gloomy*
But to his herte it was ful greet plesance.

This ugly sergeant, in the same wyse
That he hire doghter caughte, right so he,

643 Behave distractedly in your grief.
646–7 I wish for nothing, nor ever will, certainly, unless you also wish it.
658 Do what you please, and I shall obey your will.
663 I shall firmly obey your every wish.
666–7 Death cannot stand comparison with your love.

675 Or worse, if men worse kan devyse,   *conceive of*
    Hath hent hire sone, that ful was of beautee.   *seized*
    And evere in oon so pacient was she   *always*
    That she no chiere maade of hevynesse,
    But kiste hir sone, and after gan it blesse;

680   Save this, she preyede hym that, if he myghte,
    Hir litel sone he wolde in erthe grave,   *bury*
    His tendre lymes, delicaat to sighte,   *to behold*
    Fro foweles and fro beestes for to save.   *birds*
    But she noon answere of hym myghte have.
685 He wente his wey, as hym no thyng ne roghte;
    But to Boloigne he tendrely it broghte.

        This markys wondred, evere lenger the moore,
    Upon hir pacience, and if that he
    Ne hadde soothly knowen therbifoore
690 That parfitly hir children loved she,   *perfectly*
    He wolde have wend that of som subtiltee,
    And of malice, or for crueel corage,
    That she hadde suffred this with sad visage.

        But wel he knew that next hymself, certayn,
695 She loved hir children best in every wyse.   *way*
    But now of wommen wolde I axen fayn
    If thise assayes myghte nat suffise?   *trials*
    What koude a sturdy housbonde moore devyse   *stern*
    To preeve hir wyfhod and hir stedefast-   *prove; womanhood*
        nesse,
700 And he continuynge evere in sturdinesse?   *harshness*

        But ther been folk of swich condicion   *nature*
    That whan they have a certein purpos take,
    They kan nat stynte of hire entencion,   *give up*
    But, right as they were bounden to that stake,
705 They wol nat of that firste purpos slake.   *desist from*
    Right so this markys fulliche hath purposed
    To tempte his wyf as he was first disposed.   *test*

    678 She gave no sign of sorrow.
    685 As if it mattered nothing to him.
    687 The marquis wondered more and more as time went on.
    688-9 If he had not known for certain before this.
    691-3 He would have thought it was cunning, malice, or cruelty that
        made her suffer this with face unmoved.
    696 I should like to ask you women.
    702 Made a certain resolve.
    706 In just the same way the marquis was fully resolved.

He waiteth if by word or contenance   *watches to see*
That she to hym was changed of corage;   *heart*
710 But nevere koude he fynde variance.
She was ay oon in herte and in visage;
And ay the forther that she was in age,   *the older she grew*
The moore trewe, if that it were possible,
She was to hym in love, and moore penyble.   *painstaking*

715   For which it semed thus, that of hem two
Ther nas but o wyl; for, as Walter leste,   *desired*
The same lust was hire plesance also.   *desire; pleasure*
And, God be thanked, al fil for the beste.   *happened*
She shewed wel, for no worldly unreste
720 A wyf, as of hirself, nothing ne sholde
Wille in effect, but as hir housbonde wolde.

The sclaundre of Walter ofte and wyde   *evil report*
    spradde,   *spread*
That of a crueel herte he wikkedly,
For he a povre womman wedded hadde,   *because*
725 Hath mordred bothe his children prively.   *secretly*
Swich murmur was among hem comunly.
No wonder is, for to the peples ere   *ear*
Ther cam no word, but that they mordred were.

For which, where as his peple therbifore   *before this*
730 Hadde loved hym wel, the sclaundre of his diffame   *ill fame*
Made hem that they hym hatede therfore.   *for it*
To been a mordrere is an hateful name;
But nathelees, for ernest ne for game,
He of his crueel purpos nolde stente;   *give up*
735 To tempte his wyf was set al his entente.

Whan that his doghter twelve yeer was of age,
He to the court of Rome, in subtil wyse   *secret*
Enformed of his wyl, sente his message,   *messengers*
Comaundynge hem swiche bulles to devyse   *papal bulls*
740 As to his crueel purpos may suffyse,
How that the pope, as for his peples reste,   *peace of mind*
Bad hym to wedde another, if hym leste.   *he wished*

711 Her face and heart remained unchanged.
715–16 And so it seemed there was but one will between them.
719–21 She showed clearly that no wife, of her own accord or indeed for
    any earthly discomfort, should desire anything but what her husband
    desires.
733 i.e. on no account.
735 He could think of nothing else but testing his wife.

I seye, he bad they sholde countrefete
The popes bulles, makynge mencion
745 That he hath leve his firste wyf to lete,   *permission; leave*
As by the popes dispensacion,   *as if*
To stynte rancour and dissencion   *end*
Bitwixe his peple and hym; thus seyde the bulle,
The which they han publiced atte fulle.

750 The rude peple, as it no wonder is,   *ignorant*
Wenden ful wel that it hadde be right so;
But whan thise tidynges came to Grisildis,
I deeme that hire herte was ful wo.   *suppose; very sad*
But she, ylike sad for everemo,
755 Disposed was, this humble creature,
The adversitee of Fortune al t'endure,

Abidynge evere his lust and his plesance,   *will; pleasure*
To whom that she was yeven herte and al,   *given*
As to hire verray worldly suffisance.
760 But shortly if this storie I tellen shal,
This markys writen hath in special
A lettre, in which he sheweth his entente,
And secreely he to Boloigne it sente.

To the Erl of Panyk, which that hadde tho   *who; then*
765 Wedded his suster, preyde he specially
To bryngen hoom agayn his children two
In honurable estaat al openly.   *state*
But o thyng he hym preyede outrely,   *most particularly*
That he to no wight, though men wolde enquere,   *no one*
770 Sholde nat telle whos children that they were,

But seye, the mayden sholde ywedded be
Unto the Markys of Saluce anon.
And as this erl was preyed, so dide he;   *asked*
For at day set he on his wey is goon   *appointed*
775 Toward Saluce, and lordes many oon   *many a lord*
In riche array, this mayden for to gyde,   *escort*
Hir yonge brother ridynge hire bisyde.

Arrayed was toward hir mariage
This fresshe mayde, ful of gemmes cleere;
780 Hir brother, which that seven yeer was of age,
Arrayed eek ful fressh in his manere.

751 Really thought it was so.
754 As steadfast now as always.
759 As to one who was her true source of worldly contentment.
778 She wore a dress, in preparation for her marriage.
781 Was also gaily dressed in his own fashion.

And thus in greet noblesse and with glad cheere,
Toward Saluces shapynge hir journey,
Fro day to day they ryden in hir wey.

EXPLICIT QUARTA PARS

SEQUITUR PARS QUINTA

785   Among al this, after his wikke usage,   *meanwhile; custom*
This markys, yet his wyf to tempte moore
To the outtreste preeve of hir corage,
Fully to han experience and loore   *knowledge*
If that she were as stidefast as bifoore,
790   He on a day, in open audience,
Ful boistously hath seyd hire this sentence:

'Certes, Grisilde, I hadde ynogh plesance
To han yow to my wyf for youre goodnesse,
As for youre trouthe and for youre obeisance,
795   Noght for youre lynage, ne for youre   *lineage*
    richesse;   *wealth*
But now knowe I in verray soothfastnesse   *very truth*
That in greet lordshipe, if I wel avyse,
Ther is greet servitute in sondry wyse.

'I may nat doon as every plowman may.
800   My peple me constreyneth for to take
Another wyf, and crien day by day;   *clamour*
And eek the pope, rancour for to slake,   *end*
Consenteth it, that dar I undertake;
And trewely thus muche I wol yow seye,
805   My newe wyf is comynge by the weye.

'Be strong of herte, and voyde anon hir place,   *vacate*
And thilke dowere that ye broghten me,   *dowry*
Taak it agayn; I graunte it of my grace.   *back again*
Retourneth to youre fadres hous,' quod he;
810   'No man may alwey han prosperitee.
With evene herte I rede yow t'endure   *tranquil; advise*
The strook of Fortune or of aventure.'   *chance*

782 In great magnificence and in joyful mood.
787 With the ultimate test of her spirit.
791 Roughly spoke these words to her.
792 Certainly, Griselda, I was well enough pleased.
797-8 That greatness of rank, if I'm not mistaken, is in many ways
    great servitude.
803 Gives his consent to it, I assure you.

And she agayn answerde in pacience,
'My lord,' quod she, 'I woot, and wiste alway,   *know; knew*
815 How that bitwixen youre magnificence
And my poverte no wight kan ne may
Maken comparison; it is no nay.   *it cannot be denied*
I ne heeld me nevere digne in no manere
To be youre wyf, no, ne youre chamberere.   *chambermaid*

820   'And in this hous, ther ye me lady maade—   *where*
The heighe God take I for my witnesse,
And also wysly he my soule glaade—
I nevere heeld me lady ne maistresse,
But humble servant to youre worthynesse,   *worship*
825 And evere shal, whil that my lyf may dure,   *last*
Aboven every worldly creature.

'That ye so longe of youre benignitee
Han holden me in honour and nobleye,   *noble condition*
Where as I was noght worthy for to bee,
830 That thonke I God and yow, to whom I preye
Foryelde it yow; ther is namoore to seye.
Unto my fader gladly wol I wende,   *go*
And with hym dwelle unto my lyves ende.

'Ther I was fostred of a child ful smal,
835 Til I be deed my lyf ther wol I lede,
A wydwe clene in body, herte, and al.
For sith I yaf to yow my maydenhede,   *gave*
And am youre trewe wyf, it is no drede,   *without a doubt*
God shilde swich a lordes wyf to take   *forbid*
840 Another man to housbonde or to make!   *mate*

'And of youre newe wyf God of his grace
So graunte yow wele and prosperitee!   *happiness*
For I wol gladly yelden hire my place,   *yield*
In which that I was blisful wont to bee.
845 For sith it liketh yow, my lord,' quod shee,   *since; pleases*
'That whilom weren al myn hertes reste,
That I shal goon, I wol goon whan yow leste.   *you wish*

818 I never considered myself worthy in any way.
822 Even as I hope He may comfort my soul.
826 Above all other worldly creatures. (This line goes with 824.)
830–1 And I pray Him to reward you for it.
834–5 Where I was brought up from earliest childhood, there will I
   live my life until I die.
844 I used to be so happy.
846 Who once were my whole heart's-ease.

'But ther as ye me profre swich dowaire
As I first broghte, it is wel in my mynde
850 It were my wrecched clothes, nothyng faire,
The whiche to me were hard now for to fynde.
O goode God! how gentil and how kynde
Ye semed by youre speche and youre visage
The day that maked was oure mariage!

855 'But sooth is seyd—algate I fynde it trewe,
For in effect it preeved is on me—   *proved*
Love is noght oold as whan that it is newe.
But certes, lord, for noon adversitee,
To dyen in the cas, it shal nat bee
860 That evere in word or werk I shal repente   *deed*
That I yow yaf myn herte in hool entente.   *without reserve*

'My lord, ye woot that in my fadres place   *know*
Ye dide me streepe out of my povre weede,
And richely me cladden, of youre grace.
865 To yow broghte I noght elles, out of drede,   *without doubt*
But feith, and nakednesse, and maydenhede;
And heere agayn your clothyng I restoore,
And eek your weddyng ryng, for everemore.

'The remenant of youre jueles redy be   *rest*
870 Inwith youre chambre, dar I saufly sayn.   *in; safely*
Naked out of my fadres hous,' quod she,
'I cam, and naked moot I turne agayn.   *return*
Al youre plesance wol I folwen fayn;
But yet I hope it be nat youre entente
875 That I smoklees out of youre paleys wente.

'Ye koude nat doon so dishonest a thyng,   *dishonourable*
That thilke wombe in which youre children leye
Sholde biforn the peple, in my walkyng,
Be seyn al bare; wherfore I yow preye,
880 Lat me nat lyk a worm go by the weye.
Remembre yow, myn owene lord so deere,
I was youre wyf, though I unworthy weere.

848-9 But since you offer me such dowry as I first brought with me, I
well remember.
850 It was my wretched, ugly clothing.
855 But it is truly said—at least I find it true.
857 Love grown old is not the same as when it's new.
859 Even though I were to die for it.
863 You had me stripped out of my poor clothes.
873 I will gladly do all your pleasure.
875 That I should go out of your palace without a smock.

'Wherfore, in gerdon of my maydenhede   *reward for*
Which that I broghte, and noght agayn I bere,   *back again*
885 As voucheth sauf to yeve me, to my meede,
But swich a smok as I was wont to were,
That I therwith may wrye the wombe of here   *cover; her*
That was youre wyf. And heer take I my leeve
Of yow, myn owene lord, lest I yow greve.'   *offend*

890 'The smok,' quod he, 'that thou hast on thy bak,
Lat it be stille, and bere it forth with thee.'   *leave it on*
But wel unnethes thilke word he spak,
But wente his wey, for routhe and for pitee.
Biforn the folk hirselven strepeth she,   *strips*
895 And in hir smok, with heed and foot al bare,
Toward hir fader hous forth is she fare.

The folk hire folwe, wepynge in hir weye,   *follow*
And Fortune ay they cursen as they goon;
But she fro wepyng kepte hire eyen dreye,   *dry*
900 Ne in this tyme word ne spak she noon.
Hir fader, that this tidynge herde anoon,   *at once*
Curseth the day and tyme that Nature
Shoop hym to been a lyves creature.

For out of doute this olde poure man
905 Was evere in suspect of hir mariage;   *suspicious*
For evere he demed, sith that it bigan,   *thought*
That whan the lord fulfild hadde his corage,   *desire*
Hym wolde thynke it were a disparage
To his estaat so lowe for t'alighte,
910 And voyden hire as soone as ever he myghte.   *get rid of*

Agayns his doghter hastily goth he,   *to meet*
For he by noyse of folk knew hire comynge,
And with hire olde coote, as it myghte be,   *as best he could*
He covered hire, ful sorwefully wepynge.
915 But on hire body myghte he it nat brynge,
For rude was the clooth, and moore of age   *poor*
By dayes fele than at hire mariage.   *many*

885-6 Please deign to give me, as my reward, just such a smock.
892 But he found this almost more than he could say.
893 Because of the pity and compassion he felt.
903 Made him a living creature.
908-9 He would think it a disgrace to his high rank to have descended
so low.
915 But he could not make it cover all her body.

>   Thus with hire fader, for a certeyn space,   *time*
>   Dwelleth this flour of wyfly pacience,
> 920 That neither by hire wordes ne hire face,
>   Biforn the folk, ne eek in hire absence,   *their*
>   Ne shewed she that hire was doon offence;   *wrong*
>   Ne of hire heighe estaat no remembraunce
>   Ne hadde she, as by hire contenaunce.

> 925   No wonder is, for in hire grete estaat
>   Hire goost was evere in pleyn humylitee;   *spirit; complete*
>   No tendre mouth, noon herte delicaat,
>   No pompe, no semblant of roialtee,   *show of magnificence*
>   But ful of pacient benyngnytee,   *goodness*
> 930 Discreet and pridelees, ay honurable,   *without pride*
>   And to hire housbonde evere meke and stable.   *constant*

>   Men speke of Job, and moost for his   *particularly*
>   humblesse,
>   As clerkes, whan hem list, konne wel endite,
>   Namely of men, but as in soothfastnesse,
> 935 Though clerkes preise wommen but a lite,   *but little*
>   Ther kan no man in humblesse hym acquite
>   As womman kan, ne kan been half so trewe
>   As wommen been, but it be falle of newe.

[PART VI.]

>   Fro Boloigne is this Erl of Panyk come,
> 940 Of which the fame up sprang to moore and lesse,
>   And to the peples eres, alle and some,   *one and all*
>   Was kouth eek that a newe markysesse   *known*
>   He with hym broghte, in swich pompe and richesse
>   That nevere was ther seyn with mannes ye   *eye*
> 945 So noble array in al West Lumbardye.

>   The markys, which that shoop and   *who had arranged*
>   knew al this,
>   Er that this erl was come, sente his message   *messengers*
>   For thilke sely povre Grisildis;   *innocent*
>   And she with humble herte and glad visage,   *face*

924 To judge by her demeanour.
927 No delicate palate, no pleasure-loving heart.
933-4 And clerics, when they like, can highly praise this virtue in others
    —in men especially—but yet in truth.
936 There is no man who can behave as humbly as a woman can.
938 Unless it has happened recently (i.e. too recently for me to have
    heard of it).

950 Nat with no swollen thoght in hire corage,   *mind*
    Cam at his heste, and on hire knees hire sette,
    And reverently and wisely she hym grette.

    'Grisilde,' quod he, 'my wyl is outrely,   *absolutely*
    This mayden, that shal wedded been to me,
955 Received be to-morwe as roially
    As it possible is in myn hous to be,
    And eek that every wight in his degree
    Have his estaat, in sittyng and servyse
    And heigh plesaunce, as I kan best devyse.

960 'I have no wommen suffisaunt, certayn,
    The chambres for t'arraye in ordinaunce
    After my lust, and therfore wolde I fayn
    That thyn were al swich manere governaunce.
    Thou knowest eek of old al my plesaunce;
965 Thogh thyn array be badde and yvel biseye,
    Do thou thy devoir at the leeste weye.'

    'Nat oonly, lord, that I am glad,' quod she,
    'To doon youre lust, but I desire also
    Yow for to serve and plese in my degree
970 Withouten feyntyng, and shal everemo;   *fail*
    Ne nevere, for no wele ne no wo,
    Ne shal the goost withinne myn herte stente
    To love yow best with al my trewe entente.'

    And with that word she gan the hous
        to dighte,   *put in order*
975 And tables for to sette, and beddes make;
    And peyned hire to doon al that she myghte,   *took pains*
    Preyynge the chambereres, for Goddes sake,   *chambermaids*
    To hasten hem, and faste swepe and shake;
    And she, the mooste servysable of alle,   *willing to serve*
980 Hath every chambre arrayed and his halle.   *arranged*

    Abouten undren gan this erl alighte,   *mid morning*
    That with hym broghte thise noble children tweye,
    For which the peple ran to seen the sighte
    Of hire array, so richely biseye;   *rich looking*

951 Came at his command, and knelt down.
957–9 And also that everyone, according to his rank, shall be seated,
    served, and entertained as well as I can arrange it.
960–3 I certainly have no women capable of putting the rooms in good
    order, as I want them, and so I should be glad if you would take
    complete charge of such things.
965–6 Although your clothes are poor and wretched looking, I hope at
    least you will do your duty.
971–3 Never, come weal or woe, shall the spirit in my heart stop loving
    you best with all my true endeavour.

985 And thanne at erst amonges hem they seye
   That Walter was no fool, thogh that hym leste   *he wished*
   To chaunge his wyf, for it was for the beste.

   For she is fairer, as they deemen alle,   *decide*
   Than is Grisilde, and moore tendre of age,
990 And fairer fruyt bitwene hem sholde falle,
   And moore plesant, for hire heigh lynage.
   Hir brother eek so fair was of visage
   That hem to seen the peple hath caught plesaunce,
   Commendynge now the markys governaunce.—   *conduct*

995 'O stormy peple! unsad and evere untrewe!   *inconstant*
   Ay undiscreet and chaungynge as a fane!
   Delitynge evere in rumbul that is newe,   *rumour*
   For lyk the moone ay wexe ye and wane!   *wax*
   Ay ful of clappyng, deere ynogh a jane!
1000 Youre doom is fals, youre constance yvele preeveth;
   A ful greet fool is he that on yow leeveth.'   *believes in you*

   Thus seyden sadde folk in that citee,   *serious-minded*
   Whan that the peple gazed up and doun;
   For they were glad, right for the noveltee,
1005 To han a newe lady of hir toun.
   Namoore of this make I now mencioun,
   But to Grisilde agayn wol I me dresse,   *turn*
   And telle hir constance and hir bisynesse.—

   Ful bisy was Grisilde in every thyng
1010 That to the feeste was apertinent.
   Right noght was she abayst of hire clothyng,   *abashed*
   Thogh it were rude and somdeel eek torent;
   But with glad cheere to the yate is went   *cheerful face*
   With oother folk, to greete the markysesse,
1015 And after that dooth forth hire bisynesse.

985 And then for the first time they say among themselves.
990-1 And fairer and more pleasing children would be born to them because of her noble lineage.
993 That the people got pleasure from just looking at them.
996 Without discernment and always changing like a weather-vane.
999 Always full of noisy chatter which is not worth a farthing. (A *jane* was a Genoese coin of small value.)
1000 Your judgment is false, your constancy shows up badly when put to the test.
1012 Although it was coarse and also rather torn.
1015 Afterwards goes on with her work.

With so glad chiere his gestes she receyveth,
And so konnyngly, everich in his degree,
That no defaute no man aperceyveth,
But ay they wondren what she myghte bee
1020 That in so povre array was for to see,
And koude swich honour and reverence,   *knew how to do*
And worthily they preisen hire prudence.   *justly*

In al this meene while she ne stente   *did not stop*
This mayde and eek hir brother to commende   *praise*
1025 With al hir herte, in ful benyngne entente,   *kindly*
So wel that no man koude hir pris amende.
But atte laste, whan that thise lordes wende   *go*
To sitten doun to mete, he gan to calle
Grisilde, as she was bisy in his halle.

1030 'Grisilde,' quod he, as it were in his pley,   *jest*
'How liketh thee my wyf and hire beautee?'   *pleases*
'Right wel,' quod she, 'my lord; for, in good fey,   *faith*
A fairer saugh I nevere noon than she.   *saw*
I prey to God yeve hire prosperitee;
1035 And so hope I that he wol to yow sende
Plesance ynogh unto youre lyves ende.

'O thyng biseke I yow, and warne also,   *beseech*
That ye ne prikke with no tormentynge
This tendre mayden, as ye han doon mo;   *others*
1040 For she is fostred in hire norissynge   *bringing up*
Moore tendrely, and, to my supposynge,
She koude nat adversitee endure
As koude a povre fostred creature.'

And whan this Walter saugh hire pacience,
1045 Hir glade chiere, and no malice at al,
And he so ofte had doon to hire offence,   *harm*
And she ay sad and constant as a wal,   *firm*
Continuynge evere hire innocence overal,
This sturdy markys gan his herte dresse   *stern; inclined*
1050 To rewen upon hire wyfly stedfastnesse.   *have pity on*

'This is ynogh, Grisilde myn,' quod he;
'Be now namoore agast ne yvele   *frightened; displeased*
     apayed.
I have thy feith and thy benyngnytee,
As wel as evere womman was, assayed,

1017 Expertly, each one according to his rank.
1026 So well that no one could have bettered her words of praise.
1038 That you should never goad or torment.
1043 A person brought up in poverty.
1048 Maintaining her innocence in all circumstances.

1055 In greet estaat, and povreliche arrayed.
Now knowe I, dere wyf, thy stedfastnesse,'—
And hire in armes took and gan hire kesse.   *kissed*

And she for wonder took of it no keep;   *notice*
She herde nat what thyng he to hire seyde;
1060 She ferde as she had stert out of a sleep,
Til she out of hire mazednesse abreyde.
'Grisilde,' quod he, 'by God, that for us deyde,
Thou art my wyf, ne noon oother I have,
Ne nevere hadde, as God my soule save!

1065 'This is thy doghter, which thou hast supposed
To be my wyf; that oother feithfully   *assuredly*
Shal be myn heir, as I have ay disposed;   *intended*
Thou bare hym in thy body trewely.
At Boloigne have I kept hem prively;   *secretly*
1070 Taak hem agayn, for now maystow nat seye   *say*
That thou hast lorn noon of thy children tweye.

'And folk that ootherweys han seyd of me,   *otherwise*
I warne hem wel that I have doon this deede
For no malice, ne for no crueltee,
1075 But for t'assaye in thee thy wommanheede,   *test*
And nat to sleen my children—God forbeede!—   *slay*
But for to kepe hem pryvely and stille,
Til I thy purpos knewe and al thy wille.'   *resolution*

Whan she this herde, aswowne doun she falleth   *in a swoon*
1080 For pitous joye, and after hire swownynge
She bothe hire yonge children to hire calleth,
And in hire armes, pitously wepynge,
Embraceth hem, and tendrely kissynge
Ful lyk a mooder, with hire salte teeres
1085 She bathed bothe hire visage and hire heeres.

O which a pitous thyng it was to se
Hir swownyng, and hire humble voys to heere!
'Grauntmercy, lord, God thanke it yow,' quod she,
'That ye han saved me my children deere!
1090 Now rekke I nevere to been deed right heere;
Sith I stonde in youre love and in youre grace,
No fors of deeth, ne whan my spirit pace!

1055 i.e. in both wealth and poverty.
1060–1 She behaved as if she had just started out of sleep, until at last
     she recovered from her stupor.
1071 Lost either of your two children.
1077 But to keep them secretly hidden.
1090 Now I don't care if I die here and now.
1092 Death does not matter, nor when my spirit leaves me.

'O tendre, o deere, o yonge children myne!
Youre woful mooder wende stedfastly   *thought*
1095 That crueel houndes or som foul vermyne
Hadde eten yow; but God, of his mercy,
And youre benyngne fader tendrely
Hath doon yow kept,'—and in that same stounde   *moment*
Al sodeynly she swapte adoun to grounde.   *fell*

1100 And in hire swough so sadly holdeth she   *swoon; tightly*
Hire children two, whan she gan hem t'embrace,
That with greet sleighte and greet difficultee   *skill*
The children from hire arm they gonne arace.   *removed*
O many a teere on many a pitous face
1105 Doun ran of hem that stooden hire bisyde;
Unnethe abouten hire myghte they abyde.

Walter hire gladeth, and hire sorwe   *comforts*
    slaketh;   *assuages*
She riseth up, abaysed, from hire traunce,   *abashed*
And every wight hire joye and feeste maketh
1110 Til she hath caught agayn hire contenaunce.
Walter hire dooth so feithfully plesaunce
That it was deyntee for to seen the cheere   *a joy; gladness*
Bitwixe hem two, now they been met yfeere.   *together*

Thise ladyes, whan that they hir tyme say,   *saw*
1115 Han taken hire and into chambre gon,
And strepen hire out of hire rude array,
And in a clooth of gold that brighte shoon,   *brightly shone*
With a coroune of many a riche stoon
Upon hire heed, they into halle hire broghte,
1120 And ther she was honured as hire oghte.   *was her right*

Thus hath this pitous day a blisful ende,
For every man and womman dooth his myght   *best*
This day in murthe and revel to dispende   *spend*
Til on the welkne shoon the sterres lyght.   *sky; shone*
1125 For moore solempne in every mannes syght   *magnificent*
This feste was, and gretter of costage,   *of greater richness*
Than was the revel of hire mariage.

Ful many a yeer in heigh prosperitee   *great*
Lyven thise two in concord and in reste,   *harmony; peace*
1130 And richely his doghter maryed he
Unto a lord, oon of the worthieste

1098 Has had you taken care of.
1106 They could hardly bear to stay near her.
1109–10 And everyone congratulates and makes much of her until she
    has regained her composure.
1111 Walter tries so hard to please her.

Of al Ytaille; and thanne in pees and reste   *quiet*
His wyves fader in his court he kepeth,
Til that the soule out of his body crepeth.

1135 His sone succedeth in his heritage
In reste and pees, after his fader day,   *father's*
And fortunat was eek in mariage,
Al putte he nat his wyf in greet assay.
This world is nat so strong, it is no nay,   *there's no denying*
1140 As it hath been in olde tymes yoore,
And herkneth what this auctour seith therfoore.

This storie is seyd, nat for that wyves sholde
Folwen Grisilde as in humylitee,
For it were inportable, though they wolde;
1145 But for that every wight, in his degree,
Sholde be constant in adversitee
As was Grisilde; therfore Petrak writeth
This storie, which with heigh stile he enditeth.   *composes*

For, sith a womman was so pacient
1150 Unto a mortal man, wel moore us oghte
Receyven al in gree that God us sent;   *gladly*
For greet skile is, he preeve that he wroghte.
But he ne tempteth no man that he boghte,
As seith Seint Jame, if ye his pistel rede;   *epistle*
1155 He preeveth folk al day, it is no drede,

And suffreth us, as for oure exercise,
With sharpe scourges of adversitee
Ful ofte to be bete in sondry wise;   *beaten; various ways*
Nat for to knowe oure wyl, for certes he,
1160 Er we were born, knew al oure freletee;   *frailty*
And for oure beste is al his governaunce.
Lat us thanne lyve in vertuous suffraunce.   *patience*

But o word, lordynges, herkneth er I go:
It were ful hard to fynde now-a-dayes
1165 In al a toun Grisildis thre or two;   *Griseldas*
For if that they were put to swiche assayes,   *trials*

1138 Although he did not put his wife to any great test.
1144 For they would find it intolerable, with the best will in the world.
1150 All the more ought we.
1152 For it is very reasonable that He should test what He has created.
1153-5 He tempts no one whom He has redeemed, as St James says, if
you read his epistle (Jas. i. 13-14); but, undoubtedly, He is always
testing us. (A distinction is made here between 'tempting with evil'
and 'testing.')
1159 Not simply to test our will power.

The gold of hem hath now so badde alayes   *such; alloys*
With bras, that thogh the coyne be fair at ye,   *to view*
It wolde rather breste a-two than plye.

1170   For which heere, for the Wyves love of Bathe—
Whos lyf and al hire secte God mayntene
In heigh maistrie, and elles were it scathe—
I wol with lusty herte, fressh and grene,
Seyn yow a song to glade yow, I wene;
1175 And lat us stynte of ernestful matere.
Herkneth my song that seith in this manere:

LENVOY DE CHAUCER

Grisilde is deed, and eek hire pacience,   *dead*
And bothe atones buryed in Ytaille;
For which I crie in open audience,
1180 No wedded man so hardy be t'assaille
His wyves pacience in trust to fynde
Grisildis, for in certein he shal faille.   *certainly*

O noble wyves, ful of heigh prudence,
Lat noon humylitee youre tonge naille,   *nail down*
1185 Ne lat no clerk have cause or diligence
To write of yow a storie of swich mervaille
As of Grisildis pacient and kynde,
Lest Chichevache yow swelwe in hire   *swallow*
        entraille!   *inside*

Folweth Ekko, that holdeth no silence,
1190 But evere answereth at the countretaille.
Beth nat bidaffed for youre innocence,   *fooled*
But sharply taak on yow the governaille.
Emprenteth wel this lessoun in youre mynde,
For commune profit sith it may availle.

1169 It would sooner break in two than bend.
1170-4 And so, for love of the Wife of Bath, whose mastery and that
    of all her sex may God maintain—a pity else—with young and
    joyful heart I'll sing you a song I think will cheer you.
1175 And let us have done with this serious subject.
1179 For which reason I say in the hearing of you all.
1180-2 Let no married man be so foolhardy as to test his wife's patience
    in the hope of finding a Griselda.
1186-7 Such a marvellous story as that of Griselda.
1188 *Chichevache*, 'lean cow,' the name of a fabulous monster who
    lives on a diet of patient wives, and is very thin in consequence.
1189-90 Be like Echo, who is never silent, but always answers back.
1192 But peremptorily take charge of things.
1194 Since it may promote the public good.

1195   Ye archewyves, stondeth at defense,   *masterly wives*
        Syn ye be strong as is a greet camaille;   *camel*
        Ne suffreth nat that men yow doon offense.   *harm*
        And sklendre wyves, fieble as in bataille,   *slender*
        Beth egre as is a tygre yond in Ynde;
1200   Ay clappeth as a mille, I yow consaille.   *clatter*

        Ne dreed hem nat, doth hem no reverence,
        For though thyn housbonde armed be in maille,   *mail*
        The arwes of thy crabbed eloquence
        Shal perce his brest, and eek his aventaille.
1205   In jalousie I rede eek thou hym bynde,   *advise*
        And thou shalt make hym couche as doth a quaille.   *cower*

        If thou be fair, ther folk been in presence   *where; present*
        Shewe thou thy visage and thyn apparaille;   *apparel*
        If thou be foul, be fre of thy dispence;
1210   To gete thee freendes ay do thy travaille;
        Be ay of chiere as light as leef on lynde,
        And lat hym care, and wepe, and wrynge, and waille!

HEERE ENDETH THE TALE OF THE
CLERK OF OXENFORD

1199 Be fierce as a tiger far away in India.
1204 *aventaille*, the movable front of a helmet.
1209-10 If you are ugly, be free in your spending, and work hard to get
    yourself friends.
1211 Always be as light of heart as a leaf on a linden-tree (proverbial).

THE MERCHANT'S PROLOGUE

The Prologe of the Marchantes Tale

'WEPYNG and waylyng, care and oother sorwe
I knowe ynogh, on even and a-morwe,'
1215 Quod the Marchant, 'and so doon other mo   *others besides*
That wedded been. I trowe that it be so,
For wel I woot it fareth so with me.   *know; goes*
I have a wyf, the worste that may be;
For thogh the feend to hire ycoupled were,
1220 She wolde hym overmacche, I dar wel swere.   *outmatch*
What sholde I yow reherce in special
Hir hye malice? She is a shrewe at al.
Ther is a long and large difference   *broad*
Bitwix Grisildis grete pacience
1225 And of my wyf the passyng crueltee.   *surpassing*
Were I unbounden, also moot I thee!
I wolde nevere eft comen in the snare.   *again*
We wedded men lyven in sorwe and care.
Assaye whoso wole, and he shal fynde
1230 That I seye sooth, by Seint Thomas of Ynde,   *truth; India*
As for the moore part, I sey nat alle.
God shilde that it sholde so bifalle!   *forbid*
  A! goode sire Hoost, I have ywedded bee
Thise monthes two, and moore nat, pardee;   *indeed*
1235 And yet, I trowe, he that al his lyve   *life*
Wyflees hath been, though that men wolde him
    ryve   *pierce*
Unto the herte, ne koude in no manere   *possibly*
Tellen so muchel sorwe as I now heere   *much*
Koude tellen of my wyves cursednesse!'   *shrewishness*
1240   'Now,' quod oure Hoost, 'Marchaunt, so God
    yow blesse,

1213 Here (and possibly in 1381) the Merchant is repeating bitterly the
    last words spoken by the Clerk.
1214 I know all about, both night and morning.
1221–2 Why should I give you the details of her great malice? She is
    an out-and-out shrew.
1226 If I were free, as I hope to prosper!
1229 Let him try it who will.
1231 Concerning the majority of marriages.

Syn ye so muchel knowen of that art,
Ful hertely I pray yow telle us part.'
  'Gladly,' quod he, 'but of myn owene soore,   *misery*
For soory herte, I telle may namoore.'

THE MERCHANT'S TALE

HEERE BIGYNNETH THE MARCHANTES TALE

1245   WHILOM ther was dwellynge in Lumbardye
        A worthy knyght, that born was of Pavye,   *Pavia*
        In which he lyved in greet prosperitee;
        And sixty yeer a wyflees man was hee,
        And folwed ay his bodily delyt
1250   On wommen, ther as was his appetyt,
        As doon thise fooles that been seculeer.
        And whan that he was passed sixty yeer,
        Were it for hoolynesse or for dotage,
        I kan nat seye, but swich a greet corage   *desire*
1255   Hadde this knyght to been a wedded man
        That day and nyghte he dooth al that he kan
        T'espien where he myghte wedded be;
        Preyinge oure Lord to graunten him that he
        Mighte ones knowe of thilke blisful lyf
1260   That is bitwixe an housbonde and his wyf,
        And for to lyve under that hooly boond   *bond*
        With which that first God man and womman bond.   *bound*
        'Noon oother lyf,' seyde he, 'is worth a bene;   *bean*
        For wedlok is so esy and so clene,   *comfortable; pure*
1265   That in this world it is a paradys.'
        Thus seyde this olde knyght, that was so wys.

1241 Since you know so much about that art (i.e. the art of being
     unhappily married).
1244 For sorrow of heart I can say no more.
1250 Where his appetite led him.
1251 As foolish laymen do.
1257 To discover a wife for himself.
1259 For once learn something of that blissful life.

And certeinly, as sooth as God is kyng,   *truly*
To take a wyf it is a glorious thyng,
And namely whan a man is oold and hoor;   *especially; grey*
1270 Thanne is a wyf the fruyt of his tresor.
Thanne sholde he take a yong wyf and a feir,   *fair*
On which he myghte engendren hym an heir,
And lede his lyf in joye and in solas,   *pleasure*
Where as thise bacheleris synge 'allas,'
1275 Whan that they fynden any adversitee
In love, which nys but childyssh vanytee.
And trewely it sit wel to be so,
That bacheleris have often peyne and wo;
On brotel ground they buylde, and brotelnesse
1280 They fynde, whan they wene sikernesse.
They lyve but as a bryd or as a beest,   *bird*
In libertee, and under noon arreest,   *restraint*
Ther as a wedded man in his estaat   *position*
Lyveth a lyf blisful and ordinaat,   *ordered*
1285 Under this yok of mariage ybounde.
Wel may his herte in joy and blisse habounde,   *abound*
For who kan be so buxom as a wyf?   *obedient*
Who is so trewe, and eek so ententyf   *careful*
To kepe hym, syk and hool, as is his make?
1290 For wele or wo she wole hym nat forsake;
She nys nat wery hym to love and serve,   *weary*
Thogh that he lye bedrede, til he sterve.   *bedridden; die*
And yet somme clerkes seyn it nys nat so,   *learned men*
Of whiche he Theofraste is oon of tho.
1295 What force though Theofraste liste lye?
'Ne take no wyf,' quod he, 'for housbondrye,   *economy*
As for to spare in houshold thy dispence.   *expense*
A trewe servant dooth moore diligence   *takes more trouble*
Thy good to kepe, than thyn owene wyf,
1300 For she wol clayme half part al hir lyf.
And if that thou be syk, so God me save,
Thy verray freendes, or a trewe knave,
Wol kepe thee bet than she that waiteth ay
After thy good and hath doon many a day.

1270 The flower of his possessions.
1276 Which is nothing but childish folly.
1277 It is quite right it should be so.
1279–80 They build on unstable ground, and instability is what they
    find, when they expect security.
1289 To look after him, in sickness and in health, as his mate is.
1294 One of whom is Theophrastus.
1295 What does it matter if Theophrastus chose to lie?
1299 To look after your property.
1302–4 Your true friends, or a faithful servant, will take better care of
    you than a wife who looks forward all the time to enjoying your
    possessions.

1305 And if thou take a wyf unto thyn hoold,   *keeping*
     Ful lightly maystow been a cokewold.'
     This sentence, and an hundred thynges worse,   *opinion*
     Writeth this man, ther God his bones corse!   *curse*
     But take no kep of al swich vanytee;   *folly*
1310 Deffie Theofraste, and herke me.   *defy*
        A wyf is Goddes yifte verraily;
     Alle othere manere yiftes hardily,   *kinds of; certainly*
     As londes, rentes, pasture, or commune,   *common land*
     Or moebles, alle been yiftes of Fortune,   *movable goods*
1315 That passen as a shadwe upon a wal.
     But drede nat, if pleynly speke I shal,
     A wyf wol laste, and in thyn hous endure,
     Wel lenger than thee list, paraventure.
        Mariage is a ful greet sacrement.
1320 He which that hath no wyf, I holde hym shent;
     He lyveth helplees and al desolat,—
     I speke of folk in seculer estaat.
     And herke why, I sey nat this for noght,
     That womman is for mannes helpe ywroght.
1325 The hye God, whan he hadde Adam maked,
     And saugh him al allone, bely-naked,   *saw; stark naked*
     God of his grete goodnesse seyde than,
     'Lat us now make an helpe unto this man
     Lyk to hymself'; and thanne he made him Eve.   *for him*
1330 Heere may ye se, and heerby may ye preve,   *prove*
     That wyf is mannes helpe and his confort,
     His paradys terrestre, and his disport.   *diversion*
     So buxom and so vertuous is she,
     They moste nedes lyve in unitee.
1335 O flessh they been, and o flessh, as I gesse,   *one*
     Hath but oon herte, in wele and in distresse.   *happiness*
        A wyf! a, Seinte Marie, *benedicite!*   *bless us*
     How myghte a man han any adversitee
     That hath a wyf?   Certes, I kan nat seye.   *certainly*
1340 The blisse which that is bitwixe hem tweye   *two*
     Ther may no tonge telle, or herte thynke.
     If he be povre, she helpeth hym to swynke;   *toil*
     She kepeth his good, and wasteth never   *looks after*
        a deel;   *bit*
     Al that hire housbonde lust, hire liketh weel;
1345 She seith nat ones 'nay,' whan he seith 'ye.'
     'Do this,' seith he; 'Al redy, sire,' seith she.

     1306 You may very easily find yourself a cuckold.
     1318 Much longer than you wish, perhaps.
     1320 I regard him as lost.
     1323-4 I don't say this for nothing; listen why woman was made to be
        man's helpmate.
     1344 All that her husband wishes is a great pleasure to her.

O blisful ordre of wedlok precious,
Thou art so murye, and eek so vertuous,   *pleasant*
And so commended and approved eek   *approved of*
1350 That every man that halt hym worth a leek,
Upon his bare knees oughte al his lyf
Thanken his God that hym hath sent a wyf,
Or elles preye to God hym for to sende
A wyf, to laste unto his lyves ende.
1355 For thanne his lyf is set in sikernesse;   *security*
He may nat be deceyved, as I gesse,
So that he werke after his wyves reed.
Thanne may he boldely beren up his heed,   *hold*
They been so trewe, and therwithal so wyse;
1360 For which, if thou wolt werken as the wyse,
Do alwey so as wommen wol thee rede.   *advise*
   Lo, how that Jacob, as thise clerkes rede,
By good conseil of his mooder Rebekke,   *Rebecca*
Boond the kydes skyn aboute his nekke,   *fastened; kid's*
1365 For which his fadres benyson he wan.   *blessing; won*
   Lo Judith, as the storie eek telle kan,
By wys conseil she Goddes peple kepte,   *saved*
And slow hym Olofernus, whil he slepte.   *slew; Holofernes*
   Lo Abigayl, by good conseil, how she   *Abigail*
1370 Saved hir housbonde Nabal, whan that he
Sholde han be slayn; and looke, Ester also
By good conseil delyvered out of wo
The peple of God, and made hym Mardochee
Of Assuere enhaunced for to be.
1375 Ther nys no thyng in gree superlatyf,   *degree*
As seith Senek, above an humble wyf.   *Seneca*
   Suffre thy wyves tonge, as Catoun bit;   *Cato; bids*
She shal comande, and thou shalt suffren it,
And yet she wole obeye of curteisye.   *out of courtesy*
1380 A wyf is kepere of thyn housbondrye;   *household goods*
Wel may the sike man biwaille and wepe,
Ther as ther nys no wyf the hous to kepe.
I warne thee, if wisely thou wolt wirche,   *act*
Love wel thy wyf, as Crist loved his chirche.
1385 If thou lovest thyself, thou lovest thy wyf;
No man hateth his flessh, but in his lyf
He fostreth it, and therfore bidde I thee,   *fosters*
Cherisse thy wyf, or thou shalt nevere thee.   *cherish; prosper*

1350 That holds himself worth a leek, i.e. who sets any value on himself.
1357 So long as he acts on his wife's advice.
1362 As clerics tell us.
1371 Was going to be slain; and think how Esther, too.
1373-4 And brought it about that Mordecai was advanced by Ahasuerus.
1377 *Catoun.* See I. 3227.

Housbonde and wyf, what so men jape or pleye,
1390 Of worldly folk holden the siker weye;   *safe*
They been so knyt ther may noon harm bityde,
And namely upon the wyves syde.   *especially*
For which this Januarie, of whom I tolde,
Considered hath, inwith his dayes olde,   *in*
1395 The lusty lyf, the vertuous quyete,   *repose*
That is in mariage hony-sweete;
And for his freendes on a day he sente,
To tellen hem th'effect of his entente.
     With face sad his tale he hath hem toold.   *serious*
1400 He seyde, 'Freendes, I am hoor and oold,   *grey*
And almoost, God woot, on my pittes brynke;
Upon my soule somwhat moste I thynke.   *must*
I have my body folily despended;   *foolishly expended*
Blessed be God that it shal been amended!
1405 For I wol be, certeyn, a wedded man,
And that anoon in al the haste I kan.
Unto som mayde fair and tendre of age,   *of tender years*
I prey yow, shapeth for my mariage   *prepare*
Al sodeynly, for I wol nat abyde;   *promptly*
1410 And I wol fonde t'espien, on my syde,
To whom I may be wedded hastily.
But forasmuche as ye been mo than I,
Ye shullen rather swich a thyng espyen   *sooner*
Than I, and where me best were to allyen.
1415   But o thyng warne I yow, my freendes deere,
I wol noon oold wyf han in no manere.   *on any account*
She shal nat passe twenty yeer, certayn;
Oold fissh and yong flessh wolde I have   *gladly*
     fayn.
Bet is,' quod he, 'a pyk than a pykerel,
1420 And bet than old boef is the tendre veel.
I wol no womman thritty yeer of age;
It is but bene-straw and greet forage.   *coarse fodder*
And eek thise olde wydwes, God it woot,
They konne so muchel craft on Wades boot,

1389 Whatever jokes are made at their expense.
1391 They are so closely joined that no harm can befall them.
1398 The drift of what he had in mind.
1401 On the brink of the grave.
1410 I will try to find out, for my part.
1412 You are many to my one.
1414 Where it would be best for me to make an alliance.
1419-20 A pike is better than a pickerel, and tender veal is better than
     old beef.
1424 They are so expert at handling Wade's boat. (The allusion is to
     a famous Germanic hero, first mentioned in the Old English poem
     Widsith; but the point of the allusion is lost.)

1425 So muchel broken harm, whan that hem leste,
      That with hem sholde I nevere lyve in reste.   *peace*
      For sondry scoles maken sotile clerkis;
      Womman of manye scoles half a clerk is.
      But certeynly, a yong thyng may men gye,   *guide*
1430 Right as men may warm wex with handes plye.   *mould*
      Wherfore I sey yow pleynly, in a clause,   *briefly*
      I wol noon oold wyf han right for this cause.   *reason*
      For if so were I hadde swich myschaunce,
      That I in hire ne koude han no plesaunce,
1435 Thanne sholde I lede my lyf in avoutrye,   *adultery*
      And go streight to the devel, whan I dye.
      Ne children sholde I none upon hire geten;   *beget*
      Yet were me levere houndes had me eten,
      Than that myn heritage sholde falle
1440 In straunge hand, and this I telle yow alle.
      I dote nat, I woot the cause why   *know*
      Men sholde wedde, and forthermoore woot I,
      Ther speketh many a man of mariage
      That woot namoore of it than woot my page,
1445 For whiche causes man sholde take a wyf.   *why a man*
      If he ne may nat lyven chaast his lyf,   *chaste*
      Take hym a wyf with greet devocioun,
      By cause of leveful procreacioun   *lawful*
      Of children, to th'onour of God above,
1450 And nat oonly for paramour or love;   *lust*
      And for they sholde leccherye eschue,   *avoid*
      And yelde hir dette whan that it is due;
      Or for that ech of hem sholde helpen oother
      In meschief, as a suster shal the brother;   *misfortune*
1455 And lyve in chastitee ful holily.
      But sires, by youre leve, that am nat I   *leave*
      For, God be thanked! I dar make avaunt,   *boast*
      I feele my lymes stark and suffisaunt   *strong; sufficient*
      To do al that a man bilongeth to;
1460 I woot myselven best what I may do.
      Though I be hoor, I fare as dooth a tree
      That blosmeth er that fruyt ywoxen bee;
      And blosmy tree nys neither drye ne deed.   *blossoming; dead*
      I feele me nowhere hoor but on myn heed;

1425 So many petty annoyances, when they like.
1427 Instruction in different schools (i.e. universities or university
      faculties) produces expert scholars.
1433–4 If I were unfortunate enough to marry someone in whom I
      could take no pleasure.
1438 I'd rather be eaten by dogs.
1447 Let him take a wife with great devoutness.
1461–2 Though I'm white-haired, I'm like a tree that blossoms (white)
      before the fruit can grow.

1465 Myn herte and alle my lymes been as grene
     As laurer thurgh the yeer is for to sene.
     And syn that ye han herd al myn entente,
     I prey yow to my wyl ye wole assente.'
          Diverse men diversely hym tolde
1470 Of mariage manye ensamples olde.   *instances*
     Somme blamed it, somme preysed it, certeyn;
     But atte laste, shortly for to seyn,   *briefly*
     As al day falleth altercacioun
     Bitwixen freendes in disputisoun,   *argument*
1475 Ther fil a stryf bitwixe his bretheren two,
     Of whiche that oon was cleped Placebo,
     Justinus soothly called was that oother.   *truly*
          Placebo seyde, 'O Januarie, brother,
     Ful litel nede hadde ye, my lord so deere,
1480 Conseil to axe of any that is heere,   *advice; ask*
     But that ye been so ful of sapience   *except; wisdom*
     That yow ne liketh, for youre heighe prudence,
     To weyven fro the word of Salomon.   *turn aside*
     This word seyde he unto us everychon:
1485 "Wirk alle thyng by conseil," thus seyde he,
     "And thanne shaltow nat repente thee."
     But though that Salomon spak swich a word,
     Myn owene deere brother and my lord,
     So wysly God my soule brynge at reste,
1490 I holde youre owene conseil is the beste.
     For, brother myn, of me taak this motyf,
     I have now been a court-man al my lyf,   *courtier*
     And God it woot, though I unworthy be,
     I have stonden in ful greet degree
1495 Abouten lordes of ful heigh estaat;
     Yet hadde I nevere with noon of hem debaat.   *a quarrel*
     I nevere hem contraried, trewely;   *contradicted*
     I woot wel that my lord kan moore than I.
     What that he seith, I holde it ferme and stable;
1500 I seye the same, or elles thyng semblable.   *similar*
     A ful greet fool is any conseillour
     That serveth any lord of heigh honour,

1466 As laurel looks the whole year through.
1473 As an altercation always arises.
1475 A quarrel broke out between his two brothers.
1476 Of whom one was called Placebo, i.e. sycophant. (See III. 2075.)
1482 That you are unwilling, for your great prudence.
1485-6 See I. 3530.
1489 God rest my soul.
1491 Take this suggestion from me, i.e. take it from me.
1494-5 I have held great positions of trust under lords of high degree.
1498 I am well aware that my lord knows more than I.
1499 Whatever he says I confirm it.

That dar presume, or elles thenken it,
That his conseil sholde passe his lordes wit.   *exceed*
1505 Nay, lordes been no fooles, by my fay!   *faith*
Ye han youreselven shewed heer to-day   *shown*
So heigh sentence, so holily and weel,
That I consente and conferme everydeel
Youre wordes alle and youre opinioun.
1510 By God, ther nys no man in al this toun,
Ne in Ytaille, that koude bet han sayd!   *Italy; better*
Crist halt hym of this conseil ful wel apayd.
And trewely, it is an heigh corage
Of any man that stapen is in age
1515 To take a yong wyf; by my fader kyn,   *father's*
Youre herte hangeth on a joly pyn!
Dooth now in this matiere right as yow leste,   *matter; please*
For finally I holde it for the beste.'
    Justinus, that ay stille sat and herde,
1520 Right in this wise he to Placebo answerde:
'Now, brother myn, be pacient, I preye,
Syn ye han seyd, and herkneth what I seye.   *since*
Senek, amonges othere wordes wyse,
Seith that a man oghte hym right wel   *carefully consider*
    avyse
1525 To whom he yeveth his lond or his catel.   *property*
And syn I oghte avyse me right wel
To whom I yeve my good awey fro me,
Wel muchel moore I oghte avysed be   *very much*
To whom I yeve my body for alwey.   *always*
1530 I warne yow wel, it is no childes pley
To take a wyf withouten avysement.   *deliberation*
Men moste enquere, this is myn assent,   *opinion*
Wher she be wys, or sobre, or dronkelewe,
Or proud, or elles ootherweys a shrewe;
1535 A chidestere, or wastour of thy good,   *scold*
Or riche, or poore, or elles mannyssh wood.   *man-mad*
Al be it so that no man fynden shal
Noon in this world that trotteth hool in al,

1503 Who dares to presume, or even imagine.
1507–8 Such noble sentiments, in such an excellent and holy manner,
    that I agree to and confirm completely.
1512 Christ will be well pleased with your intention.
1513–15 It is a noble desire in any man advanced in years to want to
    take a young wife.
1516 Your heart hangs on a jolly peg, i.e. you have a merry heart.
1527 To whom I give away my goods.
1533 Whether she is prudent, or sober, or addicted to drink.
1534 Or bad in other ways.
1538 Anyone in this world who is faultless (lit. trots sound) in all
    respects.

Ne man, ne beest, swich as men koude devyse;
1540 But nathelees it oghte ynough suffise
With any wyf, if so were that she hadde
Mo goode thewes than hire vices badde;
And al this axeth leyser for t'enquere.
For, God it woot, I have wept many a teere
1545 Ful pryvely, syn I have had a wyf,   *in secret*
Preyse whoso wole a wedded mannes lyf,
Certein I fynde in it but cost and care
And observances, of alle blisses bare.
And yet, God woot, my neighebores aboute,   *round about*
1550 And namely of wommen many a route,   *especially; crowd*
Seyn that I have the mooste stedefast wyf,   *say*
And eek the mekeste oon that bereth lyf;   *meekest one*
But I woot best where wryngeth me my sho.   *pinches*
Ye mowe, for me, right as yow liketh do;
1555 Avyseth yow—ye been a man of age—
How that ye entren into mariage,
And namely with a yong wyf and a fair.
By hym that made water, erthe, and air,
The yongeste man that is in al this route   *company*
1560 Is bisy ynough to bryngen it aboute
To han his wyf allone.   Trusteth me,
Ye shul nat plesen hire fully yeres thre,—
This is to seyn, to doon hire ful pleasaunce.
A wyf axeth ful many an observaunce.
1565 I prey yow that ye be nat yvele apayd.'   *displeased*
'Wel,' quod this Januarie, 'and hastow ysayd
Straw for thy Senek, and for thy proverbes!
I counte nat a panyer ful of herbes
Of scole-termes.   Wyser men than thow,
1570 As thou hast herd, assenteden right now
To my purpos.   Placebo, what sey ye?'
'I seye it is a cursed man,' quod he,
'That letteth matrimoigne, sikerly.'   *hinders matrimony*
And with that word they rysen sodeynly,
1575 And been assented fully that he sholde

1539 Neither man nor beast that we are capable of imagining.
1540-2 Nevertheless it ought to satisfy us if a wife has more good
   qualities than bad.
1541 And all this demands leisure for investigation.
1546 Let him who will praise a married man's life.
1548 And duties, utterly devoid of joy.
1554 You can do as you like, as far as I'm concerned.
1555-6 You're old enough to stop and think before you enter into
   marriage.
1560-1 Has his work cut out to keep his wife to himself.
1564 A wife demands a lot of attention.
1568 I wouldn't give a basketful of weeds for your school terms (i.e.
   propositions and syllogisms).

Be wedded whanne hym liste, and where   *he pleased*
    he wolde.
    Heigh fantasye and curious bisynesse
Fro day to day gan in the soule impresse
Of Januarie aboute his mariage.
1580 Many fair shap and many a fair visage   *form; face*
Ther passeth thurgh his herte nyght by nyght,
As whoso tooke a mirour, polisshed bryght,
And sette it in a commune market-place,
Thanne sholde he se ful many a figure pace   *pass*
1585 By his mirour; and in the same wyse   *way*
Gan Januarie inwith his thoght devyse
Of maydens whiche that dwelten hym bisyde.
He wiste nat wher that he myghte abyde.
For if that oon have beaute in hir face,
1590 Another stant so in the peples grace   *stands; favour*
For hire sadnesse and hire benyngnytee   *sobriety; goodness*
That of the peple grettest voys hath she;   *praise*
And somme were riche, and hadden badde name.
But nathelees, bitwixe ernest and game,
1595 He atte laste apoynted hym on oon,   *fixed on one*
And leet alle othere from his herte goon,   *let; go*
And chees hire of his owene auctoritee;   *chose; on*
For love is blynd alday, and may nat see.   *always*
And whan that he was in his bed ybroght,
1600 He purtreyed in his herte and in his thoght   *pictured*
Hir fresshe beautee and hir age tendre,
Hir myddel smal, hire armes longe and sklendre,   *waist; slender*
Hir wise governaunce, hir gentillesse,
Hir wommanly berynge, and hire sadnesse.   *bearing*
1605 And whan that he on hire was condescended,   *settled*
Hym thoughte his choys myghte nat ben amended.   *bettered*
For whan that he hymself concluded hadde,
Hym thoughte ech oother mannes wit so badde   *every*
That inpossible it were to repplye
1610 Agayn his choys, this was his fantasye.
His freendes sente he to, at his instaunce,   *urgent request*
And preyed hem to doon hym that plesaunce,
That hastily they wolden to hym come;

1577-9 High-flown fancies and fussy, anxious thoughts about his
    marriage were thronging all the time in January's soul.
1582 Just as if someone were to take a mirror.
1586-7 January let his inward eye rove over the maidens who lived near
    him.
1588 He didn't know where to settle his affections.
1594 Half seriously and half jokingly.
1603 Her prudent demeanour, her good breeding.
1607 When he had made up his own mind.
1609-10 That there could not possibly be any objection to his choice—
    so he fancied.

He wolde abregge hir labour, alle and some.
1615 Nedeth namoore for hym to go ne ryde;
He was apoynted ther he wolde abyde.
    Placebo cam, and eek his freendes soone,
And alderfirst he bad hem alle a boone,
That noon of hem none argumentes make
1620 Agayn the purpos which that he hath take,
Which purpos was plesant to God, seyde he,
And verray ground of his prosperitee.   *very*
    He seyde ther was a mayden in the toun,
Which that of beautee hadde greet renoun,   *for*
1625 Al were it so she were of smal degree;
Suffiseth hym hir yowthe and hir beautee.
Which mayde, he seyde, he wolde han to his wyf,
To lede in ese and hoolynesse his lyf;
And thanked God that he myghte han hire al,   *all to himself*
1630 That no wight his blisse parten shal.   *no one; share*
And preyed hem to laboure in this nede,
And shapen that he faille nat to spede;
For thanne, he seyde, his spirit was at ese.
'Thanne is,' quod he, 'no thyng may me displese,
1635 Save o thyng priketh in my conscience,
The which I wol reherce in youre presence.   *mention*
    I have,' quod he, 'herd seyd, ful yoore ago,
Ther may no man han parfite blisses two,—   *perfect*
This is to seye, in erthe and eek in hevene.
1640 For though he kepe hym fro the synnes sevene,   *himself*
And eek from every branche of thilke tree,   *that*
Yet is ther so parfit felicitee
And so greet ese and lust in mariage,   *pleasure; delight*
That evere I am agast now in myn age
1645 That I shal lede now so myrie a lyf,   *pleasant*
So delicat, withouten wo and stryf,   *delicious*
That I shal have myn hevene in erthe heere.   *on*
For sith that verray hevene is boght so deere
With tribulacion and greet penaunce,
1650 How sholde I thanne, that lyve in swich plesaunce   *then*
As alle wedded men doon with hire wyvys,

1614 He would end their labours, one and all.
1615–16 There was no more need for him to go on searching; he had
    made up his mind where he would settle his affections.
1618 And to begin with he requested them all.
1620 Against the resolve he had made.
1625 Although she was of humble rank.
1631–2 To exert themselves in this matter and help to ensure his success.
1637 I have long since heard it said.
1641 An allusion to the numerous subdivisions of the seven deadly
    sins; see the *Parson's Tale.*
1644 That now at my time of life I'm always afraid.
1648 For since the true heavenly life is bought so dearly.

Come to the blisse ther Crist eterne on lyve ys?
This is my drede, and ye, my bretheren tweye,
Assoilleth me this question, I preye.'   *answer*
1655 Justinus, which that hated his folye,   *who*
Answerde anon right in his japerye;
And for he wolde his longe tale abregge,   *cut short*
He wolde noon auctoritee allegge,
But seyde, 'Sire, so ther be noon obstacle
1660 Oother than this, God of his hygh myracle
And of his mercy may so for yow wirche
That, er ye have youre right of hooly chirche,
Ye may repente of wedded mannes lyf,
In which ye seyn ther is no wo ne stryf.
1665 And elles, God forbede but he sente
A wedded man hym grace to repente
Wel ofte rather than a sengle man!
And therfore, sire—the beste reed I kan—   *advice; know*
Dispeire yow noght, but have in youre memorie,   *despair*
1670 Paraunter she may be youre purgatorie!
She may be Goddes meene and Goddes whippe;   *instrument*
Thanne shal youre soule up to hevene skippe   *leap*
Swifter than dooth an arwe out of a bowe.
I hope to God, herafter shul ye knowe
1675 That ther nys no so greet felicitee   *is not such*
In mariage, ne nevere mo shal bee,
That yow shal lette of youre savacion,
So that ye use, as skile is and reson,
The lustes of youre wyf attemprely,
1680 And that ye plese hire nat to amorously,
And that ye kepe yow eek from oother synne.
My tale is doon, for my wit is thynne.
Beth nat agast herof, my brother deere,   *afraid*
But lat us waden out of this mateere.   *leave*
1685 The Wyf of Bathe, if ye han understonde,

1652 Where Christ Eternal lives.
1656 Immediately answered in his usual jesting vein.
1658 He would not cite any authority (for his statements).
1659–60 i.e. if there is no obstacle other than wedded happiness to
    prevent January from attaining heavenly bliss.
1660–3 God in His mercy may work such a mighty miracle for you
    that, before you receive the last sacrament of the Church, you may
    have reason to repent of married life.
1665–7 God forbid that He should not send a married man grace to
    repent sooner than a single man.
1677 That it will hinder your salvation.
1678–9 So long as you indulge your wife's desires in moderation, as
    reason demands.
1685–7 The Wife of Bath, if you have understood (her), has spoken
    very well and succinctly about the business of marriage which we have
    in hand. (These words are apparently meant to be a comment inter-
    polated by the Merchant.)

Of mariage, which we have on honde,
Declared hath ful wel in litel space.
Fareth now wel, God have yow in his grace.'
    And with this word this Justyn and his brother
1690 Han take hir leve, and ech of hem of oother.
For whan they saughe that it moste nedes be,
They wroghten so, by sly and wys tretee,
That she, this mayden, which that Mayus   *May*
    hyghte,   *was called*
As hastily as evere that she myghte,
1695 Shal wedded be unto this Januarie.
I trowe it were to longe yow to tarie,
If I yow tolde of every scrit and bond   *deed*
By which that she was feffed in his lond,
Or for to herknen of hir riche array.
1700 But finally ycomen is the day
That to the chirche bothe be they went   *gone*
For to receyve the hooly sacrement.
Forth comth the preest, with stole about his nekke,
And bad hire be lyk Sarra and Rebekke   *Sarah; Rebecca*
1705 In wysdom and in trouthe of mariage;
And seyde his orisons, as is usage,   *custom*
And croucheth hem, and bad God sholde hem blesse,
And made al siker ynogh with hoolynesse.
    Thus been they wedded with solempnitee,
1710 And at the feeste sitteth he and she
With othere worthy folk upon the deys.   *dais*
Al ful of joye and blisse is the paleys,
And ful of instrumentz and of vitaille,
The mooste deyntevous of al Ytaille.   *dainty*
1715 Biforn hem stoode instrumentz of swich soun
That Orpheus, ne of Thebes Amphioun,
Ne maden nevere swich a melodye.
At every cours thanne cam loud mynstralcye,   *course*
That nevere tromped Joab for to heere,
1720 Nor he Theodomas, yet half so cleere,
At Thebes, whan the citee was in doute.   *peril*
Bacus the wyn hem shynketh al aboute,
And Venus laugheth upon every wight,   *everyone*
For Januarie was bicome hir knyght,

1689 *his brother*, i.e. Placebo.
1692 They brought it about, by skilful and prudent negotiation.
1696 I think it would take up too much of your time.
1698 By which she was put in legal possession of his land.
1707 Marked them with the sign of the cross.
1708 Made it all well and truly binding with holy rites.
1719–20 So that Joab never sounded his trumpet in men's ears, nor did Thiodamas, half so clearly.
1722 Bacchus pours out the wine for them all round.

1725 And wolde bothe assayen his corage
     In libertee, and eek in mariage;
     And with hire fyrbrond in hire hand aboute
     Daunceth biforn the bryde and al the route.   *company*
     And certeinly, I dar right wel seyn this,
1730 Ymeneus, that god of weddyng is,   *Hymen*
     Saugh nevere his lyf so myrie a wedded man.   *in his life*
     Hoold thy pees, thou poete Marcian,
     That writest us that ilke weddyng murie
     Of hire Philologie and hym Mercurie,
1735 And of the songes that the Muses songe!   *sang*
     To smal is bothe thy penne, and eek thy tonge,
     For to descryven of this mariage.   *describe*
     Whan tendre youthe hath wedded stoupyng age,   *stooping*
     Ther is swich myrthe that it may nat be writen.
1740 Assayeth it youreself, thanne may ye witen
     If that I lye or noon in this matiere.   *not*
         Mayus, that sit with so benyngne a chiere,
     Hire to biholde it semed fayerye.
     Queene Ester looked nevere with swich an ye   *Esther; eye*
1745 On Assuer, so meke a look hath she.   *Ahasuerus*
     I may yow nat devyse al hir beautee;   *describe*
     But thus muche of hire beautee telle I may,
     That she was lyk the brighte morwe of May,
     Fulfild of alle beautee and plesaunce.   *full*
1750   This Januarie is ravysshed in a traunce   *rapt; trance*
     At every tyme he looked on hir face;
     But in his herte he gan hire to manace   *threaten*
     That he that nyght in armes wolde hire streyne
     Harder than evere Parys dide Eleyne.
1755 But nathelees yet hadde he greet pitee
     That thilke nyght offenden hire moste he,
     And thoughte, 'Allas!   O tendre creature,
     Now wolde God ye myghte wel endure
     Al my corage, it is so sharp and keene!   *desire*
1760 I am agast ye shul it nat susteene.   *bear*
     But God forbede that I dide al my myght!
     Now wolde God that it were woxen nyght,   *become*
     And that the nyght wolde lasten everemo.
     I wolde that al this peple were ago.'

1725-6 i.e. he wished to try his mettle in the married state, as he had
    already done in his free bachelor days.
1727 *fyrbrond*, torch of the marriage procession.
1732 *Marcian*, Martianus Capella, author of the *Nuptials of Philology
    and Mercury* (fifth century).
1742-3 May sat there with so demure an air that she was enchanting
    to look at.
1756 That he must do offence to her that very night.

1765 And finally he dooth al his labour,
      As he best myghte, savynge his honour,
      To haste hem fro the mete in subtil wyse.
        The tyme cam that resoun was to ryse;
      And after that men daunce and drynken faste,
1770 And spices al aboute the hous they caste,
      And ful of joye and blisse is every man,—
      Al but a squyer, highte Damyan,   *called*
      Which carf biforn the knyght ful many a day. *who carved*
      He was so ravysshed on his lady May   *by*
1775 That for the verray peyne he was ny wood.
      Almoost he swelte and swowned ther he stood, *died*
      So soore hath Venus hurt hym with hire brond, *torch*
      As that she bar it daunsynge in hire hond;   *carried*
      And to his bed he wente hym hastily.
1780 Namoore of hym at this tyme speke I.
      But there I lete hym wepe ynogh and pleyne,
      Til fresshe May wol rewen on his peyne.   *take pity*
        O perilous fyr, that in the bedstraw bredeth! *springs up*
      O famulier foo, that his servyce bedeth!
1785 O servant traytour, false hoomly hewe,
      Lyk to the naddre in bosom sly untrewe,
      God shilde us alle from youre aqueyntaunce!   *shield*
      O Januarie, dronken in plesaunce
      In mariage, se how thy Damyan,
1790 Thyn owene squier and thy borne man,   *vassal*
      Entendeth for to do thee vileynye.   *means*
      God graunte thee thyn hoomly fo t'espye! *domestic*
      For in this world nys worse pestilence
      Than hoomly foo al day in thy presence.
1795   Parfourned hath the sonne his ark diurne;
      No lenger may the body of hym sojurne
      On th'orisonte, as in that latitude.   *horizon*
      Night with his mantel, that is derk and rude,
      Gan oversprede the hemysperie aboute;
1800 For which departed is this lusty route   *merry crowd*
      Fro Januarie, with thank on every syde.
      Hoom to hir houses lustily they ryde,
      Where as they doon hir thynges as hem leste,

1765–7 He does all he can, short of risking his good name, to hurry
    them from the feast by every artful means.
1768 The time came when reason told them they should rise.
1775 He was nearly mad with the torment of it.
1781 I leave him weeping and complaining bitterly.
1784 O household foe, who offers his service.
1785 O treacherous servant, false domestic.
1786 Like a sly, insidious viper in the bosom.
1795 The sun has completed his diurnal arc.
1799 Covered the hemisphere all round.
1803 Where they did whatever took their fancy.

And whan they sye hir tyme, goon to reste.
1805 Soone after that, this hastif Januarie   *eager*
Wolde go to bedde, he wolde no lenger tarye.
He drynketh ypocras, clarree, and vernage
Of spices hoote, t'encreessen his corage;   *desire*
And many a letuarie hath he ful fyn,
1810 Swiche as the cursed monk, daun Constantyn,   *sir*
Hath writen in his book *De Coitu*;
To eten hem alle he nas no thyng eschu.   *averse*
And to his privee freendes thus seyde he: *intimate*
'For Goddes love, as soone as it may be,
1815 Lat voyden al this hous in curteys wyse.'
And they han doon right as he wol devyse.
Men drynken, and the travers drawe anon.   *curtain*
The bryde was broght abedde as stille as stoon;   *a stone*
And whan the bed was with the preest yblessed,   *by*
1820 Out of the chambre hath every wight hym   *everyone; gone*
  dressed;
And Januarie hath faste in armes take
His fresshe May, his paradys, his make.   *mate*
He lulleth hire, he kisseth hire ful ofte;
With thikke brustles of his berd unsofte,   *rough*
1825 Lyk to the skyn of houndfyssh, sharp as   *dogfish*
  brere—   *briar*
For he was shave al newe in his manere—
He rubbeth hire aboute hir tendre face,
And seyde thus, 'Allas! I moot trespace   *must trespass*
To yow, my spouse, and yow greetly offende,   *against*
1830 Er tyme come that I wil doun descende.
But nathelees, considereth this,' quod he,
'Ther nys no werkman, whatsoevere he be,
That may bothe werke wel and hastily;
This wol be doon at leyser parfitly.
1835 It is no fors how longe that we pleye;   *does not matter*
In trewe wedlok coupled be we tweye;   *two*
And blessed be the yok that we been inne,
For in oure actes we mowe do no synne.   *may*
A man may do no synne with his wyf,
1840 Ne hurte hymselven with his owene knyf;
For we han leve to pleye us by the lawe.'
Thus laboureth he til that the day gan dawe;   *dawned*

1804 When they thought it time, they went to rest.
1807 He has a cordial drink, a honeyed beverage, and sweet white wine.
1809 He has many a fine medicinal syrup.
1815 Clear all the house as politely as you can.
1816 They did exactly as he said.
1826 He was newly shaven after his own fashion.
1834 This shall be done perfectly at leisure.
1841 For the law allows us to amuse ourselves.

And thanne he taketh a sop in fyn claree,   *sop (of bread)*
And upright in his bed thanne sitteth he,
1845 And after that he sang ful loude and cleere,
And kiste his wyf, and made wantown cheere.   *wanton*
He was al coltissh, ful of ragerye,   *lust*
And ful of jargon as a flekked pye.
The slakke skyn aboute his nekke shaketh,
1850 Whil that he sang, so chaunteth he and craketh.
But God woot what that May thoughte in hir herte,
Whan she hym saugh up sittynge in his sherte,
In his nyghte-cappe, and with his nekke lene;
She preyseth nat his pleyyng worth a bene.
1855 Thanne seide he thus, 'My reste wol I take;
Now day is come, I may no lenger wake.'
And doun he leyde his heed, and sleep til pryme.
And afterward, whan that he saugh his tyme,
Up ryseth Januarie; but fresshe May
1860 Heeld hire chambre unto the fourthe day,
As usage is of wyves for the beste.
For every labour somtyme moot han reste,
Or elles longe may he nat endure;
This is to seyn, no lyves creature,   *living*
1865 Be it of fyssh, or bryd, or beest, or man.   *bird*
   Now wol I speke of woful Damyan,
That langwissheth for love, as ye shul heere;
Therfore I speke to hym in this manere:
I seye, 'O sely Damyan, allas!   *poor*
1870 Andswere to my demaunde, as in this cas.
How shaltow to thy lady, fresshe May,
Telle thy wo?   She wole alwey seye nay.
Eek if thou speke, she wol thy wo biwreye.   *betray*
God be thyn helpe!   I kan no bettre seye.'
1875   This sike Damyan in Venus fyr
So brenneth that he dyeth for desyr,   *burns*
For which he putte his lyf in aventure.   *jeopardy*
No lenger myghte he in this wise endure,
But prively a penner gan he borwe,
1880 And in a lettre wroot he al his sorwe,
In manere of a compleynt or a lay,
Unto his faire, fresshe lady May;

1848 Full of chatter as a spotted magpie.
1850 He chants and sings so raucously.
1854 She didn't think his capers worth a bean.
1857 Slept till prime (i.e. 9 a.m.).
1861 As wives have the sensible custom of doing.
1862–3 Every labour must sometime be followed by rest, or else no one
  can last for long.
1870 Answer the question I put to you in this predicament of yours.
1879 Secretly he borrowed a pen-case.

And in a purs of sylk, heng on his sherte,   *(which) hung*
He hath it put, and leyde it at his herte.

1885 The moone, that at noon was thilke day
That Januarie hath wedded fresshe May
In two of Tawr, was into Cancre glyden;
So longe hath Mayus in hir chambre abyden,
As custume is unto thise nobles alle.

1890 A bryde shal nat eten in the halle
Til dayes foure, or thre dayes atte leeste,
Ypassed been; thanne lat hire go to feeste.
The fourthe day compleet fro noon to noon,   *complete*
Whan that the heighe masse was ydoon,

1895 In halle sit this Januarie and May,   *sits*
As fressh as is the brighte someres day.
And so bifel how that this goode man
Remembred hym upon this Damyan,
And seyde, 'Seynte Marie! how may this be,

1900 That Damyan entendeth nat to me?   *attends*
Is he ay syk, or how may this bityde?'
His squieres, whiche that stooden ther bisyde,
Excused hym by cause of his siknesse,
Which letted hym to doon his bisynesse;

1905 Noon oother cause myghte make hym tarye.
     'That me forthynketh,' quod this Januarie,
'He is a gentil squier, by my trouthe!   *upon my word*
If that he deyde, it were harm and routhe.   *a sad thing*
He is as wys, discreet, and as secree   *trusty*

1910 As any man I woot of his degree,   *know*
And therto manly, and eek servysable,   *willing to serve*
And for to been a thrifty man right able.
But after mete, as soone as evere I may,
I wol myself visite hym, and eek May,

1915 To doon hym al the confort that I kan.'
And for that word hym blessed every man,
That of his bountee and his gentillesse   *kindness; courtesy*
He wolde so conforten in siknesse   *comfort*
His squier, for it was a gentil dede.

1920 'Dame,' quod this Januarie, 'taak good hede,
At after-mete ye with youre wommen alle,
Whan ye han been in chambre out of this halle,

1885-7 The moon, which at noon on the day that January married
fresh young May was in the second degree of Taurus, had glided into
Cancer (i.e. four days passed by).
1901 Is he still ill, or what's the reason for it?
1904 Which prevented him from doing his duty.
1906 I'm sorry to hear that.
1912 And most deserving of success.
1921 During the interval after dinner.
1922 *chambre*, i.e. the private room of January and May, adjoining the
hall.

That alle ye go se this Damyan.
Dooth hym disport—he is a gentil man;   *cheer him up*
1925 And telleth hym that I wol hym visite,
Have I no thyng but rested me a lite;
And spede yow faste, for I wole abyde   *be quick*
Til that ye slepe faste by my syde.'
And with that word he gan to hym to calle   *called*
1930 A squier, that was marchal of his halle,
And tolde hym certeyn thynges, what he wolde.   *wanted*
     This fresshe May hath streight hir wey yholde,   *made*
With alle hir wommen, unto Damyan.
Doun by his beddes syde sit she than,
1935 Confortynge hym as goodly as she may.   *kindly*
This Damyan, whan that his tyme he say,
In secree wise his purs and eek his bille,   *letter*
In which that he ywriten hadde his wille,   *longing*
Hath put into hire hand, withouten moore,   *more ado*
1940 Save that he siketh wonder depe and soore,   *sighs*
And softely to hire right thus seyde he:
'Mercy! and that ye nat discovere me,
For I am deed if that this thyng be kyd.'
This purs hath she inwith hir bosom hyd,   *in*
1945 And wente hire wey; ye gete namoore of me.
But unto Januarie ycomen is she,
That on his beddes syde sit ful softe,   *is sitting*
He taketh hire, and kisseth hire ful ofte,
And leyde hym doun to slepe, and that anon.
1950 She feyned hire as that she moste gon
Ther as ye woot that every wight moot neede;
And whan she of this bille hath taken heede,
She rente it al to cloutes atte laste,   *tore; pieces*
And in the pryvee softely it caste.   *privy*
1955   Who studieth now but faire fresshe May?   *wonders*
Adoun by olde Januarie she lay,
That sleep til that the coughe hath hym awaked.   *slept*
Anon he preyde hire strepen hire al naked;   *strip herself*
He wolde of hire, he seyde, han som plesaunce,
1960 He seyde hir clothes dide hym encombraunce.
And she obeyeth, be hire lief or looth.
But lest that precious folk be with me wrooth,   *prim*

1926 When I've just rested a little while.
1930 *marchal.* See I. 752.
1936 When he saw his chance.
1942 And pray don't give me away.
1943 For I'm as good as dead if this thing is ever known.
1945 You'll get no more from me.
1950–1 She pretended she had to go to the place where everyone, as you
     know, is bound to pay a call.
1961 Whether she likes it or not.

How that he wroghte, I dar nat to yow telle; *performed*
Or wheither hire thoughte it paradys or helle.
1965 But heere I lete hem werken in hir wyse
Til evensong rong, and that they moste aryse.
  Were it by destynee or by aventure. *chance*
Were it by influence or by nature,
Or constellacion, that in swich estaat
1970 The hevene stood, that tyme fortunaat
Was for to putte a bille of Venus werkes—
For alle thyng hath tyme, as seyn thise clerkes—
To any womman, for to gete hire love, *win*
I kan nat seye; but grete God above,
1975 That knoweth that noon act is causelees,
He deme of al, for I wole holde my pees.
But sooth is this, how that this fresshe May
Hath take swich impression that day
Of pitee of this sike Damyan,
1980 That from hire herte she ne dryve kan
The remembrance for to doon hym ese.
'Certeyn,' thoghte she, 'whom that this thyng
  displese,
I rekke noght, for heere I hym assure *care*
To love hym best of any creature,
1985 Though he namoore hadde than his sherte.'
Lo, pitee renneth soone in gentil herte!
  Heere may ye se how excellent franchise *generosity*
In wommen is, whan they hem narwe avyse.
Som tyrant is, as ther be many oon,
1990 That hath an herte as hard as any stoon,
Which wolde han lat hym sterven in the place
Wel rather than han graunted hym hire grace; *much*
And hem rejoysen in hire crueel pryde, *rejoice*
And rekke nat to been an homycide.
1995 This gentil May, fulfilled of pitee, *full of*
Right of hire hand a lettre made she,
In which she graunteth hym hire verray grace. *true*
Ther lakketh noght, oonly but day and place,

1966 Till the bell rang for evensong.
1968–71 Whether it was by the influence of the stars or of nature, or
of some constellation, that the heavens were placed in a position
which made it a fortunate time for conveying a letter on Venus'
business.
1972 There's a time for everything, as the learned say.
1976 Let Him be sole judge.
1981 The memory or the desire to comfort him.
1982 Whoever is displeased by this.
1988 When they think things over carefully.
1989 There is more than one (female) tyrant.
1991 Who would have let him die on the spot.
1996 Wrote a letter with her own hand.

Wher that she myghte unto his lust suffise;   *desire; satisfy*
2000 For it shal be right as he wole devyse.
And whan she saugh hir tyme, upon a day,
To visite this Damyan gooth May,
And sotilly this lettre doun she threste   *skilfully; thrust*
Under his pilwe, rede it if hym leste.
2005 She taketh hym by the hand, and harde hym twiste   *squeezed*
So secrely that no wight of it wiste,
And bad hym been al hool, and forth she wente   *get well*
To Januarie, whan that he for hire sente.
    Up riseth Damyan the nexte morwe;
2010 Al passed was his siknesse and his sorwe,
He kembeth hym, he preyneth hym and pyketh,
He dooth al that his lady lust and lyketh;   *pleases*
And eek to Januarie he gooth as lowe   *docilely*
As evere dide a dogge for the bowe.
2015 He is so plesant unto every man
(For craft is al, whoso that do it kan)
That every wight is fayn to speke hym good;
And fully in his lady grace he stood.   *lady's*
Thus lete I Damyan aboute his nede,
2020 And in my tale forth I wol procede.
    Somme clerkes holden that felicitee   *scholars*
Stant in delit, and therfore certeyn he,   *consists; pleasure*
This noble Januarie, with al his myght,
In honest wyse, as longeth to a knyght,
2025 Shoop hym to lyve ful deliciously.
His housynge, his array, as honestly
To his degree was maked as a kynges.
Amonges othere of his honeste thynges,
He made a gardyn, walled al with stoon;
2030 So fair a gardyn woot I nowher noon.
For, out of doute, I verraily suppose   *honestly*
That he that wroot the Romance of the Rose
Ne koude of it the beautee wel devyse;   *describe*

2000 Just as he plans.
2004 Let him read it if he will.
2006 So secretly that no one knew anything about it.
2011 He combs his hair, he prinks and pranks himself.
2014 See III. 1369.
2017 Everyone is glad to speak kindly to him.
2019 I leave Damyan busy with his affairs.
2024 In honourable fashion, as befits a knight.
2025 Planned to live luxuriously.
2026-7 His house, his dress, were as nobly fashioned to his rank as are a king's.
2028 Among other noble things of his.
2032 An allusion to Guillaume de Lorris, author of the earlier part of the *Roman de la Rose* (a French allegorical love poem dating from the thirteenth century).

Ne Priapus ne myghte nat suffise,   *be able*
2035 Though he be god of gardyns, for to telle
The beautee of the gardyn and the welle,   *spring*
That stood under a laurer alwey grene.   *laurel*
Ful ofte tyme he Pluto and his queene,
Proserpina, and al hire fayerye,   *fairy band*
2040 Disporten hem and maken melodye
Aboute that welle, and daunced, as men tolde.
    This noble knyght, this Januarie the olde,
Swich deyntee hath in it to walke and pleye,   *pleasure*
That he wol no wight suffren bere the keye   *allow*
2045 Save he hymself; for of the smale wyket   *wicket-gate*
He baar alwey of silver a clyket,   *carried; key*
With which, whan that hym leste, he it unshette.
And whan he wolde paye his wyf hir dette   *(marital) dues*
In somer seson, thider wolde he go,
2050 And May his wyf, and no wight but they two;
And thynges whiche that were nat doon abedde,   *in bed*
He in the gardyn parfourned hem and   *performed*
        spedde.   *accomplished*
And in this wyse, many a murye day,
Lyved this Januarie and fresshe May.
2055 But worldly joye may nat alwey dure   *last*
To Januarie, ne to no creature.   *for*
    O sodeyn hap! o thou Fortune unstable!   *chance*
Lyk to the scorpion so deceyvable,   *deceitful*
That flaterest with thyn heed whan thou wolt stynge;
2060 Thy tayl is deeth, thurgh thyn envenymynge.   *poisoning*
O brotil joye! o sweete venym queynte!   *brittle; strange*
O monstre, that so subtilly kanst peynte
Thy yiftes under hewe of stidefastnesse,   *colour*
That thou deceyvest bothe moore and lesse!
2065 Why hastow Januarie thus deceyved,
That haddest hym for thy fulle freend receyved?
And now thou hast biraft hym bothe his yen,
For sorwe of which desireth he to dyen.
    Allas! this noble Januarie free,   *generous*
2070 Amydde his lust and his prosperitee,   *pleasure*
Is woxen blynd, and that al sodeynly.   *become*
He wepeth and he wayleth pitously;
And therwithal the fyr of jalousie,
Lest that his wyf sholde falle in som folye,
2075 So brente his herte that he wolde fayn
That som man bothe hire and hym had slayn.

2047 When he wished, he unlocked it.
2059 An allusion to the ancient belief that a scorpion has a pleasing
    countenance resembling a woman's.
2067 Deprived him of the use of both his eyes.

For neither after his deeth, nor in his lyf,
Ne wolde he that she were love ne wyf,
But evere lyve as wydwe in clothes blake,
2080 Soul as the turtle that lost hath hire make.
But atte laste, after a month or tweye,
His sorwe gan aswage, sooth to seye;   *grew less*
For whan he wiste it may noon oother be,   *knew*
He paciently took his adversitee,
2085 Save, out of doute, he may nat forgoon
That he nas jalous everemoore in oon;
Which jalousye it was so outrageous,
That neither in halle, n'yn noon oother hous,
Ne in noon oother place, neverthemo,
2090 He nolde suffre hire for to ryde or go,
But if that he had hond on hire alway;
For which ful ofte wepeth fresshe May,
That loveth Damyan so benyngnely   *sweetly*
That she moot outher dyen sodeynly,   *must*
2095 Or elles she moot han hym as hir leste.   *she desires*
She wayteth whan hir herte wolde breste.
     Upon that oother syde Damyan   *for his part*
Bicomen is the sorwefulleste man
That evere was; for neither nyght ne day
2100 Ne myghte he speke a word to fresshe May,
As to his purpos, of no swich mateere,
But if that Januarie moste it heere,   *unless; should*
That hadde an hand upon hire everemo.
But nathelees, by writyng to and fro,
2105 And privee signes, wiste he what she mente,   *secret; knew*
And she knew eek the fyn of his entente.   *object*
     O Januarie, what myghte it thee availle,
Thogh thou myghtest se as fer as shippes saille?   *far*
For as good is blynd deceyved be
2110 As to be deceyved whan a man may se.
     Lo, Argus, which that hadde an hondred yen,   *eyes*
For al that evere he koude poure or pryen,
Yet was he blent, and, God woot, so been   *deceived*
     mo,   *others*
That wenen wisly that it be nat so.

2078 Did he want her to be anyone else's mistress or wife.
2080 As solitary as the turtle-dove that has lost her mate.
2085-6 Except that, certainly, he could not help being jealous all the
     time.
2088-91 Nor to any other house, nor any other place, would he ever
     allow her to ride or walk, unless he had his hand on her always.
2096 She watched and waited for her heart to break.
2101 Or of any such thing.
2109 It's just as good to be deceived when blind.
2112 For all his peering and prying.
2114 Who confidently think they aren't.

2115 Passe over is an ese, I sey namoore.
   This fresshe May, that I spak of so yoore,   *long ago*
In warm wex hath emprented the clyket
That Januarie bar of the smale wyket,
By which into his gardyn ofte he wente;
2120 And Damyan, that knew al hire entente,
The cliket countrefeted pryvely.
Ther nys namoore to seye, but hastily
Som wonder by this clyket shal bityde,
Which ye shul heeren, if ye wole abyde.   *wait*
2125 O noble Ovyde, ful sooth seystou, God woot,
What sleighte is it, thogh it be long and hoot,
That Love nyl fynde it out in som manere?
By Piramus and Tesbee may men leere;
Thogh they were kept ful longe streite overal,
2130 They been accorded, rownynge thurgh a wal,
Ther no wight koude han founde out swich a sleighte.
   But now to purpos: er that dayes eighte   *the subject*
Were passed of the month of Juyn, bifil   *June; it happened*
That Januarie hath caught so greet a wil,
2135 Thurgh eggyng of his wyf, hym for to pleye   *urging*
In his gardyn, and no wight but they tweye,   *no one*
That in a morwe unto his May seith he: *one morning*
'Rys up, my wyf, my love, my lady free!   *noble*
The turtles voys is herd, my dowve sweete;
2140 The wynter is goon with alle his reynes weete.   *wet*
Com forth now, with thyne eyen columbyn!   *dove-like*
How fairer been thy brestes than is wyn!
The gardyn is enclosed al aboute;
Com forth, my white spouse! out of doute
2145 Thou hast me wounded in myn herte, O wyf!
No spot of thee ne knew I al my lyf.   *blemish in*
Com forth, and lat us taken oure disport;   *pleasure*
I chees thee for my wyf and my confort.'   *chose*
   Swiche olde lewed wordes used he.   *wanton*
2150 On Damyan a signe made she,

2115 It's a pleasure to skip the rest.
2117 In warm wax has taken an impression of the key.
2121 Had a copy of the key made secretly.
2122–3 But very soon a marvellous thing will happen because of this key.
2125–7 O noble Ovid, God knows you rightly ask what cunning trick
  there is, however long and hard, that Love will not somehow find it
  out.
2128 We can learn by the example of Pyramus and Thisbe.
2129–31 Though they were closely watched on all sides, they came to an
  agreement by whispering through a wall, when no one else could
  have thought of such a trick.
2132–3 A roundabout way of saying 'on the eighth of June.'
2134 Was seized with such a great desire.
2138 ff. Cf. the Song of Solomon.

That he sholde go biforn with his cliket.
This Damyan thanne hath opened the wyket,
And in he stirte, and that in swich manere   *darted*
That no wight myghte it se neither yheere,   *hear*
2155 And stille he sit under a bussh anon.
      This Januarie, as blynd as is a stoon,
With Mayus in his hand, and no wight mo,
Into his fresshe gardyn is ago,
And clapte to the wyket sodeynly.
2160 'Now wyf,' quod he, 'heere nys but thou and I,
That art the creature that I best love.
For by that Lord that sit in hevene above,   *dwells*
Levere ich hadde to dyen on a knyf,
Than thee offende, trewe deere wyf!
2165 For Goddes sake, thenk how I thee chees,
Noght for no coveitise, doutelees,   *covetousness*
But oonly for the love I had to thee.
And though that I be oold, and may nat see,
Beth to me trewe, and I wol telle yow why.   *be*
2170 Thre thynges, certes, shal ye wynne therby:
First, love of Crist, and to youreself honour,
And al myn heritage, toun and tour;
I yeve it yow, maketh chartres as yow leste;
This shal be doon to-morwe er sonne reste,   *sun sets*
2175 So wisly God my soule brynge in blisse.
I prey yow first, in covenant ye me kisse;
And though that I be jalous, wyte me noght.   *blame*
Ye been so depe enprented in my thoght   *imprinted*
That, whan that I considere youre beautee,
2180 And therwithal the unlikly elde of me,
I may nat, certes, though I sholde dye,   *die for it*
Forbere to been out of youre compaignye
For verray love; this is withouten doute.
Now kys me, wyf, and lat us rome aboute.'   *wander*
2185 This fresshe May, whan she thise wordes herde,
Benyngnely to Januarie answerde,   *graciously*
But first and forward she bigan to wepe.   *foremost*
'I have,' quod she, 'a soule for to kepe   *save*
As wel as ye, and also myn honour,
2190 And of my wyfhod thilke tendre flour,
Which that I have assured in youre hond,
Whan that the preest to yow my body bond;   *bound*

2163 I would rather die upon a knife.
2173 Draw up the agreements as you please.
2175 As surely as God, I hope, will bring my soul to bliss.
2176 Seal the covenant with a kiss.
2180 And also my unsuitable age.
2190 The tender flower of my womanhood.
2191 Placed in your safe-keeping.

Wherfore I wole answere in this manere,
By the leve of yow, my lord so deere: *by your leave*
2195 I prey to God that nevere dawe the day
That I ne sterve, as foule as womman may,
If evere I do unto my kyn that shame,
Or elles I empeyre so my name,
That I be fals; and if I do that lak   *fault*
2200 Do strepe me and put me in a sak,   *have me stripped*
And in the nexte ryver do me drenche.
I am a gentil womman and no wenche.
Why speke ye thus? but men been evere untrewe,
And wommen have repreve of yow ay newe.
2205 Ye han noon oother contenance, I leeve,
But speke to us of untrust and repreeve.'
    And with that word she saugh wher Damyan
Sat in the bussh, and coughen she bigan,   *to cough*
And with hir fynger signes made she
2210 That Damyan sholde clymbe upon a tree,
That charged was with fruyt, and up he wente.   *laden*
For verraily he knew al hire entente,
And every signe that she koude make,
Wel bet than Januarie, hir owene make;   *much better; mate*
2215 For in a lettre she hadde toold hym al
Of this matere, how he werchen shal.
And thus I lete hym sitte upon the pyrie,
And Januarie and May romynge myrie.
    Bright was the day, and blew the firmament;   *blue*
2220 Phebus hath of gold his stremes doun ysent,   *beams*
To gladen every flour with his warmnesse.
He was that tyme in Geminis, as I gesse,   *Gemini*
But litel fro his declynacion
Of Cancer, Jovis exaltacion.
2225 And so bifel, that brighte morwe-tyde,
That in that gardyn, in the ferther syde,
Pluto, that is kyng of Fayerye,   *fairyland*
And many a lady in his compaignye,

2195–9 I pray God the day may never dawn when I escape the foullest
    death a woman may suffer, if I ever shame my family or injure my
    fair name by being false.
2201 Have me drowned in the nearest river.
2204 Women are always being blamed by you (men).
2205–6 i.e. all your talk about distrust and blame is a pretence by which
    you try to hide your own infidelity.
2216 How he should set about it.
2217 I leave him sitting in the pear-tree.
2218 Happily wandering about.
2223–4 Only a little from his declination of Cancer, which is the exalta-
    tion of Jupiter. (In Chaucer's day the sun entered Cancer about 12th
    June.)

Folwynge his wyf, the queene Proserpyna,
2230 Which that he ravysshed out of Ethna
Whil that she gadered floures in the mede—
In Claudyan ye may the stories rede,
How in his grisely carte he hire fette—
This kyng of Fairye thanne adoun hym sette   *sat down*
2235 Upon a bench of turves, fressh and grene,
And right anon thus seyde he to his queene:
    'My wyf,' quod he, 'ther may no wight seye nay;
Th'experience so preveth every day
The tresons whiche that wommen doon to man.
2240 Ten hondred thousand [tales] tellen I kan
Notable of youre untrouthe and brotilnesse.   *fickleness*
O Salomon, wys, and richest of richesse,   *in wealth*
Fulfild of sapience and of worldly glorie,   *full of wisdom*
Ful worthy been thy wordes to memorie
2245 To every wight that wit and reson kan.
Thus preiseth he yet the bountee of man: *goodness*
"Amonges a thousand men yet foond I oon,   *found*
But of wommen alle foond I noon."
    Thus seith the kyng that knoweth youre wikkednesse.
2250 And Jhesus, *filius Syrak*, as I gesse,
Ne speketh of yow but seelde reverence.
A wylde fyr and corrupt pestilence   *erysipelas*
So falle upon youre bodyes yet to-nyght!
Ne se ye nat this honurable knyght,
2255 By cause, allas! that he is blynd and old,
His owene man shal make hym cokewold.   *vassal; cuckold*
Lo, where he sit, the lechour, in the tree!
Now wol I graunten, of my magestee,
Unto this olde, blynde, worthy knyght
2260 That he shal have ayeyn his eyen syght,   *again*
Whan that his wyf wold doon hym vileynye.
Thanne shal he knowen al hire harlotrye,
Bothe in repreve of hire and othere mo.'
    'Ye shal?' quod Proserpyne, 'wol ye so?
2265 Now by my moodres sires soule I swere

2230 Whom he carried off from Etna.
2232 Claudius Claudianus, the fourth-century author of an epic poem on the rape of Proserpine.
2233 How he fetched her in his grim chariot.
2237 There is one thing no one can gainsay.
2244-5 To be remembered by everyone who possesses reason and understanding.
2247 Eccles. vii. 28.
2250 i.e. the reputed author of Ecclesiasticus.
2251 Seldom speaks respectfully of you.
2261 When his wife is about to wrong him.
2263 To the reproach of her and others too.
2265 By the soul of my mother's father (i.e. Saturn).

That I shal yeven hire suffisant answere,   *sufficient*
And alle wommen after, for hir sake;
That, though they be in any gilt ytake,
With face boold they shulle hemself excuse,
2270 And bere hem doun that wolden hem accuse.
For lak of answere noon of hem shal dyen.
Al hadde man seyn a thyng with bothe his yen,
Yit shul we wommen visage it hardily,
And wepe, and swere, and chyde subtilly,   *artfully*
2275 So that ye men shul been as lewed as gees.   *ignorant*
   What rekketh me of youre auctoritees?
I woot wel that this Jew, this Salomon,
Foond of us wommen fooles many oon.
But though that he ne foond no good womman,
2280 Yet hath ther founde many another man
Wommen ful trewe, ful goode, and vertuous.
Witnesse on hem that dwelle in Cristes hous;
With martirdom they preved hire constance.
The Romayn geestes eek make remembrance   *Roman history*
2285 Of many a verray, trewe wyf also.   *faithful*
But, sire, ne be nat wrooth, al be it so,
Though that he seyde he foond no good womman,
I prey yow take the sentence of the man;
He mente thus, that in sovereyn bontee   *goodness*
2290 Nis noon but God, but neither he ne she.
Ey! for verray God, that nys but oon,
What make ye so muche of Salomon?   *why*
What though he made a temple, Goddes hous?
What though he were riche and glorious?
2295 So made he eek a temple of false goddis.
How myghte he do a thyng that moore forbode is?   *forbidden*
Pardee, as faire as ye his name emplastre,
He was a lecchour and an ydolastre,   *lecher; idolater*
And in his elde he verray God forsook;   *old age*
2300 And if God ne hadde, as seith the book,
Yspared him for his fadres sake, he sholde
Have lost his regne rather than he wolde.
I sette right noght, of al the vileynye
That ye of wommen write, a boterflye!

2272 Though a man has seen.
2273 Boldly face it out.
2276 What do I care for your authorities?
2278 Found many of us women fools.
2288 Grasp the man's real meaning.
2290 But neither man nor woman, i.e. none of God's creatures.
2291 By the one true God.
2297 Indeed, however much you whitewash his name.
2302 Have lost his kingdom sooner than he wished.
2303–4 I don't care a butterfly for all the shameful things you men write
   about women.

2305 I am a womman, nedes moot I speke,
     Or elles swelle til myn herte breke.
     For sithen he seyde that we been   *since*
          jangleresses,   *chatterboxes*
     As evere hool I moote brouke my tresses,
     I shal nat spare, for no curteisye,
2310 To speke hym harm that wolde us vileynye.'
          'Dame,' quod this Pluto, 'be no lenger wrooth;
     I yeve it up! but sith I swoor myn ooth
     That I wolde graunten hym his sighte ageyn,
     My word shal stonde, I warne yow certeyn.
2315 I am a kyng, it sit me noght to lye.'
          'And I,' quod she, 'a queene of Fayerye!
     Hir answere shal she have, I undertake.
     Lat us namoore wordes heerof make;
     For sothe, I wol no lenger yow contrarie.'   *oppose*
2320   Now lat us turne agayn to Januarie,
     That in the gardyn with his faire May
     Syngeth ful murier than the papejay,
     'Yow love I best, and shal, and oother noon.'   *none other*
     So longe aboute the aleyes is he goon,
2325 Til he was come agaynes thilke pyrie
     Where as this Damyan sitteth ful myrie
     An heigh among the fresshe leves grene.   *on*
          This fresshe May, that is so bright and sheene, *beautiful*
     Gan for to syke, and seyde, 'Allas, my syde!   *sighed*
2330 Now sire,' quod she, 'for aught that may   *whatever happens*
          bityde,
     I moste han of the peres that I see,
     Or I moot dye, so soore longeth me
     To eten of the smale peres grene.
     Help, for hir love that is of hevene queene!
2335 I telle yow wel, a womman in my plit   *condition*
     May han to fruyt so greet an appetit   *for*
     That she may dyen, but she of it have.'
          'Allas!' quod he, 'that I ne had heer a knave   *boy*
     That koude clymbe!   Allas, allas,' quod he,
2340 'For I am blynd!'   'Ye, sire, no fors,' quod she; *matter*
     'But wolde ye vouche sauf, for Goddes sake,
     The pyrie inwith youre armes for to take,
     For wel I woot that ye mystruste me,

2308 As surely as I hope to keep my tresses.
2310 To speak ill of any man who wants to do us wrong.
2315 It is not fitting that I should tell a lie.
2322 Sings much more merrily than a popinjay.
2324-5 He went on wandering round the garden paths until at length
     he reached the very pear-tree.
2332 Or I shall die, I long so terribly.
2334 For the love of her who is queen of heaven.

Thanne sholde I clymbe wel ynogh,' quod she,
2345 'So I my foot myghte sette upon youre bak.'
'Certes,' quod he, 'theron shal be no lak,
Mighte I yow helpen with myn herte blood.'
He stoupeth doun, and on his bak she stood,
And caughte hire by a twiste, and up she gooth—
2350 Ladyes, I prey yow that ye be nat wrooth;
I kan nat glose, I am a rude man—
And sodeynly anon this Damyan
Gan pullen up the smok, and in he throng.   *thrust*
And whan that Pluto saugh this grete wrong,
2355 To Januarie he gaf agayn his sighte,
And made hym se as wel as evere he myghte.
And whan that he hadde caught his sighte agayn,
Ne was ther nevere man of thyng so fayn,
But on his wyf his thoght was everemo.
2360 Up to the tree he caste his eyen two,
And saugh that Damyan his wyf had dressed
In swich manere it may nat been expressed,
But if I wolde speke uncurteisly;   *unless; rudely*
And up he yaf a roryng and a cry,
2365 As dooth the mooder whan the child shal dye: *mother*
'Out! help! allas! harrow!' he gan to crye,
'O stronge lady stoore, what dostow?'
And she answerde, 'Sire, what eyleth yow?   *ails*
Have pacience and resoun in youre mynde!
2370 I have yow holpe on bothe youre eyen blynde.   *helped*
Up peril of my soule, I shal nat lyen,
As me was taught, to heele with youre eyen,
Was no thyng bet, to make yow to see,
Than strugle with a man upon a tree.
2375 God woot, I dide it in ful good entente.'
'Strugle!' quod he, 'ye, algate in it wente!   *all the same*
God yeve yow bothe on shames deth to dyen!
He swyved thee, I saugh it with myne yen,
And elles be I hanged by the hals!'   *neck*
2380 'Thanne is,' quod she, 'my medicyne fals;   *wrong*
For certeinly, if that ye myghte se,
Ye wolde nat seyn thise wordes unto me.

2346 You shan't want for anything.
2349 And caught hold of a branch.
2351 I can't gloss over it, I'm a plain man.
2358 Never was a man so pleased about anything.
2361-2 Saw that Damyan had dealt with his wife in such a way.
2367 O bold, bad woman, what are you doing?
2371-4 Upon my soul—I'm not lying—I was told there was no better
        way to heal your eyes and make you see than to struggle with a man
        in a tree.
2375 With the best of intentions.
2377 God grant you may both die a shameful death.

Ye han som glymsyng, and no parfit sighte.'
  'I se,' quod he, 'as wel as evere I myghte,
2385 Thonked be God! with bothe myne eyen two,
  And by my trouthe, me thoughte he dide   *upon my word*
    thee so.'
  'Ye maze, maze, goode sire,' quod she;   *are confused*
'This thank have I for I have maad yow see.   *thanks*
Allas,' quod she, 'that evere I was so kynde!'
2390   'Now, dame,' quod he, 'lat al passe out of mynde.
Com doun, my lief, and if I have myssayd,   *love; said wrong*
God helpe me so, as I am yvele apayd.
But, by my fader soule, I wende han seyn   *thought I saw*
How that this Damyan hadde by thee leyn,   *lain*
2395 And that thy smok hadde leyn upon his brest.'
  'Ye, sire,' quod she, 'ye may wene as   *think*
    yow lest.   *please*
But, sire, a man that waketh out of his sleep,
He may nat sodeynly wel taken keep   *notice*
Upon a thyng, ne seen it parfitly,   *perfectly*
2400 Til that he be adawed verraily.
Right so a man that longe hath blynd ybe,   *been*
Ne may nat sodeynly so wel yse,   *see*
First whan his sighte is newe come ageyn,   *newly*
As he that hath a day or two yseyn.
2405 Til that youre sighte ysatled be a while,
Ther may ful many a sighte yow bigile.   *deceive*
Beth war, I prey yow; for, by hevene kyng,
Ful many a man weneth to seen a thyng,
And it is al another than it semeth.
2410 He that mysconceyveth, he mysdemeth.'
  And with that word she leep doun fro the tree.   *leapt*
  This Januarie, who is glad but he?
He kisseth hire, and clippeth hire ful ofte,   *embraces*
And on hire wombe he stroketh hire ful softe,
2415 And to his palays hoom he hath hire lad.   *led*
Now, goode men, I pray yow to be glad.
Thus endeth heere my tale of Januarie;
God blesse us, and his mooder Seinte Marie!

HEERE IS ENDED THE MARCHANTES
TALE OF JANUARIE

2383 You have some glimmerings, but not perfect sight.
2390 Let's forget about it.
2392 So help me God, I'm sorry for it.
2400 Till he is really awake.
2405 Until your sight has settled down a bit.
2408 Many a man thinks he sees a certain thing.
2410 He who misunderstands a thing misjudges it.

EPILOGUE TO THE MERCHANT'S TALE

       'EY!   Goddes mercy!' seyde oure Hooste tho,   *then*
2420 'Now swich a wyf I pray God kepe me fro!   *preserve*
       Lo, whiche sleightes and subtilitees   *what tricks*
       In wommen been! for ay as bisy as bees
       Been they, us sely men for to deceyve,   *foolish*
       And from the soothe evere wol they weyve;
2425 By this Marchauntes tale it preveth weel.
       But doutelees, as trewe as any steel
       I have a wyf, though that she povre be,   *poor*
       But of hir tonge a labbyng shrewe is she,   *babbling*
       And yet she hath an heep of vices mo;
2430 Therof no fors! lat alle swiche thynges go.
       But wyte ye what?   In conseil be it seyd,   *know; secret*
       Me reweth soore I am unto hire teyd,
       For, and I sholde rekenen every vice   *if*
       Which that she hath, ywis I were to nyce;
2435 And cause why, it sholde reported be   *for this reason*
       And toold to hire of somme of this meynee,—   *by; company*
       Of whom, it nedeth nat for to declare,
       Syn wommen konnen outen swich chaffare;
       And eek my wit suffiseth nat therto,
2440 To tellen al, wherfore my tale is do.'   *done*

2424 They're always trying to dodge the truth.
2425 This is well shown by the Merchant's tale.
2429 A heap of other vices.
2430 No matter! let it go.
2432 I'm mighty sorry I'm tied to her.
2434 I'd be a fool indeed.
2438 Since women are good at peddling this sort of merchandise.
    (Apparently a dig at the Wife of Bath, as being the most likely informant.)

Fragment V (Group F)

INTRODUCTION TO THE SQUIRE'S TALE

'Squier, com neer, if it youre wille be,
And sey somwhat of love; for certes ye
Konnen theron as muche as any man.'   *know*
  'Nay, sire,' quod he, 'but I wol seye as I kan
5 With hertly wyl; for I wol nat rebelle   *goodwill*
Agayn youre lust; a tale wol I telle.   *wish*
Have me excused if I speke amys;
My wyl is good, and lo, my tale is this.'

THE SQUIRE'S TALE

Heere bigynneth the Squieres Tale

At Sarray, in the land of Tartarye,
10 Ther dwelte a kyng that werreyed Russye,   *warred against*
Thurgh which ther dyde many a doughty man.   *died*
This noble kyng was cleped Cambyuskan,
Which in his tyme was of so greet renoun
That ther was nowher in no regioun
15 So excellent a lord in alle thyng.
Hym lakked noght that longeth to a kyng.
As of the secte of which that he was born   *religion*
He kepte his lay, to which that he was sworn;   *creed*

---

10 An allusion to the invasion of Russia and eastern Europe by the
Tartars in the thirteenth century.
12 *Cambyuskan*, Genghis Khan, grandfather of Kublai Khan.
16 He lacked nothing that befits a king.

And therto he was hardy, wys, and riche,
20 And pitous and just, alwey yliche;
Sooth of his word, benigne, and honurable,　　　*true*
Of his corage as any centre stable;
Yong, fressh, and strong, in armes desirous　　　*healthy; eager*
As any bacheler of al his hous.　　　*young knight*
25 A fair persone he was and fortunat,　　　*hansome*
And kepte alwey so wel roial estat
That ther was nowher swich another man.
　　This noble kyng, this Tartre Cambyuskan,
Hadde two sones on Elpheta his wyf,
30 Of whiche the eldeste highte Algarsyf,　　　*was named*
That oother sone was cleped Cambalo.　　　*called*
A doghter hadde this worthy kyng also,
That yongest was, and highte Canacee.
But for to telle yow al hir beautee,
35 It lyth nat in my tonge, n'yn my konnyng;
I dar nat undertake so heigh a thyng.　　　*ambitious*
Myn Englissh eek is insufficient.
It moste been a rethor excellent,
That koude his colours longynge for that art,
40 If he sholde hire discryven every part.
I am noon swich, I moot speke as I kan.　　　*must*
　　And so bifel that whan this Cambyuskan
Hath twenty wynter born his diademe,
As he was wont fro yeer to yeer, I deme,　　　*think*
45 He leet the feeste of his nativitee
Doon cryen thurghout Sarray his citee,
The laste Idus of March, after the yeer.
Phebus the sonne ful joly was and cleer;　　　*joyful*
For he was neigh his exaltacioun
50 In Martes face, and in his mansioun
In Aries, the colerik hoote signe.
Ful lusty was the weder and benigne,　　　*pleasant*
For which the foweles, agayn the sonne sheene,
What for the sesoun and the yonge grene,　　　*with*

20 Unvaryingly just and merciful.
22 As steadfast in disposition as a fulcrum.
26 Always maintained such very royal state.
35 i.e. I haven't the eloquence or skill.
38-40 It would take an excellent master of rhetoric, knowing all the
stylistic ornaments of his art, to give a full picture of her.
45-6 He had the feast of his nativity proclaimed.
47 i.e. 15th March; *after the yeer*, according to the calendar.
49-51 The zodiacal sign Aries (described by the astrologers as hot and
dry, and therefore 'choleric') was the 'exaltation' of the sun. It was
also one of the two 'mansions' of Mars, and was divided into three
'faces' of ten degrees each, the first being known as the 'face of Mars.'
53 The birds, looking towards the bright sun.

55 Ful loude songen hire affecciouns.   *loudly sang*
   Hem semed han geten hem protecciouns
   Agayn the swerd of wynter, keene and coold.   *sword*
      This Cambyuskan, of which I have yow toold,
   In roial vestiment sit on his deys,   *sits; dais*
60 With diademe, ful heighe in his paleys,
   And halt his feeste so solempne and so ryche   *holds*
   That in this world ne was ther noon it lyche;   *like*
   Of which if I shal tellen al th'array,   *arrangement*
   Thanne wolde it occupie a someres day;
65 And eek it nedeth nat for to devyse   *describe*
   At every cours the ordre of hire servyse.   *serving*
   I wol nat tellen of hir strange sewes,   *broths*
   Ne of hir swannes, ne of hire heronsewes.   *young herons*
   Eek in that lond, as tellen knyghtes olde.
70 Ther is som mete that is ful deynte holde,
   That in this lond men recche of it but smal;
   Ther nys no man that may reporten al.
   I wol nat taryen yow, for it is pryme,
   And for it is no fruyt, but los of tyme;
75 Unto my firste I wole have my recours.
      And so bifel that after the thridde cours,
   Whil that this kyng sit thus in his nobleye,   *state*
   Herknynge his mynstralles hir thynges pleye   *songs*
   Biforn hym at the bord deliciously,   *delightfully*
80 In at the halle dore al sodeynly
   Ther cam a knyght upon a steede of bras,
   And in his hand a brood mirour of glas.   *broad*
   Upon his thombe he hadde of gold a ryng,
   And by his syde a naked swerd hangyng;
85 And up he rideth to the heighe bord.   *table*
   In al the halle ne was ther spoken a word
   For merveille of this knyght; hym to biholde
   Ful bisily they wayten, yonge and olde.
      This strange knyght, that cam thus sodeynly,
90 Al armed, save his heed, ful richely,   *head*
   Saleweth kyng and queene and lordes alle,   *greets*
   By ordre, as they seten in the halle,   *sat*
   With so heigh reverence and obeisaunce,
   As wel in speche as in contenaunce,
95 That Gawayn, with his olde curteisye,

56 It seemed to them they had found protection for themselves.
70-1 There are some foods considered a great luxury, which are thought
      little of in this land.
73 I don't want to delay you, because it is prime (i.e. 9 a.m.).
74 It is not essential, but a waste of time.
75 I will return to my original subject.
87-8 They watch him all agog.
93 With such deep reverence and submission.

Though he were comen ayeyn out of Fairye,   *fairyland*
Ne koude hym nat amende with a word.
And after this, biforn the heighe bord,
He with a manly voys seide his message,
100 After the forme used in his langage,
Withouten vice of silable or of lettre;   *fault*
And, for his tale sholde seme the bettre,
Accordant to his wordes was his cheere,
As techeth art of speche hem that it leere.
105 Al be that I kan nat sowne his stile,   *imitate; style*
Ne kan nat clymben over so heigh a style,   *stile*
Yet seye I this, as to commune entente,   *general meaning*
Thus muche amounteth al that evere he mente,
If it so be that I have it in mynde.
110   He seyde, 'The kyng of Arabe and of   *Arabia*
      Inde,   *India*
My lige lord, on this solempne day   *liege; festive*
Saleweth yow, as he best kan and may,
And sendeth yow, in honour of youre feeste,
By me, that am al redy at youre heeste,   *command*
115 This steede of bras, that esily and weel
Kan in the space of o day natureel—   *natural*
This is to seyn, in foure and twenty houres—
Wher-so yow lyst, in droghte or elles shoures,
Beren youre body into every place   *carry*
120 To which youre herte wilneth for to pace,   *desires; go*
Withouten wem of yow, thurgh foul or fair;
Or, if yow lyst to fleen as hye in the air   *fly*
As dooth an egle, whan hym list to soore,   *soar*
This same steede shal bere yow evere moore,
125 Withouten harm, til ye be ther yow leste,   *where you wish*
Though that ye slepen on his bak or reste,
And turne ayeyn, with writhyng of a pyn.   *twisting*
He that it wroghte koude ful many a gyn.
He wayted many a constellacion
130 Er he had doon this operacion,
And knew ful many a seel and many a bond.

97 Could not improve on a single word of his.
100 According to the form of words in his language.
103–4 He suited his looks and gestures to his words, as those who study
    the art of speaking learn to do.
108 What he had to say really amounted to this.
118 Wherever you please, in drought or else in showers (i.e. in any
    circumstances).
121 Without hurt to yourself, through thick and thin.
128 The man who made it knew many a cunning contrivance.
129–30 He watched for a favourable combination of the planets before
    he performed this operation. (Cf. I. 415–18.)
131 The use of 'seals' and 'bonds' (to compel the service of spirits)
    was common in medieval magic.

This mirour eek, that I have in myn hond,
Hath swich a myght that men may in it see   *power*
Whan ther shal fallen any adversitee   *befall*
135 Unto youre regne or to youreself also,   *realm*
And openly who is youre freend or foo.
And over al this, if any lady bright   *over and above*
Hath set hire herte on any maner wight,   *sort of person*
If he be fals, she shal his tresoun see,
140 His newe love, and al his subtiltee,   *guile*
So openly that ther shal no thyng hyde.
Wherfore, ageyn this lusty someres tyde,
This mirour and this ryng, that ye may see,
He hath sent to my lady Canacee,
145 Youre excellente doghter that is heere.
The vertu of the ryng, if ye wol heere,
Is this, that if hire lust it for to were   *she pleases*
Upon hir thombe, or in hir purs it bere,
Ther is no fowel that fleeth under the hevene   *bird*
150 That she ne shal wel understonde his stevene,   *language*
And knowe his menyng openly and pleyn,
And answere hym in his langage ageyn;
And every gras that groweth upon roote
She shal eek knowe, and whom it wol do boote,   *good*
155 Al be his woundes never so depe and wyde.   *although*
This naked swerd, that hangeth by my syde,
Swich vertu hath that, what man so ye smyte,   *whatever*
Thurgh out his armure it wole kerve and byte,   *cut*
Were it as thikke as is a branched ook;
160 And what man that is wounded with the strook
Shal never be hool til that yow list, of grace,   *well*
To stroke hym with the plat in thilke place
Ther he is hurt; this is as muche to seyn,   *where*
Ye moote with the platte swerd ageyn
165 Stroke hym in the wounde, and it wol close.
This is a verray sooth, withouten glose;   *truth; deceit*
It failleth nat whils it is in youre hoold.'
And whan this knyght hath thus his tale toold,
He rideth out of halle, and doun he lighte.   *alighted*
170 His steede, which that shoon as sonne brighte,
Stant in the court, stille as any stoon.   *stands; courtyard*
This knyght is to his chambre lad anoon,   *led*
And is unarmed, and to mete yset.   *seated at table*
The presentes been ful roially yfet,—   *fetched*
175 This is to seyn, the swerd and the mirour,
And born anon into the heighe tour

142 Near the beginning of this joyful summer season.
162 With the flat (of the sword) in the same place.

With certeine officers ordeyned therfore;
And unto Canacee this ryng is bore   *carried*
Solempnely, ther she sit at the table.   *where; sits*
180 But sikerly, withouten any fable,   *truly*
The hors of bras, that may nat be remewed,   *removed*
It stant as it were to the ground yglewed.   *glued*
Ther may no man out of the place it dryve
For noon engyn of wyndas or polyve;
185 And cause why? for they kan nat the craft.
And therfore in the place they han it laft,   *left*
Til that the knyght hath taught hem the manere
To voyden hym, as ye shal after heere.   *remove*
Greet was the prees that swarmeth to and fro   *crowd*
190 To gauren on this hors that stondeth so;   *stare*
For it so heigh was, and so brood and long,
So wel proporcioned for to been strong,
Right as it were a steede of Lumbardye;
Therwith so horsly, and so quyk of ye,
195 As it a gentil Poilleys courser were.
For certes, fro his tayl unto his ere,
Nature ne art ne koude hym nat amende   *improve on*
In no degree, as al the peple wende.   *thought*
But everemoore hir mooste wonder was   *greatest*
200 How that it koude gon, and was of bras;   *move*
It was a fairye, as the peple semed.
Diverse folk diversely they demed;   *thought*
As many heddes, as manye wittes ther been.
They murmureden as dooth a swarm of been,   *bees*
205 And maden skiles after hir fantasies,
Rehersynge of thise olde poetries,
And seyden it was lyk the Pegasee,   *Pegasus*
The hors that hadde wynges for to flee;   *fly*
Or elles it was the Grekes hors Synon,
210 That broghte Troie to destruccion,
As men in thise olde geestes rede.   *may; stories*
'Myn herte,' quod oon, 'is everemoore in drede;
I trowe som men of armes been therinne,
That shapen hem this citee for to wynne.   *plot*

177 By certain officers appointed for this purpose.
183–4 No one can drive it out of the place by using any device like a
    windlass or pulley.
185 And why was that? Because they don't know the method.
194 At the same time it was so completely all that a horse should be,
    and so quick of eye.
195 As if it were a well-bred Apulian steed.
201 Of fairy origin, it seemed to the people.
203 Many heads, as many notions.
205 And invented reasons according to their fancy.
206 Quoting bits from old poems.
209 The horse of Sinon the Greek, i.e. the Trojan horse.

215 It were right good that al swich thyng were knowe.'   *known*
    Another rowned to his felawe lowe,   *whispered; softly*
    And seyde, 'He lyeth, for it is rather lyk   *lies*
    An apparence ymaad by som magyk,   *illusion*
    As jogelours pleyen at thise feestes grete.'   *jugglers*
220 Of sondry doutes thus they jangle and trete,
    As lewed peple demeth comunly
    Of thynges that been maad moore subtilly
    Than kan in hir lewednesse comprehende;   *ignorance*
    They demen gladly to the badder ende.
225   And somme of hem wondred on the mirour,   *wondered at*
    That born was up into the maister-tour,   *chief tower*
    Hou men myghte in it swiche thynges se.
       Another answerde, and seyde it myghte wel be
    Naturelly, by composicions
230 Of anglis and of slye reflexiouns,
    And seyde that in Rome was swich oon.
    They speken of Alocen, and Vitulon,
    And Aristotle, that writen in hir lyves
    Of queynte mirours and of perspectives,   *curious*
235 As knowen they that han hir bookes herd.
       And oother folk han wondred on the swerd
    That wolde percen thurghout every thyng;
    And fille in speche of Thelophus the kyng,   *fell to talking*
    And of Achilles with his queynte spere,
240 For he koude with it bothe heele and dere,   *heal; wound*
    Right in swich wise as men may with the swerd
    Of which right now ye han youreselven herd.
    They speken of sondry hardyng of metal,
    And speke of medicynes therwithal,
245 And how and whanne it sholde yharded be,   *hardened*
    Which is unknowe, algates unto me.   *at any rate*
       Tho speeke they of Canacees ryng,
    And seyden alle that swich a wonder thyng
    Of craft of rynges herde they nevere noon,
250 Save that he Moyses and kyng Salomon
    Hadde a name of konnyng in swich art.   *for*

220–1 Thus they wrangle and give voice to their various fears, as ignorant people commonly will.
224 They gladly imagine the worst possible explanation.
229–30 By combinations of angles and artfully contrived reflections.
231 An allusion to the magic mirror supposed to have been set up in Rome by Virgil, who was more famous as a magician than as a poet in the Middle Ages.
233 Who wrote during their lifetime.
235 Who have heard their books (read aloud).
243–4 Of various ways of hardening metal, and of the medicaments used for this purpose.
248–9 They had never heard of such a wonderful example of the goldsmith's craft.

Thus seyn the peple, and drawen hem apart.
But nathelees somme seiden that it was   *nevertheless*
Wonder to maken of fern-asshen glas,
255 And yet nys glas nat lyk asshen of fern;
But, for they han yknowen it so fern,
Therfore cesseth hir janglyng and hir wonder.
As soore wondren somme on cause of thonder,
On ebbe, on flood, on gossomer, and on myst,
260 And alle thyng, til that the cause is wyst.   *known*
Thus jangle they, and demen, and devyse,
Til that the kyng gan fro the bord aryse.   *rose from table*
   Phebus hath laft the angle meridional,
And yet ascendynge was the beest roial,
265 The gentil Leon, with his Aldiran,
Whan that Tartre kyng, this Cambyuskan,
Roos fro his bord, ther as he sat ful hye.
Toforn hym gooth the loude mynstralcye,   *before*
Til he cam to his chambre of parementz,   *presence chamber*
270 Ther as they sownen diverse instrumentz,   *play on*
That it is lyk an hevene for to heere.
Now dauncen lusty Venus children deere,
For in the Fyssh hir lady sat ful hye,
And looketh on hem with a freendly ye.   *eye*
275 This noble kyng is set upon his trone.
This strange knyght is fet to hym ful soone,   *fetched*
And on the daunce he gooth with Canacee.
Heere is the revel and the jolitee   *revelry*
That is nat able a dul man to devyse.   *describe*
280 He moste han knowen love and his servyse,   *its*
And been a feestlych man as fressh as May,   *convivial*
That sholde yow devysen swich array.   *festivities*
   Who koude telle yow the forme of daunces
So unkouthe, and swiche fresshe contenaunces,
285 Swich subtil lookyng and dissymulynges
For drede of jalouse mennes aperceyvynges?

254 A wonderful thing to make glass from fern-ashes.
256-7 But because men have known it (i.e. the art of glass-making) for
   so long, they have stopped chattering and wondering about it.
258 Some will wonder just as much about the cause of thunder.
261 They chatter, guess, and speculate.
263-5 This elaborate description of the relative positions of the sun and
   the zodiacal sign Leo is equivalent to saying that it was nearly two
   hours past noon.
267 Where he sat high up (on the dais).
272 The beloved subjects of lusty Venus, i.e. lovers.
273 Their lady (i.e. the planet Venus) was 'exalted' in Pisces (in which
   sign, according to astrologers, she has the greatest influence).
284-5 So strange, and the youthful faces (of the dancers) so alive with
   secret glances and dissemblings.

No man but Launcelot, and he is deed.
Therfore I passe of al this lustiheed;   *pass over; merriment*
I sey namoore, but in this jolynesse   *jollity*
290 I lete hem, til men to the soper dresse.   *leave; go*
    The styward bit the spices for to hye,
And eek the wyn, in al this melodye.   *amid*
The usshers and the squiers been ygoon,   *gone*
The spices and the wyn is come anoon.   *at once*
295 They ete and drynke; and whan this hadde an ende,
Unto the temple, as reson was, they wende.   *go*
The service doon, they soupen al by day.
What nedeth yow rehercen hire array?
Ech man woot wel that a kynges feeste
300 Hath plentee to the meeste and to the leeste,   *greatest*
And deyntees mo than been in my knowyng.   *delicacies*
At after-soper gooth this noble kyng
To seen this hors of bras, with al a route   *company*
Of lordes and of ladyes hym aboute.
305   Swich wondryng was ther on this hors of bras
That syn the grete sege of Troie was,   *since*
Theras men wondreden on an hors also,   *where*
Ne was ther swich a wondryng as was tho.   *then*
But fynally the kyng axeth this knyght
310 The vertu of this courser and the myght,   *steed*
And preyde hym to telle his governaunce.
    This hors anoon bigan to trippe and daunce,
Whan that this knyght leyde hand upon his reyne,   *its*
And seyde, 'Sire, ther is namoore to seyne,   *be said*
315 But, whan yow list to ryden anywhere,
Ye mooten trille a pyn, stant in his ere,
Which I shall yow telle bitwix us two.
Ye moote nempne hym to what place also,   *tell*
Or to what contree, that yow list to ryde.
320 And whan ye come ther as yow list abyde,   *stay*
Bidde hym descende, and trille another pyn,
For therin lith th'effect of al the gyn,
And he wol doun descende and doon youre wille,
And in that place he wol abyde stille.
325 Though al the world the contrarie hadde yswore,   *sworn*
He shal nat thennes been ydrawe ne ybore.   *dragged; carried*

287 *Launcelot.* See VII. 3212.
291 Orders the spices to be quickly brought.
297 They feast all day long.
298 What need is there to give you every detail of their festivities?
302 *At after-soper*, i.e. during the interval between supper and bedtime.
311 To explain how it was controlled.
316-17 You must twirl a pin that's fixed in its ear, which I shall tell
    you about when we are by ourselves.
322 The efficacy of the whole contrivance lies in that.

Or, if yow liste bidde hym thennes goon,
Trille this pyn, and he wol vanysshe anoon
Out of the sighte of every maner wight,
330 And come agayn, be it by day or nyght,
Whan that yow list to clepen hym ageyn
In swich a gyse as I shal to yow seyn   *manner*
Bitwixe yow and me, and that ful soone.
Ride whan yow list, ther is namoore to doone.'   *be done*
335   Enformed whan the kyng was of that knyght,   *by*
And hath conceyved in his wit aright
The manere and the forme of al this thyng,
Ful glad and blithe, this noble doughty kyng
Repeireth to his revel as biforn.   *returns; before*
340 The brydel is unto the tour yborn
And kept among his jueles leeve and deere.
The hors vanysshed, I noot in what manere,   *know not*
Out of hir sighte; ye gete namoore of me.
But thus I lete in lust and jolitee   *leave; joy*
345 This Cambyuskan his lordes festeiynge,   *feasting*
Til wel ny the day bigan to sprynge.   *dawn*

EXPLICIT PRIMA PARS

SEQUITUR PARS SECUNDA

The norice of digestioun, the sleep,   *nurse*
Gan on hem wynke and bad hem taken keep
That muchel drynke and labour wolde han reste;   *much*
350 And with a galpyng mouth hem alle he keste, *yawning; kissed*
And seyde that it was tyme to lye adoun,   *down*
For blood was in his domynacioun.
'Cherisseth blood, natures freend,' quod he.
They thanken hym galpynge, by two, by   *in twos and threes*
thre,
355 And every wight gan drawe hym to his reste,
As sleep hem bad; they tooke it for the beste.
Hire dremes shul nat now been toold for me;
Ful were hire heddes of fumositee,

329 Of everyone (lit. of every sort of person).
336 And has properly grasped.
341 Among his most precious jewels.
348 Blinked at them and bade them take note.
352 According to the old physiologists, each of the four humours (see
I. 420) was dominant for a part of the day. The domination of the
blood, it was held by some, lasted for six hours after midnight.
355 And everyone went to rest.
356 They thought it the best thing to do.
358 *fumositee*, fumes rising into the head from the stomach.

That causeth dreem of which ther nys no charge.
360 They slepen til that it was pryme large,
The mooste part, but it were Canacee.   *except*
She was ful mesurable, as wommen be;   *temperate*
For of hir fader hadde she take leve
To goon to reste soone after it was eve.
365 Hir liste nat appalled for to be,
Ne on the morwe unfeestlich for to se,
And slepte hire firste sleep, and thanne awook.
For swich a joye she in hir herte took
Bothe of hir queynte ryng and hire mirour,
370 That twenty tyme she changed hir colour;
And in hire sleep, right for impressioun
Of hire mirour, she hadde a visioun.
Wherfore, er that the sonne gan up glyde,   *before the sun rose*
She cleped on hir maistresse hire bisyde,
375 And seyde that hire liste for to ryse.   *she wished*
    Thise olde wommen that been gladly wyse,
As is hire maistresse, answerde hire anon,
And seyde, 'Madame, whider wil ye goon   *where*
Thus erly, for the folk been alle on reste?'
380 'I wol,' quod she, 'arise, for me leste
Ne lenger for to slepe, and walke aboute.'
    Hire maistresse clepeth wommen a greet route,   *company*
And up they rysen, wel a ten or twelve;   *fully*
Up riseth fresshe Canacee hirselve,
385 As rody and bright as dooth the yonge sonne,   *ruddy*
That in the Ram is foure degrees up ronne—
Noon hyer was he whan she redy was—
And forth she walketh esily a pas,   *at an easy pace*
Arrayed after the lusty seson soote
390 Lightly, for to pleye and walke on foote,
Nat but with fyve or sixe of hir meynee;
And in a trench forth in the park gooth she.   *alley*
    The vapour which that fro the erthe glood   *glided*
Made the sonne to seme rody and brood;
395 But nathelees it was so fair a sighte
That it made alle hire hertes for to lighte,   *feel light*

359 Dreams which have no weight.
360 They slept till it was fully prime (i.e. 9 a.m.).
365–6 She had no wish to look pale or jaded on the morrow.
371–2 Because of the deep impression made by her mirror.
374 She called to her governess who lay beside her.
376–7 Her governess, who was inquisitive, as old women usually are,
    answered at once.
385 *yonge sonne.* Cf. I. 7.
386–7 The sun had not risen higher than four degrees above the horizon,
    i.e. it was just after 6 a.m.
389–90 Lightly dressed to suit the sweet and joyful season.
391 With not more than five or six of her retinue.

What for the seson and the morwenynge,
And for the foweles that she herde synge.   *birds*
For right anon she wiste what they mente, *all at once; knew*
400 Right by hir song, and knew al hire entente.
    The knotte why that every tale is toold,   *point*
If it be taried til that lust be coold   *delayed; interest*
Of hem that han it after herkned yoore,
The savour passeth ever lenger the moore,
405 For fulsomnesse of his prolixitee;
And by the same resoun, thynketh me,
I sholde to the knotte condescende,   *come*
And maken of hir walkyng soone an ende.
    Amydde a tree, for drye as whit as chalk,
410 As Canacee was pleyyng in hir walk,
Ther sat a faucon over hire heed ful hye,   *falcon*
That with a pitous voys so gan to crye
That all the wode resouned of hire cry.   *resounded with*
Ybeten hadde she hirself so pitously   *beaten*
415 With bothe hir wynges, til the rede blood
Ran endelong the tree ther-as she stood.   *down along*
And evere in oon she cryde alwey and shrighte,
And with hir beek hirselven so she prighte,
That ther nys tygre, ne noon so crueel beest,
420 That dwelleth outher in wode or in forest,
That nolde han wept, if that he wepe koude,
For sorwe of hire, she shrighte alwey so loude.
For ther nas nevere yet no man on lyve,   *alive*
If that I koude a faucon wel discryve,   *describe*
425 That herde of swich another of fairnesse,
As wel of plumage as of gentillesse
Of shap, of al that myghte yrekened be.
A faucon peregryn thanne semed she   *peregrine*
Of fremde land; and everemoore, as she stood,   *foreign*
430 She swowneth now and now for lak of blood,
Til wel neigh is she fallen fro the tree.
    This faire kynges doghter, Canacee,
That on hir fynger baar the queynte ryng,   *wore*
Thurgh which she understood wel every thyng
435 That any fowel may in his leden seyn,   *language; say*
And koude answeren hym in his ledene ageyn,

397 What with the season and the early morning.
403 Of those who have long been listening for it.
404–5 Its savour gradually wears off because of the excessive prolixity
with which it is told.
409 So dried up it looked as white as chalk.
417 And all the time she kept up her crying and shrieking.
425–7 Who has heard of another bird as beautiful in plumage and in
nobleness of form, and indeed in every possible way.
430 She swoons again and again.

Hath understonde what this faucon seyde,
And wel neigh for the routhe almoost she deyde.   *pity*
And to the tree she gooth ful hastily,
440 And on this faucon looketh pitously,
And heeld hir lappe abroad, for wel she wiste
The faukon moste fallen fro the twiste,   *branch*
Whan that it swowned next, for lak of blood.
A longe whil to wayten hire she stood,   *watching*
445 Til atte laste she spak in this manere
Unto the hauk, as ye shal after heere: *hawk*
     'What is the cause, if it be for to telle,   *can be told*
That ye be in this furial pyne of helle?'   *furious pain*
Quod Canacee unto this hauk above.
450 'Is this for sorwe of deeth or los of love?
For, as I trowe, thise been causes two   *think*
That causen moost a gentil herte wo;
Of oother harm it nedeth nat to speke.
For ye youreself upon yourself yow wreke,
455 Which proveth wel that outher ire or drede   *anger; fear*
Moot been enchesoun of youre cruel dede,
Syn that I see noon oother wight yow chace.   *pursues*
For love of God, as dooth youreselven grace,
Or what may been youre help? for west nor est
460 Ne saugh I nevere er now no bryd ne beest   *saw; before*
That ferde with hymself so pitously.
Ye sle me with youre sorwe verraily,   *slay*
I have of yow so greet compassioun.   *such*
For Goddes love, com from the tree adoun;
465 And as I am a kynges doghter trewe,
If that I verraily the cause knewe
Of youre disese, if it lay in my myght,   *grief*
I wolde amenden it er that it were nyght,   *cure*
As wisly helpe me grete God of kynde!
470 And herbes shal I right ynowe yfynde
To heele with youre hurtes hastily.'
     Tho shrighte this faucon yet moore pitously   *then shrieked*
Than ever she dide, and fil to grounde anon,
And lith aswowne, deed and lyk a stoon,
475 Til Canacee hath in hire lappe hire take

441 Held out her lap, for she well knew.
452 That give a noble heart most sorrow.
454 For you take vengeance on your own self.
456 Must be the reason for your cruelty.
458 Please have mercy on yourself.
461 Who treated himself so pitiably.
469 So help me the great God of nature.
470 Find in plenty.
471 To heal your wounds with quickly.
474 Lies in a deathly swoon, stone-still.

Unto the tyme she gan of swough awake.
And after that she of hir swough gan breyde,   *awoke*
Right in hir haukes ledene thus she seyde:
'That pitee renneth soone in gentil herte,
480 Feelynge his similitude in peynes smerte,
Is preved alday, as men may it see,
As wel by werk as by auctoritee;
For gentil herte kitheth gentillesse.
I se wel that ye han of my distresse
485 Compassion, my faire Canacee,
Of verray wommanly benignytee
That Nature in youre principles hath set.
But for noon hope for to fare the bet,
But for to obeye unto youre herte free,   *noble*
490 And for to maken othere be war by me,
As by the whelp chasted is the leon,
Right for that cause and that conclusion,
Whil that I have a leyser and a space, *leisure; opportunity*
Myn harm I wol confessen er I pace.'
495 And evere, whil that oon hir sorwe tolde,
That oother weep as she to water wolde,
Til that the faucon bad hire to be stille,
And, with a syk, right thus she seyde hir wille: *sigh*
'Ther I was bred—allas, that ilke day!— *where*
500 And fostred in a roche of marbul gray   *rock*
So tendrely that no thyng eyled me,   *troubled*
I nyste nat what was adversitee,   *knew not*
Til I koude flee ful hye under the sky.   *fly*
Tho dwelte a tercelet me faste by,   *male falcon*
505 That semed welle of alle gentillesse;   *source*
Al were he ful of treson and falsnesse, *although he was*
It was so wrapped under humble cheere, *bearing*
And under hewe of trouthe in swich manere,
Under plesance, and under bisy peyne,
510 That no wight koude han wend he koude feyne, *imagined*
So depe in greyn he dyed his coloures.

476 Until she awoke from her swoon.
480 Finding its complement in another's suffering.
481-2 Is continually proved . . . both by experience and authority.
483 For a noble heart shows itself in noble deeds.
486-7 Springing from the true womanly grace that nature has implanted
  in your disposition.
488 But with no hope of improving my condition.
491 As the lion is chastised by means of the dog. (The allusion is to
  the old proverb, 'Beat the dog before the lion,' i.e. teach a great man
  a lesson by punishing a humble man in his presence.)
496 The other wept as if she would turn to water.
508-9 Under an outward show of truthfulness, of pleasure and whole-
  hearted devotion in all his dealings with me.
511 His (false) colours were dyed so fast.

Right as a serpent hit hym under floures   *hides himself*
Til he may seen his tyme for to byte,
Right so this god of loves ypocryte
515 Dooth so his cerymonyes and obeisaunces,
And kepeth in semblaunt alle his observaunces
That sownen into gentillesse of love.
As in a toumbe is al the faire above,   *beauty*
And under is the corps, swich as ye woot,   *know*
520 Swich was this ypocrite, bothe coold and hoot.
And in this wise he served his entente,   *purpose*
That, save the feend, noon wiste what he mente,
Til he so longe hadde wopen and compleyned,   *wept*
And many a yeer his service to me feyned,
525 Til that myn herte, to pitous and to nyce,
Al innocent of his crouned malice,   *consummate*
Forfered of his deeth, as thoughte me,
Upon his othes and his seuretee,   *pledge*
Graunted hym love, upon this condicioun,
530 That everemoore myn honour and renoun
Were saved, bothe privee and apert;
This is to seyn, that after his desert,   *deserts*
I yaf hym al myn herte and al my thoght—
God woot and he, that ootherwise noght—
535 And took his herte in chaunge of myn for ay.
But sooth is seyd, goon sithen many a day,
"A trewe wight and a theef thenken nat oon."
And whan he saugh the thyng so fer ygoon
That I hadde graunted hym fully my love,
540 In swich a gyse as I have seyd above,   *way*
And yeven hym my trewe herte as free   *freely*
As he swoor he yaf his herte to me;
Anon this tigre, ful of doublenesse,   *duplicity*
Fil on his knees with so devout humblesse,
545 With so heigh reverence, and, as by his cheere,
So lyk a gentil lovere of manere,
So ravysshed, as it semed, for the joye,
That nevere Jason ne Parys of Troye—

515-17 Did homage in ceremonious fashion, and kept up the appearance
     of all those practices that accord with noble love.
520 Just so this hypocrite blew hot and cold.
525 Too pitiful and foolish.
527 Fearful of his death, for so it seemed to me.
531 Were kept safe, both in public and in private.
534 That I gave nothing else.
536 But there has long been a true saying.
537 An honest person and a scoundrel don't think alike.
545 With such deep reverence, and in his bearing.
548 Jason deserted Medea for Glauce, and Paris deserted Oenone for
     Helen.

Jason? certes, ne noon oother man

550 Syn Lameth was, that alderfirst bigan   *Lamech; first of all*
To loven two, as writen folk biforn—
Ne nevere, syn the firste man was born,   *since*
Ne koude man, by twenty thousand part,
Countrefete the sophymes of his art,

555 Ne were worthy unbokelen his galoche,   *shoe*
Ther doublenesse or feynyng sholde approche,
Ne so koude thonke a wight as he dide me!   *thank*
His manere was an hevene for to see
Til any womman, were she never so wys,   *to; prudent*

560 So peynted he and kembde at point-devys
As wel his wordes as his contenaunce.
And I so loved hym for his obeisaunce,   *obedience*
And for the trouthe I demed in his herte,   *supposed*
That if so were that any thyng hym smerte,   *grieved*

565 Al were it never so lite, and I it wiste,
Me thoughte I felte deeth myn herte twiste.   *wring*
And shortly, so ferforth this thyng is went,
That my wyl was his willes instrument;
This is to seyn, my wyl obeyed his wyl

570 In alle thyng, as fer as reson fil,   *allowed*
Kepynge the boundes of my worshipe evere.
Ne nevere hadde I thyng so lief, ne levere,   *dear; dearer*
As hym, God woot! ne nevere shal namo.   *again*
   This laste lenger than a yeer or two,

575 That I supposed of hym noght but good.
But finally, thus atte laste it stood,
That Fortune wolde that he moste twynne   *depart*
Out of that place which that I was inne.
Wher me was wo, that is no questioun;

580 I kan nat make of it discripsioun;
For o thyng dar I tellen boldely,
I knowe what is the peyne of deeth therby;
Swich harm I felte for he ne myghte bileve.
So on a day of me he took his leve,

585 So sorwefully eek that I wende verraily   *believed*
That he had felt as muche harm as I,
Whan that I herde hym speke, and saugh his hewe.

---

551 As ancient authors have written.
554 Imitate his artful deceits.
555 An echo of Mark i. 7.
556 Where duplicity or pretence were called for.
560 Trimmed to perfection.
565 However trivial it might be, and I knew of it.
567 And briefly, this thing went to such lengths.
571 Always observing the bounds of honour.
579 Whether I was unhappy, you need not ask.
583 Such grief I felt because he could not stay.
587 And saw his colour, i.e. saw how pale he was.

But nathelees, I thoughte he was so trewe,
And eek that he repaire sholde ageyn   *return*
590 Withinne a litel while, sooth to seyn;   *truth*
And resoun wolde eek that he moste go
For his honour, as ofte it happeth so,   *happens*
That I made vertu of necessitee,
And took it wel, syn that it moste be.   *had to*
595 As I best myghte, I hidde fro hym my sorwe,
And took hym by the hond, Seint John to   *as my pledge*
         borwe,
And seyde hym thus: "Lo, I am youres al;
Beth swich as I to yow have been and shal."
What he answerde, it nedeth noght reherce;   *repeat*
600 Who kan sey bet than he, who kan do werse?   *better*
Whan he hath al wel seyd, thanne hath he doon.
"Therfore bihoveth hire a ful long spoon   *she needs*
That shal ete with a feend," thus herde I seye.   *devil*
So atte laste he moste forth his weye,
605 And forth he fleeth til he cam ther hym leste.
Whan it cam hym to purpos for to reste,
I trowe he hadde thilke text in mynde,   *that*
That "alle thyng, repeirynge to his kynde,
Gladeth hymself;" thus seyn men, as I gesse.
610 Men loven of propre kynde newefangelnesse,   *by nature*
As briddes doon that men in cages fede.   *birds*
For though thou nyght and day take of hem hede,   *care*
And strawe hir cage faire and softe as silk,
And yeve hem sugre, hony, breed and milk,
615 Yet right anon as that his dore is uppe,
He with his feet wol spurne adoun his cuppe,
And to the wode he wole, and wormes ete;   *will go*
So newefangel been they of hire mete,
And loven novelries of propre kynde;   *novelties*
620 No gentillesse of blood ne may hem bynde.   *nobleness*
     So ferde this tercelet, allas the day!   *behaved*
Though he were gentil born, and fressh and gay,
And goodlich for to seen, and humble and   *handsome*
         free,   *generous*
He saugh upon a tyme a kyte flee,   *fly past*

591-2 Also reasons of honour compelled him to go.
601 After talking so well, he behaved shamefully.
604 At last he had to go away.
605 Away he flew till he came where he longed to be.
606 When it suited his purpose to come to rest.
608-9 Everything gladly reverts to its own true nature.
613 And line their cage with straw.
615 Yet immediately the door of his cage is left open.
618 They have such newfangled whims about food.

625 And sodeynly he loved this kyte so
That al his love his clene fro me ago;
And hath his trouthe falsed in this wyse.
Thus hath the kyte my love in hire servyse,
And I am lorn withouten remedie!'   *lost*
630 And with that word this faucon gan to crie,
And swowned eft in Canacees barm.   *again; lap*
  Greet was the sorwe for the haukes harm
That Canacee and alle hir wommen made;
They nyste hou they myghte the faucon   *knew not*
      glade.   *comfort*
635 But Canacee hom bereth hire in hir lappe,   *home*
And softely in plastres gan hire wrappe,   *plasters*
Ther as she with hire beek hadde hurt hirselve. *where; beak*
Now kan nat Canacee but herbes delve
Out of the ground, and make salves newe
640 Of herbes preciouse and fyne of hewe,
To heelen with this hauk. Fro day to nyght   *heal*
She dooth hire bisynesse and al hire myght,
And by hire beddes heed she made a mewe,
And covered it with veluettes blewe,   *velvet*
645 In signe of trouthe that is in wommen sene.
And al withoute, the mewe is peynted grene,
In which were peynted alle thise false fowles,
As ben thise tidyves, tercelettes, and owles;
Right for despit were peynted hem bisyde,   *in scorn*
650 Pyes, on hem for to crie and chyde.
    Thus lete I Canacee hir hauk kepyng;   *leave; tending*
I wol namoore as now speke of hir ryng,
Til it come eft to purpos for to seyn
How that this faucon gat hire love ageyn
655 Repentant, as the storie telleth us,
By mediacion of Cambalus,
The kynges sone, of which I yow tolde.
But hennesforth I wol my proces holde   *will proceed*
To speken of aventures and of batailles,
660 That nevere yet was herd so grete mervailles.   *such*
    First wol I telle yow of Cambyuskan,
That in his tyme many a citee wan;   *won*
And after wol I speke of Algarsif,
How that he wan Theodora to his wif,   *for*
665 For whom ful ofte in greet peril he was,

627 And this is how he broke faith with me.
638 Now all that Canace can do is to dig herbs.
642 She made every effort she could.
645 As a sign of the faithfulness seen in women. (Blue was the colour of truth and constancy.)
648 *tidyves*, small birds; *tercelettes*, male falcons.
653 Until it is again relevant to tell.

Ne hadde he ben holpen by the steede of bras; *helped*
And after wol I speke of Cambalo,
That faught in lystes with the brethren two
For Canacee er that he myghte hire wynne.
670 And ther I lefte I wol ayeyn bigynne. *where I left off*

EXPLICIT SECUNDA PARS

INCIPIT PARS TERCIA

Appollo whirleth up his chaar so hye, *chariot*
Til that the god Mercurius hous, the slye—

Heere folwen the wordes of the Frankeleyn to the
Squier, and the wordes of the Hoost to the Frankeleyn.

'In feith, Squier, thow hast thee wel *acquitted yourself*
    yquit
And gentilly.   I preise wel thy wit,' *nobly*
675 Quod the Frankeleyn, 'considerynge thy yowthe,
So feelyngly thou spekest, sire, I allow the! *congratulate*
As to my doom, ther is noon that is heere *in my judgment*
Of eloquence that shal be thy peere, *equal*
If that thou lyve; God yeve thee good chaunce, *luck*
680 And in vertu sende thee continuaunce!
For of thy speche I have greet deyntee. *pleasure*
I have a sone, and by the Trinitee,
I hadde levere than twenty pound worth lond, *rather*
Though it right now were fallen in myn hond,
685 He were a man of swich discrecioun
As that ye been!   Fy on possessioun,
But if a man be vertuous withal! *unless*
I have my sone snybbed, and yet shal, *rebuked*
For he to vertu listeth nat entende;
690 But for to pleye at dees, and to despende *waste*
And lese al that he hath, is his usage. *lose*
And he hath levere talken with a page *would rather*
Than to comune with any gentil wight
Where he myghte lerne gentillesse aright.'
695   'Straw for youre gentillesse!' quod oure Hoost.
'What, Frankeleyn! pardee, sire, wel thou woost *know*
That ech of yow moot tellen atte leste *must*
A tale or two, or breken his biheste.' *promise*

672 Until (he enters) the mansion of the god Mercury, the cunning.
689 Because he shows no desire to learn virtuous ways.
693 Than converse with a gentleman.

     'That knowe I wel, sire,' quod the Frankeleyn.
700 'I prey yow, haveth me nat in desdeyn,   *disdain*
Though to this man I speke a word or two.'
     'Telle on thy tale withouten wordes mo.'
     'Gladly, sire Hoost,' quod he, 'I wole obeye
Unto your wyl; now herkneth what I seye.
705 I wol yow nat contrarien in no wyse   *oppose*
As fer as that my wittes wol suffyse.
I prey to God that it may plesen yow;
Thanne woot I wel that it is good ynow.'   *enough*

701 *this man*, i.e. the Squire.

THE FRANKLIN'S PROLOGUE

The Prologe of the Frankeleyns Tale

THISE olde gentil Britouns in hir dayes   *noble Bretons*
710 Of diverse aventures maden layes,
      Rymeyed in hir firste Briton tonge;   *original*
      Whiche layes with hir instrumentz they songe,
      Or elles redden hem for hir plesaunce,   *read; pleasure*
      And oon of hem have I in remembraunce,
715 Which I shal seyn with good wyl as I kan.
      But, sires, by cause I am a burel man,   *uneducated*
      At my bigynnyng first I yow biseche,
      Have me excused of my rude speche.   *rough*
      I lerned nevere rethorik, certeyn;   *rhetoric*
720 Thyng that I speke, it moot be bare and pleyn. *must*
      I sleep nevere on the Mount of Pernaso,   *Parnassus*
      Ne lerned Marcus Tullius Scithero.   *Cicero*
      Colours ne knowe I none, withouten drede,   *doubt*
      But swiche colours as growen in the mede,
725 Or elles swiche as men dye or peynte.
      Colours of rethoryk been to me queynte;   *strange*
      My spirit feeleth noght of swich mateere.
      But if yow list, my tale shul ye heere.   *wish*

THE FRANKLIN'S TALE

Heere bigynneth the Frankeleyns Tale

IN ARMORIK, that called is Britayne,   *Armorica; Brittany*
730 Ther was a knyght that loved and dide his payne   *utmost*
      To serve a lady in his beste wise;
      And many a labour, many a greet emprise   *enterprise*

724 Such colours as grow in the meadow, i.e. the colours of flowers.
726 *Colours of rethoryk*, rhetorical ornaments.
727 I have no feeling for such things.

310

He for his lady wroghte, er she were wonne.   *performed*
For she was oon the faireste under sonne,   *one of*
735 And eek therto comen of so heigh kynrede
That wel unnethes dorste this knyght, for drede,
Telle hire his wo, his peyne, and his distresse.
But atte laste she, for his worthynesse,
And namely for his meke obeysaunce,   *obedience*
740 Hath swich a pitee caught of his penaunce
That pryvely she fil of his accord
To take hym for hir housbonde and hir lord,
Of swich lordshipe as men han over hir wyves.
And for to lede the moore in blisse hir lyves,
745 Of his free wyl he swoor hire as a knyght   *swore*
That nevere in al his lyf he, day ne nyght,
Ne sholde upon hym take no maistrie
Agayn hir wyl, ne kithe hire jalousie,   *against; show*
But hire obeye, and folwe hir wyl in al,   *follow*
750 As any lovere to his lady shal,   *must*
Save that the name of soveraynetee,
That wolde he have for shame of his degree.
     She thanked hym, and with ful greet humblesse   *humility*
She seyde, 'Sire, sith of youre gentillesse
755 Ye profre me to have so large a reyne,
Ne wolde nevere God bitwixe us tweyne,
As in my gilt, were outher werre or stryf.
Sire, I wol be youre humble trewe wyf,
Have heer my trouthe, til that myn herte breste.'   *pledge; break*
760 Thus been they bothe in quiete and in reste.
     For o thyng, sires, saufly dar I seye,   *safely*
That freendes everych oother moot obeye,
If they wol longe holden compaignye.   *keep company*
Love wol nat been constreyned by maistrye.
765 Whan maistrie comth, the God of Love anon
Beteth his wynges, and farewel, he is gon!   *beats*
Love is a thyng as any spirit free.
Wommen, of kynde, desiren libertee,   *by nature*
And nat to been constreyned as a thral;
770 And so doon men, if I sooth seyen shal.   *truth*

735-6 And, moreover, come of such noble family that this knight hardly
   dared, for fear (of her).
740-1 Felt such pity for his suffering that secretly she came to an agreement with him.
743 The sort of lordship men have over their wives.
747 Would he take any authority on himself.
751-2 Except that he wanted the sovereignty in name, lest he should
   shame his rank (as husband).
754-7 Since you are courteous enough to offer me so free a rein, God
   grant there may never be trouble or strife between us two through any
   fault of mine.
762 Friends must obey each other.

Looke who that is moost pacient in love,   *whoever is*
He is at his avantage al above.
Pacience is an heigh vertu, certeyn,
For it venquysseth, as thise clerkes seyn,
775 Thynges that rigour sholde nevere atteyne.
For every word men may nat chide or pleyne.   *complain*
Lerneth to suffre, or elles, so moot I goon,
Ye shul it lerne, wher so ye wole or noon;   *no*
For in this world, certein, ther no wight is   *person*
780 That he ne dooth or seith somtyme amys.
Ire, siknesse, or constellacioun,
Wyn, wo, or chaungynge of complexioun
Causeth ful ofte to doon amys or speken.
On every wrong a man may nat be wreken.   *avenged*
785 After the tyme moste be temperaunce
To every wight that kan on governaunce.
And therfore hath this wise, worthy knyght,
To lyve in ese, suffrance hire bihight,
And she to hym ful wisly gan to swere   *truly swore*
790 That nevere sholde ther be defaute in here.   *fault; her*
    Heere may men seen an humble, wys accord;
Thus hath she take hir servant and hir lord,—
Servant in love and lord in mariage.
Thanne was he bothe in lordshipe and servage.   *servitude*
795 Servage? nay, but in lordshipe above,
Sith he hath bothe his lady and his love;   *since*
His lady, certes, and his wyf also,   *certainly*
The which that lawe of love acordeth to.
And whan he was in this prosperitee,
800 Hoom with his wyf he gooth to his contree,   *home*
Nat fer fro Pedmark, ther his dwellyng was,   *far from; where*
Where as he lyveth in blisse and in solas.   *pleasure*
    Who koude telle, but he hadde wedded be,
The joye, the ese, and the prosperitee   *contentment; well-being*
805 That is bitwixe an housbonde and his wyf?   *between*
A yeer and moore lasted this blisful lyf,

772 He has the advantage over all others.
774-5 For, as men of learning say, it vanquishes things that force could
     never reach.
777 Learn forbearance, or else, upon my life.
780 Who does not sometimes do or say the wrong thing.
781 *constellacioun*, i.e. the position of the planets, especially at the time
     of a man's birth.
782-3 Wine, sorrow, or some change in the mixture of humours in the
     body very often makes a man act or speak wrongly.
785-6 According to the occasion, everyone capable of self-control must
     practise moderation.
788 In order to live in peace, promised to be forbearing with her.
798 Who has assented to the law of love.

Til that the knyght of which I speke of thus,
That of Kayrrud was cleped Arveragus,
Shoop hym to goon and dwelle a yeer or   *prepared to go*
      tweyne
810 In Engelond, that cleped was eek Briteyne,
To seke in armes worshipe and honour;
For al his lust he sette in swich labour;   *pleasure*
And dwelled there two yeer, the book seith thus.
      Now wol I stynten of this Arveragus,
815 And speken I wole of Dorigen his wyf,
That loveth hire housbonde as hire hertes lyf.
For his absence wepeth she and siketh,   *sighs*
As doon thise noble wyves whan hem liketh.   *they please*
She moorneth, waketh, wayleth, fasteth, pleyneth;
820 Desir of his presence hire so destreyneth   *distresses*
That al this wyde world she sette at noght.
Hire freendes, whiche that knewe hir hevy thoght,   *sad*
Conforten hire in al that ever they may.
They prechen hire, they telle hire nyght and day
825 That causelees she sleeth hirself, allas!
And every confort possible in this cas
They doon to hire with al hire bisynesse,
Al for to make hire leve hire hevynesse.   *sorrow*
      By proces, as ye knowen everichoon,
830 Men may so longe graven in a stoon   *engrave on*
Til som figure therinne emprented be.   *imprinted*
So longe han they conforted hire, til she
Receyved hath, by hope and by resoun,
The emprentyng of hire consolacioun,   *imprint*
835 Thurgh which hir grete sorwe gan aswage;   *grew less*
She may nat alwey duren in swich rage.
      And eek Arveragus, in al this care,   *also*
Hath sent hire lettres hoom of his welfare,
And that he wol come hastily agayn;
840 Or elles hadde this sorwe hir herte slayn.
      Hire freendes sawe hir sorwe gan to slake,   *abate*
And preyde hire on knees, for Goddes sake,
To come and romen hire in compaignye,
Awey to dryve hire derke fantasye.   *gloomy*

808 Who was called Arveragus of Kayrrud.
814 Now I will say no more about Arveragus.
816 As her own heart's life, i.e. as dearly as life itself.
819 She mourns, lies awake at night.
821 That she cared nothing for the things of this world.
825 That she is killing herself for nothing.
827 They give her with the utmost diligence.
829 In due course, as you all know.
836 She can't go on suffering such anguish.
843 Roam about with them.

845 And finally she graunted that requeste,
  For wel she saugh that it was for the beste. *saw*
   Now stood hire castel faste by the see,
  And often with hire freendes walketh shee,
  Hire to disporte, upon the bank an heigh,
850 Where as she many a ship and barge seigh *saw*
  Seillynge hir cours, where as hem liste go.
  But thanne was that a parcel of hire wo,
  For to hirself ful ofte, 'Allas!' seith she,
  'Is ther no ship, of so manye as I se,
855 Wol bryngen hom my lord?   Thanne were myn herte *home*
  Al warisshed of his bittre peynes smerte.'
   Another tyme ther wolde she sitte and thynke,
  And caste hir eyen dounward fro the brynke.
  But whan she saugh the grisly rokkes blake, *black*
860 For verray feere so wolde hir herte quake *very fear*
  That on hire feet she myghte hire noght sustene.
  Thanne wolde she sitte adoun upon the grene, *grass*
  And pitously into the see biholde,
  And seyn right thus, with sorweful sikes colde: *say; sighs*
865 'Eterne God, that thurgh thy *eternal*
   purveiaunce *providence*
  Ledest the world by certein governaunce,
  In ydel, as men seyn, ye no thyng make. *in vain*
  But, Lord, thise grisly feendly rokkes blake, *fiendish*
  That semen rather a foul confusion
870 Of werk than any fair creacion
  Of swich a parfit wys God and a stable,
  Why han ye wroght this werk unresonable?
  For by this werk, south, north, ne west, ne eest,
  Ther nys yfostred man, ne bryd, ne beest; *sustained*
875 It dooth no good, to my wit, but anoyeth.
  Se ye nat, Lord, how mankynde it destroyeth?
  An hundred thousand bodyes of mankynde
  Han rokkes slayn, al be they nat in mynde,
  Which mankynde is so fair part of thy werk
880 That thou it madest lyk to thyn owene merk. *in; image*
  Thanne semed it ye hadde a greet chiertee *love*
  Toward mankynde; but how thanne may it bee
  That ye swiche meenes make it to destroyen, *means*
  Whiche meenes do no good, but evere anoyen? *do harm*

849 For her recreation, on the cliff-top.
851 Wherever they chose to go.
852 Then that became part and parcel of her woe.
856 All cured of its bitter, grievous pain.
863 And gaze piteously at the sea.
866 Guidest the world by thy sure government.
869–70 A work of vile destruction.
875 It does no good, to my mind, but only harm.
878 Although they are no more remembered.

885 I woot wel clerkes wol seyn as hem leste,
By argumentz, that al is for the beste,
Though I ne kan the causes nat yknowe.
But thilke God that made wynd to blowe
As kepe my lord! this my conclusion.
890 To clerkes lete I al disputison. *leave; disputation*
But wolde God that alle thise rokkes blake
Were sonken into helle for his sake!
Thise rokkes sleen myn herte for the feere.'
Thus wolde she seyn, with many a pitous teere.

895　Hire freendes sawe that it was no disport *pleasure*
To romen by the see, but disconfort, *sorrow*
And shopen for to pleyen somwher elles. *arranged*
They leden hire by ryveres and by welles,
And eek in othere places delitables; *delightful*
900 They dauncen, and they pleyen at ches *chess*
　　and tables. *backgammon*
　So on a day, right in the morwe-tyde, *morning*
Unto a gardyn that was ther bisyde, *nearby*
In which that they hadde maad hir ordinaunce
Of vitaille and of oother purveiaunce,
905 They goon and pleye hem al the longe day. *amuse themselves*
And this was on the sixte morwe of May, *sixth*
Which May hadde peynted with his softe shoures
This gardyn ful of leves and of floures; *leaves*
And craft of mannes hand so curiously *skilfully*
910 Arrayed hadde this gardyn, trewely, *adorned*
That nevere was ther gardyn of swich prys, *excellence*
But if it were the verray paradys.
The odour of floures and the fresshe sighte
Wolde han maked any herte lighte *feel happy*
915 That evere was born, but if to greet siknesse,
Or to greet sorwe, helde it in distresse;
So ful it was of beautee with plesaunce. *pleasure*
At after-dyner gonne they to daunce,
And synge also, save Dorigen allone,
920 Which made alwey hir compleint and hir moone, *lament*
For she ne saugh hym on the daunce go
That was hir housbonde and hir love also.
But nathelees she moste a tyme abyde,

885–6 I know it pleases scholars to claim in argument.
888–9 But may that God who made the wind blow be pleased to keep my lord safe. This is my conclusion.
893 Kill my heart with fear.
903–4 In which they had provided themselves with food and other necessaries.
912 Except paradise itself.
915 Unless too great a sickness.
918 *At after-dyner*, i.e. during the interval after dinner.
923 Nevertheless she had to go on waiting for a time.

	And with good hope lete hir sorwe slyde.	*let*
925	Upon this daunce, amonges othere men,	
	Daunced a squier biforn Dorigen,	*squire*
	That fressher was and jolyer of array,	
	As to my doom, than is the month of May.	*in my opinion*
	He syngeth, daunceth, passynge any man	*surpassing*
930	That is, or was, sith that the world bigan.	*since*
	Therwith he was, if men sholde hym discryve,	*describe*
	Oon of the beste farynge man on lyve;	
	Yong, strong, right vertuous, and riche, and wys,	
	And wel biloved, and holden in greet prys.	*high esteem*
935	And shortly, if the sothe I tellen shal,	*truth*
	Unwityng of this Dorigen at al,	
	This lusty squier, servant to Venus,	
	Which that ycleped was Aurelius,	*called*
	Hadde loved hire best of any creature	
940	Two yeer and moore, as was his aventure,	
	But nevere dorste he tellen hire his grevaunce.	*dared* *suffering*
	Withouten coppe he drank al his penaunce.	
	He was despeyred; no thyng dorste he seye,	*filled with despair*
	Save in his songes somwhat wolde he wreye	*reveal*
945	His wo, as in a general compleynyng;	
	He seyde he lovede, and was biloved no thyng.	*not at all*
	Of swich matere made he manye layes,	
	Songes, compleintes, roundels, virelayes,	
	How that he dorste nat his sorwe telle,	
950	But langwissheth as a furye dooth in helle;	*Fury*
	And dye he moste, he seyde, as dide Ekko	*die; Echo*
	For Narcisus, that dorste nat telle hir wo.	
	In oother manere than ye heere me seye,	
	Ne dorste he nat to hire his wo biwreye,	*reveal*
955	Save that, paraventure, somtyme at daunces,	*perhaps*
	Ther yonge folk kepen hir observaunces,	
	It may wel be he looked on hir face	
	In swich a wise as man that asketh grace;	*mercy*
	But nothyng wiste she of his entente.	*knew; intention*

927 More bravely dressed.
932 One of the handsomest men alive.
936 All unknown to Dorigen
940 Two years or more, as it chanced.
942 i.e. he drank his fill of sorrow.
945 Making his complaint in general terms.
947 On such a theme he wrote many lyrics.
948 *compleintes*, formal expressions of grief in verse; *roundels, virelayes,*
     short lyrical poems with a set metrical pattern.
956 Where young people keep love's ritual.

960 Nathelees it happed, er they thennes wente,
    By cause that he was hire neighebour,
    And was a man of worshipe and honour,
    And hadde yknowen hym of tyme yoore,
    They fille in speche; and forth, moore and moore,
965 Unto his purpos drough Aurelius,   *drew*
    And whan he saugh his tyme, he seyde thus:
        'Madame,' quod he, 'by God that this world made,
    So that I wiste it myghte youre herte glade,
    I wolde that day that youre Arveragus
970 Wente over the see, that I, Aurelius,
    Hadde went ther nevere I sholde have come agayn.
    For wel I woot my servyce is in vayn;   *know*
    My gerdon is but brestyng of myn herte.   *reward; breaking*
    Madame, reweth upon my peynes smerte;
975 For with a word ye may me sleen or save.   *slay*
    Heere at youre feet God wolde that I were grave!   *buried*
    I ne have as now no leyser moore to seye;   *opportunity*
    Have mercy, sweete, or ye wol do me deye!'   *make; die*
        She gan to looke upon Aurelius:
980 'Is this youre wyl,' quod she, 'and sey ye thus?
    Nevere erst,' quod she, 'ne wiste I what ye   *before; knew*
        mente.
    But now, Aurelie, I knowe youre entente,
    By thilke God that yaf me soule and lyf,   *gave*
    Ne shal I nevere been untrewe wyf
985 In word ne werk, as fer as I have wit;
    I wol been his to whom that I am knyt.   *joined (in marriage)*
    Taak this for fynal answere as of me.'
    But after that in pley thus seyde she: *playfully*
        'Aurelie,' quod she, 'by heighe God above,
990 Yet wolde I graunte yow to been youre love,
    Syn I yow se so pitously complayne.   *since*
    Looke what day that endelong Britayne
    Ye remoeve alle the rokkes, stoon by stoon,
    That they ne lette ship ne boot to goon,—
995 I seye, whan ye han maad the coost so clene
    Of rokkes that ther nys no stoon ysene,   *to be seen*
    Thanne wol I love yow best of any man,

---

960 Nevertheless it happened, before they went from there (i.e. from
    the garden).
963 And (she) had known him for a long time.
968 If I had known it would gladden your heart.
971 Had gone to a place from where I should never have returned, i.e.
    had died.
974 Have pity on my grievous suffering.
985 In word or deed, if I can help it.
992 Whenever the day comes that all along the coast of Brittany.
994 So that they no more obstruct the passage of ship or boat.

Have heer my trouthe, in al that evere I kan.'
'Is ther noon oother grace in yow?' quod he.

1000 'No, by that Lord,' quod she, 'that maked me!   *made*
For wel I woot that it shal never bityde.   *happen*
Lat swiche folies out of youre herte slyde.   *foolish notions*
What deyntee sholde a man han in his lyf
For to go love another mannes wyf,

1005 That hath hir body whan so that hym liketh?'
Aurelius ful ofte soore siketh;   *sighs*
Wo was Aurelie whan that he this herde,
And with a sorweful herte he thus answerde:
'Madame,' quod he, 'this were an
inpossible!   *impossible thing*

1010 Thanne moot I dye of sodeyn deth horrible.'   *must*
And with that word he turned hym anon.   *turned away*
Tho coome hir othere freendes many oon,
And in the aleyes romeden up and doun,   *walks; wandered*
And nothyng wiste of this conclusioun,

1015 But sodeynly bigonne revel newe   *revelry; anew*
Til that the brighte sonne loste his hewe;   *its colour*
For th'orisonte hath reft the sonne his lyght,—
This is as muche to seye as it was nyght!—
And hoom they goon in joye and in solas,   *contentment*

1020 Save oonly wrecche Aurelius, allas!   *wretched*
He to his hous is goon with sorweful herte.
He seeth he may nat fro his deeth asterte;   *escape*
Hym semed that he felte his herte colde.
Up to the hevene his handes he gan holde,

1025 And on his knowes bare he sette hym doun,   *knees*
And in his ravyng seyde his orisoun.   *frenzy; prayer*
For verray wo out of his wit he breyde.
He nyste what he spak, but thus he seyde;   *knew not*
With pitous herte his pleynt hath he bigonne

1030 Unto the goddes, and first unto the sonne:
He seyde, 'Apollo, god and governour
Of every plaunte, herbe, tree, and flour,   *flower*
That yevest, after thy declinacion,
To ech of hem his tyme and his seson,

998 I give you my word, in every way I can.
1003-4 What pleasure can a man get out of life by loving another man's
wife.
1012 Then came many of her other friends.
1014 i.e. they knew nothing of the outcome of Dorigen's conversation
with Aurelius.
1017 For the horizon had robbed the sun of its light.
1023 It seemed to him he felt his heart grow cold.
1027 For sheer sorrow he went out of his mind.
1033 You who give, according to your declination (i.e. distance from
the celestial equator).

1035 As thyn herberwe chaungeth lowe or heighe,
     Lord Phebus, cast thy merciable eighe   *merciful eye*
     On wrecche Aurelie, which that am but lorn.
     Lo, lord! my lady hath my deeth ysworn
     Withoute gilt, but thy benignytee
1040 Upon my dedly herte have som pitee.   *dying*
     For wel I woot, lord Phebus, if yow lest,   *you will*
     Ye may me helpen, save my lady, best.
     Now voucheth sauf that I may yow devyse   *tell*
     How that I may been holpen and in what   *helped*
         wyse.   *way*
1045   Youre blisful suster, Lucina the sheene,
     That of the see is chief goddesse and queene
     (Though Neptunus have deitee in the see,   *godship*
     Yet emperisse aboven hym is she),   *empress*
     Ye knowen wel, lord, that right as hir desir   *just*
1050 Is to be quyked and lighted of youre fir,
     For which she folweth yow ful bisily,
     Right so the see desireth naturelly
     To folwen hire, as she that is goddesse
     Bothe in the see and ryveres moore and lesse. *great and small*
1055 Wherfore, lord Phebus, this is my requeste—
     Do this miracle, or do myn herte breste—
     That now next at this opposicion
     Which in the signe shal be of the Leon,
     As prieth hire so greet a flood to brynge   *pray*
1060 That fyve fadme at the leeste it over-   *fathom; rise above*
         sprynge
     The hyeste rokke in Armorik Briteyne;   *Armorican Brittany*
     And lat this flood endure yeres tweyne.   *two*
     Thanne certes to my lady may I seye,
     "Holdeth youre heste, the rokkes been aweye."   *promise*
1065   Lord Phebus, dooth this miracle for me.   *do*
     Preye hire she go no faster cours than ye;
     I seye, preyeth your suster that she go
     No faster cours than ye thise yeres two.
     Thanne shal she been evene atte fulle alway,
1070 And spryng flood laste bothe nyght and day.

     1035 According as your position is high or low (in the sky).
     1037 Who is surely lost.
     1038-9 My lady has decreed my death, innocent though I am.
     1045 Lucina the fair, i.e. the moon.
     1050 Is to be quickened and illumined by your fire.
     1056 Or break my heart.
     1057-8 Even now at your next opposition in the sign Leo. (Exception-
         ally high tides are to be expected when the sun and moon are in
         opposition.)
     1066 Beseech her to move in her orbit no faster than you.
     1069 Then she will remain exactly at the full.

And but she vouche sauf in swich manere
To graunte me my sovereyn lady deere,
Prey hire to synken every rok adoun
Into hir owene dirke regioun
1075 Under the ground, ther Pluto dwelleth inne,
Or nevere mo shal I my lady wynne.
Thy temple in Delphos wol I barefoot seke.   *Delphi*
Lord Phebus, se the teeris on my cheke,
And of my peyne have som compassioun.'   *on*
1080 And with that word in swowne he fil adoun,
And longe tyme he lay forth in a traunce.
   His brother, which that knew of his penaunce,   *suffering*
Up caughte hym, and to bedde he hath hym broght.
Dispeyred in this torment and this thoght
1085 Lete I this woful creature lye;   *leave*
Chese he, for me, wheither he wol lyve or dye.
   Arveragus, with heele and greet honour,   *health*
As he that was of chivalrie the flour,   *flower*
Is comen hoom, and othere worthy men.
1090 O blisful artow now, thou Dorigen,
That hast thy lusty housbonde in thyne armes,
The fresshe knyght, the worthy man of armes,
That loveth thee as his owene hertes lyf.
No thyng list hym to been ymaginatyf,
1095 If any wight hadde spoke, whil he was oute,
To hire of love; he hadde of it no doute.   *fear*
He noght entendeth to no swich mateere,
But daunceth, justeth, maketh hire good cheere;
And thus in joye and blisse I lete hem dwelle,
1100 And of the sike Aurelius wol I telle.   *sick*
   In langour and in torment furyus   *sickness*
Two yeer and moore lay wrecche Aurelyus,
Er any foot he myghte on erthe gon;
Ne confort in this tyme hadde he noon,
1105 Save of his brother, which that was a clerk.   *learned man*
He knew of al this wo and al this werk;   *trouble*
For to noon oother creature, certeyn,
Of this matere he dorste no word seyn.
Under his brest he baar it moore secree   *kept; secret*
1110 Than evere dide Pamphilus for Galathee.

1071 And if she will not agree in such a manner
1075 Wherein Pluto dwells.
1084 Desperate with pain and anxiety.
1086 Let him choose, as far as I'm concerned.
1094–6 He had no desire to wonder suspiciously whether anyone had
    spoken to her of love while he was away.
1097 He gives no thought to such things.
1098 Jousts, and entertains her well.
1103 Before he could walk a single step.

His brest was hool, withoute for to sene,
But in his herte ay was the arwe kene.
And wel ye knowe that of a sursanure
In surgerye is perilous the cure,
1115 But men myghte touche the arwe, or come therby.   *unless*
His brother weep and wayled pryvely,   *wept*
Til atte laste hym fil in remembraunce,   *he remembered*
That whiles he was at Orliens in Fraunce,
As yonge clerkes, that been lykerous
1120 To reden artes that been curious,   *recondite*
Seken in every halke and every herne   *nook; corner*
Particuler sciences for to lerne—   *special*
He hym remembred that, upon a day,
At Orliens in studie a book he say
1125 Of magyk natureel, which his felawe,   *friend*
That was that tyme a bacheler of lawe,
Al were he ther to lerne another craft,
Hadde prively upon his desk ylaft;   *left*
Which book spak muchel of the operaciouns   *much about*
1130 Touchynge the eighte and twenty mansiouns
That longen to the moone, and swich folye   *belong*
As in oure dayes is nat worth a flye,—
For hooly chirches feith in oure bileve
Ne suffreth noon illusioun us to greve.
1135 And whan this book was in his remembraunce,
Anon for joye his herte gan to daunce,
And to hymself he seyde pryvely:
'My brother shal be warisshed hastily;   *cured quickly*
For I am siker that ther be sciences   *sure*
1140 By whiche men make diverse apparences,   *illusions*
Swiche as thise subtile tregetoures pleye.
For ofte at feestes have I wel herd seye   *feasts*
That tregetours, withinne an halle large,
Have maad come in a water and a barge,   *sea*
1145 And in the halle rowen up and doun.
Somtyme hath semed come a grym leoun;   *fierce lion*

1111 Seen from without, his heart was whole.
1112 *arwe*, i.e. the arrow shot from love's bow.
1113 *sursanure*, a wound healed superficially, but not inwardly.
1118 *Orliens*, i.e. the University of Orleans.
1119 Just as most young students, who are eager.
1124 In his study he saw a book.
1125 *magyk natureel*. See I. 416.
1127 Although he was actually there to learn another subject.
1130 Astrologers divided the zodiac into twenty-eight 'mansions' or 'stations,' each representing the portion traversed by the moon in one day.
1133-4 For our belief in the faith of holy church will not allow an illusion to harm us.
1141 Such as skilful jugglers conjure up.

And somtyme floures sprynge as in a   *spring up*
      mede;   *meadow*
Somtyme a vyne, and grapes white and rede;
Somtyme a castel, al of lym and stoon;   *lime*
1150 And whan hem lyked, voyded it anon.
Thus semed it to every mannes sighte.
    Now thanne conclude I thus, that if I myghte
At Orliens som oold felawe yfynde   *friend*
That hadde thise moones mansions in mynde,
1155 Or oother magyk natureel above,
He sholde wel make my brother han his love.
For with an apparence a clerk may make,
To mannes sighte, that alle the rokkes blake
Of Britaigne weren yvoyded everichon,   *removed*
1160 And shippes by the brynke comen and gon,
And in swich forme enduren a wowke or two.
Thanne were my brother warisshed of his wo;   *cured*
Thanne moste she nedes holden hire biheste,
Or elles he shal shame hire atte leeste.'   *at least*
1165   What sholde I make a lenger tale of this?   *why*
Unto his brotheres bed he comen is,
And swich confort he yaf hym for to gon   *encouragement*
To Orliens that he up stirte anon,   *got up quickly*
And on his wey forthward thanne is he fare   *gone*
1170 In hope for to been lissed of his care.   *relieved; sorrow*
    Whan they were come almoost to that citee,
But if it were a two furlong or thre,
A yong clerk romynge by hymself they mette,   *met*
Which that in Latyn thriftily hem grette,   *politely; greeted*
1175 And after that he seyde a wonder thyng: *wondrous*
'I knowe,' quod he, 'the cause of youre comyng.'
And er they ferther any foote wente,   *a single foot*
He tolde hem al that was in hire entente.
    This Briton clerk hym asked of felawes
1180 The whiche that he had knowe in olde dawes,   *days*
And he answerde hym that they dede were,
For which he weep ful ofte many a teere.   *wept*
    Doun of his hors Aurelius lighte anon,   *alighted*
And with this magicien forth is he gon
1185 Hoom to his hous, and maden hem wel at ese.
Hem lakked no vitaille that myghte hem plese.   *food*

1150 And when they wished, it straightway disappeared.
1155 Or some other higher natural magic.
1157 For by means of an illusion a learned man could make it appear.
1160 And ships (safely) coming and going near the shore.
1161 And make things last like this a week or two.
1172 With only two or three furlongs still to go
1185 And they (Aurelius and his brother) made themselves very com-
      fortable.

So wel arrayed hous as ther was oon
Aurelius in his lyf saugh nevere noon.

He shewed hym, er he wente to sopeer,   *supper*
1190 Forestes, parkes ful of wilde deer;   *animals*
Ther saugh he hertes with hir hornes hye,   *harts*
The gretteste that evere were seyn with ye.   *eye*
He saugh of hem an hondred slayn with houndes,
And somme with arwes blede of bittre woundes.

1195 He saugh, whan voyded were thise wilde deer,   *removed*
Thise fauconers upon a fair ryver,
That with hir haukes han the heron slayn.

Tho saugh he knyghtes justyng in a playn;   *jousting*
And after this he dide hym swich plesaunce

1200 That he hym shewed his lady on a daunce,
On which hymself he daunced, as hym thoughte.
And whan this maister that this magyk wroughte
Saugh it was tyme, he clapte his handes two,
And farewel! al oure revel was ago.   *revelry; gone*

1205 And yet remoeved they nevere out of the hous,   *moved*
Whil they saugh al this sighte marveillous,
But in his studie, ther as his bookes be,   *where*
They seten stille, and no wight but they thre.   *sat; no one*

To hym this maister called his squier,   *servant*

1210 And seyde hym thus: 'Is redy oure soper?
Almoost an houre it is, I undertake,   *warrant*
Sith I yow bad oure soper for to make,   *since*
Whan that thise worthy men wenten with me
Into my studie, ther as my bookes be.'   *where*

1215 'Sire,' quod this squier, 'whan it liketh yow,   *pleases*
It is al redy, though ye wol right now.'
'Go we thanne soupe,' quod he, 'as for the beste.
Thise amorous folk somtyme moote han hir reste.'   *must have*

At after-soper fille they in tretee

1220 What somme sholde this maistres gerdon be,   *reward*
To remoeven alle the rokkes of Britayne,
And eek from Gerounde to the mouth of   *Gironde*
   Sayne.   *Seine*

He made it straunge, and swoor, so God   *made difficulties*
   hym save,
Lasse than a thousand pound he wolde nat have,
1225 Ne gladly for that somme he wolde nat goon.

1187–8 Such a well-appointed house as that one was Aurelius had never
   seen in his life before.
1194 Some bled with grievous arrow-wounds.
1196 Falconers hunting on a fine hawking-ground.
1199–1200 He did him the great pleasure of showing him.
1216 This very moment, if you wish.
1219 After supper they began to discuss.
1225 And even for that sum he wasn't eager to go.

Aurelius, with blisful herte anoon,   *at once*
Answerde thus: 'Fy on a thousand pound!
This wyde world, which that men seye is round,
I wolde it yeve, if I were lord of it.   *give*
1230 This bargayn is ful dryve, for we been knyt.
Ye shal be payed trewely, by my trouthe!   *upon my word*
But looketh now, for no necligence or slouthe   *take care*
Ye tarie us heere no lenger than to-morwe.'
   'Nay,' quod this clerk, 'have heer my feith to borwe.'
1235   To bedde is goon Aurelius whan hym leste,   *he wished*
And wel ny al that nyght he hadde his reste.   *well-nigh*
What for his labour and his hope of blisse,   *what with*
His woful herte of penaunce hadde a lisse.   *suffering; relief*
   Upon the morwe, whan that it was day,
1240 To Britaigne tooke they the righte way,   *shortest*
Aurelius and this magicien bisyde,   *by his side*
And been descended ther they wolde abyde.
And this was, as thise bookes me remembre,   *remind*
The colde, frosty seson of Decembre.
1245   Phebus wax old, and hewed lyk laton,   *copper-coloured*
That in his hoote declynacion
Shoon as the burned gold with stremes brighte;
But now in Capricorn adoun he lighte,
Where as he shoon ful pale, I dar wel seyn.
1250 The bittre frostes, with the sleet and reyn,
Destroyed hath the grene in every yerd.   *garden*
Janus sit by the fyr, with double berd,   *sits*
And drynketh of his bugle horn the wyn;
Biforn hym stant brawen of the tusked swyn,
1255 And 'Nowel' crieth every lusty man.   *Noel; joyful*
   Aurelius, in al that evere he kan,
Dooth to this maister chiere and reverence,
And preyeth hym to doon his diligence   *utmost*
To bryngen hym out of his peynes smerte,   *grievous*
1260 Or with a swerd that he wolde slitte his herte.   *pierce*
   This subtil clerk swich routhe had of this man   *pity; on*
That nyght and day he spedde hym that he kan
To wayten a tyme of his conclusioun;
This is to seye, to maken illusioun,

1230 It's a bargain then, for we're agreed.
1233 You keep us waiting here.
1234 I give you my word.
1242 And dismounted at the place where they had a mind to stay.
1246 i.e. in the sign of Cancer (at the summer solstice).
1247 Shone like burnished gold with radiant beams.
1248 But now he descended into Capricorn (at the winter solstice).
1252 i.e. January, the month of double-headed Janus.
1256–7 Aurelius, in every way he can, makes the master welcome and
    treats him with respect.
1262–3 He hurried to find the most propitious time for his experiment.

1265 By swich an apparence or jogelrye—
     I ne kan no termes of astrologye—   *know*
     That she and every wight sholde wene and   *everyone; think*
        seye
     That of Britaigne the rokkes were aweye,
     Or ellis they were sonken under grounde.
1270 So atte laste he hath his tyme yfounde
     To maken his japes and his wrecchednesse
     Of swich a supersticious cursednesse.
     His tables Tolletanes forth he brought,
     Ful wel corrected, ne ther lakked   *nothing was lacking*
        nought,
1275 Neither his collect ne his expans yeeris,
     Ne his rootes, ne his othere geeris,   *contrivances*
     As been his centris and his argumentz
     And his proporcioneles convenientz
     For his equacions in every thyng.
1280 And by his eighte speere in his wirkyng
     He knew ful wel how fer Alnath was shove   *far; advanced*
     Fro the heed of thilke fixe Aries above,   *head; fixed*
     That in the ninthe speere considered is;
     Ful subtilly he kalkuled al this.   *calculated*
1285   Whan he hadde founde his first mansioun,
     He knew the remenaunt by proporcioun,
     And knew the arisyng of his moone weel,
     And in whos face, and terme, and everydeel;
     And knew ful weel the moones mansioun
1290 Acordaunt to his operacioun,
     And knew also his othere observaunces
     For swiche illusiouns and swiche meschaunces
     As hethen folk useden in thilke dayes.   *practised; those*
     For which no lenger maked he delayes,
1295 But thurgh his magik, for a wyke or tweye,   *week*
     It semed that alle the rokkes were aweye.

     1265 By such a show of magic or legerdemain.
      1271-2 To play his tricks and stage his miserable performance of wicked
        superstition.
      1273 *tables Tolletanes*, astronomical tables.
      1275 ff. The astronomical terms in these lines have to do with data for
        calculating the motions of the planets during given periods.
      1280 And by observing the movement of the eighth sphere (i.e. the
        sphere of the fixed stars).
      1281 *Alnath*, the name of a star of the first magnitude.
      1285 i.e. the first mansion of the moon (see 1130).
      1286 He was able to calculate the other mansions proportionally.
      1287-8 The moon's rising he knew well, and in which divisions of the
        zodiacal signs it would be, and everything else about it.
      1290 Favourable to his experiment.
      1291-2 The other observations necessary for such illusions and evil
        doings.

Aurelius, which that yet despeired is   *filled with despair*
Wher he shal han his love or fare amys,   *whether*
Awaiteth nyght and day on this myracle;   *waits . . . for*
1300 And whan he knew that ther was noon obstacle,
That voyded were thise rokkes everychon,   *removed*
Doun to his maistres feet he fil anon,
And seyde, 'I, woful wrecche, Aurelius,
Thanke yow, lord, and lady myn Venus,
1305 That me han holpen fro my cares colde.'
And to the temple his wey forth hath he holde,   *taken*
Where as he knew he sholde his lady see.
And whan he saugh his tyme, anon-right hee,
With dredful herte and with ful humble   *fearful*
cheere,   *mien*
1310 Salewed hath his sovereyn lady deere: *greeted*
'My righte lady,' quod this woful man,
'Whom I moost drede and love as I best kan,
And lothest were of al this world displese,   *most loath*
Nere it that I for yow have swich disese
1315 That I moste dyen heere at youre foot anon,   *must*
Noght wolde I telle how me is wo bigon.
But certes outher moste I dye or pleyne;
Ye sle me giltelees for verray peyne.
But of my deeth thogh that ye have no routhe,   *pity*
1320 Avyseth yow er that ye breke youre   *think well*
trouthe.   *word*
Repenteth yow, for thilke God above,
Er ye me sleen by cause that I yow love.
For, madame, wel ye woot what ye han   *know*
hight—   *promised*
Nat that I chalange any thyng of right
1325 Of yow, my sovereyn lady, but youre grace—
But in a gardyn yond, at swich a place,   *yonder*
Ye woot right wel what ye bihighten me;
And in myn hand youre trouthe plighten ye   *pledged*
To love me best—God woot, ye seyde so,
1330 Al be that I unworthy am therto.   *of it*
Madame, I speke it for the honour of yow
Moore than to save myn hertes lyf right now,—

1305 Who have rescued me from my fatal misery.
1308 When he saw his chance, he at once.
1314 If I did not suffer such great distress for love of you.
1316 I would not tell you how miserable I am.
1317 Certainly I must either die or give voice to my complaint.
1318 You murder me, an innocent man, with sheer suffering.
1321 Repent, by the God above you.
1324–5 Not that I claim anything from you as a right, but rather beg
it as a favour.
1331 Out of regard for your honour.

I have do so as ye comanded me;   *done as*
And if ye vouche sauf, ye may go see.   *deign to*
1335 Dooth as yow list; have youre biheste in   *please; promise*
            mynde,
For, quyk or deed, right there ye shal me fynde.
In yow lith al to do me lyve or deye,—
But wel I woot the rokkes been aweye.'
      He taketh his leve, and she astoned stood;   *bewildered*
1340 In al hir face nas a drope of blood.   *was not*
She wende nevere han come in swich a trappe.
'Allas,' quod she, 'that evere this sholde happe!   *happen*
For wende I nevere by possibilitee
That swich a monstre or merveille myghte   *monstrous thing*
            be!
1345 It is agayns the proces of nature.'   *course*
And hoom she goth a sorweful creature;
For verray feere unnethe may she go.
She wepeth, wailleth, al a day or two,
And swowneth, that it routhe was to see.
1350 But why it was to no wight tolde shee,   *no one*
For out of towne was goon Arveragus.   *gone*
But to hirself she spak, and seyde thus,
With face pale and with ful sorweful cheere,   *expression*
In hire compleynt, as ye shal after heere: *next hear*
1355   'Allas,' quod she, 'on thee, Fortune, I pleyne,   *complain*
That unwar wrapped hast me in thy cheyne,   *unawares*
Fro which t'escape woot I no socour,   *help*
Save oonly deeth or elles dishonour;
Oon of thise two bihoveth me to chese.   *choose*
1360 But nathelees, yet have I levere to lese   *I would rather lose*
My lif than of my body to have a shame,
Or knowe myselven fals, or lese my name;   *(good) name*
And with my deth I may be quyt, ywis.
Hath ther nat many a noble wyf er this,
1365 And many a mayde, yslayn hirself, allas!
Rather than with hir body doon trespas?   *do wrong*
      Yis, certes, lo, thise stories beren witnesse:
Whan thritty tirauntz, ful of cursednesse,   *wickedness*
Hadde slayn Phidon in Atthenes atte feste,   *at the feast*
1370 They comanded his doghtres for t'areste,   *to be arrested*
And bryngen hem biforn hem in despit,
Al naked, to fulfille hir foul delit,   *delight*

1336 For you will find me, alive or dead, there (in the garden).
1337 It lies in your power to make me live or die.
1343 For I never imagined it possible.
1347 She can hardly walk for her great fear.
1349 So that it was pitiful to see.
1363 I may be released (from my promise), truly.
1371 And to be brought shamefully before them.

And in hir fadres blood they made hem daunce
Upon the pavement, God yeve hem meschaunce!   *misfortune*
1375 For which thise woful maydens, ful of drede,   *fear*
Rather than they wolde lese hir maydenhede,
They prively been stirt into a welle,   *leapt*
And dreynte hemselven, as the bookes telle.   *drowned*
They of Mecene leete enquere and seke
1380 Of Lacedomye fifty maydens eke,
On whiche they wolden doon hir lecherye.   *sate their lust*
But was ther noon of al that compaignye
That she nas slayn, and with a good entente
Chees rather for to dye than assente
1385 To been oppressed of hir maydenhede.   *ravished*
Why sholde I thanne to dye been in drede?
Lo, eek, the tiraunt Aristoclides,
That loved a mayden, heet Stymphalides,   *(who) was called*
Whan that hir fader slayn was on a nyght,
1390 Unto Dianes temple goth she right,   *straight*
And hente the ymage in hir handes two,   *seized*
Fro which ymage wolde she nevere go.
No wight ne myghte hir handes of it arace   *tear*
Til she was slayn, right in the selve place.   *selfsame*
1395   Now sith that maydens hadden swich despit   *scorn*
To been defouled with mannes foul delit,
Wel oghte a wyf rather hirselven slee
Than be defouled, as it thynketh me.
What shal I seyn of Hasdrubales wyf,
1400 That at Cartage birafte hirself hir lyf?
For whan she saugh that Romayns wan the toun,   *won*
She took hir children alle, and skipte adoun   *jumped*
Into the fyr, and chees rather to dye   *chose*
Than any Romayn dide hire vileynye.   *should do*
1405 Hath nat Lucresse yslayn hirself, allas!   *Lucretia*
At Rome, whan that she oppressed was   *ravished*
Of Tarquyn, for hire thoughte it was a shame
To lyven whan she had lost hir name?
The sevene maydens of Milesie also   *Miletus*
1410 Han slayn hemself, for verrey drede and wo,
Rather than folk of Gawle hem sholde oppresse.   *Gaul*
Mo than a thousand stories, as I gesse,
Koude I now telle as touchynge this mateere.   *concerning*
Whan Habradate was slayn, his wyf so deere   *Abradates*

1379–80 The people of Messene sent for fifty Spartan maidens.
1383–4 Who was not slain, and who did not willingly choose to die
    rather than consent.
1396 To be defiled by man's foul lust.
1397–8 A wife should surely kill herself rather than be defiled.
1400 At Carthage took her own life.
1407 By Tarquin, because it seemed to her a shame.

1415 Hirselven slow, and leet hir blood to glyde
      In Habradates woundes depe and wyde,
      And seyde, "My body, at the leeste way,   *at the very least*
      Ther shal no wight defoulen, if I may."
      What sholde I mo ensamples heerof sayn,
1420 Sith that so manye han hemselven slayn
      Wel rather than they wolde defouled be?   *much*
      I wol conclude that it is bet for me   *better*
      To sleen myself than been defouled thus.
      I wol be trewe unto Arveragus,
1425 Or rather sleen myself in som manere,
      As dide Demociones doghter deere   *Demotion's*
      By cause that she wolde nat defouled be.
      O Cedasus, it is ful greet pitee
      To reden how thy doghtren deyde, allas!   *daughters died*
1430 That slowe hemself for swich manere cas.
      As greet a pitee was it, or wel moore,   *much greater*
      The Theban mayden that for Nichanore *because of Nicanor*
      Hirselven slow, right for swich manere wo.
      Another Theban mayden dide right so;   *just the same*
1435 For oon of Macidonye hadde hire oppressed,
      She with hire deeth hir maydenhede redressed.   *vindicated*
      What shal I seye of Nicerates wyf,
      That for swich cas birafte hirself hir lyf?   *took her own life*
      How trewe eek was to Alcebiades
1440 His love, that rather for to dyen chees
      Than for to suffre his body unburyed be.
      Lo, which a wyf was Alceste,' quod she.   *what; Alcestis*
      'What seith Omer of goode Penalopee?   *Homer*
      Al Grece knoweth of hire chastitee.
1445 Pardee, of Laodomya is writen thus,   *indeed; Laodamia*
      That whan at Troie was slayn Protheselaus,   *Protesilaus*
      Ne lenger wolde she lyve after his day.
      The same of noble Porcia telle I may;   *Portia*
      Withoute Brutus koude she nat lyve,
1450 To whom she hadde al hool hir herte yive.   *wholly; given*
      The parfit wyfhod of Arthemesie   *Artemisia*
      Honured is thurgh al the Barbarie.   *barbarian lands*
      O Teuta, queene! thy wyfly chastitee
      To alle wyves may a mirour bee.
1455 The same thyng I seye of Bilyea,
      Of Rodogone, and eek Valeria.'

1418 Shall no man defile, if I can prevent it.
1419 Why should I give more instances of this.
1430 Who slew themselves because they were in the same sort of plight.
1435 Because a Macedonian had ravished her.
1440-1 His beloved, who chose to die rather than allow his body to be
    unburied.

Thus pleyned Dorigen a day or tweye, *lamented*
Purposynge evere that she wolde deye.
But nathelees, upon the thridde nyght,
1460 Hoom cam Arveragus, this worthy knyght,
And asked hire why that she weep so soore; *wept*
And she gan wepen ever lenger the moore.
'Allas,' quod she, 'that evere was I born!
Thus have I seyd,' quod she, 'thus have I sworn'—
1465 And toold hym al as ye han herd bifore; *heard*
It nedeth nat reherce it yow namoore. *repeat*
This housbonde, with glad chiere, in freendly wyse
Answerde and seyde as I shal yow devyse: *tell*
'Is ther oght elles, Dorigen, but this?' *anything*
1470 'Nay, nay,' quod she, 'God helpe me so as wys!
This is to muche, and it were Goddes wille.'
'Ye, wyf,' quod he, 'lat slepen that is stille.
It may be wel, paraventure, yet to day.
Ye shul youre trouthe holden, by my fay!
1475 For God so wisly have mercy upon me,
I hadde wel levere ystiked for to be
For verray love which that I to yow have,
But if ye sholde youre trouthe kepe and save.
Trouthe is the hyeste thyng that man may kepe'— *a promise*
1480 But with that word he brast anon to wepe, *burst into tears*
And seyde, 'I yow forbede, up peyne of deeth, *forbid*
That nevere, whil thee lasteth lyf ne breeth, *or breath*
To no wight telle thou of this aventure,—
As I may best, I wol my wo endure,—
1485 Ne make no contenance of hevynesse, *sign; grief*
That folk of yow may demen harm or gesse.' *think*
And forth he cleped a squier and a *called*
mayde: *maidservant*
'Gooth forth anon with Dorigen,' he sayde,
'And bryngeth hire to swich a place anon.'
1490 They take hir leve, and on hir wey they gon,
But they ne wiste why she thider wente. *knew*
He nolde no wight tellen his entente.
Paraventure an heep of yow, ywis, *lot*
Wol holden hym a lewed man in this *foolish*

1462 And she went on weeping all the more.
1470 So help me God.
1471 This is (already) too much, even if it be God's will.
1472 Cf. 'Let sleeping dogs lie.'
1473 Perhaps this thing may yet go well to-day.
1474 You must keep your promise, by my faith.
1475-8 For God have mercy on me, I would much rather be stabbed to death for the true love I bear you than that you should fail to keep your promise.
1483 Tell no one of this misfortune.

1495 That he wol putte his wyf in jupartie.   *jeopardy*
     Herkneth the tale er ye upon hire crie.
     She may have bettre fortune than yow semeth;   *suppose*
     And whan that ye han herd the tale, demeth.   *judge*
         This squier, which that highte Aurelius,
1500 On Dorigen that was so amorus,
     Of aventure happed hire to meete
     Amydde the toun, right in the quykkest strete,   *busiest*
     As she was bown to goon the wey forth right
     Toward the gardyn ther as she had hight.
1505 And he was to the gardyn-ward also;
     For wel he spyed whan she wolde go
     Out of hir hous to any maner place.   *sort of*
     But thus they mette, of aventure or grace,
     And he saleweth hire with glad entente,   *greets*
1510 And asked of hire whiderward she wente;
     And she answerde, half as she were mad,
     'Unto the gardyn, as myn housbonde bad,
     My trouthe for to holde, allas! allas!'
         Aurelius gan wondren on this cas,
1515 And in his herte hadde greet compassioun
     Of hire and of hire lamentacioun,   *on*
     And of Arveragus, the worthy knyght,
     That bad hire holden al that she had hight,   *promised*
     So looth hym was his wyf sholde breke hir   *loath he was*
         trouthe;
1520 And in his herte he caughte of this greet routhe,
     Considerynge the beste on every syde,
     That fro his lust yet were hym levere abyde
     Than doon so heigh a cherlyssh wrecchednesse
     Agayns franchise and alle gentillesse;
1525 For which in fewe wordes seyde he thus:
         'Madame, seyth to youre lord Arveragus,
     That sith I se his grete gentillesse
     To yow, and eek I se wel youre distresse,
     That him were levere han shame (and that were routhe)
1530 Than ye to me sholde breke thus youre trouthe,

1496 Listen to the end of the tale before you exclaim against her.
1501 (As if) by chance happened to meet her.
1503 As she was all ready to make her way straight.
1504 Where she had made her promise.
1505 On his way to the garden also.
1506 For he noticed carefully whenever she went.
1510 And asked her where she was going.
1514 Aurelius wondered at this turn of events.
1520–4 And this moved his heart to great pity and made him anxious
     to do what was right, so that he felt he would rather forgo his pleasure
     than be guilty of such a mean act against nobleness and courtesy.
1529 In that he would rather suffer shame (and that would be a pity).

I have wel levere evere to suffre wo
Than I departe the love bitwix yow two.
I yow relesse, madame, into youre hond
Quyt every serement and every bond
1535 That ye han maad to me as heerbiforn,
Sith thilke tyme which that ye were born.   *since the*
My trouthe I plighte, I shal yow never repreve
Of no biheste, and heere I take my leve,
As of the treweste and the beste wyf
1540 That evere yet I knew in al my lyf.'
But every wyf be war of hire biheeste!
On Dorigen remembreth, atte leeste.
Thus kan a squier doon a gentil dede   *noble*
As wel as kan a knyght, withouten drede.   *doubt*
1545   She thonketh hym upon hir knees al bare,
And hoom unto hir housbonde is she fare,   *she went*
And tolde hym al, as ye han herd me sayd;
And be ye siker, he was so weel apayd   *sure; pleased*
That it were inpossible me to wryte.   *impossible for me*
1550 What sholde I lenger of this cas endyte?
    Arveragus and Dorigen his wyf
In sovereyn blisse leden forth hir lyf.
Nevere eft ne was ther angre hem bitwene.   *again; trouble*
He cherisseth hire as though she were a queene,
1555 And she was to hym trewe for everemoore.
Of thise two folk ye gete of me namoore.   *get from*
    Aurelius, that his cost hath al forlorn,
Curseth the tyme that evere he was born:
'Allas,' quod he, 'allas, that I bihighte   *promised*
1560 Of pured gold a thousand pound of wighte   *pure; weight*
Unto this philosophre!   How shal I do?   *astrologer*
I se namoore but that I am fordo.   *ruined*
Myn heritage moot I nedes selle,
And been a beggere; heere may I nat dwelle,
1565 And shamen al my kynrede in this place,   *kindred*
But I of hym may gete bettre grace.
But nathelees, I wole of hym assaye,
At certeyn dayes, yeer by yeer, to paye,
And thanke hym of his grete curteisye.   *for*
1570 My trouthe wol I kepe, I wol nat lye.'

1532 Than that I should divide.
1533-5 Madam, I release you from every oath and every bond you
    have given me up till now.
1537-8 I shall never reproach you for any promise you have made.
1541 Let every wife be careful of her promises.
1550 Why should I write about this affair any longer?
1557 Whose expense had all been wasted.
1566 i.e. unless he (the astrologer) has mercy on me.
1567-8 Nevertheless, I'll see whether he will let me pay him back on
    certain days each year.

With herte soor he gooth unto his cofre,   *coffer*
And broghte gold unto this philosophre,
The value of fyve hundred pound, I gesse,
And hym bisecheth, of his gentillesse,   *nobleness*
1575 To graunte hym dayes of the remenaunt;
And seyde, 'Maister, I dar wel make avaunt,   *boast*
I failled nevere of my trouthe as yit.
For sikerly my dette shal be quyt   *truly; paid*
Towardes yow, howevere that I fare
1580 To goon a-begged in my kirtle bare.
But wolde ye vouche sauf, upon seuretee,
Two yeer or thre for to respiten me,
Thanne were I wel; for elles moot I selle   *happy; must*
Myn heritage; ther is namoore to telle.'
1585 This philosophre sobrely answerde,   *gravely*
And seyde thus, whan he thise wordes herde:
'Have I nat holden covenant unto thee?'
'Yes, certes, wel and trewely,' quod he.
'Hastow nat had thy lady as thee liketh?'   *as you desire*
1590 'No, no,' quod he, and sorwefully he siketh.   *sighs*
'What was the cause? tel me if thou kan.'
Aurelius his tale anon bigan,
And tolde hym al, as ye han herd bifoore;
It nedeth nat to yow reherce it moore.   *tell*
1595 He seide, 'Arveragus, of gentillesse,
Hadde levere dye in sorwe and in distresse   *rather*
Than that his wyf were of hir trouthe fals.'
The sorwe of Dorigen he tolde hym als;   *also*
How looth hire was to been a wikked wyf,   *loath she was*
1600 And that she levere had lost that day hir lyf,
And that hir trouthe she swoor thurgh innocence,
She nevere erst hadde herd speke of apparence.
'That made me han of hire so greet pitee;   *have*
And right as frely as he sente hire me,
1605 As frely sente I hire to hym ageyn.
This al and som; ther is namoore to seyn.'
This philosophre answerde, 'Leeve brother,   *dear*
Everich of yow dide gentilly til oother.   *each; nobly*
Thou art a squier, and he is a knyght;
1610 But God forbede, for his blisful myght,

1575 Give him time to pay the rest by instalments.
1579–80 Even if I have to go begging, clad only in my coat.
1582 To grant me a respite of two or three years.
1597 His wife should be untrue to her word.
1601–2 And that she had made her promise in all innocence, for she had
    never heard before of magical illusion.
1604 And just as freely as he (Arveragus).
1606 This is the long and short of it.

But if a clerk koude doon a gentil dede
As wel as any of yow, it is no drede!   *doubt*
    Sire, I releesse thee thy thousand pound,
As thou right now were cropen out of the ground,
1615 Ne nevere er now ne haddest knowen me.
For, sire, I wol nat taken a peny of thee
For al my craft, ne noght for my travaille.   *skill*
Thou hast ypayed wel for my vitaille.   *food*
It is ynogh, and farewel, have good day!'
1620 And took his hors, and forth he goth his way.
Lordynges, this question, thanne wol I aske now,
Which was the mooste fre, as thynketh yow?   *noble*
Now telleth me, er that ye ferther wende.   *go*
I kan namoore; my tale is at an ende.   *know*

HEERE IS ENDED THE FRANKELEYNS TALE

1611 That a scholar should not do a noble deed.
1614 i.e. as though you were newly born. (Cf. 1536.)

Fragment VI (Group C)

THE PHYSICIAN'S TALE

HEERE FOLWETH THE PHISICIENS TALE

THER was, as telleth Titus Livius,   *Livy*
A knyght that called was Virginius,
Fulfild of honour and of worthynesse,   *full of*
And strong of freendes, and of greet richesse.   *wealth*
5   This knyght a doghter hadde by his wyf;
No children hadde he mo in al his lyf.   *more*
Fair was this mayde in excellent beautee
Aboven every wight that man may see;
For Nature hath with sovereyn diligence
10 Yformed hire in so greet excellence,   *formed*
As though she wolde seyn, 'Lo! I, Nature,
Thus kan I forme and peynte a creature,
Whan that me list; who kan me countrefete?
Pigmalion noght, though he ay forge and bete,
15 Or grave, or peynte; for I dar wel seyn,   *carve*
Apelles, Zanzis, sholde werche in veyn
Outher to grave, or peynte, or forge, or bete,   *either*
If they presumed me to countrefete.
For He that is the formere principal   *Creator*
20 Hath maked me his vicaire general,
To forme and peynten erthely creaturis
Right as me list, and ech thyng in my cure is   *care*
Under the moone, that may wane and waxe;
And for my werk right no thyng wol I axe;   *ask*
25 My lord and I been ful of oon accord.
I made hire to the worshipe of my lord;
So do I alle myne othere creatures,
What colour that they han, or what figures.'   *whatever*
Thus semeth me that Nature wolde seye.
30   This mayde of age twelve yeer was and tweye,
In which that Nature hadde swich delit.   *in whom; delight*
For right as she kan peynte a lilie whit,

7-8 Excelling in beauty all other creatures to be seen.
13 When I desire; who can imitate me?
14 Not Pygmalion, though he for ever forge and hammer.
20 'Vicar General' (i.e. chief deputy) was a title often given to the Pope, as head of the Church under Christ.

335

And reed a rose, right with swich peynture
She peynted hath this noble creature,
35 Er she were born, upon hir lymes fre,   *graceful*
Where as by right swiche colours sholde be;
And Phebus dyed hath hire tresses grete
Lyk to the stremes of his burned heete.
And if that excellent was hire beautee,
40 A thousand foold moore vertuous was she.
In hire ne lakked no condicioun
That is to preyse, as by discrecioun.
As wel in goost as body chast was she;   *spirit; chaste*
For which she floured in virginitee   *flowered*
45 With alle humylitee and abstinence,
With alle attemperaunce and pacience,   *temperance*
With mesure eek of beryng and array.
Discreet she was in answeryng alway;
Though she were wis as Pallas, dar I seyn,
50 Hir facound eek ful wommanly and pleyn,
No countrefeted termes hadde she   *artificial phrases*
To seme wys; but after hir degree
She spak, and alle hire wordes, moore and lesse,
Sownynge in vertu and in gentillesse.
55 Shamefast she was in maydens shamefastnesse,   *modest*
Constant in herte, and evere in bisynesse
To dryve hire out of ydel slogardye.
Bacus hadde of hir mouth right no maistrie;
For wyn and youthe dooth Venus encresse,
60 As men in fyr wol casten oille or greesse.
And of hir owene vertu, unconstreyned,
She hath ful ofte tyme syk hire feyned,
For that she wolde fleen the compaignye   *escape from*
Where likly was to treten of folye,
65 As is at feestes, revels, and at daunces,
That been occasions of daliaunces,   *wanton play*
Swich thynges maken children for to be
To soone rype and boold, as men may se,
Which is ful perilous, and hath been yoore.   *of old*

33 With just such art.
36 Where such colours should rightly be.
38 (A colour) like that of his own hot burnished beams.
41–2 No quality was lacking in her that a serious person would wish
    to praise.
47 With moderation in bearing and in dress.
50 Her eloquence of a simple, womanly kind.
52 According to her station.
54 Were conducive to virtue and good breeding.
56–7 And always diligent in shunning idleness and sloth.
58 Bacchus had no power over her mouth.
62 Often pretended to feel ill.
64 Where there was any likelihood of folly.

70 For al to soone may she lerne loore
   Of booldnesse, whan she woxen is a wyf.
      And ye maistresses, in youre olde lyf,   *governesses*
   That lordes doghtres han in governaunce,   *charge*
   Ne taketh of my wordes no displesaunce.   *displeasure*
75 Thenketh that ye been set in governynges   *put in charge*
   Of lordes doghtres, oonly for two thynges:
   Outher for ye han kept youre honestee,   *virtue*
   Or elles ye han falle in freletee,
   And knowen wel ynough the olde daunce,
80 And han forsaken fully swich meschaunce   *bad ways*
   For everemo; therfore, for Cristes sake,
   To teche hem vertu looke that ye ne slake.
      A theef of venysoun, that hath forlaft   *given up*
   His likerousnesse and al his olde craft,   *gluttonous appetite*
85 Kan kepe a forest best of any man.   *take care of*
   Now kepeth wel, for if ye wole, ye kan.
   Looke wel that ye unto no vice assente,
   Lest ye be dampned for youre wikke entente;   *condemned*
   For whoso dooth, a traitour is, certeyn.
90 And taketh kep of that that I shal seyn: *heed*
   Of alle tresons sovereyn pestilence
   Is whan a wight bitrayseth innocence.   *betrays*
      Ye fadres and ye moodres eek also,
   Though ye han children, be it oon or mo,
95 Youre is the charge of al hir surveiaunce,
   Whil that they been under youre governaunce.
   Beth war, if by ensample of youre lyvynge,
   Or by youre necligence in chastisynge,
   That they ne perisse; for I dar wel seye,   *perish*
100 If that they doon, ye shul it deere abeye.
   Under a shepherde softe and necligent
   The wolf hath many a sheep and lamb torent.   *torn to pieces*
   Suffiseth oon ensample now as heere,
   For I moot turne agayn to my matere.
105   This mayde, of which I wol this tale expresse,
   So kepte hirself hir neded no maistresse;
   For in hir lyvyng maydens myghten rede,   *way of life*
   As in a book, every good word or dede

70–1 Learn to be brazen when she becomes a wife.
78–9 Or else because you have been weak enough to fall, and so know
      all the tricks of the trade.
82 See that you do not slacken in your efforts to teach them virtue.
91 The most pestilential sort of treason.
95 Yours is the responsibility for seeing that they get proper supervision.
100 You shall pay for it dearly.
103 One parable is enough for now.
105 Of whom I wish to tell this tale.
106 Governed herself so well that she needed no governess.

That longeth to a mayden vertuous,   *belongs*
110 She was so prudent and so bountevous.   *bounteous*
For which the fame out sprong on every syde,
Bothe of hir beautee and hir bountee wyde,   *ample goodness*
That thurgh that land they preised hire echone   *all*
That loved vertu, save Envye allone,
115 That sory is of oother mennes wele,   *good fortune*
And glad is of his sorwe and his unheele.   *misfortune*
(The doctour maketh this descripcioun).
    This mayde upon a day wente in the toun
Toward a temple, with hire mooder deere,   *mother*
120 As is of yonge maydens the manere.
Now was ther thanne a justice in that toun,   *judge*
That governour was of that regioun.
And so bifel this juge his eyen caste   *eyes*
Upon this mayde, avysynge hym ful faste,
125 As she cam forby ther as this juge stood.   *by where*
Anon his herte chaunged and his mood,
So was he caught with beautee of this mayde,
And to hymself ful pryvely he sayde,   *secretly*
'This mayde shal be myn, for any man!'
130   Anon the feend into his herte ran,   *devil*
And taughte hym sodeynly that he by slyghte   *cunning*
The mayden to his purpos wynne myghte.
For certes, by no force ne by no meede,   *bribery*
Hym thoughte, he was nat able for to speede;
135 For she was strong of freendes, and eek she
Confermed was in swich soverayn bountee,   *firm*
That wel he wiste he myghte hire nevere wynne
As for to make hire with hir body synne.
For which, by greet deliberacioun,
140 He sente after a cherl, was in the toun,
Which that he knew for subtil and for boold.
This juge unto this cherl his tale hath toold
In secree wise, and made hym to ensure   *promise*
He sholde telle it to no creature,
145 And if he dide, he sholde lese his heed.   *lose*
Whan that assented was this cursed reed,
Glad was this juge, and maked him greet   *made much of him*
    cheere,

111 For which reason the fame spread far and wide.
117 *doctour*, i.e. St Augustine.
124 Narrowly appraising her.
129 In spite of everyone.
134 It seemed to him, would he be able to succeed.
137–8 Well he knew he could never prevail on her to sin with her **body**.
140–1 He sent for a low fellow (who) lived in the town, well known to
    him for his craftiness and impudence.
146 When this wicked plan was agreed on.

And yaf hym yiftes preciouse and deere.   *gave*
Whan shapen was al hire conspiracie   *planned*
150 Fro point to point, how that his lecherie   *in detail*
Parfourned sholde been ful subtilly,   *accomplished*
As ye shul heere it after openly,
Hoom gooth the cherl, that highte Claudius.   *was called*
This false juge, that highte Apius,
155 (So was his name, for this is no fable,
But knowen for historial thyng notable;
The sentence of it sooth is, out of doute),
This false juge gooth now faste aboute
To hasten his delit al that he may.
160 And so bifel soone after, on a day,
This false juge, as telleth us the storie,
As he was wont, sat in his consistorie,   *court*
And yaf his doomes upon sondry cas.   *judgments; cases*
This false cherl cam forth a ful greet pas,
165 And seyde, 'Lord, if that it be youre wille,
As dooth me right upon this pitous bille,
In which I pleyne upon Virginius;   *complain against*
And if that he wol seyn it is nat thus,
I wol it preeve, and fynde good witnesse,   *prove*
170 That sooth is that my bille wol expresse.'
The juge answerde, 'Of this, in his absence,
I may nat yeve diffynytyf sentence.   *final*
Lat do hym calle, and I wol gladly heere;   *have him summoned*
Thou shalt have al right, and no wrong heere.'
175 Virginius cam to wite the juges wille,   *learn*
And right anon was rad this cursed bille;   *read*
The sentence of it was as ye shul heere: *content*
'To yow, my lord, sire Apius so deere,
Sheweth youre povre servant Claudius   *poor*
180 How that a knyght, called Virginius,
Agayns the lawe, agayn al equitee,
Holdeth, expres agayn the wyl of me,   *expressly*
My servant, which that is my thral by right,   *who is*
Which fro myn hous was stole upon a nyght,   *stolen*
185 Whil that she was ful yong; this wol I preeve
By witnesse, lord, so that it nat yow greeve.
She nys his doghter nat, what so he seye.
Wherfore to yow, my lord the juge, I preye,

156 As a notable historical fact.
157 The substance of it is true, beyond a doubt.
158-9 Quickly sets about hastening his pleasure in every way he can.
164 Came forward quickly.
166 Do me justice in my pitiful petition.
170 That what is set down in my petition is true.
186 If it will not offend you.
187 She is not his daughter, whatever he may say.

Yeld me my thral, if that it be youre wille.'   *give*
190 Lo, this was al the sentence of his bille.
 Virginius gan upon the cherl biholde,   *looked at*
But hastily, er he his tale tolde,
And wolde have preeved it as sholde a knyght,
And eek by witnessyng of many a wight,   *person*
195 That al was fals that seyde his adversarie,
This cursed juge wolde no thyng tarie,
Ne heere a word moore of Virginius,
But yaf his juggement, and seyde thus:
 'I deeme anon this cherl his servant have;
200 Thou shalt no lenger in thyn hous hir save.   *keep*
Go bryng hire forth, and put hire in oure warde.
The cherl shal have his thral, this I awarde.'
 And whan this worthy knyght Virginius,
Thurgh sentence of this justice Apius,
205 Moste by force his deere doghter yiven
Unto the juge, in lecherie to lyven,
He gooth hym hoom, and sette him in his   *home; sat down*
  halle,
And leet anon his deere doghter calle,
And with a face deed as asshen colde
210 Upon hir humble face he gan biholde,
With fadres pitee stikynge thurgh his herte,   *piercing*
Al wolde he from his purpos nat converte.
 'Doghter,' quod he, 'Virginia, by thy name,
Ther been two weyes, outher deeth or shame,
215 That thou most suffre; allas, that I was bore!   *born*
For nevere thou deservedest wherfore   *for any cause*
To dyen with a swerd or with a knyf.
O deere doghter, endere of my lyf,   *ender*
Which I have fostred up with swich pleasaunce   *pleasure*
220 That thou were nevere out of my remembraunce!
O doghter, which that art my laste wo,
And in my lyf my laste joye also,
O gemme of chastitee, in pacience
Take thou thy deeth, for this is my sentence.
225 For love, and nat for hate, thou most be deed;   *must die*
My pitous hand moot smyten of thyn heed.   *head*
Allas, that evere Apius the say!   *saw thee*
Thus hath he falsly jugged the to-day'—   *judged*
And tolde hire al the cas, as ye bifore
230 Han herd; nat nedeth for to telle it moore.

192 But quickly, before he (Virginius) had time to speak.
196 This wicked judge would not brook a moment's delay.
199 I rule forthwith this fellow must have his servant.
208 And at once sent for his dear daughter.
212 Although he would not be deflected from his purpose.

'O mercy, deere fader!' quod this mayde,
And with that word she bothe hir armes layde
Aboute his nekke, as she was wont to do.
The teeris bruste out of hir eyen two,   *burst*
235 And seyde, 'Goode fader, shal I dye?
Is ther no grace, is ther no remedye?'
    'No, certes, deere doghter myn,' quod he.
    'Thanne yif me leyser, fader myn,' quod she,   *time*
'My deeth for to compleyne a litel space;   *while*
240 For, pardee, Jepte yaf his doghter grace   *Jephthah*
For to compleyne, er he hir slow, allas!   *slew*
And, God it woot, no thyng was hir trespas,
But for she ran hir fader first to see,
To welcome hym with greet solempnitee.'
245 And with that word she fil aswowne anon,   *in a swoon*
And after, whan hir swownyng is agon,   *passed*
She riseth up, and to hir fader sayde,
'Blissed be God, that I shal dye a mayde!
Yif me my deeth, er that I have a shame;
250 Dooth with youre child youre wyl, a Goddes name!'   *in*
    And with that word she preyed hym ful ofte
That with his swerd he wolde smyte softe;   *gently*
And with that word aswowne doun she fil.
Hir fader, with ful sorweful herte and wil,
255 Hir heed of smoot, and by the top it hente,
And to the juge he gan it to presente,   *presented it*
As he sat yet in doom in consistorie.   *judgment; court*
And whan the juge it saugh, as seith the storie,
He bad to take hym and anhange hym faste;
260 But right anon a thousand peple in thraste,   *thrust*
To save the knyght, for routhe and for pitee,   *compassion*
For knowen was the false iniquitee.
The peple anon had suspect in this thyng,   *suspicion*
By manere of the cherles chalangyng,
265 That it was by the assent of Apius;
They wisten wel that he was lecherus.   *knew*
For which unto this Apius they gon,
And caste hym in a prisoun right anon,
Ther as he slow hymself; and Claudius,   *where*
270 That servant was unto this Apius,
Was demed for to hange upon a tree,   *sentenced*
But that Virginius, of his pitee,
So preyde for hym that he was exiled;
And elles, certes, he had been bigyled.   *destroyed*

242–3 God knows, her only crime was that she ran.
255 Smote off her head, and took it by the hair.
259 He ordered him to be seized and hanged forthwith.
264 Because of the way in which the fellow had brought his charge.

275 The remenant were anhanged, moore and   *rest; hanged*
        lesse,
    That were consentant of this cursednesse.
        Heere may men seen how synne hath his merite.   *its deserts*
    Beth war, for no man woot whom God wol   *beware; knows*
        smyte
    In no degree, ne in which manere wyse
280 The worm of conscience may agryse
    Of wikked lyf, though it so pryvee be   *secret*
    That no man woot therof but God and he.
    For be he lewed man, or ellis lered,
    He noot how soone that he shal been afered.
285 Therfore I rede yow this conseil take: *advice*
    Forsaketh synne, er synne yow forsake.

HEERE ENDETH THE PHISICIENS TALE

276 Who had been party to this wickedness.
279–81 In any rank of society, nor how the worm of conscience may
    shudder at a man's wicked life.
283 *lewed . . . lered,* ignorant . . . educated, i.e. layman or cleric.
284 He doesn't know how soon he will be terrified (by the approach
    of death).
286 Forsake sin before sin forsakes you, i.e. before you die.

THE INTRODUCTION TO THE PARDONER'S TALE

The Wordes of the Hoost to the Phisicien and the Pardoner

OURE HOOSTE gan to swere as he were wood; *like mad*
'Harrow!' quod he, 'by nayles and by blood!
This was a fals cherl and a fals justise.
290 As shameful deeth as herte may devyse
Come to thise juges and hire advocatz!
Algate this sely mayde is slayn, allas!
Allas, to deere boughte she beautee!
Wherfore I seye al day that men may see *always*
295 That yiftes of Fortune and of Nature *gifts*
Been cause of deeth to many a creature.
Hire beautee was hire deth, I dar wel sayn.
Allas, so pitously as she was slayn!
Of bothe yiftes that I speke of now
300 Men han ful ofte moore for harm than prow.
But trewely, myn owene maister deere,
This is a pitous tale for to heere. *pitiful*
But nathelees, passe over, is no fors.
I pray to God so save thy gentil cors, *body*
305 And eek thyne urynals and thy jurdones,
Thyn ypocras, and eek thy galiones,
And every boyste ful of thy letuarie; *box; medicament*
God blesse hem, and oure lady Seinte Mari,
So moot I theen, thou art a propre man,
310 And lyk a prelat, by Seint Ronyan!
Seyde I nat wel? I kan nat speke in terme; *learned terms*
But wel I woot thou doost myn herte to erme,
That I almoost have caught a cardynacle.

288 Help! . . . by the nails of the Cross and the blood of Christ.
292 All the same this innocent maid was killed.
293 She (Virginia of the *Physician's Tale*) paid too dearly for her beauty.
298 Alas, how pitifully she was slain.
300 People very often get more harm than benefit.
303 However, never mind; let's pass over it.
305 *urynals*, glass vessels used to hold urine for the purpose of diagnosis; *jurdones*, chamber-pots.
306 *ypocras*, a kind of cordial; *galiones*, remedies named after Galen.
309 As I hope to prosper. you're a fine fellow.
312-13 But well I know you've made my heart feel sad (i.e. with your tale of Virginia), so that I've almost got palpitations.

343

By corpus bones! but I have triacle,
315 Or elles a draughte of moyste and corny ale,
Or but I heere anon a myrie tale,   *at once*
Myn herte is lost for pitee of this mayde.
Thou beel amy, thou Pardoner,' he sayde,   *good friend*
'Telle us som myrthe or japes right anon.' *amusing tale; jest*
320 'It shal be doon,' quod he, 'by Seint Ronyon!
But first,' quod he, 'heere at this ale-stake
I wol bothe drynke, and eten of a cake.'   *loaf*
But right anon thise gentils gonne to crye,
'Nay, lat hym telle us of no ribaudye!   *ribald jest*
325 Telle us som moral thyng, that we may leere   *learn*
Som wit, and thanne wol we gladly heere.'   *wisdom*
'I graunte, ywis,' quod he, 'but I moot thynke
Upon som honest thyng while that I drynke.'   *respectable*

THE PARDONER'S PROLOGUE

Heere folweth the Prologe of
the Pardoners Tale

Radix malorum est Cupiditas.   Ad Thimotheum, 6°.

'Lordynges,' quod he, 'in chirches whan I preche,   *sirs*
330 I peyne me to han an hauteyn speche,
And rynge it out as round as gooth a belle,   *sonorously*
For I kan al by rote that I telle.   *know*
My theme is alwey oon, and evere was—   *text*
Radix malorum est Cupiditas.

314 *By corpus bones* (a confusion of *by corpus domini* and *by Goddes
bones*), unless I have a remedy.
315 New and corny ale, i.e. ale tasting strongly of corn or malt
321 *ale-stake.* See I. 667.
323 But immediately the gentlefolk cried out.
327 Certainly I will . . . but I must think
330 I take pains to speak loudly.
334 1 Tim. vi. 10: 'The love of money is the root of all evil.'

335   First I pronounce whennes that I come,   *declare*
      And thanne my bulles shewe I, alle and some.
      Oure lige lordes seel on my patente,
      That shewe I first, my body to warente,
      That no man be so boold, ne preest ne clerk,   *cleric*
340   Me to destourbe of Cristes hooly werk.   *from*
      And after that thanne telle I forth my tales;
      Bulles of popes and of cardynales,
      Of patriarkes and bishopes I shewe,
      And in Latyn I speke a wordes fewe,
345   To saffron with my predicacioun,
      And for to stire hem to devocioun.
      Thanne shewe I forth my longe cristal stones,   *glass cases*
      Ycrammed ful of cloutes and of bones,—   *rags*
      Relikes been they, as wenen they echoon.   *suppose; all*
350   Thanne have I in latoun a sholder-boon   *brass*
      Which that was of an hooly Jewes sheep.
      "Goode men," I seye, "taak of my wordes keep;   *note*
      If that this boon be wasshe in any welle,   *washed*
      If cow, or calf, or sheep, or oxe swelle
355   That any worm hath ete, or worm ystonge,
      Taak water of that welle and wassh his tonge,   *its*
      And it is hool anon; and forthermoore,   *restored to health*
      Of pokkes and of scabbe, and every soore   *pustules*
      Shal every sheep be hool that of this welle
360   Drynketh a draughte.   Taak kep eek what I telle: *also*
      If that the good-man that the beestes oweth
      Wol every wyke, er that the cok hym croweth,   *week; crows*
      Fastynge, drynken of this welle a draughte,
      As thilke hooly Jew oure eldres taughte,   *that (same); ancestors*
365   His beestes and his stoor shal multiplie.   *stock*
          And, sires, also it heeleth jalousie;   *cures*
      For though a man be falle in jalous rage,   *fallen into*
      Lat maken with this water his potage,
      And nevere shal he moore his wyf mystriste,   *mistrust*
370   Though he the soothe of hir defaute wiste,
      Al had she taken prestes two or thre.   *although*
          Heere is a miteyn eek, that ye may se.   *glove*
      He that his hand wol putte in this mitayn,

---

336 I show my papal mandates, one and all.
337-8 First I show our liege lord's (i.e. bishop's) seal on my licence to
      sell indulgences, in order to protect myself.
345 To flavour my sermon with.
350-1 Divination by means of the shoulder-bone of a sheep is referred
      to in the *Parson's Tale*, X. 1585.   The 'holy Jew' may be Jacob.
355 That has eaten any snake, or that any snake has stung.
361 If the master of the house who owns the beasts.
368 Have his soup made with this water.
370 Though he knew the truth about her misdemeanour.

He shal have multipliyng of his grayn,
375 Whan he hath sowen, be it whete or otes,
So that he offre pens, or elles grotes.   *groats*
    Goode men and wommen, o thyng warne I yow:
If any wight be in this chirche now   *person*
That hath doon synne horrible, that he
380 Dar nat, for shame, of it yshryven be,   *shriven*
Or any womman, be she yong or old,
That hath ymaked hir housbonde cokewold.   *cuckold*
Swich folk shal have no power ne no grace
To offren to my relikes in this place.
385 And whoso fyndeth hym out of swich blame,
He wol come up and offre a Goddes name.
And I assoille him by the auctoritee   *absolve*
Which that by bulle ygraunted was to me."
    By this gaude have I wonne, yeer by yeer,   *trick*
390 An hundred mark sith I was pardoner.   *since*
I stonde lyk a clerk in my pulpet,
And whan the lewed peple is doun yset,   *ignorant; seated*
I preche so as ye han herd bifoore,
And telle an hundred false japes moore.   *idle tales*
395 Thanne peyne I me to strecche forth the nekke,
And est and west upon the peple I bekke,   *nod*
As dooth a dowve sittynge on a berne.   *barn*
Myne handes and my tonge goon so yerne   *eagerly*
That it is joye to se my bisynesse.   *industry*
400 Of avarice and of swich cursednesse   *wickedness*
Is al my prechyng, for to make hem free   *generous*
To yeven hir pens, and namely unto me.   *give; especially*
For myn entente is nat but for to wynne,
And nothyng for correccioun of synne.   *not at all*
405 I rekke nevere, whan that they been beryed,   *buried*
Though that hir soules goon a-blakeberyed!
For certes, many a predicacioun   *certainly; sermon*
Comth ofte tyme of yvel entencioun;   *comes*
Som for plesance of folk and flaterye,
410 To been avaunced by ypocrisye,
And som for veyne glorie, and som for hate.
For whan I dar noon oother weyes debate,
Thanne wol I stynge hym with my tonge smerte   *sharply*
In prechyng, so that he shal nat asterte   *escape*

390 *mark*, coin worth two-thirds of a pound.
403 Is only to gain money.
406 Go a-blackberrying, i.e. go to blazes.
409 One for the purpose of pleasing and flattering folk.
411 *som* (twice), another.
412 When I dare quarrel in no other way, i.e. when I dare not quarrel
openly.
413 *hym*, i.e. someone whom the Pardoner hates.

415 To been defamed falsly, if that he   *slandered*
    Hath trespased to my bretheren or to me.
    For though I telle noght his propre name,   *individual*
    Men shal wel knowe that it is the same,
    By signes, and by othere circumstances.
420 Thus quyte I folk that doon us displesances;
    Thus spitte I out my venym under hewe   *pretence*
    Of hoolynesse, to semen hooly and trewe.
        But shortly myn entente I wol devyse: *describe*
    I preche of no thyng but for coveityse.   *covetousness*
425 Therfore my theme is yet, and evere was,
    Radix malorum est Cupiditas.
    Thus kan I preche agayn that same vice
    Which that I use, and that is avarice.   *practise*
    But though myself be gilty in that synne,
430 Yet kan I maken oother folk to twynne   *cease*
    From avarice, and soore to repente.
    But that is nat my principal entente;
    I preche nothyng but for coveitise.
    Of this mateere it oghte ynogh suffise.
435   Thanne telle I hem ensamples many oon
    Of olde stories longe tyme agoon.
    For lewed peple loven tales olde;
    Swiche thynges kan they wel reporte   *relate*
            and holde.   *keep in mind*
    What, trowe ye, that whiles I may preche,   *suppose*
440 And wynne gold and silver for I teche,   *by my teaching*
    That I wol lyve in poverte wilfully?   *poverty; voluntarily*
    Nay, nay, I thoghte it nevere, trewely!   *thought of*
    For I wol preche and begge in sondry landes;
    I wol nat do no labour with myne handes,
445 Ne make baskettes, and lyve therby,
    By cause I wol nat beggen ydelly.   *in idleness*
    I wol noon of the apostles countrefete;   *imitate*
    I wol have moneie, wolle, chese, and whete,   *wool*
    Al were it yeven of the povereste page,
450 Or of the povereste wydwe in a village,
    Al sholde hir children sterve for famyne.   *although; die*
    Nay, I wol drynke licour of the vyne,   *juice*
    And have a joly wenche in every toun.
    But herkneth, lordynges, in conclusioun:
455 Youre likyng is that I shal telle a tale.   *desire*

---

420 Thus I pay back people who offend us.
434 i.e. enough has been said about my motives for preaching.
435 *ensamples*, moral tales used by preachers to illustrate their sermons.
445 A reference to Paul the Hermit, who plied the trade of basket-maker.
449 Although it were given by the poorest servant.

Now have I dronke a draughte of corny ale,
By God, I hope I shal yow telle a thyng
That shal by reson been at youre likyng.
For though myself be a ful vicious man,
460 A moral tale yet I yow telle kan,
Which I am wont to preche for to wynne.   *win (money)*
Now hoold youre pees! my tale I wol bigynne.'

THE PARDONER'S TALE

HEERE BIGYNNETH THE PARDONERS TALE

IN FLAUNDRES whilom was a compaignye   *once*
Of yonge folk that haunteden folye,   *practised*
465 As riot, hasard, stywes, and tavernes,
Where as with harpes, lutes, and gyternes,   *where; guitars*
They daunce and pleyen at dees bothe day and nyght,
And eten also and drynken over hir myght,
Thurgh which they doon the devel sacrifise
470 Withinne that develes temple, in cursed wise,
By superfluytee abhomynable.   *excess; unnatural*
Hir othes been so grete and so dampnable
That it is grisly for to heere hem swere.   *terrible*
Oure blissed Lordes body they totere,—   *tear to pieces*
475 Hem thoughte that Jewes rente hym noght   *it seemed to them*
      ynough;
And ech of hem at otheres synne lough.   *laughed*
And right anon thanne comen tombesteres
Fetys and smale, and yonge frutesteres,

456 *corny,* tasting strongly of corn or malt.
458 That shall in consequence be to your liking.
465 Such as riotous living, gambling, brothels.
474 The reference is to swearing by the parts of Christ's body (e.g. 651).
477–8 And then straightway came graceful and slender dancing girls
      and young fruit-sellers.

Syngeres with harpes, baudes, wafereres, *sellers of wafer-cakes*
480 Whiche been the verray develes officeres   *very*
That is annexed unto glotonye.   *attached*
The hooly writ take I to my witnesse
That luxurie is in wyn and dronkenesse.   *lechery*
485   Lo, how that dronken Looth, unkyndely,   *unnaturally*
Lay by his doghtres two, unwityngly;
So dronke he was, he nyste what he wroghte.   *knew not*
  Herodes, whoso wel the stories soghte,   *Herod*
Whan he of wyn was repleet at his feeste,
490 Right at his owene table he yaf his heeste   *command*
To sleen the Baptist John, ful giltelees.   *slay*
  Senec seith a good word doutelees;   *Seneca*
He seith he kan no difference fynde
Bitwix a man that is out of his mynde
495 And a man which that is dronkelewe,   *drunk*
But that woodnesse, yfallen in a shrewe,
Persevereth lenger than dooth dronkenesse.   *lasts*
O glotonye, ful of cursednesse!   *wickedness*
O cause first of oure confusioun!   *ruin*
500 O original of oure dampnacioun,   *origin*
Til Crist hadde boght us with his blood agayn!   *redeemed*
Lo, how deere, shortly for to sayn,
Aboght was thilke cursed vileynye!
Corrupt was al this world for glotonye.   *corrupted*
505   Adam oure fader, and his wyf also,
Fro Paradys to labour and to wo
Were dryven for that vice, it is no drede.
For whil that Adam fasted, as I rede,
He was in Paradys; and whan that he
510 Eet of the fruyt deffended on the tree,   *forbidden*
Anon he was out cast to wo and peyne.
O glotonye, on thee wel oghte us pleyne!
O, wiste a man how manye maladyes   *if a man knew*
Folwen of excesse and of glotonyes,   *follow from*
515 He wolde been the moore mesurable   *temperate*
Of his diete, sittynge at his table.
Allas! the shorte throte, the tendre mouth,
Maketh that est and west and north and south,
In erthe, in eir, in water, men to swynke

483-4 Eph. v. 18.
485 Gen. xix. 30-6.
488 As anyone could see who consulted the histories carefully.
496 Except that madness, when it has befallen a wretched creature.
502-3 In short, how dearly paid for was that execrable wickedness.
512 We have good reason to complain against you.
517 The short-lived pleasure of swallowing, the delicate mouth.
518-19 *Maketh that . . . men to swynke*, causes men to toil.

520 To gete a glotoun deyntee mete and drynke!
Of this matiere, o Paul, wel kanstow trete:
'Mete unto wombe, and wombe eek unto mete,
Shal God destroyen bothe,' as Paulus seith.
Allas! a foul thyng is it, by my feith,
525 To seye this word, and fouler is the dede,
Whan man so drynketh of the white and rede   *red (wine)*
That of his throte he maketh his pryvee,   *privy*
Thurgh thilke cursed superfluitee.
    The apostel wepyng seith ful pitously,   *sorrowfully*
530 'Ther walken manye of whiche yow toold have I—
I seye it now wepyng, with pitous voys—
They been enemys of Cristes croys.
Of whiche the ende is deeth, wombe is hir god!'   *belly*
O wombe! O bely! O stynkyng cod,   *stomach*
535 Fulfilled of dong and of corrupcioun!   *filled full*
At either ende of thee foul is the soun.   *sound*
How greet labour and cost is thee to fynde!
Thise cookes, how they stampe, and streyne, and grynde,
And turnen substaunce into accident,
540 To fulfille al thy likerous talent!
Out of the harde bones knokke they
The mary, for they caste noght awey
That may go thurgh the golet softe and swoote.   *sweetly*
Of spicerie of leef, and bark, and roote   *spices*
545 Shal been his sauce ymaked by delit,
To make hym yet a newer appetit.
But, certes, he that haunteth swiche delices
Is deed, whil that he lyveth in tho vices.   *those*
A lecherous thyng is wyn, and dronkenesse
550 Is ful of stryvyng and of wrecchednesse.   *strife*
O dronke man, disfigured is thy face,   *drunken*
Sour is thy breeth, foul artow to embrace,
And thurgh thy dronke nose semeth the soun
As though thou seydest ay 'Sampsoun, Sampsoun!'

522–3 1 Cor. vi. 13: 'Meats for the belly, and the belly for meats: but
    God shall destroy both it and them.'
530–3 Phil. iii. 18–19: 'For many walk, of whom I have told you often,
    and now tell you even weeping, that they are the enemies of the cross
    of Christ: Whose end is destruction, whose god is their belly.'
537 What a great labour and cost it is to provide for you.
538 How they pound (in a mortar) and strain (through a sieve).
539 *substaunce* and *accident* are philosophical terms for (*a*) the real
    essence of a thing and (*b*) its external form. 'To turn substance into
    accident' therefore means in this context 'to turn food, the true
    purpose of which is to sustain the body, into a means of tickling the
    palate.'
540 To gratify your dainty appetite.
545–6 His sauce shall be delightfully made, to give him a still sharper
    appetite. (*his* and *hym* are used indefinitely.)
547 He who makes a practice of such pleasures (1 Tim. v. 6).

555 And yet, God woot, Sampsoun drank nevere no wyn.
    Thou fallest as it were a styked swyn;   *stuck*
    Thy tonge is lost, and al thyn honeste cure;   *sense of decency*
    For dronkenesse is verray sepulture   *tomb*
    Of mannes wit and his discrecioun.   *wisdom*
560 In whom that drynke hath dominacioun
    He kan no conseil kepe, it is no drede.   *secret; doubt*
    Now kepe yow fro the white and fro the rede,
    And namely fro the white wyn of Lepe,
    That is to selle in Fysshstrete or in Chepe. *for sale; Cheapside*
565 This wyn of Spaigne crepeth subtilly   *insidiously*
    In othere wynes, growynge faste by,   *into; near*
    Of which ther ryseth swich fumositee
    That whan a man hath dronken draughtes thre,
    And weneth that he be at hoom in Chepe,
570 He is in Spaigne, right at the toune of Lepe,—
    Nat at the Rochele, ne at Burdeux toun;
    And thanne wol he seye 'Sampsoun, Sampsoun!'   *then*
      But herkneth, lordynges, o word, I yow preye,
    That alle the sovereyn actes, dar I seye,   *most notable records*
575 Of victories in the Olde Testament,
    Thurgh verray God, that is omnipotent,   *true*
    Were doon in abstinence and in preyere.
    Looketh the Bible, and ther ye may it leere.   *look at; learn*
      Looke, Attilla, the grete conquerour,   *behold*
580 Deyde in his sleep, with shame and dishonour,
    Bledynge ay at his nose in dronkenesse.
    A capitayn sholde lyve in sobrenesse.
    And over al this, avyseth yow right wel   *consider*
    What was comaunded unto Lamuel—
585 Nat Samuel, but Lamuel, seye I—
    Redeth the Bible, and fynde it expresly   *read*
    Of wyn-yevyng to hem that han justise.
    Namoore of this, for it may wel suffise.
      And now that I have spoken of glotonye,
590 Now wol I yow deffenden hasardrye.   *forbid gambling*
    Hasard is verray mooder of lesynges,   *lies*
    And of deceite, and cursed forswerynges,   *perjury*
    Blaspheme of Crist, manslaughtre, and wast also *blasphemy*
    Of catel and of tyme; and forthermo,   *property; furthermore*
595 It is repreeve and contrarie of honour   *reproach*
    For to ben holde a commune hasardour.   *gambler*

---

563 *namely*, especially; *Lepe*, town in Spain, near Cadiz.
565 ff. A humorous allusion to the vintner's illicit practice of mixing
    the cheaper (and stronger) wines of Spain with the dearer wines of
    France.
567 *fumositee*. See V. 358.
586–7 And find the explicit statement about the giving of wine to those
    who have the administration of justice (Prov. xxxi. 4–6).

And ever the hyer he is of estaat,   *rank*
The moore is he yholden desolaat.   *considered abandoned*
If that a prynce useth hasardrye,   *practises*
600 In alle governaunce and policye
He is, as by commune opinioun,
Yholde the lasse in reputacioun.
    Stilboun, that was a wys embassadour,
Was sent to Corynthe, in ful greet honour,
605 Fro Lacidomye, to make hire alliaunce.   *Lacedaemon*
And whan he cam, hym happede, par chaunce,
That alle the gretteste that were of that lond,
Pleyynge atte hasard he hem fond.   *found*
For which, as soone as it myghte be,
610 He stal hym hoom agayn to his contree,
And seyde, 'Ther wol I nat lese my name,   *reputation*
Ne I wol nat take on me so greet defame,   *dishonour*
Yow for to allie unto none hasardours.
Sendeth othere wise embassadours;
615 For, by my trouthe, me were levere dye   *I would rather*
Than I yow sholde to hasardours allye.
For ye, that been so glorious in honours,
Shul nat allyen yow with hasardours
As by my wyl, ne as by my tretee.'   *treaty*
620 This wise philosophre, thus seyde hee.
    Looke eek that to the kyng Demetrius
The kyng of Parthes, as the book seith us,   *Parthians*
Sente him a paire of dees of gold in scorn,
For he hadde used hasard ther-biforn;   *previously*
625 For which he heeld his glorie or his renoun
At no value or reputacioun.   *repute*
Lordes may fynden oother maner pley
Honest ynough to dryve the day awey.
    Now wol I speke of othes false and grete
630 A word or two, as olde bookes trete.   *treat (of them)*
Gret sweryng is a thyng abhominable,   *unnatural*
And fals sweryng is yet moore reprevable.   *reprehensible*
The heighe God forbad sweryng at al,   *altogether*
Witnesse on Mathew; but in special
635 Of sweryng seith the hooly Jeremye,   *Jeremiah*
'Thou shalt swere sooth thyne othes, and nat lye,   *truly*
And swere in doom, and eek in rightwisnesse';   *judgment*
But ydel sweryng is a cursednesse.   *wicked thing*
Bihoold and se that in the firste table
640 Of heighe Goddes heestes honurable,   *commandments*

600 In all government and political affairs.
606 It happened to him, by chance.
634 Matt. v. 36.
636–7 Jer. iv. 2.
639 i.e. in the first five commandments.

Hou that the seconde heeste of hym is this:
'Take nat my name in ydel or amys.'   *vain*
Lo, rather he forbedeth swich sweryng   *sooner*
Than homycide or many a cursed thyng;
645 I seye that, as by ordre, thus it stondeth;
This knoweth, that his heestes understondeth,
How that the seconde heeste of God is that.
And forther over, I wol thee telle al plat,   *furthermore; bluntly*
That vengeance shal nat parten from his hous   *depart*
650 That of his othes is to outrageous.
'By Goddes precious herte,' and 'By his nayles,'
And 'By the blood of Crist that is in Hayles,
Sevene is my chaunce, and thyn is cynk and treye!'
'By Goddes armes, if thou falsly pleye,
655 This daggere shal thurghout thyn herte go!'
This fruyt cometh of the bicched bones two,
Forsweryng, ire, falsnesse, homycide.   *perjury*
Now, for the love of Crist, that for us dyde,
Lete youre othes, bothe grete and smale.
660 But, sires, now wol I telle forth my tale.
      Thise riotoures thre of whiche I telle,   *profligates*
Longe erst er prime rong of any belle,
Were set hem in a taverne to drynke,   *seated*
And as they sat, they herde a belle clynke
665 Biforn a cors, was caried to his grave.   *(which) was; its*
That oon of hem gan callen to his knave:
'Go bet,' quod he, 'and axe redily
What cors is this that passeth heer forby;   *by*
And looke that thou reporte his name weel.'
670   'Sire,' quod this boy, 'it nedeth never-a-deel;
It was me toold er ye cam heer two houres.
He was, pardee, an old felawe of youres;   *(by God), indeed*
And sodeynly he was yslayn to-nyght,
Fordronke, as he sat on his bench upright.   *very drunk*
675 Ther cam a privee theef, men clepeth Deeth,   *privy; call*
That in this contree al the peple sleeth,

641 The second commandment according to the Vulgate numbering,
    but the third in the A.V.
645-6 Thus, I say, is the order in which the commandments stand;
    those who understand His commandments know this.
652 The Abbey of Hailes in Gloucestershire, where the monks dis-
    played a phial containing what was believed to be some of Christ's
    blood.
653 The allusion is to the game of hazard.
656 *bicched bones*, cursed bones, i.e. dice.
662 Long before any bell rang for prime (the canonical office sung at
    sunrise).
666 One of them called out to his servant.
667 Go as quickly as you can . . . and ask at once.
670 It isn't at all necessary.

And with his spere he smoot his herte atwo,   *in two*
And wente his wey withouten wordes mo.   *more*
He hath a thousand slayn this pestilence.   *during this plague*
680 And, maister, er ye come in his presence,
Me thynketh that it were necessarie
For to be war of swich an adversarie.
Beth redy for to meete hym everemoore;
Thus taughte me my dame; I sey namoore.'   *mother*
685 'By seinte Marie!' seyde this taverner   *the innkeeper*
'The child seith sooth, for he hath slayn this yeer,   *truth*
Henne over a mile, withinne a greet village,
Bothe man and womman, child, and hyne, and page;   *servant*
I trowe his habitacioun be there.
690 To been avysed greet wysdom it were,   *forewarned*
Er that he dide a man a dishonour.'
   'Ye, Goddes armes!' quod this riotour,
'Is it swich peril with hym for to meete?
I shal hym seke by wey and eek by strete,
695 I make avow to Goddes digne bones!   *a vow; worthy*
Herkneth, felawes, we thre been al ones;   *of one mind*
Lat ech of us holde up his hand til oother,   *to*
And ech of us bicomen otheres brother,
And we wol sleen this false traytour Deeth.
700 He shal be slayn, he that so manye sleeth,
By Goddes dignitee, er it be nyght!'
   Togidres han thise thre hir trouthes plight   *together; troth*
To lyve and dyen ech of hem for oother,
As though he were his owene ybore brother.   *born*
705 And up they stirte, al dronken in this rage,   *frenzy*
And forth they goon towardes that village
Of which the taverner hadde spoke biforn.   *before*
And many a grisly ooth thanne han they sworn,
And Cristes blessed body they torente—   *torn to pieces*
710 Deeth shal be deed, if that they may hym hente! *die; catch*
   Whan they han goon nat fully half a mile,
Right as they wolde han troden over a stile,   *stepped*
An oold man and a povre with hem mette.   *poor*
This olde man ful mekely hem grette,   *greeted*
715 And seyde thus, 'Now, lordes, God yow see!'   *keep you*
   The proudeste of thise riotoures three
Answerde agayn, 'What, carl, with sory grace!
Why artow al forwrapped save they face?   *wrapped up*
Why lyvestow so longe in so greet age?'.   *do you live*
720 This olde man gan looke in his visage,   *looked; face*
And seyde thus: 'For I ne kan nat fynde
A man, though that I walked into Ynde,   *India*

687 Over a mile from here.
717 *carl*, fellow; *with sory grace*, bad luck to you!

Neither in citee ne in no village,
That wolde chaunge his youthe for myn age;   *exchange*
725 And therfore moot I han myn age stille,   *must; have*
As longe tyme as it is Goddes wille.
Ne Deeth, allas! ne wol nat han my lyf.
Thus walke I, lyk a restelees kaityf,   *wretch*
And on the ground, which is my moodres gate,
730 I knokke with my staf, bothe erly and late,
And seye "Leeve mooder, leet me in!   *dear mother*
Lo how I vanysshe, flessh, and blood, and skyn!
Allas! whan shul my bones been at reste?
Mooder, with yow wolde I chaunge my cheste
735 That in my chambre longe tyme hath be,   *been*
Ye, for an heyre clowt to wrappe me!"
But yet to me she wol nat do that grace,
For which ful pale and welked is my face.   *withered*
  But, sires, to yow it is no curteisye
740 To speken to an old man vileynye,
But he trespasse in word, or elles in dede.   *unless*
In Hooly Writ ye may yourself wel rede:
"Agayns an oold man, hoor upon his heed,
Ye sholde arise;" wherfore I yeve yow reed,   *advice*
745 Ne dooth unto an oold man noon harm now,
Namoore than that ye wolde men did to yow
In age, if that ye so longe abyde.
And God be with yow, where ye go or ryde!
I moot go thider as I have to go.'   *where*
750   'Nay, olde cherl, by God, thou shalt nat so,'
Seyde this oother hasardour anon;   *gambler; at once*
'Thou partest nat so lightly, by Seint John!   *depart; easily*
Thou spak right now of thilke traytour Deeth,   *that (same)*
That in this contree alle oure freendes sleeth.
755 Have heer my trouthe, as thou art his espye,   *promise; spy*
Telle where he is, or thou shalt it abye,   *pay for*
By God, and by the hooly sacrement!
For soothly thou art oon of his assent
To sleen us yonge folk, thou false theef!'
760   'Now, sires,' quod he, 'if that yow be so leef   *desirous*
To fynde Deeth, turne up this croked wey,
For in that grove I lafte hym, by my fey,   *faith*
Under a tree, and there he wole abyde;

734–6 i.e. he is willing to exchange the chest containing all his worldly
  goods for a shroud of hair-cloth to wrap himself in.
740 To speak rudely to an old man.
743–4 Lev. xix. 32: 'Thou shalt rise up before the hoary head, and
  honour the face of the old man.'
748 Whether you walk or ride, i.e. in all circumstances.
758 For truly you are in conspiracy with him.

Noght for youre boost he wole him no thyng hyde.
765 Se ye that ook?   Right there ye shal hym fynde.
    God save yow, that boghte agayn mankynde,   *redeemed*
    And yow amende!'   Thus seyde this olde man;
    And everich of thise riotoures ran   *each*
    Til he cam to that tree, and ther they founde
770 Of floryns fyne of gold ycoyned rounde
    Wel ny an eighte busshels, as hem thoughte.
    No lenger thanne after Deeth they soughte,
    But ech of hem so glad was of that sighte,
    For that the floryns been so faire and brighte,
775 That doun they sette hem by this precious hoord.
    The worste of hem, he spak the firste word.
    'Bretheren,' quod he, 'taak kep what that I seye;   *note*
    My wit is greet, though that I bourde and pleye.   *jest*
    This tresor hath Fortune unto us yiven,
780 In myrthe and joliftee oure lyf to lyven,   *jollity*
    And lightly as it comth, so wol we spende.
    Ey! Goddes precious dignitee! who
            wende   *would have supposed*
    To-day that we sholde han so fair a grace?   *fortune*
    But myghte this gold be caried fro this place
785 Hoom to myn hous, or elles unto youres—   *else*
    For wel ye woot that al this gold is oures—   *know*
    Thanne were we in heigh felicitee.
    But trewely, by daye it may nat bee.
    Men wolde seyn that we were theves stronge,   *violent*
790 And for oure owene tresor doon us honge.   *have us hanged*
    This tresor moste ycaried be by nyghte
    As wisely and as slyly as it myghte.   *craftily as possible*
    Wherfore I rede that cut among us alle   *advise; lots*
    Be drawe, and lat se wher the cut wol falle;   *drawn*
795 And he that hath the cut with herte blithe
    Shal renne to the town, and that ful swithe,   *quickly*
    And brynge us breed and wyn ful prively.
    And two of us shul kepen subtilly   *guard secretly*
    This tresor wel; and if he wol nat tarie,
800 Whan it is nyght, we wol this tresor carie,
    By oon assent, where as us thynketh best.'
    That oon of hem the cut broghte in his fest,
    And bad hem drawe, and looke where it wol falle;
    And it fil on the yongeste of hem alle,
805 And forth toward the toun he wente anon.
    And also soone as that he was gon,   *as*

    764 He will not hide himself at all for your boasting.
    770-1 Very nearly eight bushels, it seemed to them, of fine gold florins
        coined round.
    781 And as easily as it came, so will we spend it.
    801 With one accord, to where it seems best to us.

That oon of hem spak thus unto that oother:
'Thow knowest wel thou art my sworen brother;
Thy profit wol I telle thee anon.   *advantage*
810 Thou woost wel that oure felawe is agon,
And heere is gold, and that ful greet plentee,
That shal departed been among us thre.   *divided*
But nathelees, if I kan shape it so   *nevertheless; plan*
That it departed were among us two,
815 Hadde I nat doon a freendes torn to thee?'
    That oother answerde, 'I noot hou that may be. *know not*
He woot that the gold is with us tweye;   *two*
What shal we doon? What shal we to hym seye?'
    'Shal it be conseil?' seyde the firste   *a secret*
        shrewe,   *scoundrel*
820 'And I shal tellen in a wordes fewe
What we shal doon, and brynge it wel aboute.'
    'I graunte,' quod that oother, 'out of doute,   *promise*
That, by my trouthe, I wol thee nat biwreye.'   *betray*
    'Now,' quod the firste, 'thou woost wel we be tweye, *know*
825 And two of us shul strenger be than oon.
Looke whan that he is set, that right anoon   *seated*
Arys as though thou woldest with hym pleye,
And I shal ryve hym thurgh the sydes tweye   *pierce*
Whil that thou strogelest with hym as in game,
830 And with thy daggere looke thou do the same;
And thanne shal al this gold departed be,
My deere freend, bitwixen me and thee.   *between*
Thanne may we bothe oure lustes all fulfille,   *desires*
And pleye at dees right at oure owene wille.'
835 And thus acorded been thise shrewes tweye
To sleen the thridde, as ye han herd me seye.
    This yongeste, which that wente to the toun,
Ful ofte in herte he rolleth up and doun   *turns over and over*
The beautee of thise floryns newe and brighte.
840 'O Lord!' quod he, 'if so were that I myghte *if only I could*
Have al this tresor to myself allone,
Ther is no man that lyveth under the trone
Of God that sholde lyve so murye as I!'
And atte laste the feend, oure enemy,
845 Putte in his thought that he sholde poyson beye,   *buy*
With which he myghte sleen his felawes tweye;
For-why the feend foond hym in swich lyvynge
That he hadde leve him to sorwe brynge.
For this was outrely his fulle entente,
850 To sleen hem bothe, and nevere to repente.

821 And bring it about successfully.
829 While you're struggling with him as if in sport.
847-8 Because the fiend found him living such a life that he had per-
    mission to bring him to sorrow.

And forth he gooth, no lenger wolde he tarie,
Into the toun, unto a pothecarie,   *apothecary*
And preyde hym that he hym wolde selle
Som poyson, that he myghte his rattes quelle;   *kill*
855 And eek ther was a polcat in his hawe,   *yard*
That, as he seyde, his capouns hadde yslawe,   *capons; killed*
And fayn he wolde wreke hym, if he myghte,
On vermyn that destroyed hym by nyghte.   *annoyed*
     The pothecarie answerde, 'And thou shalt have
860 A thyng that, also God my soule save,
In al this world ther is no creature,
That eten or dronken hath of this confiture   *concoction*
Noght but the montance of a corn of whete,
That he ne shal his lif anon forlete;
865 Ye, sterve he shal, and that in lasse while   *die*
Than thou wolt goon a paas nat but a mile,
This poysoun is so strong and violent.'
     This cursed man hath in his hond yhent   *taken*
This poysoun in a box, and sith he ran   *afterwards*
870 Into the nexte strete unto a man,
And borwed of hym large botelles thre;
And in the two his poyson poured he;
The thridde he kepte clene for his drynke.
For al the nyght he shoop hym for to swynke
875 In cariynge of the gold out of that place.
And whan this riotour, with sory grace,   *bad luck to him*
Hadde filled with wyn his grete botels thre,
To his felawes agayn repaireth he.
     What nedeth it to sermone of it moore?   *preach*
880 For right as they hadde cast his deeth bifoore,   *planned*
Right so they han hym slayn, and that anon.
And whan that this was doon, thus spak that oon:
'Now lat us sitte and drynke, and make us merie,
And afterward we wol his body berie.'
885 And with that word it happed hym, par cas,
To take the botel ther the poyson was,
And drank, and yaf his felawe drynke also,
For which anon they storven bothe two.
     But certes, I suppose that Avycen

857 And he would gladly avenge himself.
860 God save my soul.
863-4 No bigger amount than a grain of wheat, who shall not give up
   his life immediately.
866 Than it would take you to walk a mile.
874-5 He planned to toil at carrying the gold.
885 It happened to him, by chance.
889 *Avycen*, Avicenna, the eleventh-century Arab physician, whose
   celebrated treatise on medicine, known as the 'Book of the Canon in
   Medicine,' was divided into 'fens' or chapters.

890 Wroot nevere in no canon, ne in no fen,
    Mo wonder signes of empoisonyng   *symptoms*
    Than hadde thise wrecches two, er hir endyng.
    Thus ended been thise homycides two,
    And eek the false empoysonere also.
895   O cursed synne of alle cursednesse!
    O traytours homycide, O wikkednesse!   *treacherous*
    O glotonye, luxurie, and hasardrye!   *lechery; gambling*
    Thou blasphemour of Crist with vileynye   *vile language*
    And othes grete, of usage and of pride!   *from habit*
900 Allas! mankynde, how may it bitide
    That to thy creatour, which that the wroghte,
    And with his precious herte-blood thee boghte,   *redeemed*
    Thou art so fals and so unkynde, allas?   *ungrateful*
        Now, goode men, God foryeve yow youre trespas,
905 And ware yow fro the synne of avarice!   *keep*
    Myn hooly pardoun may yow alle warice,   *cure*
    So that ye offre nobles or sterlynges,
    Or elles silver broches, spoones, rynges.
    Boweth youre heed under this hooly bulle!   *bow*
910 Cometh up, ye wyves, offreth of youre wolle!   *wool*
    Youre names I entre heer in my rolle anon;
    Into the blisse of hevene shul ye gon.   *go*
    I yow assoille, by myn heigh power,   *absolve*
    Yow that wol offre, as clene and eek as cleer
915 As ye were born.—And lo, sires, thus I preche.
    And Jhesu Crist, that is oure soules leche,   *physician*
    So graunte yow his pardoun to receyve,
    For that is best; I wol yow nat deceyve.
        But, sires, o word forgat I in my tale:
920 I have relikes and pardoun in my male,   *bag*
    As faire as any man in Engelond,   *excellent*
    Whiche were me yeven by the popes hond.
    If any of yow wole, of devocion,
    Offren, and han myn absolucion,
925 Com forth anon, and kneleth heere adoun,
    And mekely receyveth my pardoun;
    Or elles taketh pardoun as ye wende,
    Al newe and fressh at every miles ende,
    So that ye offren, alwey newe and newe,   *again and again*
930 Nobles or pens, whiche that be goode and trewe.
    It is an honour to everich that is heer   *everyone*
    That ye mowe have a suffisant pardoneer   *competent*
    T'assoille yow, in contree as ye ryde,
    For aventures whiche that may bityde.   *because of accidents*

895 O most accursed of all sins!
907 Provided you offer gold and silver coins.
915 The Pardoner now addresses his fellow pilgrims.

935 Paraventure ther may fallen oon or two
Doun of his hors, and breke his nekke atwo.   *in two*
Looke which a seuretee is it to yow alle
That I am in youre felaweshipe yfalle,   *come by chance*
That may assoille yow, bothe moore and lasse,   *high and low*
940 Whan that the soule shal fro the body passe.
I rede that oure Hoost heere shal bigynne,   *advise*
For he is moost envoluped in synne.   *enveloped*
Com forth, sire Hoost, and offre first anon,
And thou shalt kisse the relikes everychon,
945 Ye, for a grote!   Unbokele anon thy purs.'
          'Nay, nay!' quod he, 'thanne have I Cristes   *may I have*
          curs!
Lat be,' quod he, 'it shal nat be, so theech!
Thou woldest make me kisse thyn olde breech,
And swere it were a relyk of a seint,
950 Though it were with thy fundement depeint!   *stained*
But, by the croys which that Seint Eleyne fond,   *found*
I wolde I hadde thy coillons in myn hond   *testicles*
In stide of relikes or of seintuarie.   *holy things*
Lat kutte hem of, I wol thee helpe hem carie;
955 They shul be shryned in an hogges toord!'   *enshrined*
          This Pardoner answerde nat a word;
So wrooth he was, no word ne wolde he seye.
          'Now,' quod oure Hoost, 'I wol no lenger pleye
With thee, ne with noon oother angry man.'
960 But right anon the worthy Knyght bigan,
Whan that he saugh that al the peple lough,   *laughed*
'Namoore of this, for it is right ynough!   *quite*
Sire Pardoner, be glad and myrie of cheere;   *cheerful*
And ye, sire Hoost, that been to me so deere,
965 I prey yow that ye kisse the Pardoner.
And Pardoner, I prey thee, drawe thee neer,   *nearer*
And, as we diden, lat us laughe and pleye.'   *did (before)*
Anon they kiste, and ryden forth hir weye.

HEERE IS ENDED THE PARDONERS TALE

937 See what a safeguard it is.
947 As I hope to prosper.
951 A reference to the finding of the Cross by St Helen, the mother of
    Constantine.

THE SHIPMAN'S TALE

HEERE BIGYNNETH THE SHIPMANNES TALE

A MARCHANT whilom dwelled at Seint-Denys,   *once*
That riche was, for which men helde hym wys.   *prudent*
A wyf he hadde of excellent beautee;
And compaignable and revelous was she,
5 Which is a thyng that causeth more dispence   *expense*
Than worth is al the chiere and reverence
That men hem doon at festes and at daunces.   *feasts*
Swiche salutaciouns and contenaunces   *pretences*
Passen as dooth a shadwe upon the wal;
10 But wo is hym that payen moot for al!   *must*
The sely housbonde, algate he moot paye,
He moot us clothe, and he moot us arraye,
Al for his owene worshipe richely,
In which array we daunce jolily.   *merrily*
15 And if that he noght may, par aventure,   *perhaps*
Or ellis list no swich dispence endure,
But thynketh it is wasted and ylost,
Thanne moot another payen for oure cost,
Or lene us gold, and that is perilous.   *lend*
20   This noble marchaunt heeld a worthy hous,
For which he hadde alday so greet repair
For his largesse, and for his wyf was fair,   *liberality*
That wonder is; but herkneth to my tale.
Amonges alle his gestes, grete and smale,
25 Ther was a monk, a fair man and a boold—
I trowe a thritty wynter he was oold—
That evere in oon was drawynge to that place.
This yonge monk, that was so fair of face,

4 She was sociable and fond of revelry.
6 Than all the greetings and compliments are worth.
11 The wretched husband always foots the bill.
12–13 He must dress us handsomely if only to do himself credit. (*us*
apparently means 'us women'; it therefore looks as if this tale was
originally meant for a woman, probably the Wife of Bath.)
16 Or else will not put up with such expense.
21 And so he was always having visitors.
26 I should think he was some thirty years old.
27 Who was continually visiting that place.

361

Aqueynted was so with the goode man,
30 Sith that hir firste knoweliche bigan,
That in his hous as famulier was he   *at home*
As it is possible any freend to be.
    And for as muchel as this goode man,   *much*
And eek this monk, of which that I bigan,
35 Were bothe two yborn in o village,
The monk hym claymeth as for cosynage;
And he agayn, he seith nat ones nay,
But was as glad therof as fowel of day;
For to his herte it was a greet plesaunce.   *pleasure*
40 Thus been they knyt with eterne alliaunce,   *joined; eternal*
And ech of hem gan oother for t'assure
Of bretherhede, whil that hir lyf may dure.
    Free was daun John, and manly of dispence,
As in that hous, and ful of diligence
45 To doon plesaunce, and also greet costage.
He noght forgat to yeve the leeste page
In al that hous; but after hir degree,   *according to their rank*
He yaf the lord, and sitthe al his meynee,   *then; household*
Whan that he cam, som manere honest thyng;
50 For which they were as glad of his comyng
As fowel is fayn whan that the sonne up riseth.   *glad*
Na moore of this as now, for it suffiseth.
    But so bifel, this marchant on a day
Shoop hym to make redy his array
55 Toward the toun of Brugges for to fare,   *Bruges; go*
To byen there a porcioun of ware;
For which he hath to Parys sent anon
A messenger, and preyed hath daun John   *messenger*
That he sholde come to Seint-Denys to pleye   *take a holiday*
60 With hym and with his wyf a day or tweye,
Er he to Brugges wente, in alle wise.
    This noble monk, of which I yow devyse,   *tell*
Hath of his abbot, as hym list, licence,

29–30 Had become so friendly with the good man since their first
    acquaintance.
35 Both born in the same village.
36 Claims kinship with him.
37–8 And he (the merchant) did not once deny it, but welcomed it as
    gladly as a bird the dawn.
41–2 They swore brotherhood with each other.
43 Sir John was open-handed, and generous in spending.
45 And also to go to great expense.
46 He did not forget to give something to the humblest page.
49 Some decent sort of present.
54 Set about making preparations.
56 To buy there a certain quantity of merchandise.
57 And so he immediately sent to Paris.
63 Has permission from his abbot, whenever he pleases.

By cause he was a man of heigh prudence,
65 And eek an officer, out for to ryde,
To seen hir graunges and hire bernes wyde,
And unto Seint-Denys he comth anon.
Who was so welcome as my lord daun John,
Oure deere cosyn, ful of curteisye?
70 With hym broghte he a jubbe of malvesye, *jug; malmsey*
And eek another, ful of fyn vernage,
And volatyl, as ay was his usage.
And thus I lete hem ete and drynke and pleye, *leave*
This marchant and this monk, a day or tweye.
75 The thridde day, this marchant up ariseth,
And on his nedes sadly hym avyseth,
And up into his countour-hous gooth he *counting-house*
To rekene with hymself, wel may be,
Of thilke yeer how that it with hym stood,
80 And how that he despended hadde his good, *spent; money*
And if that he encressed were or noon. *richer; not*
His bookes and his bagges many oon *a one*
He leith biforn hym on his countyng- *counting-house table*
  bord.
Ful riche was his tresor and his hord, *hoarded wealth*
85 For which ful faste his countour-dore he shette;
And eek he nolde that no man sholde hym lette
Of his acountes, for the meene tyme;
And thus he sit til it was passed pryme. *sits; 9 a.m.*
 Daun John was rysen in the morwe also, *early morning*
90 And in the gardyn walketh to and fro,
And hath his thynges seyd ful curteisly.
 This goode wyf cam walkynge pryvely *stealthily*
Into the gardyn, there he walketh softe, *softly*
And hym saleweth, as she hath doon ofte. *greets*
95 A mayde child cam in hire compaignye,
Which as hir list she may governe and gye,
For yet under the yerde was the mayde.
'O deere cosyn myn, daun John,' she sayde,

---

65 *out for to ryde.* See I. 166.
66 To supervise their granges and their spacious barns.
71 *vernage,* an Italian wine.
72 And wild-fowl, as he always did.
76 And gives serious thought to his affairs.
78–9 To reckon up by himself, as near as he could, how things stood
 with him that year.
85 And so he shut fast his counting-house door.
86–7 He wanted no one to disturb him at his reckoning in the mean
 time.
91 Reverently said the things he had to say, i.e. the divine office in the
 breviary.
96–7 Whom she can instruct and govern as she likes, for the maiden was
 still under her authority.

'What eyleth yow so rathe for to ryse?'

100   'Nece,' quod he, 'it oghte ynough   *ought to be enough*
      suffise
    Fyve houres for to slepe upon a nyght,
    But it were for an old appalled wight,
    As been thise wedded men, that lye and dare   *cower*
    As in a fourme sit a wery hare,
105 Were al forstraught with houndes grete and smale.
    But deere nece, why be ye so pale?
    I trowe, certes, that oure goode man
    Hath yow laboured sith the nyght bigan,
    That yow were nede to resten hastily.'
110 And with that word he lough ful murily,   *laughed*
    And of his owene thought he wax al reed.
      This faire wyf gan for to shake hir heed
    And seyde thus, 'Ye, God woot al,' quod she.
    'Nay, cosyn myn, it stant nat so with me;   *stands*
115 For, by that God that yaf me soule and lyf,   *gave*
    In al the reawme of France is ther no wyf   *realm*
    That lasse lust hath to that sory pley.
    For I may synge "allas and weylawey,
    That I was born," but to no wight,' quod she,   *no one*
120 'Dar I nat telle how that it stant with me.
    Wherfore I thynke out of this land to wende,   *go*
    Or elles of myself to make an ende,
    So ful am I of drede and eek of care.'   *fear; sorrow*
      This monk bigan upon this wyf to stare,
125 And seyde, 'Allas, my nece, God forbede
    That ye, for any sorwe or any drede,
    Fordo youreself; but telleth me youre grief.   *destroy*
    Paraventure I may, in youre meschief,   *perhaps; misfortune*
    Conseille or helpe; and therfore telleth me
130 Al youre anoy, for it shal been secree.   *trouble; secret*
    For on my porthors I make an ooth   *breviary*
    That nevere in my lyf, for lief ne looth,   *friend or foe*
    Ne shal I of no conseil yow biwreye.'
      'The same agayn to yow,' quod she, 'I seye.
135 By God and by this porthors I yow swere,
    Though men me wolde al into pieces tere,   *tear*

    99 What's wrong with you that you are up so early?
    102 Except for a decrepit old creature.
    104 Like a weary hare in its form.
    105 Which is distracted by hounds.
    109 So that you have urgent need to rest.
    111 And blushed a bright red at his own thoughts.
    113 God knows all, i.e. God knows it is not what you imagine.
    117 Who takes less pleasure in that wretched sport.
    133 Shall I betray any secret of yours.

Ne shal I nevere, for to goon to helle,
Biwreye a word of thyng that ye me telle,   *anything*
Nat for no cosynage ne alliance,
140 But verraily, for love and affiance.'   *trust*
Thus been they sworn, and heerupon they kiste,
And ech of hem tolde oother what hem liste.   *they pleased*
    'Cosyn,' quod she, 'if that I hadde a space,   *opportunity*
As I have noon, and namely in this place,   *none; especially*
145 Thanne wolde I telle a legende of my lyf,   *story*
What I have suffred sith I was a wyf   *since*
With myn housbonde, al be he youre cosyn.'   *although he is*
    'Nay,' quod this monk, 'by God and seint Martyn,
He is na moore cosyn unto me
150 Than is this leef that hangeth on the tree!
I clepe hym so, by Seint Denys of Fraunce,   *call*
To have the moore cause of aqueyntaunce
Of yow, which I have loved specially
Aboven alle wommen, sikerly.   *truly*
155 This swere I yow on my professioun.
Telleth youre grief, lest that he come adoun;   *down*
And hasteth yow, and gooth youre wey anon.'   *be quick*
    'My deere love,' quod she, 'O my daun John,
Ful lief were me this conseil for to hyde,
160 But out it moot, I may namoore abyde.   *must; bear it*
Myn housbonde is to me the worste man
That evere was sith that the world bigan.
But sith I am a wyf, it sit nat me
To tellen no wight of oure privetee,   *anyone; private affairs*
165 Neither abedde, ne in noon oother place;
God shilde I sholde it tellen, for his grace!
A wyf ne shal nat seyn of hir housbonde
But al honour, as I kan understonde;
Save unto yow thus muche I tellen shal: *except*
170 As helpe me God, he is noght worth at al   *so*
In no degree the value of a flye.
But yet me greveth moost his nygardye.   *miserliness*
And wel ye woot that wommen naturelly
Desiren thynges sixe as wel as I: *six*
175 They wolde that hir housbondes sholde be
Hardy, and wise, and riche, and therto free,   *brave; generous*
And buxom unto his wyf, and fressh abedde.   *obedient; lively*
But by that ilke Lord that for us bledde,

137 Though I went to hell for it.
139 And this I do, not for kinship.
152-3 To have a better excuse for knowing you.
159 I'd dearly like to keep this secret hidden.
163 It's unbecoming of me.
166 God forbid I should tell it, by His grace!
168 Anything but what is honourable.

For his honour, myself for to arraye,
180 A Sonday next I moste nedes paye   *on*
An hundred frankes, or ellis I am lorn.   *ruined*
Yet were me levere that I were unborn
Than me were doon a sclaundre or vileynye;
And if myn housbonde eek it myghte espye,
185 I nere but lost; and therfore I yow preye,
Lene me this somme, or ellis moot I deye.   *lend; must*
Daun John, I seye, lene me thise hundred frankes.
Pardee, I wol nat faille yow my thankes,
If that yow list to doon that I yow praye.
190 For at a certeyn day I wol yow paye,
And doon to yow what plesance and service   *pleasure*
That I may doon, right as yow list devise.
And but I do, God take on me vengeance,   *unless*
As foul as evere hadde Genylon of France.'
195   This gentil monk answerde in this manere: *noble*
'Now trewely, myn owene lady deere,
I have,' quod he, 'on yow so greet a routhe   *pity*
That I yow swere, and plighte yow my trouthe,   *troth*
That whan youre housbonde is to Flaundres fare,   *gone*
200 I wol delyvere yow out of this care;   *anxiety*
For I wol brynge yow an hundred frankes.'
And with that word he caughte hire by the flankes,
And hire embraceth harde, and kiste hire ofte.
'Gooth now youre wey,' quod he, 'al stille and softe,   *quietly*
205 And lat us dyne as soone as that ye may;
For by my chilyndre it is pryme of day.
Gooth now, and beeth as trewe as I shal be.'
   'Now elles God forbede, sire,' quod she;
And forth she gooth as jolif as a pye,   *merry; magpie*
210 And bad the cookes that they sholde hem hye,   *hurry*
So that men myghte dyne, and that anon.
Up to hir housbonde is this wyf ygon,
And knokketh at his countour boldely.
   '*Quy la?*' quod he.   'Peter! it am I,'   *who's there?*
215 Quod she, 'what, sire, how longe wol ye faste?
How longe tyme wol ye rekene and caste
Youre sommes, and youre bookes, and youre thynges?

179 In order to dress myself in a way that will do him credit.
182-3 I'd rather never have been born than expose myself to slander
   or reproach.
184-5 If my husband were to find out, I'd be as good as lost
188-9 Indeed, I shan't fail to thank you, if you are willing to do what
   I ask.
192 Just as you care to suggest.
194 *Genylon.* See VII. 3227.
206 For by my cylinder (i.e. portable sun-dial) it is 9 a.m.

The devel have part on alle swiche rekenynges!
Ye have ynough, pardee, of Goddes sonde;   *gifts*
220 Com doun to-day, and lat youre bagges stonde.
Ne be ye nat ashamed that daun John
Shal fasting al this day alenge goon?   *miserable*
What! lat us heere a messe, and go we dyne.'   *mass*
'Wyf,' quod this man, 'litel kanstow devyne   *guess*
225 The curious bisynesse that we have.   *complicated*
For of us chapmen, also God me save,   *merchants*
And by that lord that clepid is Seint Yve,   *called*
Scarsly amonges twelve tweye shul thryve
Continuelly, lastynge unto oure age.
230 We may wel make chiere and good visage,
And dryve forth the world as it may be,
And kepen oure estaat in pryvetee,
Til we be deed, or elles that we pleye
A pilgrymage, or goon out of the weye.
235 And therfore have I greet necessitee
Upon this queynte world t'avyse me;
For everemoore we moote stonde in drede   *fear*
Of hap and fortune in oure chapmanhede.   *chance; trading*
To Flaundres wol I go to-morwe at day,   *daybreak*
240 And come agayn, as soone as evere I may.
For which, my deere wyf, I thee biseke,
As be to every wight buxom and meke,   *everyone; obedient*
And for to kepe oure good be curious,
And honestly governe wel oure hous.   *honourably*
245 Thou hast ynough, in every maner wise,   *way*
That to a thrifty houshold may suffise.
Thee lakketh noon array ne no vitaille;   *clothes; food*
Of silver in thy purs shaltow nat faille.'
And with that word his countour-dore he shette,   *shut*
250 And doun he gooth, no lenger wolde he lette.   *delay*
But hastily a messe was ther seyd,
And spedily the tables were yleyd,   *laid*
And to the dyner faste they hem spedde,   *hurried*
And richely this monk the chapman fedde.
255   At after-dyner daun John sobrely
This chapman took apart, and pryvely

218 May the devil have a share in all such reckonings.
228-9 Hardly two in twelve will stay prosperous till old age.
230-4 Well may we try to be cheerful and put a good face on things,
   and make what show we can in the world, and keep our affairs secret
   till we die; or, failing all this, try to find relaxation on a pilgrimage,
   or go somewhere out of the way (of creditors).
236 To consider this curious world with care.
243 And be careful to look after our goods.
254 The merchant fed the monk with sumptuous fare.
255-6 During the interval after dinner Sir John gravely took the merchant aside.

He seyde hym thus: 'Cosyn, it standeth so,
That wel I se to Brugges wol ye go.
God and seint Austyn spede yow and gyde!   *prosper*
260 I prey yow, cosyn, wisely that ye ryde.   *prudently*
Governeth yow also of youre diete
Atemprely, and namely in this hete.
Bitwix us two nedeth no strange fare;
Farewel, cosyn; God shilde yow fro care!   *shield*
265 And if that any thyng by day or nyght,
If it lye in my power and my myghte,
That ye me wol comande in any wyse,
It shal be doon, right as ye wol devyse.   *exactly; say*
    O thyng, er that ye goon, if it may be,
270 I wolde prey yow; for to lene me   *lend*
An hundred frankes, for a wyke or tweye,   *week*
For certein beestes that I moste beye,   *must buy*
To stoore with a place that is oures.
God helpe me so, I wolde it were youres!
275 I shal nat faille surely of my day,
Nat for a thousand frankes, a mile way.
But lat this thyng be secree, I yow preye,   *secret*
For yet to-nyght thise beestes moot I beye.
And fare now wel, myn owene cosyn deere;
280 Graunt mercy of youre cost and of youre cheere.'
    This noble marchant gentilly anon   *kindly*
Answerde and seyde, 'O cosyn myn, daun John,
Now sikerly this is a smal requeste.   *certainly*
My gold is youres, whan that it yow leste,   *you like*
285 And nat oonly my gold, but my chaffare.   *wares*
Take what yow list, God shilde that ye spare.
    But o thyng is, ye knowe it wel ynogh,
Of chapmen, that hir moneie is hir plogh.   *money; plough*
We may creaunce whil we have a name;
290 But goldlees for to be, it is no game.
Paye it agayn whan it lith in youre ese;
After my myght ful fayn wolde I yow plese.'
    Thise hundred frankes he fette forth anon,   *fetched out*
And prively he took hem to daun John.   *secretly; gave*

261-2 Be moderate in your diet, especially in this heat.
263 Between us two there's no need for reserve.
273 To stock up a place of ours.
275 I will not fail to keep my day (for payment).
276 By as much as twenty minutes (i.e. the average time for walking a
mile).
280 Many thanks for your generosity and hospitality.
286 God forbid you should be sparing.
289 We can get credit while our name is good.
291 When it's convenient to you.
292 I'm very glad to do what I can to please you.

295 No wight in al this world wiste of this loone,   *knew; loan*
    Savynge this marchant and daun John allone.
    They drynke, and speke, and rome a while and pleye,   *loiter*
    Til that daun John rideth to his abbeye.
      The morwe cam, and forth this marchant rideth
300 To Flaundres-ward; his prentys wel hym gydeth,
    Til he cam into Brugges murily.   *happily*
    Now gooth this marchant faste and bisily
    Aboute his nede, and byeth and   *business*
      creaunceth.   *obtains credit*
    He neither pleyeth at the dees ne daunceth,   *dice*
305 But as a marchaunt, shortly for to telle,   *briefly*
    He let his lyf, and there I lete hym dwelle.   *leads; leave*
      The Sonday next the marchant was agon,
    To Seint-Denys ycomen is daun John,
    With crowne and berd al fressh and newe yshave.   *shaven*
310 In al the hous ther nas so litel a knave,
    Ne no wight elles, that he nas ful fayn
    That my lord daun John was come agayn.
    And shortly to the point right for to gon
    This faire wyf acorded with daun John   *agreed*
315 That for thise hundred frankes he sholde al nyght
    Have hire in his armes bolt upright;   *flat on her back*
    And this acord parfourned was in dede.
    In myrthe al nyght a bisy lyf they lede
    Til it was day, that daun John wente his way,   *when*
320 And bad the meynee 'farewel, have good day!'   *household*
    For noon of hem, ne no wight in the toun,
    Hath of daun John right no suspecioun.
    And forth he rydeth hoom to his abbeye,
    Or where hym list; namoore of hym I seye.   *he pleases*
325   This marchant, whan that ended was the faire,
    To Seint-Denys he gan for to repaire,   *went home*
    And with his wyf he maketh feeste and cheere,
    And telleth hire that chaffare is so deere   *merchandise*
    That nedes moste he make a chevyssaunce;
330 For he was bounden in a reconyssaunce
    To paye twenty thousand sheeld anon.   *crowns*
    For which this marchant is to Parys gon

300 Towards Flanders; his apprentice guides him well.
307 The very next Sunday after the merchant had gone.
310-11 There was no serving-lad, however small, nor anyone else, who
     was not very glad.
317 This agreement was carried out to the letter.
322 Has the least suspicion of Sir John.
327 He feasts and makes merry.
329 That he would have to raise a loan.
330 For he was bound by a recognizance.

To borwe of certeine freendes that he hadde   *from*
A certeyn frankes; and somme with him he ladde.
335 And whan that he was come into the toun,
For greet chiertee and greet affeccioun,   *fondness*
Unto daun John he first gooth hym to   *to enjoy himself*
    pleye;
Nat for to axe or borwe of hym moneye,   *ask*
But for to wite and seen of his welfare,
340 And for to tellen hym of his chaffare,   *trading*
As freendes doon whan they been met yfeere.   *together*
Daun John hym maketh feeste and murye cheere,
And he hym tolde agayn, ful specially,
How he hadde wel yboght and graciously,   *favourably*
345 Thanked be God, al hool his marchandise;
Save that he moste, in alle maner wise,   *by all means*
Maken a chevyssaunce, as for his beste,
And thanne he sholde been in joye and reste.   *peace of mind*
    Daun John answerde, 'Certes, I am fayn   *glad*
350 That ye in heele ar comen hom agayn.   *safe and sound*
And if that I were riche, as have I blisse,
Of twenty thousand sheeld sholde ye nat mysse,   *crowns; lack*
For ye so kyndely this oother day
Lente me gold; and as I kan and may,
355 I thanke yow, by God and by seint Jame!   *James*
But nathelees, I took unto oure dame,   *gave; lady*
Youre wyf, at hom, the same gold ageyn   *home*
Upon youre bench; she woot it wel, certeyn,
By certeyn tokenes that I kan hire telle.
360 Now, by youre leve, I may no lenger dwelle;
Oure abbot wole out of this toun anon,   *intends to leave*
And in his compaignye moot I goon.   *must*
Grete wel oure dame, myn owene nece sweete,   *greet*
And fare wel, deere cosyn, til we meete!'   *meet (again)*
365   This marchant, which that was ful war   *cautious; prudent*
    and wys,
Creanced hath, and payd eek in Parys   *obtained credit*
To certeyn Lumbardes, redy in hir hond,
The somme of gold, and gat of hem his bond;

334 A certain number of francs; and some (francs) he took with him.
339 But to ask and see about his welfare.
342 Sir John receives him warmly and entertains him well.
343 And he (the merchant), in return, makes a point of telling him.
345 Thanks be to God, the whole of his marchandise.
347 Raise a loan in his own best interests.
351 As I hope for (eternal) bliss.
354 As well as I am able.
358–9 (And put it back) on your counting-house table; she knows all
    about it by reason of certain vouchers I gave her.
367 *Lumbardes*, Lombards, the moneylenders of medieval Europe.
368 i.e. he recovered his bond for the money he had borrowed.

And hoom he gooth, murie as a papejay,   *popinjay*
370 For wel he knew he stood in swich array
That nedes moste he wynne in that viage
A thousand frankes aboven al his costage.   *expenses*
   His wyf ful redy mette hym atte gate,
As she was wont of oold usage algate,
375 And al that nyght in myrthe they bisette;
For he was riche and cleerly out of dette.   *completely*
Whan it was day, this marchant gan embrace
His wyf al newe, and kiste hire on hir face,   *all over again*
And up he gooth and maketh it ful tough.
380 'Namoore,' quod she, 'by God, ye have
        ynough!'
And wantownly agayn with hym she pleyde,
Til atte laste thus this marchant seyde:
'By God,' quod he, 'I am a litel wrooth   *angry*
With yow my wyf, although it be me   *unwilling though I am*
      looth.
385 And woot ye why? by God, as that I gesse
That ye han maad a manere straungenesse
Bitwixen me and my cosyn daun John.
Ye sholde han warned me, er I had gon,
That he yow hadde an hundred frankes payed
390 By redy token; and heeld hym yvele apayed,
For that I to hym spak of chevyssaunce;   *borrowing money*
Me semed so, as by his contenaunce.
But natheles, by God, oure hevene kyng,
I thoughte nat to axen hym no thyng.
395 I prey thee, wyf, ne do namoore so;
Telle me alwey, er that I fro thee go,
If any dettour hath in myn absence   *debtor*
Ypayed thee, lest thurgh thy necligence
I myghte hym axe a thing that he hath payed.'   *ask for*
400   This wyf was nat afered nor affrayed,   *frightened; dismayed*
But boldely she seyde, and that anon:
'Marie, I deffie the false monk, daun John!   *marry; defy*
I kepe nat of his tokenes never a deel;
He took me certeyn gold, that woot I weel,—   *gave; know*

370–1 He was so placed that he was sure to make money out of that
    business trip.
374 As she had long been in the habit of doing.
375 And they spent all that night in jollification.
379 And has an energetic time of it.
385–6 Because I have an idea you caused some unfriendliness.
390 And he was not very pleased.
392 So it seemed to me, by the look on his face.
394 I had no intention of asking him for anything.
395 Don't ever do it again.
403 I care nothing for his vouchers.

405 What! yvel thedam on his monkes snowte!
    For, God it woot, I wende, withouten doute,   *supposed*
    That he hadde yeve it me bycause of yow,   *given*
    To doon therwith myn honour and my prow,   *benefit*
    For cosynage, and eek for beele cheere   *kinship; hospitality*
410 That he hath had ful ofte tymes heere.
    But sith I se I stonde in this disjoynt,   *difficult position*
    I wol answere yow shortly to the poynt.
    Ye han mo slakkere dettours than am I!   *slacker*
    For I wol paye yow wel and redily
415 Fro day to day, and if so be I faille,
    I am youre wyf; score it upon my taille,
    And I shal paye as soone as ever I may.
    For by my trouthe, I have on myn array,   *clothes*
    And nat on wast, bistowed every deel;   *bit*
420 And for I have bistowed it so weel
    For youre honour, for Goddes sake, I seye,
    As be nat wrooth, but lat us laughe and pleye.
    Ye shal my joly body have to wedde;   *as a pledge*
    By God, I wol nat paye yow but abedde!   *except in bed*
425 Forgyve it me, myn owene spouse deere;
    Turne hiderward, and maketh bettre cheere.'
        This marchant saugh ther was no remedie,   *saw*
    And for to chide it nere but folie,
    Sith that the thyng may nat amended be.
430 'Now wyf,' he seyde, 'and I foryeve it thee;
    But, by thy lyf, ne be namoore so large.   *extravagant*
    Keep bet thy good, this yeve I thee incharge.'
    Thus endeth my tale, and God us sende
    Taillynge ynough unto oure lyves ende.   Amen.

HEERE ENDETH THE SHIPMANNES TALE

    405 Bad luck to his monkish snout!
    416 Score it on my tally, i.e. charge it to my account.
    426 Turn this way, and cheer up.
    428 And that it would be silly to scold her.
    432 Take better care of my money, I implore you.
    434 *Taillynge*, tallying.   Both here and in 416 a comic pun is no doubt
        intended on *taille*, 'tally,' and *tail*, 'tail' (see *Oxford English Dictionary*,
        sub. Tail, *sb.*¹, sense 5c).

Bihoold the murie wordes of the Hoost to the Shipman and to the lady Prioresse.

435   'WEL SEYD, by *corpus dominus*,' quod oure Hoost,
      'Now longe moote thou saille by the cost,   *may; coast*
      Sire gentil maister, gentil maryneer!   *noble*
      God yeve the monk a thousand last quade yeer!
      A ha! felawes! beth ware of swich a jape!   *trick*
440   The monk putte in the mannes hood an ape,
      And in his wyves eek, by Seint Austyn!
      Draweth no monkes moore unto youre in.
        But now passe over, and lat us seke aboute,
      Who shal now telle first of al this route
445   Another tale;' and with that word he sayde,
      As curteisly as it had been a mayde,   *as if he*
      'My lady Prioresse, by youre leve,
      So that I wiste I sholde yow nat greve,
      I wolde demen that ye tellen sholde
450   A tale next, if so were that ye wolde.
      Now wol ye vouche sauf, my lady deere?'   *condescend*
      'Gladly,' quod she, and seyde as ye shal heere.

435 *corpus dominus*. This is the Host's ungrammatical version of *corpus domini*, the Lord's body. (Cf. VI. 314.)
438 God give the monk a thousand cartloads of bad years. (The Host is referring to the monk of the *Shipman's Tale*.)
440–1 The monk made dupes of the man and his wife.
442 Invite no more monks to your house.
448–50 If I knew it wouldn't offend you, I should like to ask you to tell the next tale, if you're quite sure you don't mind.

THE PROLOGE OF THE PRIORESSES TALE

    'O Lord, oure Lord, thy name how merveillous
    Is in this large world ysprad,' quod she;   *spread*
455 'For noght oonly thy laude precious   *praise*
    Parfourned is by men of dignitee,   *celebrated*
    But by the mouth of children thy bountee   *excellence*
    Parfourned is, for on the brest soukynge   *sucking*
    Somtyme shewen they thyn heriynge.

460 Wherfore in laude, as I best kan or may,
    Of thee and of the white lylye flour
    Which that the bar, and is a mayde alway,
    To telle a storie I wol do my labour;   *take pains*
    Nat that I may encressen hir honour,   *increase*
465 For she hirself is honour and the roote
    Of bountee, next hir Sone, and soules boote. *soul's salvation*

    O mooder Mayde! o mayde Mooder free!   *gracious*
    O bussh unbrent, brennynge in Moyses *unburnt; burning*
        sighte,
    That ravyshedest doun fro the Deitee,   *drew*
470 Thurgh thyn humblesse, the Goost that in th'alighte,
    Of whos vertu, whan he thyn herte lighte,
    Conceyved was the Fadres sapience,
    Help me to telle it in thy reverence!

    Lady, thy bountee, thy magnificence,
475 Thy vertu, and thy grete humylitee,
    Ther may no tonge expresse in no science;
    For somtyme, Lady, er men praye to thee,   *before*

459 Sometimes they declare thy praise.
460 As well as I possibly can.
461 ff. The white lily and the burning bush were both symbols of Mary's
    unsullied purity.
462 Who bore thee, and remained a virgin.
465 For she is honour itself.
470 Through thy humility, the Holy Ghost that alighted in thee.
471 By whose power, when He illumined thy heart.
472 The wisdom of the Father, i.e. the Son.
476 No tongue can express even in learned terms.

Thou goost biforn of thy benyngnytee,
And getest us the lyght, of thy preyere,
480 To gyden us unto thy Sone so deere.

My konnyng is so wayk, o blisful Queene,   *skill; weak*
For to declare thy grete worthynesse
That I ne may the weighte nat susteene;   *support*
But as a child of twelf month oold, or lesse,
485 That kan unnethes any word expresse,   *hardly*
Right so fare I, and therfore I yow preye,
Gydeth my song that I shal of yow seye.'   *guide*

EXPLICIT

THE PRIORESS'S TALE

HEERE BIGYNNETH THE PRIORESSES TALE

THER was in Asye, in a greet citee,   *Asia*
Amonges Cristene folk, a Jewerye,   *Jewish quarter*
490 Sustened by a lord of that contree
For foule usure and lucre of vileynye,
Hateful to Crist and to his compaignye;
And thurgh the strete men myghte ride or wende,   *walk*
For it was free and open at eyther ende.

495 A litel scole of Cristen folk ther stood   *school*
Doun at the ferther ende, in which ther were
Children an heep, ycomen of Cristen blood,

478 Thou art gracious enough to anticipate our prayers.
491 For the sake of vile usury and filthy lucre.
492 *compaignye*, followers, i.e. the Church.
494 For it was a thoroughfare.
497 A large number of children.

That lerned in that scole yeer by yere
Swich manere doctrine as men used there,
500 This is to seyn, to syngen and to rede,   *read*
As smale children doon in hire childhede.   *childhood*

Among thise children was a wydwes sone,   *widow's son*
A litel clergeon, seven yeer of age,   *choir-boy*
That day by day to scole was his wone,
505 And eek also, where as he saugh th'ymage   *where he saw*
Of Cristes mooder, hadde he in usage,
As hym was taught, to knele adoun and seye
His *Ave Marie*, as he goth by the weye.

Thus hath this wydwe hir litel sone ytaught
510 Oure blisful Lady, Cristes mooder deere,
To worshipe ay, and he forgat it naught,   *forgot; not*
For sely child wol alday soone leere.
But ay, whan I remembre on this mateere,   *matter*
Seint Nicholas stant evere in my presence,
515 For he so yong to Crist dide reverence.

This litel child, his litel book lernynge,
As he sat in the scole at his prymer,
He *Alma redemptoris* herde synge,
As children lerned hire antiphoner;   *anthem-book*
520 And as he dorste, he drough hym ner and ner,
And herkned ay the wordes and the noote,   *notes*
Til he the firste vers koude al by rote.   *knew all by heart*

Noght wiste he what this Latyn was to seye,
For he so yong and tendre was of age.
525 But on a day his felawe gan he preye
T'expounden hym this song in his langage,
Or telle hym why this song was in usage;

499 The kind of lesson that was usually taught there.
504 Whose practice it was to go to school every day.
506–7 It was his habit, as he had been taught.
508 *Ave Marie*, Hail Mary (a Latin prayer to the Virgin based on Luke i. 28, 42).
512 For a good child will always learn quickly.
514 St Nicholas is always present to me. (St Nicholas was the patron saint of schoolboys.)
517 *prymer*, prayer book used as a first reading-book.
518 *Alma redemptoris* (*mater*), loving mother of the Redeemer. (A reference to the anthem sung during Advent.)
520 And as far as he dared he drew nearer and nearer.
523 He did not know what the Latin meant.
525–6 But one day he begged his friend to explain this song to him in his own language.
527 *in usage*, in use, i.e. being practised at that season of the church year.

This preyde he hym to construe and declare   *explain*
Ful often tyme upon his knowes bare.   *knees*

530 His felawe, which that elder was than he,
Answerde hym thus: 'This song, I have herd seye,
Was maked of our blisful Lady free,
Hire to salue, and eek hire for to preye   *greet; also*
To been oure help and socour whan we deye.
535 I kan namoore expounde in this mateere;
I lerne song, I kan but smal grammeere.'

'And is this song maked in reverence
Of Cristes mooder?' seyde this innocent.
'Now, certes, I wol do my diligence   *best*
540 To konne it al er Cristemasse be went.
Though that I for my prymer shal be shent,
And shal be beten thries in an houre,
I wol it konne Oure Lady for to honoure!'

His felawe taughte hym homward prively,
545 Fro day to day, til he koude it by rote,
And thanne he song it wel and boldely,
Fro word to word, acordynge with the note.
Twies a day it passed thurgh his throte,
To scoleward and homward whan he   *on the way to school*
        wente;
550 On Cristes mooder set was his entente.

As I have seyd, thurghout the Juerie,
This litel child, as he cam to and fro,
Ful murily than wolde he synge and crie   *sweetly*
O *Alma redemptoris* everemo.   *all the time*
555 The swetnesse his herte perced so
Of Cristes mooder that, to hire to preye,
He kan nat stynte of syngyng by the weye.   *keep from*

Oure firste foo, the serpent Sathanas,
That hath in Jues herte his waspes nest,   *Jew's*
560 Up swal, and seide, 'O Hebrayk peple, allas!   *swelled up*
Is this to yow a thyng that is honest,   *honourable*

532 Was made in honour of our blessed, gracious Lady.
536 I know but little grammar.
540 To learn it all before Christmas has gone.
541 Though I shall be punished for not knowing my primer.
544 Taught him secretly on the way home.
547 Word by word, with all the right notes.
550 His whole mind was fixed on Christ's mother.

That swich a boy shal walken as hym lest
In youre despit, and synge of swich sentence,
Which is agayn youre lawes reverence?'

565 Fro thennes forth the Jues han conspired   *have*
This innocent out of this world to chace.   *drive*
An homycide therto han they hyred,   *murderer*
That in an aleye hadde a privee place;   *secret*
And as the child gan forby for to pace,   *passed by*
570 This cursed Jew hym hente, and heeld hym faste,   *seized*
And kitte his throte, and in a pit hym caste.   *cut*

I seye that in a wardrobe they hym threwe   *privy*
Where as thise Jewes purgen hire entraille.
O cursed folk of Herodes al newe,
575 What may youre yvel entente yow availle?   *purpose*
Mordre wol out, certeyn, it wol nat faille,
And namely ther th'onour of God shal sprede;
The blood out crieth on youre cursed dede.

O martir, sowded to virginitee,   *united*
580 Now maystow syngen, folwynge evere in   *following always*
        oon
The white Lamb celestial—quod she—
Of which the grete evaungelist, Seint John,
In Pathmos wroot, which seith that they that goon
Biforn this Lamb, and synge a song al newe,   *before*
585 That nevere, flesshly, wommen they ne knewe.

This poure wydwe awaiteth al that nyght   *watches*
After hir litel child, but he cam noght;   *for*
For which, as soone as it was dayes lyght,
With face pale of drede and bisy thoght,
590 She hath at scole and elleswhere hym soght,
Til finally she gan so fer espie   *found out*
That he last seyn was in the Juerie.   *seen*

With moodres pitee in hir brest enclosed,
She gooth, as she were half out of hir mynde,

562–3 That such a boy should walk about as he likes in contempt of
    you, and sing of such a subject.
564 Which is against the respect due to your law.
573 Where the Jews purge their bowels.
574 O accursed people, reborn Herods.
576–7 Murder will out, unfailingly, and especially where the honour of
    God can be magnified.
579 ff. Rev. xiv. 3–4.
583 Wrote in Patmos, saying that they who go.
585 'Are they which were not defiled with women' (Rev. xiv. 4).
589 Pale with fear and anxiety.

595 To every place where she hath supposed
     By liklihede hir litel child to fynde;   *in all likelihood*
     And evere on Cristes mooder meeke and kynde
     She cride, and atte laste thus she wroghte: *did*
     Among the cursed Jues she hym soghte.

600 She frayneth and she preyeth pitously   *asks; piteously*
     To every Jew that dwelte in thilke place,   *that (same)*
     To telle hire if hir child wente oght forby.
     They seyde 'nay'; but Jhesu, of his grace,
     Yaf in hir thoght, inwith a litel space,
605 That in that place after hir sone she cryde,
     Where he was casten in a pit bisyde.

     O grete God, that parfournest thy   *dost celebrate*
             laude   *praise*
     By mouth of innocentz, lo, heere thy myght!
     This gemme of chastite, this emeraude,
610 And eek of martirdom the ruby bright,
     Ther he with throte ykorven lay upright,
     He *Alma redemptoris* gan to synge   *began*
     So loude that al the place gan to rynge.   *loudly*

     The Cristene folk that thurgh the strete wente
615 In coomen for to wondre upon this thyng,   *came*
     And hastily they for the provost sente;   *chief magistrate*
     He cam anon withouten tariyng,   *delay*
     And herieth Crist that is of hevene kyng,   *praises*
     And eek his mooder, honour of mankynde,
620 And after that the Jewes leet he bynde.   *he had bound*

     This child with pitous lamentacioun
     Up taken was, syngynge his song alway,   *all the while*
     And with honour of greet processioun
     They carien hym unto the nexte abbay.   *nearest*
625 His mooder swownynge by his beere lay;   *bier*
     Unnethe myghte the peple that was theere   *hardly*
     This newe Rachel brynge fro his beere.

     With torment and with shameful deeth echon
     This provost dooth thise Jewes for to sterve
630 That of this mordre wiste, and that anon.

     602 If her child had passed by at all.
     604–6 Put it into her head after a short while to cry out for her son near
         the place where he had been thrown into a pit.
     608 Here is an instance of thy might.
     611 Where he lay on his back with his throat cut.
     627 This second Rachel. (Cf. Matt. ii. 18.)
     629–30 The chief magistrate at once had every Jew put to death who
         knew anything about this murder.

He nolde no swich cursednesse observe.
'Yvele shal have that yvele wol deserve';
Therfore with wilde hors he dide hem drawe,
And after that he heng hem by the lawe.

635   Upon this beere ay lith this innocent   *all the time; lies*
    Biforn the chief auter, whil the masse laste;   *altar; lasted*
    And after that, the abbot with his covent   *monks*
    Han sped hem for to burien hym ful faste;   *hastened*
    And whan they hooly water on hym caste,
640 Yet spak this child, whan spreynd was hooly water,   *sprinkled*
    And song *O Alma redemptoris mater!*

    This abbot, which that was an hooly man,
    As monkes been—or elles oghte be—
    This yonge child to conjure he bigan,
645 And seyde, 'O deere child, I halse thee,   *beseech*
    In vertu of the hooly Trinitee,
    Tel me what is thy cause for to synge,
    Sith that thy throte is kut to my semynge?'

    'My throte is kut unto my nekke boon,'
650 Seyde this child, 'and, as by wey of kynde,
    I sholde have dyed, ye, longe tyme agon.   *yea; ago*
    But Jesu Crist, as ye in bookes fynde,
    Wil that his glorie laste and be in mynde,   *desires*
    And for the worship of his Mooder deere
655 Yet may I synge *O Alma* loude and cleere.

    'This welle of mercy, Cristes mooder sweete,
    I loved alwey, as after my konnynge;
    And whan that I my lyf sholde forlete,
    To me she cam, and bad me for to synge
660 This anthem verraily in my deyynge,   *as I lay dying*
    As ye han herd, and whan that I hadde songe,   *sung*
    Me thoughte she leyde a greyn upon my tonge.

631 He would not countenance such wickedness.
633 He had them torn apart by wild horses.
634 He hanged them as the law decreed.
643 A disapproving allusion to the monk of the *Shipman's Tale* or even,
    possibly, to the Monk on pilgrimage.
647 What it is that causes you to sing.
648 Since your throat is cut, it seems to me.
650 In the natural course of things.
657 To the best of my ability.
658 I had to give up my life.
662 It seemed to me she laid a grain upon my tongue.

'Wherfore I synge, and synge moot certeyn,   *must; certainly*
In honour of that blisful Mayden free,
665 Til fro my tonge of taken is the greyn;
And after that thus seyde she to me:
"My litel child, now wol I fecche thee,
Whan that the greyn is fro thy tonge ytake.
Be nat agast, I wol thee nat forsake." '

670   This hooly monk, this abbot, hym meene I,
His tonge out caughte, and took awey the greyn,   *drew out*
And he yaf up the goost ful softely.
And whan this abbot hadde this wonder seyn,   *seen*
His salte teeris trikled doun as reyn,
675 And gruf he fil al plat upon the grounde,
And stille he lay as he had ben ybounde.

The covent eek lay on the pavement   *also*
Wepynge, and herying Cristes mooder deere,   *praising*
And after that they ryse, and forth been went,   *went out*
680 And tooken awey this martir from his beere;   *took*
And in a tombe of marbul stones cleere   *bright*
Enclosen they his litel body sweete.
Ther he is now, God leve us for to meete!

O yonge Hugh of Lyncoln, slayn also
685 With cursed Jewes, as it is notable,   *by; well known*
For it is but a litel while ago,
Preye eek for us, we synful folk unstable,   *fickle*
That, of his mercy, God so merciable   *merciful*
On us his grete mercy mutliplie,
690 For reverence of his mooder Marie.   Amen.

HEERE IS ENDED THE PRIORESSES TALE

665 Till the grain is taken from my tongue.
675 And headlong he fell flat on the ground.
683 Where he is now, God grant we may meet him.
684 Hugh of Lincoln was a boy believed to have been murdered by the
Jews at Lincoln in 1255.

PROLOGUE TO SIR THOPAS

Bihoold the murye wordes of the Hoost to Chaucer

WHAN seyd was al this miracle, every man
As sobre was that wonder was to se,
Til that oure Hooste japen tho bigan,   *joke; then*
And thanne at erst he looked upon me,   *for the first time*
695 And seyde thus, 'What man artow?' quod he;
'Thou lookest as thou woldest fynde an hare,   *wanted to*
For evere upon the ground I se thee stare.

'Approche neer, and looke up murily.   *nearer; cheerfully*
Now war yow, sires, and lat this man have *mind yourselves*
    place!
700 He in the waast is shape as wel as I;   *waist; shaped*
This were a popet in an arm t'enbrace
For any womman, smal and fair of face.
He semeth elvyssh by his contenaunce,
For unto no wight dooth he daliaunce.

705 'Sey now somwhat, syn oother folk han sayd; *something*
Telle us a tale of myrthe, and that anon.'
'Hooste,' quod I, 'ne beth nat yvele apayd,   *displeased*
For oother tale certes kan I noon,
But of a rym I lerned longe agoon.'
710 'Ye, that is good,' quod he; 'now shul we heere *yea*
Som deyntee thyng, me thynketh by his cheere.'

692 Was so serious that it was marvellous to see.
695 What sort of man are you?
700 An allusion to Chaucer's plumpness, for the Host himself was a
    large man (see I. 753).
701 He'd make a cuddlesome pet.
703 *elvyssh*, elf-like (with reference to Chaucer's air of abstraction).
704 He doesn't chat with anyone.
708 For certainly I know no other tale.
711 Something choice, judging by his face.

SIR THOPAS

Heere bigynneth Chaucers Tale of Thopas

The First Fit. *canto*

LISTETH, lordes, in good entent,
And I wol telle verrayment   *truly*
    Of myrthe and of solas;
715 Al of a knyght was fair and gent
In bataille and in tourneyment,
    His name was sire Thopas.

Yborn he was in fer contree,
In Flaundres, al biyonde the see,
720   At Poperyng, in the place.
His fader was a man ful free,   *most noble*
And lord he was of that contree,
    As it was Goddes grace.

Sire Thopas wax a doghty swayn;
725 Whit was his face as payndemayn,
    His lippes rede as rose;
His rode is lyk scarlet in grayn,
And I yow telle in good certayn,   *for a fact*
    He hadde a semely nose.   *fine*

730   His heer, his berd was lyk saffroun,
That to his girdel raughte adoun;   *reached down*
    His shoon of cordewane.
Of Brugges were his hosen broun,   *from; brown hose*
His robe was of syklatoun,
735   That coste many a jane.

712 Listen, lords, with goodwill.
714 A pleasant and diverting tale.
715 (Who) was handsome and graceful.
717 *Thopas* is the same word as 'topaz' and so is 'an excellent title
    for such a gem of a knight' (Skeat). The whole poem, with its iog-
    trot metre and otiose diction, is Chaucer's burlesque of the poorer
    rhymed romances of his day.
720 At Poperinghe, in the manor-house.
724 Grew up a valiant young man.
725 *payndemayn*, a fine white bread.
727 His colouring is bright scarlet.
730 Like saffron, i.e. of an orange-red colour.
732 His shoes of Cordova leather.
734 *syklatoun*, a costly cloth.
735 *jane*, a Genoese coin of small value.

He koude hunte at wilde deer,   *after; animals*
And ride an haukyng for river
   With grey goshauk on honde;   *goshawk*
Therto he was a good archeer;
740 Of wrastlyng was ther noon his peer,   *equal*
   Ther any ram shal stonde.

Ful many a mayde, bright in bour,   *bower*
They moorne for hym paramour,   *passionately*
   Whan hem were bet to slepe;
745 But he was chaast and no lechour,   *lecher*
And sweete as is the brembul flour   *bramble*
   That bereth the rede hepe.   *red hip*

And so bifel upon a day,
For sothe, as I yow telle may,   *in truth*
750   Sire Thopas wolde out ride.
He worth upon his steede gray,   *gets on*
And in his hand a launcegay,   *lance*
   A long swerd by his side.

He priketh thurgh a fair forest,   *rides*
755 Therinne is many a wilde best,
   Ye, bothe bukke and hare;   *buck*
And as he priketh north and est,
I telle it yow, hym hadde almest
   Bitid a sory care.

760   Ther spryngen herbes grete and smale,   *grow*
The lycorys and the cetewale,   *liquorice; ginger*
   And many a clowe-gylofre;   *clove*
And notemuge to putte in ale,   *nutmeg*
Wheither it be moyste or stale,   *fresh*
765   Or for to leye in cofre.

The briddes synge, it is no nay,
The sparhauk and the papejay,   *sparrowhawk; popinjay*
   That joye it was to heere;
The thrustelcok made eek hir lay,
770 The wodedowve upon the spray   *wood-pigeon*
   She sang ful loude and cleere.

737 And ride a-hawking for waterfowl.
741 Where any ram was set up as the prize.   (See I. 548.)
744 When it would do them more good to sleep.
750 *out ride*, go on an expedition.   (Cf. I. 45.)
758-9 A grievous mishap nearly befell him.
765 To put in a chest (for the sake of the scent).
769 The thrush also made its lay.

Sire Thopas fil in love-longynge,
Al whan he herde the thrustel synge,   *just*
And pryked as he were wood.
775 His faire steede in his prikynge   *its hard riding*
So swatte that men myghte him wrynge;
His sydes were al blood.

Sire Thopas eek so wery was
For prikyng on the softe gras,
780 So fiers was his corage,
That doun he leyde him in that plas   *lay*
To make his steede som solas,   *relief*
And yaf hym good forage.   *gave; fodder*

'O seinte Marie, *benedicite!*
785 What eyleth this love at me
To bynde me so soore?
Me dremed al this nyght, pardee,   *I dreamt; indeed*
An elf-queene shal my lemman be   *sweetheart*
And slepe under my goore.   *robe*

790 'An elf-queene wol I love, ywis,   *truly*
For in this world no womman is
Worthy to be my make   *mate*
     In towne;
Alle othere wommen I forsake,
795 And to an elf-queene I me take
     By dale and eek by downe!'   *hill*

Into his sadel he clamb anon,   *climbed forthwith*
And priketh over stile and stoon   *stone*
An elf-queene for t'espye,   *look for*
800 Til he so longe hath riden and goon
That he foond, in a pryve woon,
     The contree of Fairye   *fairyland*
        So wilde;
For in that contree was ther noon
805 That to him durste ride or goon,   *walk*
     Neither wyf ne childe;

Til that ther cam a greet geaunt,
His name was sire Olifaunt,   *Elephant*
     A perilous man of dede.   *in deed*

772 Fell victim to a lover's longing.
774 And rode like mad.
776 Sweated so much that you could have wrung him out.
784 *benedicite*, bless us.
785 What has love got against me that it so painfully enthrals me?
793 *In towne*, i.e. among ordinary mortals.
801 In a secret dwelling-place.

810 He seyde, 'Child, by Termagaunt!
    But if thou prike out of myn haunt,   *unless; abode*
      Anon I sle thy steede   *will slay*
          With mace.
    Heere is the queene of Fayerye,
815 With harpe and pipe and symphonye,
      Dwellynge in this place.'

    The child seyde, 'Also moote I thee,
    Tomorwe wol I meete with thee,
      Whan I have myn armoure;
820   And yet I hope, *par ma fay*,   *faith*
    That thou shalt with this launcegay
      Abyen it ful sowre.
          Thy mawe   *belly*
    Shal I percen, if I may,
825 Er it be fully pryme of day,
      For heere thow shalt be slawe.'   *slain*

    Sire Thopas drow abak ful faste;   *drew*
    This geant at hym stones caste
      Out of a fel staf-slynge.
830 But faire escapeth child Thopas,
    And al it was thurgh Goddes gras,   *grace*
      And thurgh his fair berynge.   *noble bearing*

    Yet listeth, lordes, to my tale   *listen*
    Murier than the nightyngale,
835   For now I wol yow rowne   *whisper*
    How sir Thopas, with sydes smale,   *slender waist*
    Prikyng over hill and dale,
      Is comen agayn to towne.

    His myrie men comanded he
840 To make hym bothe game and glee,   *entertainment*
      For nedes moste he fighte
    With a geaunt with hevedes three,   *heads*
    For paramour and jolitee
      Of oon that shoon ful brighte.

    810 *Child*, a general term for a young knight or squire in medieval
        English romances; *Termagaunt*, an imaginary deity believed by
        medieval Christians to be a god of the Saracens.
    815 *symphonye*, a kind of tabor.
    817 As I hope to prosper.
    822 Pay dearly for it.
    825 *fully pryme*, 9 a.m.
    829 *fel staf-slynge*, deadly sling attached to a staff.
    834 That's pleasanter to listen to than the nightingale.
    843-4 For the love and pleasure of one who was radiantly beautiful.

845   'Do come,' he seyde, 'my mynstrales,   *summon*
      And geestours for to tellen tales,   *story-tellers*
        Anon in myn armynge,
      Of romances that been roiales,
      Of popes and of cardinales,
850   And eek of love-likynge.'   *loving*

      They fette hym first the sweete wyn,   *fetched*
      And mede eek in a mazelyn,
        And roial spicerye   *mixture of spices*
      Of gyngebreed that was ful fyn,
855 And lycorys, and eek comyn,   *cummin*
        With sugre that is trye.   *excellent*

      He dide next his white leere,
      Of clooth of lake fyn and cleere,
        A breech and eek a sherte;   *breeches*
860 And next his sherte an aketoun,
      And over that an haubergeoun   *coat of mail*
        For percynge of his herte;

      And over that a fyn hawberk,
      Was al ywroght of Jewes werk,
865   Ful strong it was of plate;
      And over that his cote-armour
      As whit as is a lilye flour,
        In which he wol debate.   *fight*

      His sheeld was al of gold so reed,   *red*
870 And therinne was a bores heed,   *boar's*
        A charbocle bisyde;
      And there he swoor on ale and breed
      How that the geaunt shal be deed,
        Bityde what bityde!   *come what may*

875   His jambeaux were of quyrboilly,
      His swerdes shethe of yvory,
        His helm of latoun bright;   *brass*

847 While I am being armed.
848 Romances about royalty.
852 Also mead in a bowl.
857–8 He put next to his white flesh a fine white linen cloth.
860 *aketoun*, a wadded jacket worn under the coat of mail.
862 To prevent his heart from being pierced.
863 *hawberk*, breastplate and backplate.
864 Of Jewish workmanship.
866 *cote-armour*. See I. 1016.
871 *charbocle*, carbuncle (i.e. the precious stone).
875 His leg-pieces were of hardened leather.

His sadel was of rewel boon,   *ivory*
His brydel as the sonne shoon,
880   Or as the moone light.

His spere was of fyn ciprees,   *cypress-wood*
That bodeth werre, and nothyng pees,
    The heed ful sharpe ygrounde;
His steede was al dappull gray,
885 It gooth an ambil in the way
        Ful softely and rounde
            In londe.
        Loo, lordes myne, heere is a fit!
    If ye wol any moore of it,
890   To telle it wol I fonde.   *try*

The Second Fit.

Now holde youre mouth, *par charitee,*   *for charity's sake*
Bothe knyght and lady free,   *noble*
    And herkneth to my spelle;   *story*
Of bataille and of chivalry,
895 And of ladyes love-drury   *passionate love*
    Anon I wol yow telle.

Men speken of romances of prys,   *great value*
Of Horn child and of Ypotys,
    Of Beves and sir Gy,
900 Of sir Lybeux and Pleyndamour,—
But sir Thopas, he bereth the flour
    Of roial chivalry!

His goode steede al be bistrood,
And forth upon his wey he glood   *glided*
905   As sparcle out of the bronde;
Upon his creest he bar a tour,
And therinne stiked a lilie flour,—   *stuck*
    God shilde his cors fro shonde!   *body; shame*

And for he was a knyght auntrous,   *adventurous*
910 He nolde slepen in noon hous,
    But liggen in his hoode;   *lie*

882–3 Boding war, not peace, the head all sharply ground.
885–6 It ambles along at a gentle, easy pace.
887 *In londe,* across country. (This is a tag which is commonly used
    with little meaning in the popular poetry of Chaucer's day.)
888 Here is one canto finished.
898 ff. These are the names of medieval romances.
905 Like a spark from a firebrand.
906 i.e. the crest of his helm was as high as a tower.

His brighte helm was his wonger,   *pillow*
And by hym baiteth his dextrer
    Of herbes fyne and goode.

915 Hymself drank water of the well,
    As dide the knyght sire Percyvell
        So worly under wede,
    Til on a day—   *one day*

Heere the Hoost stynteth Chaucer of his Tale of Thopas.

    'Namoore of this, for Goddes dignitee,'
920 Quod oure Hooste, 'for thou makest me
    So wery of thy verray lewednesse   *utter ignorance*
    That, also wisly God my soule blesse,
    Myne eres aken of thy drasty speche.   *ache; filthy*
    Now swich a rym the devel I biteche!   *consign to*
925 This may wel be rym dogerel,' quod he.
        'Why so?' quod I, 'why wiltow lette me   *hinder*
    Moore of my tale than another man,
    Syn that it is the beste rym I kan?'   *know*
        'By God,' quod he, 'for pleynly, at a word,   *because*
930 Thy drasty rymyng is nat worth a toord!
    Thou doost noght elles but despendest tyme.   *waste*
    Sire, at o word, thou shalt no lenger ryme.   *longer*
    Lat se wher thou kanst tellen aught in geeste,
    Or telle in prose somwhat, at the leeste,   *something*
935 In which ther be som murthe or som doctryne.'   *instruction*
        'Gladly,' quod I, 'by Goddes sweete pyne!   *passion*
    I wol yow telle a litel thyng in prose
    That oghte liken yow, as I suppose,   *please*
    Or elles, certes, ye been to daungerous.   *difficult to please*
940 It is a moral tale vertuous,
    Al be it told somtyme in sondry wyse
    Of sondry folk, as I shal yow devyse.
        As thus: ye woot that every Evaungelist,
    That telleth us the peyne of Jhesu Crist,
945 Ne seth nat alle thyng as his felawe dooth;   *everything*
    But nathelees hir sentence is al sooth,
    And alle acorden as in hire sentence,
    Al be ther in hir tellyng difference.

913 And his war-horse grazes beside him.
917 So worthy in his armour (a common alliterative phrase).
933 Let's see whether you can tell a story in alliterative verse (i.e. as
    distinct from one in rhymed verse or prose). Cf. X. 43.
941–2 Although it is sometimes told in different ways by different people,
    as I shall explain to you.
946–7 But nevertheless the essential meaning they express is quite true,
    and they all agree as far as their meaning is concerned.

For somme of hem seyn moore, and somme seyn lesse,
950 Whan they his pitous passioun expresse—   *pitiful*
I meene of Mark, Mathew, Luc, and John—   *I refer to*
But doutelees hir sentence is al oon.   *one and the same*
Therfore, lordynges alle, I yow biseche,
If that yow thynke I varie as in my speche,
955 As thus, though that I telle somwhat moore
Of proverbes than ye han herd bifoore
Comprehended in this litel tretys heere,
To enforce with th'effect of my mateere,
And though I nat the same wordes seye
960 As ye han herd, yet to yow alle I preye
Blameth me nat; for, as in my sentence,   *meaning*
Shul ye nowher fynden difference
Fro the sentence of this tretys lyte
After the which this murye tale I write.   *pleasant*
965 And therfore herkneth what that I shal seye,
And lat me tellen al my tale, I preye.'

EXPLICIT

958 To reinforce my theme and make it more effective.
963 'This little treatise' is the French work from which Chaucer
translated his *Tale of Melibee*.

THE TALE OF MELIBEE

HEERE BIGYNNETH CHAUCERS TALE OF MELIBEE

A YONG man called Melibeus, myghty and riche, bigat upon
his wyf, that called was Prudence, a doghter which that called
was Sophie.

970   Upon a day bifel that he for his desport [*pleasure*] is went
into the feeldes hym to pleye. His wyf and eek his doghter
hath he left inwith [*within*] his hous, of which the dores weren
faste yshette [*shut*]. Thre of his olde foes han it espyed, and
setten laddres to the walles of his hous, and by wyndowes been
entred, and betten [*beat*] his wyf, and wounded his doghter
with fyve mortal woundes in fyve sondry places,—this is to
seyn, in hir feet, in hire handes, in hir erys [*ears*], in hir nose,
and in hire mouth,—and leften hire for deed, and wenten awey.

Whan Melibeus retourned was in to his hous, and saugh
980 [*saw*] al this meschief [*evil*], he, lyk a mad man, rentynge his
clothes, gan to wepe and crie.

Prudence, his wyf, as ferforth [*far*] as she dorste [*dared*],
bisoghte hym of his wepyng for to stynte [*stop*]; but nat forthy
he gan to crie and wepen evere lenger the moore.

This noble wyf Prudence remembred hire upon the sentence
[*saying*] of Ovide, in his book that cleped [*called*] is the Remedie
of Love, where as he seith: 'He is a fool that destourbeth the
mooder [*mother*] to wepen in the deeth of hire child, til she
have wept hir fille as for a certein tyme; and thanne shal man
990 doon his diligence [*utmost*] with amyable wordes hire to
reconforte [*comfort*], and preyen hire of hir wepyng for to
stynte.' For which resoun this noble wyf Prudence suffred
hir housbonde for to wepe and crie as for a certein space; and
whan she saugh hir tyme, she seyde hym in this wise: 'Allas,
my lord,' quod she, 'why make ye youreself for to be lyk a
fool? For sothe it aperteneth [*befits*] nat to a wys man to
maken swich a sorwe. Youre doghter, with the grace of God,
shal warisshe [*recover*] and escape. And, al were it so that
[*even though*] she right now were deed, ye ne oughte nat, as for
1000 hir deeth, youreself to destroye. Senek [*Seneca*] seith: "The

---

973 *Thre of his olde foes*, i.e. the world, the flesh, and the devil; see
1922 below.
983–4 But nevertheless he began to cry and weep all the more.

wise man shal nat take to greet disconfort [*grief*] for the deeth of his children; but, certes, he sholde suffren it in pacience as wel as he abideth the deeth of his owene propre persone.'''

This Melibeus answerde anon, and seyde, 'What man,' quod he, 'sholde of his wepyng stente [*stop*] that hath so greet a cause for to wepe? Jhesu Crist, oure Lord, hymself wepte for the deeth of Lazarus hys freend.'

Prudence answerde: 'Certes, wel I woot attempree wepyng is no thyng deffended to hym that sorweful is, amonges folk 1010 in sorwe, but it is rather graunted hym to wepe. The Apostle Paul unto the Romayns writeth, "Man shal rejoyse with hem that maken joye, and wepen with swich folk as wepen." But though attempree wepyng be ygraunted, outrageous [*excessive*] wepyng certes [*certainly*] is deffended. Mesure of [*moderation in*] wepyng sholde be considered, after the loore that techeth us Senek: "Whan that thy frend is deed," quod he, "lat nat thyne eyen to [*too*] moyste been of teeris, ne to muche drye; although the teeris come to thyne eyen, lat hem nat falle; and whan thou hast forgoon [*lost*] thy freend, 1020 do diligence [*your utmost*] to gete another freend; and this is moore wysdom than for to wepe for thy freend which that thou hast lorn [*lost*], for therinne is no boote [*use*]." And therfore, if ye governe yow by sapience [*wisdom*], put awey sorwe out of youre herte. Remembre yow that Jhesus Syrak [*son of Sirach*] seith, "A man that is joyous and glad in herte, it hym conserveth florissynge [*keeps flourishing*] in his age; but soothly [*truly*] sorweful herte maketh his bones drye." He seith eek thus, that sorwe in herte sleeth [*slays*] ful many a man. Salomon seith that right as motthes [*moths*] in the 1030 shepes [*sheep's*] flees anoyeth [*does harm*] to the clothes, and the smale wormes to the tree, right so anoyeth sorwe to the herte. Wherfore us oghte [*we ought*], as wel in the deeth of oure children as in the los of oure othere goodes temporels [*temporal*], have pacience. Remembre yow upon the pacient Job. Whan he hadde lost his children and his temporeel substance, and in his body endured and receyved ful many a grevous tribulacion, yet seyde he thus: "Oure Lord hath yeve [*given*] it me; oure Lord hath biraft it [*taken it from*] me; right as oure Lord hath wold [*willed*], right so it is doon; 1040 blessed be the name of oure Lord!"''

To thise forseide thynges answerde Melibeus unto his wyf Prudence: 'Alle thy wordes,' quod he, 'been sothe [*true*], and therto [*also*] profitable; but trewely myn herte is troubled with this sorwe so grevously that I noot [*know not*] what to doone [*do*].

'Lat calle,' quod Prudence, 'thy trewe freendes alle, and

1008–9 I well know that moderate weeping is not at all forbidden.
1015–16 According to the doctrine that Seneca teaches us.

thy lynage [kinsmen] whiche that been wise. Telleth youre
cas, and herkneth what they seye in conseillyng, and yow
governe after hire sentence. Salomon seith, "Werk [do] alle
1050 thy thynges by conseil, and thou shalt never repente."'

Thanne, by the conseil of his wyf Prudence, this Melibeus
leet callen [summoned] a greet congregacion of folk; as surgiens, phisiciens, olde folk and yonge, and somme of his olde
enemys reconsiled [brought back] as by hir semblaunt [appar-
ently] to his love and into his grace; and therwithal ther
coomen [came] somme of his neighebores that diden hym
reverence moore for drede [fear] than for love, as it happeth
[happens] ofte. Ther coomen also ful many subtille [cunning]
flatereres, and wise advocatz lerned in the lawe.
1060 And whan this folk togidre assembled weren, this Melibeus
in sorweful wise shewed hem his cas. And by the manere
of his speche it semed that in herte he baar a crueel ire [anger],
redy to doon vengeaunce upon his foes, and sodeynly [eagerly]
desired that the werre [war] sholde bigynne; but nathelees
[nevertheless], yet axed [asked] he hire conseil upon this
matiere. A surgien, by licence [permission] and assent of
swiche as weren wise, up roos [rose], and to Melibeus seyde
as ye may heere:

'Sire,' quod he, 'as to us surgiens aperteneth that we do to
1070 every wight the beste that we kan, where as we been withholde,
and to oure pacientz that we do no damage; wherfore it
happeth many tyme and ofte that whan twey [two] men han
everich [have each] wounded oother, oon same [one and the
same] surgien heeleth hem bothe; wherfore unto oure art it
is nat pertinent to norice werre ne parties to supporte. But
certes, as to the warisshynge [healing] of youre doghter, al be
it so that [although] she perilously be wounded, we shullen do
so ententif bisynesse fro day to nyght that with the grace of
God she shal be hool [safe] and sound as soone as is possible.'
1080 Almoost right in the same wise [manner] the phisiciens
answerden, save that they seyden a fewe woordes moore: that
right as maladies been cured by hir contraries [opposites],
right so shul men warisshe werre by vengeaunce.

His neighebores ful of envye, his feyned freendes that
semeden reconsiled, and his flatereres maden semblant [pre-
tence] of wepyng, and empeireden and agreggeden muchel of
this matiere in preisynge greetly Melibee of [for his] myght,

1047-9 Explain your situation, and listen to what advice they have to
  give you, and be guided by their opinion.
1069-70 As for us surgeons it is right that we do the best we can for every
  person, where we are engaged (by him).
1074-5 It is not in keeping with our profession to foment war or support
  opposing factions.
1077-8 We shall do such devoted work from morning till night.
1083 Just so shall men put a stop to war by taking vengeance.
1086-7 Made the matter worse and much aggravated it.

of power, of richesse [*wealth*], and of freendes, despisynge the power of his adversaries, and seiden outrely [*decidedly*] that
1090 he anon sholde wreken hym [*avenge himself*] on his foes, and bigynne werre.

Up roos thanne an advocat that was wys, by leve and by conseil of othere that were wise, and seide: 'Lordynges, the nede [*business*] for which we been assembled in this place is a ful hevy [*grave*] thyng and an heigh [*important*] matiere, by cause of the wrong and of the wikkednesse that hath be [*been*] doon, and eek by resoun of the grete damages that in tyme comynge been possible to fallen [*may possibly happen*] for this same cause, and eek by resoun of the grete richesse and power of
1100 the parties bothe; for the whiche resouns it were a ful greet peril to erren [*err*] in this matiere. Wherfore, Melibeus, this is oure sentence [*opinion*]: we conseille yow aboven alle thyng that right anon thou do thy diligence in kepynge of thy propre persone in swich a wise that thou ne wante noon espie ne wacche, thy persone for to save. And after that, we conseille that in thyn hous thou sette sufficeant garnisoun [*garrison*] so that they may as wel thy body as thyn hous defende. But certes, for to moeve [*begin*] werre, ne sodeynly for to doon vengeaunce, we may nat demen [*judge*] in so litel
1110 tyme that it were [*would be*] profitable. Wherfore we axen leyser [*leisure*] and espace [*opportunity*] to have deliberacion in this cas to deme. For the commune proverbe seith thus: "He that soone deemeth, soone shal repente." And eek men seyn [*say*] that thilke juge is wys that soone understondeth a matiere and juggeth by [*at*] leyser; for, al be it so that alle tariyng be anoyful, algates it is nat to repreve in yevynge of juggement ne in vengeance takyng, whan it is sufficeant and resonable. And that shewed oure Lord Jhesu Crist by ensample [*parable*]; for whan that the womman that was taken in avowtrie
1120 [*adultery*] was broght in his presence to knowen what sholde be doon with hire persone, al be it so that he wiste [*knew*] wel hymself what that he wolde answere, yet ne wolde he nat answere sodeynly, but he wolde have deliberacion, and in the ground he wroot twies [*wrote twice*]. And by thise causes we axen [*ask for*] deliberacioun, and we shal thanne, by the grace of God, conseille thee thyng that shal be profitable.

Up stirten [*jumped*] thanne the yonge folk atones, and the mooste partie of that compaignye han scorned this olde wise
1130 man, and bigonnen to make noyse, and seyden that right so as [*just as*], whil that iren [*iron*] is hoot [*hot*], men sholden

---

1103-5 You should immediately do your utmost to defend yourself in such a way that you are not without spy or sentinel to keep you safe.
1115-16 Although all delay is annoying, nevertheless it is not to be scorned.

smyte, right so men sholde wreken hir wronges whil
that they been fresshe and newe; and with loud voys they
criden 'Werre! werre!'

Up roos tho oon of thise olde wise, and with his hand made
contenaunce [*sign*] that men sholde holden hem stille [*keep
quiet*] and yeven hym audience. 'Lordynges,' quod he, 'ther
is ful many a man that crieth "Werre! werre!" that woot ful
litel what werre amounteth [*amounts to*]. Werre at his [*its*]
1140 bigynnyng hath so greet an entryng [*entry*] and so large, that
every wight may entre whan hym liketh, and lightly [*easily*]
fynde werre; but certes, what ende that shal therof bifalle, it
is nat light [*easy*] to knowe. For soothly [*truly*], whan that
werre is ones bigonne, ther is ful many a child unborn of his
mooder that shal sterve yong [*die young*] by cause of thilke
werre, or elles lyve in sorwe and dye in wrecchednesse. And
therfore, er that any werre bigynne, men moste have greet
conseil [*consultation*] and greet deliberacion.' And whan this
olde man wende [*thought*] to enforcen his tale by resons
1150 [*arguments*], wel ny alle atones bigonne they to rise for to
breken his tale, and beden hym ful ofte his wordes for to
abregge. For soothly, he that precheth to hem that listen
[*wish*] nat heeren his wordes, his sermon hem anoieth [*annoys*]
For Jhesus Syrak seith that 'musik in wepynge [*mourning*] is
a noyous [*troublesome*] thyng'; this is to seyn: as muche
availleth [*it is as much use*] to speken bifore folk to which
[*whom*] his speche anoyeth, as it is to synge biforn hym that
wepeth. And whan this wise man saugh that hym wanted
audience, al shamefast [*shamefaced*] he sette hym doun agayn.
1160 For Salomon seith: 'Ther as thou ne mayst have noon
audience, enforce thee nat to speke.' 'I see wel,' quod this
wise man, 'that the commune proverbe is sooth [*true*], that
"good conseil [*advice*] wanteth [*is wanting*] whan it is moost
nede."'

Yet hadde this Melibeus in his conseil [*council*] many
folk that prively [*privately*] in his eere conseilled hym certeyn
thyng, and conseilled hym the contrarie in general [*public*]
audience.

When Melibeus hadde herd that the gretteste partie of his
1170 conseil weren accorded [*agreed*] that he sholde maken werre,
anoon he consented to hir conseillyng, and fully affermed hire
sentence [*opinion*]. Thanne dame Prudence, whan that she
saugh how that hir housbonde shoop hym [*prepared*] for to
wreken hym [*avenge himself*] on his foes, and to bigynne
werre, she in ful humble wise, whan she saugh [*saw*] hir tyme,
seide to hym thise wordes: 'My lord,' quod she, 'I yow biseche

1150-2 Nearly all of them at once got up to interrupt what he was saying,
and repeatedly told him to cut short his words.
1160-1 Where you can't get a hearing, don't insist on speaking.

as hertely [*earnestly*] as I dar and kan, ne haste yow nat to faste, and for alle gerdons, as yeveth me audience. For Piers Alfonce [*Petrus Alfonsi*] seith, "Whoso that dooth to
1180 thee oother [*either*] good or harm, haste thee nat to quiten [*repay*] it; for in this wise thy freend wole abyde [*remain*], and thyn enemy shal the lenger lyve in drede [*fear*]." The proverbe seith, "He hasteth wel that wisely kan abyde," and in wikked haste is no profit.'

This Melibee answerde unto his wyf Prudence: 'I purpose nat,' quod he, 'to werke by thy conseil [*act on your advice*], for many causes and resouns. For certes, every wight [*one*] wolde holde me thanne a fool; this is to seyn [*say*], if I, for thy conseillyng, wolde chaungen thynges that been ordeyned
1190 and affermed by so manye wyse [*wise men*]. Secoundely, I seye that alle wommen been wikke [*wicked*], and noon good of hem alle. For "of a thousand men," seith Salomon, "I foond o good man, but certes, of alle wommen, good womman foond I nevere." And also, certes, if I governed me by thy conseil, it sholde seme that I hadde yeve [*given*] to thee over me the maistrie [*mastery*]; and God forbede that it so weere [*should be so*]! For Jhesus Syrak seith that "if the wyf have maistrie, she is contrarious [*contrary*] to hir housbonde." And Salomon seith: "Nevere in thy lyf to thy wyf, ne to thy
1200 child, ne to thy freend, ne yeve no power over thyself; for bettre it were that thy children aske of thy persone [*of you*] thynges that hem nedeth [*they need*], than thou see thyself in the handes of thy children." And also if I wolde werke by thy conseillyng, certes, my conseil moste som tyme be secree, til it were tyme that it moste be knowe, and this ne may noght be. [*Car il est escript, la genglerie des femmes ne puet riens celler fors ce qu'elle ne scet. Apres, le philosophre dit, en mauvais conseil les femmes vainquent les hommes: et par ces raisons je ne dois point user de ton conseil.*]

1210 Whanne dame Prudence, ful debonairly [*gently*] and with greet pacience, hadde herd al that hir housbonde liked for to seye, thanne axed she of hym licence [*permission*] for to speke, and seyde in this wise: 'My lord,' quod she, 'as to youre firste resoun, certes it may lightly [*easily*] been answered. For I seye that it is no folie to chaunge conseil [*purpose*] whan the

---

1177-8 Don't go too fast, and for all my services (to you) please listen to me.

1183 He makes good speed who can wisely wait.

1203-6 If I were to act on your advice, it is certain that my purpose, which should be kept secret until the time comes to make it known, could not remain hidden.

1206-9 For it is written that the babbling of women can hide only things they do not know. Furthermore, the philosopher says, women outdo men at giving bad advice; and for these reasons I ought not to follow your advice.

thyng is chaunged, or elles whan the thyng semeth ootherweyes [*otherwise*] than it was biforn. And mooreover, I seye
that though ye han sworn and bihight [*promised*] to perfourne
youre emprise [*undertaking*], and nathelees ye weyve [*omit*] to
1220 perfourne thilke same emprise by juste cause, men sholde nat
seyn therfore that ye were a liere [*liar*] ne forsworn. For the
book seith that "the wise man maketh no lesyng whan he
turneth his corage to the bettre." And al be it so that youre
emprise be establissed and ordeyned by greet multitude of folk,
yet thar [*need*] ye nat accomplice [*carry out*] thilke ordinaunce,
but [*unless*] yow like. For the trouthe of thynges and the
profit been rather founden in fewe folk that been wise and
ful of resoun, than by greet multitude of folk ther every man
crieth and clatereth what that hym liketh. Soothly swich
1230 multitude is nat honest [*worthy of respect*]. And as to the
seconde resoun, where as ye seyn that alle wommen been
wikke; save [*saving*] youre grace, certes ye despisen alle
wommen in this wyse, and "he that al despiseth, al displeseth,"
as seith the book. And Senec seith that "whoso wole have
sapience shal no man dispreyse [*disparage*], but he shal gladly
techen the science [*knowledge*] that he kan withouten presumpcion or pride; and swiche thynges as he noght ne kan [*does
not know*], he shal nat been ashamed to lerne hem, and
enquere of lasse [*lesser*] folk than hymself." And, sire, that
1240 ther hath been many a good womman, may lightly [*easily*] be
preved. For certes, sire, oure Lord Jhesu Crist wolde nevere
have descended to be born of a womman, if alle wommen
hadden ben wikke. And after that, for the grete bountee
[*goodness*] that is in wommen, oure Lord Jhesu Crist, whan
he was risen fro deeth to lyve, appeered rather [*sooner*] to a
womman than to his Apostles. And though that Salomon
seith that he ne foond nevere womman good, it folweth nat
therfore that alle wommen ben wikke. For though that he
ne foond no good womman, certes, many another man hath
1250 founden many a womman ful good and trewe. Or elles,
per aventure [*perhaps*], the entente [*meaning*] of Salomon
was this, that, as in sovereyn [*supreme*] bountee, he foond no
womman; this is to seyn, that ther is no wight [*creature*] that
hath sovereyn bountee save God allone, as he hymself re-
cordeth in hys Evaungelie [*gospel*]. For ther nys no creature
so good that hym ne wanteth somwhat of the perfeccioun of
God, that is his makere. Youre thridde [*third*] reson is this:
ye seyn that if ye governe yow [*yourself*] by my conseil, it
sholde seme that ye hadde yeve [*given*] me the maistrie and the
1260 lordshipe over youre persone. Sire, save youre grace, it is
nat so. For if it so were that no man sholde be conseilled

1222-3 The wise man tells no lie when he changes his mind.
1228-9 Where every man jabbers and cries out whatever he likes.

but [*except*] oonly of [*by*] hem that hadden lordshipe and
maistrie of his persone, men wolden nat be conseilled so ofte.
For soothly thilke man that asketh conseil of [*advice about*]
a purpos, yet hath he free choys wheither he wole werke by
[*act on*] that conseil or noon [*not*].   And as to youre fourthe
resoun, ther ye seyn that the janglerie of wommen kan hyde
thynges that they wot noght, as who seith that a womman kan
nat hyde that she woot; sire, thise wordes been understonde
1270 of [*apply to*] wommen that been jangleresses [*babblers*] and
wikked; of whiche wommen men seyn that thre thynges dryven
a man out of his hous,—that is to seyn [*say*], smoke, droppyng
of reyn [*rain*], and wikked wyves; and of swiche wommen
seith Salomon that "it were bettre dwelle in desert than with
a womman that is riotous [*wanton*]."   And sire, by youre leve,
that am nat I; for ye han ful ofte assayed my grete silence and
my grete pacience, and eek how wel that I kan hyde, and hele
[*conceal*] thynges that men oghte secreely to hyde.   And
soothly, as to youre fifthe resoun, where as ye seyn that in
1280 wikked conseil wommen venquisshe men, God woot, thilke
resoun stant heere in no stede.   For understoond now, ye
asken conseil to do wikkednesse; and if ye wole werken
wikkednesse [*do evil*], and youre wif restreyneth thilke wikked
purpos, and overcometh yow by reson and by good conseil,
certes youre wyf oghte rather to be preised than yblamed.
Thus sholde ye understonde the philosophre that seith, "In
wikked conseil wommen venquisshen hir housbondes."   And
ther as [*whereas*] ye blamen alle wommen and hir resouns, I
shal shewe yow by manye ensamples that many a womman
1290 hath ben ful good, and yet been [*still are*], and hir conseils ful
hoolsome and profitable.   Eek som men han seyd that the
conseillynge of wommen is outher to deere [*either too dear*], or
elles to litel of pris [*value*].   But al be it so that ful many a
womman is badde, and hir conseil vile and noght worth, yet
han men founde ful many a good womman, and ful discret
and wis in conseillynge.   Loo, Jacob, by good conseil of his
mooder Rebekka, wan [*won*] the benysoun [*blessing*] of Ysaak
his fader, and the lordshipe over alle his bretheren.   Judith,
by hire good conseil, delivered the citee of Bethulie, in which
1300 she dwelled, out of the handes of Olofernus [*Holofernes*], that
hadde it biseged and wolde have al destroyed it.   Abygail
delivered Nabal hir housbonde fro David the kyng, that wolde
have slayn hym, and apaysed [*appeased*] the ire [*anger*] of the
kyng by hir wit [*wisdom*] and by hir good conseillyng.   Hester
[*Esther*], by hir good conseil, enhaunced [*raised up*] greetly the
peple of God in the regne of Assuerus the kyng.   And the

1267–9 The babbling of women can hide only things they do not know,
    which is as good as saying that a woman cannot hide what she does
    know.
1280–1 God knows, that particular reason counts for nothing in this case.

same bountee [*excellence*] in good conseillyng of many a good womman may men telle. And mooreover, whan oure Lord hadde creat [*created*] Adam, oure forme fader [*first father*], he
1310 seyde in this wise: "It is nat good to been a man alloone; make we to hym an helpe [*helper*] semblable [*similar*] to hymself." Heere may ye se that if that wommen were nat goode, and hir conseils goode and profitable, oure Lord God of hevene wolde nevere han wroght hem, ne called hem help of man, but rather confusioun [*ruin*] of man. And ther seyde oones a clerk in two vers [*verses*], "What is bettre than gold? Jaspre. What is bettre than jaspre? Wisedoom. And what is better than wisedoom? Womman. And what is bettre than a good womman? Nothyng." And, sire, by manye
1320 of othre resons may ye seen that manye wommen been goode, and hir conseils goode and profitable. And therfore, sire, if ye wol triste [*trust*] to my conseil, I shal restoore yow youre doghter hool [*safe*] and sound. And eek I wol do to yow [*for you*] so muche that ye shul have honour in this cause [*matter*].'

When Melibee hadde herd the wordes of his wyf Prudence, he seyde thus: 'I se wel that the word of Salomon is sooth [*true*]. He seith that "wordes that been spoken discreetly by ordinaunce [*in order*] been honycombes, for they yeven
1330 swetnesse to the soule and hoolsomnesse [*health*] to the body." And, wyf, by cause of thy sweete wordes, and eek for I have assayed [*tried*] and preved thy grete sapience and thy grete trouthe, I wol governe me by thy conseil in alle thyng.'

'Now, sire,' quod dame Prudence, 'and syn ye vouche sauf to been governed by my conseil, I wol enforme yow how ye shul governe yourself in chesynge [*choosing*] of youre conseillours. Ye shul first in alle youre werkes mekely biseken [*beseech*] to the heighe [*high*] God that he wol be youre conseillour; and shapeth yow to swich entente that he yeve yow
1340 conseil and confort, as taughte Thobie [*Tobit*] his sone: "At alle tymes thou shalt blesse God, and praye hym to dresse [*direct*] thy weyes, and looke that alle thy conseils been in hym for everemoore." Seint Jame [*James*] eek seith: "If any of yow have nede of sapience [*wisdom*], axe [*ask*] it of God." And afterward thanne shul ye taken conseil in youreself, and examyne wel youre thoghtes of swich thyng as yow thynketh that is best for youre profit. And thanne shul ye dryve fro youre herte thre thynges that been contrariouse [*contrary*] to good conseil; that is to seyn, ire, coveitise
1350 [*covetousness*], and hastifnesse [*rashness*].

1310 It is not good for a man to be alone.
1339 And prepare yourself to the end that He may give you.
1342-3 See that all your counsels are sought from Him.
1346-7 Your thoughts about the thing that seems most profitable to you.

First, he that axeth conseil of hymself, certes he moste been
withouten ire, for manye causes.   The first is this: he that
hath greet ire and wratthe in hymself, he weneth [*thinks*]
alwey that he may do thyng that he may nat do.   And
secoundely, he that is irous [*angry*] and wrooth, he ne may nat
wel deme [*judge*]; and he that may nat wel deme, may nat wel
conseille.   The thridde is this, that he that is irous and wrooth,
as seith Senec [*Seneca*], ne may nat speke but blameful thynges,
and with his viciouse wordes he stireth [*stirs up*] oother folk to
1360 angre and to ire.   And eek, sire, ye moste dryve coveitise out
of youre herte.   For the Apostle seith that coveitise is roote
of alle harmes.   And trust wel that a coveitous man ne kan
noght deme ne thynke, but oonly to fulfille the ende of his
coveitise; and certes, that ne may nevere been accompliced;
for evere the moore habundaunce that he hath of richesse
[*wealth*], the moore he desireth.   And, sire, ye moste also
dryve out of youre herte hastifnesse; for certes, ye ne may
nat deeme for the beste by a sodeyn thought that falleth in
youre herte, but ye moste avyse yow on [*think about*] it ful
1370 ofte.   For, as ye herde her biforn, the commune proverbe
is this, that "he that soone deemeth [*judges*], soone repenteth."
Sire, ye ne be nat alwey in lyk disposicioun; for certes, somthyng that somtyme semeth to yow that it is good for to do,
another tyme it semeth to yow the contrarie.

    Whan ye han taken conseil in [*of*] yourself, and han
deemed by good deliberacion swich thyng as you semeth best,
thanne rede [*advise*] I yow that ye kepe it secree.   Biwrey
[*reveal*] nat youre conseil [*purpose*] to no persone, but if so
be that ye wenen sikerly that thurgh youre biwreyyng youre
1380 condicioun shal be to yow the moore profitable.   For Jhesus
Syrak seith, "Neither to thy foo, ne to thy frend, discovere
nat thy secree ne thy folie; for they wol yeve yow audience
and lookynge [*attention*] and supportacioun [*support*] in thy
presence, and scorne thee in thyn absence."   Another clerk
[*writer*] seith that "scarsly shaltou fynden any persone that
may kepe conseil secrely [*secretly*]."   The book seith, "Whil
that thou kepest thy conseil in thyn herte, thou kepest it in
thy prisoun; and whan thou biwreyest thy conseil to any
wight, he holdeth thee in his snare."   And therfore yow [*for
1390 you*] is bettre to hyde youre conseil in youre herte than praye
him to whom ye han biwreyed youre conseil that he wole
kepen it cloos [*secret*] and stille [*quiet*].   For Seneca seith:
"If so be that thou ne mayst nat thyn owene conseil hyde, how
darstou prayen any oother wight thy conseil secrely to kepe?"
But nathelees, if thou wene sikerly [*really think*] that the
biwreiyng of thy conseil to a persone wol make thy condicion
to stonden in the bettre plyt [*state*], thanne shaltou tellen hym

---

1372 You are not always in the same frame of mind.

thy conseil in this wise. First thou shalt make no semblant
wheither thee were levere pees or werre, or this or that, ne
1400 shewe hym nat thy wille and thyn entente. For trust wel that
comunli [*commonly*] thise conseillours been flatereres, namely
[*especially*] the conseillours of grete lordes; for they enforcen
hem [*try*] alwey rather to speken plesante wordes, enclynynge
to the lordes lust [*desire*], than wordes that been trewe or
profitable. And therfore men seyn that the riche man hath
seeld [*seldom*] good conseil, but if [*unless*] he have it of hymself.

And after that thou shalt considere thy freendes and thyne
enemys. And as touchynge thy freendes, thou shalt considere which of hem been moost feithful and moost wise and
1410 eldest and most approved in conseillyng; and of hem shalt
thou aske thy conseil, as the caas requireth. I seye that
first ye shul clepe [*summon*] to youre conseil youre freendes
that been trewe. For Salomon seith that "right as the herte
of a man deliteth [*delights*] in savour that is soote [*sweet*],
right so the conseil of trewe freendes yeveth [*gives*] swetnesse
to the soule." He seith also, "Ther may no thyng be likned
to the trewe freend; for certes gold ne silver ben nat so muche
worth as the goode wyl of a trewe freend." And eek he seith
that "a trewe freend is a strong deffense; who so that it
1420 fyndeth, certes he fyndeth a greet tresour." Thanne shul ye
eek considere if that youre trewe freendes been discrete and
wise. For the book seith, "Axe alwey thy conseil of hem
that been wise." And by [*for*] this same resoun shul ye
clepen to youre conseil of [*those of*] youre freendes that been
of age, swiche as han seyn [*seen*] and been expert in manye
thynges and been approved in conseillynges. For the book
seith that "in olde men is the sapience, and in longe tyme the
prudence." And Tullius [*i.e. Cicero*] seith that "grete thynges
ne been nat ay accompliced by strengthe, ne by delivernesse
1430 [*dexterity*] of body, but by good conseil, by auctoritee of
persones, and by science [*knowledge*]; the whiche thre thynges
ne been nat fieble [*feeble*] by age, but certes they enforcen
[*grow stronger*] and encreescen day by day." And thanne
shul ye kepe this for a general reule: First shul ye clepen to
youre conseil a fewe of youre freendes that been especiale;
for Salomon seith, "Manye freendes have thou, but among a
thousand chese [*choose*] thee oon to be thy conseillour." For
al be it so that [*although*] thou first ne telle thy conseil but to
a fewe, thou mayst afterward telle it to mo [*more*] folk if it
1440 be nede. But looke alwey that thy conseillours have thilke
thre condiciouns [*qualities*] that I have seyd bifore, that is to
seyn, that they be trewe, wise, and of oold experience. And
werke [*act*] nat alwey in every nede by oon counseillour

1398-9 You must not let it appear whether you prefer peace or war.
1416-17 Nothing can compare with a true friend.

allone; for somtyme bihooveth it [*it is necessary*] to been
conseilled by manye. For Salomon seith, "Salvacion of
thynges is where as ther been manye conseillours."

Now, sith that I have toold yow of [*by*] which folk ye sholde
been counseilled, now wol I teche yow which conseil ye oghte to
eschewe [*avoid*]. First, ye shul eschue the conseillyng of
1450 fooles; for Salomon seith, "Taak no conseil of a fool, for he
ne kan noght conseille but after his owene lust [*desire*] and his
affeccioun [*inclination*]." The book seith that "the propretee
[*character*] of a fool is this: he troweth lightly [*believes easily*]
harm of every wight, and lightly troweth alle bountee in
[*good of*] hymself." Thou shalt eek eschue the conseillyng of
alle flatereres, swiche as enforcen hem rather to preise youre
persone by flaterye than for to telle yow the soothfastnesse
[*truth*] of thynges. Wherfore Tullius seith, "Amonges alle
the pestilences [*ills*] that been in freendshipe the gretteste is
1460 flaterie." And therfore is it moore [*greater*] nede that thou
eschue and drede flatereres than any oother peple. The
book seith, "Thou shalt rather drede and flee fro the sweete
wordes of flaterynge preiseres [*praisers*] than fro the egre
[*sharp*] wordes of thy freend that seith thee thy sothes."
Salomon seith that "the wordes of a flaterere is a snare to
cacche with innocentz." He seith also that "he that speketh
to his freend wordes of swetnesse and of plesaunce [*pleasure*],
setteth a net biforn his feet to cacche hym." And therfore
seith Tullius, "Enclyne nat thyne eres to flatereres, ne taak
1470 no conseil of the wordes of flaterye." And Caton [*Cato*] seith,
"Avyse thee wel, and eschue the wordes of swetnesse and of
plesaunce." And eek thou shalt eschue the conseillyng of
thyne olde enemys that been reconsiled. The book seith
that "no wight retourneth saufly [*safely*] into the grace of his
olde enemy." And Isope [*Aesop*] seith, "Ne trust nat to
hem to whiche thou hast had som tyme werre or enemytee,
ne telle hem nat thy conseil." And Seneca telleth the cause
[*reason*] why: "It may nat be,' seith he, "that where greet fyr
hath longe tyme endured, that ther ne dwelleth som vapour
1480 [*breath*] of warmnesse." And therfore seith Salomon, "In
thyn olde foo trust nevere." For sikerly [*surely*], though thyn
enemy be reconsiled, and maketh thee chiere [*show*] of
humylitee, and lowteth [*bows*] to thee with his heed, ne trust
hym nevere. For certes he maketh thilke [*that*] feyned
humilitee moore for his profit than for any love of thy persone,
by cause that he deemeth [*thinks*] to have victorie over thy
persone by swich feyned contenance [*show*], the which victorie
he myghte nat have by strif or werre. And Peter Alfonce
seith, "Make no felawshipe with thyne olde enemys; for if

1445-6 'In the multitude of counsellors there is safety' (Prov. xi. 14).
1465-6 To catch innocent men with.

1490 thou do hem bountee [*good*], they wol perverten it into
wikkednesse." And eek thou most eschue the conseillyng of
hem that been thy servantz and beren thee greet reverence,
for peraventure they seyn it moore for drede than for love.
And therfore seith a philosophre in this wise: "Ther is no
wight parfitly [*perfectly*] trewe to hym that he to soore [*too
greatly*] dredeth." And Tullius seith, "Ther nys no myght
so greet of any emperour that longe may endure, but if [*unless*]
he have moore love of [*from*] the peple than drede." Thou
shalt also eschue the conseiling of folk that been dronkelewe
1500 [*addicted to drink*], for they ne kan no conseil hyde. For
Salomon seith, "Ther is no privetee [*privacy*] ther as regneth
[*reigns*] dronkenesse." Ye shul also han in suspect [*suspicion*] the conseillyng of swich folk as conseille yow o thyng
prively, and conseille yow the contrarie openly. For Cassi-
dorie [*Cassiodorus*] seith that "it is a manere sleighte to
hyndre, whan he sheweth [*pretends*] to doon o thyng openly
and werketh prively the contrarie." Thou shalt also have in
suspect the conseillyng of wikked folk. For the book seith,
"The conseillyng of wikked folk is alwey ful of fraude."
1510 And David seith, "Blisful is that man that hath nat folwed the
conseilyng of shrewes [*scoundrels*]." Thou shalt also eschue
the conseillyng of yong folk, for hir conseil is nat rype.
Now, sire, sith I have shewed yow of which folk ye shul
take youre conseil, and of which folk ye shul folwe the conseil,
now wol I teche yow how ye shal examyne youre conseil, after
the doctrine of Tullius. In the examynynge thanne of youre
conseillour ye shul considere manye thynges. Alderfirst
[*first of all*] thou shalt considere that in thilke thyng that thou
purposest, and upon what thyng thou wolt have conseil, that
1520 verray [*real*] trouthe be seyd and conserved [*observed*]; this is
to seyn, telle trewely thy tale. For he that seith fals may nat
wel be conseilled in that cas of which he lieth [*tells lies*].
And after this thou shalt considere the thynges that acorden
to that thou purposest for to do by thy conseillours, if resoun
accorde therto; and eek if thy myght [*power*] may atteine therto;
and if the moore part and the bettre part of thy conseillours
acorde therto, or noon [*not*]. Thanne shaltou considere what
thyng shal folwe of [*from*] that conseillyng, as hate, pees,
werre, grace, profit, or damage, and manye othere thynges.
1530 And in alle thise thynges thou shalt chese the beste, and weyve
[*reject*] alle othere thynges. Thanne shaltow considere of
what roote is engendred the matiere of thy conseil, and what
fruyt it may conceyve and engendre [*produce*]. Thou shalt

1505-6 A kind of trick to hinder you.
1519 And about which you wish to have advice.
1523-5 You must consider whether the things you intend to do on the
advice of your counsellors are reasonable.
1531-2 From what root the substance of your advice springs.

eek considere alle thise causes, fro whennes they been
sprongen. And whan ye han examyned youre conseil, as I
have seyd, and which partie is the bettre and moore profitable,
and han approved it by manye wise folk and olde, thanne
shaltou considere if thou mayst parfourne it and maken of it
a good ende. For certes, resoun wol nat that any man sholde
1540 bigynne a thyng, but if [*unless*] he myghte parfourne it as hym
oghte; ne no wight sholde take upon hym so hevy a charge
[*burden*] that he myghte nat bere it. For the proverbe seith,
"He that to muche embraceth, distreyneth [*grasps*] litel."
And Catoun seith, "Assay to do swich thyng as thou hast
power to doon, lest that the charge oppresse thee so soore that
thee bihoveth to weyve [*abandon*] thyng that thou hast bigonne."
And if so be that thou be in doute wheither thou mayst parfourne a thing or noon, chese rather to suffre [*endure*] than
bigynne. And Piers Alphonce seith, "If thou hast myght to
1550 doon a thyng of which thou most [*might*] repente, it is bettre
'nay' than 'ye.'" This is to seyn, that thee is bettre holde thy
tonge stille than for to speke. Thanne may ye understonde
by strenger [*stronger*] resons that if thou hast power to parfourne a werk of which thou shalt repente, thanne is it bettre
that thou suffre than bigynne. Wel seyn they that defenden
[*forbid*] every wight to assaye a thyng of which he is in doute
[*doubt*] wheither he may parfourne it or noon. And after,
whan ye han examyned youre conseil [*purpose*], as I have seyd
biforn, and knowen wel that ye may parfourne youre emprise
1560 [*undertaking*], conferme it thanne sadly [*firmly*] til it be at an
ende.

Now is it resoun and tyme that I shewe yow whanne and
wherefore that ye may chaunge youre counseil withouten
youre repreve. Soothly [*truly*], a man may chaungen his
purpos and his conseil if the cause cesseth, or whan a newe
caas bitydeth [*situation arises*]. For the lawe seith that
"upon thynges that newely bityden bihoveth newe conseil."
And Senec seith, "If thy conseil is comen to the eeris of thyn
enemy, chaunge thy conseil." Thou mayst also chaunge thy
1570 conseil if so be that thou fynde that by errour, or by oother
cause, harm or damage may bityde. Also if thy conseil be
dishonest, or ellis cometh of dishonest cause, chaunge thy
conseil. For the lawes seyn that "alle bihestes [*promises*] that
been dishoneste been of no value"; and eek if so be that it
be inpossible [*impossible*], or may nat goodly [*well*] be parfourned or kept.

And take this for a general reule, that every conseil that is
affermed so strongly that it may nat be chaunged for no

1538-9 If you can carry it out and bring it to a successful conclusion.
1563-4 Without reproaching yourself.
1578-9 That it cannot be changed, whatever new circumstances arise.

condicioun that may bityde, I seye that thilke conseil is
1580 wikked.'

This Melibeus, whanne he hadde herd the doctrine of his
wyf dame Prudence, answerde in this wyse: 'Dame,' quod
he, 'as yet into this tyme [*up till now*] ye han wel and coven-
ably taught me as in general, how I shal governe me in the chesynge, and in the withholdynge [*retaining*] of my conseillours. But now wolde I fayn that ye wolde condescende
in especial, and telle me how liketh yow, or what semeth
yow, by oure conseillours that we han chosen in oure present
nede.'

1590   'My lord,' quod she, 'I biseke yow in al humblesse that ye
wol nat wilfully replie agayn my resouns, ne distempre youre
herte, thogh I speke thyng that yow displese. For God woot
that, as in myn entente [*intention*], I speke it for youre beste,
for youre honour, and for youre profite eke [*also*]. And
soothly, I hope that youre benyngnytee [*kindness*] wol taken
it in pacience. Trusteth me wel,' quod she, 'that youre
conseil [*purpose*] as in this caas ne sholde nat, as to speke
properly, be called a conseillyng, but a mocioun or a moevyng
of folye, in which conseil ye han erred in many a sondry
1600 wise [*different ways*].

First and forward [*foremost*], ye han erred in th'assemblynge
of youre conseillours. For ye sholde first have cleped
[*summoned*] a fewe folk to youre conseil, and after ye myghte
han shewed it to mo folk, if it hadde been nede. But certes,
ye han sodeynly cleped to youre conseil a greet multitude of
peple, ful chargeant [*wearisome*] and ful anoyous [*tedious*] for
to heere. Also ye han erred, for theras ye sholden oonly have
cleped to youre conseil youre trewe frendes olde and wise,
ye han ycleped straunge folk, yonge folk, false flatereres, and
1610 enemys reconsiled, and folk that doon yow reverence withouten love. And eek also ye have erred, for ye han broght
with yow to youre conseil ire, coveitise, and hastifnesse, the
whiche thre thinges been contrariouse to every conseil honest
and profitable; the whiche thre thinges ye han nat anientissed
[*annihilated*] or destroyed hem, neither in youreself, ne in
youre conseillours, as yow oghte. Ye han erred also, for ye
han shewed to youre conseillours youre talent [*desire*] and
youre affeccioun [*inclination*] to make werre anon, and for to
do vengeance. They han espied by youre wordes to what
1620 thyng ye been enclyned; and therfore han they rather conseilled
yow to youre talent than to youre profit. Ye han erred also,
for it semeth that yow suffiseth [*are satisfied*] to han been

1586 I should be glad if you would especially condescend.
1587-8 How you like, or what you think of, our counsellors.
1591-2 Nor be disturbed in heart.
1598-9 Be called the result of deliberation, but rather a gesture or
    motion of folly.

conseilled by thise conseillours oonly, and with litel avys, whereas in so greet and so heigh a nede it hadde been necessarie mo conseillours and moore deliberacion to parfourne youre emprise.   Ye han erred also, for ye ne han nat examyned youre conseil in the forseyde manere, ne in due manere, as the caas requireth.   Ye han erred also, for ye han maked no division [*distinction*] bitwixe youre conseillours; this is to

1630   seyn, bitwixen youre trewe freendes and youre feyned conseillours; ne ye han nat knowe the wil [*wishes*] of youre trewe freendes olde and wise; but ye han cast alle hire wordes in an hochepot [*hotchpotch*], and enclyned youre herte to the moore part and to the gretter nombre, and there been ye condescended.   And sith ye woot wel that men shal alwey fynde a gretter nombre of fooles than of wise men, and therfore the conseils that been at congregaciouns and multitudes of folk, there as men take moore reward to the nombre than to the sapience of persones, ye se wel that in swiche conseillynges

1640   fooles han the maistrie.'

Melibeus answerde agayn, and seyde, 'I graunte wel [*freely*] that I have erred; but there as thou hast toold me heerbiforn that he nys nat to blame that chaungeth his conseillours in certein caas [*cases*] and for certeine juste causes, I am al redy to chaunge my conseillours right as thow wolt devyse.   The proverbe seith that "for to do synne is mannyssh [*human*], but certes for to persevere [*continue*] longe in synne is werk of the devel."'

To this sentence [*opinion*] answered anon dame Prudence,

1650   and seyde: 'Examineth,' quod she, 'youre conseil, and lat us see the whiche of hem han spoken most resonably, and taught yow best conseil.   And for as muche as that the examynacion is necessarie, lat us bigynne at the surgiens and at the phisiciens, that first speeken [*spoke*] in this matiere.   I sey yow that the surgiens and phisiciens han seyd yow in youre conseil discreetly, as hem oughte; and in hir speche seyden ful wisely that to the office of hem aperteneth to doon to every wight honour and profit, and no wight for to anoye; and after hir craft to doon greet diligence unto the cure of hem which that

1660   they han in hir governaunce.   And, sire, right as they han answered wisely and discreetly, right so rede [*advise*] I that they been heighly and sovereynly gerdoned [*rewarded*] for hir

1624-5 More counsellors were needed.
1636-40 For that reason in the counsels offered at gatherings and multitudes of people, where men have more regard for the number than the wisdom of persons, you can well see that fools have the mastery.
1650 Examine the advice given you.
1655-6 Have advised you with discretion, as they ought.
1657-8 That it is a part of their duty to respect and do good to everyone.
1658-60 And, according to their skill, to do their utmost to cure those whom they have in their charge.

noble speche; and eek for they sholde do the moore ententif bisynesse [*attentive care*] in the curacion [*curing*] of youre doghter deere. For al be it so that they been youre freendes, therfore shal ye nat suffren [*allow*] that they serve yow for noght, but ye oghte the rather gerdone hem and shewe hem youre largesse [*generosity*]. And as touchynge the proposicioun which that the phisiciens encreesceden [*advanced*] in
1670 this caas, this is to seyn, that in maladies that oon contrarie is warisshed [*cured*] by another contrarie, I wolde fayn knowe hou ye understonde thilke text, and what is youre sentence [*opinion*].

'Certes,' quod Melibeus, 'I understonde it in this wise: that right as they han doon me a contrarie, right so sholde I doon hem another. For right as they han venged [*revenged*] hem on me and doon me wrong, right so shal I venge me upon hem and doon hem wrong; and thanne have I cured oon contrarie [*one act of hostility*] by another.'

1680 'Lo, lo,' quod dame Prudence, 'how lightly [*easily*] is every man enclined to his owene desir and to his owene plesaunce. Certes,' quod she, 'the wordes of the phisiciens ne sholde nat han been understonden in thys wise. For certes, wikkednesse is nat contrarie to wikkednesse, ne vengeance to venveaunce, ne wrong to wrong, but they been semblable [*similar*]. And therfore o [*one*] vengeaunce is nat warisshed by another vengeaunce, ne o wroong by another wroong, but everich [*each*] of hem encreesceth and aggreggeth [*aggravates*] oother. But certes, the wordes of the phisiciens sholde been under-
1690 stonden in this wise: For good [*goodness*] and wikkednesse been two contraries, and pees and werre, vengeaunce and suffraunce [*long-suffering*], discord and accord, and manye othere thynges. But certes, wikkednesse shal be warisshed by goodnesse, discord by accord, werre by pees, and so forth of othere thynges. And heerto accordeth [*agrees*] Seint Paul the Apostle in manye places. He seith: "Ne yeldeth [*give*] nat harm for harm, ne wikked speche for wikked speche; but do wel to hym that dooth thee harm, and blesse hym that seith to thee harm.' And in manye othere places he amonesteth
1700 [*recommends*] pees and accord. But now wol I speke to yow of the conseil which that was yeven to yow by the men of lawe and the wise folk, that seyden alle by [*with*] oon accord, as ye han herd bifore, that over alle thynges ye shal doon youre diligence to kepen [*protect*] youre persone and to warnestoore [*defend*] youre hous; and seyden also that in this caas yow oghten for to werken ful avysely [*advisedly*] and with greet deliberacioun. And, sire, as to the firste point, that toucheth [*concerns*] to the kepyng of youre persone, ye shul understonde

1675–6 Just as they have shown hostility to me, so should I to them.
1694–5 And similarly with other things.

that he that hath werre shal everemoore mekely and devoutly
1710 preyen, biforn alle thynges, that Jhesus Crist of his mercy wol
han hym in his proteccion and been his sovereyn helpyng
[*help*] at his nede.   For certes, in this world ther is no wight
that may be conseilled ne kept sufficeantly withouten the
kepyng [*protection*] of oure Lord Jhesu Crist.   To this sentence [*opinion*] accordeth the prophete David, that seith, "If
God ne kepe the citee, in ydel waketh he that it kepeth."
Now, sire, thanne shul ye committe the kepyng of youre
persone to youre trewe freendes, that been approved and
yknowe, and of hem shul ye axen help youre persone for to
1720 kepe.   For Catoun seith: "If thou hast nede of help, axe it
of thy freendes; for ther nys noon so good a phisicien as thy
trewe freend."   And after this thanne shul ye kepe yow fro alle
straunge folk, and fro lyeres [*liars*], and have alwey in suspect
hire compaignye.   For Piers Alfonce seith, "Ne taak [*keep*]
no compaignye by the weye [*along the way*] of a straunge man,
but if so be that thou have knowe hym of a lenger [*longer*]
tyme.   And if so be that he falle into thy compaignye paraventure [*by chance*], withouten thyn assent, enquere thanne
as subtilly [*skilfully*] as thou mayst of his conversacion
1730 [*behaviour*], and of his lyf bifore, and feyne thy wey; seye that
thou wolt thider as thou wolt nat go; and if he bereth [*carries*]
a spere, hoold thee [*keep*] on the right syde, and if he bere a
swerd, hoold thee on the lift syde."   And after this thanne
shul ye kepe yow wisely from all swich manere peple as I have
seyd bifore, and hem and hir conseil eschewe [*shun*].   And
after this thanne shul ye kepe yow in swich manere that, for
any presumpcion of youre strengthe, that ye ne dispise nat,
ne accompte nat the myght of youre adversarie so litel,
that ye lete [*neglect*] the kepyng of youre persone for
1740 youre presumpcioun; for every wys man dredeth his enemy.
And Salomon seith: "Weleful [*happy*] is he that of alle hath
drede; for certes, he that thurgh the hardynesse [*audacity*] of
his herte, and thurgh the hardynesse of hymself, hath to greet
presumpcioun, hym shal yvel bityde."   Thanne shul ye
everemoore contrewayte embusshementz and alle espiaille.
For Senec seith that "the wise man that dredeth harmes,
eschueth [*avoid*] harmes, ne he ne falleth into perils that perils
eschueth."   And al be it so that it seme that thou art in

1716 He who guards it watches in vain.
1723–4 Always suspect their fellowship.
1730–1 Make up a story about the way you are going; say you are on
 your way to a place you have no intention of going to.
1736–8 Protect yourself in such a manner that, through presuming on
 your strength, you do not despise or take so little account of the
 power of your adversary.
1744–5 Then you must always watch out for ambushes and all kinds of
 spies.

siker [*safe*] place, yet shaltow alwey do thy diligence in kepynge
1750 of thy persone; this is to seyn, ne be nat necligent to kepe thy
persone, nat oonly fro thy gretteste enemys, but fro thy
leeste enemy. Senek seith: "A man that is well avysed
[*advised*], he dredeth his leste enemy." Ovyde seith that "the
litel wesele [*weasel*] wol slee the grete bole [*bull*] and the wilde
hert [*hart*]." And the book seith, "A litel thorn may prikke
a kyng ful soore, and an hound wol holde the wilde boor
[*boar*]." But nathelees, I sey nat thou shalt be so coward that
thou doute [*fear*] ther wher as is no drede. The book seith
that "somme folk han greet lust [*desire*] to deceyve, but yet
1760 they dreden hem [*fear*] to be deceyved." Yet shaltou drede to
been empoisoned [*poisoned*], and kepe the from the compaignye
of scorneres. For the book seith, "With scorneres make no
compaignye, but flee hire wordes as venym."

Now, as to the seconde point, where as youre wise conseillours conseilled yow to warnestoore youre hous with gret
diligence, I wolde fayn knowe how that ye understonde thilke
wordes and what is youre sentence.'

Melibeus answerde, and seyde, 'Certes, I understande it in
this wise: That I shal warnestoore myn hous with toures
1770 [*towers*], swiche as han castelles and othere manere edifices,
and armure, and artelries; by whiche thynges I may my
persone and myn hous so kepen and deffenden that myne
enemys shul been in drede myn hous for to approche.'

To this sentence answerde anon Prudence: 'Warnestooryng
[*fortifying*],' quod she, 'of heighe toures and of grete edifices
apperteyneth somtyme to pryde. And eek men make heighe
toures, and grete edifices with grete costages [*expense*] and
with greet travaille; and whan that they been accompliced
[*finished*], yet be they nat worth a stree [*straw*], but if they be
1780 defended by trewe freendes that been olde and wise. And
understoond wel that the gretteste and strongeste garnysoun
that a riche man may have, as wel to kepen his persone as his
goodes, is that he be biloved with [*by*] hys subgetz and with his
neighebores. For thus seith Tullius, that "ther is a manere
garnysoun [*one kind of garrison*] that no man may venquysse
ne disconfite [*overthrow*], and that is a lord to be biloved of
his citezeins and of his peple."

Now, sire, as to the thridde point, where as youre olde and
wise conseillours seyden that yow ne oghte nat sodeynly ne
1790 hastily proceden in this nede, but that yow oghte purveyen
and apparaillen yow in this caas with greet diligence and greet
deliberacioun; trewely, I trowe that they seyden right wisely
and right sooth. For Tullius seith: "In every nede, er thou

1771 And with defensive armour and artillery.
1776 Is sometimes related to pride.
1790-1 You should provide and prepare in this case.

bigynne it, apparaille thee with greet diligence." Thanne
seye I that in vengeance-takyng, in werre, in bataille, and in
warnestooryng, er thow bigynne, I rede that thou apparaille
thee therto, and do it with greet deliberacion.   For Tullius
seith that "longe apparaillyng [*preparation*] biforn the bataille
maketh short victorie."   And Cassidorus seith, "The garny-
1800 soun is stronger, whan it is longe tyme avysed [*forewarned*]."
    But now lat us speken of the conseil that was accorded by
youre neighbores, swiche as doon yow reverence withouten
love, youre olde enemys reconsiled, youre flatereres, that
conseilled yow certeyne thynges prively, and openly conseilleden yow the contrarie; the yonge folk also, that conseilleden
yow to venge yow, and make werre anon.   And certes, sire,
as I have seyd biforn, ye han greetly erred to han cleped swich
manere folk to youre conseil, which conseillours been ynogh
repreved by the resouns aforeseyd.   But nathelees, lat us now
1810 descende to the special [*particular*].   Ye shuln first procede
after the doctrine of Tullius.   Certes, the trouthe of this
matiere, or of this conseil, nedeth nat diligently enquere; for
it is wel wist whiche they been that han doon to yow this
trespas [*wrong*] and vileynye [*shameful deed*], and how manye
trespassours, and in what manere they han to yow doon al
this wrong and al this vileynye.   And after this, thanne shul
ye examyne the seconde condicion which that the same
Tullius addeth in this matiere.   For Tullius put [*puts*] a thyng
which that he clepeth "consentynge"; this is to seyn, who been
1820 they, and whiche been they and how manye, that consenten
to thy conseil in thy wilfulnesse [*stubborn resolve*] to doon
hastif [*rash*] vengeance.   And lat us considere also who been
they, and how manye been they, and whiche been they, that
consenteden to youre adversaries.   And certes, as to the firste
poynt, it is wel knowen whiche folk been they that consenteden
to youre hastif wilfulnesse; for trewely, alle tho that conseilleden yow to maken sodeyn werre ne been nat youre freendes.
Lat us now considere whiche been they that ye holde so greetly
youre freendes as to youre persone.   For al be it so that ye
1830 be myghty and riche, certes ye ne been but allone, for certes
ye ne han no child but a doghter, ne ye ne han bretheren, ne
cosyns germayns [*first cousins*], ne noon oother neigh kynrede
[*near kindred*], wherfore that youre enemys for drede sholde
stinte to plede with yow, or to destroye youre persone.   Ye
knowen also that youre richesses mooten [*may*] been dis-

1812-13 Need not be diligently inquired into; for it is well known who
    they are.
1820 What sort of men they are and how many.
1828-9 Who they are that you take to be your personal friends.
1830 You are as good as alone.
1833-4 On whose account your enemies would for fear desist from
    disputing with you or destroying you.

pended [*divided*] in diverse parties [*parts*], and whan that every wight hath his part [*share*], they ne wollen taken but litel reward to venge thy deeth. But thyne enemys been thre, and they han manie children, bretheren, cosyns, and oother ny
1840 kynrede. And though so were that thou haddest slayn of hem two or three, yet dwellen ther ynowe [*enough*] to wreken [*avenge*] hir deeth, and to sle thy persone. And though so be that youre kynrede be moore siker [*sure*] and stedefast than the kyn of youre adversarie, yet nathelees youre kynrede nys but a fer [*distant*] kynrede; they been but litel syb [*slightly related*] to yow, and the kyn of youre enemys been ny syb to hem. And certes, as in that, hir condicioun is bet than youres. Thanne lat us considere also if the conseillyng of hem that conseilleden yow to taken sodeyn vengeaunce,
1850 wheither it accorde to resoun. And certes, ye knowe wel "nay." For, as by right and resoun, ther may no man taken vengeance on no wight but the juge that hath the jurisdiccioun of it, whan it is graunted hym to take thilke vengeance hastily [*swiftly*] or attemprely [*with moderation*], as the lawe requireth. And yet mooreover of thilke word that Tullius clepeth "consentynge," thou shalt considere if thy myght and thy power may consenten and suffise to thy wilfulnesse and to thy conseillours. And certes thou mayst wel seyn that "nay." For sikerly [*surely*], as for to speke proprely, we may do no
1860 thyng, but oonly swich thyng as we may doon rightfully. And certes rightfully ne mowe ye take no vengeance, as of youre propre [*own*] auctoritee. Thanne mowe [*may*] ye seen that youre power ne consenteth nat, ne accordeth [*agrees*] nat, with youre wilfulnesse.

Lat us now examyne the thridde point, that Tullius clepeth "Consequent." Thou shalt understonde that the vengeance that thou purposest for to take is the consequent; and therof folweth another vengeaunce, peril, and werre, and othere damages [*harms*] withoute nombre, of whiche we be nat war
1870 [*aware*], as at this tyme.

And as touchynge the fourthe point, that Tullius clepeth "engendrynge," thou shalt considere that this wrong which that is doon to thee is engendred of [*produced by*] the hate of thyne enemys, and of the vengeance-takynge upon that wolde engendre another vengeance, and muchel [*much*] sorwe and wastynge of richesses, as I seyde.

Now, sire, as to the point that Tullius clepeth "causes," which that is the laste point, thou shalt understonde that the wrong that thou hast receyved hath certeine causes, whiche
1880 that clerkes clepen *Oriens* and *Efficiens*, and *Causa longinqua* and *Causa propinqua*, this is to seyn, the fer [*remote*] cause and

1837-8 They will give but little attention to avenging your death.
1874-5 And that avenging it would produce more vengeance.

the ny [*immediate*] cause.   The fer cause is almyghty God that
is cause of alle thynges.   The neer cause is thy thre enemys.
The cause accidental was hate.   The cause material been the
fyve woundes of thy doghter.   The cause formal is the manere
of hir werkynge that broghten laddres and cloumben [*climbed*]
in at thy wyndowes.   The cause final was for to sle [*slay*] thy
doghter.   It letted nat in as muche as in hem was.   But for
to speken of the fer cause, as to what ende they shul come, or
1890 what shal finally bityde of [*happen to*] hem in this caas, ne kan
I nat deeme [*judge*] but by conjectynge [*conjecture*] and by
supposynge.   For we shul suppose that they shul come to a
wikked ende, by cause that the Book of Decrees seith, "Seel-
den, or with greet peyne, been causes ybroght to good ende
whanne they been baddely bigonne."
    Now, sire, if men wolde axe me why that God suffred men
to do yow this vileynye, certes, I kan nat wel answere, as for
no soothfastnesse.   For th'apostle seith that "the sciences
[*knowledge*] and the juggementz of oure Lord God almyghty
1900 been ful depe; ther may no man comprehende ne serchen hem
suffisantly."   Nathelees, by certeyne presumpciouns and
conjectynges, I holde and bileeve that God, which that is ful
of justice and of rightwisnesse, hath suffred this bityde by
juste cause resonable.
    Thy name is Melibee, this is to seyn, "a man that drynketh
hony."   Thou hast ydronke so muchel hony of sweete
temporeel richesses [*wealth*], and delices [*delights*] and honours
of this world, that thou art dronken, and hast forgeten Jhesu
Crist thy creatour.   Thou ne hast nat doon to hym swich
1910 honour and reverence as thee oughte, ne thou ne hast nat wel
ytaken kep [*heed*] to the wordes of Ovide, that seith, "Under
the hony of the goodes of the body is hyd the venym that sleeth
[*slays*] the soule."   And Salomon seith, "If thou hast founden
hony, ete of it that suffiseth; for if thou ete of it out of mesure
[*immoderately*], thou shalt spewe," and be nedy and povre
[*poor*].   And peraventure Crist hath thee in despit [*contempt*],
and hath turned awey fro thee his face and his eeris [*ears*] of
misericorde [*mercy*]; and also he hath suffred that thou hast
been punysshed in the manere that thow hast ytrespassed
1920 [*sinned*].   Thou hast doon synne agayn oure Lord Crist;
for certes, the three enemys of mankynde, that is to seyn,
the flessh, the feend, and the world, thou hast suffred hem entre
in to thyn herte wilfully by the wyndowes of thy body, and
hast nat defended thyself suffisantly agayns hire assautes
[*assaults*] and hire temptaciouns, so that they han wounded

1888 They did not delay in this any more than they could help.
1893 *Book of Decrees*, a book of papal decrees compiled by Gratian.
1897–8 I cannot very well answer, in truth.
1903–4 Has allowed this to happen for a just and reasonable cause.

thy soule in fyve places; this is to seyn, the deedly synnes
that been entred into thyn herte by thy fyve wittes [*senses*].
And in the same manere oure Lord Crist hath woold [*willed*]
and suffred [*permitted*] that thy three enemys been entred into
1930 thyn hous by the wyndowes, and han ywounded thy doghter in
the forseyde manere.'

'Certes,' quod Melibee, 'I se wel that ye enforce yow muchel
[*try hard*] by wordes to overcome me in swich manere that I
shal nat venge me of myne enemys, shewynge me the perils
and the yveles that myghten falle of [*come from*] this vengeance.
But whoso wolde considere in alle vengeances the perils and
yveles that myghte sewe of [*ensue from*] vengeance-takynge, a
man wolde never take vengeance, and that were harm [*a pity*];
for by the vengeance-takyng been the wikked men disseuered
1940 [*separated*] fro the goode men, and they that han wyl to do
wikkednesse restreyne hir wikked purpos, whan they seen the
punyssynge and chastisynge of the trespassours.'

[*Et a ce respont dame Prudence, 'Certes,' dist elle, 'je
t'ottroye que de vengence vient molt de maulx et de biens; Mais
vengence n'appartient pas a un chascun fors seulement aux
juges et a ceulx qui ont la juridicion sur les malfaitteurs.*] And
yet seye I moore, that right as a singuler [*private*] persone
synneth in takynge vengeance of another man, right so
synneth the juge if he do no vengeance of hem that it han
1950 disserved [*deserved*]. For Senec seith thus: "That maister,"
he seith, "is good that proveth shrewes." And as Cassidore
seith, "A man dredeth to do outrages whan he woot and
knoweth that it displeseth [*is displeasing*] to the juges and the
sovereyns." And another seith, "The juge that dredeth to
do right, maketh men shrewes." And Seint Paul the Apostle
seith in his Epistle, whan he writeth unto the Romayns, that
"the juges beren nat the spere withouten cause, but they
beren it to punysse the shrewes and mysdoeres, and for to
defende the goode men." If ye wol thanne take vengeance
1960 of [*on*] youre enemys, ye shul retourne or have youre recours
to the juge that hath the jurisdiccion upon hem, and he shal
punysse hem as the lawe axeth and requireth.'

'A!' quod Melibee, 'this vengeance liketh me no thyng.
I bithenke me [*recollect*] now and take heede how Fortune
hath norissed [*nourished*] me fro my childhede, and hath
holpen [*helped*] me to passe many a stroong paas [*critical
situation*]. Now wol I assayen [*test*] hire, trowynge [*believing*],

---

1943–6 And to this dame Prudence replied 'Certainly,' said she, 'I
grant that from vengeance comes much evil and much good; but
vengeance does not rightfully belong to everyone, but only to judges
and to those who have jurisdiction over wrongdoers.'
1950–1 That master . . . is good who finds out the wicked.
1963 This sort of vengeance does not appeal to me at all.

with Goddes help, that she shal helpe me my shame for to venge.'

1970 'Certes,' quod Prudence, 'if ye wol werke by my conseil, ye shul nat assaye Fortune by no wey [*in any way*], ne ye shul nat lene or bowe unto hire, after the word of Senec; for "thynges that been folily [*foolishly*] doon, and that been in hope of Fortune, shullen nevere come to good ende." And, as the same Senec seith, "The moore cleer and the moore shynyng that Fortune is, the moore brotil [*brittle*] and the sonner [*sooner*] broken she is." Trusteth nat in hire, for she nys nat [*is not*] stidefast ne stable; for whan thow trowest to be moost seur [*sure*] or siker [*certain*] of hire help, she wol 1980 faille thee and deceyve thee. And where as ye seyn that Fortune hath norissed yow fro youre childhede, I seye that in so muchel shul ye the lasse [*less*] truste in hire and in hir wit [*wisdom*]. For Senec seith, "What man that is norissed by Fortune, she maketh hym a greet fool." Now thanne, syn ye desire and axe vengeance, and the vengeance that is doon after [*according to*] the lawe and bifore the juge ne liketh yow nat, and the vengeance that is doon in hope of Fortune is perilous and uncertein, thanne have ye noon oother remedie but for to have youre recours unto the sovereyn Juge that 1990 vengeth alle vileynyes and wronges. And he shal venge yow after that hymself witnesseth, where as he seith, "Leveth the vengeance to me, and I shal do it."'

Melibee answerde, 'If I ne venge me nat of the vileynye that men han doon to me, I sompne [*summon*] or warne hem that han doon to me that vileynye, and alle othere, to do me another vileynye. For it is writen, "If thou take no vengeance of an oold vileynye, thou sompnest thyne adversaries to do thee a newe vileynye." And also for my suffrance [*long-suffering*] men wolden do me so muchel vileynye that I myghte 2000 neither bere it ne susteene [*endure*], and so sholde I been put and holden overlowe [*esteemed too lightly*]. For men seyn, "In muchel suffrynge shul manye thynges falle [*happen*] unto thee whiche thou shalt nat mowe suffre."'

'Certes,' quod Prudence, 'I graunte yow that over-muchel [*too much*] suffraunce is nat good. But yet ne folweth it nat therof that every persone to whom men doon vileynye take of it vengeance; for that aperteneth and longeth al oonly to the juges, for they shul venge the vileynyes and injuries. And therfore tho two auctoritees that ye han seyd above been oonly

1971-2 Nor shall you bend or bow to her, according to the words of Seneca.
1981-2 I say that by the same token.
1990-1 He shall avenge you as He Himself testifies.
2003 Which you will not be able to endure.
2009-10 The two authorities you have quoted above refer only to the judges.

2010 understonden in the juges. For whan they suffren over-
muchel the wronges and the vileynyes to be doon withouten
punysshynge, they sompne nat a man al oonly for to do newe
wronges, but they comanden it. Also a wys man seith that
"the juge that correcteth nat the synnere comandeth and
biddeth hym do synne." And the juges and sovereyns
myghten in hir land so muchel suffre of the shrewes and
mysdoeres that they sholden, by swich suffrance, by proces of
tyme wexen of swich power and myght that they sholden putte
out the juges and the sovereyns from hir places, and atte laste
2020 maken hem lesen [*lose*] hire lordshipes [*authority*].

But lat us now putte [*suppose*] that ye have leve [*permission*]
to venge yow. I seye ye been nat of myght and power as now
to venge yow; for if ye wole maken comparisoun unto the
myght of youre adversaries, ye shul fynde in manye thynges
that I have shewed yow er this that hire condicion is bettre
than youres. And therfore seye I that it is good as now that
ye suffre and be pacient.

Forthermoore, ye knowen wel that after the comune sawe
[*saying*], "it is a woodnesse [*madness*] a man to stryve with a
2030 strenger or a moore myghty man than he is hymself; and for
to stryve with a man of evene [*equal*] strengthe, that is to seyn,
with as strong a man as he is, it is peril; and for to stryve with
a weyker man, it is folie [*folly*]." And therfore sholde a man
flee stryvynge [*strife*] as muchel as he myghte. For Salomon
seith, "It is a greet worshipe [*honour*] to a man to kepen hym
fro noyse and stryf." And if it so bifalle or happe that a man
of gretter myght and strengthe than thou art do thee grevaunce
[*wrong*], studie and bisye thee [*busy yourself*] rather to stille
[*mitigate*] the same grevaunce than for to venge thee. For
2040 Senec seith that "he putteth hym [*himself*] in greet peril that
stryveth with a gretter man than he is hymself." And Catoun
seith, "If a man of hyer estaat or degree, or moore myghty
than thou, do thee anoy or grevaunce, suffre hym; for he that
oones hath greved [*wronged*] thee, may another tyme releeve
thee and helpe." Yet sette I caas, ye have bothe myght and
licence [*permission*] for to venge yow, I seye that ther be ful
manye thynges that shul restreyne yow of vengeance-takynge,
and make yow for to enclyne to suffre [*endure*], and for to han
pacience in the wronges that han been doon to yow. First
2050 and forward, if ye wole considere the defautes [*faults*] that
been in youre owene persone, for whiche defautes God hath

2012-13 They not only summon men to do new wrongs, but they
command it.
2016-17 Tolerate so much from wicked men and evil-doers.
2017-18 In course of time grow to such power.
2022-3 I say you have not at present the power and might to avenge
yourself.
2045 Again I will suppose.

suffred yow have this tribulacioun, as I have seyd yow heer-
biforn. For the poete seith that "we oghte paciently taken
the tribulacions that comen to us whan we thynken and consideren that we han disserved [*deserved*] to have hem."   And
Seint Gregorie seith that "whan a man considereth wel the
nombre of his defautes and of his synnes, the peynes and the
tribulaciouns that he suffreth semen the lesse unto hym; and
in as muche as hym thynketh his synnes moore hevy and
2060 grevous, in so muche semeth his peyne the lighter and the esier
unto hym."   Also ye owen to enclyne and bowe youre herte
to take the pacience of oure Lord Jhesu Crist, as seith Seint
Peter in his Epistles. "Jhesu Crist," he seith, "hath suffred
for us and yeven ensample to every man to folwe and sewe
[*imitate*] hym; for he dide nevere synne, ne nevere cam ther a
vileyns [*evil*] word out of his mouth. Whan men cursed hym,
he cursed hem noght; and whan men betten [*beat*] hym, he
manaced [*threatened*] hem noght."   Also the grete pacience
which the seintes that been in Paradys han had in tribulaciouns
2070 that they han ysuffred, withouten hir desert or gilt, oghte
muchel stiren [*move*] yow to pacience.   Forthermoore ye
sholde enforce yow [*try*] to have pacience, considerynge that
the tribulaciouns of this world but litel while endure, and
soone passed been and goon, and the joye that a man seketh
to have by pacience in tribulaciouns is perdurable [*everlasting*], after that the Apostle seith in his epistle.   "The joye
of God," he seith, "is perdurable," that is to seyn, evere-
lastynge.   Also troweth [*trust*] and bileveth stedefastly that
he nys nat wel ynorissed [*bred*], ne wel ytaught, that kan nat
2080 have pacience, or wol nat receyve pacience.   For Salomon
seith that "the doctrine [*learning*] and the wit [*wisdom*] of a
man is knowen by pacience."   And in another place he seith
that "he that is pacient governeth hym by greet prudence."
And the same Salomon seith, "The angry and wrathful man
maketh noyses, and the pacient man atempreth hem and
stilleth."   He seith also, "It is moore worth to be pacient
than for to be right strong; and he that may have the lordshipe
of his owene herte is moore to preyse [*be praised*] than he that
by his force or strengthe taketh grete citees."   And therfore
2090 seith Seint Jame in his Epistle that "pacience is a greet vertu
of perfeccioun."'
    'Certes,' quod Melibee, 'I graunte yow, dame Prudence,
that pacience is a greet vertu of perfeccioun; but every man
may nat have the perfeccioun that ye seken; ne I nam nat of
the nombre of right parfite men, for myn herte may nevere
been in pees unto the tyme it be venged.   And al be it so that
[*although*] it was greet peril to myne enemys to do me a

2070 Undeservedly and innocently.
2085-6 Moderates them and keeps silence.

vileynye in takynge vengeance upon me, yet tooken [*took*] they
noon heede of the peril, but fulfilleden hir wikked wyl and hir
2100 corage [*desire*].   And therfore me thynketh men oghten nat
repreve me, though I putte me in a litel peril for to venge me,
and though I do a greet excesse, that is to seyn, that I venge
oon outrage by another.'
'A,' quod dame Prudence, 'ye seyn youre wyl and as yow
liketh, but in no caas of the world a man sholde nat doon
outrage ne excesse for to vengen hym.   For Cassidore seith
that "as yvele dooth he that vengeth hym by outrage as he
that dooth the outrage."   And therfore ye shul venge yow
after the ordre of [*according to*] right, that is to seyn, by the
2110 lawe, and noght by excesse ne by outrage.   And also, if ye
wol venge yow of the outrage of youre adversaries in oother
manere than right comandeth, ye synnen.   And therfore
seith Senec that "a man shal nevere vengen shrewednesse
[*evil*] by shrewednesse."   And if ye seye that right axeth
[*demands*] a man to defenden violence by violence, and
fightyng by fightyng, certes ye seye sooth [*truth*], whan the
defense is doon anon withouten intervalle or withouten
tariyng or delay, for to deffenden hym and nat for to vengen
hym.   And it bihoveth that a man putte swich attemperance
2120 in his deffense that men have no cause ne matiere to repreven
hym that deffendeth hym of excesse and outrage, for ellis
were it agayn resoun.   Pardee [*indeed*], ye knowen wel that
ye maken no deffense [*resistance*] as now for to deffende yow,
but for to venge yow; and so seweth it that ye han no wyl to
do youre dede attemprely.   And therfore me thynketh that
pacience is good; for Salomon seith that "he that is nat
pacient shal have greet harm."'
'Certes,' quod Melibee, 'I graunte yow that whan a man is
inpacient and wrooth, of that that toucheth hym noght and
2130 that aperteneth nat unto hym, though it harme hym, it is no
wonder.   For the lawe seith that "he is coupable [*guilty*] that
entremetteth hym [*interferes*] or medleth with swych thyng
as aperteneth [*belongs*] nat unto hym."   And Salomon seith
that "he that entremetteth hym of the noyse or strif of another
man is lyk to hym that taketh an hound by the eris [*ears*]."
For right as he that taketh a straunge hound by the eris is
outherwhile [*sometimes*] biten with [*by*] the hound, right in
the same wise is it resoun that he have harm that by his

2104–6 You speak your mind as you please, but in no circumstances
   in this world should a man commit violence.
2119–21 And a man should defend himself with such moderation that
   others have no cause to reproach him with excess and cruelty.
2124–5 And so it follows that you have no desire to take action in a
   moderate manner.
2128–31 When a man is impatient and angry in a matter that does not
   concern him, it is not to be wondered at if he comes to harm.

inpacience medleth hym of the noyse of another man, wheras
2140 it aperteneth nat unto hym.   But ye knowen wel that this
dede, that is to seyn, my grief and my disese [*distress*], toucheth
me right ny [*very closely*].   And therfore, though I be wrooth
and inpacient, it is no merveille.   And, savynge youre grace,
I kan nat seen that it myghte greetly harme me though I tooke
vengeaunce.   For I am richer and moore myghty than myne
enemys been; and wel knowen ye that by moneye and by
havynge grete possessions been alle the thynges of this world
governed.   And Salomon seith that "alle thynges obeyen to
moneye.'"
2150   Whan Prudence hadde herd hir housbonde avanten hym
[*boast*] of his richesse and of his moneye, dispreisynge [*disparag-
ing*] the power of his adversaries, she spak, and seyde in this
wise: 'Certes, deere sire, I graunte yow that ye been riche and
myghty, and that the richesses been goode to hem that han
wel ygeten [*got*] hem and wel konne usen hem.   For right as
the body of a man may nat lyven withoute the soule, namoore
may it lyve withouten temporeel goodes.   And by richesses
may a man gete hym grete freendes.   And therfore seith
Pamphilles: "If a net-herdes [*cowherd's*] doghter," seith he,
2160 "be riche, she may chesen of a thousand men which she wol
take to [*for*] hir housbonde; for, of a thousand men, oon wol
nat forsaken hire ne refusen hire."   And this Pamphilles
seith also: "If thow be right happy"—that is to seyn, if thou
be right riche—"thou shalt fynde a greet nombre of felawes
[*companions*] and freendes.   And if thy fortune change that
[*so that*] thou wexe povre, farewel freendshipe and felaweshipe;
for thou shalt be alloone withouten any compaignye, but if it
be the compaignye of povre folk."   And yet seith this Pamphilles moreover that "they that been thralle and bonde of
2170 lynage [*by birth*] shullen been maad worthy and noble by the
richesses."   And right so as by richesses ther comen manye
goodes, right so by poverte come ther manye harmes and
yveles.   For greet poverte constreyneth a man to do manye
yveles.   And therfore clepeth [*calls*] Cassidore poverte the
mooder of ruyne, that is to seyn, the mooder of overthrowynge
or fallynge doun.   And therfore seith Piers Alfonce: "Oon
of the gretteste adversitees of this world is whan a free man by
kynde [*nature*] or of burthe is constreyned by poverte to eten
the almesse [*alms*] of his enemy," and the same seith Innocent
2180 in oon of his bookes.   He seith that "sorweful and myshappy
[*unhappy*] is the condicioun of a povre beggere; for if he
axe [*begs*] nat his mete [*food*], he dyeth for hunger; and if he
axe, he dyeth for shame; and algates [*in any case*] necessitee
constreyneth hym to axe."   And therfore seith Salomon that
"bet [*better*] it is to dye than for to have swich poverte."   And
as the same Salomon seith, "Bettre it is to dye of bitter deeth
than for to lyven in swich wise."   By thise resons that I have

seid unto yow, and by manye othere resons that I koude seye, I graunte yow that richesses been goode to hem that geten
2190 hem wel, and to hem that wel usen tho [*those*] richesses. And therfore wol I shewe yow hou ye shul have yow and how ye shul bere yow in gaderynge of richesses, and in what manere ye shul usen hem.

First, ye shul geten hem withouten greet desir, by good leyser, sokyngly and nat over-hastily. For a man that is to desirynge to gete richesses abaundoneth hym first to thefte, and to alle othere yveles; and therfore seith Salomon, "He that hasteth hym to bisily to wexe riche shal be noon inno-cent." He seith also that "the richesse that hastily cometh to
2200 a man, soone and lightly [*easily*] gooth and passeth fro a man; but that richesse that cometh litel and [*by*] litel, wexeth alwey and multiplieth." And, sire, ye shul geten richesses by youre wit [*intelligence*] and by youre travaille unto youre profit; and that withouten wrong or harm doynge to any oother persone. For the lawe seith that "ther maketh no man himselven riche, if he do harm to another wight." This is to seyn, that nature deffendeth [*prohibits*] and forbedeth by right [*rightly*] that no man make hymself riche unto the harm of another persone. And Tullius seith that "no sorwe, ne no drede of deeth, ne no
2210 thyng that may falle [*happen*] unto a man, is so muchel agayns [*against*] nature as a man to encressen his owene profit to the harm of another man. And though the grete men and the myghty men geten richesses moore lightly than thou, yet shaltou nat been ydel ne slow to do thy profit, for thou shalt in alle wise flee [*shun*] ydelnesse." For Salomon seith that "ydelnesse techeth a man to do manye yveles." And the same Salomon seith that "he that travailleth and bisieth hym to tilien [*till*] his land, shal eten breed; but he that is ydel and casteth hym [*applies himself*] to no bisynesse ne occupacioun,
2220 shal falle into poverte, and dye for hunger." And he that is ydel and slow kan nevere fynde convenable [*suitable*] tyme for to doon his profit. For ther is a versifiour [*versifier*] seith that "the ydel man excuseth hym in wynter by cause of the grete coold, and in somer by enchesoun [*reason*] of the greete heete." For thise causes seith Caton, "Waketh and enclyneth nat yow over-muchel for to slepe, for over-muchel reste norisseth and causeth manye vices." And therfore seith Seint Jerome, "Dooth somme goode dedes that the devel, which is oure enemy, ne fynde yow nat unocupied." For the devel ne

2191–2 How you should behave and conduct yourself.
2194–5 In a leisurely way, gradually.
2197–9 He who makes haste too eagerly to get rich shall not be innocent.
2205 No man makes himself rich.
2214 To work for your own profit.
2225–6 Be wakeful and not too much inclined to sleep.

2230 taketh nat lightly unto his werkynge [*service*] swiche as he
fyndeth occupied in goode werkes.

Thanne thus, in getynge richesses, ye mosten flee ydelnesse.
And afterward, ye shul use the richesses which ye have geten
by youre wit and by youre travaille, in swich a manere that
men holde yow nat to scars, ne to sparynge, ne to fool-large,
that is to seyen, over-large a spendere. For right as men
blamen an avaricious man by cause of his scarsetee [*parsi-
moniousness*] and chyncherie [*miserliness*], in the same wise is
he to blame that spendeth over-largely. And therfore seith
2240 Caton: "Use," he seith, "thy richesses that thou hast geten
in swich a manere that men have no matiere [*reason*] ne cause
to calle thee neither wrecche ne chynche [*miser*]; for it is a
greet shame to a man to have a povere herte and a riche purs."
He seith also: "The goodes that thou hast ygeten, use hem by
mesure [*in moderation*]," that is to seyn, spende hem mesurably;
for they that folily [*foolishly*] wasten and despenden [*spend*] the
goodes that they han, whan they han namoore propre [*possessions*] of hir owene, they shapen hem [*plan*] to take the goodes
of another man. I seye thanne that ye shul fleen [*shun*]
2250 avarice; usynge youre richesses in swich manere that men seye
nat that youre richesses been yburyed [*buried*], but that ye
have hem in youre myght and in youre weeldynge [*control*].
For a wys man repreveth the avaricious man, and seith thus
in two vers [*verses*]: "Wherto [*wherefore*] and why burieth a
man his goodes by his grete avarice, and knoweth wel that
nedes moste he [*he must needs*] dye? For deeth is the ende
of every man as in this present lyf." And for what cause or
enchesoun [*reason*] joyneth he hym or knytteth he hym so faste
unto his goodes that alle hise wittes mowen nat disseveren
2260 [*separate*] hym or departen [*part*] hym from his goodes, and
knoweth wel, or oghte knowe, that whan he is deed he shal
no thyng bere with hym out of this world? And therfore
seith Seint Austyn [*Augustine*] that "the avaricious man is
likned unto helle, that the moore it swelweth [*swallows*], the
moore desir it hath to swelwe and devoure." And as wel as
ye wolde eschewe [*avoid*] to be called an avaricious man or
chynche [*miser*], as wel sholde ye kepe yow and governe yow
in swich a wise that men calle yow nat fool-large. Therfore
seith Tullius: "The goodes," he seith, "of thyn hous ne
2270 sholde nat been hyd ne kept so cloos, but that they myghte
been opened by pitee and debonairetee [*gentleness*];" that is
to seyn, to yeven [*give*] part to hem that han greet nede; "ne
thy goodes shullen nat been so opene to been every mannes
goodes." Afterward, in getynge of youre richesses and in

2235 Men consider you neither too parsimonious, nor too sparing, nor
too foolishly generous.
2272-4 Nor shall your goods be so free as to be every man's goods.

usynge hem, ye shul alwey have thre thynges in youre herte,
that is to seyn, oure Lord God, conscience, and good name.
First, ye shul have God in youre herte, and for no richesse ye
shullen do no thyng which may in any manere displese God,
that is youre creatour and makere.   For after [*according to*]
2280 the word of Salomon, "It is bettre to have a litel good with
the love of God, than to have muchel good and tresour, and
lese [*lose*] the love of his Lord God."   And the prophete seith
that "bettre it is to been a good man and have litel good and
tresour, than to been holden a shrewe [*wicked person*] and have
grete richesses."   And yet seye I ferthermoore, that ye sholde
alwey doon youre bisynesse [*take pains*] to gete yow richesses,
so that ye gete hem with good conscience.   And th'apostle
seith that "ther nys thyng in this world of which we sholden
have so [*such*] greet joye as whan oure conscience bereth us
2290 good witnesse."   And the wise man seith, "The substance of
a man is ful good, whan synne is nat in mannes conscience."
Afterward, in getynge of youre richesses and in usynge of
hem, yow moste have greet bisynesse and greet diligence that
youre goode name be alwey kept and conserved [*preserved*].
For Salomon seith that "bettre it is and moore it availleth
[*profits*] a man to have a good name, than for to have grete
richesses."   And therfore he seith in another place, "Do
greet diligence [*do your utmost*]," seith Salomon, "in kepyng
of thy freend and of thy goode name; for it shal lenger abide
2300 with thee than any tresour, be it never so precious."   And
certes [*certainly*] he sholde nat be called a gentil [*noble*] man
that after God and good conscience, alle thynges left, ne dooth
his diligence and bisynesse to kepen his goode name.   And
Cassidore seith that "it is signe of a gentil herte, whan a man
loveth and desireth to han a good name."   And therfore seith
Seint Austyn that "ther been two thynges that arn necessarie
and nedefulle, and that is good conscience and good loos
[*reputation*]; that is to seyn, good conscience to thyn owene
persone inward, and good loos for thy neighebor outward."
2310 And he that trusteth hym so muchel [*trusts so much*] in his
goode conscience that he displeseth, and setteth at noght
[*naught*] his goode name or loos, and rekketh [*cares*] noght
though he kepe nat his goode name, nys but a crueel cherl
[*cruel fellow*].

Sire, now have I shewed yow how ye shul do in getynge
richesses, and how ye shullen usen hem, and I se wel that for
the trust that ye han in youre richesses ye wole moeve [*begin*]
werre and bataille.   I conseille yow that ye bigynne no werre

2293 You must exert yourself diligently.
2302 In accord with God and a good conscience, all other things laid
aside.
2309-10 A good conscience within yourself, and a good reputation
among your neighbours outside.

in trust of youre richesses, for they ne suffisen noght werres
2320 to mayntene. And therfore seith a philosophre, "That man
that desireth and wole algates [*at any price*] han werre, shal
never have suffisaunce [*sufficiency*]; for the richer that he is,
the gretter despenses [*expenditure*] moste he make, if he wole
have worshipe [*honour*] and victorie." And Salomon seith
that "the gretter richesses that a man hath, the mo despendours
[*spenders*] he hath." And, deere sire, al be it so that for youre
richesses ye mowe have muchel folk, yet bihoveth it nat [*it
is not necessary*], ne it is nat good, to bigynne werre, whereas
[*seeing that*] ye mowe in oother manere have pees unto youre
2330 worshipe and profit. For the victorie of batailles that been
in this world lyth nat in greet nombre or multitude of the
peple, ne in the vertu of man, but it lith in the wyl and in the
hand of oure Lord God Almyghty. And therfore Judas
Machabeus, which was Goddes knyght, whan he sholde fighte
agayn his adversarie that hadde a gretter nombre and a gretter
multitude of folk and strenger than was this peple of Machabee, yet he reconforted [*encouraged*] his litel compaignye, and
seyde right in this wise: "Als lightly [*as easily*]," quod he,
"may oure Lord God Almyghty yeve victorie to a fewe folk
2340 as to many folk; for the victorie of a bataile comth nat by the
grete nombre of peple, but it cometh from oure Lord God of
hevene." And, deere sire, for as muchel as ther is no man
certein if he be worthy that God yeve [*should give*] hym victorie,
[*ne plus que il est certain se il est digne de l'amour de Dieu*],
or naught, after that Salomon seith, therfore every man
sholde greetly drede werres to bigynne. And by cause that
in batailles fallen [*occur*] manye perils, and happeth outher
while [*sometimes*] that as soone is the grete man slayn as the
litel man; and as it is writen in the seconde Book of Kynges,
2350 "The dedes of batailles been aventurouse [*risky*] and nothyng
certeyne, for as lightly is oon hurt with a spere as another";
and for [*because*] ther is gret peril in werre; therfore sholde a
man flee and eschue [*avoid*] werre, in as muchel as a man may
goodly. For Salomon seith, "He that loveth peril shal falle
in peril."'

After that Dame Prudence hadde spoken in this manere,
Melibee answerde, and seyde: 'I see wel, dame Prudence,
that by youre faire wordes, and by youre resouns that ye han
shewed me, that the werre liketh yow no thyng; but I have nat
2360 yet herd youre conseil, how I shal do in this nede.'

2326-7 Although because of your wealth you may have many people (at
your command).
2330-1 For victory by battle in this world does not lie with.
2344-5 Any more than he is certain whether he is worthy or not of God's
love, according to what Solomon says.
2353-4 As far as he properly can.
2359 War does not please you at all.

'Certes,' quod she, 'I conseille yow that ye accorde with youre adversaries and that ye have pees with hem. For Seint Jame seith in his Epistles that "by concord and pees the smale richesses wexen grete, and by debaat [*strife*] and discord the grete richesses fallen doun." And ye knowen wel that oon of the gretteste and moost sovereyn thyng that is in this world is unytee [*unity*] and pees. And therfore seyde oure Lord Jhesu Crist to his apostles in this wise: "Wel happy and blessed been they that loven and purchacen [*promote*] pees, for they
2370 been called children of God."'

'A,' quod Melibee, 'now se I wel that ye loven nat myn honour ne my worshipe. Ye knowen wel that myne adversaries han bigonnen this debaat and bryge [*contention*] by hire outrage, and ye se wel that they ne requeren [*beg*] ne preyen me nat of pees, ne they asken nat to be reconsiled. Wol ye thanne that I go and meke me [*humble myself*] and obeye me to hem, and crie hem mercy? For sothe, that were nat my worshipe. For right as men seyn that "over-greet hoomlynesse [*familiarity*] engendreth dispreisyng [*contempt*],"
2380 so fareth it by to greet humylitee or mekenesse.'

Thanne bigan dame Prudence to maken semblant of wratthe, and seyde: 'Certes, sire, sauf [*saving*] youre grace, I love youre honour and youre profit as I do myn owene, and evere have doon; ne ye, ne noon oother, seyn nevere the contrarie. And yit if I hadde seyd that ye sholde han purchaced [*obtained*] the pees and the reconsiliacioun, I ne hadde nat muchel mystaken me, ne seyd amys. For the wise man seith, "The dissensioun bigynneth by [*with*] another man, and the reconsilyng bygynneth by thyself." And the prophete
2390 seith, "Flee shrewednesse [*evil*] and do goodnesse; seke pees and folwe it, as muchel as in thee is." Yet seye I nat that ye shul rather pursue [*sooner appeal*] to youre adversaries for pees than they shuln [*shall*] to yow. For I knowe wel that ye been so hard-herted that ye wol do no thyng for me. And Salomon seith, "He that hath over-hard an herte, atte laste he shal myshappe and mystyde."'

Whanne Melibee hadde herd dame Prudence maken semblant of wratthe, he seyde in this wise: 'Dame I prey yow that ye be nat displeased of [*with*] thynges that I seye, for ye
2400 knowe wel that I am angry and wrooth, and that is no wonder; and they that been wrothe witen [*know*] nat wel what they don, ne what they seyn. Therfore the prophete seith that

2377–8 In truth, that would not be to my honour.
2380 So it is with too great humility or meekness.
2381–2 Then dame Prudence began to make a show of being angry.
2386–7 I would not have been far wrong.
2389 *the prophete*, i.e. David.
2396 He shall meet with misfortune and come to grief.

"troubled eyen han no cleer sighte." But seyeth and con-
seileth me as yow liketh, for I am redy to do right as ye wol
desire; and if ye repreve me of my folye, I am the moore holden
[*bound*] to love yow and to preyse yow. For Salomon seith
that "he that repreveth hym that dooth folye, he shal fynde
gretter grace than he that deceyveth hym by sweete words."'

Thanne seide dame Prudence, 'I make no semblant of
2410 wratthe ne anger, but for youre grete profit' For Salomon
seith, "He is moore worth that repreveth or chideth a fool
for his folye, shewynge hym semblant of wratthe, than he that
supporteth hym and preyseth hym in his mysdoynge, and
laugheth at his folye." And this same Salomon seith afterward that "by the sorweful visage [*face*] of a man," that is to
seyn by the sory and hevy contenaunce of a man, "the fool correcteth and amendeth hymself."'

Thanne seyde Melibee, 'I shal nat konne [*be able to*] answere
to so manye faire resouns as ye putten to me and shewen.
2420 Seyeth shortly youre wyl and youre conseil, and I am al redy
to fulfille and parfourne it.'

Thanne dame Prudence discovered [*made known*] al hir
wyl to hym, and seyde, 'I conseille yow,' quod she, 'aboven
alle thynges, that ye make pees bitwene God and yow; and
beth reconsiled unto hym and to his grace. For, as I have
seyd yow heer biforn, God hath suffred yow to have this
tribulacioun and disese [*misery*] for youre synnes. And if
ye do as I sey yow, God wol sende youre adversaries unto yow,
and maken hem fallen at youre feet, redy to do youre wyl and
2430 youre comandementz. For Salomon seith, "Whan the
condicioun of man is plesaunt and likynge [*pleasing*] to God,
he chaungeth the hertes of the mannes adversaries and constreyneth hem to biseken [*beseech*] hym of pees and of grace."
And I prey yow lat me speke with youre adversaries in privee
[*private*] place; for they shul nat knowe that it be of youre wyl
or of youre assent. And thanne, whan I knowe hir wil and
hire entente, I may conseille yow the moore seurely [*surely*].'

'Dame,' quod Melibee, 'dooth youre wil and youre likynge;
for I putte me hoolly in youre disposicioun and ordinaunce.'
2440 Thanne dame Prudence, whan she saugh [*saw*] the good wyl
of hir housbonde, delibered and took avys in hirself, thinkinge
how she myghte brynge this nede [*difficult matter*] unto a good
conclusioun and to a good ende. And whan she saugh hir
tyme, she sente for thise adversaries to come unto hire into a
pryvee place, and shewed wisely unto hem the grete goodes
[*benefits*] that comen of pees, and the grete harmes and perils

2412 Making a show of anger for his benefit.
2435-6 That it is with your will and assent.
2439 I put myself wholly at your disposal and command.
2441 Deliberated with herself.

that been in werre; and seyde to hem in a goodly manere hou
that hem oughten have greet repentaunce of the injurie and
wrong that they hadden doon to Melibee hir lord, and unto
2450 hire, and to hire doghter.

And whan they herden the goodliche [*kindly*] wordes of
dame Prudence, they weren so supprised and ravysshed, and
hadden so greet joye of hire that wonder was to telle. 'A,
lady,' quod they, 'ye han shewed unto us the blessynge of
swetnesse, after [*according to*] the sawe [*saying*] of David the
prophete; for the reconsilynge which we been nat worthy to
have in no manere, but we oghte requeren it with greet
contricioun and humylitee, ye of youre grete goodnesse have
presented unto us. Now se we wel that the science [*learning*]
2460 and the konnynge [*wisdom*] of Salomon is ful trewe. For he
seith that "sweete wordes multiplien and encreescen freendes,
and maken shrewes [*wicked persons*] to be debonaire [*gentle*]
and meeke."

'Certes,' quod they, 'we putten oure dede [*action*] and al
oure matere and cause al hoolly in youre goode wyl and been
redy to obeye to the speche and comandement of my lord
Melibee. And therfore, deere and benynge lady, we preien
yow and biseke yow as mekely as we konne and mowen, that
it lyke [*please*] unto youre grete goodnesse to fulfillen in dede
2470 youre goodliche [*kindly*] wordes. For we consideren and
knowelichen [*acknowledge*] that we han offended and greved
my lord Melibee out of mesure, so ferforth that we be nat
of power to maken his amendes. And therfore we oblige
and bynden us [*ourselves*] and oure freendes for to doon al his
wyl and his comandementz. But peraventure [*perhaps*] he hath
swich hevynesse [*resentment*] and swich wratthe to us-ward
[*towards us*], by cause of oure offense, that he wole enjoyne
us swich a peyne as we mowe nat bere ne susteene. And
therfore, noble lady, we biseke [*beseech*] to youre wommanly
2480 pitee to taken swich avysement in this nede that we, ne oure
freendes be nat desherited [*disinherited*] ne destroyed thurgh
oure folye.'

'Certes,' quod Prudence, 'it is an hard thyng and right
perilous that a man putte [*should put*] hym al outrely [*utterly*]
in the arbitracioun and juggement, and in the myght and

2447–8 And told them in a kindly manner that they should greatly
repent the injury.

2452–3 They were so surprised and enraptured, and so highly delighted
with her, that it is marvellous to relate.

2456–8 For the reconciliation which we are not at all worthy to have,
but which we ought to beg with great contrition.

2468 As humbly as we possibly can.

2472–3 To such a degree that we lack the power to make him amends.

2477–8 That he will lay such a penalty on us.

2480 To take such counsel in this extremity.

power of his enemys. For Salomon seith, "Leeveth [*believe*]
me, and yeveth credence to that I shal seyn: I seye," quod he,
"ye peple, folk and governours of hooly chirche, to thy sone,
to thy wyf, to thy freend, ne to thy broother, ne yeve thou
2490 nevere myght ne maistre of thy body whil thou lyvest."   Now
sithen he deffendeth [*forbids*] that man sholde nat yeven to his
broother ne to his freend the myght of his body, by a strenger
resoun he deffendeth and forbedeth a man to yeven hymself
to his enemy.   And nathelees I conseille you that ye mystruste
nat my lord, for I woot wel and knowe verraily that he is
debonaire and meeke, large, curteys, and nothyng desirous ne
coveitous of good ne richesse.   For ther nys nothyng in this
world that he desireth, save oonly worshipe and honour.
Forthermoore I knowe wel and am right seur [*sure*] that he
2500 shal nothyng doon in this nede withouten my conseil; and I
shal so werken in this cause [*matter*] that, by the grace of oure
Lord God, ye shul been reconsiled unto us.'

Thanne seyden they with o [*one*] voys, 'Worshipful lady, we
putten us and oure goodes al fully in youre wil and disposicioun, and been redy to comen, what day that it like
unto youre noblesse to lymyte us or assigne us, for to maken
oure obligacioun and boond as strong as it liketh unto youre
goodnesse, that we mowe fulfille the wille of yow and of my
lord Melibee.'

2510 When dame Prudence hadde herd the answeres of thise
men, she bad hem goon agayn prively [*secretly*]; and she
retourned to hir lord Melibee, and tolde hym how she foond
his adversaries ful repentant, knowelechynge [*acknowledging*]
ful lowely [*humbly*] hir synnes and trespas, and how they
were redy to suffren all peyne [*penalty*], requirynge [*begging*]
and preiynge hym of mercy and pitee.

Thanne seyde Melibee: 'He is wel worthy to have pardoun
and foryifnesse of his synne, that excuseth nat his synne,
but knowelecheth it and repenteth hym, axinge indulgence.
2520 For Senec seith, "Ther is the remissioun and foryifnesse,
where as the confessioun is"; for confessioun is neighebor to
innocence.   And he seith in another place that "he that hath
shame of his synne and knowlecheth it, is worthy remissioun."
And therfore I assente and conferme me to have pees; but
it is good that we do it nat withouten the assent and wyl of
oure freendes.'

Thanne was Prudence right glad and joyeful, and seyde:
'Certes, sire,' quod she, 'ye han wel and goodly [*rightly*]
answered; for right [*just*] as by the conseil, assent, and help

---

2489–90 Never give power over your body as long as you live.
2495–7 I know well and truly that he is gentle and meek, generous,
    courteous, and not at all desirous or covetous of goods or wealth.
2505–6 On whatever day it pleases your nobleness to allot or assign to us.
2524 I consent and firmly resolve to have peace.

2530 of youre freendes ye han been stired [*moved*] to venge yow and maken werre, right so withouten hire conseil shul ye nat accorden yow [*reconcile yourself*] ne have pees with youre adversaries. For the lawe seith: "Ther nys no thyng so good by wey of kynde as a thyng to be unbounde by hym that it was ybounde."'

And thanne dame Prudence, withouten delay or tariynge, sente anon hire messages for hire kyn, and for hir olde freendes which that were trewe and wyse, and tolde hem by ordre [*in order*] in the presence of Melibee al this mateere as it is aboven
2540 expressed and declared, and preyden hem that they wolde yeven hire avys [*advice*] and conseil what best were to doon in this nede. And whan Melibees freendes hadde taken hire avys and deliberacioun of the forseide mateere, and hadden examyned it by greet bisynesse [*care*] and greet diligence, they yave ful conseil [*unanimous advice*] for to have pees and reste [*quiet*], and that Melibee sholde receyve with good herte his adversaries to foryifnesse and mercy.

And whan dame Prudence hadde herd [*heard*] the assent of hir lord Melibee, and the conseil of his freendes, accorde with
2550 hire wille and hire entencioun, she was wonderly [*wondrously*] glad in hire herte, and seyde: 'Ther is an old proverbe,' quod she, 'seith that "the goodnesse that thou mayst do this day, do it, and abide nat ne delaye it nat til to-morwe." And therfore I conseille that ye sende youre messages [*messengers*], swiche as been discrete and wise, unto youre adversaries, tellynge hem on youre bihalve [*behalf*] that if they wole trete [*treat*] of pees and of accord, that they shape hem [*prepare*] withouten delay or tariyng to comen unto us.' Which thyng parfourned was in dede. And whanne thise trespassours and
2560 repentynge folk of hire folies, that is to seyn, the adversaries of Melibee, hadden herd what thise messagers seyden unto hem, they weren right glad and joyeful, and answereden ful mekely and benignely, yeldynge graces [*giving thanks*] and thankynges to hir lord Melibee and to al his compaignye; and shopen hem [*prepared*] withouten delay to go with the messagers, and obeye to the comandement of hir lord Melibee.

And right anon they tooken hire wey to the court of Melibee, and tooken with hem somme of hire trewe freendes to maken feith for hem and for to been hire borwes. And whan they
2570 were comen to the presence of Melibee, he seyde hem thise wordes: 'It standeth thus,' quod Melibee, 'and sooth [*true*] it is, that ye, causelees and withouten skile [*cause*] and resoun,

2533–5 There is nothing so good by way of nature as for a thing to be undone by him who did it.
2542–3 When Melibeus' friends had consulted and deliberated.
2559–60 These offenders and people repenting of their follies.
2568–9 To swear to their good faith and stand surety for them.

han doon grete injuries and wronges to me and to my wyf
Prudence, and to my doghter also. For ye han entred into myn
hous by violence, and have doon swich outrage that alle men
knowen wel that ye have disserved the deeth. And therfore
wol I knowe and wite [*learn*] of yow wheither ye wol putte the
punyssement and the chastisynge and the vengeance of this
outrage in the wyl of me and of my wyf Prudence, or ye wol
2580 nat?'

Thanne the wiseste of hem thre answerde for hem alle, and
seyde, 'Sire,' quod he, 'we knowen wel that we been unworthy
to comen unto the court of so greet a lord and so worthy as
ye been. For we han so greetly mystaken us, and han
offended and agilt [*sinned*] in swich a wise agayn youre heigh
lordshipe, that trewely we han disserved the deeth. But yet,
for the grete goodnesse and debonairetee [*gentleness*] that
al the world witnesseth of youre persone, we submytten us to
the excellence and benignitee of youre gracious lordshipe,
2590 and been redy to obeie to alle youre comandementz; bisekynge
yow that of youre merciable [*merciful*] pitee ye wol considere
oure grete repentaunce and lowe [*humble*] submyssioun, and
graunten us foryevenesse of oure outrageous trespas and
offense. For wel we knowe that youre liberal grace and
mercy strecchen hem [*reach*] ferther into goodnesse than doon
oure outrageouse giltes and trespas into wikkednesse, al be
it that cursedly [*wickedly*] and dampnablely we han agilt
agayn youre heigh lordshipe.'

Thanne Melibee took hem up fro the ground ful benignely,
2600 and receyved hire obligaciouns and hir boondes by hire othes
upon hire plegges and borwes, and assigned hem a certeyn day
to retourne unto his court, for to accepte and receyve the
sentence and juggement that Melibee wolde comande to be
doon [*passed*] on hem by [*for*] the causes aforeseyd. Whiche
thynges ordeyned, every man retourned to his hous.

And whan that dame Prudence saugh hir tyme, she freyned
and axed hir lord Melibee what vengeance he thoughte to
taken of his adversaries.

To which Melibee answerde, and seyde: 'Certes,' quod he,
2610 'I thynke and purpose me fully to desherite hem of al that
evere they han, and for to putte hem in exil for evere.'

'Certes,' quod dame Prudence, 'this were a crueel sentence
and muchel agayn resoun. For ye been riche ynough, and
han no nede of oother mennes good; and ye myghte lightly
[*easily*] in this wise gete yow a coveitous name, which is a
vicious thyng, and oghte been eschued of [*avoided by*] every

2584 For we have erred so greatly.
2600-1 Received their sureties and their bonds confirmed by oaths and
    pledges.
2606-7 She asked and inquired of her lord Melibeus.
2615 A reputation for covetousness.

good man. For after the sawe of the word of the Apostle,
"Coveitise is roote of alle harmes."   And therfore it were
bettre for yow to lese so muchel good [*as much property*] of
2620 youre owene, than for to taken of hir good in this manere;
for bettre it is to lesen good with worshipe [*honour*], than it is
to wynne good with vileynye and shame.   And everi man
oghte to doon his diligence and his bisynesse to geten hym a
good name.   And yet shal he nat oonly bisie hym in kepynge
of his good name, but he shal also enforcen hym [*endeavour*]
alwey to do somthyng by which he may renovelle [*renew*] his
good name.   For it is writen that "the olde good loos
[*reputation*] or good name of a man is soone goon and passed,
whan it is nat newed [*renewed*] ne renovelled."   And as
2630 touchynge that ye seyn ye wole exile youre adversaries, that
thynketh me muchel agayn resoun and out of mesure [*moderation*], considered [*considering*] the power that they han yeve
yow upon hemself.   And it is writen that "he is worthy to
lesen his privilege, that mysuseth the myght and the power
that is yeven hym."   And I sette cas ye myghte enjoyne hem
that peyne by right and by lawe, which I trowe ye mowe [*may*]
nat do, I seye ye mighte nat putten it to [*into*] execucioun
peraventure, and thanne were it likly to retourne to the werre
as it was biforn.   And therfore, if ye wole that men do yow
2640 obeisance [*homage*], ye moste deemen moore curteisly; this
is to seyn, ye moste yeven moore esy sentences and juggementz.
For it is writen that "he that moost [*most*] curteisly comandeth,
to hym men moost obeyen."   And therfore I prey yow that in
this necessitee and in this nede ye caste yow to overcome youre
herte.   For Senec seith that "he that overcometh his herte,
overcometh twies [*twice*]."   And Tullius seith: "Ther is no
thyng so comendable in a greet lord as whan he is debonaire
[*gentle*] and meeke, and appeseth him lightly."   And I prey
yow that ye wole forbere now to do vengeance, in swich
2650 a manere that youre goode name may be kept and conserved [*preserved*], and that men mowe have cause and
mateere [*reason*] to preyse yow of [*for*] pitee and of mercy, and
that ye have no cause to repente yow of thyng that ye doon.
For Senec seith, "He overcometh in an yvel manere that
repenteth hym of his victorie."   Wherfore I pray yow, lat
mercy been in youre herte, to th'effect [*end*] and entente
[*purpose*] that God Almighty have mercy on yow in his laste

2622-4 Everyone should exert himself diligently to get himself a good
    name.
2629-30 And as for your statement that you will exile your adversaries.
2635-6 And even supposing you could impose that penalty by right and
    law.
2640 You must judge more graciously.
2648 And is easily appeased.
2654-5 He is a poor victor that repents of his victory.

juggement. For Seint Jame seith in his Epistle: "Juggement
withouten mercy shal be doon to hym that hath no mercy of
2660 [on] another wight [person]."

Whan Melibee hadde herd the grete skiles [arguments] and
resouns of dame Prudence, and hire wise informaciouns and
techynges, his herte gan enclyne to the wil of his wif, considerynge hir trewe entente, and conformed hym anon, and
assented fully to werken after [act on] hir conseil; and thonked
God, of whom procedeth al vertu and alle goodnesse, that
hym sente a wyf of so greet discrecioun. And whan the day
cam that his adversaries sholde appieren in his presence, he
spak unto hem ful goodly [very kindly], and seyde in this wyse:
2670 'Al be it so that of youre pride and heigh presumpcioun and
folie, and of youre necligence and unkonnynge [ignorance],
ye have mysborn yow [misbehaved] and trespassed unto me,
yet for as muche as I see and biholde youre grete humylitee,
and that ye been sory and repentant of youre giltes, it constreyneth me to doon yow grace and mercy. Wherfore I
receyve yow to my grace, and foryeve yow outrely [entirely]
alle the offenses, injuries, and wronges that ye have doon
agayn me and myne, to this effect and to this ende that God
of his endelees mercy wole at the tyme of oure diynge [dying]
2680 foryeven us oure giltes that we han trespassed to hym in this
wrecched world. For doutelees, if we be sory and repentant
of the synnes and giltes which we han trespassed in the sighte
of oure Lord God, he is so free [generous] and so merciable
[merciful] that he wole foryeven us oure giltes, and bryngen
us to the blisse that nevere hath ende. Amen.

HEERE IS ENDED CHAUCERS TALE OF MELIBEE AND
OF DAME PRUDENCE

2664 And he at once conformed.
2680 Forgive us the sins we have committed against Him.

THE PROLOGUE OF THE MONK'S TALE

THE MURYE WORDES OF THE HOOST TO THE MONK

WHAN ended was my tale of Melibee,
And of Prudence and hire benignytee,   *goodness*
Oure Hooste seyde, 'As I am feithful man,
And by that precious corpus Madrian,
2690 I hadde levere than a barel ale   *rather*
That Goodelief, my wyf, hadde herd this tale!
For she nys no thyng of swich pacience   *is not*
As was this Melibeus wyf Prudence.
By Goddes bones! whan I bete my knaves, *serving-lads*
2695 She bryngeth me forth the grete clobbed staves,
And crieth, "Slee the dogges everichoon, *slay; every one*
And brek hem, bothe bak and every boon!" *break*
 And if that any neighebor of myne
Wol nat in chirche to my wyf enclyne,   *bow*
2700 Or be so hardy to hire to trespace,
Whan she comth hoom she rampeth in my face, *flies*
And crieth, "False coward, wrek thy wyf! *avenge*
By corpus bones, I wol have thy knyf,
And thou shalt have my distaf and go spynne!"
2705 Fro day to nyght right thus she wol bigynne. *dawn*
"Allas!" she seith, "that evere I was shape *destined*
To wedden a milksop, or a coward ape,   *cowardly*
That wol been overlad with every wight!
Thou darst nat stonden by thy wyves right!"
2710 This is my lif, but if that I wol fighte;
And out at dore anon I moot me dighte,
Or elles I am but lost, but if that I
Be lik a wilde leoun, fool-hardy.
I woot wel she wol do me slee som day
2715 Som neighebor, and thanne go my way;
For I am perilous with knyf in honde,   *dangerous*
Al be it that I dar nat hire withstonde,   *although*

2688 As I am a true believer.
2689 *corpus Madrian*, body of Madrian (an unknown saint, probably
 the Host's perversion of an authentic name).
2700 Or is rash enough to offend her.
2708 Put upon by everyone.
2709 You dare not stand up for your wife's rights.
2710 Unless I'm willing to fight.
2711–13 And I must take myself out of doors in a hurry or I'm as good as
 lost, unless indeed I'm rash enough to play the lion.
2714–15 One day I'm sure she'll egg me on to kill a neighbour, and then
 leave me to run for it.

431

For she is byg in armes, by my feith: *upon my word*
That shal he fynde that hire mysdooth or seith,—

2720 But lat us passe awey from this mateere.
My lord, the Monk,' quod he, 'be myrie of cheere,   *cheer up*
For ye shul telle a tale trewely.
Loo, Rouchestre stant heer faste by!   *Rochester; near*
Ryde forth, myn owene lord, brek nat oure game.

2725 But, by my trouthe, I knowe nat youre name.   *on my honour*
Wher shal I calle yow my lord daun John,
Or daun Thomas, or elles daun Albon?
Of what hous be ye, by youre fader kyn?
I vowe to God, thou hast a ful fair skyn;

2730 It is a gentil pasture ther thow goost.   *fine; where*
Thou art nat lyk a penant or a goost: *penitent; ghost*
Upon my feith, thou art som officer,
Som worthy sexteyn, or som celerer,   *sacristan; cellarer*
For by my fader soule, as to my doom,

2735 Thou art a maister whan thou art at hoom;
No povre cloysterer, ne no novys,   *poor*
But a governour, wily and wys,   *presiding officer*
And therwithal of brawnes and of bones,
A wel-farynge persone for the nones.

2740 I pray to God, yeve hym confusioun
That first thee broghte unto religioun!
Thou woldest han been a tredefowel aright.
Haddestow as greet a leeve, as thou hast myght,   *permission*
To parfourne al thy lust in engendrure,

2745 Thou haddest bigeten ful many a creature.
Allas, why werestow so wyd a cope?
God yeve me sorwe, but, and I were a pope,   *give; if*
Nat oonly thou, but every myghty man,
Though he were shorn ful hye upon his pan,

2750 Sholde have a wyf; for al the world is lorn!
Religioun hath take up al the corn
Of tredyng, and we borel men been shrympes.
Of fieble trees ther comen wrecched ympes.   *miserable shoots*
This maketh that oure heires been so sklendre   *slender*

2719 He'll find that out who does or says the wrong thing to her.
2724 Don't spoil our game, i.e. the game of story-telling.
2726 Shall I call you my lord sir John.
2728 What (religious) house do you belong to, by the honour of your ancestors?
2734–5 In my opinion you're a person in authority when you're at home.
2736 No poor cloistered monk, no novice.
2739 A very good-looking person.
2742 You would have made a brave cock (lit. treader of fowls).
2744 To satisfy your joy in procreation.
2749 Though he is shaven on top of his pate (a reference to the tonsure).
2751–3 Religion has grabbed the best part of procreation, and we lay-men are puny creatures.

2755 And feble that they may nat wel engendre.
This maketh that oure wyves wole assaye   *try*
Religious folk, for ye mowe bettre paye   *can*
Of Venus paiementz than mowe we;   *debts*
God woot, no lussheburghes payen ye!
2760 But be nat wrooth, my lord, though that I pleye.
Ful ofte in game a sooth I have herd seye!'   *truth*
     This worthy Monk took al in pacience.
And seyde, 'I wol doon al my diligence,   *utmost*
As fer as sowneth into honestee,
2765 To telle yow a tale, or two, or three.
And if yow list to herkne hyderward,   *listen to me*
I wol yow seyn the lyf of Seint Edward;
Or ellis, first, tragedies wol I telle,
Of whiche I have an hundred in my celle.
2770 Tragedie is to seyn a certeyn storie,   *means*
As olde bookes maken us memorie,   *remind us*
Of hym that stood in greet prosperitee,
And is yfallen out of heigh degree
Into myserie, and endeth wrecchedly.
2775 And they ben versified communely   *commonly*
Of six feet, which men clepen *exametron*.
In prose eek been endited many oon,   *composed*
And eek in meetre, in many a sondry wyse.
Lo, this declaryng oghte ynogh suffise.
2780   Now herkneth, if yow liketh for to heere.   *you would like*
But first I yow biseeke in this mateere,   *beseech*
Though I by ordre telle nat thise thynges,
Be it of popes, emperours, or kynges,
After hir ages, as men writen fynde,
2785 But tellen hem som bifore and som bihynde,
As it now comth unto my remembraunce
Have me excused of myn ignoraunce.'

EXPLICIT

2759 God knows you pass no spurious coins.
2764 As far as is consistent with decency.
2767 i.e. Edward the Confessor.
2769 *celle.* See I. 172.
2776 In six feet, which are called *hexameters*.
2778 And also in many different kinds of metre.
2779 This description ought to be enough.
2782 *by ordre*, in chronological order.
2784 According to the ages in which they lived.

THE MONK'S TALE

HEERE BIGYNNETH THE MONKES TALE DE CASIBUS VIRORUM ILLUSTRIUM

    I WOL biwaille, in manere of tragedie,   *lament*
    The harm of hem that stoode in heigh degree,   *suffering*
2790 And fillen so that ther nas no remedie   *fell*
    To brynge hem out of hir adversitee.
    For certein, whan that Fortune list to flee,   *chooses*
    Ther may no man the cours of hire withholde.
    Lat no man truste on blynd prosperitee;   *in*
2795 Be war by thise ensamples trewe and olde.

Lucifer

    At Lucifer, though he an angel were,
    And nat a man, at hym wol I bigynne.
    For though Fortune may noon angel dere,   *harm*
    From heigh degree yet fel he for his synne
2800 Doun into helle, where he yet is inne.
    O Lucifer, brightest of angels alle,
    Now artow Sathanas, that mayst nat twynne
    Out of miserie, in which that thou art falle.

Adam

    Loo Adam, in the feeld of Damyssene,
2805 With Goddes owene fynger wroght was he,
    And nat bigeten of mannes sperme unclene,   *seed*
    And welte al paradys savynge o tree.   *ruled; except*
    Hadde nevere worldly man so heigh degree   *such*
    As Adam, til he for mysgovernaunce   *misconduct*
2810 Was dryven out of hys hye prosperitee
    To labour, and to helle, and to meschaunce.   *misfortune*

Sampson

    Loo Sampsoun, which that was annunciat
    By th'angel, longe er his nativitee,
    And was to God Almyghty consecrat,   *consecrated*
2815 And stood in noblesse whil he myghte see.

2793 No one can stay her course.
2802 Now you are Satan, and can never escape.
2804 A reference to the legend that Adam was created in the place where
    Damascus afterwards stood.
2812 Whose birth was foretold.
2815 And stood high in honour as long as he could see.

Was nevere swich another as was hee,
To speke of strengthe, and therwith hardynesse;
But to his wyves toolde he his secree,   *secret*
Thurgh which he slow hymself for wrecched-   *slew; misery*
    nesse.

2820 Sampsoun, this noble almyghty champioun,
Withouten wepen, save his handes tweye,   *two*
He slow and al torente the leoun,   *tore apart*
Toward his weddyng walkynge by the weye.
His false wyf koude hym so plese and preye
2825 Til she his conseil knew; and she, untrewe,   *secret*
Unto his foos his conseil gan biwreye,   *betrayed*
And hym forsook, and took another newe.

Thre hundred foxes took Sampson for ire,
And alle hir tayles he togydre bond,   *fastened*
2830 And sette the foxes tayles alle on fire,
For he on every tayl had knyt a brond;   *tied; firebrand*
And they brende alle the cornes in that lond,   *burned; crops*
And alle hire olyveres, and vynes eke.   *olive-trees; also*
A thousand men he slow eek with his hond,
2835 And hadde no wepen but an asses cheke.   *jaw-bone*

Whan they were slayn, so thursted hym that he
Was wel ny lorn, for which he gan to preye
That God wolde on his peyne han some pitee,
And sende hym drynke, or elles moste he deye;   *must; die*
2840 And of this asses cheke, that was dreye,   *dry*
Out of a wang-tooth sprang anon a welle,   *molar tooth*
Of which he drank ynogh, shortly to seye;
Thus heelp hym God, as *Judicum* can telle.   *helped*

By verray force at Gazan, on a nyght,   *sheer; Gaza*
2845 Maugree Philistiens of that citee,
The gates of the toun he hath up plyght,   *torn*
And on his bak ycaryed hem hath hee   *carried*
Hye on an hill whereas men myghte hem see.   *where*
O noble, almyghty Sampsoun, lief and deere,   *beloved*
2850 Had thou nat toold to wommen thy secree,
In al this world ne hadde been thy peere!

2817 In respect of strength and boldness.
2823 While on his way to his wedding.
2836–7 He had so great a thirst that he was all but lost, and he there-
    fore prayed.
2842 From which he drank his fill, to speak briefly.
2843 *Judicum*, the Book of Judges.
2845 In spite of all the Philistines living in that city.
2851 There would not have been your equal.

This Sampson nevere ciser drank ne wyn,   *strong drink*
Ne on his heed cam rasour noon ne sheere,
By precept of the messager divyn,   *messenger*
2855 For alle his strengthes in his heeres weere.
And fully twenty wynter, yeer by yeere,   *year*
He hadde of Israel the governaunce.   *rule*
But soone shal he wepe many a teere,
For wommen shal hym bryngen to meschaunce!

2860 Unto his lemman Dalida he tolde   *sweetheart; Delilah*
That in his heeris al his strengthe lay,
And falsly to his foomen she hym solde.
And slepynge in hir barm, upon a day,   *bosom; one day*
She made to clippe or shere his heres away,
2865 And made his foomen al his craft espyen;
And whan that they hym foond in this array,   *found; condition*
They bounde hym faste and putten out his yen.   *eyes*

But er his heer were clipped or yshave,   *before*
Ther was no boond with which men myghte him   *bond*
        bynde;
2870 But now is he in prison in a cave,
Where-as they made hym at the queerne   *where; hand-mill*
        grynde.
O noble Sampsoun, strongest of mankynde.
O whilom juge, in glorie and in richesse!   *sometime; wealth*
Now maystow wepen with thyne eyen blynde,
2875 Sith thou fro wele art falle in wrecchednesse.   *since; prosperity*

The ende of this caytyf was as I shal seye.   *captive wretch*
His foomen made a feeste upon a day,
And made hym as hire fool biforn hem pleye;   *before*
And this was in a temple of greet array.   *splendour*
2880 But atte laste he made a foul affray;
For he two pilers shook and made hem falle,
And doun fil temple and al, and ther it lay,—
And slow hymself, and eek his foomen alle.

This is to seyn, the prynces everichoon,   *every one*
2885 And eek thre thousand bodyes, were ther slayn
With fallynge of the grete temple of stoon.
Of Sampson now wol I namoore sayn.
Beth war by this ensample oold and playn

2853 Neither razor nor shears touched his head.
2864 She had all his locks clipped or cut off.
2865 And so let his enemies see where his strength lay.
2880 But at last he made a terrible assault.

That no men telle hir conseil til hir wyves
2890 Of swich thyng as they wolde han secree fayn,
If that it touche hir lymes or hir lyves.

Hercules

Of Hercules, the sovereyn conquerour,
Syngen his werkes laude and heigh renoun;
For in his tyme of strengthe he was the flour.
2895 He slow, and rafte the skyn of the leoun;
He of Centauros leyde the boost adoun;
He Arpies slow, the crueel bryddes felle;   *Harpies; deadly*
He golden apples rafte of the dragoun;   *stole from*
He drow out Cerberus, the hound of helle;   *dragged*

2900 He slow the crueel tyrant Busirus,
And made his hors to frete hym, flessh and   *horses; devour*
    boon;
He slow the firy serpent venymus;
Of Acheloys two hornes he brak oon;
And he slow Cacus in a cave of stoon;
2905 He slow the geant Antheus the stronge;   *Antaeus*
He slow the grisly boor, and that anon;   *boar*
And bar the hevene on his nekke longe.

Was nevere wight, sith that this world bigan,   *man*
That slow so manye monstres as dide he.
2910 Thurghout this wyde world his name ran,
What for his strengthe and for his heigh   *great*
    bountee,   *goodness*
And every reawme wente he for to see.   *realm*
He was so stroong that no man myghte hym lette.   *oppose*
At bothe the worldes endes, seith Trophee,
2915 In stide of boundes he a pileer sette.

A lemman hadde this noble champioun,
That highte Dianira, fressh as May;
And as thise clerkes maken mencioun,   *the learned*
She hath hym sent a sherte, fressh and gay.   *shirt*

2889–90 That no men should confide to their wives those things they
    would like to keep secret.
2892–3 As for Hercules . . . his labours sing his praise and high renown.
2894 In his day he was the flower of strength.
2895 He slew the (Nemean) lion and took away its skin.
2896 He laid low the pride of the Centaurs.
2903 He broke one of the two horns of Achelous.
2907 And long he bore the heavens upon his neck.
2914–15 At both ends of the world, Tropheus says, he set up a pillar
    as a boundary.

2920 Allas! this sherte, allas and weylaway!
Envenymed was so subtilly withalle,
That er that he had wered it half a day,   *worn*
It made his flessh al from his bones falle.

But nathelees somme clerkes hire excusen
2925 By oon that highte Nessus, that it maked.
Be as be may, I wol hire noght accusen;   *be that as it may*
But on his bak this sherte he wered al naked,   *wore*
Til that his flessh was for the venym blaked.   *blackened*
And whan he saugh noon oother remedye,
2930 In hoote coles he hath hymselven raked,
For with no venym deigned hym to dye.

Thus starf this worthy, myghty Hercules.   *died*
Lo, who may truste on Fortune any throwe?   *length of time*
For hym that folweth al this world of prees,
2935 Er he be war, is ofte yleyd ful lowe.   *aware; laid*
Ful wys is he that kan hymselven knowe!
Beth war, for whan that Fortune list to   *chooses*
     glose,   *deceive*
Thanne wayteth she her man to overthrowe
By swich a wey as he wolde leest suppose.   *least expect*

Nabugodonosor   Nebuchadnezzar

2940   The myghty trone, the precious tresor,   *throne*
The glorious ceptre, and roial magestee   *sceptre*
That hadde the kyng Nabugodonosor
With tonge unnethe may discryved bee.
He twyes wan Jerusalem the citee;   *conquered*
2945 The vessel of the temple he with hym ladde.   *vessels; took*
At Babiloigne was his sovereyn see,
In which his glorie and his delit he hadde.   *delight*

The faireste children of the blood roial
Of Israel he leet do gelde anoon,
2950 And maked ech of hem to been his thral.   *made; thrall*
Amonges othere Daniel was oon,
That was the wiseste child of everychon;

2921 Was so cunningly poisoned.
2925 On the grounds that a person called Nessus made the shirt.
2930-1 He raked hot coals upon himself, for he would not deign to die
     by poison.
2934 For he whom this turbulent world follows.
2938 She watches for a chance to overthrow her victim.
2943 The tongue can scarce describe.
2946 His chief seat of government was at Babylon.
2949 He had castrated without delay.
2951-2 Among others was Daniel, the wisest youth of them all.

For he the dremes of the kyng expowned,   *explained*
Whereas in Chaldeye clerk ne was ther noon
2955 That wiste to what fyn his dremes sowned.

This proude kyng leet maken a statue of gold,   *had made*
Sixty cubites long and sevene in brede;   *breadth*
To which ymage bothe yong and oold
Comanded he to loute, and have in drede,   *bow; awe*
2960 Or in a fourneys, ful of flambes rede,   *furnace; flames*
He shal be brent that wolde noght obeye.   *burnt*
But nevere wolde assente to that dede
Daniel, ne his yonge felawes tweye.   *two young companions*

This kyng of kynges proud was and elaat;   *elated*
2965 He wende that God, that sit in magestee,   *thought; dwells*
Ne myghte hym nat bireve of his estaat. *deprive; (high) estate*
But sodeynly he loste his dignytee,
And lyk a beest hym semed for to bee,
And eet hey as an oxe, and lay theroute   *ate; out of doors*
2970 In reyn; with wilde beestes walked hee,
Til certein tyme was ycome aboute.

And lik an egles fetheres wax his heres;   *grew; hairs*
His nayles lyk a briddes clawes weere;   *bird's; were*
Til God relessed hym a certeyn yeres,
2975 And yaf hym wit, and thanne with many a teere
He thanked God, and evere his lyf in feere
Was he to doon amys or moore trespace;
And til that tyme he leyd was on his beere,   *bier*
He knew that God was ful of myght and grace.

Balthasar   Belshazzar

2980 His sone, which that highte Balthasar,   *was called*
That heeld the regne after his fader day, *kingdom; father's*
He by his fader koude noght be war,
For proud he was of herte and of array;   *display*
And eek an ydolastre was he ay.   *idolater; always*
2985 His hye estaat assured hym in pryde;
But Fortune caste hym doun, and ther he lay,
And sodeynly his regne gan divide.   *was divided*

2954-5 Although there was no learned man in Chaldea who knew what
    his dreams signified.
2968 And imagined himself to be an animal.
2974 After a certain number of years.
2975 And restored his sanity.
2976-7 And for the rest of his life he was afraid to do wrong again.
2982 He could not take warning by his father.
2985 His high estate confirmed him in his pride.

A feeste he made unto his lordes alle,   *feast*
Upon a tyme, and bad hem blithe bee;   *be merry*
2990 And thanne his officeres gan he calle:
'Gooth, bryngeth forth the vesseles,' quod he,
'Whiche that my fader in his prosperitee
Out of the temple of Jerusalem birafte;   *stole*
And to oure hye goddes thanke we
2995 Of honour that oure eldres with us lafte.'

Hys wyf, his lordes, and his concubynes
Ay dronken, whil hire appetites laste,   *drank; lasted*
Out of thise noble vessels sondry wynes.
And on a wal this kyng his eyen caste,
3000 And saugh an hand, armlees, that wroot   *saw; wrote*
ful faste,
For feere of which he quook and siked   *trembled; sighed*
soore.
This hand, that Balthasar so soore agaste,
Wroot *Mane, techel, phares,* and namoore.   *no more*

In all that land magicien was noon
3005 That koude expoune what this lettre mente;   *writing*
But Daniel expowned it anoon,
And seyde, 'Kyng, God to thy fader lente
Glorie and honour, regne, tresour, rente;   *revenue*
And he was proud, and nothyng God ne dradde,
3010 And therfore God greet wreche upon hym sente,   *vengeance*
And hym birafte the regne that he hadde.

He was out cast of mannes compaignye;   *cast out from*
With asses was his habitacioun,
And eet hey as a beest in weet and drye,
3015 Til that he knew, by grace and by resoun,
That God of hevene hath domynacioun
Over every regne and every creature;
And thanne hadde God of hym compassioun,
And hym restored his regne and his figure.   *(human) form*

3020 Eek thou, that art his sone, art proud also,
And knowest alle thise thynges verraily,
And art rebel to God, and art his foo.
Thou drank eek of his vessels boldely;
Thy wyf eek, and thy wenches, synfully

2995 For the honour our ancestors bequeathed to us.
2999 And the king glanced at a wall.
3009 And had no fear of God.
3014 And like a beast ate hay in sun and rain.

3025 Dronke of the same vessels sondry wynys;   *drank from*
      And heryest false goddes cursedly;
      Therfore to thee yshapen ful greet pyne ys.   *ordained; torment*

      This hand was sent from God that on the wal
      Wroot *Mane, techel, phares,* truste me;
3030 Thy regne is doon, thou weyest noght at al.
      Dyvyded is thy regne, and it shal be
      To Medes and to Perses yeven,' quod he.   *Persians*
      And thilke same nyght this kyng was slawe,   *that; slain*
      And Darius occupieth his degree,   *position*
3035 Thogh he therto hadde neither right ne lawe.   *legal claim*

      Lordynges, ensample heerby may ye take   *sirs*
      How that in lordshipe is no sikernesse;   *security*
      For whan Fortune wole a man forsake,
      She bereth awey his regne and his richesse,
3040 And eek his freendes, bothe moore and lesse.
      For what man that hath freendes thurgh Fortune,   *whoever*
      Mishap wol maken hem enemys, I gesse;
      This proverbe is ful sooth and ful commune.   *very true*

              Cenobia   *Zenobia*

      Cenobia, of Palymerie queene,   *Palmyra*
3045 As writen Persiens of hir noblesse,   *nobility*
      So worthy was in armes and so keene,
      That no wight passed hire in hardynesse,
      Ne in lynage, ne in oother gentillesse.   *lineage; noble breeding*
      Of kynges blood of Perce is she descended.
3050 I seye nat that she hadde moost fairnesse,
      But of hir shap she myghte nat been amended.

      From hire childhede I fynde that she fledde
      Office of wommen, and to wode she wente,   *duties; wood*
      And many a wilde hertes blood she shedde   *hart's*
3055 With arwes brode that she to hem sente.
      She was so swift that she anon hem hente;   *caught*
      And whan that she was elder, she wolde kille   *older*
      Leouns, leopardes, and beres al torente,
      And in hir armes weelde hem at hir wille.   *control*

3026 And you wickedly praise false gods.
3030 Your reign is done, you have no weight at all.
3047 That no one surpassed her in valour.
3049 Of royal Persian blood.
3051 But her figure could not be bettered.
3058 And tear bears apart.

3060 She dorste wilde beestes dennes seke,
     And rennen in the montaignes al the nyght,   *run; mountains*
     And slepen under a bussh, and she koude eke
     Wrastlen, by verray force and verray myght,
     With any yong man, were he never so wight.   *active*
3065 Ther myghte no thyng in hir armes stonde.
     She kepte hir maydenhod from every wight;
     To no man deigned hire for to be bonde.

     But atte last hir freendes han hire maried
     To Odenake, a prynce of that contree,
3070 Al were it so that she hem longe taried.
     And ye shul understonde how that he
     Hadde swiche fantasies as hadde she.
     But nathelees, whan they were knyt in-feere,   *joined together*
     They lyved in joye and in felicitee;
3075 For ech of hem hadde oother lief and deere.   *held; beloved*

     Save o thyng, that she wolde nevere assente,   *except for*
     By no wey, that he sholde by hire lye   *on any account*
     But ones, for it was hir pleyn entente   *plain*
     To have a child, the world to multiplye;
3080 And also soone as that she myghte espye   *see*
     That she was nat with childe with that dede,   *act*
     Thanne wolde she suffre hym doon his fantasye
     Eft-soone, and nat but oones, out of drede.

     And if she were with childe at thilke cast,   *attempt*
3085 Namoore sholde he pleyen thilke game
     Til fully fourty wikes weren past;   *weeks*
     Thanne wolde she ones suffre hym do the same.
     Al were this Odenake wilde or tame,
     He gat namoore of hire, for thus she seyde,
3090 It was to wyves lecherie and shame,
     In oother caas, if that men with hem pleyde.

     Two sones by this Odenake hadde she,
     The whiche she kepte in vertu and lettrure;
     But now unto oure tale turne we.

3060 She dared to seek out wild beasts in their dens.
3063 Wrestle, by sheer strength.
3065 No one crushed in her arms could stay standing.
3067 To no man would she deign to be bound (in marriage).
3070 Although she put them off for a long time.
3072 Had fancies similar to hers, i.e. he too was unwilling to get married.
3082-3 She was willing to allow him to indulge his desire once again,
    but not more than once, certainly.
3088 Whether Odenathus felt lustful or not (lit. wild or tame).
3090-1 It was otherwise a lecherous and shameful thing for wives.
3093 Whom she brought up in virtue and learning.

3095 I seye, so worshipful a creature,
     And wys therwith, and large with mesure,
     So penyble in the werre, and curteis eke,   *painstaking*
     Ne moore labour myghte in werre endure,
     Was noon, though al this world men sholde seke.

3100 Hir riche array ne myghte nat be told,
     As wel in vessel as in hire clothyng.
     She was al clad in perree and in gold,   *gems*
     And eek she lafte noght, for noon huntyng,
     To have of sondry tonges ful knowyng,
3105 Whan that she leyser hadde; and for to entende   *leisure*
     To lerne bookes was al hire likyng,
     How she in vertu myghte hir lyf dispende.   *spend*

     And shortly of this storie for to trete,   *tell*
     So doghty was hir housbonde and eek she,   *valiant*
3110 That they conquered manye regnes grete   *kingdoms*
     In the orient, with many a fair citee
     Apertenaunt unto the magestee   *belonging*
     Of Rome, and with strong hond held hem ful faste,
     Ne nevere myghte hir foomen doon hem flee,   *make*
3115 Ay whil that Odenakes dayes laste.

     Hir batailles, whoso list hem for to rede,
     Agayn Sapor the kyng and othere mo,   *against*
     And how that al this proces fil in dede,
     Why she conquered, and what title had therto,
3120 And after, of hir meschief and hire wo,   *misfortune*
     How that she was biseged and ytake,—   *captured*
     Lat hym unto my maister Petrak go,   *Petrarch*
     That writ ynough of this, I undertake.

     Whan Odenake was deed, she myghtily
3125 The regnes heeld, and with hire propre hond   *held; own*
     Agayn hir foos she faught so cruelly
     That ther nas kyng ne prynce in al that lond

3095–6 A creature so deserving praise, and wise as well, and generous
     in moderation.
3098 Or able to endure more toil in war.
3101 Not only in precious vessels but in her apparel.
3103–4 And for all her hunting, she did not neglect to learn various
     languages.
3105–6 To devote herself to the study of books was her delight.
3115 As long as Odenathus was alive.
3116 Should you wish to read about them.
3118 And how all these things turned out.
3119 And what title she had to her conquests.
3123 Who writes a lot about this, I promise you.

That he nas glad, if he that grace fond,
That she ne wolde upon his lond werreye.
3130 With hire they maden alliance by bond   *treaty*
To been in pees, and lete hire ride and pleye.   *let*

The Emperour of Rome, Claudius
Ne hym bifore, the Romayn Galien,
Ne dorste nevere been so corageus,
3135 Ne noon Ermyn, ne noon Egipcien,   *Armenian*
Ne Surrien, ne noon Arabyen,   *Syrian*
Withinne the feeld that dorste with hire fighte,
Lest that she wolde hem with hir handes slen,   *slay*
Or with hir meignee putten hem to flighte.   *army*

3140 In kynges habit wente hir sones two,   *raiment*
As heires of hir fadres regnes alle,
And Hermanno and Thymalao
Hir names were, as Persiens hem calle.
But ay Fortune hath in hire hony galle;
3145 This myghty queene may no while endure.   *last no longer*
Fortune out of hir regne made hire falle
To wrecchednesse and to mysaventure.   *misfortune*

Aurelian, whan that the governaunce   *government*
Of Rome cam into his handes tweye,   *two*
3150 He shoop upon this queene to doon vengeaunce. *prepared*
And with his legions he took his weye
Toward Cenobie, and, shortly for to seye,
He made hire flee, and atte laste hire hente,   *captured*
And fettred hire, and eek hire children tweye,
3155 And wan the land, and hoom to Rome he wente.   *won*

Amonges othere thynges that he wan,
Hir chaar, that was with gold wroght and   *chariot*
    perree,   *gems*
This grete Romayn, this Aurelian,
Hath with hym lad, for that men sholde it see.   *led*
3160 Biforen his triumphe walketh shee,   *before*
With gilte cheynes on hire nekke hangynge.   *golden*
Coroned was she, as after hir degree,
And ful of perree charged hire clothynge.

3128-9 Who was not glad, if he had the good fortune to find that she
    had no wish to make war on his land.
3137 That dared fight with her on the battle-field.
3146 Fortune made her fall from her dominion.
3162-3 She wore a crown, in keeping with her rank, and her garments
    were laden with gems.

Allas, Fortune! she that whilom was
3165 Dredeful to kynges and to emperoures,
Now gaureth al the peple on hire, allas!⁣   *stare*
And she that helmed was in starke stoures,
And wan by force townes stronge and toures,
Shal on hir heed now were a vitremyte;   *woman's cap*
3170 And she that bar the ceptre ful of floures
Shal bere a distaf, hire cost for to quyte.

De Petro Rege Ispannie

O noble, O worthy Petro, glorie of Spayne,   *Pedro*
Whom Fortune heeld so hye in magestee,
Wel oghten men thy pitous deeth complayne!   *pitiful*
3175 Out of thy land thy brother made thee flee,
And after, at a seege, by subtiltee,   *siege; guile*
Thou were bitraysed and lad unto his tente,   *betrayed; led*
Where as he with his owene hand slow thee,   *slew*
Succedynge in thy regne and in thy rente.

3180 The feeld of snow, with th'egle of blak therinne,
Caught with the lymrod coloured as the gleede,
He brew this cursednesse and al this   *contrived; wickedness*
  synne
The wikked nest was werker of this nede.   *peril*
Noght Charles Olyver, that took ay heede
3185 Of trouthe and honour, but of Armorike
Genylon-Olyver, corrupt for meede,
Broghte this worthy kyng in swich a brike.   *trap*

De Petro Rege de Cipro

O worthy Petro, kyng of Cipre, also,   *Peter; Cyprus*
That Alisandre wan by heigh maistrie,
3190 Ful many an hethen wroghtestow ful wo,
Of which thyne owene liges hadde envie,   *lieges*
And for no thyng but for thy chivalrie

3167 She who had worn a helmet in stern combats.
3171 Must carry a distaff, to earn her keep.
3179 Succeeding to your realm and révenues.
3180-1 A description of the coat of arms of Bertrand du Guesclin
who lured Pedro to his brother's tent.
3181 Caught by a lime-twig of bright red.
3183 *wikked nest*, a pun on the name of the Armorican knight Sir
Oliver de Mauny (cf. O.F. *mau ni*), an accomplice of du Guesclin.
3184-6 i.e. not Charlemagne's Oliver, but an Armorican Oliver, a
traitor like Ganelon, corrupted by bribes.
3189 Who captured Alexandria with outstanding skill.
3190 You did great harm to many a heathen.

They in thy bed han slayn thee by the   *early in the morning*
       morwe.
Thus kan Fortune hir wheel governe and gye,   *control*
3195 And out of joye brynge men to sorwe.

De Barnabo de Lumbardia

Off Melan grete Barnabo Viscounte,
God of delit, and scourge of Lumbardye,   *pleasure*
Why sholde I nat thyn infortune acounte,
Sith in estaat thow cloumbe were so hye?
3200 Thy brother sone, that was thy double allye,
For he thy nevew was, and sone-in-lawe,   *nephew*
Withinne his prisoun made thee to dye,—
But why, ne how, noot I that thou were slawe.

De Hugelino Comite de Pize

Off the Erl Hugelyn of Pyze the langour
3205 Ther may no tonge telle for pitee.
But litel out of Pize stant a tour,   *stands*
In which tour in prisoun put was he,
And with hym been his litel children thre;
The eldest scarsly fyf yeer was of age.
3210 Allas, Fortune! it was greet crueltee
Swiche briddes for to putte in swich a cage!

Dampned was he to dyen in that prisoun,
For Roger, which that bisshop was of Pize,
Hadde on hym maad a fals suggestioun,
3215 Thurgh which the peple gan upon hym rise,   *rose against him*
And putten hym to prisoun, in swich wise
As ye han herd, and mete and drynke he hadde   *food*
So smal, that wel unnethe it may suffise,
And therwithal it was ful povre and badde.   *poor*

3220 And on a day bifil that in that hour
Whan that his mete wont was to be broght,
The gayler shette the dores of the tour.   *jailer; shut*
He herde it wel, but he spak right noght,
And in his herte anon ther fil a thoght   *came*

3196 Great Bernabo, viscount of Milan.
3198 Take account of your misfortune.
3199 Since you climbed up to such high estate.
3200 Your brother's son, who was doubly related to you.
3203 But I don't know why or how you were slain.
3204 Concerning the sad plight of Earl Ugolino of Pisa.
3214 Had brought a false charge against him.
3218 That it was barely enough (to keep them alive).

3225 That they for hunger wolde doon hym dyen.
'Allas!' quod he, 'allas, that I was wroght!'   *born*
Therwith the teeris fillen from his yen.   *fell; eyes*

His yonge sone, that thre yeer was of age,
Unto hym seyde, 'Fader, why do ye wepe?
3230 Whanne wol the gayler bryngen oure potage?   *soup*
Is ther no morsel breed that ye do kepe?
I am so hungry that I may nat slepe.
Now wolde God that I myghte slepen evere!
Thanne sholde nat hunger in my wombe crepe;   *belly*
3235 Ther is no thyng, but breed, that me were levere.'

Thus day by day this child bigan to crye,
Til in his fadres barm adoun it lay,   *lap*
And seyde, 'Farewel, fader, I moot dye!'
And kiste his fader, and dyde the same day.
3240 And whan the woful fader deed it say,   *dead; saw*
For wo his armes two he gan to byte,
And seyde, 'Allas, Fortune, and weylaway!
Thy false wheel my wo al may I wyte.'

His children wende that it for hunger was   *thought*
3245 That he his armes gnow, and nat for wo,   *gnawed*
And seyde, 'Fader, do nat so, allas!
But rather ete the flessh upon us two.
Oure flessh thou yaf us, take oure flessh us fro,   *gave*
And ete ynogh,'—right thus they to hym seyde,
3250 And after that, withinne a day or two,
They leyde hem in his lappe adoun and deyde.

Hymself, despeired, eek for hunger starf;
Thus ended is this myghty Erl of Pize.
From heigh estaat Fortune awey hym carf.   *cut*
3255 Of this tragedie it oghte ynough suffise;
Whoso wol here it in a lenger wise,   *at greater length*
Redeth the grete poete of Ytaille   *Italy*
That highte Dant, for he kan al devyse
Fro point to point, nat o word wol he faille.

3225 They intended to make him die of hunger.
3231 Is there no morsel of bread you're saving?
3235 There's nothing I'd rather have, except bread.
3243 I can blame your false wheel for all my woe. (Cf. I. 925.)
3252 He, in despair, also died of hunger.
3255 This should be enough of such a tragic tale.
3258-9 Who is called Dante, for he can tell the whole of it from beginning to end, without falling short in a single word.

Nero

3260 Although that Nero were as vicius
 As any feend that lith ful lowe adoun,
 Yet he, as telleth us Swetonius,   *Suetonius*
 This wyde world hadde in subjeccioun
 Bothe est and west, [south], and septemtrioun. *north*
3265 Of rubies, saphires, and of peerles white
 Were alle his clothes brouded up *embroidered; everywhere*
   and doun;
 For he in gemmes greetly gan delite.   *took delight*

 Moore delicaat, moore pompous of array, *fastidious*
 Moore proud was nevere emperour than he;
3270 That ilke clooth that he hadde wered o day,
 After that tyme he nolde it nevere see.
 Nettes of gold threed hadde he greet plentee *in great number*
 To fisshe in Tybre, whan hym liste pleye.
 His lustes were al lawe in his decree,   *wishes*
3275 For Fortune as his freend hym wolde obeye.

 He Rome brende for his delicasie;   *amusement*
 The senatours he slow upon a day,
 To heere how that men wolde wepe and crie;
 And slow his brother, and by his suster lay.
3280 His mooder made he in pitous array,
 For he hire wombe slitte to biholde   *slit*
 Where he conceyved was; so weilaway! *alas*
 That he so litel of his mooder tolde.

 No teere out of his eyen for that sighte
3285 Ne cam, but seyde, 'A fair womman was she!'
 Greet wonder is how that he koude or myghte
 Be domesman of hire dede beautee.
 The wyn to bryngen hym comanded he,
 And drank anon,—noon oother wo he made.
3290 Whan myght is joyned unto crueltee,
 Allas, to depe wol the venym wade!

  3261 As any devil that lives in deepest hell.
  3270-1 Those clothes he had worn for one day he never wished to see
   again.
  3273 To fish the Tiber with, when he wanted to amuse himself.
  3280 He reduced his mother to a pitiful state.
  3283 That he set such little store by his mother.
  3287 Make himself the judge of her dead beauty.
  3289 And showed no other grief.
  3291 The poison will go too deep.

In yowthe a maister hadde this emperour
To teche hym letterure and curteisye,   *knowledge of books*
For of moralitee he was the flour,
3295 As in his tyme, but if bookes lye;
And whil this maister hadde of hym maistrye, *authority over*
He maked hym so konnyng and so sowple *skilful; compliant*
That longe tyme it was er tirannye
Or any vice dorste on hym uncowple.

3300 This Seneca, of which that I devyse   *tell*
By cause Nero hadde of hym swich drede,
For he fro vices wolde hym ay chastise
Discreetly, as by word and nat by dede,—
'Sire,' wolde he seyn, 'an emperour moot nede   *must needs*
3305 Be vertuous and hate tirannye—'
For which he in a bath made hym to blede   *bleed*
On bothe his armes, til he moste dye.   *was made to*

This Nero hadde eek of acustumaunce   *was accustomed*
In youthe agayns his maister for to ryse,
3310 Which afterward hym thoughte a greet grevaunce; *hardship*
Therefore he made hym dyen in this wise.
But nathelees this Seneca the wise
Chees in a bath to dye in this manere   *chose*
Rather than han another tormentise;   *torture*
3315 And thus hath Nero slayn his maister deere.

Now fil it so that Fortune liste no lenger   *happened; cared*
The hye pryde of Nero to cherice,   *cherish*
For though that he were strong, yet was she strenger.
She thoughte thus, 'By God! I am to nyce   *too foolish*
3320 To sette a man that is fulfild of vice   *full*
In heigh degree, and emperour hym calle.
By God! out of his sete I wol hym trice;   *seat; pull*
Whan he leest weneth, sonnest shal he falle.'

The peple roos upon hym on a nyght   *rose against*
3325 For his defaute, and whan he it espied   *wickedness*
Out of his dores anon he hath hym dight   *hurried*
Allone, and ther he wende han been allied,

3292 *a maister*, i.e. Seneca.
3294-5 He was the flower of moral wisdom in his day, if the books
don't lie.
3299 Dared unloose itself on him.
3302 For he would always punish him for his vices.
3309 To stand up in the presence of his master.
3323 When he least expects it, soonest shall he fall.
3327 Where he thought he would receive aid.

He knokked faste, and ay the moore he cried,
The fastere shette they the dores alle.   *shut*
3330 Tho wiste he wel, he hadde himself mysgyed,
And wente his wey; no lenger dorste he calle.

The peple cride and rombled up and doun,   *muttered*
That with his erys herde he how they seyde,
'Where is this false tiraunt, this Neroun?'
3335 For fere almoost out of his wit he breyde,   *went*
And to his goddes pitously he preyde
For socour, but it myghte nat bityde.   *be*
For drede of this, hym thoughte that he deyde,
And ran into a gardyn hym to hyde.

3340 And in this gardyn foond he cherles   *he found two churls*
        tweye
That seten by a fyr greet and reed.   *sat*
And to thise cherles two he gan to preye
To sleen hym, and to girden of his heed,   *strike off*
That to his body, whan that he were deed,
3345 Were no despit ydoon for his defame.
Hymself he slow, he koude no bettre reed,
Of which Fortune lough, and hadde a game.

                    De Oloferno   *Holofernes*

Was nevere capitayn under a kyng
That regnes mo putte in subjeccioun,   *more*
3350 Ne strenger was in feeld of alle thyng,
As in his tyme, ne gretter of renoun,
Ne moore pompous in heigh presumpcioun
Than Oloferne, which Fortune ay kiste
So likerously, and ladde hym up and doun,   *lecherously*
3355 Til that his heed was of, er that he wiste.

Nat oonly that this world hadde hym in awe
For lesynge of richesse or libertee,
But he made every man reneyen his lawe.   *renounce his faith*
'Nabugodonosor was god,' seyde hee;

3330 Then he knew well he had misbehaved.
3338 For fear of this, he thought he would die.
3345 No shameful outrage should be done.
3346 He could not think of anything better to do.
3347 At which Fortune laughed and enjoyed herself.
3350 Or was stronger in all things on the battle-field.
3352 Or more magnificently presumptuous.
3355 Until his head was off before he knew it.
3357 For fear of losing wealth.

3360 'Noon oother god sholde adoured bee.'   *adored*
     Agayns his heeste no wight trespace
     Save in Bethulia, a strong citee,
     Where Eliachim a preest was of that place.

     But taak kep of the deth of Oloferne: *note*
3365 Amydde his hoost he dronke lay a-nyght,
     Withinne his tente, large as is a berne,   *barn*
     And yet, for al his pompe and al his myght,
     Judith, a womman, as he lay upright   *on his back*
     Slepynge, his heed of smoot, and from his tente   *smote*
3370 Ful pryvely she stal from every wight,
     And with his heed unto hir toun she wente.

De Rege Antiocho illustri

     What nedeth it of kyng Anthiochus
     To telle his hye roial magestee,
     His hye pride, his werkes venymus?   *deeds*
3375 For swich another was ther noon as he.
     Rede which that he was in Machabee,
     And rede the proude wordes that he seyde,
     And why he fil fro heigh prosperitee,
     And in an hill how wrecchedly he deyde.   *on*

3380 Fortune hym hadde enhaunced so in pride   *exalted*
     That verraily he wende he myghte attayne
     Unto the sterres upon every syde,
     And in balance weyen ech montayne,   *weigh*
     And alle the floodes of the see restrayne.
3385 And Goddes peple hadde he moost in hate;
     Hem wolde he sleen in torment and in payne,
     Wenynge that God ne myghte his pride abate.   *thinking*

     And for that Nichanore and Thymothee   *because*
     Of Jewes weren venquysshed myghtily,
3390 Unto the Jewes swich an hate hadde he
     That he bad greithen his chaar ful hastily,
     And swoor, and seyde ful despitously   *swore; scornfully*
     Unto Jerusalem he wolde eftsoone,
     To wreken his ire on it ful cruelly;   *wreak*
3395 But of his purpos he was let ful soone.   *thwarted*

     3361 No one dared transgress his command.
     3365 In the midst of his army he lay drunk one night.
     3376 Read what sort of man he was in Maccabees.
     3391 He commanded his chariot to be made ready with all speed.
     3393 He would very soon go.

God for his manace hym so soore smoot   *threat*
With invisible wounde, ay incurable,
That in his guttes carf it so and boot
That his peynes weren importable.   *insufferable*
3400 And certeinly the wreche was resonable,   *vengeance*
For many a mannes guttes dide he peyne.   *torture*
But from his purpos cursed and dampnable,
For al his smert, he wolde hym nat restreyne,   *anguish*

But bad anon apparaillen his hoost;   *prepare*
3405 And sodeynly, er he was of it war,   *aware*
God daunted al his pride and al his boost.   *boasting*
For he so soore fil out of his char   *violently*
That it his limes and his skyn totar,
So that he neyther myghte go ne ryde,   *walk*
3410 But in a chayer men aboute hym bar,   *chair*
Al forbrused, bothe bak and syde.

The wreche of God hym smoot so cruelly
That thurgh his body wikked wormes crepte,
And therwithal he stank so horribly
3415 That noon of al his meynee that hym kepte,
Wheither so he wook, or ellis slepte,   *was awake*
Ne myghte noght the stynk of hym endure.
In this meschief he wayled and eek wepte,   *misfortune*
And knew God lord of every creature.

3420 To al his hoost and to hymself also
Ful wlatsom was the stynk of his careyne;
No man ne myghte hym bere to ne fro.
And in this stynk and this horrible peyne,
He starf ful wrecchedly in a monteyne.   *died*
3425 Thus hath this robbour and this homycide,   *murderer*
That many a man made to wepe and pleyne,
Swich gerdoun as bilongeth unto pryde.   *reward*

De Alexandro

The storie of Alisaundre is so commune
That every wight that hath discrecioun
3430 Hath herd somwhat or al of his fortune.
This wyde world, as in conclusioun,   *in the end*
He wan by strengthe, or for his hye renoun

3398 Which cut and bit into his entrails so deeply.
3408 It tore his limbs and skin to pieces.
3411 Terribly bruised all over.
3415 None of all his servants who looked after him.
3421 The stench of his carcass was as loathsome as could be.

They weren glad for pees unto hym sende.   *to sue*
The pride of man and beest he leyde adoun,
3435 Wherso he cam, unto the worldes ende.

Comparisoun myghte nevere yet been maked
Bitwixe hym and another conquerour;   *between*
For al this world for drede of hym hath quaked.   *trembled*
He was of knyghthod and of fredom flour;   *nobility; flower*
3440 Fortune hym made the heir of hire honour.
Save wyn and wommen, no thing myghte aswage   *lessen*
His hye entente in armes and labour,   *endeavour*
So was he ful of leonyn corage.

What pris were it to hym, though I yow tolde
3445 Of Darius, and an hundred thousand mo
Of kynges, princes, dukes, erles bolde
Whiche he conquered, and broghte hem into wo?
I seye, as fer as man may ryde or go,
The world was his,—what sholde I moore devyse?
3450 For though I write or tolde yow everemo   *wrote*
Of his knyghthod, it myghte nat suffise.

Twelf yeer he regned, as seith Machabee.
Philippes sone of Macidoyne he was,
That first was kyng in Grece the contree.
3455 O worthy, gentil Alisandre, allas,   *noble*
That evere sholde fallen swich a cas!
Empoysoned of thyn owene folk thou weere;   *by*
Thy sys Fortune hath turned into aas,
And for thee ne weep she never a teere.   *wept*

3460 Who shal me yeven teeris to compleyne   *lament*
The deeth of gentillesse and of franchise,
That al the world weelded in his demeyne,
And yet hym thoughte it myghte nat suffise?
So ful was his corage of heigh emprise.
3465 Allas! who shal me helpe to endite   *indict*
False Fortune, and poyson to despise,
The whiche two of al this wo I wyte?

3443 He was so lion-hearted.
3444 What praise would it be to him.
3449 Why should I say more?
3452 *Machabee*, i.e. the first book of Maccabees.
3453 He was the son of King Philip of Macedon.
3456 That ever such a misfortune should befall.
3458 i.e. Fortune turned your six (the highest throw at dice) into an
      ace (the lowest).
3461-3 The death of one so noble and magnanimous, who ruled the
      whole world and yet thought it not enough.
3467 I blame for all this harm.

De Julio Cesare

By wisedom, manhede, and by greet labour,   *manhood*
From humble bed to roial magestee
3470 Up roos he Julius, the conquerour,
That wan al th'occident by land and see,
By strengthe of hand, or elles by tretee,   *treaty*
And unto Rome made hem tributarie;
And sitthe of Rome the emperour was he,   *afterwards*
3475 Til that Fortune weex his adversarie.

O myghty Cesar, that in Thessalie
Agayn Pompeus, fader thyn in lawe,
That of the orient hadde al the chivalrie   *men-at-arms*
As fer as that the day bigynneth dawe,
3480 Thou thurgh thy knyghthod hast hem take and slawe,   *slain*
Save fewe folk that with Pompeus fledde,
Thurgh which thou puttest al th'orient in awe.
Thanke Fortune, that so wel thee spedde!   *served*

But now a litel while I wol biwaille
3485 This Pompeus, this noble governour
Of Rome, which that fleigh at this bataille.   *fled*
I seye, oon of his men, a fals traitour,
His heed of smoot, to wynnen hym favour   *smote; for himself*
Of Julius, and hym the heed he broghte.
3490 Allas, Pompeye, of th'orient conquerour,
That Fortune unto swich a fyn thee broghte!   *end*

To Rome agayn repaireth Julius   *goes*
With his triumphe, lauriat ful hye;
But on a tyme Brutus Cassius,
3495 That evere hadde of his hye estaat envye,
Ful prively hath maad conspiracye   *secretly*
Agayns this Julius in subtil wise,   *cunning fashion*
And caste the place in which he sholde dye   *planned*
With boydekyns, as I shal yow devyse.   *daggers; tell*

3500 This Julius to the Capitolie wente   *Capitol*
Upon a day, as he was wont to goon,
And in the Capitolie anon hym hente   *seized*
This false Brutus and his othere foon,   *foes*
And stiked hym with boydekyns anoon   *stabbed*
3505 With many a wounde, and thus they lete hym lye;
But nevere gronte he at no strook but oon,   *groaned*
Or elles at two, but if his storie lye.

3477 Against Pompey, your father-in-law.
3479 As far as where the day begins to dawn.
3493 Wearing a high crown of laurel.
3507 Unless the story of his life is false.

So manly was this Julius of herte,
And so wel lovede estaatly honestee,
3510 That though his deedly woundes soore smerte,   *hurt*
His mantel over his hypes caste he,   *threw*
For no man sholde seen his privetee;   *privy parts*
And as he lay of diying in a traunce,
And wiste verraily that deed was hee,
3515 Of honestee yet hadde he remembraunce.

Lucan, to thee this storie I recomende,   *refer*
And to Swetoun, and to Valerius also,   *Suetonius*
That of this storie writen word and ende,
How that to thise grete conqueroures two
3520 Fortune was first freend, and sitthe foo.   *afterwards*
No man ne truste upon hire favour longe,
But have hire in awayt for everemoo;
Witnesse on alle thise conqueroures stronge.

Cresus   *Croesus*

    This riche Cresus, whilom kyng of Lyde,   *once; Lydia*
3525 Of which Cresus Cirus soore him dradde,
Yet was he caught amyddes al his pryde,   *in*
And to be brent men to the fyr hym ladde.   *burnt; led*
But swich a reyn doun fro the welkne shadde   *sky; poured*
That slow the fyr, and made hym to escape;   *quenched*
3530 But to be war no grace yet he hadde,
Til Fortune on the galwes made hym gape.   *gallows*

Whanne he escaped was, he kan nat stente   *stop*
For to bigynne a newe werre agayn.
He wende wel, for that Fortune hym sente   *thought; because*
3535 Swich hap that he escaped thurgh the rayn,   *luck*
That of his foos he myghte nat be slayn;   *by*
And eek a sweven upon a nyght he mette,   *dream; dreamt*
Of which he was so proud and eek so fayn   *glad*
That in vengeance he al his herte sette.   *on*

3540 Upon a tree he was, as that hym thoughte,   *it seemed to him*
Ther Juppiter hym wessh, bothe bak and syde,
And Phebus eek a fair towaille hym broughte   *towel*
To dryen hym with; and therfore wax his pryde,   *grew*

3509 And cared so much for dignity and decency.
3513 As he lay in his dying swoon.
3514 And knew for certain he would die.
3518 Who tell this story from beginning to end.
3521 Let no man trust her favour long.
3522 But always keep an eye on her.
3525 Whom Cyrus greatly feared.
3530 But he had not the grace to take warning.
3541 Where Jupiter washed all his body.

And to his doghter, that stood hym bisyde,
3545 Which that he knew in heigh sentence habounde
He bad hire telle hym what it signyfyde,
And she his dreem bigan right thus expounde:

'The tree,' quod she, 'the galwes is to meene,
And Juppiter bitokneth snow and reyn,
3550 And Phebus, with his towaille so clene,
Tho been the sonne stremes for to seyn.
Thou shalt anhanged be, fader, certeyn;   *hanged*
Reyn shal thee wasshe, and sonne shal thee drye.'
Thus warned hym ful plat and eek ful pleyn   *bluntly*
3555 His doghter, which that called was Phanye.

Anhanged was Cresus, the proude kyng;
His roial trone myghte hym nat availle.
Tragediës noon oother maner thyng
Ne kan in syngyng crie ne biwaille
3560 But that Fortune alwey wole assaille
With unwar strook the regnes that been proude;
For whan men trusteth hire, thanne wol she faille,
And covere hire brighte face with a clowde.

Explicit Tragedia

Heere stynteth the Knyght the Monk of his Tale

3545 Whom he knew to possess deep insight.
3548 By the tree is meant the gallows.
3551 Those signify the sun's rays.
3558–61 Tragedies lament in song just this—that Fortune is always ready
to assail proud kingdoms with a sudden stroke.

THE PROLOGUE OF THE NUN'S PRIEST'S TALE

THE PROLOGE OF THE NONNES PREESTES TALE

'Hoo!' quod the Knyght, 'good sire, namoore of this!
3565 That ye han seyd is right ynough, ywis,
 And muchel moore; for litel hevynesse   *sorrow*
 Is right ynough to muche folk, I gesse.   *many*
 I seye for me, it is a greet disese,
 Whereas men han been in greet welthe   *where*
  and ese,   *comfort*
3570 To heeren of hire sodeyn fal, allas!   *hear; sudden*
 And the contrarie is joye and greet solas,   *pleasure*
 As whan a man hath been in povre estaat, *poor*
 And clymbeth up and wexeth fortunat,   *becomes*
 And there abideth in prosperitee
3575 Swich thyng is gladsom, as it thynketh me,
 And of swich thyng were goodly for to telle.'
  'Ye,' quod oure Hooste, 'by seint Poules *yes; St Paul's*
  belle!
 Ye seye right sooth; this Monk he clappeth lowde.
 He spak how Fortune covered with a clowde
3580 I noot nevere what; and als of a tragedie
 Right now ye herde, and, pardee, no remedie *(by God), indeed*
 It is for to biwaille ne compleyne
 That that is doon, and als it is a peyne,   *that which*
 As ye han seyd, to heere of hevynesse.
3585 Sire Monk, namoore of this, so God yow blesse!
 Youre tale anoyeth al this compaignye.   *wearies*
 Swich talkyng is nat worth a boterflye,
 For therinne is ther no desport ne game. *amusement*
 Wherfore, sire Monk, or daun Piers by youre *Sir Peter*
  name,

3565 What you have said is quite enough, to be sure.
3568 Speaking for myself, it is very painful.
3575 Such a thing is pleasant, it seems to me.
3576 It would be good to tell.
3578 What you say is quite true; this Monk prattles loudly.
3579 See 3563.
3580 I don't know what; and also of a tragedy. (The Monk has told several stories which conform to the medieval idea of tragedy by beginning in joy and ending in sorrow.)

3590 I pray yow hertely telle us somwhat elles;   *with all my heart*
For sikerly, nere clynkyng of youre belles,
That on youre bridel hange on every syde,
By hevene kyng, that for us alle dyde,   *died*
I sholde er this han fallen doun for sleep,   *before*
3595 Althogh the slough had never been so deep;
Thanne hadde your tale al be toold in veyn.   *vain*
For certeinly, as that thise clerkes seyn,   *as the learned say*
Whereas a man may have noon audience,   *where*
Noght helpeth it to tellen his sentence.
3600 And wel I woot the substance is in me,
If any thyng shal wel reported be.   *told*
Sir, sey somwhat of huntyng, I yow preye.'   *something about*
'Nay,' quod this Monk, 'I have no lust to pleye.   *desire*
Now lat another telle, as I have toold.'   *let*
3605 Thanne spak oure Hoost with rude speche and boold,   *rough*
And seyde unto the Nonnes Preest anon,
'Com neer, thou preest, com hyder, thou sir John!
Telle us swich thyng as may oure hertes glade.   *gladden*
Be blithe, though thou ryde upon a jade.
3610 What thogh thyn hors be bothe foul and lene?   *wretched*
If he wol serve thee, rekke nat a bene.   *care; bean*
Looke that thyn herte be murie everemo.'   *evermore*
'Yis, sir,' quod he, 'yis, Hoost, so moot I go,
But I be myrie, ywis I wol be blamed.'   *unless; certainly*
3615 And right anon his tale he hath attamed,   *begun*
And thus he seyde unto us everichon,   *every one*
This sweete preest, this goodly man sir John.   *excellent*

EXPLICIT

3591 For certainly, if it weren't for the jingling of your bells.
3599 It does no good to voice his opinions.
3600 And well I know I have the stuff of a good listener in me.
3606 *Nonnes Preest.* See I. 164.
3607 *sir John,* a nickname for a priest, though here it appears to be the Nun's Priest's real name; cf. 3617 below.
3613 *Yis,* yes (more emphatic than *ye*); *so moot I go,* so may I walk, i.e. as I hope to enjoy the use of my legs.

HEERE BIGYNNETH THE NONNES PREESTES TALE OF THE COK AND HEN, CHAUNTECLEER AND PERTELOTE

A POVRE wydwe, somdeel stape in age   *somewhat advanced*
Was whilom dwellyng in a narwe cotage,   *once; small*
3620 Biside a grove, stondynge in a dale.
This wydwe, of which I telle yow my tale,
Syn thilke day that she was last a wyf,   *that (same)*
In pacience ladde a ful symple lyf,
For litel was hir catel and hir rente.   *property; income*
3625 By housbondrie of swich as God hire sente   *economical use*
She foond hirself and eek hir doghtren two.
Thre large sowes hadde she, and namo,   *no more*
Three keen, and eek a sheep that highte Malle.
Ful sooty was hire bour and eek hir halle,   *bower*
3630 In which she eet ful many a sklendre meel.   *slender*
Of poynaunt sauce hir neded never a deel.
No deyntee morsel passed thurgh hir throte;
Hir diete was accordant to hir cote.   *in keeping with; cottage*
Repleccioun ne made hire nevere sik;   *over-eating*
3635 Attempree diete was al hir phisik,   *moderate*
And exercise, and hertes suffisaunce.   *contentment*
The goute lette hire nothyng for to daunce,
N'apoplexie shente nat hir heed.   *injured*
No wyn ne drank she, neither whit ne reed;
3640 Hir bord was served moost with whit and blak,—
Milk and broun breed, in which she foond no lak,—   *fault*
Seynd bacoun, and somtyme an ey or tweye;   *broiled; egg*
For she was, as it were, a maner deye.   *sort of dairy woman*
A yeerd she hadde, enclosed al aboute
3645 With stikkes, and a drye dych withoute,   *stakes*
In which she hadde a cok, hight Chaunte-   *(who) was called*
   cleer.
In al the land, of crowyng nas his peer.
His voys was murier than the murie orgon   *pleasanter*
On messe-dayes that in the chirche gon.

3626 She provided for herself and her two daughters as well.
3628 Three cows, and also a sheep that was called Moll.
3629 The widow's two-roomed cottage is described in terms of a great
    house, with its large public hall and its private room or 'bower' for
    the lord and lady. A mock-heroic style is frequently used elsewhere
    in this poem, as for example in the description of Chauntecleer,
    3656 ff., or in the allusion to the fall of Troy, 4152 ff.
3631 She had no need of sharp-flavoured sauces.
3637 The gout did not stop her dancing at all.
3647 In all the land there was none his equal in crowing.
3649 That plays in church on feast-days.

3650 Wel sikerer was his crowyng in his logge
Than is a clokke or an abbey orlogge.   *clock*
By nature he knew ech ascencioun
Of the equynoxial in thilke toun;
For whan degrees fiftene weren ascended,
3655 Thanne crew he, that it myghte nat been
          amended.   *bettered*
His coomb was redder than the fyn coral,   *comb*
And batailled as it were a castel wal;   *crenellated*
His byle was blak, and as the jeet it shoon;   *jet*
Lyk asure were his legges and his toon;   *toes*
3660 His nayles whitter than the lylye flour,
And lyk the burned gold was his colour.   *burnished*
This gentil cok hadde in his governaunce   *noble; control*
Sevene hennes for to doon al his plesaunce,   *pleasure*
Whiche were his sustres and his paramours,   *concubines*
3665 And wonder lyk to hym, as of colours;   *wonderfully; in colour*
Of whiche the faireste hewed on hir throte
Was cleped faire damoysele Pertelote.   *called; mistress*
Curteys she was, discreet, and debonaire,
And compaignable, and bar hyrself so faire,
3670 Syn thilke day that she was seven nyght oold,   *since*
That trewely she hath the herte in hoold
Of Chauntecleer, loken in every lith;
He loved hire so that wel was hym therwith.
But swich a joye was it to here hem synge,   *such*
3675 Whan that the brighte sonne gan to sprynge,   *rose*
In sweete accord, 'My lief is faren in londe!'
For thilke tyme, as I have understonde,
Beestes and briddes koude speke and synge.
          And so bifel that in a dawenynge,   *dawn*
3680 As Chauntecleer among his wyves alle
Sat on his perche, that was in the halle,
And next hym sat this faire Pertelote,
This Chauntecleer gan gronen in his throte,   *groaned*
As man that in his dreem is drecched soore.   *troubled*
3685 And whan that Pertelote thus herde hym roore,   *roar*
She was agast, and seyde, 'Herte deere,   *frightened*
What eyleth yow, to grone in this manere?   *ails*

3650 The crowing heard in his abode was much more trustworthy.
3652-3 By instinct he could measure the movement of the equinoctial
    circle above the horizon in that village.
3666 Of whom the one with the brightest feathers on her throat.
3668-9 She was courteous, discreet, gracious, and friendly, and had
    behaved so well.
3671-2 That truly she has complete possession of Chauntecleer's heart;
    loken in every lith means literally 'locked in every limb.'
3673 He loved her so much that it made him very happy.
3676 In sweet harmony, 'My love has gone away.'

Ye been a verray sleper; fy, for shame!'   *fine*
      And he answerde, and seyde thus: 'Madame,
3690 I pray yow that ye take it nat agrief.
      By God, me mette I was in swich meschief   *I dreamt; trouble*
      Right now, that yet myn herte is soore afright.
      Now God,' quod he, 'my swevene recche aright
      And kepe my body out of foul prisoun!
3695 Me mette how that I romed up and doun   *wandered*
      Withinne our yeerd, wheer as I saugh a beest   *saw*
      Was lyk an hound, and wolde han maad areest   *seized*
      Upon my body, and wolde han had me deed.   *killed me*
      His colour was bitwixe yelow and reed,
3700 And tipped was his tayl and bothe his eeris
      With blak, unlyk the remenant of his heeris;   *rest*
      His snowte smal, with glowynge eyen tweye.   *narrow; two*
      Yet of his look for feere almoost I deye;   *fear; die*
      This caused me my gronyng, doutelees.'
3705 'Avoy!' quod she, 'fy on yow, hertelees!   *fie; coward*
      Allas!' quod she, 'for, by that God above,
      Now han ye lost myn herte and al my love.
      I kan nat love a coward, by my feith!
      For certes, what so any womman seith,   *certainly*
3710 We alle desiren, if it myghte bee,
      To han housbondes hardy, wise, and free,   *brave; noble*
      And secree, and no nygard, ne no fool,   *discreet; miser*
      Ne hym that is agast of every tool,   *weapon*
      Ne noon avauntour, by that God above!   *boaster*
3715 How dorste ye seyn, for shame, unto youre love
      That any thyng myghte make yow aferd?   *afraid*
      Have ye no mannes herte, and han a berd?
      Allas! and konne ye been agast of swevenys?   *dreams*
      Nothyng, God woot, but vanitee in   *knows; futility*
            sweven is.
3720 Swevenes engendren of replecciouns,
      And ofte of fume and of complecciouns,
      Whan humours been to habundant in a   *abundant*
            wight.   *person*
      Certes this dreem, which ye han met to-nyght, *this night*
      Cometh of the greete superfluytee   *excess*
3725 Of youre rede colera, pardee,   *choler*

3690 I beg you not to be offended.
3693 Interpret my dream favourably, i.e. make its outcome favourable.
3705 *Avoy*, an exclamation of reproach.
3720–1 Dreams are produced by over-eating, and often by noxious
    vapours rising from the stomach and by an unbalanced mixture of
    the humours. (In the following verses Pertelote gives an accurate
    description of the symptoms of choler and melancholy and of the
    method of treating them. For the 'humours' see I. 420.)

Which causeth folk to dreden in hir dremes
Of arwes, and of fyr with rede lemes,   *flames*
Of rede beestes, that they wol hem byte,
Of contek, and of whelpes, grete and lyte;
3730 Right as the humour of malencolie   *melancholy*
Causeth ful many a man in sleep to crie
For feere of blake beres, or boles blake,   *bears; bulls*
Or elles blake develes wol him take.
Of othere humours koude I telle also
3735 That werken many a man in sleep ful wo;
But I wol passe as lightly as I kan.
     Lo Catoun, which that was so wys a man,
Seyde he nat thus, "Ne do no fors of dremes?"
     Now sire,' quod she, 'whan we flee fro the bemes,
3740 For Goddes love, as taak som laxatyf.
Up peril of my soule and of my lyf,
I conseille yow the beste, I wol nat lye,   *for the best*
That bothe of colere and of malencolye
Ye purge yow; and for ye shal nat tarie,
3745 Though in this toun is noon apothecarie,
I shal myself to herbes techen yow   *direct*
That shul been for youre hele and for youre   *health*
     prow;   *benefit*
And in oure yeerd tho herbes shal I fynde
The whiche han of hire propretee by kynde
3750 To purge yow bynethe and eek above.
Foryet nat this, for Goddes owene love!   *forget*
Ye been ful coleryk of compleccioun;   *temperament*
Ware the sonne in his ascencioun
Ne fynde yow nat repleet of humours hoote.   *full*
3755 And if it do, I dar wel leye a grote,
That ye shul have a fevere terciane,   *tertian*
Or an agu, that may be youre bane.   *death*
A day or two ye shul have digestyves   *must*
Of wormes, er ye take youre laxatyves   *before*
3760 Of lawriol, centaure, and fumetere,
Or elles of ellebor, that groweth there,   *hellebore*

3729 Of strife, and of dogs, big and small.
3733 Or else of black devils who try to seize them.
3735 That cause many a man great distress in his sleep.
3737 *Catoun*, Dionysius Cato.   (See I. 3227.)
3738 Don't attach any importance to dreams.
3740 For the love of God, please take some laxative.
3744 You purge yourself; and so that you shan't delay.
3749–50 Which have naturally the special power to purge you down-
     wards and upwards.
3753 Beware lest the sun in its ascension.
3755 I'll wager a groat (fourpenny-bit).
3760 Laurel, centaury, and fumitory.

Of katapuce, or of gaitrys beryis,
Of herbe yve, growyng in oure yeerd, ther mery is;
Pekke hem up right as they growe and ete hem yn.   *peck*
3765 Be myrie, housbonde, for youre fader kyn!
Dredeth no dreem, I kan sey yow namoore.'
   'Madame,' quod he, 'graunt mercy of youre loore.   *advice*
But nathelees, as touchyng daun Catoun,   *as for*
That hath of wysdom swich a greet renoun,
3770 Though that he bad no dremes for to drede,
By God, men may in olde bookes rede   *read*
Of many a man moore of auctorite
Than evere Caton was, so moot I thee,
That al the revers seyn of this sentence,
3775 And han wel founden by experience
That dremes been significaciouns
As wel of joye as of tribulaciouns   *signs*
That folk enduren in this lif present.
Ther nedeth make of this noon argument;
3780 The verray preeve sheweth it in dede.
   Oon of the gretteste auctour that men rede
Seith thus: that whilom two felawes wente   *once; friends*
On pilgrimage, in a ful good entente;
And happed so, they coomen in a toun   *happened*
3785 Wher as ther was swich congregacioun   *where*
Of peple, and eek so streit of herbergage,
That they ne founde as muche as o cotage
In which they bothe myghte ylogged bee.   *put up*
Wherfore they mosten of necessitee,
3790 As for that nyght, departen compaignye;   *part*
And ech of hem gooth to his hostelrye,
And took his loggyng as it wolde falle.   *as chance decided*
That oon of hem was logged in a stalle,   *one*
Fer in a yeerd, with oxen of the plough;   *far down a yard*
3795 That oother man was logged wel ynough,
As was his aventure or his fortune,   *luck; good fortune*
That us governeth alle as in commune.   *in common*
   And so bifel that, longe er it were day,   *before*
This man mette in his bed, ther as he lay,   *dreamt; where*
3800 How that his felawe gan upon hym calle,   *called*
And seyde, "Allas! for in an oxes stalle

3762 Catapuce, or buckthorn berries.
3763 Buck's-horn, growing in a pleasant spot in our garden.
3765 For the honour of your father's family.
3773 As I hope to prosper.
3774 Who express exactly the opposite of this opinion.
3780 Actual experience shows it to be a fact.
3781 'One of the greatest authors' is a reference to either Cicero or
Valerius Maximus.
3783 In a most devout frame of mind.
3786 And (which) was also so short of accommodation.

This nyght I shal be mordred ther I lye.   *murdered*
Now help me, deere brother, or I dye.
In alle haste com to me!" he sayde.
3805 This man out of his sleep for feere abrayde;   *woke with a start*
But whan that he was wakened of his sleep,
He turned hym, and took of this no keep.   *turned over; notice*
Hym thoughte his dreem nas but a vanitee.
Thus twies in his slepyng dremed hee;
3810 And atte thridde tyme yet his felawe   *again*
Cam, as hym thoughte, and seide, "I am now slawe.   *slain*
Bihoold my bloody woundes depe and wyde!
Arys up erly in the morwe tyde,   *morning*
And at the west gate of the toun," quod he,
3815 "A carte ful of dong ther shaltow se,
In which my body is hid ful prively;   *secretly*
Do thilke carte arresten boldely.
My gold caused my mordre, sooth to sayn."   *to tell the truth*
And tolde hym every point how he was slayn,
3820 With a ful pitous face, pale of hewe.
And truste wel, his dreem he foond ful trewe,
For on the morwe, as soone as it was day,
To his felawes in he took the way;   *inn*
And whan that he cam to this oxes stalle,
3825 After his felawe he bigan to calle.
     The hostiler answerede hym anon,
And seyde, "Sire, your felawe is agon.   *gone*
As soone as day he wente out of the toun."
     This man gan fallen in suspecioun,   *became suspicious*
3830 Remembrynge on his dremes that he mette,   *dreamt*
And forth he gooth—no lenger wolde he lette—   *delay*
Unto the west gate of the toun, and fond
A dong-carte, wente as it were to donge lond,
That was arrayed in that same wise   *got ready; way*
3835 As ye han herd the dede man devyse.   *describe*
And with an hardy herte he gan to crye   *brave; called for*
Vengeance and justice of this felonye.
"My felawe mordred is this same nyght,
And in this carte he lith gapyng upright.
3840 I crye out on the ministres," quod he,
"That sholden kepe and reulen this citee.   *watch over*
Harrow! allas! heere lith my felawe slayn!"
What sholde I moore unto this tale sayn?   *why*

3808 It seemed to him his dream was nothing but an idle fancy.
3817 Have that cart stopped boldly.
3833 (Which) went as if to manure the land.
3839 He lies on his back with gaping mouth.
3840 I call on the magistrates.
3842 *Harrow*, a cry for help.

The peple out sterte and caste the cart to grounde,
3845 And in the myddel of the dong they founde
The dede man, that mordred was al newe.   *newly*
O blisful God, that art so just and trewe,   *blessed*
Lo, how that thou biwreyest mordre alway!   *reveal; always*
Mordre wol out, that se we day by day.
3850 Mordre is so wlatsom and abhomynable
To God, that is so just and resonable,
That he ne wol nat suffre it heled be,   *concealed*
Though it abyde a yeer, or two, or thre.
Mordre wol out, this my conclusioun.   *this (is)*
3855 And right anon, ministres of that toun
Han hent the carter and so soore hym pyned,   *tortured*
And eek the hostiler so soore engyned,   *racked*
That they biknewe hire wikkednesse anon,   *confessed*
And were anhanged by the nekke-bon.   *hanged*
3860   Heere may men seen that dremes been   *are*
                    to drede.   *to be feared*
And certes in the same book I rede,
Right in the nexte chapitre after this—
I gabbe nat, so have I joye or blis—
Two men that wolde han passed over see,
3865 For certeyn cause, into a fer contree,
If that the wynd ne hadde been contrarie,
That made hem in a citee for to tarie
That stood ful myrie upon an haven-syde;
But on a day, agayn the even-tyde,
3870 The wynd gan chaunge, and blew right as hem leste.
Jolif and glad they wente unto hir reste,   *cheerful*
And casten hem ful erly for to saille.   *resolved*
But herkneth! To that o man fil a greet mervaille:
That oon of hem, in slepyng as he lay,
3875 Hym mette a wonder dreem agayn the day.
Hym thoughte a man stood by his beddes   *it seemed to him*
                    syde,
And hym comanded that he sholde abyde,
And seyde hym thus; "If thou tomorwe wende,
Thow shalt be dreynt; my tale is at an ende."   *drowned*
3880 He wook, and tolde his felawe what he mette,
And preyde hym his viage for to lette;

3850 Murder is so heinous and unnatural.
3863 I do not lie, as I hope for happiness.
3868 That was pleasantly situated on the shore of a haven.
3869–70 But one day, towards evening, the wind changed and blew just
  as they wished.
3873–5 But to one of them a marvellous thing happened: as he lay
  sleeping he dreamt a strange dream just before dawn.
3881 And begged him to postpone his voyage.

As for that day, he preyde hym to byde.   *wait*
His felawe, that lay by his beddes syde,
Gan for to laughe, and scorned him ful faste.
3885 "No dreem," quod he, "may so myn herte agaste   *terrify*
That I wol lette for to do my thynges.
I sette nat a straw by thy dremynges,
For swevenes been but vanytees and japes.
Men dreme alday of owles and of apes,   *constantly*
3890 And of many a maze therwithal;   *delusive thing*
Men dreme of thyng that nevere was ne shal.   *shall (be)*
But sith I see that thou wolt heere abyde,   *since*
And thus forslewthen wilfully thy tyde,
God woot, it reweth me; and have good day!"
3895 And thus he took his leve, and wente his way.
But er that he hadde half his cours yseyled,   *voyage*
Noot I nat why, ne what myschaunce it eyled,
But casuelly the shippes botme rente,
And ship and man under the water wente
3900 In sighte of othere shippes it bisyde,
That with hem seyled at the same tyde.   *time*
And therfore, faire Pertelote so deere,
By swiche ensamples olde maistow leere
That no man sholde been to recchelees   *disregardful*
3905 Of dremes; for I seye thee, doutelees,
That many a dreem ful soore is   *is greatly*
        for to drede.   *to be feared*
    Lo, in the lyf of Seint Kenelm I rede,
That was Kenulphus sone, the noble kyng
Of Mercenrike, how Kenelm mette a thyng.   *Mercia*
3910 A lite er he was mordred, on a day,   *short time before*
His mordre in his avysioun he say.   *vision; saw*
His norice hym expowned every deel
His swevene, and bad hym for to kepe hym weel
For traisoun; but he nas but seven yeer oold,
3915 And therfore litel tale hath he toold   *he took little account*
Of any dreem, so hooly was his herte.
By God! I hadde levere than my sherte   *rather*

3884 Laughed and poured scorn on him.
3886 That I will delay doing my business.
3887-8 I don't care a straw for your dreaming, for dreams are nothing
    but tricks and idle fancies.
3893 And so wilfully waste your time in idleness.
3894 God knows, I'm sorry for it, and so farewell.
3897 I don't know why, nor what went wrong.
3898 By some mischance the ship's bottom was torn open.
3903 From such old stories you may learn.
3912-14 His nurse expounded his dream to him in detail, and begged
    him to guard himself well for fear of treason.
3917-18 i.e. I'd give my shirt to know that you had read the story of
    his life.

That ye hadde rad his legende, as have I.   *read*
   Dame Pertelote, I sey yow trewely,
3920 Macrobeus, that writ the avisioun
In Affrike of the worthy Cipioun,   *Africa; Scipio*
Affermeth dremes, and seith that they been
Warnynge of thynges that men after seen.   *afterwards*
And forthermoore, I pray yow, looketh wel
3925 In the olde testament, of Daniel,   *concerning*
If he heeld dremes any vanitee.   *idle fancy*
Reed eek of Joseph, and ther shul ye see   *also*
Wher dremes be somtyme—I sey nat alle—   *whether*
Warnynge of thynges that shul after falle.   *happen*
3930 Looke of Egipte the kyng, daun Pharao,
His bakere and his butiller also,   *butler*
Wher they ne felte noon effect in dremes.
Whoso wol seken actes of sondry remes
May rede of dremes many a wonder thyng.
3935 Lo Cresus, which that was of Lyde kyng,   *Croesus; Lydia*
Mette he nat that he sat upon a tree,   *not*
Which signified he sholde anhanged bee?
Lo heere Andromacha, Ectores wyf,   *Andromache*
That day that Ector sholde lese his lyf,   *was to lose*
3940 She dremed on the same nyght biforn
How that the lyf of Ector sholde be lorn,   *would be lost*
If thilke day he wente into bataille.   *that*
She warned hym, but it myghte nat availle;
He wente for to fighte natheles,   *nevertheless*
3945 But he was slayn anon of Achilles.
But thilke tale is al to longe to telle,
And eek it is ny day, I may nat dwelle.   *near*
Shortly I seye, as for conclusioun,
That I shal han of this avisioun   *have from*
3950 Adversitee; and I seye forthermoor,
That I ne telle of laxatyves no stoor,
For they been venymes, I woot it weel;
I hem diffye, I love hem never a deel!
   Now let us speke of myrthe, and stynte al this.   *stop*
3955 Madame Pertelote, so have I blis,
Of o thyng God hath sent me large grace;
For whan I se the beautee of youre face,

3920 Macrobius was the author of a commentary (*c.* A.D. 400) on
   Cicero's *Somnium Scipionis*.
3925 Dan. vii ff.
3930 Consider the king of Egypt, lord Pharaoh (Gen. xl, xli).
3932 Whether they felt no consequences of dreams.
3933 Anyone who will search the histories of various realms.
3951 That I set no store by laxatives.
3953 I spurn them—I don't like them a bit!
3956 In one thing God has sent me great good fortune.

Ye been so scarlet reed aboute youre yen,   *eyes*
It maketh al my drede for to dyen;
3960 For al so siker as *In principio*,
Mulier est hominis confusio,—
Madame, the sentence of this Latyn is,   *meaning*
"Womman is mannes joye and al his blis."
For whan I feele a-nyght your softe syde,   *at night*
3965 Al be it that I may nat on yow ryde,
For that oure perche is maad so narwe, allas!   *narrow*
I am so ful of joye and of solas,   *delight*
That I diffye bothe sweven and dreem.'
And with that word he fley doun fro the beem,   *flew*
3970 For it was day, and eke his hennes alle,
And with a chuk he gan hem for to calle,   *cluck*
For he hadde founde a corn, lay in the yerd.
Real he was, he was namoore aferd.   *regal*
He fethered Pertelote twenty tyme,
3975 And trad hire eke as ofte, er it was pryme.
He looketh as it were a grym leoun,   *like a fierce lion*
And on his toos he rometh up and doun;   *stalks*
Hym deigned nat to sette his foot to grounde.   *he did not deign*
He chukketh whan he hath a corn yfounde,
3980 And to hym rennen thanne his wyves alle.
Thus roial, as a prince is in his halle,
Leve I this Chauntecleer in his pasture,
And after wol I telle his aventure.
        Whan that the month in which the world bigan,
3985 That highte March, whan God first maked man,   *is called*
Was compleet, and passed were also,
Syn March was gon, thritty dayes and two,
Bifel that Chauntecleer in al his pryde,
His sevene wyves walkynge by his syde,
3990 Caste up his eyen to the brighte sonne,
That in the signe of Taurus hadde yronne
Twenty degrees and oon, and somwhat moore,
And knew by kynde, and by noon oother   *instinct*
    loore,   *learning*

3959 It makes all my fear die away.
3960–1 For it's as true as the gospel (*In principio* are the opening words of St John's Gospel) that 'Woman is man's ruin.'
3968 I defy both vision and dream.
3972 A grain of corn which lay in the yard.
3975 *pryme*, first division of the day (6–9 a.m.).   Here and in 3994 the later hour of 9 a.m. is meant.
3982 I leave Chauntecleer feeding.
3984–7 A roundabout way of saying 'When it was May 3rd.' *Syn March bigan* may be understood as meaning 'since March began (and ended).'
3990–2 i.e. the sun in its annual course (according to the Ptolemaic system of astronomy) was in the 22nd degree of the zodiacal sign Taurus; this again points to May 3rd.

That it was pryme, and crew with blisful stevene.
3995 'The sonne,' he seyde, 'is clomben up on hevene   *climbed*
Fourty degrees and oon, and moore ywis.
Madame Pertelote, my worldes blis,
Herkneth thise blisful briddes how they synge,
And se the fresshe floures how they sprynge;   *grow*
4000 Ful is myn herte of revel and solas!'   *joy*
But sodeynly hym fil a sorweful cas,   *mischance*
For evere the latter ende of joye is wo.
God woot that worldly joye is soone ago;   *gone*
And if a rethor koude faire endite,
4005 He in a cronycle saufly myghte it write
As for a sovereyn notabilitee.
Now every wys man, lat him herkne me:
This storie is also trewe, I undertake,
As is the book of Launcelot de Lake,
4010 That wommen holde in ful greet reverence.   *whom*
Now wol I torne agayn to my sentence.   *subject*
  A col-fox, ful of sly iniquitee,
That in the grove hadde woned yeres three,
By heigh ymaginacioun forncast,
4015 The same nyght thurghout the hegges brast   *burst*
Into the yerd ther Chauntecleer the faire
Was wont, and eek his wyves, to repaire;
And in a bed of wortes still he lay,   *cabbages*
Til it was passed undren of the day,   *noon*
4020 Waitynge his tyme on Chauntecleer   *watching his opportunity*
  to falle,
As gladly doon thise homycides alle
That in await liggen to mordre men.
O false mordrour, lurkynge in thy den!
O newe Scariot, newe Genylon,
4025 False dissymulour, o Greek Synon,   *dissembler*
That broghtest Troye al outrely to sorwe!   *utterly*
O Chauntecleer, acursed be that morwe

3995-6 The sun's altitude at 9 a.m. on May 3rd is correctly given by
    Chauntecleer as rather more than 41°.
4002 For joy always ends in sorrow.
4004-6 And if a master of rhetoric knew his job, he could confidently
    write it down in a chronicle as a most notable fact.
4008 This story is as true, I give you my word.
4009 An allusion to the story of Lancelot, the lover of Queen Guinevere.
4012 *col-fox*, 'coal fox,' i.e. fox with black markings.
4014 As foreseen by divine foreknowledge.
4021-2 As all assassins usually do that lie in wait to murder men.
4024 *Scariot*, Judas Iscariot; *Genylon*, Ganelon, the man who betrays
    Roland in the *Chanson de Roland*.
4025 *Synon*, Sinon, the Greek who persuaded the Trojans to receive the
    wooden horse into Troy.

That thou into that yerd flaugh fro the bemes!   *flew*
Thou were ful wel ywarned by thy dremes
4030 That thilke day was perilous to thee;
But what that God forwoot moot nedes bee,
After the opinioun of certein clerkis.   *according; scholars*
Witnesse on hym that any parfit clerk is,
That in scole is greet altercacioun
4035 In this mateere, and greet disputisoun,   *debate*
And hath been of an hundred thousand men.
But I ne kan nat bulte it to the bren,
As kan the hooly doctour Augustyn,
Or Boece, or the Bisshop Bradwardyn,
4040 Wheither that Goddes worthy forwityng   *foreknowledge*
Streyneth me nedely for to doon a   *constrains; necessarily*
        thyng,—
'Nedely' clepe I symple necessitee;   *call*
Or elles, if free choys be graunted me
To do that same thyng, or do it noght,   *not*
4045 Though God forwoot it er that I was wroght;
Or if his wityng streyneth never a deel
But by necessitee condicioneel.
I wol nat han to do of swich mateere;
My tale is of a cok, as ye may heere,
4050 That tok his conseil of his wyf, with sorwe,
To walken in the yerd upon that morwe
That he hadde met that dreem that I yow tolde.
Wommennes conseils been ful ofte colde;   *very often fatal*
Wommannes conseil broghte us first to wo,
4055 And made Adam fro Paradys to go,
Ther as he was ful myrie and wel at ese.
But for I noot to whom it myght displese,   *know not*
If I conseil of wommen wolde blame,
Passe over, for I seyde it in my game.   *in fun*
4060 Rede auctours, where they trete of swich mateere,
And what they seyn of wommen ye may heere.

4031 But whatever God foreknows must necessarily be.
4033–4 Take any accomplished scholar as witness that in the schools
    (i.e. universities).
4037 But I cannot sift the flour from the bran, i.e. find out the truth of
    the matter.
4038–9 *Augustyn*, St Augustine of Hippo (345–430); *Boece*, Boethius
    (d. 524), author of *De Consolatione Philosophiae*, which Chaucer
    translated; *Bradwardyn*, Thomas Bradwardine, Archbishop of
    Canterbury (d. 1349). These three are named here as authorities
    on the problem of the relationship between free will and predestination.
4045 Though God foreknows it before I was born.
4046–7 Or if His knowledge involves no constraint at all, except that
    of conditional necessity (i.e. the necessity implied by divine fore-
    knowledge that a thing will come to pass).
4050 Who took his wife's advice—bad luck to him!
4056 Where he was very happy and comfortable.

Thise been the cokkes wordes, and nat myne;
I kan noon harm of no womman divyne.
    Faire in the soond, to bathe hire myrily,

4065 Lith Pertelote, and alle hire sustres by,
Agayn the sonne, and Chauntecleer so free   *noble*
Soong murier than the mermayde in the see;   *more sweetly*
For Phisiologus seith sikerly   *truly*
How that they syngen wel and myrily.

4070 And so bifel that, as he caste his ye
Among the wortes on a boterflye,
He was war of this fox, that lay ful lowe.
Nothyng ne liste hym thanne for to crowe,
But cride anon, 'Cok! cok!' and up he sterte

4075 As man that was affrayed in his herte.
For natureelly a beest desireth flee
Fro his contrarie, if he may it see,
Though he never erst hadde seyn it with his ye.   *previously*
    This Chauntecleer, whan he gan hym   *caught sight of him*
        espye,

4080 He wolde han fled, but that the fox anon
Seyde, 'Gentil sire, allas! wher wol ye gon?
Be ye affrayed of me that am youre freend?
Now, certes, I were worse than a feend,
If I to yow wolde harm or vileynye!   *intended; bad turn*

4085 I am nat come youre conseil for t'espye,   *secrets; spy out*
But trewely, the cause of my comynge
Was oonly for to herkne how that ye synge.
For trewely, ye have as myrie a stevene
As any aungel hath that is in hevene.

4090 Therwith ye han in musyk moore feelynge
Than hadde Boece, or any that kan synge.
My lord youre fader—God his soule blesse!—
And eek youre mooder, of hire gentillesse,
Han in myn hous ybeen to my greet ese;

4095 And certes, sire, ful fayn wolde I yow plese.
But, for men speke of syngyng, I wol seye,—
So moote I brouke wel myne eyen tweye,—

4063 I can think no harm of any woman.
4064–6 Pertelote, with all her sisters beside her, lies elegantly in the sand
    and there, in the sunshine, takes a pleasant bath.
4068 *Phisiologus*, the medieval Latin bestiary or book of beasts, in
    which the song of the Sirens (identified with mermaids in Chaucer's
    tale) is interpreted as a symbol of deceitful worldly pleasure.
4073 Then he had no desire at all to crow.
4091 Boethius wrote a treatise on music which was a standard text-book
    in the Middle Ages.
4093–4 (They) did me the courtesy of visiting me in my house, to my
    great satisfaction.
4097 As I hope to make good use of my two eyes.

Save yow, I herde nevere man so synge   *except for*
As dide youre fader in the morwenynge.
4100 Certes, it was of herte, al that he song.   *from the heart*
And for to make his voys the moore strong,
He wolde so peyne hym that with bothe his yen
He moste wynke, so loude he wolde cryen,
And stonden on his tiptoon therwithal,   *tiptoes*
4105 And strecche forth his nekke long and smal.   *slender*
And eek he was of swich discrecioun   *discernment*
That ther nas no man in no regioun
That hym in song or wisedom myghte passe.   *surpass*
I have wel rad in "Daun Burnel the Asse,"
4110 Among his vers, how that ther was a cok,
For that a preestes sone yaf hym a knok   *because*
Upon his leg whil he was yong and nyce,
He made hym for to lese his benefice.   *lose*
But certeyn, ther nys no comparisoun
4115 Bitwixe the wisedom and discrecioun
Of youre fader and of his subtiltee.
Now syngeth, sire, for seinte charitee;   *holy*
Lat se, konne ye youre fader countrefete?'
    This Chauntecleer his wynges gan to bete,
4120 As man that koude his traysoun nat espie,   *one*
So was he ravysshed with his flaterie.
    Allas! ye lordes, many a fals flatour   *flatterer*
Is in youre courtes, and many a losengeour,   *deceiver*
That plesen yow wel moore, by my feith,   *much*
4125 Than he that soothfastnesse unto yow seith.   *truth*
Redeth Ecclesiaste of flaterye;
Beth war, ye lordes, of hir trecherye.
    This Chauntecleer stood hye upon his toos,
Strecchynge his nekke, and heeld his eyen cloos,
4130 And gan to crowe loude for the nones.   *for the occasion*
And daun Russell the fox stirte up atones,
And by the gargat hente Chauntecleer,   *throat; seized*
And on his bak toward the wode hym beer,   *carried*
For yet ne was ther no man that hym sewed.   *pursued*
4135   O destinee, that mayst nat been eschewed!   *avoided*
Allas, that Chauntecleer fleigh fro the bemes!   *flew*

4102–3 He would exert himself so much that he had to close both his eyes.
4109 I have read indeed in 'Lord Burnel the Ass.' (A donkey named Burnellus is the hero of a Latin satirical poem on the regular clergy written by Nigel Wireker, a twelfth-century monk of Christ Church, Canterbury.)
4112 While he (i.e. the priest's son) was young and foolish.
4116 And his (i.e. that cock's) ingenuity.
4118 Show me whether you can imitate your father.
4126 Ecclus. xxvii. 26; Prov. xxix. 5.

Allas, his wyf ne roghte nat of dremes!
And on a Friday fil al this meschaunce.   *misfortune*
   O Venus, that art goddesse of plesaunce,   *pleasure*
4140 Syn that thy servant was this Chauntecleer,
And in thy servyce dide al his poweer,   *did his utmost*
Moore for delit than world to multiplye,   *delight*
Why woldestow suffre hym on thy day to dye?
   O Gaufred, deere maister soverayn,
4145 That whan thy worthy kyng Richard was slayn
With shot, compleynedest his deeth so soore,
Why ne hadde I now thy sentence and thy loore,
The Friday for to chide, as diden ye?
For on a Friday, soothly, slayn was he.
4150 Thanne wolde I shewe yow how that I koude
    pleyne
For Chauntecleres drede and for his peyne.   *fear; suffering*
Certes, swich cry ne lamentacion,
Was nevere of ladyes maad whan Ylion   *Ilion*
Was wonne, and Pirrus with his streite swerd,
4155 Whan he hadde hent kyng Priam by the berd,
And slayn hym, as seith us *Eneydos*,
As maden alle the hennes in the clos,   *yard*
Whan they had seyn of Chauntecleer the sighte.
But sovereynly dame Pertelote shrighte,
4160 Ful louder than dide Hasdrubales wyf,
Whan that hir housbonde hadde lost his lyf,
And that the Romayns hadde brend Cartage.   *burnt*
She was so ful of torment and of rage   *anguish; frenzy*
That wilfully into the fyr she sterte,   *deliberately; leapt*
4165 And brende hirselven with a stedefast herte.
   O woful hennes, right so criden ye,
As, whan that Nero brende the citee
Of Rome, cryden senatoures wyves
For that hir husbondes losten alle hir lyves,—
4170 Withouten gilt this Nero hath hem slayn.
Now wole I turne to my tale agayn.

4137 Alas, that his wife took no heed of dreams.
4144 *Gaufred*, Geoffrey de Vinsauf, whose *Poetria Nova*, an early
    thirteenth-century treatise on the art of poetry, had considerable
    influence on Chaucer as a young poet. The maturer Chaucer, as
    the irony of this allusion shows, had outgrown Geoffrey's precepts
    and models.
4145 Richard I (*d.* 1199).
4146 By the shooting of an arrow, lamented his death so bitterly.
4147 Why haven't I now your noble sentiments and learning.
4154-5 And when Pyrrhus with his drawn sword had seized King Priam.
4156 *Aeneid*, ii. 550 ff.
4159 But madam Pertelote shrieked above all the others.
4160 Hasdrubal was the king of Carthage when the Romans burnt it
    in 146 B.C.

This sely wydwe and eek hir doghtres two   *poor*
Herden thise hennes crie and maken wo,   *lamentation*
And out at dores stirten they anon,   *rushed*
4175 And syen the fox toward the grove gon,   *saw*
And bar upon his bak the cok away,
And cryden, 'Out! harrow! and weylaway!   *alas*
Ha! ha! the fox!' and after hym they ran,
And eek with staves many another man.
4180 Ran Colle oure dogge, and Talbot, and Gerland,
And Malkyn, with a dystaf in hir hand;
Ran cow and calf, and eek the verray hogges,
So fered for the berkyng of the dogges *frightened because of*
And shoutyng of the men and wommen eeke,
4185 They ronne so hem thoughte hir herte breeke.
They yolleden as feendes doon in helle;   *yelled*
The dokes cryden as men wolde hem quelle;   *ducks; kill*
The gees for feere flowen over the trees;
Out of the hyve cam the swarm of bees.
4190 So hydous was the noyse, a, *benedicitee*!   *hideous; bless us*
Certes, he Jakke Straw and his meynee
Ne made nevere shoutes half so shrille
Whan that they wolden any Flemyng kille,
As thilke day was maad upon the fox.
4195 Of bras they broghten bemes, and of box,   *trumpets; boxwood*
Of horn, of boon, in whiche they blewe and   *bone*
      powped,   *tooted*
And therwithal they skriked and they   *shrieked*
      howped.   *whooped*
It semed as that hevene sholde falle.
      Now, goode men, I prey yow herkneth alle:
4200 Lo, how Fortune turneth sodeynly   *overturns*
The hope and pryde eek of hir enemy!
This cok, that lay upon the foxes bak,
In al his drede unto the fox he spak,
And seyde, 'Sire, if that I were as ye,
4205 Yet sholde I seyn, as wys God helpe me,
"Turneth agayn, ye proude cherles alle!   *back; churls*
A verray pestilence upon yow falle!
Now I am come unto the wodes syde;
Maugree youre heed, the cok shal heere abyde.

4180 *Talbot* and *Gerland* are dogs' names.
4181 *Malkyn*, diminutive of *Moll*.
4185 They ran so hard it seemed to them their hearts would break.
4191 Surely Jack Straw and his following. (Jack Straw was one of the
     leaders of the Peasants' Revolt in 1381.   The massacre of the Flemings
     by the London mob was due to envy of their success as woollen
     merchants and manufacturers.)
4204-5 If I were you . . . so help me God.
4209 In spite of all you can do (lit. in spite of your head), the cock
     shall stay here.

4210 I wol hym ete, in feith, and that anon!'''   *immediately*
    The fox answerde, 'In feith, it shal be don.'
And as he spak that word, al sodeynly
This cok brak from his mouth delyverly,
And heighe upon a tree he fleigh anon.
4215 And whan the fox saugh that the cok was gon,
    'Allas!' quod he, 'O Chauntecleer, allas!
I have to yow,' quod he, 'ydoon trespas,   *done wrong*
In as muche as I maked yow aferd
Whan I yow hente and broghte out of the yerd.
4220 But, sire, I dide it in no wikke entente.
Com doun, and I shal telle yow what I mente;
I shal seye sooth to yow, God help me so!'
    'Nay thanne,' quod he, 'I shrewe us bothe two.   *curse*
And first I shrewe myself, bothe blood and bones,
4225 If thou bigyle me ofter than ones.   *fool*
Thou shalt namoore, thurgh thy flaterye,
Do me to synge and wynke with myn ye;
For he that wynketh, whan he sholde see,
Al wilfully, God lat him nevere thee!'   *prosper*
4230   'Nay,' quod the fox, 'but God yeve hym meschaunce,
That is so undiscreet of governaunce
That jangleth holde his pees.'   *chatters*
    Lo, swich it is for to be recchelees
And necligent, and truste on flaterye.
4235   But ye that holden this tale a folye,   *silly thing*
As of a fox, or of a cok and hen,
Taketh the moralite, goode men.
For seint Paul seith that al that writen is,
To oure doctrine it is ywrite, ywis;
4240 Taketh the fruyt, and lat the chaf be stille.
Now, goode God, if that it be thy wille,
As seith my lord, so make us alle goode men,
And brynge us to his heighe blisse!   Amen.

HEERE IS ENDED THE NONNES PREESTES TALE

4213 Nimbly escaped from his mouth.
4224 I curse myself utterly.
4227 Make me sing and shut my eyes.
4231 So lacking in self-control.
4233 See, this is what happens when you are thoughtless.
4239 Is written for our instruction, certainly.   (See Rom. xv. 4.)
4242 *my lord.* A marginal note in the Ellesmere MS. explains this as
    an allusion to the Archbishop of Canterbury; but the point of the
    allusion is lost.

EPILOGUE TO THE NUN'S PRIEST'S TALE

'Sire Nonnes Preest,' oure Hooste seide anoon,
4245 'I-blessed be thy breche, and every stoon!   *breeches*
This was a murie tale of Chauntecleer.
But by my trouthe, if thou were seculer,
Thou woldest ben a trede-foul aright.
For if thou have corage as thou hast myght,   *desire*
4250 Thee were nede of hennes, as I wene,
Ya, moo than seven tymes seventene.   *yea*
See, whiche braunes hath this gentil preest,   *what muscles*
So gret a nekke, and swich a large breest!
He loketh as a sperhauk with his yen;   *sparrow-hawk; eyes*
4255 Him nedeth nat his colour for to dyen
With brasile, ne with greyn of Portyngale.
Now, sire, faire falle yow for youre tale!'   *good luck to you*
    And after that he, with ful merie chere,   *cheerfully*
Seide unto another, as ye shuln heere.

4248 See 2742 above.
4250 You would have need of hens.
4255-6 He doesn't need to put colour into his face by using red dyes
    made from brazil-wood or cochineal.

THE SECOND NUN'S PROLOGUE

The Prologe of the Seconde Nonnes Tale

THE MINISTRE and the norice unto vices,   *nurse*
Which that men clepe in Englissh ydelnesse,   *call*
That porter of the gate is of delices,
To eschue, and by hire contrarie hire oppresse,
5 That is to seyn, by leveful bisynesse,
Wel oghten we to doon al oure entente,
Lest that the feend thurgh ydelnesse us hente.

For he that with his thousand cordes slye
Continuelly us waiteth to biclappe,
10 Whan he may man in ydelnesse espye,
He kan so lightly cacche hym in his trappe,
Til that a man be hent right by the lappe,
He nys nat war the feend hath hym in honde.
Wel oghte us werche, and ydelnesse withstonde.   *work*

15 And though men dradden nevere for to dye,
Yet seen men wel by resoun, doutelees,
That ydelnesse is roten slogardye,   *slothfulness*
Of which ther nevere comth no good n'encrees;   *profit*
And syn that slouthe hire holdeth in a lees
20 Oonly to slepe, and for to ete and drynke,
And to devouren al that othere swynke,   *others toil for*

And for to putte us fro swich ydelnesse,
That cause is of so greet confusioun,   *much ruin*

---

3 Who is portress at the gateway to sinful pleasures.
4–7 We ought to make every effort to avoid her and crush her by means of her opposite, that is to say, by lawful industry, lest through our idleness the devil seize us.
8 i.e. idleness is the devil's net.
9 Watches out to catch us.
12–13 Till a man is seized by the hem of his garment he is not aware the devil has hold of him.
15 Even if men never feared to die, i.e. if they thought only of this life.
19 Since sloth holds her (i.e. idleness) in a leash.

I have heer doon my feithful bisynesse
25 After the legende, in translacioun
Right of thy glorious lif and passioun,
Thou with thy gerland wroght with rose and lilie,—   *made*
Thee meene I, mayde and martyr, Seint Cecilie.   *mean*

Invocacio ad Mariam

And thow that flour of virgines art alle   *flower*
30 Of whom that Bernard list so wel to write,
To thee at my bigynnyng first I calle;
Thou confort of us wrecches, do me endite   *help me to relate*
Thy maydens deeth, that wan thurgh hire merite   *won*
The eterneel lyf, and of the feend victorie, *victory over the devil*
35 As man may after reden in hire storie.   *read*

Thow Mayde and Mooder, doghter of thy Sone,
Thow welle of mercy, synful soules cure,
In whom that God for bountee chees to wone,
Thow humble, and heigh over every creature,   *high*
40 Thow nobledest so ferforth oure nature,
That no desdeyn the Makere hadde of kynde
His Sone in blood and flessh to clothe and wynde.   *wrap*

Withinne the cloistre blisful of thy sydis   *blessed cloister*
Took mannes shap the eterneel love and pees,
45 That of the tryne compas lord and gyde is,   *threefold world*
Whom erthe and see and hevene, out of   *without ceasing*
    relees,
Ay heryen; and thou, Virgine wemmelees,   *praise; spotless*
Baar of thy body—and dweltest mayden pure—   *bore*
The Creatour of every creature.

50 Assembled is in thee magnificence
With mercy, goodnesse, and with swich pitee
That thou, that art the sonne of excellence,   *sun*
Nat oonly helpest hem that preyen thee,   *pray to*
But often tyme, of thy benygnytee,
55 Ful frely, er that men thyn help biseche,   *beseech*
Thou goost biforn, and art hir lyves leche.

24-6 I have faithfully done my best, following the legend (i.e. the life
of St Cecilia), to translate the story of your glorious passion.
27 In medieval art St Cecilia is always shown wearing a garland of roses.
30 Of whom St Bernard loves so much to write.
38 In whom for goodness God chose to dwell.
40-1 You so far ennobled our nature that the Maker (of human nature)
did not disdain.
56 You anticipate their prayers, and are their life's physician.

Now help, thow meeke and blisful faire mayde,
Me, flemed wrecche, in this desert of galle;   *banished exile*
Thynk on the womman Cananee, that sayde
60 That whelpes eten somme of the crommes alle   *dogs may eat*
That from hir lordes table been yfalle;   *fallen*
And though that I, unworthy sone of Eve,
By synful, yet accepte my bileve.   *belief*

And, for that feith is deed withouten werkis,
65 So for to werken yif me wit and space,   *wisdom; opportunity*
That I be quit fro thennes that most derk is!
O thou, that art so fair and ful of grace,
Be myn advocat in that heighe place
Theras withouten ende is songe 'Osanne,'
70 Thow Cristes mooder, doghter deere of Anne!

And of thy light my soule in prison lighte,   *lighten*
That troubled is by the contagioun
Of my body, and also by the wighte   *weight*
Of erthely lust and fals affeccioun;   *desire*
75 O havene of refut, o salvacioun   *refuge*
Of hem that been in sorwe and in distresse,
Now help, for to my werk I wol me dresse.   *address myself*

Yet preye I yow that reden that I write,   *what*
Foryeve me that I do no diligence
80 This ilke storie subtilly to endite,
For bothe have I the wordes and sentence   *meaning*
Of hym that at the seintes reverence
The storie wroot, and folwen hire legende,   *wrote; follow*
And pray yow that ye wole my werk amende.   *improve*

Interpretacio nominis Cecilie quam ponit
Frater Jacobus Januensis in Legenda

85 First wolde I yow the name of Seint Cecilie
Expowne, as men may in hir storie see.   *explain*
It is to seye in Englissh 'hevenes lilie,'
For pure chaastnesse of virginitee;
Or, for she whitnesse hadde of honestee,
90 And grene of conscience, and of good fame
The soote savour, 'lilie' was hir name.   *sweet*

59 Think of the woman of Canaan.
66 That I may be delivered from darkness.
69 Where 'Hosanna' endlessly is sung.
79-80 That I take no pains to tell this story in a subtle fashion.
82 From him (i.e. Jacobus Januensis) who out of reverence for the saint.
87 It signifies in English.
89-90 Because she had the whiteness of purity and the green of tenderness.

Or Cecilie is to seye 'the wey to blynde,' *path for the blind*
For she ensample was by good techynge;   *example*
Or elles Cecile, as I writen fynde,
95 Is joyned, by a manere conjoynynge
Of 'hevene' and 'Lia'; and heere, in figurynge, *figuratively*
The 'hevene' is set for thoght of hoolynesse,
And 'Lia' for hire lastynge bisynesse.   *ceaseless labour*

Cecile may eek be seyd in this manere,
100 'Wantynge of blyndnesse,' for hir grete light   *lack*
Of sapience, and for hire thewes cleere;   *wisdom; virtues*
Or elles, loo, this maydens name bright
Of 'hevene' and 'leos' comth, for which by right
Men myghte hire wel 'the hevene of peple' calle,
105 Ensample of goode and wise werkes alle.

For 'leos' 'peple' in Englissh is to seye,
And right as men may in the hevene see
The sonne and moone and sterres every weye,   *on all sides*
Right so men goostly in this mayden free
110 Seyen of feith the magnanymytee,
And eek the cleernesse hool of sapience,
And sondry werkes, brighte of excellence.

And right so as thise philosophres write
That hevene is swift and round and eek brennynge, *burning*
115 Right so was faire Cecilie the white
Ful swift and bisy evere in good werkynge,
And round and hool in good perseverynge,   *perfect*
And brennynge evere in charite ful brighte.
Now have I yow declared what she highte.

EXPLICIT

95–6 Is a compound formed by joining 'heaven' and 'Leah.'
99 May also be said to mean.
109–11 So in this noble maiden, spiritually, are seen the magnanimity
of faith and the perfect radiance of wisdom.
119 Now I have explained her name to you.

THE SECOND NUN'S TALE

HERE BIGYNNETH THE SECONDE NONNES TALE OF THE LYF OF SEINTE CECILE

120   THIS mayden bright Cecilie, as hir lif seith,
    Was comen of Romayns, and of noble kynde,
    And from hir cradel up fostred in the feith   *brought up*
    Of Crist and bar his gospel in hir mynde.   *bore*
    She nevere cessed, as I writen fynde,   *ceased*
125 Of hir preyere, and God to love and drede,   *fear*
    Bisekynge hym to kepe hir maydenhede.   *guard*

    And whan this mayden sholde unto a man
    Ywedded be, that was ful yong of age,
    Which that ycleped was Valerian,
130 And day was comen of hir marriage,
    She, ful devout and humble in hir corage,   *heart*
    Under hir robe of gold, that sat ful faire,
    Hadde next hire flessh yclad hire in an haire.

    And whil the organs maden melodie,
135 To God allone in herte thus sang she:
    'O Lord, my soule and eek my body gye   *keep*
    Unwemmed, lest that I confounded be.'   *unblemished*
    And, for his love that dyde upon a tree,   *cross*
    Every seconde and thridde day she faste,   *fasted*
140 Ay biddynge in hire orisons ful faste.

    The nyght cam, and to bedde moste she gon
    With hire housbonde, as ofte is the manere,
    And pryvely to hym she seyde anon,   *privately*
    'O sweete and wel biloved spouse deere,
145 Ther is a conseil, and ye wolde it heere,
    Which that right fayn I wolde unto yow seye,   *gladly*
    So that ye swere ye shul it nat biwreye.'   *betray*

    Valerian gan faste unto hire swere
    That for no cas, ne thyng that myghte be,   *in no case*
150 He sholde nevere mo biwreyen here;   *her*
    And thanne at erst to hym thus seyde she: *for the first time*

---

121 Was Roman born, and of noble lineage.
132 That fitted (her) most beautifully.
133 Had put on a hair-shirt next to her flesh.
140 Offering earnestly her prayers.
145 There is a secret, if you will hear it.
148 Valerian solemnly swore to her.

'I have an aungel which that loveth me,
That with greet love, wher so I wake or sleepe,   *wherever*
Is redy ay my body for to kepe.

155 'And if that he may feelen, out of drede,   *without doubt*
That ye me touche, or love in vileynye,   *wickedly*
He right anon wol sle yow with the dede,
And in youre yowthe thus ye shullen dye;   *youth; shall*
And if that ye in clene me gye,   *keep*
160 He wol yow loven as me, for youre clennesse,
And shewen yow his joye and his brightnesse.'

    Valerian, corrected as God wolde,
Answerde agayn, 'If I shal trusten thee,
Lat me that aungel se, and hym biholde;
165 And if that it a verray angel bee,   *real*
Thanne wol I doon as thou hast prayed me;
And if thou love another man, for sothe
Right with this swerd thanne wol I sle yow bothe.'

    Cecile answerde anon-right in this wise:
170 'If that yow list, the angel shul ye see,   *wish*
So that ye trowe on Crist and yow baptize.   *believe in*
Gooth forth to Via Apia,' quod shee,
'That fro this toun ne stant but miles three,   *stands*
And to the povre folkes that ther dwelle,   *poor*
175 Sey hem right thus, as that I shal yow telle.

    'Telle hem that I, Cecile, yow to hem sente,
To shewen yow the goode Urban the olde,
For secree nedes and for good entente.
And whan that ye Seint Urban han biholde,   *have beheld*
180 Telle hym the wordes whiche I to yow tolde;
And whan that he hath purged yow fro synne,
Thanne shul ye se that angel, er ye twynne.'   *depart*

    Valerian is to the place ygon,   *gone*
And right as hym was taught by his lernynge,   *instruction*
185 He foond this hooly olde Urban anon
Among the seintes buryeles lotynge.
And he anon, withouten tariynge,   *delay*
Dide his message; and whan that he it tolde,   *delivered*
Urban for joye his handes gan up holde.   *held up*

157 He will instantly kill you in the act.
177 That they might show you.
178 For a secret need and devout purpose.
186 Lying hid among the burial-places of the saints (i.e. the catacombs).

190 The teeris from his eyen leet he falle.   *let*
    'Almyghty Lord, o Jhesu Crist,' quod he,
    'Sower of chaast conseil, hierde of us alle,   *counsel; shepherd*
    The fruyt of thilke seed of chastitee
    That thou hast sowe in Cecile, taak to thee!   *sown; take*
195 Lo, lyk a bisy bee, withouten gile,   *guile*
    Thee serveth ay thyn owene thral Cecile.   *thrall*

    'For thilke spouse that she took but now   *that husband*
    Ful lyk a fiers leoun, she sendeth heere,
    As meke as evere was any lomb, to yow!'   *lamb*
200 And with that word anon ther gan appeere
    An oold man, clad in white clothes cleere,   *shining*
    That hadde a book with lettre of gold in honde,
    And gan bifore Valerian to stonde.   *stood*

    Valerian as deed fil doun for drede   *dead*
205 Whan he hym saugh, and he up hente hym tho,
    And on his book right thus he gan to rede:
    'O Lord, o feith, o God, withouten mo,
    O Cristendom, and Fader of alle also,
    Aboven alle and over alle everywhere.'
210 Thise wordes al with gold ywriten were.

    Whan this was rad, thanne seyde this olde man,   *read*
    'Leevestow this thyng or no? Sey ye or nay.'   *do you believe*
    'I leeve al this thyng,' quod Valerian,
    'For sother thyng than this, I dar wel say,   *truer*
215 Under this hevene no wight thynke may.'   *no one*
    Tho vanysshed the olde man, he nyste where,
    And Pope Urban hym cristned right there.

        Valerian gooth hoom and fynt Cecilie   *finds*
    Withinne his chambre with an angel stonde.   *standing*
220 This angel hadde of roses and of lilie
    Corones two, the which he bar in honde;   *crowns*
    And first to Cecile, as I understonde,
    He yaf that oon, and after gan he take
    That oother to Valerian, hir make.   *mate*

225 'With body clene and with unwemmed thoght   *unblemished*
    Kepeth ay wel thise corones,' quod he;
    'Fro paradys to yow have I hem broght,
    Ne nevere mo ne shal they roten bee,   *more*

    201 *An oold man*, i.e. St Paul.
    205 When he saw him, and then he (i.e. the old man) lifted him up.
    207-8 One Lord, one faith, one God alone, one baptism.
    216 He (Valerian) knew not where.
    223 He gave the one, and then he gave.

Ne lese hir soote savour, trusteth me;   *lose; sweet*
230 Ne nevere wight shal seen hem with his ye,
But he be chaast and hate vileynye.   *unless*

'And thow, Valerian, for thow so soone
Assentedest to good conseil also,
Sey what thee list, and thou shalt han thy boone.'
235 'I have a brother,' quod Valerian tho,
'That in this world I love no man so.
I pray yow that my brother may han grace
To knowe the trouthe, as I do in this place.'

The angel seyde, 'God liketh thy requeste,   *is pleased with*
240 And bothe, with the palm of martirdom,
Ye shullen come unto his blisful feste.'   *feast*
And with that word Tiburce his brother coom.   *came*
And whan that he the savour undernoom,
Which that the roses and the lilies caste   *shed*
245 Withinne his herte, he gan to wondre faste,   *marvelled greatly*

And seyde, 'I wondre, this tyme of the yeer,
Whennes that soote savour cometh so   *whence*
Of rose and lilies that I smelle heer.
For though I hadde hem in myne handes two,
250 The savour myghte in me no depper go.   *deeper*
The sweete smel that in myn herte I fynde
Hath chaunged me al in another kynde.'

Valerian seyde: 'Two corones han we,
Snow white and rose reed, that shynen cleere,
255 Whiche that thyne eyen han no myght to see;   *eyes*
And as thou smellest hem thurgh my preyere,
So shaltow seen hem, leeve brother deere,   *beloved*
If it so be thou wolt, withouten slouthe,
Bileve aright and knowen verray trouthe.'

260   Tiburce answerde, 'Seistow this to me
In soothnesse, or in dreem I herkne this?'   *truth; listen to*
'In dremes,' quod Valerian, 'han we be
Unto this tyme, brother myn, ywis.   *certainly*
But now at erst in trouthe oure dwellyng is.' *for the first time*
265 'How woostow this?' quod Tiburce, 'and in   *do you know*
        what wyse?'
Quod Valerian, 'That shal I thee devyse.   *tell*

234 Say what you would like, and your request shall be granted.
243 When he became aware of the fragrance.
252 Has completely changed my nature.
258-9 If you are willing, without sloth, to believe what is right and
    acknowledge the truth.

'The aungel of God hath me the trouthe ytaught
Which thou shalt seen, if that thou wolt reneye   *renounce*
The ydoles and be clene, and elles naught.'   *not otherwise*
270 And of the myracle of thise corones tweye
Seint Ambrose in his preface list to seye;
Solempnely this noble doctour deere
Commendeth it, and seith in this manere:

'The palm of martirdom for to receyve,
275 Seinte Cecile, fulfild of Goddes yifte,   *filled with*
The world and eek hire chambre gan she weyve;
Witnesse Tyburces and Valerians shrifte,   *confession*
To whiche God of his bountee wolde shifte
Corones two of floures wel smellynge,
280 And make his angel hem the corones brynge.

The mayde hath broght thise men to blisse above;
The world hath wist what it is worth, certeyn,
Devocioun of chastitee to love.'
Tho shewed hym Cecile al open and pleyn   *then; plainly*
285 That alle ydoles nys but a thyng in veyn,   *are but useless things*
For they been dombe, and therto they
    been deve,   *deaf*
And charged hym his ydoles for to leve.   *leave*

'Whoso that troweth nat this, a beest he is,'   *believes; beast*
Quod tho Tiburce, 'if that I shal nat lye.'   *lie*
290 And she gan kisse his brest, that herde this,
And was ful glad he koude trouthe espye.
'This day I take thee for myn allye,'   *kinsman*
Seyde this blisful faire mayde deere,
And after that she seyde as ye may heere:

295 'Lo, right so as the love of Crist,' quod she,
'Made me thy brotheres wyf, right in that wise
Anon for myn allye heer take I thee,
Syn that thou wolt thyne ydoles despise.
Go with thy brother now, and thee baptise,
300 And make thee clene, so that thou mowe biholde   *may*
The angels face of which thy brother tolde.

271 Chooses to speak.
276 Forsook the world and also her marriage-chamber.
278 To whom God in His goodness chose to assign.
282-3 The world has learnt (by their example) the value of chaste
    devotion to (spiritual) love.
296 In exactly the same way.

Tiburce answerde and seyde, 'Brother deere,
First tel me whider I shal, and to what man?' *where I must go*
'To whom?' quod he, 'com forth with right good *joyfully*
   cheere,
305 I wol thee lede unto the Pope Urban.'
'Til Urban? brother myn Valerian,' *my brother*
Quod tho Tiburce, 'woltow me thider lede?
Me thynketh that it were a wonder dede.

'Ne menestow nat Urban,' quod he tho,
310 'That is so ofte dampned to be deed,
And woneth in halkes alwey to and fro,
And dar nat ones putte forth his heed?
Men sholde hym brennen in a fyr so reed *would; burn*
If he were founde, or that men myghte hym spye,
315 And we also, to bere hym compaignye; *for bearing*

'And whil we seken thilke divinitee
That is yhid in hevene pryvely, *secretly*
Algate ybrend in this world shul we be!'
To whom Cecile answerde boldely,
320 'Men myghten dreden wel and skilfully *reasonably*
This lyf to lese, myn owene deere brother, *lose*
If this were lyvynge oonly and noon oother. *the only life*

'But ther is bettre lif in oother place,
That nevere shal be lost, ne drede thee noght,
325 Which Goddes Sone us tolde thurgh his grace.
That Fadres Sone hath alle thyng ywroght, *made*
And al that wroght is with a skilful thoght,
The Goost, that fro the Fader gan procede, *Holy Ghost*
Hath sowled hem, withouten any drede.

330 By word and by myracle heigh Goddes Sone,
Whan he was in this world, declared heere
That ther was oother lyf ther men may wone.' *where; dwell*
To whom answerde Tiburce, 'O suster deere,
Ne seydestow right now in this manere,
335 Ther nys but o God, lord in soothfastnesse? *one; truth*
And now of three how maystow bere witnesse?'

308 That would be a strange thing to do, it seems to me.
310 Who has so often been condemned to death.
311 And lives in holes and corners, always on the run.
318 We shall at any rate be burnt on earth.
325 Of which God's Son has told us through His grace.
327 And all creatures with a mind capable of reasoning.
329 Has endued them with a soul, without any doubt.
334 Did you not say just now.

'That shal I telle,' quod she, 'er I go.
Right as a man hath sapiences three,   *kinds of wisdom*
Memorie, engyn, and intellect also,   *mother wit*
340 So in o beynge of divinitee,
Thre persones may ther right wel bee.'
Tho gan she hym ful bisily to preche
Of Cristes come, and of his peynes teche,   *coming; sufferings*

And manye pointes of his passioun;   *details*
345 How Goddes Sone in this world was withholde   *kept*
To doon mankynde pleyn remissioun,   *give*
That was ybounde in synne and cares colde;   *fatal*
Al this thyng she unto Tiburce tolde.
And after this Tiburce in good entente   *with goodwill*
350 With Valerian to Pope Urban he wente,

That thanked God, and with glad herte and light   *who*
He cristned hym, and made hym in that place
Parfit in his lernynge, Goddes knyght.
And after this Tiburce gat swich grace
355 That every day he saugh, in tyme and space,
The aungel of God; and every maner boone   *kind of boon*
That he God axed, it was sped ful soone.   *granted*

It were ful hard by ordre for to seyn   *in order*
How manye wondres Jhesus for hem wroghte;   *miracles*
360 But atte laste, to tellen short and pleyn,
The sergeantz of the toun of Rome hem soghte,   *officers*
And hem biforn Almache, the prefect, broghte,
Which hem apposed, and knew al hire entente,   *questioned*
And to the ymage of Juppiter hem sente,

365 And seyde, 'Whoso wol nat sacrifise,
Swape of his heed; this my sentence heer.'   *strike; this (is)*
Anon thise martirs that I yow devyse,   *tell you of*
Oon Maximus, that was an officer
Of the prefectes, and his corniculer,
370 Hem hente, and whan he forth the seintes ladde,   *seized; led*
Hymself he weep for pitee that he hadde.   *wept*

Whan Maximus had herd the seintes loore,
He gat hym of the tormentoures leve,
And ladde hem to his hous withoute moore,   *delay*

353 Perfect in Christian knowledge, as God's knight.
355 *in tyme and space*, i.e. at the appointed time.
360 To make my story short and plain.
369 Of the prefect's, and his secretary.
372 The teaching of these saints.
373 He got leave from the executioners.

375 And with hir prechyng, er that it were eve,
    They gonnen fro the tormentours to reve,
    And fro Maxime, and fro his folk echone,
    The false feith, to trowe in God allone.

        Cecile cam, whan it was woxen nyght,   *night had fallen*
380 With preestes that hem cristned alle yfeere;   *together*
    And afterward, whan day was woxen light,
    Cecile hem seyde with a ful stedefast cheere,   *mien*
    'Now, Cristes owene knyghtes leeve and deere,   *beloved*
    Cast alle awey the werkes of derknesse,
385 And armeth yow in armure of brightnesse.

    'Ye han for sothe ydoon a greet bataille,
    Youre cours is doon, youre feith han ye conserved.   *preserved*
    Gooth to the corone of lif that may nat faille;
    The rightful Juge, which that ye han served,   *whom*
390 Shal yeve it yow, as ye han it deserved.'   *give*
    And whan this thyng was seyd as I devyse,   *describe*
    Men ledde hem forth to doon the sacrefise.

    But whan they weren to the place broght,
    To tellen shortly the conclusioun,
395 They nolde encense ne sacrifise right noght,
    But on hir knees they setten hem adoun   *went down*
    With humble herte and sad devocioun,   *steadfast*
    And losten bothe hir hevedes in the place.
    Hir soules wenten to the Kyng of grace.

400 This Maximus, that saugh this thyng bityde,   *happen*
    With pitous teeris tolde it anonright,   *immediately*
    That he hir soules saugh to hevene glyde
    With aungels ful of cleernesse and of light,   *splendour*
    And with his word converted many a wight;   *person*
405 For which Almachius dide hym so bete
    With whippe of leed, til he his lif gan lete.

    Cecile hym took and buryed hym anon
    By Tiburce and Valerian softely
    Withinne hire buriyng place, under the stoon;   *gently*
                                                        stone

---

375-8 And by their preaching, before evening came, they had converted
    the executioners, as well as Maximus and all his men, from the false
    faith to a belief in God alone.
386 You have in truth waged a great battle.
394 To tell briefly what happened.
395 They would not offer incense or make any sacrifice.
398 And both lost their heads there and then.
405-6 Had him severely beaten with whips of lead until he died.

410 And after this Almachius hastily
    Bad his ministres fecchen openly   *officers*
    Cecile, so that she myghte in his presence
    Doon sacrifice, and Juppiter encense.

    But they, converted at hir wise loore,   *by; teaching*
415 Wepten ful soore, and yaven ful credence
    Unto hire word, and cryden moore and moore,
    'Crist, Goddes Sone, withouten difference,
    Is verray God—this is al oure sentence—   *opinion*
    That hath so good a servant hym to serve.
420 This with o voys we trowen, thogh we sterve!'

    Almachius, that herde of this doynge,
    Bad fecchen Cecile, that he myghte hire see,
    And alderfirst, lo! this was his axynge:
    'What maner womman artow?' tho quod he.   *sort of*
425 'I am a gentil womman born,' quod she.
    'I axe thee,' quod he, 'though it thee greeve,   *grieve*
    Of thy religioun and of thy bileeve.'   *about*

    'Ye han bigonne youre questioun folily,'   *foolishly*
    Quod she, 'that wolden two answeres conclude   *include*
430 In o demande; ye axed lewedly.'   *ignorantly*
    Almache answerde unto that similitude,   *statement*
    'Of whennes comth thyn answeryng so rude?'
    'Of whennes?' quod she, whan that she was freyned,   *asked*
    'Of conscience and of good feith unfeyned.'

435 Almachius seyde, 'Ne takestow noon heede   *do you take*
    Of my power?'   And she answerde hym this:
    'Youre myght,' quod she, 'ful litel is to dreede, *be feared*
    For every mortal mannes power nys
    But lyk a bladdre ful of wynd, ywys.
440 For with a nedles poynt, whan it is blowe,   *needle's; blown up*
    May al the boost of it be leyd ful lowe.'

    'Ful wrongfully bigonne thow,' quod he,   *began*
    'And yet in wrong is thy perseveraunce.
    Wostow nat how oure myghty princes free   *noble*

417 *withouten difference*, i.e. the same in majesty and might.
420 This we all believe, though we die for it.
422 Ordered Cecilia to be fetched.
423 And this was the question he first put to her.
441 May all its vainglory be deflated.
443 And still you persevere in the wrong.

445 Han thus comanded and maad ordinaunce,
    That every Cristen wight shal han penaunce   *punishment*
    But if that he his Cristendom withseye,
    And goon al quit, if he wole it reneye?'   *free; deny*

    'Yowre princes erren, as youre nobleye dooth,'   *nobles*
450 Quod tho Cecile, 'and with a wood sentence   *mad*
    Ye make us gilty, and it is nat sooth.   *true*
    For ye, that knowen wel oure innocence,
    For as muche as we doon a reverence
    To Crist, and for we bere a Cristen name,
455 Ye putte on us a cryme, and eek a blame.

    But we that knowen thilke name so
    For vertuous, we may it nat withseye.'
    Almache answerde, 'Chees oon of thise two: *choose*
    Do sacrifice, or Cristendom reneye,
460 That thou mowe now escapen by that weye.'
    At which the hooly blisful faire mayde
    Gan for to laughe, and to the juge sayde:

    'O juge, confus in thy nycetee,   *confused; folly*
    Woltow that I reneye innocence,
465 To make me a wikked wight?' quod shee.
    'Lo, he dissymuleth heere in audience;
    He stareth, and woodeth in his advertence!'
    To whom Almachius, 'Unsely wrecche,   *unhappy*
    Ne woostow nat how fer my myght may strecche?

470 'Han noght oure myghty princes to me yiven,
    Ye, bothe power and auctoritee   *yea*
    To maken folk to dyen or to lyven?
    Why spekestow so proudly thanne to me?'
    'I speke noght but stedfastly,' quod she;
475 'Nat proudly, for I seye, as for my syde,   *part*
    We haten deedly thilke vice of pryde.

    'And if thou drede nat a sooth to heere,   *truth*
    Thanne wol I shewe al openly, by right,
    That thou hast maad a ful gret lesyng heere.   *told; lie*

    447 Unless he renounces his Christian faith.
    453–4 Because we hold Christ in reverence.
    456–7 We, who know that name to be virtuous, cannot renounce it.
    465 In order to make a wicked person of me.
    466 See, he dissembles here in open court.
    467 He stares and raves in delivering his judgment.
    469 Don't you know how far my power can stretch?
    476 We have deadly hatred for that sin of pride.

480 Thou seyst thy princes han thee yeven myght   *given*
    Bothe for to sleen and for to quyken a wight;
    Thou, that ne mayst but oonly lyf bireve,
    Thou hast noon oother power ne no leve.

    'But thou mayst seyn thy princes han thee maked   *say*
485 Ministre of deeth; for if thou speke of mo,   *more*
    Thou lyest, for thy power is ful naked.'   *weak*
    'Do wey thy booldnesse,' seyde Almachius tho,
    'And sacrifice to oure goddes, er thou go!
    I recche nat what wrong that thou me profre,   *care; insult*
490 For I kan suffre it as a philosophre;

        'But thilke wronges may I nat endure
    That thou spekest of our goddes heere,' quod he.
    Cecile answerde, 'O nyce creature!   *foolish*
    Thou seydest no word syn thou spak to me
495 That I ne knew therwith thy nycetee;
    And that thou were, in every maner wise,   *every way*
    A lewed officer and a veyn justise.

    'Ther lakketh no thyng to thyne outter yën
    That thou n'art blynd; for thyng that we seen alle
500 That it is stoon,—that men may wel espyen,—
    That ilke stoon a god thow wolt it calle.
    I rede thee, lat thyn hand upon it falle,   *advise*
    And taste it wel, and stoon thou shalt it fynde,   *feel*
    Syn that thou seest nat with thyne eyen blynde.   *since*

505 'It is a shame that the peple shal
    So scorne thee, and laughe at thy folye;
    For communly men woot it wel overal
    That myghty God is in his hevenes hye,
    And thise ymages, wel thou mayst espye,
510 To thee ne to hemself mowen noght profite,
    For in effect they been nat worth a myte.'   *mite*

481 Both to kill a person and to give him life.
482-3 You, who cannot do more than take a life, have no power nor
    warrant other than this.
487 Enough of your impudence.
494-5 Since you started talking to me you've not said a single word
    that did not convince me of your folly.
497 An ignorant official and a foolish judge.
498-501 Your bodily eyes are totally blind, for something we can all
    easily see is made of stone you want to call a god.
507 For it is commonly known by men everywhere.
510 Do you no good or themselves either.

Thise wordes and swiche othere seyde she,
And he weex wrooth, and bad men sholde hir lede   *got angry*
Hom til hir hous, and 'In hire hous,' quod he,
515 'Brenne hire right in a bath of flambes rede.'   *burn; flames*
And as he bad, right so was doon the dede;
For in a bath they gonne hire faste shetten,   *shut*
And nyght and day greet fyr they under betten.   *kindled*

The longe nyght, and eek a day also,
520 For al the fyr, and eek the bathes heete,   *heat*
She sat al coold, and feelede no wo.   *felt*
It made hire nat a drope for to sweete.   *sweat*
But in that bath hir lyf she moste lete,   *give up*
For he Almachius, with ful wikke entente,
525 To sleen hire in the bath his sonde sente.   *kill; messenger*

Thre strokes in the nekke he smoot hire tho,   *then*
The tormentour, but for no maner chaunce
He myghte noght smyte al hir nekke atwo;   *in two*
And for ther was that tyme an ordinaunce
530 That no man sholde doon man swich penaunce
The ferthe strook to smyten, softe or soore,
This tormentour ne dorste do namoore,

But half deed, with hir nekke ycorven there,   *cut*
He lefte hir lye, and on his wey he went.   *gone*
535 The Cristen folk, which that aboute hire were,
With sheetes han the blood ful faire yhent.   *caught*
Thre dayes lyved she in this torment,
And nevere cessed hem the feith to teche
That she hadde fostred; hem she gan to preche,

540 And hem she yaf hir moebles and hir thyng,
And to the Pope Urban bitook hem tho,
And seyde, 'I axed this of hevene kyng,   *asked*
To han respit thre dayes and namo,
To recomende to yow, er that I go,   *commend*
545 Thise soules, lo! and that I myghte do werche
Heere of myn hous perpetuelly a cherche.'

527 The executioner, but on no account.
530–1 No man could make anyone suffer a fourth stroke, gentle or hard.
539 Whom she had fostered, i.e. converted.
540 She gave them her personal effects and property.
541 And then entrusted them to Pope Urban's care.
545 And so that I might make.

Seint Urban, with his deknes, prively   *deacons; secretly*
The body fette, and buryed it by nyghte   *fetched*
Among his othere seintes honestly.   *honourably*
550 Hir hous the chirche of Seint Cecilie highte;   *was called*
Seint Urban halwed it, as he wel myghte;   *hallowed*
In which, into this day, in noble wyse,
Men doon to Crist and to his seint servyse.

HEERE IS ENDED THE SECONDE NONNES TALE

THE CANON'S YEOMAN'S PROLOGUE

The Prologe of the Chanouns Yemannes Tale

WHAN ended was the lyf of Seinte Cecile,
555 Er we hadde riden fully fyve mile,
At Boghtoun under Blee us gan atake
A man that clothed was in clothes blake,
And undernethe he hadde a whyt surplys.
His hakeney, that was al pomely grys,
560 So swatte that it wonder was to see;   *sweated*
It semed as he had priked miles three.   *ridden hard*
The hors eek that his yeman rood upon   *servant*
So swatte that unnethe myghte it gon.
Aboute the peytrel stood the foom ful hye;
565 He was of foom al flekked as a pye.
A male tweyfoold on his croper lay;
It semed that he caried lite array.   *little clothing*
Al light for somer rood this worthy man,   *summer*
And in myn herte wondren I bigan
570 What that he was, til that I understood   *realized*
How that his cloke was sowed to his hood;   *sewn*
For which, whan I hadde longe avysed me,   *thought it over*
I demed hym som chanoun for to be.   *judged; canon*
His hat heeng at his bak doun by a laas,   *hung; cord*
575 For he hadde riden moore than trot or paas;   *ambling pace*
He hadde ay priked lik as he were wood.   *mad*
A clote-leef he hadde under his hood   *burdock-leaf*
For swoot, and for to keep his heed from heete.
But it was joye for to seen hym swete!
580 His forheed dropped as a stillatorie,
Were ful of plantayne and of paritorie.
And whan that he was come, he gan to crye,
'God save,' quod he, 'this joly compaignye!

556 At Boughton-under-Blean there overtook us.
557 i.e. the Canon.
559 His hack, that was all dapple-grey.
563 Sweated so much that it could hardly keep going.
564 The foam frothed up high round its breast-piece.
565 He (the Canon) was all flecked with foam, so that he looked like
 a magpie.
566 A bag, folded double, lay on his crupper.
578 To prevent sweating, and to protect his head from the heat.
580–1 Dripped like a still full of plantain and pellitory.

Faste have I priked,' quod he, 'for youre sake,
585 By cause that I wolde yow atake,
To riden in this myrie compaignye.'
His yeman eek was ful of curteisye,
And seyde, 'Sires, now in the morwe-tyde   *morning*
Out of youre hostelrie I saugh yow ryde,   *saw*
590 And warned heer my lord and my soverayn,   *told*
Which that to ryden with yow is ful fayn   *glad*
For his desport; he loveth daliaunce.'   *amusement; a chat*
       'Freend, for thy warnyng God yeve thee good
              chaunce!'   *luck*
Thanne seyde oure Hoost, 'for certein it would seme
595 Thy lord were wys, and so I may wel deme.
He is ful jocunde also, dar I leye!   *I'll wager*
Can he oght telle a myrie tale or tweye,
With which he glade may this compaignye?'   *gladden*
       'Who, sire? my lord? ye, ye, withouten lye, *yes, truly*
600 He kan of murthe and eek of jolitee
Nat but ynough; also, sire, trusteth me,
And ye hym knewe as wel as do I,
Ye wolde wondre how wel and craftily   *skilfully*
He koude werke, and that in sondry wise.   *various ways*
605 He hath take on hym many a greet emprise,
Which were ful hard for any that is heere
To brynge aboute, but they of hym it leere.
As hoomly as he rit amonges yow,
If ye hym knewe, it wolde be for youre prow.   *advantage*
610 Ye wolde nat forgoon his aqueyntaunce   *forgo*
For muchel good, I dar leye in balaunce
Al that I have in my possessioun.
He is a man of heigh discrecioun;   *great*
I warne yow wel, he is a passyng man.'   *excellent*
615 'Wel,' quod oure Hoost, 'I pray thee, tel me than,
Is he a clerk, or noon? telle what he is.'   *cleric; not*
       'Nay, he is gretter than a clerk, ywis,'
Seyde this Yeman, 'and in wordes fewe,
Hoost, of his craft somwhat I wol yow shewe.
620 I seye, my lord kan swich subtilitee—
But al his craft ye may nat wite at me,   *learn from*
And somwhat helpe I yet to his wirkyng—
That al this ground on which we been ridyng,

597 Can he by any chance tell a merry tale or two.
600-1 He knows more than enough funny stories.
605 He has taken on many a great enterprise.
607 Unless they learn it from him.
608 However informally he rides among you.
611 For a lot of money, I'll wager.
620 Has such abstruse knowledge.
622 Although I give him some assistance in his work.

Til that we come to Caunterbury toun,
625 He koude al clene turnen up-so-doun,
And pave it al of silver and of gold.'
    And whan this Yeman hadde this tale ytold
Unto oure Hoost, he seyde, '*Benedicitee*!   *bless us*
This thyng is wonder merveillous to me,   *very*
630 Syn that thy lord is of so heigh prudence,
By cause of which men sholde hym reverence,   *respect*
That of his worshipe rekketh he so lite.
His overslope nys nat worth a myte,   *gown*
As in effect, to hym, so moot I go!
635 It is al baudy and totore also.   *dirty; tattered*
Why is thy lord so sluttissh, I the preye,
And is of power bettre clooth to beye,
If that his dede accorde with thy speche?
Telle me that, and that I thee biseche.'
540   'Why?' quod this Yeman, 'wherto axe   *wherefore; ask*
          ye me?
God help me so, for he shal nevere thee!
(But I wol nat avowe that I seye,
And therfore keepe it secree, I yow preye.)   *secret*
He is to wys, in feith, as I bileeve.
645 That that is overdoon, it wol nat preeve
Aright, as clerkes seyn; it is a vice.   *the learned*
Wherfore in that I holde hym lewed and   *ignorant*
          nyce.   *foolish*
For whan a man hath over-greet a wit,
Ful oft hym happeth to mysusen it.
650 So dooth my lord, and that me greveth soore;
God it amende! I kan sey yow namoore.'
    'Ther-of no fors, good Yeman,' quod   *never mind about that*
          oure Hoost;
'Syn of the konnyng of thy lord thow woost,   *skill; know*
Telle how he dooth, I pray thee hertely,   *cordially*
655 Syn that he is so crafty and so sly.
Where dwelle ye, if it to telle be?'
    'In the suburbes of a toun,' quod he,
'Lurkynge in hernes and in lanes blynde,   *corners*
Whereas thise robbours and thise theves by   *where*
          kynde   *nature*

625 Turn it clean upside-down.
632 That he cares so little for his dignity.
634 In fact, for a man like him; *so moot I go*, so may I walk, on my life.
637 When he is able to buy better clothes.
638 If his performance tallies with your description.
641 For he (i.e. the Canon) will never prosper. (The Canon's Yeoman
     is blurting out the truth about his master.)
642 But I don't want to own up to saying this.
645 That which is overdone will not succeed.
649 It very often happens that he misuses it.

660 Holden hir pryvee fereful residence,   *secret*
     As they that dar nat shewen hir presence;
     So faren we, if I shal seye the sothe.'   *truth*
          'Now,' quod oure Hoost, 'yit lat me talke to the. *let*
     Why artow so discoloured of thy face?'
665   'Peter!' quod he, 'God yeve it harde grace,
     I am so used in the fyr to blowe
     That it hath chaunged my colour, I trowe.
     I am nat wont in no mirour to prie,   *peer*
     But swynke soore and lerne multiplie.
670 We blondren evere and pouren in the fir,
     And for al that we faille of oure desir,   *in*
     For evere we lakken oure conclusioun,
     To muchel folk we doon illusioun,
     And borwe gold, be it a pound or two,   *borrow*
675 Or ten, or twelve, or manye sommes mo,   *more*
     And make hem wenen, at the leeste weye,
     That of a pound we koude make tweye.   *two*
     Yet is it fals, but ay we han good hope
     It for to doon, and after it we grope.   *of doing it*
680 But that science is so fer us biforn,   *ahead of us*
     We mowen nat, although we hadden it sworn,   *cannot*
     It overtake, it slit awey so faste.   *slips*
     It wole us maken beggers atte laste.'
          Whil this Yeman was thus in his talkyng,
685 This Chanoun drough hym neer, and herde   *drew near*
          al thyng
     Which this Yeman spak, for suspecioun
     Of mennes speche evere hadde this Chanoun.
     For Catoun seith that he that gilty is
     Demeth alle thyng be spoke of hym, ywis.   *imagines*
690 That was the cause he gan so ny hym drawe
     To his Yeman, to herknen al his sawe.
     And thus he seyde unto his Yeman tho: *then*
     'Hoold thou thy pees, and spek no wordes mo,
     For if thou do, thou shalt it deere abye.   *pay for it dearly*
695 Thou sclaundrest me heere in this compaignye,   *slander*
     And eek discoverest that thou sholdest hyde.'   *reveal*
          'Ye,' quod oure Hoost, 'telle on, what   *whatever happens*
          so bityde.

     665 By St Peter . . . bad luck to it.
     669 But I toil away and learn to multiply (the technical term for trans-
          muting baser metals into gold).
     670 We blunder away and gape into the fire.
     672 For we never get a successful result.
     673 We deceive many people.
     676 And make them believe, at the very least.
     690 That was the reason he drew so near.
     691 To listen to all he was saying.

Of al his thretyng rekke nat a myte!'   *threatening; care*
'In feith,' quod he, 'namoore I do but lyte.'   *little*
700 And whan this Chanon saugh it wolde nat bee,
But his Yeman wolde telle his pryvetee,   *secrets*
He fledde awey for verray sorwe and shame.   *very*
'A!' quod the Yeman, 'heere shal arise game;
Al that I kan anon now wol I telle.   *know*
705 Syn he is goon, the foule feend hym quelle!   *kill*
For nevere heerafter wol I with hym meete   *meet*
For peny ne for pound, I yow biheete.   *promise*
He that me broghte first unto that game,
Er that he dye, sorwe have he and shame!
710 For it is ernest to me, by my feith;
That feele I wel, what so any man seith.
And yet, for al my smert and al my grief,   *pain*
For al my sorwe, labour, and meschief,   *misfortune*
I koude nevere leve it in no wise.
715 Now wolde God my wit myghte suffise
To tellen al that longeth to that art!   *belongs*
But nathelees yow wol I tellen part.
Syn that my lord is goon, I wol nat spare;
Swich thyng as that I knowe, I wol declare.

HEERE ENDETH THE PROLOGE OF THE CHANOUNS
YEMANNES TALE

THE CANON'S YEOMAN'S TALE

HEERE BIGYNNETH THE CHANOUNS YEMAN HIS TALE

[Prima Pars]

720 WITH this Chanoun I dwelt have seven yeer,
And of his science am I never the neer.   *nearer*
Al that I hadde I have lost therby,
And, God woot, so hath many mo than I.   *more*

703 i.e. now for some fun.
710 It's a serious thing for me, upon my word.
714 I could never leave it at any price.

Ther I was wont to be right fressh and gay   *where*
725 Of clothyng and of oother good array,
Now may I were an hose upon myn heed;
And wher my colour was bothe fressh and reed,
Now is it wan and of a leden hewe—   *leaden hue*
Whoso it useth, soore shal he rewe!—
730 And of my swynk yet blered is myn ye.
Lo! which avantage is to multiplie!
That slidynge science hath me maad so bare   *slippery*
That I have no good, wher that evere I fare;
And yet I am endetted so therby,   *indebted*
735 Of gold that I have borwed, trewely,
That whil I lyve I shal it quite nevere.   *repay*
Lat every man be war by me for evere!
What maner man that casteth hym therto,
If he continue, I holde his thrift ydo.
740 For so helpe me God, therby shal he nat wynne,
But empte his purs, and make his wittes thynne.
And whan he, thurgh his madnesse and folye,
Hath lost his owene good thurgh jupartye,
Thanne he exciteth oother folk therto,
745 To lesen hir good, as he hymself hath do.   *lose; done*
For unto shrewes joye it is and ese   *wicked people*
To have hir felawes in peyne and disese.   *misery*
Thus was I ones lerned of a clerk.
Of that no charge, I wol speke of oure werk.
750   Whan we been there as we shul exercise   *are where*
Oure elvysshe craft, we semen   *mysterious*
          wonder wise,   *wonderfully*
Oure termes been so clergial and so queynte. *learned; curious*
I blowe the fir til that myn herte feynte.   *feels faint*
What sholde I tellen ech proporcion   *why*
755 Of thynges whiche that we werche upon—   *work*
As on fyve or sixe ounces, may wel be,
Of silver, or som oother quantitee—
And bisye me to telle yow the names   *trouble*
Of orpyment, brent bones, iren squames,   *burnt; iron scales*
760 That into poudre grounden been ful smal;
And in an erthen pot how put is al,

726 Now I must wear an old stocking on my head.
729 Anyone who meddles with it will be sorry.
730 And, in return for my labour, I'm blear-eyed.
731 See what advantage comes from multiplying!
733 I have nothing left, whichever way I turn.
738-9 Whoever tries his hand at it, if he continues, I reckon his prosperous days are over.
741 But empty his purse, and addle his brains.
743 Has gambled away his own money.
748 So a learned man once taught me.
749 That doesn't matter.

And salt yput in, and also papeer,   *paper*
Biforn thise poudres that I speke of heer,   *before*
And wel ycovered with a lampe of glas;   *plate*
765 And of muche oother thyng which that ther
          was;
And of the pot and glasses enlutyng,
That of the eyr myghte passe out nothyng;   *gas*
And of the esy fir, and smart also,   *slow; brisk*
Which that was maad, and of the care and wo
770 That we hadde in oure matires sublymyng,
And in amalgamyng and calcenyng
Of quyksilver, yclept mercurie crude?   *called*
For alle oure sleightes we kan nat conclude.
Oure orpyment and sublymed mercurie,
775 Oure grounden litarge eek on the porfurie,
Of ech of thise of ounces a certeyn—   *certain (number)*
Noght helpeth us, oure labour is in veyn.   *nothing*
Ne eek oure spirites ascencioun,
Ne oure materes that lyen al fix adoun,
780 Mowe in oure werkyng no thyng us availle,   *can*
For lost is al oure labour and travaille;
And al the cost, a twenty devel waye,   *confound it*
Is lost also, which we upon it laye.   *lay out*
    Ther is also ful many another thyng
785 That is unto oure craft apertenyng.   *pertaining*
Though I by ordre hem nat reherce kan,
By cause that I am a lewed man,   *uneducated*
Yet wol I telle hem as they come to mynde,
Thogh I ne kan nat sette hem in hir kynde:
790 As boole armonyak, verdegrees, boras,
And sondry vessels maad of erthe and glas,
Oure urynales and oure descensories,
Violes, crosletz, and sublymatories,
Cucurbites and alambikes eek,
795 And othere swiche, deere ynough a leek.

765 And of all the other things there were.
766 And how the pot and glass were daubed with clay.
770 In sublimating our materials.
771 In the amalgamation and calcination.
773 For all our tricks we can't succeed.
775 Our litharge ground on a slab of porphyry.
778 Neither the rising of our gases.
779 Nor our solid substances lying at the bottom (of the pot).
786 Though I can't recite them in order.
789 Though I don't know how to classify them.
790 Such as Armenian clay (a medicinal earth or clay), verdigris, borax.
792 Our urinals (pear-shaped glass vessels) and our descensories (used
    in distillation).
793 Phials, crucibles, and vessels used in sublimation.
794 Our cucurbits (for distillation) and alembics.
795 And other such things, just as worthless.

Nat nedeth it for to reherce hem alle,—
Watres rubifiyng, and boles galle,
Arsenyk, sal armonyak, and brymstoon; *ammoniac*
And herbes koude I telle eek many oon,
800 As egremoyne, valerian, and lunarie,   *agrimony*
And othere swiche, if that me liste tarie; *I wished to linger*
Oure lampes brennyng bothe nyght and day,
To brynge aboute oure purpos, if we may;
Oure fourneys eek of calcinacioun,   *furnace*
805 And of watres albificacioun; *whitening of waters*
Unslekked lym, chalk, and gleyre of an ey,
Poudres diverse, asshes, donge, pisse, and cley, *clay*
Cered pokkets, sal peter, vitriole,
And diverse fires maad of wode and cole; *charcoal*
810 Sal tartre, alkaly, and sal preparat,
And combust materes and coagulat;   *burnt*
Cley maad with hors or mannes heer, and oille *mixed; hair*
Of tartre, alum glas, berme, wort, and argoille,
Resalgar, and oure materes enbibyng,   *absorption*
815 And eek of oure materes encorporyng, *incorporation*
And of oure silver citrinacioun,   *citronizing*
Oure cementyng and fermentacioun,
Oure yngottes, testes, and many mo.
 I wol yow telle, as was me taught also,
820 The foure spirites and the bodies sevene,
By ordre, as ofte I herde my lord hem nevene.
 The firste spirit quyksilver called is,
The seconde orpyment, the thridde, ywis,
Sal armonyak, and the ferthe brymstoon.
625 The bodyes sevene eek, lo! hem heere anoon:
Sol gold is, and Luna silver we threpe,   *affirm*
Mars iren, Mercurie quyksilver we clepe,
Saturnus leed, and Juppiter is tyn,
And Venus coper, by my fader kyn!   *father's*
830 This cursed craft whoso wole excercise, *practise*
He shal no good han that hym may suffise;
For al the good he spendeth theraboute
He lese shal; therof have I no doute.   *lose*
Whoso that listeth outen his folie,
835 Lat hym come forth and lerne multiplie;

---

797 Reddening of waters, and bull's gall.
806 Unslaked lime, chalk, and white of egg.
808 Little bags closed with wax, saltpetre, vitriol.
810 Salt of tartar, alkali, and prepared (common) salt.
813 Crystallized alum, yeast, unfermented beer, and crude tartar.
814 *Resalgar*, realgar (disulphide of arsenic).
818 Our moulds, our vessels for assaying metals, and many more.
831 He'll have nothing like enough money.
834 Anyone who wants to show his folly.

And every man that oght hath in his cofre,   *anything*
Lat hym appiere, and wexe a   *become*
 philosophre.   *alchemist*
Ascaunce that craft is so light to leere?
Nay, nay, God woot, al be he monk or frere, *although*
840 Preest or chanoun, or any oother wyght, *person*
Though he sitte at his book bothe day and nyght
In lernyng of this elvysshe nyce loore,
Al is in veyn, and parde! muchel moore. *indeed; much*
To lerne a lewed man this subtiltee—
845 Fy! spek nat therof, for it wol nat bee;
And konne he letterure, or konne he noon,
As in effect, he shal fynde it al oon.   *in practice; one*
For bothe two, by my savacioun,   *salvation*
Concluden in multiplicacioun
850 Ylike wel, whan they han al ydo;
This is to seyn, they faillen bothe two.
 Yet forgat I to maken rehersaille   *enumeration*
Of watres corosif, and of lymaille,
And of bodies mollificacioun,
855 And also of hire induracioun;
Oilles, ablucions, and metal fusible,—
To tellen al wolde passen any bible
That owher is; wherfore, as for the beste,
Of alle thise names now wol I me reste.
860 For, as I trowe, I have yow toold ynowe *enough*
To reyse a feend, al looke he never so rowe.
 A! nay! lat be; the philosophres stoon,
Elixer clept, we sechen faste echoon;
For hadde we hym, thanne were we siker ynow. *safe*
865 But unto God of hevene I make avow, *I swear*
For al oure craft, whan we han al ydo, *skill; done*
And al oure sleighte, he wol nat come us to. *cunning*
He hath ymaad us spenden muchel good, *much money*
For sorwe of which almoost we wexen wood, *go mad*
870 But that good hope crepeth in oure herte,
Supposynge evere, though we sore smerte, *suffer*

838 Perhaps you think this trade is an easy one to learn?
842 This silly elvish lore.
844 To teach an ignorant man such abstruse knowledge.
846 And whether he has book-learning or not.
848 *bothe two*, i.e. both the ignorant and the learned man.
849-50 Will have the same success in multiplying by the time they're
 finished.
853 Of acids and metal filings.
854-5 Of the softening and hardening of metals.
857-8 To tell all this would beat any book existing anywhere.
861 However rough he looks. (An allusion to the portrayal of the
 devil by medieval artists as a satyr with hairy skin.)
863 Called the elixir, we seek it eagerly, all of us.

To be releeved by hym afterward.
Swich supposyng and hope is sharp and hard;
I warne yow wel, it is to seken evere.

875 That futur temps hath maad men to dissevere,   *tense; part*
In trust therof, from al that evere they hadde.
Yet of that art they kan nat wexen sadde,   *grow weary*
For unto hem it is a bitter sweete,—
So semeth it,—for nadde they but a sheete,

880 Which that they myghte wrappe hem inne a-nyght,   *at night*
And a brat to walken inne by daylyght,   *cloak of cloth*
They wolde hem selle and spenden on this craft.
They kan nat stynte til no thyng be laft.   *stop; left*
And everemoore, where that evere they goon,

885 Men may hem knowe by smel of brymstoon.
For al the world they stynken as a goot;   *goat*
Hir savour is so rammyssh and so hoot   *smell; rank*
That though a man from hem a mile be,
The savour wole infecte hym, trusteth me.

890 Lo, thus by smellyng and threedbare array,   *clothing*
If that men liste, this folk they knowe may.   *like*
And if a man wole aske hem pryvely   *privately*
Why they been clothed so unthriftily,   *poorly*
They right anon wol rownen in his ere,   *whisper*

895 And seyn that if that they espied were,   *observed*
Men wolde hem slee by cause of hir science.   *kill; learning*
Lo, thus this folk bitrayen innocence!
   Passe over this; I go my tale unto.
Er that the pot be on the fir ydo,   *placed*

900 Of metals with a certeyn quantitee,
My lord hem tempreth, and no man but he—   *tempers*
Now he is goon, I dar seyn boldely—
For, as men seyn, he kan doon craftily.
Algate I woot wel he hath swich a name,

905 And yet ful ofte he renneth in a blame.
And wite ye how? ful ofte it happeth so,   *know*
The pot tobreketh, and farewel, al is go!   *bursts*
Thise metals been of so greet violence,
Oure walles mowe nat make hem resistence,   *cannot*

910 But if they weren wroght of lym and stoon;   *unless*
They percen so, and thurgh the wal they goon.
And somme of hem synken into the ground—
Thus han we lost by tymes many a pound—   *at*
And somme are scatered al the floor aboute;

915 Somme lepe into the roof.   Withouten doute,   *doubt*

874 It is always to be sought, i.e. never to be found.
879 If they had nothing but a sheet.
903-4 He can work skilfully. At any rate I know he has a name for
    doing so.
905 He lays himself open to blame.

Though that the feend noght in oure sighte hym
    shewe,
I trowe he with us be, that ilke shrewe!   *scoundrel*
In helle, where that he is lord and sire,
Nis ther moore wo, ne moore rancour ne ire.   *anger*
920 Whan that oure pot is broke, as I have sayd,
Every man chit, and halt hym yvele apayd.
    Somme seyde it was long on the fir makyng;
Somme seyde nay, it was on the blowyng,—
Thanne was I fered, for that was myn office.   *afraid*
925 'Straw!' quod the thridde, 'ye been lewed   *ignorant*
    and nyce.   *foolish*
It was nat tempred as it oghte be.'   *tempered*
'Nay,' quod the fourthe, 'stynt and herkne me.   *shut up*
By cause oure fir ne was nat maad of beech,
That is the cause, and oother noon, so thee'ch!'
930 I kan nat telle wheron it was long,
But wel I woot greet strif is us among.
    'What,' quod my lord, 'ther is namoore to doone;   *be done*
Of thise perils I wol be war eftsoone.   *after this*
I am right siker that the pot was crased.   *sure; cracked*
935 Be as be may, be ye no thyng amased;
As usage is, lat swepe the floor as swithe,
Plukke up youre hertes, and beeth glad and   *lift; happy*
    blithe.'
    The mullok on an heep ysweped was,
And on the floor ycast a canevas,   *thrown; canvas*
940 And al this mullok in a syve ythrowe,   *sieve*
And sifted, and ypiked many a throwe.
    'Pardee,' quod oon, 'somwhat of oure metal
Yet is ther heere, though that we han nat al.
And though this thyng myshapped have as now,   *come to grief*
945 Another tyme it may be well ynow.   *enough*
Us moste putte oure good in aventure.
A marchant, pardee, may nat ay endure,   *always stay*
Trusteth me wel, in his prosperitee.
Somtyme his good is drowned in the see,
950 And somtyme comth it sauf unto the londe.'   *safe*
    'Pees!' quod my lord, 'the nexte tyme I wol fonde   *try*

916 Though the devil does not show himself to us.
921 Everyone is abusive, and anything but pleased.
922 One said it was owing to the way the fire had been made.
923 *blowyng*, i.e. with the bellows.
929 As I hope to prosper.
930 I can't say what it was due to.
935 Be that as it may, don't get alarmed.
936 As usual, let's sweep up the floor immediately.
938 The rubbish was swept into a heap.
941 And picked over many times.
946 We're bound to risk our money.

To bryngen oure craft al in another plite,
And but I do, sires, lat me han the wite.
Ther was defaute in somwhat, wel I woot.'   *defect*
955   Another seyde the fir was over-hoot,—
But, be it hoot or coold, I dar seye this,
That we concluden everemoore amys.
We faille of that which that we wolden have,
And in oure madnesse everemoore we rave.
960 And whan we been togidres everichoon,
Every man semeth a Salomon.
But al thyng which that shineth as the gold
Nis nat gold, as that I have herd told;
Ne every appul that is fair at eye   *apple; to*
965 Ne is nat good, what so men clappe or crye.
Right so, lo, fareth it amonges us:
He that semeth the wiseste, by Jhesus!
Is moost fool, whan it cometh to the preef;   *proof*
And he that semeth trewest is a theef.   *rascal*
970 That shul ye knowe, er that I fro yow wende,
By that I of my tale have maad an ende.

EXPLICIT PRIMA PARS

ET SEQUITUR PARS SECUNDA

Ther is a chanoun of religioun
Amonges us, wolde infecte al a toun,
Thogh it as greet were as was Nynyvee,   *Nineveh*
975 Rome, Alisaundre, Troye, and othere three.
His sleightes and his infinite falsnesse   *tricks*
Ther koude no man writen, as I gesse,
Though that he myghte lyve a thousand yeer.
In al this world of falshede nis his peer;
980 For in his termes he wol hym so wynde,
And speke his wordes in so sly a kynde,   *manner*
Whanne he commune shal with any wight,   *converse*
That he wol make hym doten anonright,   *act foolishly*

952 i.e. to conduct our experiment more successfully.
953 Unless I do so, sirs, let me have the blame.
957 That we always come to a bad end.
960 When we are all (talking) together.
965 Whatever men shout or prattle.
971 By the time I have finished my tale.
975 Alexandria . . . or any other three.
977 No one could write (in full), I suppose.
979 There's none on earth to equal him in falseness.
980 He'll use such involved expressions.

But it a feend be, as hymselven is.
985 Ful many a man hath he bigiled er this,
And wole, if that he lyve may a while;
And yet men ride and goon ful many a mile   *walk*
Hym for to seke and have his aqueyntaunce,   *visit*
Noght knowynge of his false governaunce.   *conduct*
990 And if yow list to yeve me audience,
I wol it tellen heere in youre presence.
    But worshipful chanons religious,
Ne demeth nat that I sclaundre youre hous,   *think; slander*
Although that my tale of a chanoun bee.
995 Of every ordre som shrewe is, pardee,
And God forbede that al a compaignye   *forbid*
Sholde rewe o singuleer mannes folye.
To sclaundre yow is no thyng myn entente,   *not at all*
But to correcten that is mys I mente.
1000 This tale was nat oonly toold for yow,
But eek for othere mo; ye woot wel how   *others as well*
That among Cristes apostelles twelve
Ther nas no traytour but Judas hymselve.
Thanne why sholde al the remenant have a   *bear the blame*
    blame
1005 That giltlees were?   By yow I seye the same,   *of*
Save oonly this, if ye wol herkne me:
If any Judas in youre covent be,
Remoeveth hym bitymes, I yow rede,
If shame or los may causen any drede.
1010 And beeth no thyng displesed, I yow preye,
But in this cas herkneth what I shal seye.
    In Londoun was a preest, an annueleer,
That therinne dwelled hadde many a yeer,
Which was so plesaunt and so servysable   *who; useful*
1015 Unto the wyf, where as he was at table,
That she wolde suffre hym no thyng for to paye
For bord ne clothyng, wente he never so gaye;
And spendyng silver hadde he right ynow.   *ready money*
Therof no fors; I wol procede as now,   *never mind about that*
1020 And telle forth my tale of the chanoun
That broghte this preest to confusioun.   *ruin*

---

984 Unless the other man's a devil like himself.
995 There is some rascal in every (religious) order, indeed.
997 Should pay for a single man's folly.
999 But I meant to correct what is wrong.
1008 Remove him in good time, I advise you.
1009 If you fear (and wish to avoid) loss or shame.
1012 *annueleer*, a priest employed in singing anniversary masses for the
    dead.
1015 At whose house he boarded.
1017 However fine his clothes were.

This false chanon cam upon a day
Unto this preestes chambre, wher he lay,
Bisechynge hym to lene hym a certeyn
1025 Of gold, and he wolde quite it hym ageyn.   *pay*
'Leene me a marc,' quod he, 'but dayes three,
And at my day I wol it quiten thee.   *on the appointed day*
And if so be that thow me fynde fals,
Another day do hange me by the hals!'
1030 This preest hym took a marc, and that as swithe,
And this chanoun hym thanked ofte sithe,   *many times*
And took his leve, and wente forth his weye,   *leave*
And at the thridde day broghte his moneye,
And to the preest he took his gold agayn,   *gave*
1035 Wherof this preest was wonder glad and fayn.
'Certes,' quod he, 'no thyng anoyeth me
To lene a man a noble, or two, or thre,
Or what thyng were in my possessioun,   *whatever*
Whan he so trewe is of condicioun   *character*
1040 That in no wise he breke wole his day;
To swich a man I kan never seye nay.'
'What!' quod this chanoun, 'sholde I be untrewe?
Nay, that were thyng yfallen al of newe.
Trouthe is a thyng that I wol evere kepe   *a promise*
1045 Unto that day in which that I shal crepe
Into my grave, and ellis God forbede.
Bileveth this as siker as your Crede.   *surely*
God thanke I, and in good tyme be it sayd,
That ther was nevere man yet yvele apayd   *displeased*
1050 For gold ne silver that he to me lente,
Ne nevere falshede in myn herte I mente.
And sire,' quod he, 'now of my pryvetee,   *secrets*
Syn ye so goodlich han been unto me,   *since; kind*
And kithed to me so greet gentillesse,   *shown; courtesy*
1055 Somwhat to quyte with youre kyndenesse   *repay*
I wol yow shewe, and if yow list to leere,   *wish; learn*
I wol yow teche pleynly the manere
How I kan werken in philosophie.   *alchemy*
Taketh good heede, ye shul wel seen   *see with your own eyes*
          at yë
1060 That I wol doon a maistrie er I go.'
'Ye,' quod the preest, 'ye, sire, and wol ye so?   *yea*

1024 To lend him a certain sum of gold.
1029 Have me hanged by the neck.
1030 The priest at once gave him a mark.
1036 Certainly, . . . it doesn't bother me at all.
1040 That he will on no account fail to pay on the day agreed.
1043 That would be something altogether new.
1048 At a good time be it said.   (A formula meant to ensure good luck.)
1060 Perform a masterly feat before I go.

Marie! therof I pray yow hertely.'
   'At youre comandement, sire, trewely,'
Quod the chanoun, 'and ellis God forbeede!'
1065   Loo, how this theef koude his service beede!   *rascal; offer*
Ful sooth it is that swich profred servyse
Stynketh, as witnessen thise olde wyse,
And that, ful soone I wol it verifie
In this chanoun, roote of al trecherie,
1070 That everemoore delit hath and gladnesse—
Swiche feendly thoghtes in his herte impresse—
How Cristes peple he may to meschief brynge.   *ruin*
God kepe us from his false dissymulynge!
   Noght wiste this preest with whom that   *knew*
      he delte,   *dealt*
1075 Ne of his harm comynge he no thyng felte.
O sely preest! o sely innocent!   *foolish*
With coveitise anon thou shalt be blent!
O gracelees, ful blynd is thy conceite,   *understanding*
No thyng ne artow war of the deceite
1080 Which that this fox yshapen hath to thee!   *prepared for*
His wily wrenches thou ne mayst nat flee.   *tricks*
Wherfore, to go to the conclusion,
That refereth to thy confusion,
Unhappy man, anon I wol me hye   *hasten*
1085 To tellen thyn unwit and thy folye,   *stupidity*
And eek the falsnesse of that oother wrecche,
As ferforth as that my konnyng wol strecche.
   This chanon was my lord, ye wolden weene?   *suppose*
Sire hoost, in feith, and by the hevenes queene,
1090 It was another chanoun, and nat hee,
That kan an hundred foold moore subtiltee.
He hath bitrayed folkes many tyme;
Of his falsnesse it dulleth me to ryme.   *wearies*
Evere whan that I speke of his falshede,
1095 For shame of hym my chekes wexen rede.   *grow*
Algates they bigynnen for to glowe,   *at any rate*
For reednesse have I noon, right wel I knowe,
In my visage; for fumes diverse
Of metals, whiche ye han herd me reherce,
1100 Consumed and wasted han my reednesse.

1062 Marry! I cordially invite you to.
1066–7 It is quite true, as wise old people vouch, that proffered (i.e. uninvited) service stinks.
1071 Such devilish thoughts throng in his heart.
1077 By covetousness you shall soon be blinded.
1079 You aren't at all aware of the deception.
1083 Which concerns your undoing.
1087 As far as my ability will stretch.
1089 *Sire hoost*, i.e. Harry Bailly.
1091 Who is a hundred times more cunning.

Now taak heede of this chanons cursednesse!   *wickedness*
　'Sire,' quod he to the preest, 'lat youre man gon
For quyksilver, that we it hadde anon;
And lat hym bryngen ounces two or three;
1105 And whan he comth, as faste shal ye see   *very quickly*
A wonder thyng, which ye saugh nevere er this.'   *wonderful*
　'Sire,' quod the preest,' 'it shal be doon, ywis.'   *certainly*
He bad his servant fecchen hym this thyng,   *fetch*
And he al redy was at his biddyng,
1110 And wente hym forth, and cam anon agayn
With this quyksilver, shortly for to sayn,   *briefly*
And took thise ounces thre to the chanoun;
And he hem leyde faire and wel adoun,
And bad the servant coles for to brynge,   *charcoal*
1115 That he anon myghte go to his werkynge.
　The coles right anon weren yfet,   *fetched*
And this chanoun took out a crosselet   *crucible*
Of his bosom, and shewed it to the preest.
'This instrument,' quod he, 'which that thou seest,
1120 Taak in thyn hand, and put thyself therinne
Of this quyksilver an ounce, and heer bigynne,
In name of Crist, to wexe a philosofre.
Ther been ful fewe to whiche I wolde profre   *offer*
To shewen hem thus muche of my science.
1125 For ye shul seen heer, by experience,   *experiment*
That this quyksilver I wol mortifye
Right in youre sighte anon, withouten lye,   *truly*
And make it as good silver and as fyn   *fine*
As ther is any in youre purs or myn,
1130 Or elleswhere, and make it malliable;
And elles holdeth me fals and unable   *unfit*
Amonges folk for evere to appeere.
I have a poudre heer, that coste me deere,   *owder*
Shal make al good, for it is cause of al
1135 My konnyng, which that I yow shewen shal.   *skill*
Voyde youre man, and lat hym be theroute,   *send away*
And shette the dore, whils we been aboute   *shut*
Oure pryvetee, that no man us espie,   *private business*
Whils that we werke in this philosophie.'   *alchemy*
1140 　Al as he bad fulfilled was in dede.
This ilke servant anonright out yede   *at once; went*
And his maister shette the dore anon,
And to hire labour spedily they gon.

　1103 So that we can have it at once.
　1113 He laid them down carefully.
　1115 So that he could at once begin his experiment.
　1122 To become an alchemist.
　1126 *mortifye*, change by chemical action.
　1134 Which will make good my promise.

           This preest, at this cursed chanons biddyng,   *wicked*
1145 Upon the fir anon sette this thyng,
           And blew the fir, and bisyed hym ful faste.   *worked very hard*
           And this chanoun into the crosselet caste   *crucible; threw*
           A poudre, noot I wherof that it was   *know not*
           Ymaad, outher of chalk, outher of glas,   *either . . . or*
1150 Or somwhat elles, was nat worth a flye,
           To blynde with this preest; and bad hym hye
           The coles for to couchen al above
           The crosselet. 'For in tokenyng I thee love,'   *token*
           Quod this chanoun, 'thyne owene handes two
1155 Shul werche al thyng which that shal heer   *perform*
              be do.'   *done*
           'Graunt mercy,' quod the preest, and was ful glad,
           And couched coles as the chanoun bad.
           And while he bisy was, this feendly wrecche,   *fiendish*
           This false chanoun—the foule feend hym fecche!—
1160 Out of his bosom took a bechen cole,
           In which ful subtilly was maad an hole,   *ingeniously*
           And therinne put was of silver lemaille   *filings*
           An ounce, and stopped was, withouten faille,
           This hole with wex, to kepe the lemaille in.   *wax*
1165 And understondeth that this false gyn   *contrivance*
           Was nat maad ther, but it was maad bifore;
           And othere thynges I shal tellen moore
           Herafterward, whiche that he with hym broghte.
           Er he cam there, hym to bigile he thoghte,   *planned*
1170 And so he dide, er that they wente atwynne;   *apart*
           Til he had terved hym, koude he nat blynne.
           It dulleth me whan that I of hym speke.   *wearies*
           On his falshede fayn wolde I me wreke,
           If I wiste how, but he is heere and there;   *knew*
1175 He is so variaunt, he abit nowhere.   *shifty; stays*
              But taketh heede now, sires, for Goddes love!
           He took his cole of which I spak above,
           And in his hand he baar it pryvely,   *held; secretly*
           And whiles the preest couched bisily
1180 The coles, as I tolde yow er this,
           This chanoun seyde, 'Freend, ye doon amys.   *wrong*
           This is nat couched as it oghte be;
           But soone I shal amenden it,' quod he.   *put it right*
           'Now lat me medle therwith but a while,

           1150–3 Or something else not worth a fly, to blind the priest with; and
              told him to hurry up and lay the charcoal right on top of the crucible.
           1160 *bechen cole,* charcoal made from beech-wood.
           1171 He couldn't rest till he had fleeced him.
           1173 I would gladly avenge myself on him for his falseness.
           1184 Let me have a hand in it for a little while.

1185 For of yow have I pitee, by Seint Gile!   *Giles*
     Ye been right hoot; I se wel how ye swete.   *sweat*
     Have heere a clooth, and wipe awey the wete.'
     And whiles that the preest wiped his face,
     This chanoun took his cole—with sory   *bad luck to him!*
     grace!—
1190 And leyde it above upon the myddeward
     Of the crosselet, and blew wel afterward,
     Til that the coles gonne faste brenne.
       'Now yeve us drynke,' quod the chanoun thenne;
     'As swithe al shal be wel, I undertake.
1195 Sitte we doun, and lat us myrie make.'
     And whan that this chanounes bechen cole
     Was brent, al the lemaille out of the hole
     Into the crosselet fil anon adoun;   *fell down*
     And so it moste nedes, by resoun,
1200 Syn it so evene above couched was.   *exactly above*
     But therof wiste the preest nothyng, alas!   *knew*
     He demed alle the coles yliche good;
     For of that sleighte he nothyng understood.   *trick*
     And whan this alkamystre saugh his tyme,   *alchemist*
1205 'Ris up,' quod he, 'sire preest, and stondeth by me;
     And for I woot wel ingot have ye noon,
     Gooth, walketh forth, and bryngeth a chalk   *piece of chalk*
     stoon;
     For I wol make it of the same shap   *shape*
     That is an ingot, if I may han hap.   *mould; luck*
1210 And bryngeth eek with yow a bolle or a panne   *bowl*
     Ful of water, and ye shul se wel thanne
     How that oure bisynesse shal thryve and preeve.   *succeed*
     And yet, for ye shul han no mysbileeve   *suspicion*
     Ne wrong conceite of me in youre absence,   *notion*
1215 I ne wol nat been out of youre presence,
     But go with yow, and come with yow ageyn.'
     The chambre dore, shortly for to seyn,
     They opened and shette, and wente hir weye.
     And forth with hem they carieden the keye,
1220 And coome agayn withouten any delay.
     What sholde I tarien al the longe day?
     He took the chalk, and shoop it in the wise   *shaped*
     Of an ingot, as I shal yow devyse.   *describe*

1190–1 And laid it on top of the crucible, right in the middle.
1194 Very soon all will be well, I'll warrant.
1199 And so it was bound to do, naturally enough.
1202 He thought all the coals were equally good.
1206 And since I'm certain you haven't any mould (for pouring metal into).
1221 Why should I drag out my story the whole day?

I seye, he took out of his owene sleeve
1225 A teyne of silver—yvele moot he cheeve!—
Which that ne was nat but an ounce of weighte.
And taaketh heede now of his cursed sleighte!   *wicked trick*
He shoop his ingot, in lengthe and in breede
Of this teyne, withouten any drede,
1230 So slyly that the preest it nat espide,
And in his sleve agayn he gan it hide,
And fro the fir he took up his mateere,   *material*
And in th'yngot putte it with myrie cheere,
And in the water-vessel he it caste,   *threw*
1235 Whan that hym luste, and bad the preest as faste,
'Loke what ther is, put in thyn hand and grope.
Thow fynde shalt ther silver, as I hope.
What, devel of helle! sholde it elles be?
Shaving of silver silver is, pardee!'
1240 He putte his hand in and took up a teyne   *thin plate*
Of silver fyn, and glad in every veyne   *vein*
Was this preest, whan he saugh it was so.   *saw*
'Goddes blessyng, and his moodres also,
And alle halwes, have ye, sire chanoun,'   *saints*
1245 Seyde the preest, 'and I hir malisoun,   *their curse*
But, and ye vouche-sauf to techen me
This noble craft and this subtilitee,
I wol be youre in al that evere I may.'
     Quod the chanoun, 'Yet wol I make assay
1250 The seconde tyme, that ye may taken heede
And been expert of this, and in youre neede   *in*
Another day assaye in myn absence
This disciplyne and this crafty science.   *skilful*
Lat take another ounce,' quod he tho,   *let's; then*
1255 'Of quyksilver, withouten wordes mo,   *more*
And do therwith as ye han doon er this
With that oother, which that now silver is.'
     This preest hym bisieth in al that he kan
To doon as this chanoun, this cursed man,
1260 Comanded hym, and faste blew the fir,
For to come to th'effect of his desir.

1224–31 These lines anticipate the third trick played on the priest by
    the canon; cf. 1317–18.
1225 A thin plate of silver—a bad ending to him!
1228–9 He made his mould of the same length and breadth as this
    plate of silver, without a doubt.
1233 And cheerfully put it in the mould.
1235 When he chose to, and quickly asked the priest.
1238 What else, in the devil's name, could it be?
1239 A sliver of silver is silver right enough.
1246–8 If, supposing you agree to teach me this noble craft and abstruse
    science, I'm unwilling to serve you in every way I can.
1261 In order to achieve his desire.

And this chanon, right in the meene while,
Al redy was this preest eft to bigile,   *again*
And for a contenaunce in his hand he bar
1265 An holwe stikke—taak kep and be war!—   *hollow; heed*
In the ende of which an ounce, and namoore,
Of silver lemaille put was, as bifore   *filings*
Was in his cole, and stopped with wex weel
For to kepe in his lemaille every deel.
1270 And whil this preest was in his bisynesse,
This chanoun with his stikke gan hym dresse
To hym anon, and his poudre caste in
As he dide er—the devel out of his skyn
Hym terve, I pray to God, for his falshede!   *flay*
1275 For he was evere fals in thoght and dede—
And with this stikke, above the crosselet,   *crucible*
That was ordeyned with that false jet,
He stired the coles til relente gan   *melted*
The wex agayn the fir, as every man,   *in*
1280 But it a fool be, woot wel it moot nede,
And al that in the stikke was out yede,   *ran out*
And in the crosselet hastily it fel.
    'Now, goode sires, what wol ye bet than wel?
Whan that this preest thus was bigiled ageyn,
1285 Supposynge noght but treuthe, sooth to seyn,
He was so glad that I kan nat expresse
In no manere his myrthe and his gladnesse;
And to the chanoun he profred eftsoone   *once again*
Body and good. 'Ye,' quod the chanoun soone,   *goods*
1290 'Though poure I be, crafty thou shalt me   *poor; skilful*
    fynde.
I warne thee, yet is ther moore bihynde.
Is ther any coper herinne?' seyde he.   *copper*
    'Ye,' quod the preest, 'sire, I trowe wel ther be.'
    'Elles go bye us som, and that as swithe;
1295 Now, goode sire, go forth thy wey and hy the.'   *hurry*
He wente his wey, and with the coper cam,
And this chanon it in his handes nam,   *took*
And of that coper weyed out but an ounce.   *weighed*
    Al to symple is my tonge to pronounce,

1264 And for the look of the thing he held in his hand.
1267–9 Just as before it had been hidden in his piece of charcoal, and the stick was well stopped with wax to keep all his filings in.
1270 And while the priest was busy (blowing the fire).
1271–2 Straightway went up to him.
1277 That (i.e. the stick) was fitted with that false contrivance.
1280 Unless he is a fool, well knows it must.
1283 i.e. what more do you want?
1285 i.e. without the least suspicion of the canon's honesty.
1291 I tell you, there is still more to come.
1294 If not, go quickly and buy us some.

1300 As ministre of my wit, the doublenesse   *duplicity*
     Of this chanoun, roote of alle cursednesse!   *wickedness*
     He semed freendly to hem that knewe hym noght,
     But he was feendly bothe in werk and thoght.   *fiendish*
     It weerieth me to telle of his falsnesse,   *wearies*
1305 And nathelees yet wol I it expresse,   *nevertheless*
     To th'entente that men may be war therby,
     And for noon oother cause, trewely.

        He putte this ounce of coper in the crosselet,
     And on the fir as swithe he hath it set,   *immediately*
1310 And cast in poudre, and made the preest to blowe,
     And in his werkyng for to stoupe lowe,
     As he dide er,—and al nas but a jape;
     Right as hym liste, the preest he made his ape!
     And afterward in the ingot he it caste,
1315 And in the panne putte it at the laste   *finally*
     Of water, and in he putte his owene hand,
     And in his sleve (as ye biforen-hand
     Herde me telle) he hadde a silver teyne.
     He slyly took it out, this cursed heyne,   *wretch*
1320 Unwityng this preest of his false craft,
     And in the pannes botme he hath it laft;   *left*
     And in the water rombled to and fro,   *fumbled*
     And wonder pryvely took up also   *with amazing stealth*
     The coper teyne, noght knowynge this preest,
1325 And hidde it, and hym hente by the breest,   *grasped; breast*
     And to hym spak, and thus seyde in his game: *jokingly*
     'Stoupeth adoun, by God, ye be to blame!   *bend*
     Helpeth me now, as I dide yow whileer;   *before*
     Putte in youre hand, and looketh what is theer.'   *see*
1330   This preest took up this silver teyne anon,
     And thanne seyde the chanoun, 'Lat us gon
     With thise thre teynes, whiche that we han wroght,   *made*
     To som goldsmyth, and wite if they been oght.
     For, by my feith, I nolde, for myn hood,
1335 But if that they were silver fyn and good,
     And that as swithe preeved it shal bee.'
        Unto the goldsmyth with thise teynes three
     They wente, and putte thise teynes in assay
     To fir and hamer; myghte no man seye nay,   *deny*
1340 But that they weren as hem oghte be.   *they should*

1311 And to bend down low over his work.
1312 And it was all a hoax.
1313 He cheated the priest just as he liked.
1320 The priest being unaware of his artful trick.
1324 Without the priest knowing.
1333 And find out if they're worth anything.
1334-6 For, upon my honour, I'll wager my hood they're nothing but
     good fine silver, and that shall be proved immediately.

This sotted preest, who was gladder than he?   *stupid*
Was nevere brid gladder agayn the day,
Ne nyghtyngale, in the sesoun of May,
Was nevere noon that luste bet to synge;
1345 Ne lady lustier in carolynge,
Or for to speke of love and wommanhede,
Ne knyght in armes to doon an hardy dede,   *brave*
To stonden in grace of his lady deere,
Than hadde this preest this soory craft to leere.   *learn*
1350 And to the chanoun thus he spak and seyde:
'For love of God, that for us alle deyde,   *died*
And as I may deserve it unto yow,   *of you*
What shal this receite coste? telleth now!'   *recipe*
'By oure Lady,' quod this chanon, 'it is deere,
1355 I warne yow wel; for save I and a frere,
In Engelond ther kan no man it make.'
'No fors,' quod he, 'now, sire, for Goddes sake,   *matter*
What shal I paye? telleth me, I preye.'
'Ywis,' quod he, 'it is ful deere, I seye.   *certainly*
1360 Sire, at o word, if that thee list it have,   *wish*
Ye shul paye fourty pound, so God me save!
And nere the freendshipe that ye dide er this
To me, ye sholde paye moore, ywis.'
This preest the somme of fourty pound anon
1365 Of nobles fette, and took hem everichon   *all*
To this chanoun, for this ilke receite.   *same*
Al his werkyng nas but fraude and deceite.
'Sire preest,' he seyde, 'I kepe han no loos
Of my craft, for I wolde it kept were cloos;   *secret*
1370 And, as ye love me, kepeth it secree.
For, and men knewen al my soutiltee,   *if; skill*
By God, they wolden han so greet envye
To me, by cause of my philosophye,
I sholde be deed; ther were noon oother weye.'   *die*
1375 'God it forbeede,' quod the preest, 'what sey ye?   *forbid*
Yet hadde I levere spenden al the good
Which that I have, and elles wexe I wood,
Than that ye sholden falle in swich mescheef.'   *harm*
'For youre good wyl, sire, have ye right good preef,'

1342 Never was bird more glad to greet the day.
1343–4 Nor any nightingale . . . more desirous of singing.
1345 Nor lady more joyful in singing and dancing a carol (a ring-dance
    accompanied by song).
1348 Cf. I. 88.
1362–3 If it weren't for the friendship you showed me a short while ago.
1367 Everything he did was sheer fraud and deceit.
1368–9 I don't care to win fame by my skill.
1376 Yet I would rather spend all the money.
1377 And may I go mad if I wouldn't.
1379 Good luck to you, sir, for your goodwill.

1380 Quod the chanoun, 'and farwel, grant mercy!'
     He wente his wey, and never the preest hym sy   *saw*
     After that day; and whan that this preest shoolde
     Maken assay, at swich tyme as he wolde,
     Of this receit, farwel! it wolde nat be.
1385 Lo, thus byjaped and bigiled was he!   *tricked*
     Thus maketh he his introduccioun,
     To brynge folk to hir destruccioun.
         Considereth, sires, how that, in ech estaat,   *every rank*
     Bitwixe men and gold ther is debaat   *between; strife*
1390 So ferforth that unnethes is ther noon.
     This multiplying blent so many oon   *blinds*
     That in good feith I trowe that it bee
     The cause grettest of swich scarsetee.
     Philosophres speken so mystily   *vaguely*
1395 In this craft that men kan nat come therby,
     For any wit that men han now-a-dayes.
     They mowe wel chiteren as doon jayes,   *may; chatter*
     And in hir termes sette hir lust and peyne,
     But to hir purpos shul they nevere atteyne.
1400 A man may lightly lerne, if he have aught,   *easily*
     To multiplie, and brynge his good to naught!
         Lo! swich a lucre is in this lusty game,
     A mannes myrthe it wol turne unto grame,   *grief*
     And empten also grete and hevye purses,   *empty*
1405 And maken folk for to purchacen curses   *earn*
     Of hem that han hir good therto ylent.
     O! fy, for shame! they that han been brent,   *burnt*
     Allas! kan they nat flee the fires heete?   *heat*
     Ye that it use, I rede ye it leete,
1410 Lest ye lese al; for bet than nevere is late.   *lose*
     Nevere to thryve were to long a date.
     Though ye prolle ay, ye shul it nevere fynde.
     Ye been as boold as is Bayard the blynde,
     That blondreth forth, and peril casteth noon.
1415 He is as boold to renne agayn a stoon   *against*
     As for to goon bisides in the weye.

1386 Thus he (the canon) effects an introduction.
1390 To such an extent that there is hardly any (gold) left.
1396 Not with the intelligence we have nowadays.
1398 And take delight and trouble in their jargon.
1402 There's so much money in this merry game.
1406 Of those who have lent their money for that purpose.
1409 You who practise it, I advise you to give it up.
1411 Never to prosper would be too long a time.
1412 Though you prowl about for ever.
1413 As bold as blind Bayard. (A proverbial phrase, *Bayard* being a
     common name for a horse.)
1414 That blunders on, and has no thought of danger.
1416 As to turn aside and pass it on the way.

So faren ye that multiplie, I seye.

If that youre eyen kan nat seen aright,   *eyes*

Looke that youre mynde lakke noght his sight.   *its*

1420 For though ye looken never so brode and stare,

Ye shul nothyng wynne on that chaffare,   *trade*

But wasten al that ye may rape and renne.

Withdraweth the fir, lest it to faste brenne;

Medleth namoore with that art, I mene,

1425 For if ye doon, youre thrift is goon ful clene.

And right as swithe I wol yow tellen heere   *right away*

What philosophres seyn in this mateere.   *alchemists*

   Lo, thus seith Arnold of the Newe Toun,

As his Rosarie maketh mencioun;

1430 He seith right thus, withouten any lye: *truly*

'Ther may no man mercurie mortifie

But it be with his brother knowlechyng.'

How be that he which that first seyde this thyng

Of philosophres fader was, Hermes—

1435 He seith how that the dragon, doutelees,

Ne dyeth nat, but if that he be slayn   *unless*

With his brother; and that is for to sayn,   *by*

By the dragon, Mercurie, and noon oother

He understood, and brymstoon by his brother,

1440 That out of Sol and Luna were ydrawe.

'And therfore,' seyde he,—taak heede to my sawe—

'Lat no man bisye hym this art for to seche,

But if that he th'entencioun and speche

Of philosophres understonde kan;

1445 And if he do, he is a lewed man.   *ignorant*

For this science and this konnyng,' quod he,   *knowledge; skill*

'Is of the secree of the secretes, pardee.'   *secret; indeed*

   Also ther was a disciple of Plato,

That on a tyme seyde his maister to,

1450 As his book Senior wol bere wittnesse,

And this was his demande in soothfastnesse: *question; truth*

'Telle me the name of the privee stoon.'   *secret stone*

   And Plato answerde unto hym anoon,

1420 Though you look with eyes wide open.
1422 All that you seize and lay hold of.
1425 Your savings are clean gone.
1428 Arnoldus de Villa Nova, a thirteenth-century French physician and alchemist.
1431–2 No one can mortify mercury except with the help of its brother. (The 'brother' of mercury was brimstone or sulphur.)
1434 Was Hermes (Trismegistus), the father of alchemists.
1438–9 By the dragon he meant mercury, and nothing else.
1440 Which are taken from gold (*Sol*) and quicksilver (*Luna*).
1441 Pay heed to what I say.
1442 Let no man busy himself exploring this art.
1450 *Senior*, the name of a medieval treatise on alchemy.

'Take the stoon that Titanos men name.'
1455   'Which is that?' quod he. 'Magnasia is   *magnesia*
          the same,'
        Seyde Plato. 'Ye, sire, and is it thus?
        This is *ignotum per ignocius.*
        What is Magnasia, good sire, I yow preye?'
          'It is a water that is maad, I seye,
1460   Of elementes foure,' quod Plato.
          'Telle me the roote, good sire,' quod he tho,   *then*
        'Of that water, if it be youre wil.'
          'Nay, nay,' quod Plato, 'certein, that I nyl.   *will not*
        The philosophres sworn were everychoon   *all*
1465   That they sholden discovere it unto noon,   *reveal*
        Ne in no book it write in no manere.
        For unto Crist it is so lief and deere   *precious*
        That he wol nat that it discovered bee,
        But where it liketh to his deitee
1470   Men for t'enspire, and eek for to deffende
        Whom that hym liketh; lo, this is the ende.'
          Thanne conclude I thus, sith that God of hevene   *since*
        Ne wil nat that the philosophres nevene   *tell*
        How that a man shal come unto this stoon,
1475   I rede, as for the beste, lete it goon.
        For whoso maketh God his adversarie,
        As for to werken any thyng in contrarie
        Of his wil, certes, never shal he thryve,
        Thogh that he multiplie terme of his lyve.   *all his life*
1480   And there a poynt; for ended is my tale.
        God sende every trewe man boote of his bale!   *remedy; ills*

HEERE IS ENDED THE CHANOUNS YEMANNES TALE

        1457 This is explaining the unknown by the more unknown.
        1469–71 Except as it pleases His deity to inspire certain men, and also
            to forbid whomever He will.
        1475 The best advice I can give is to leave it alone.
        1480 And here I come to a full stop.

Fragment IX (Group H)

THE MANCIPLE'S PROLOGUE

Heere folweth the Prologe of the Maunciples
Tale

Woot ye nat where ther stant a litel toun	*know; stands*
Which that ycleped is Bobbe-up-and-doun,	*called*
Under the Blee, in Caunterbury Weye?	
Ther gan oure Hooste for to jape and pleye,	*joke*
5 And seyde, 'Sires, what! Dun is in the myre!	
Is ther no man, for preyere ne for hyre,	
That wole awake oure felawe al bihynde?	
A theef myghte hym ful lightly robbe and bynde.	*easily*
See how he nappeth! see how, for cokkes bones,	*nods*
10 That he wol falle fro his hors atones!	
Is that a cook of Londoun, with mes-	*bad luck to him*
chaunce?	
Do hym come forth, he knoweth his penaunce;	*make*
For he shal telle a tale, by my fey,	*faith*
Although it be nat worth a botel hey.	*bottle of hay*
15 Awake, thou Cook,' quod he, 'God yeve thee sorwe!	
What eyleth thee to slepe by the morwe?	
Hastow had fleen al nyght, or artow dronke?	*fleas*
Or hastow with som quene al nyght yswonke,	*wench; toiled*
So that thow mayst nat holden up thyn heed?'	*head*
20 This Cook, that was ful pale and no thyng reed,	
Seyde to oure Hoost, 'So God my soule blesse,	
As ther is falle on me swich hevynesse,	
Noot I nat why, that me were levere slepe	
Than the beste galon wyn in Chepe.'	
25 'Wel,' quod the Maunciple, 'if it may doon ese	*help*
To thee, sire Cook, and to no wight displese,	*no one*

2 *Bobbe-up-and-doun*, possibly Harbledown, which stands close by the
Blean Forest (*Under the Blee*) on the way to Canterbury.
5 *Dun is in the myre*, a proverbial saying taken from an old game.
The Host means, in effect, 'Things are at a standstill.'
6 i.e. for love or money.
7 Our companion in the rear.
9 *for cokkes bones*, a corruption of the oath *by Goddes bones*.
16 What's wrong with you to be sleeping in the morning?
20 And with no trace of colour.
22–4 Such a heavy feeling has come over me, I don't know why, that
I'd rather sleep than have the best gallon of wine in Cheapside.

Which that heere rideth in this compaignye,
And that oure Hoost wole, of his curteisye,
I wol as now excuse thee of thy tale.   *for now*
30 For, in good feith, thy visage is ful pale,
Thyne eyen daswen eek, as that me thynketh,
And, wel I woot, thy breeth ful soure stynketh: *sour*
That sheweth wel thou art nat wel disposed.   *indisposed*
Of me, certeyn, thou shalt nat been yglosed.
35 See how he ganeth, lo! this dronken wight,   *yawns*
As though he wolde swolwe us anonright.
Hoold cloos thy mouth, man, by thy fader kyn!   *father's*
The devel of helle sette his foot therin!
Thy cursed breeth infecte wole us alle.
40 Fy, stynkyng swyn! fy, foule moote thee falle!   *bad luck to you*
A! taketh heede, sires, of this lusty man.
Now, sweete sire, wol ye justen atte fan?
Therto me thynketh ye been wel yshape!
I trowe that ye dronken han wyn ape,
45 And that is whan men pleyen with a straw.'
And with this speche the Cook wax wrooth and
                                                wraw,   *peevish*
And on the Manciple he gan nodde faste
For lakke of speche, and doun the hors hym caste,   *threw*
Where as he lay, til that men hym up took.
50 This was a fair chyvachee of a cook!
Allas! he nadde holde hym by his ladel!
And er that he agayn were in his sadel,   *before*
Ther was greet showvyng bothe to and fro   *shoving*
To lifte hym up, and muchel care and wo,
55 So unweeldy was this sory palled goost.
And to the Manciple thanne spak oure Hoost:
'By cause drynke hath dominacioun
Upon this man, by my savacioun,
I trowe he lewedly wolde telle his tale.   *badly*
60 For, were it wyn, or oold or moysty ale
That he hath dronke, he speketh in his nose,
And fneseth faste, and eek he hath the pose.

28 And if our Host is good enough to let me.
31 Your eyes are glazed too, it seems to me.
34 You'll get no flattery from me, that's certain.
36 As though he'd swallow us right off.
42 Joust at the vane (of the quintain).
43 You're in splendid shape for that, I must say!
44 I think you must have drunk ape-wine, i.e. you're as drunk as an ape.
45 That's when men start playing with a straw.
50 A fine feat of horsemanship for a cook!
51 Alas, that he did not stick to his ladle!
55 This pale and wretched ghost.
60 Whether it's wine, or old or new ale.
62 Snorts hard, as if he had a cold in the head.

He hath also to do moore than *more than enough to do*
 ynough
To kepen hym and his capul out of the slough; *nag*
65 And if he falle from his capul eftsoone, *once more*
Thanne shal we alle have ynogh to doone *do*
In liftyng up his hevy dronken cors. *carcass*
Telle on thy tale; of hym make I no fors.
 But yet, Manciple, in feith thou art to nyce, *very foolish*
70 Thus openly repreve hym of his vice. *reprove*
Another day he wole, peraventure,
Reclayme thee and brynge thee to lure;
I meene, he speke wole of smale thynges,
As for to pynchen at thy rekenynges,
75 That were nat honest, if it cam to preef.' *the proof*
 'No,' quod the Manciple, 'that were a greet
 mescheef! *misfortune*
So myghte he lightly brynge me in the snare. *easily*
Yet hadde I levere payen for the mare *I'd rather pay*
Which he rit on, than he sholde with me stryve. *rides*
80 I wol nat wratthen hym, also moot I thryve!
That that I spak, I seyde it in my bourde. *jest*
And wite ye what? I have heer in a gourde *know*
A draghte of wyn, ye, of a ripe grape,
And right anon ye shul seen a good jape. *joke*
85 This Cook shal drynke therof, if I may. *if I can manage it*
Up peyne of deeth, he wol nat seye me nay.' *on*
 And certeynly, to tellen as it was,
Of this vessel the Cook drank faste, allas! *deep*
What neded hym? he drank ynough biforn. *need had he*
90 And whan he hadde pouped in this horn,
To the Manciple he took the gourde agayn; *gave*
And of that drynke the Cook was wonder fayn,
And thanked hym in swich wise as he koude. *as best he could*
 Thanne gan oure Hoost to laughen wonder loude,
95 And seyde, 'I se wel it is necessarie,
Where that we goon, good drynke with us carie; *go*
For that wol turne rancour and disese *grievance*
T'acord and love, and many a wrong apese.

---

68 Go on and tell your tale; I don't care about him.
72 Call you back and bring you to the lure. (This metaphor, taken
 from hawking, means that the Cook will contrive to get his own back
 on the Manciple.)
74 Such as finding fault with your accounts.
80 I don't want to anger him, as I hope to prosper!
83 Yes, of an excellent vintage.
90 Blown on this horn, i.e. drunk a large draught out of the gourd.
 (A pun on *horn* 'wind instrument' and *horn* 'drinking horn.')
92 The Cook was wonderfully pleased with that drink.
98 To love and harmony, and settle many a wrong.

O Bacus, yblessed be thy name,   *Bacchus*
100 That so kanst turnen ernest into game!   *seriousness*
Worshipe and thank be to thy deitee!   *thanks*
Of that mateere ye gete namoore of me.
Telle on thy tale, Manciple, I thee preye.'
'Wel, sire,' quod he, 'now herkneth what I seye.'

THE MANCIPLE'S TALE

HEERE BIGYNNETH THE MAUNCIPLES TALE OF THE CROWE

105 WHAN Phebus dwelled heere in this erthe adoun,   *below*
As olde bookes maken mencioun,
He was the mooste lusty bachiler
In al this world, and eek the beste archer.
He slow Phitoun, the serpent, as he lay
110 Slepynge agayn the sonne upon a day;
And many another noble worthy dede
He with his bowe wroghte, as men may rede.   *performed*
    Pleyen he koude on every mynstralcie,
And syngen, that it was a melodie   *melodious*
115 To heeren of his cleere voys the soun.
Certes the kyng of Thebes, Amphioun,   *certainly*
That with his syngyng walled that citee,
Koude nevere syngen half so wel as hee.
Therto he was the semelieste man
120 That is or was, sith that the world bigan.   *since*
What nedeth it his fetures to discryve?   *describe*
For in this world was noon so faire on-lyve.   *alive*

107 He was the lustiest young knight.
109 He slew the Python.
110 Sleeping in the sun one day.
113 Every kind of musical instrument.
119 He was, besides, the handsomest man.

He was therwith fulfild of gentillesse,
Of honour, and of parfit worthynesse.
125 This Phebus, that was flour of bachilrie,
As wel in fredom as in chivalrie,
For his desport, in signe eek of victorie   *amusement*
Of Phitoun, so as telleth us the storie,   *over*
Was wont to beren in his hand a bowe.
130 Now hadde this Phebus in his hous a crowe
Which in a cage he fostred many a day,   *fed*
And taughte it speken, as men teche a jay.
Whit was this crowe as is a snow-whit swan,
And countrefete the speche of every man   *imitate*
135 He koude, whan he sholde telle a tale.
Therwith in al this world no nyghtyngale
Ne koude, by an hondred thousand deel,
Syngen so wonder myrily and weel.
 Now hadde this Phebus in his hous a wyf
140 Which that he lovede moore than his lyf,
And nyght and day dide evere his diligence   *utmost*
Hir for to plese, and doon hire reverence,
Save oonly, if the sothe that I shal sayn,   *truth*
Jalous he was, and wolde have kept hire fayn.
145 For hym were looth byjaped for to be,
And so is every wight in swich degree;
But al in ydel, for it availleth noght.   *vain*
A good wyf, that is clene of werk and thoght,
Sholde nat been kept in noon awayt, certayn;
150 And trewely, the labour is in vayn
To kepe a shrewe, for it wol nat bee.
This holde I for a verray nycetee,   *real folly*
To spille labour for to kepe wyves:
Thus writen olde clerkes in hir lyves.
155 But now to purpos, as I first bigan: *to the subject*
This worthy Phebus dooth al that he kan
To plesen hire, wenynge for swich plesaunce,
And for his manhede and his governaunce,

123–4 Full of nobleness, honour, and flawless worth.
125–6 Flower of all young knights, both in generosity and knightly
  conduct.
137–8 Could sing a hundred thousandth part so sweetly.
144 He was jealous, and would gladly have kept her under guard.
145 For he was unwilling to be tricked.
146 And so is everyone in like case.
149 Should not be kept under surveillance, that's certain.
151 To guard a bad wife, for it can't be done.
153 To waste our efforts guarding wives.
154 Thus wrote the ancients during their lifetime.
157–8 Thinking that if he gave her pleasure, and acted in a manly and
  masterful fashion.

That no man sholde han put hym from hir grace.
160 But God it woot, ther may no man embrace
As to destreyne a thyng which that nature
Hath natureelly set in a creature.
    Taak any bryd, and put it in a cage,   *bird*
And do al thyn entente and thy corage
165 To fostre it tendrely with mete and drynke
Of alle deyntees that thou kanst bithynke,   *think of*
And keep it al so clenly as thou may,
Although his cage of gold be never so gay,
Yet hath this brid, by twenty thousand foold,   *times*
170 Levere in a forest, that is rude and coold,   *rather; rough*
Goon ete wormes and swich wrecchednesse.
For evere this brid wol doon his bisynesse   *take pains*
To escape out of his cage, yif he may.   *if*
His libertee this brid desireth ay.
175   Lat take a cat, and fostre hym wel with milk
And tendre flessh, and make his couche of silk,
And lat hym seen a mous go by the wal,
Anon he weyveth milk and flessh and al,   *abandons*
And every deyntee that is in that hous,
180 Swich appetit hath he to ete a mous.
Lo, heere hath lust his dominacioun,
And appetit fleemeth discrecioun.   *drives out*
    A she-wolf hath also a vileyns kynde.   *base nature*
The lewedeste wolf that she may fynde,
185 Or leest of reputacioun, wol she take,
In tyme whan hir lust to han a make.
    Alle thise ensamples speke I by thise men
That been untrewe, and nothyng by wommen.   *not at all*
For men han evere a likerous appetit   *lecherous*
190 On lower thyng to parfourne hire delit   *fulfil*
Than on hire wyves, be they never so faire,
Ne never so trewe, ne so debonaire.   *gentle*
Flessh is so newfangel, with meschaunce,
That we ne konne in nothyng han plesaunce
195 That sowneth into vertu any while.
    This Phebus, which that thoghte upon no gile,   *guile*
Deceyved was, for al his jolitee.   *excellence*
For under hym another hadde shee,

160-2 God knows, no one can succeed in constraining something that
    nature has naturally implanted in a creature.
164 And try with all your heart and mind.
171 Go and eat worms and suchlike wretched fare.
181 Here you see that desire is dominant.
186 At a time when she desires to have a mate.
187 All these instances I give you refer to men.
193 The flesh is so fond of novelty, the devil take it.
194-5 We cannot take pleasure for long in anything that has a virtuous
    disposition.

A man of litel reputacioun,
200 Nat worth to Phebus in comparisoun.
The moore harm is; it happeth ofte so,   *more's the pity*
Of which ther cometh muchel harm and wo.
   And so bifel, whan Phebus was absent,
His wyf anon hath for hir lemman sent.   *lover*
205 Hir lemman? Certes, this is a knavyssh speche!
Foryeveth it me, and that I yow biseche.   *forgive*
   The wise Plato seith, as ye may rede,
The word moot nede accorde with the dede.
If men shal telle proprely a thyng,
210 The word moot cosyn be to the werkyng.   *deed*
I am a boystous man, right thus seye I,   *plain*
Ther nys no difference, trewely,
Bitwixe a wyf that is of heigh degree,   *between*
If of hir body dishonest she bee,   *dishonourable*
215 And a povre wenche, oother than this—   *poor*
If it so be they werke bothe amys—
But that the gentile, in estaat above,
She shal be cleped his lady, as in love;   *called*
And for that oother is a povre womman,
220 She shal be cleped his wenche or his lemman.
And, God it woot, myn owene deere brother,   *knows*
Men leyn that oon as lowe as lith that oother.
   Right so bitwixe a titlelees tiraunt
And an outlawe, or a theef erraunt,   *arrant*
225 The same I seye, ther is no difference.
To Alisaundre was toold this sentence: *opinion*
That, for the tirant is of gretter myght,
By force of meynee, for to sleen dounright,
And brennen hous and hoom, and make al playn,   *burn*
230 Lo, therfore is he cleped a capitayn;
And for the outlawe hath but smal meynee,   *following*
And may nat doon so greet an harm as he,
Ne brynge a contree to so greet mescheef,   *harm*
Men clepen hym an outlawe or a theef.
235 But, for I am a man noghte textueel,   *learned*
I wol noght telle of textes never a deel;
I wol go to my tale, as I bigan.
Whan Phebus wyf had sent for hir lemman,

200 Worth nothing by comparison with Phoebus.
208 See I. 742.
216 If it happens that they both misbehave.
217 The gentlewoman, of high degree.
222 Men lay the one as low as ever lies the other.
223 *titlelees*, without a title, i.e. usurping.
228 With the help of a strong army, to slay outright.
229 And level everything to the ground.
236 I won't quote a single authority.

Anon they wroghten al hire lust volage.   *wanton*
240   The white crowe, that heeng ay in the cage,   *hung*
Biheeld hire werk, and seyde never a word.
And whan that hoom was come Phebus. the lord,
This crowe sang 'Cokkow! cokkow! cokkow!'
   'What, bryd!' quod Phebus, 'what song syngestow?
245 Ne were thow wont so myrily to synge   *were you not*
That to myn herte it was a rejoysynge
To heere thy voys? Allas! what song is this?'
   'By God!' quod he, 'I synge nat amys.
Phebus,' quod he, 'for al thy worthynesse,
250 For al thy beautee and thy gentilesse,   *nobility*
For al thy song and al thy mynstralcye,
For al thy waityng, blered is thyn ye
With oon of litel reputacioun,
Noght worth to thee, as in comparisoun,
255 The montance of a gnat, so moote I thryve!
For on thy bed thy wyf I saugh hym swyve.'
   What wol ye moore? The crowe anon hym tolde,
By sadde tokenes and by wordes bolde,   *sure signs*
How that his wyf had doon hire lecherye,
260 Hym to greet shame and to greet vileynye;
And tolde hym ofte he saugh it with his yen.
   This Phebus gan aweyward for to wryen,   *turned away*
And thoughte his sorweful herte brast atwo.   *broke in two*
His bowe he bente, and sette therinne a flo,   *arrow*
265 And in his ire his wyf thanne hath he slayn.
This is th'effect, ther is namoore to sayn;
For sorwe of which he brak his mynstralcie,
Bothe harpe, and lute, and gyterne, and   *guitar*
   sautrie;   *psaltery*
And eek he brak his arwes and his bowe,
270 And after that thus spak he to the crowe:
   'Traitour,' quod he, 'with tonge of scorpioun,
Thou hast me broght to my confusioun,   *ruin*
Allas, that I was wroght! why nere I deed?
O deere wyf! o gemme of lustiheed!   *delight*
275 That were to me so sad and eek so trewe,   *constant*
Now listow deed, with face pale of hewe,   *you lie dead*
Ful giltelees, that dorste I swere, ywys!
O rakel hand, to doon so foule amys!

243 *Cokkow*, cuckoo, suggestive of 'cuckold.'
252-5 For all your watching, you are hoodwinked by a man of little
    repute who is not worth a gnat by comparison with you.
260 To his great shame and great disgrace.
266 This is the upshot of it all.
267 He broke his musical instruments.
273 Alas, that I was born! Why couldn't I die?
278 O rash hand, to do so foul a wrong!

O trouble wit, o ire recchelees,
280 That unavysed smyteth gilteles!
O wantrust, ful of fals suspecion,   *distrust*
Where was thy wit and thy discrecion?
O every man, be war of rakelnesse!   *rashness*
Ne trowe no thyng withouten strong witnesse.
285 Smyt nat to soone, er that ye witen why,   *before; know*
And beeth avysed wel and sobrely,
Er ye doon any execucion
Upon youre ire for suspecion.
Allas! a thousand folk hath rakel ire
290 Fully fordoon, and broght hem in the mire.   *destroyed*
Allas! for sorwe I wol myselven slee!'   *slay*
    And to the crowe, 'O false theef!' seyde he,   *wretch*
'I wol thee quite anon thy false tale.
Thou songe whilom lyk a nyghtyngale;   *sang once*
295 Now shaltow, false theef, thy song forgon,   *forgo*
And eek thy white fetheres everichon,   *every one*
Ne nevere in al thy life ne shaltou speke.
Thus shal men on a traytour been awreke;   *avenged*
Thou and thyn ofspryng evere shul be blake,
300 Ne nevere sweete noyse shul ye make,
But evere crie agayn tempest and rayn,   *iust before*
In tokenynge that thurgh thee my wyf is slayn.'   *token*
And to the crowe he stirte, and that anon,   *rushed*
And pulled his white fetheres everychon,   *plucked*
305 And made hym blak, and refte hym al his song,
And eek his speche, and out at dore hym slong   *slung*
Unto the devel, which I hym bitake;
And for this caas been alle crowes blake.   *reason*
    Lordynges, by this ensample I yow preye,   *moral story*
310 Beth war, and taketh kep what that ye seye.   *heed*
Ne telleth nevere no man in youre lyf
How that another man hath dight his wyf;   *dishonoured*
He wol yow haten mortally, certeyn.
Daun Salomon, as wise clerkes seyn,   *lord; scholars*
315 Techeth a man to kepen his tonge weel.   *guard*
But, as I seyde, I am noght textueel.   *learned*
But nathelees, thus taughte me my dame: *mother*
'My sone, thenk on the crowe, a Goddes name!   *in*
My sone, keep wel thy tonge, and keep thy freend.
320 A wikked tonge is worse than a feend;

279-80 O troubled mind, O reckless anger that rashly smote an innocent
    creature!
286-8 Think well and soberly before you act in anger merely on sus-
    picion.
293 I'll pay you back for your lying words without delay.
305 And took all his song away from him.
307 To whom I commend him.

My sone, from a feend men may hem blesse.
My sone, God of his endelees goodnesse
Walled a tonge with teeth and lippes eke,   *as well*
For man sholde hym avyse what he speeke.
325 My sone, ful ofte, for to muche speche   *too*
Hath many a man been spilt, as clerkes teche;   *ruined*
But for litel speche avysely
Is no man shent, to speke generally.   *injured*
My sone, thy tonge sholdestow restreyne
330 At alle tymes, but whan thou doost thy peyne
To speke of God, in honour and preyere.
The firste vertu, sone, if thou wolt leere,   *learn*
Is to restreyne and kepe wel thy tonge;   *guard*
Thus lerne children whan that they been yonge.
335 My sone, of muchel spekyng yvele avysed,
Ther lasse spekyng hadde ynough suffised,
Comth muchel harm; thus was me toold and taught.
In muchel speche synne wanteth naught.   *is no lack of sin*
Wostow whereof a rakel tonge serveth?
340 Right as a swerd forkutteth and forkerveth   *cuts; hews*
An arm a-two, my deere sone, right so
A tonge kutteth freendshipe al a-two.
A jangler is to God abhomynable.   *prattler*
Reed Salomon, so wys and honurable;   *read*
345 Reed David in his psalmes, reed Senekke.   *Seneca*
My sone, spek nat, but with thyn heed thou   *head*
    bekke.   *nod*
Dissimule as thou were deef, if that thou heere   *pretend*
A janglere speke of perilous mateere.
The Flemyng seith, and lerne it if thee leste,   *if you please*
350 That litel janglyng causeth muchel reste.
My sone, if thou no wikked word hast seyd,
Thee thar nat drede for to be biwreyd;
But he that hath mysseyd, I dar wel sayn,   *said amiss*
He may by no wey clepe his word agayn.
355 Thyng that is seyd is seyd, and forth it gooth,
Though hym repente, or be hym nevere so looth.
He is his thral to whom that he hath sayd

---

321 Men can cross themselves as a defence against the devil.
324 So that a man should think before he speaks.
327 But for a few words spoken advisedly.
330–1 Except when you take pains to honour God in prayer.
335–6 From ill-advised, excessive speech, where fewer words would
    have done.
339 Do you know what a rash tongue serves to do?
350 Little prattle means great peace of mind.
352 You need not fear to be betrayed.
354 He cannot possibly recall his words.
356 Though the speaker repent of it, and however hateful it is to him.

A tale of which he is now yvele apayd.
My sone, be war, and be noon auctour newe
360 Of tidynges, wheither they been false or trewe.
Whereso thou come, amonges hye or lowe,   *wherever*
Kepe wel thy tonge, and thenk upon the crowe.'   *guard*

HEERE IS ENDED THE MAUNCIPLES
TALE OF THE CROWE

358 Words for which he is now sorry.
359 Don't be the original author.

THE PARSON'S PROLOGUE

HEERE FOLWETH THE PROLOGE OF THE PERSOUNS TALE

BY THAT the Maunciple hadde his tale al ended,
The sonne fro the south lyne was descended   *meridian*
So lowe that he nas nat, to my sighte,
Degreës nyne and twenty as in highte.   *altitude*
5 Foure of the clokke it was tho, as I gesse,   *then*
For ellevene foot, or litel moore or lesse,
My shadwe was at thilke tyme, as there,
Of swiche feet as my lengthe parted were
In sixe feet equal of proporcioun.
10 Therwith the moones exaltacioun,
I meene Libra, alwey gan ascende,
As we were entryng at a thropes ende;
For which oure Hoost, as he was wont to gye,
As in this caas, oure joly compaignye,
15 Seyde in this wise: 'Lordynges everichoon,   *every one*
Now lakketh us no tales mo than oon.
Fulfilled is my sentence and my decree;   *carried out*
I trowe that we han herd of ech degree;
Almoost fulfild is al myn ordinaunce.
20 I pray to God, so yeve hym right good chaunce,
That telleth this tale to us lustily.
    Sire preest,' quod he, 'artow a vicary?   *vicar*
Or arte a person? sey sooth, by thy fey!
Be what thou be, ne breke thou nat oure pley;
25 For every man, save thou, hath toold his tale.
Unbokele, and shewe us what is in thy male;

6–9 i.e. his shadow was to his height in the proportion of 11 to 6.
11 Went on ascending (above the horizon).
12 As we were entering the outskirts of a village.
13–14 To guide our merry company in such matters.
16 We're short of only one more story.
18 I think we've heard (a story) from folk of every rank.
20–1 I pray God send the best of luck to the man who tells us this (remaining) tale in a lively manner.
23 Or are you a rector?   Tell the truth, on your honour!
24 Whichever you are, don't you spoil our fun.
26 Open your bag and show us what's inside.

For, trewely, me thynketh by thy cheere
Thou sholdest knytte up wel a greet mateere.
Telle us a fable anon, for cokkes bones!'   *tale*
30   This Persoun answerde, al atones,   *at once*
'Thou getest fable noon ytoold for me;
For Paul, that writeth unto Thymothee,   *Timothy*
Repreveth hem that weyven soothfastnesse,
And tellen fables and swich wrecchednesse.   *trash*
35 Why sholde I sowen draf out of my fest,   *chaff; fist*
When I may sowen whete, if that me lest?   *I choose*
For which I seye, if that yow list to heere   *are willing*
Moralitee and vertuous mateere,   *moral instruction*
And thanne that ye wol yeve me audience,   *give*
40 I wol ful fayn, at Cristes reverence,
Do yow plesaunce leefful, as I kan.
But trusteth wel, I am a Southren man,   *Southern*
I kan nat geeste "rum, ram, ruf," by lettre,
Ne, God woot, rym holde I but litel bettre;
45 And therfore, if yow list—I wol nat glose—
I wol yow telle a myrie tale in prose   *pleasant*
To knytte up al this feeste, and make an ende.
And Jhesu, for his grace, wit me sende
To shewe yow the wey, in this viage,
50 Of thilke parfit glorious pilgrymage
That highte Jerusalem celestial.   *is called*
And if ye vouche sauf, anon I shal
Bigynne upon my tale, for which I preye
Telle youre avys, I kan no bettre seye.
55   But nathelees, this meditacioun
I putte it ay under correccioun
Of clerkes, for I am nat textueel;
I take but the sentence, trusteth weel.

27–8 By the look of you it seems to me you should be good at concocting
    some weighty matter.
29 *for cokkes bones.*   See IX. 9.
31 *for me*, as far as I'm concerned.
33 Reproves those who set aside the truth.
40 I will most gladly, out of reverence for Christ.
41 Give you what lawful pleasure I can.
43 i.e. I cannot tell a tale in alliterative verse. (This is an allusion to
    the alliterative poems written in the Northern and West Midland
    districts of England during the fourteenth century.)
45 I won't flatter you.
47 To round off this entertainment.
49–50 To guide you, on this journey, to that perfect and glorious place
    of pilgrimage.
53–4 And so I beg you to give me your opinion, i.e. tell me whether or
    not you want to hear my moral discourse.
56–7 I submit it to the correction of scholars, for I am not a learned man.
58 I shan't give you anything but the essential meaning, believe me.

Therfore I make protestacioun
60 That I wol stonde to correccioun.'
   Upon this word we han assented soone,
For, as it seemed, it was for to doone,
To enden in som vertuous sentence,   *subject*
And for to yeve hym space and audience;
65 And bade oure Hoost he sholde to hym seye
That alle we to telle his tale hym preye.
   Oure Hoost hadde the wordes for us alle:
'Sire preest,' quod he, 'now faire yow   *good luck to you*
   bifalle!
Telleth,' quod he, 'youre meditacioun.
70 But hasteth yow, the sonne wole adoun;
Beth fructuous, and that in litel space,   *fruitful*
And to do wel God sende yow his grace!
Sey what yow list, and we wol gladly heere.'
And with that word he seyde in this manere.

                    EXPLICIT PROHEMIUM

               THE PARSON'S TALE

          HEERE BIGYNNETH THE PERSOUNS TALE

   *Jer. 6°. State super vias, et videte, et interrogate de viis
antiquis que sit via bona, et ambulate in ea; et inuenietis re-
frigerium animabus vestris, etc.*
   Oure sweete Lord God of hevene, that no man wole perisse
[*destroy*], but wole that we comen alle to the knoweleche of
hym, and to the blisful lif that is perdurable [*everlasting*],
amonesteth [*admonishes*] us by the prophete Jeremie, that
seith in thys wyse: Stondeth upon the weyes, and seeth [*look*]
80 and axeth of [*ask for*] olde pathes (that is to seyn, of olde

----

62 It seemed to be the right thing to do.
64 To give him a hearing and an opportunity (to speak).
70 But be quick, for the sun will soon set.

sentences) which is the goode wey, and walketh in that wey,
and ye shal fynde refresshynge for youre soules, etc. Manye
been the weyes espirituels [*spiritual*] that leden folk to oure
Lord Jhesu Crist, and to the regne [*kingdom*] of glorie. Of
whiche weyes, ther is a ful noble wey and a ful covenable
[*fitting*], which may nat fayle to man ne to womman that thurgh
synne hath mysgoon [*gone astray*] fro the righte wey of
Jerusalem celestial; and this wey is cleped [*called*] Penitence,
of which man sholde gladly herknen [*harken*] and enquere
90 with al his herte, to wyten [*learn*] what is Penitence, and
whennes [*why*] it is cleped Penitence, and in how manye
maneres been the acciouns or werkynges of Penitence, and
how manye speces [*kinds*] ther been of Penitence, and whiche
thynges apertenen [*belong*] and bihoven [*are necessary*] to
Penitence, and whiche thynges destourben Penitence.

Seint Ambrose seith that Penitence is the pleynynge [*lamenting*] of man for the gilt that he hath doon, and namoore to
do any thyng for which hym oghte [*he ought*] to pleyne. And
som doctour [*theologian*] seith, 'Penitence is the waymentynge
100 [*lamentation*] of man that sorweth for his synne, and pyneth
hymself for he hath mysdoon.' Penitence, with [*in*] certeyne
circumstances, is verray [*true*] repentance of a man that halt
[*holds*] hymself in sorwe and oother peyne for his giltes. And
for [*in order that*] he shal be verray penitent, he shal first
biwaylen the synnes that he hath doon, and stidefastly pur-
posen in his herte to have shrift of mouthe, and to doon
satisfaccioun, and nevere to doon thyng for which hym oghte
moore to biwayle or to compleyne, and to continue in goode
werkes, or elles his repentance may nat availle. For, as seith
110 seint Ysidre [*Isidore*], 'he is a japere [*mocker*] and a gabbere
[*liar*], and no verray repentant, that eftsoone [*soon afterwards*]
dooth thyng for which hym oghte repente.' Wepynge, and
nat for to stynte [*stop*] to do synne, may nat avayle. But
nathelees [*nevertheless*], men shal hope that every tyme that
man falleth, be it never so ofte, that he may arise thurgh
Penitence, if he have grace; but certeinly it is greet doute
[*doubt*]. For, as seith Seint Gregorie, 'unnethe [*with difficulty*] ariseth he out of his synne, that is charged with the
charge of yvel usage.' And therfore repentant folk, that
120 stynte for to synne, and forlete synne er that synne forlete
hem, hooly chirche holdeth hem siker [*sure*] of hire savacioun.
And he that synneth and verraily [*truly*] repenteth hym in his

---

100–1 And makes himself suffer because he has done wrong.
106–7 *shrift of mouthe*, i.e. auricular confession; *satisfaccioun*, satisfaction by penitential works, required as a part of the sacrament of
confession.
118–19 Who is burdened with the burden of evil habit.
120–1 And forsake sin before sin forsakes them, i.e. before they die.
(Cf. VI. 286.)

laste, hooly chirche yet hopeth [*hopes for*] his savacioun, by the grete mercy of oure Lord Jhesu Crist, for his repentaunce; but taak the siker wey.

And now, sith [*since*] I have declared yow what thyng is Penitence, now shul ye understonde that ther been three acciouns [*actions*] of Penitence.   The firste is that if a man be baptized after that he hath synned, Seint Augustyn seith, 130 'But he be penytent for his olde synful lyf, he may nat bigynne the newe clene lif.'   For, certes [*certainly*], if he be baptized withouten penitence of his olde gilt, he receyveth the mark of baptesme, but nat the grace ne the remission of his synnes, til he have repentance verray.   Another defaute [*defect*] is this, that men doon deedly synne after that they han receyved baptesme.   The thridde defaute is that men fallen in venial synnes after hir baptesme, fro day to day.   Therof seith Seint Augustyn that penitence of goode and humble folk is the penitence of every day.

140 The speces of Penitence been three.   That oon of hem is solempne [*public*], another is commune [*ordinary*], and the thridde is privee [*secret*].   Thilke [*that*] penance that is solempne is in two maneres; as to be put out of holy chirche in Lente, for slaughtre of children, and swich maner thyng [*suchlike things*].   Another is, whan a man hath synned openly, of which synne the fame [*infamy*] is openly spoken in the contree, and thanne hooly chirche by juggement destrey-neth [*compels*] hym for to do open penaunce.   Commune penaunce is that [*that which*] preestes enjoynen men communly 150 in certeyn caas [*cases*], as for to goon peraventure naked in pilgrimages, or bare-foot.   Pryvee penaunce is thilke that men doon alday [*continually*] for privee synnes, of whiche we shryve us prively and receyve privee penaunce.

Now shaltow understande what is bihovely [*useful*] and necessarie to verray perfit [*perfect*] Penitence.   And this stant on [*consists in*] three thynges: Contricioun of herte, Con-fessioun of Mouth, and Satisfaccioun.   For which seith Seint John Crisostom: 'Penitence destreyneth a man to accepte benygnely [*meekly*] every peyne [*penance*] that hym is enjoyned, 160 with contricioun of herte, and shrift of mouth, with satis-faccioun; and in werkynge of alle manere humylitee.'   And this is fruytful penitence agayn [*against*] three thynges in which we wratthe [*anger*] oure Lord Jhesu Crist: this is to seyn, by delit in thynkynge, by reccheleesnesse [*recklessness*] in spekynge, and by wikked synful werkynge [*action*].   And agayns thise wikkede giltes is Penitence, that may be likned unto a tree.

The roote of this tree is Contricioun, that hideth hym in the

150 As, perhaps, to go thinly clad.
161 And in suffering every kind of humiliation.

herte of hym that is verray repentaunt, right as the roote of
170 a tree hydeth hym in the erthe.   Of [from] the roote of Contricioun spryngeth a stalke that bereth braunches and leves
of Confessioun, and fruyt of Satisfaccioun.   For which
Crist seith in his gospel: 'Dooth digne fruyt of Penitence';
for by this fruyt may men knowe this tree, and nat by the
roote that is hyd in the herte of man, ne by the braunches, ne
by the leves of Confessioun.   And therfore oure Lord Jhesu
Crist seith thus: 'By the fruyt of hem shul ye knowen hem.'
Of this roote eek [also] spryngeth a seed of grace, the which
seed is mooder of sikernesse [security], and this seed is egre
180 [keen] and hoot [fervent].   The grace of this seed spryngeth
of [from] God thurgh remembrance of the day of doom
[judgment] and on the peynes of helle.   Of this matere seith
Salomon that in the drede of God man forleteth [forsakes] his
synne.   The heete [fervour] of this seed is the love of God,
and the desiryng of the joye perdurable [everlasting].   This
heete draweth the herte of a man to God, and dooth [makes]
hym haten his synne.   For soothly [truly] ther is nothyng that
savoureth [tastes] so wel to a child as the milk of his norice
[nurse], ne nothyng is to hym moore abhomynable than thilke
190 milk whan it is medled [mixed] with oother mete [food].
Right so the synful man that loveth his synne, hym semeth
[it seems to him] that it is to him moost sweete of any thyng;
but fro that tyme that he loveth sadly [steadfastly] oure Lord
Jhesu Crist, and desireth the lif perdurable, ther nys to him
no thyng moore abhomynable.   For soothly the lawe of God
is the love of God; for which David the prophete seith: 'I
have loved thy lawe, and hated wikkednesse and hate'; he
that loveth God kepeth his lawe and his word.   This tree
saugh [saw] the prophete Daniel in spirit, upon the avysioun
200 of the kyng Nabugodonosor, whan he conseiled hym to do
penitence.   Penaunce is the tree of lyf [life] to hem that it
receyven, and he that holdeth hym in verray penitence is
blessed, after the sentence of Salomon.

In this Penitence or Contricioun man shal understonde
foure thynges; that is to seyn, what is Contricioun, and whiche
[what] been the causes that moeven [move] a man to Contricioun, and how he sholde be contrit, and what Contricioun
availleth to the soule.   Thanne is it thus: that Contricioun is
the verray sorwe that a man receyveth in his herte for his
210 synnes, with sad [steadfast] purpos to shryve hym, and to do
penaunce, and neveremoore to do synne.   And this sorwe
shal been in this manere, as seith Seint Bernard: 'It shal been

173 'Bring forth therefore fruits meet for repentance.'   (Matt. iii. 8.)
199-201 At the time of the vision of King Nebuchadnezzar, when he
    counselled him to do penance.
203 According to the saying of Solomon.
207-8 And what good Contrition does to the soul.

hevy and grevous, and ful sharp and poynaunt [*poignant*] in herte.' First, for man hath agilt his Lord and his Creatour; and moore sharp and poynaunt, for he hath agilt hys Fader celestial; and yet moore sharp and poynaunt, for he hath wrathed [*angered*] and agilt hym that boghte [*redeemed*] hym, that with his precious blood hath delivered us fro the bondes of synne, and fro the crueltee of the devel, and fro the peynes
220 of helle.

The causes that oghte moeve a man to Contricioun been sixe. First a man shal remembre hym of his synnes; but looke he that thilke remembraunce ne be to hym no delit by no wey, but greet shame and sorwe for his gilt. For Job seith, 'Synful men doon werkes worthy of confusioun.' And therfore seith Ezechie [*Hezekiah*], 'I wol remembre me alle the yeres of my lyf in bitternesse of myn herte.' And God seith in the Apocalipse, 'Remembreth yow fro whennes that ye been falle'; for biforn [*before*] that tyme that ye synned, ye were
230 the children of God, and lymes [*members*] of the regne [*kingdom*] of God; but for youre synne ye been woxen thral, and foul, and membres of the feend, hate of aungels, sclaundre [*scandal*] of hooly chirche, and foode of the false serpent; perpetueel matere of the fir of helle; and yet moore foul and abhomynable, for ye trespassen so ofte tyme as dooth the hound that retourneth to eten his spewyng [*its vomit*]. And yet be ye fouler for youre longe continuyng in synne and youre synful usage [*habits*], for which ye be roten [*filthy*] in youre synne, as a beest in his dong. Swiche manere of thoghtes
240 maken a man to have shame of his synne, and no delit, as God seith by the prophete Ezechiel: 'Ye shal remembre yow of youre weyes, and they shuln [*shall*] displese yow.' Soothly [*truly*] synnes been the weyes that leden folk to helle.

The seconde cause that oghte make a man to have desdeyn of synne is this: that, as seith Seint Peter, 'whoso that dooth synne is thral of synne'; and synne put [*puts*] a man in greet thraldom. And therfore seith the prophete Ezechiel: 'I wente sorweful in desdayn of myself.' Certes, wel oghte a man have desdayn of synne, and withdrawe hym from that
250 thraldom and vileynye [*servitude*]. And lo, what seith Seneca in this matere? He seith thus: 'Though I wiste [*knew*] that neither God ne man ne sholde nevere knowe it, yet wolde I have desdayn for to do synne.' And the same Seneca also seith: 'I am born to gretter thynges than to be thral to my

214 Because a man has offended his Lord.
222-3 But let him take care that such remembrance does not give him any pleasure at all.
228-9 'Remember therefore from whence thou art fallen.' (Rev. ii. 5.)
231-4 You have become enslaved, and filthy, and members of Satan ... everlasting material for the fire of hell.

body, or than for to maken of my body a thral.' Ne a fouler thral may no man ne womman maken of his body than for to yeven [*give*] his body to synne. Al [*although*] were it the fouleste cherl or the fouleste womman that lyveth, and leest of value, yet is he thanne moore foul and moore in servitute 260 [*servitude*]. Evere fro the hyer degree that man falleth, the moore is he thral, and moore to God and to the world vile and abhomynable. O goode God, wel oghte man have desdayn of synne, sith that thurgh [*since through*] synne, ther [*whereas*] he was free, now is he maked bonde. And therfore seyth Seint Augustyn: 'If thou hast desdayn of thy servant, if he agilte [*offend*] or synne, have thou thanne desdayn that thou thyself sholdest do synne.' Tak reward of thy value, that thou ne be to foul to thyself. Allas! wel oghten they thanne have desdayn to been servauntz and thralles to synne, and 270 soore [*bitterly*] been ashamed of hemself, that God of his endelees goodnesse hath set hem in heigh [*high*] estaat, or yeven [*given*] hem wit, strengthe of body, heele [*health*], beautee, prosperitee, and boghte [*redeemed*] hem fro the deeth with his herte-blood, that they so unkyndely, agayns his gentilesse, quiten hym so vileynsly to slaughtre of hir owene soules. O goode God, ye wommen that been of so greet beautee, remembreth yow of the proverbe of Salomon. He seith: 'Likneth a fair womman that is a fool of hire body lyk to a ryng of gold that were in the groyn [*snout*] of a soughe 280 [*sow*].' For right as a soughe wroteth in everich ordure, so wroteth she hire beautee in the stynkynge ordure of synne.

The thridde cause that oghte moeve a man to Contricioun is drede of the day of doom and of the horrible peynes of helle. For, as Seint Jerome seith, 'At every tyme that me remembreth of the day of doom I quake [*tremble*]; for whan I ete or drynke, or what so that I do, evere semeth me that the trompe sowneth [*trumpet sounds*] in myn ere: "Riseth up, ye that been dede, and cometh to the juggement."' O goode God, muchel oghte a man to drede swich a juggement, 'ther as [*where*] we shullen 290 been alle,' as Seint Poul seith, 'biforn the seete [*seat*] of oure Lord Jhesu Crist;' whereas [*where*] he shal make a general congregacioun, whereas no man may been absent. For certes there availleth noon essoyne [*excuse*] ne excusacioun [*plea*]. And nat oonly that oure defautes shullen be jugged, but eek that alle oure werkes shullen openly be

255-6 Nor can a man or woman make a fouler slave.
267 Have regard for your own worth.
268-9 With good reason then should they disdain to be servants.
274-6 That they so unnaturally, in return for His noble goodness, repay Him so evilly as to slaughter their own souls.
280 Roots in every sort of filth.
294-6 And not only shall our faults be judged, but also all our works shall openly be known.

knowe. And, as seith Seint Bernard, 'Ther ne shal no
pledynge availle, ne no sleighte [*trickery*]; we shullen yeven
rekenynge of everich [*every*] ydel word.' Ther shul we
han a juge that may nat been deceyved ne corrupt [*corrupted*].
300 And why? For, certes, alle oure thoghtes been discovered
[*revealed*] as to hym; ne for preyere ne for meede [*bribe*]
he shal nat been corrupt. And therfore seith Salomon,
'The wratthe of God ne wol nat spare no wight [*person*],
for preyere ne for yifte'; and therfore, at the day of doom,
ther nys noon [*is not any*] hope to escape. Wherfore, as
seith Seint Anselm, 'Ful greet angwyssh shul the synful
folk have at that tyme; ther shal the stierne and wrothe
juge sitte above, and under hym the horrible pit of helle open
to destroyen hym that moot biknowen [*must acknowledge*] his
310 synnes, whiche synnes openly been shewed biforn God and
biforn every creature; and in [*on*] the left syde mo [*more*]
develes than herte may bithynke [*imagine*], for to harye
[*harry*] and drawe the synful soules to the peyne of helle; and
withinne the hertes of folk shal be the bitynge conscience, and
withoute forth shal be the world al brennynge. Whider shal
thanne the wrecched synful man flee to hiden hym? Certes,
he may nat hyden hym; he moste come forth and shewen hym.'
For certes, as seith Seint Jerome, 'the erthe shal casten hym
out of hym, and the see also, and the eyr [*air*] also, that shal
320 be ful of thonder-clappes and lightnynges.' Now soothly,
whoso wel remembreth hym of thise thynges, I gesse that his
synne shal nat turne hym into delit, but to greet sorwe, for
drede of the peyne of helle. And therfore seith Job to God:
'Suffre, Lord, that I may a while biwaille and wepe, er I go
withoute returnyng to the derke lond, covered with the derknesse of deeth; to the lond of mysese [*misery*] and of derknesse, whereas is the shadwe of deeth; whereas ther is noon
ordre or ordinaunce [*rule*], but grisly drede that evere shal
laste.' Loo, heere may ye seen that Job preyde respit a while,
330 to biwepe [*weep for*] and waille [*bewail*] his trespas; for soothly
oo day of respit is bettre than al the tresor of this world. And
forasmuche as a man may acquiten hymself biforn God by
penitence in this world, and nat by tresor, therfore sholde he
preye to God to yeve hym respit a while to biwepe and biwaillen his trespas. For certes, al the sorwe that a man
myghte make fro the bigynnyng of the world nys but a litel
thyng at regard of the sorwe of helle. The cause why that
Job clepeth helle the lond of derknesse; understondeth that he
clepeth it 'lond' or erthe, for it is stable, and nevere shal faille;

---

315 Outside shall be a world all in flames.
321-2 I don't think his sin will be any joy to him, but a great sorrow.
329 Job prayed for a short respite.
336-7 Is but a small thing by comparison with the sorrow of hell

340 'derk,' for he that is in helle hath defaute of light material.
    For certes, the derke light that shal come out of the fyr that
    evere shal brenne, shal turne hym al to peyne that is in helle;
    for it sheweth him to the horrible develes that hym tormenten.
    'Covered with the derknesse of deeth,' that is to seyn, that
    he that is in helle shal have defaute of the sighte of God; for
    certes, the sighte of God is the lyf perdurable [everlasting].
    'The derknesse of deeth' been the synnes that the wrecched
    man hath doon, whiche that destourben [prevent] hym to see
    [from seeing] the face of God, right as dooth a derk clowde
350 bitwixe us and the sonne.   'Lond of misese,' by cause that
    ther been three maneres of defautes, agayn three thynges that
    folk of this world han [have] in this present lyf, that is to seyn,
    honours, delices [pleasures], and richesses [riches].   Agayns
    honour, have they in helle shame and confusioun.   For wel
    ye woot that men clepen honour the reverence that man doth
    to man; but in helle is noon honour ne reverence.   For certes,
    namoore reverence shal be doon there to a kyng than to a
    knave [low-born man].   For which God seith by the prophete
    Jeremye, 'Thilke [those] folk that me despisen shul been in
360 despit [contempt].'   Honour is eek cleped greet lordshipe; ther
    shal no wight serven other, but of harm and torment.   Honour
    is eek cleped greet dignytee and heighnesse [high rank], but in
    helle shul they been al fortroden of [trampled on by] develes.
    And God seith, 'The horrible develes shulle goon and comen
    upon the hevedes [heads] of the dampned [damned] folk.'   And
    this is for as muche as the hyer that they were in this present
    lyf, the moore shulle they been abated and defouled in helle.
    Agayns the richesse of this world shul they han mysese
    [misery] of poverte, and this poverte shal been in foure thynges:
370 In defaute [lack] of tresor, of which that David seith, 'The
    riche folk, that embraceden and oneden al hire herte to tresor
    of this world, shul slepe in the slepynge of deeth; and nothyng
    ne shal they fynden in hir handes of al hir tresor.'   And
    mooreover the myseyse of helle shal been in defaute of mete
    and drinke.   For God seith thus by Moyses: 'They shul been
    wasted with hunger, and the briddes [birds] of helle shul
    devouren hem with bitter deeth, and the galle of the dragon
    shal been hire drynke, and the venym of the dragon hire
    morsels [portions to eat].'   And forther over [furthermore],
380 hire myseyse shal been in defaute of clothyng; for they shulle

340 Lack of material light.
342 Shall all turn to pain for him who is in hell.
351 Three kinds of deprivations, as opposed to three things.
360-1 There no man shall serve another, except with harm and torment.
366-7 And this is as good as saying that the higher . . . the more they
    shall be degraded and trampled down in hell.
371-2 Whose heart embraced and wedded itself to the wealth of this
    world.

be naked in body as of clothyng, save the fyr in which they
brenne [*burn*], and othere filthes; and naked shul they been of
soule, as of alle manere vertues, which that is the clothyng of
the soule.　Where been thanne [*then*] the gaye robes, and the
softe shetes [*sheets*], and the smale [*fine*] shertes?　Loo, what
seith God of hem by the prophete Ysaye: that 'under hem
shul been strawed [*strewn*] motthes, and hire covertures shulle
been of wormes of helle.'　And forther over, hir myseyse shal
been in defaute of freendes.　For he nys nat povre [*poor*]
390　that hath goode freendes; but there is no frend, for neither
God ne no creature shal been freend to hem, and everich of
hem shal haten oother with deedly hate.　'The sones and the
doghtren shullen rebellen agayns fader and mooder, and
kynrede agayns kynrede, and chiden and despisen everich of
hem oother [*each other*] bothe day and nyght,' as God seith by
the prophete Michias.　And the lovynge children, that whilom
[*once*] loveden so flesshly [*carnally*] everich oother, wolden
everich of hem eten oother if they myghte.　For how sholden
they love hem togidre in the peyne of helle, whan they hated
400　everich of hem oother in the prosperitee of this lyf?　For
truste wel, hir flesshly love was deedly hate, as seith the
prophete David: 'Whoso that [*whoever*] loveth wikkednesse,
he hateth his soule.'　And whoso hateth his owene soule,
certes, he may love noon oother wight [*person*] in no manere.
And therfore, in helle is no solas ne no freendshipe, but evere
the moore flesshly kynredes that been in helle, the moore
cursynges, the more chidynges, and the moore deedly hate
ther is among hem.　And forther over, they shul have
defaute of alle manere delices [*pleasures*].　For certes, delices
410　been after the appetites of the fyve wittes, as sighte, herynge,
smellynge, savorynge [*taste*], and touchynge.　But in helle
hir sighte shal be ful of derknesse and of smoke, and therfore
ful of teeres; and hir herynge ful of waymentynge [*lamentation*]
and of gryntynge [*gnashing*] of teeth, as seith Jhesu Crist.
Hir nose-thirles [*nostrils*] shullen be ful of stynkynge stynk;
and, as seith Ysaye the prophete, 'hir savoryng shal be ful of
bitter galle'; and touchynge of al hir body ycovered with 'fir
that nevere shal quenche [*be quenched*], and with wormes that
nevere shul dyen,' as God seith by the mouth of Ysaye.
420　And for as muche as they shul nat wene [*imagine*] that they
may dyen for peyne, and by hir deeth flee fro peyne, that may
they understonden by the word of Job, that seith, 'ther as is
the shadwe of deeth.'　Certes, a shadwe hath the liknesse of

386–8　Isa. xiv. 11.
398–9　For how should they love each other.
406　But the more fleshly kindred that are together in hell.
409–10　For certainly, pleasures answer to the appetites of the five senses.
417　And their bodily touch.
422–3　In that place is the shadow of death.

the thyng of which it is shadwe, but shadwe is nat the same
thyng of which it is shadwe.   Right so fareth the peyne of
helle; it is lyk deeth for the horrible angwissh, and why?   For
it peyneth hem evere, as though they sholde dye anon; but
certes, they shal nat dye.   For, as seith Seint Gregorie, 'To
wrecche caytyves [*miserable wretches*] shal be deeth withoute
430 deeth, and ende withouten ende, and defaute withoute failynge.
For hir deeth shal alwey lyven, and hir ende shal everemo
[*evermore*] bigynne, and hir defaute shal nat faille.'   And
therfore seith Seint John the Evaungelist: 'They shullen folwe
deeth, and they shul nat fynde hym; and they shul desiren to
dye, and deeth shal flee fro hem.'   And eek Job seith that in
helle is noon ordre of rule.   And al be it so that [*although*]
God hath creat [*created*] alle thynges in right ordre, and no
thyng withouten ordre, but alle thynges been ordeyned and
nombred [*numbered*]; yet, nathelees, they that been dampned
440 been nothyng in ordre, ne holden noon ordre.   For the erthe
ne shal bere hem no fruyt.   For as the prophete David seith,
'God shal destroie the fruyt of the erthe as fro hem; ne water
ne shal yeve hem no moisture, ne the eyr [*air*] no refresshyng,
ne fyr no light.'   For, as seith Seint Basilie, 'The brennynge
[*burning*] of the fyr of this world shal God yeven in helle to
hem that been dampned, but the light and the cleernesse
[*brightness*] shal be yeven in hevene to his children'; right as
the goode man yeveth flessh to his children and bones to his
houndes.   And for they shullen have noon hope to escape,
450 seith Seint Job atte laste that 'ther shal horrour and grisly
drede [*fear*] dwellen withouten ende.'   Horrour is alwey drede
of harm that is to come, and this drede shal evere dwelle in
the hertes of hem that been dampned.   And therfore han
they lorn [*lost*] al hire hope, for sevene causes.   First, for
God, that is hir juge, shal be withouten mercy to hem; and
they may nat plese hym ne noon of his halwes [*saints*]; ne they
ne may yeve no thyng for hir raunsoun; ne they have no voys
to speke to hym; ne they may nat fle fro peyne; ne they have
no goodnesse in hem, that they mowe [*can*] shewe to delivere
460 hem fro peyne.   And therfore seith Salomon: 'The wikked
man dyeth, and whan he is deed, he shal have noon hope to
escape fro peyne.'   Whoso thanne wolde wel understande thise
peynes, and bithynke hym weel [*consider well*] that he hath
deserved thilke [*those*] peynes for his synnes, certes, he sholde
have moore talent [*desire*] to siken [*sigh*] and to wepe, than for
to syngen and to pleye.   For, as that seith Salomon, 'Whoso
that hadde the science to knowe the peynes that been establissed and ordeyned for synne, he wolde make sorwe.'   'Thilke

425-6 Just so it is with the torment of hell.
430 And a want that shall never cease.
440 Are in no kind of order, nor is any order acceptable to them.
450 St Job declares finally.

science,' as seith Seint Augustyn, 'maketh a man to waymenten
470 [*lament*] in his herte.'

The fourthe point that oghte maken a man to have contricion is the sorweful remembraunce of the good that he hath
left [*omitted*] to doon heere in erthe, and eek the good that he
hath lorn. Soothly, the goode werkes that he hath lost,
outher they been the goode werkes that he wroghte er [*before*]
he fel into deedly synne, or elles the goode werkes that he
wroghte while he lay in synne. Soothly, the goode werkes that
he dide biforn that he fil [*fell*] in synne been al mortefied and
astoned and dulled by the ofte synnyng. The othere goode
480 werkes, that he wroghte whil he lay in deedly synne, thei been
outrely dede, as to the lyf perdurable in hevene. Thanne
thilke goode werkes that been mortefied by ofte synnyng,
whiche goode werkes he dide whil he was in charitee, ne mowe
[*can*] nevere quyken [*come alive*] agayn withouten verray
penitence. And therof seith God by the mouth of Ezechiel,
that 'if the rightful man returne agayn from [*go back on*] his
rightwisnesse and werke wikkednesse, shal he lyve?' Nay,
for all the goode werkes that he hath wroght ne shul nevere
been in remembraunce, for he shal dyen in his synne. And
490 upon thilke chapitre [*subject*] seith Seint Gregorie thus: that
'we shulle understonde this principally; that whan we doon
deedly synne, it is for noght [*nothing*] thanne to rehercen or
drawen into memorie the goode werkes that we han wroght
biforn.' For certes, in the werkynge of the deedly synne, ther
is no trust to no good werk that we han doon biforn; that is
to seyn, as for to have therby the lyf perdurable in hevene.
But nathelees, the goode werkes quyken agayn, and comen
agayn, and helpen, and availlen to have the lyf perdurable in
hevene, whan we han contricoun. But soothly, the goode
500 werkes that men doon whil they been in deedly synne, for as
muche as they were doon in deedly synne, they may nevere
quyke agayn. For certes, thyng that nevere hadde lyf may
nevere quykene; and nathelees, al be it that they ne availle
noght to han the lyf perdurable, yet availlen they to abregge
of the peyne of helle, or elles to geten temporal richesse, or
elles that God wole the rather enlumyne and lightne the herte
of the synful man to have repentaunce; and eek they availlen
for to usen [*accustom*] a man to doon goode werkes, that the

478–9 Mortified and paralysed and stultified by frequent sinning.
481 Utterly dead, as regards the eternal life in heaven.
483 While he was in the Christian state of charity.
494–5 For certainly, having done deadly sin, we can put no trust in any
good work we did before.
503–7 Although they are of no help in gaining the eternal life, yet they
do help to shorten the torments of hell, or to get temporal wealth,
or else through them God will the sooner illumine the heart of the
sinful man and light his way to repentance.

feend have the lasse [*less*] power of his soule. And thus the
510 curteis Lord Jhesu Crist ne wole that no good werk be lost;
for in somewhat [*some degree*] it shal availle. But, for as
muche as the goode werkes that men doon whil they been in
good lyf been al mortefied by synne folwynge, and eek sith
that [*also since*] alle the goode werkes that men doon whil
they been in deedly synne been outrely dede as for to have
the lyf perdurable; wel may that man that no good werk ne
dooth [*does*] synge thilke newe Frenshe song, '*Jay tout perdu
mon temps et mon labour.*' For certes, synne bireveth [*deprives*]
a man bothe goodnesse of nature and eek the goodnesse of
520 grace. For soothly, the grace of the Hooly Goost fareth
[*behaves*] lyk fyr, that may nat been ydel; for fyr fayleth anoon
as it forleteth his wirkynge, and right so grace fayleth anoon
as it forleteth his werkynge. Then leseth [*loses*] the synful man
the goodnesse of glorie, that oonly is bihight [*promised*] to
goode men that labouren and werken. Wel may he be sory
thanne, that oweth al his lif to God as longe as he hath lyved,
and eek as longe as he shal lyve, that no goodnesse ne hath
to paye with his dette to God to whom he oweth al his lyf.
For trust wel, 'he shal yeven acountes [*give account*],' as seith
530 Seint Bernard, 'of alle the goodes that han be yeven hym in
this present lyf, and how he hath hem despended [*spent*]; in
so muche that ther shal nat perisse [*perish*] an heer of his heed,
ne a moment of an houre ne shal nat perisse of his tyme, that
he ne shal yeve of it a rekenyng.'

The fifthe thyng that oghte moeve [*move*] a man to contricioun
is remembrance of the passioun that oure Lord Jhesu Crist
suffred for oure synnes. For, as seith Seint Bernard, 'Whil
that I lyve I shal have remembrance of the travailles [*hardships*] that oure Lord Crist suffred in prechyng; his werynesse
540 in travaillyng [*toiling*], his temptaciouns whan he fasted, his
longe wakynges [*vigils*] whan he preyde, hise teeres whan
that he weep [*wept*] for pitee of good peple; the wo and the
shame and the filthe that men seyden to hym; of the foule
spittyng that men spitte in his face, of the buffettes that men
yaven [*gave*] hym, of the foule mowes [*grimaces*], and of the
repreves [*insults*] that men to hym seyden; of the nayles with
which he was nayled to the croys, and of al the remenant
[*rest*] of his passioun that he suffred for my synnes, and no
thyng [*not at all*] for his gilt.' And ye shul understonde that
550 in mannes synne is every manere of ordre or ordinaunce
turned up-so-doun [*upside-down*]. For it is sooth that God,
and resoun, and sensualitee, and the body of man been so
ordeyned that everich [*each*] of thise foure thynges sholde

517–18 These French words are used by Chaucer in his ballade on
Fortune.
521–2 For fire goes out as soon as it ceases to be active.
528 To pay his debt with to God.

have lordshipe over that oother; as thus : God sholde have
lordshipe over resoun, and resoun over sensualitee, and
sensualitee over the body of man.   But soothly, whan man
synneth, al this ordre or ordinaunce is turned up-so-doun.
And therfore, thanne, for as muche as the resoun of man ne
wol nat be subget [*subject*] ne obeisant [*obedient*] to God, that
560 is his lord by right, therfore leseth [*loses*] it the lordshipe that
it sholde have over sensualitee, and eek over the body of man.
And why?   For sensualitee rebelleth thanne agayns resoun,
and by that wey leseth resoun the lordshipe over sensualitee
and over the body.   For right as resoun is rebel to God,
right so is bothe sensualitee rebel to resoun and the body also.
And certes this disordinaunce [*disorder*] and this rebellioun
oure Lord Jhesu Crist aboghte [*atoned for*] upon his precious
body ful deere, and herkneth in which wise [*what manner*].
For as muche thanne as resoun is rebel to God, therfore is
570 man worthy to have sorwe and to be deed [*to die*].   This
suffred oure Lord Jhesu Crist for man, after that he hadde be
bitraysed of [*betrayed by*] of his disciple, and distreyned
[*seized*] and bounde, so that his blood brast [*burst*] out at
every nayl of his handes, as seith Seint Augustyn.   And
forther over, for as muchel as resoun of man ne wol nat
daunte [*subdue*] sensualitee whan it may, therfore is man
worthy to have shame; and this suffred oure Lord Jhesu Crist
for man, whan they spetten [*spat*] in his visage.   And forther
over, for as muchel thanne as the caytyf body of man is rebel
580 bothe to resoun and to sensualitee, therfore is it worthy the
deeth.   And this suffred oure Lord Jhesu Crist for man upon
the croys [*cross*], where as ther was no part of his body free
withouten [*from*] greet peyne and bitter passioun.   And al
this suffred Jhesu Crist, that nevere forfeted [*did wrong*].   And
therfore resonably may be seyd of [*by*] Jhesu in this manere:
'To muchel am I peyned for the thynges that I nevere deserved,
and to muche defouled [*maltreated*] for shendshipe [*shame*]
that man is worthy to have.'   And therfore may the synful
man wel seye, as seith Seint Bernard, 'Acursed be the bitter-
590 nesse of my synne, for which ther moste be suffred so muchel
bitternesse.'   For certes, after the diverse disordinaunces of
oure wikkednesses was the passioun of Jhesu Crist ordeyned
in diverse thynges, as thus.   Certes, synful mannes soule is
bitraysed of the devel by coveitise of temporeel prosperitee,
and scorned by deceite whan he cheseth [*chooses*] flesshly
delices [*delights*]; and yet is it tormented by inpacience [*im-*

565 In just the same way is sensuality rebellious both to reason and the
     body.
591–2 For certainly, in a manner answering to the various disorders of
     our wickedness.
594–8 Betrayed by the devil through its coveting of temporal prosperity
     . . . and spat upon by servitude and subjection to sin.

patience] of adversitee, and bispet by servage and subjeccioun of synne; and atte laste it is slayn fynally. For this dis-ordinaunce [*disorder*] of synful man was Jhesu Crist first
600 bitraysed, and after that was he bounde, that cam for to unbynden us of [*from*] synne and peyne. Thanne was he byscorned [*scorned*], that oonly sholde han been honoured in alle thynges and of [*by*] alle thynges. Thanne was his visage, that oghte be desired to be seyn of [*seen by*] al mankynde, in [*on*] which visage aungels desiren to looke, vileynsly bispet [*vilely spat upon*]. Thanne was he scourged, that no thyng hadde agilt [*had not sinned at all*]; and finally, thanne was he crucified and slayn. Thanne was acompliced the word of Ysaye, 'He was wounded for oure mysdedes and defouled
610 [*maltreated*] for oure felonies.' Now sith that Jhesu Crist took upon hymself the peyne of alle oure wikkednesses, muchel oghte synful man wepen and biwayle, that for his synnes Goddes sone of hevene sholde al this peyne endure.

The sixte thyng that oghte moeve a man to contricioun is the hope of three thynges; that is to seyn, foryifnesse of synne, and the yifte of grace wel for to do, and the glorie of hevene, with which God shal gerdone [*reward*] man for his goode dedes. And for as muche as Jhesu Crist yeveth us thise yiftes of his largesse [*generosity*] and of his sovereyn bountee
620 [*goodness*], therfore is he cleped [*named*] *Jhesus Nazarenus rex Judeorum*. *Jhesus* is to seyn [*signifies*] 'saveour' or 'sal-vacioun,' on whom men shul hope to have foryifnesse of synnes, which that is proprely salvacioun of [*from*] synnes. And therfore seyde the aungel to Joseph, 'Thou shalt clepen his name Jhesus, that shal saven his peple of hir synnes.' And heerof seith Seint Peter: 'Ther is noon oother name under hevene that is yeve [*given*] to any man, by which a man may be saved, but oonly Jhesus.' *Nazarenus* is as muche for to seye as 'florisshynge [*flourishing*],' in which a man shal hope
630 that he that yeveth hym remissioun of synnes shal yeve hym eek grace wel for to do. For in the flour [*flower*] is hope of fruyt in tyme comynge, and in foryifnesse of synnes hope of grace wel for to do. 'I was atte dore [*at the door*] of thyn herte,' seith Jhesus, 'and cleped [*called*] for to entre. He that openeth to me shal have foryifnesse of synne. I wol entre into hym by my grace, and soupe [*sup*] with hym,' by the goode werkes that he shal doon, whiche werkes been the foode of God; 'and he shal soupe with me,' by the grete joye that I shal yeven hym. Thus shal man hope, for his werkes of
640 penaunce, that God shal yeven hym his regne [*kingdom*], as he bihooteth [*promises*] hym in the gospel.

Now shal a man understonde in which manere shal been his contricioun. I seye that it shal been universal and total.

613 The Son of God of heaven.

This is to seyn, a man shal be verray [*truly*] repentaunt for alle his synnes that he hath doon in delit of his thoght; for delit is ful perilous. For ther been two manere of consentynges: that oon of hem is cleped consentynge of affeccioun [*feeling*], whan a man is moeved to do synne, and deliteth hym longe for to thynke on that synne; and his reson aper-
650 ceyveth it wel that it is synne agayns the lawe of God, and yet his resoun refreyneth [*curbs*] nat his foul delit or talent [*desire*], though he se wel apertly that it is agayns the reverence of God. Although his resoun ne consente noght to doon that synne in dede, yet seyn somme doctours [*learned men*] that swich delit that dwelleth longe, it is ful perilous, al be it nevere so lite [*little*]. And also a man sholde sorwe namely [*especially*] for al that evere he hath desired agayn the law of God with perfit [*full*] consentynge of his resoun; for therof is no doute, that it is deedly synne in consentynge. For certes,
660 ther is no deedly synne, that it nas [*was not*] first in mannes thought, and after that in his delit, and so forth into consentynge and into dede. Wherfore I seye that many men ne repenten hem nevere of swiche thoghtes and delites, ne nevere shryven [*shrive*] hem of it, but oonly of the dede of grete synnes outward [*external*]. Wherfore I seye that swiche wikked delites and wikked thoghtes been subtile bigileres [*deceivers*] of hem that shullen be dampned. Mooreover man oghte to sorwe for his wikkede wordes as wel as for his wikkede dedes. For certes, the repentaunce of a synguler
670 [*particular*] synne, and nat repente [*to repent*] of alle his othere synnes, or elles repenten hym of alle his othere synnes, and nat of a synguler synne, may nat availle. For certes, God almyghty is al [*wholly*] good; and therfore he foryeveth al, or elles right noght [*nothing at all*]. And heerof seith Seint Augustyn: 'I wot certeynly that God is enemy to everich [*every*] synnere'; and how thanne, he that observeth o synne, shal he have foryifnesse of the remenaunt of his othere synnes? Nay. And forther over, contricioun sholde be wonder sorweful and angwissous; and therfor yeveth hym God
680 pleynly his mercy; and therfore, whan my soule was angwissous withinne me, I hadde remembrance of God that my preyere myghte come to hym. Further over, contricioun moste be continueel [*continuous*], and that man have stedefast purpos

644-5 For all the sins he has committed in pleasurable anticipation.
646-9 There are two kinds of consent . . . and long delights to think of that sin.
652-3 Though he sees quite clearly that it is against the reverence due to God.
658-9 For there can be no doubt that there is deadly sin in such consent.
676-7 How then shall he who pays heed to only one of his sins have forgiveness for the rest of his sins?
678-9 Exceedingly sorrowful and full of anguish.
683 And a man should have the steadfast purpose.

to shriven hym [*himself*], and for to amenden hym of [*improve*]
his lyf.   For soothly, whil contricioun lasteth, man may evere
have hope of foryifnesse; and of this comth hate of synne,
that destroyeth synne, bothe in himself, and eek in oother
folk, at his power.   For which seith David: 'Ye that loven
God, hateth wikkednesse.'   For trusteth wel, to love God is
690 for to love that he loveth, and hate that he hateth.
    The laste thyng that men shal understonde in contricioun
is this: wherof avayleth contricioun.   I seye that somtyme
contricioun delivereth a man fro synne; of which that David
seith, 'I seye,' quod David (that is to seyn, I purposed fermely)
'to shryve me, and thow, Lord, relessedest [*forgave*] my synne.'
And right so as contricion availleth noght withouten sad
purpos of shrifte, if man have oportunitee, right so litel worth
is shrifte or satisfaccioun withouten contricioun.   And mooreover contricion destroyeth the prisoun of helle, and maketh
700 wayk [*weak*] and fieble [*feeble*] alle the strengthes of the
develes, and restoreth the yiftes [*gifts*] of the Hooly Goost and
of alle goode vertues; and it clenseth the soule of synne, and
delivereth the soule fro the peyne of helle, and fro the compaignye of the devel, and fro the servage [*slavery*] of synne,
and restoreth it to alle goodes espirituels [*spiritual good*], and
to the compaignye and communyoun of hooly chirche.   And
forther over, it maketh hym that whilom [*once*] was sone of
ire [*a child of wrath*] to be sone of grace; and alle thise thynges
been preved [*proved*] by hooly writ.   And therfore, he that
710 wolde sette his entente [*mind*] to thise thynges, he were ful
wys [*wise*]; for soothly he ne sholde nat thanne in al his lyf
have corage [*inclination*] to synne, but yeven his body and al
his herte to the service of Jhesu Crist, and therof doon hym
hommage.   For soothly oure sweete Lord Jhesu Crist hath
spared us so debonairly [*graciously*] in oure folies, that if
he ne hadde pitee of [*on*] mannes soule, a sory song we mygthen
alle synge.

ET SEQUITUR SECUNDA PARS EIUSDEM

EXPLICIT PRIMA PARS PENITENTIE

    The seconde partie of Penitence is Confessioun, that is
signe of contricioun.   Now shul ye understonde what is
720 Confessioun, and wheither it oghte nedes be doon or noon
[*not*], and whiche thynges been covenable [*proper*] to verray
Confessioun.

688 *at his power*, with all his might.
692 What contrition is useful for.
696–7 Without the firm intention of being shriven.
713–14 And in that way do Him homage.

First shaltow understonde that Confessioun is verray shewynge of synnes to the preest. This is to seyn 'verray,' for he moste confessen hym of alle the condiciouns that bilongen to his synne, as ferforth as he kan. Al moot [*must*] be seyd, and no thyng excused ne hyd ne forwrapped [*wrapped up*], and noght avaunte thee of thy goode werkes. And forther over [*furthermore*], it is necessarie to understonde
730 whennes [*whence*] that synnes spryngen, and how they encreessen [*increase*] and whiche [*what*] they been.

Of the spryngynge [*beginning*] of synnes seith Seint Paul in this wise: that 'right as by a man synne entred first into this world, and thurgh that synne deeth, right so thilke deeth entred into alle men that synneden.' And this man was Adam, by whom synne entred into this world, whan he brak [*broke*] the comaundementz of God. And therfore, he that first was so myghty that he sholde nat have dyed, bicam swich oon [*such a one*] that he moste nedes dye, wheither he wolde or
740 noon [*no*], and al his progenye in this world, that in thilke man synneden. Looke that [*see how*] in th'estaat [*state*] of innocence, whan Adam and Eve naked weren in Paradys, and nothyng ne hadden shame of hir nakednesse, how that the serpent, that was moost wily of alle othere beestes that God hadde maked, seyde to the womman: 'Why comaunded God to yow ye sholde nat eten of every tree in Paradys?' The womman answerde: 'Of the fruyt,' quod she, 'of the trees in Paradys we feden us, but soothly, of the fruyt of the tree that is in the myddel of Paradys, God forbad us for to ete, ne nat
750 touchen it, lest per aventure [*perhaps*] we sholde dyen.' The serpent seyde to the womman: 'Nay, nay, ye shul nat dyen of deeth; for sothe, God woot that what day that ye eten therof, youre eyen [*eyes*] shul opene, and ye shul been as goddes, knowynge good and harm [*evil*].' The womman thanne saugh [*saw*] that the tree was good to feedyng, and fair to the eyen, and delitable [*delightful*] to the sighte. She took of the fruyt of the tree, and eet [*ate*] it, and yaf [*gave*] to hire housbonde, and he eet, and anoon the eyen of hem bothe openeden. And whan that they knewe that they were naked,
760 they sowed of fige leves a maner of breches to hiden hire

724–6 'True,' that is to say, because a man must confess all the circumstances of his sin, as far as he can.
728 And do not boast of your good works.
734–5 And through that sin came death, just so death entered into all men that sinned.
740–1 And all his progeny in this world (must also die), who sinned through that man (i.e. Adam).
742–3 And had no shame at all of their nakedness.
751–3 You shall not suffer death; for truly, God knows that on the day that you eat thereof,
755 Good for eating.
760 They sewed fig leves together and made themselves breeches of a sort.

membres. There may ye seen that deedly synne hath first suggestion of the feend, as sheweth heere by the naddre; and afterward, the delit of the flessh, as sheweth heere by Eve; and after that, the consentynge of resoun, as sheweth heere by Adam. For trust wel, though so were that the feend tempted Eve, that is to seyn, the flessh, and the flessh hadde delit in the beautee of the fruyt defended [*forbidden*], yet certes, til that resoun, that is to seyn, Adam, consented to the etynge of the fruyt, yet [*still*] stood he in th'estaat of innocence.
770 Of [*from*] thilke Adam tooke we thilke synne original; for of hym flesshly [*physically*] descended be we alle, and engendred of vile and corrupt mateere [*matter*]. And whan the soule is put in oure body, right anon is contract [*contracted*] original synne; and that that was erst but oonly peyne of concupiscence, is afterward bothe peyne and synne. And therfore be we alle born sones of wratthe and of dampnacioun perdurable [*eternal*], if it nere baptesme that we receyven, which bynymeth us the culpe. But for sothe, the peyne dwelleth with us, as to temptacioun, which peyne highte concupiscence.
780 And this concupiscence, whan it is wrongfully disposed or ordeyned [*ordered*] in man, it maketh hym coveite, by coveitise [*covetousness*] of flessh, flesshly synne, by sighte of his eyen as to erthely thynges, and eek coveitise of hynesse by pride of herte.

Now, as for to speken of the firste coveitise, that is concupiscence, after [*according to*] the lawe of oure membres, that weren lawefulliche ymaked and by rightful juggement of God; I seye, forasmuche as man is nat obeisaunt [*obedient*] to God, that is his lord, therfore is the flessh to hym dis-
790 obeisaunt thurgh concupiscence, which yet is cleped norrissynge of synne and occasioun of synne. Therfore, al the while that a man hath in hym the peyne of concupiscence, it is impossible but he be tempted somtime and moeved [*moved*] in his flessh to synne. And this thyng may nat faille as longe as he lyveth; it may wel wexe [*grow*] fieble and faille by vertu of baptesme, and by the grace of God thurgh penitence; but fully ne shal it nevere quenche, that he ne shal som tyme be

---

761-3 Deadly sin was first suggested by the devil, as represented here by the serpent; and afterwards by the delight of the flesh.

765-6 Though it was the devil that tempted Eve.

774-5 And that which at first was only the torment of concupiscence is later both torment and sin.

777-9 If it were not for the baptism we receive, which takes the guilt from us. But in truth, the torment stays with us as a temptation, which torment is called concupiscence.

781-4 It makes him covet fleshly sin through fleshly covetousness . . . and also the dignity of rank through pride of heart.

797-9 It shall never be fully extinguished, nor shall he cease to be moved at times to sin, unless he is cooled down by sickness or by some evil act of sorcery.

moeved in hymself, but if he were al refreyded by siknesse, or
by malefice of sorcerie, or colde drynkes. For lo, what seith
800 Seint Paul: 'The flessh coveiteth agayn [*against*] the spirit,
and the spirit agayn the flessh; they been so contrarie and so
stryven that a man may nat alway doon as he wolde.' The
same Seint Paul, after his grete penaunce in water and in
lond,—in water, by nyght and by day in greet peril and in greet
peyne; in lond, in famyne and thurst, in coold and cloothlees
[*without clothes*], and ones [*once*] stoned almoost to the
deeth,—yet seyde he, 'Allas, I caytyf [*wretched*] man! who
shal delivere me fro the prisoun of my caytyf body?' And
Seint Jerome, whan he longe tyme hadde woned [*lived*]
810 in desert, where as he hadde no compaignye but of wilde
beestes, where as he ne hadde no mete [*food*] but herbes, and
water to his drynke, ne no bed but the naked erthe, for which
his flessh was blak as an Ethiopeen for heete, and ny destroyed
for coold, yet seyde he that 'the brennynge [*burning fire*] of
lecherie boyled in al his body.' Wherfore I woot wel sykerly
that they been deceyved that seyn that they ne be nat tempted
in hir body. Witnesse on Seint Jame the Apostel, that seith
that 'every wight is tempted in his owene concupiscence';
that is to seyn, that everich of us hath matere [*cause*] and
820 occasioun to be tempted of [*by*] the norissynge of synne that
is in his body. And therfore seith Seint John the Evaungelist:
'If that we seyn that we be withoute synne, we deceyve us
selve [*ourselves*], and trouthe is nat in us.'

Now shal ye understonde in what manere that synne wexeth
or encreesseth in man. The firste thyng is thilke norissynge
of synne of which I spak biforn, thilke flesshly concupiscence.
And after that comth the subjeccioun [*suggestion*] of the
devel, this is to seyn, the develes bely [*bellows*], with which he
bloweth in man the fir of flesshly concupiscence. And after
830 that, a man bithynketh hym [*considers*] wheither he wol doon,
or no, thilke thing to which he is tempted. And thanne, if
that a man withstonde and weyve [*avoid*] the firste entisynge
of his flessh and of the feend, thanne is it no synne; and if
it so be that he do nat so, thanne feeleth he anoon a flambe
[*flame*] of delit. And thanne is it good to be war, and kepen
hym [*guard himself*] wel, or elles he wol falle anon into consentynge of synne; and thanne wol he do it, if he may have
tyme and place. And of this matere seith Moyses by [*concerning*] the devel in this manere: 'The feend seith, "I wole
840 chace and pursue the man by wikked suggestioun, and I wole
hente [*seize*] hym by moevynge or stirynge of synne. And I
wol departe my prise or my praye by deliberacioun, and my

803-4 On sea and land.
815 Wherefore I know for a certainty.
841-3 And I will single out my prize or my prey with deliberation, and
     my desire shall be accomplished with delight.

lust shal been acompliced in delit.   I wol drawe my swerd in consentynge"—for certes, right as a swerd departeth [*divides*] a thyng in two peces, right so consentynge departeth God fro man—"and thanne wol I sleen [*slay*] hym with myn hand in dede [*act*] of synne"; thus seith the feend.'   For certes, thanne is a man al deed in soule.   And thus is synne acompliced by temptacioun, by delit [*pleasure*], and by consentynge; and
850 thanne is the synne cleped actueel [*called actual*].

For sothe [*in truth*], synne is in two maneres; outher it is venial, or deedly synne.   Soothly, whan man loveth any creature moore than Jhesu Crist oure Creatour, thanne is it deedly synne.   And venial synne is it, if man love Jhesu Crist lasse than hym oghte [*he ought*].   For sothe, the dede of this venial synne is ful perilous; for it amenuseth [*lessens*] the love that men sholde han to God moore and moore.   And therfore, if a man charge [*burden*] hymself with manye swiche venial synnes, certes, but if [*unless*] so be that he somtyme
860 descharge hym [*unburden himself*] of hem by shrifte, they mowe [*may*] ful lightly [*easily*] amenuse in hym al the love that he hath to Jhesu Crist; and in this wise skippeth [*passes quickly*] venial into deedly synne.   For certes, the moore that a man chargeth his soule with venial synnes, the moore is he enclyned to fallen into deedly synne.   And therfore lat us nat be necligent to deschargen us of venial synnes.   For the proverbe seith that 'manye smale maken a greet.'   And herkne this ensample [*illustration*].   A greet wawe [*wave*] of the see comth som tyme with so greet a violence that it drencheth [*swamps*]
870 the ship.   And the same harm doon som tyme the smale dropes of water, that entren thurgh a litel crevace [*crack*] into the thurrok [*hold*], and in the botme of the ship, if men be so necligent that they ne descharge hem nat by tyme.   And therfore, although ther be a difference bitwixe thise two causes of drenchynge, algates [*in any case*] the ship is dreynt [*swamped*].   Right so fareth it somtyme of deedly synne, and of anoyouse [*troublesome*] veniale synnes, whan they multiplie in a man so greetly that the love of thilke [*those*] worldly thynges that he loveth, thurgh whiche he synneth venyally, is as greet in his
880 herte as the love of God, or moore.   And therfore, the love of every thyng that is nat biset [*set*] in God, ne doon principally for Goddes sake, although that a man love it lasse than God, yet is it venial synne; and deedly synne whan the love of any thyng weyeth [*weighs*] in the herte of man as muchel [*much*] as the love of God, or moore.   'Deedly synne,' as seith Seint Augustyn, 'is whan a man turneth his herte fro God, which that is verray sovereyn bountee [*goodness*], that may nat chaunge, and yeveth his herte to thyng that may chaunge and

872–3 If men are so negligent that they do not empty them out in time.
876 Just so it happens sometimes with deadly sin.

flitte [*pass away*].' And certes, that is every thyng save God
890 of hevene. For sooth is that if a man yeve his love, the which
that he oweth al to God with al his herte, unto a creature,
certes, as muche of his love as he yeveth to thilke creature, so
muche he bireveth fro [*takes from*] God; and therfore dooth
he synne. For he that is dettour [*debtor*] to God ne yeldeth
[*pays*] nat to God al his dette, that is to seyn, al the love of his
herte.

Now sith man understondeth generally which [*what*] is
venial synne, thanne is it covenable [*fitting*] to tellen specially
of synnes whiche that many a man peraventure ne demeth
900 hem nat synnes, and ne shryveth him nat of the same thynges,
and yet nathelees they been synnes; soothly, as thise clerkes
[*scholars*] writen, this is to seyn, that at every tyme that a man
eteth or drynketh moore than suffiseth to the sustenaunce of
his body, in certein he dooth synne. And eek whan he
speketh moore than it nedeth, it is synne. Eke whan he
herkneth nat benignely [*kindly*] the compleint of the povre
[*poor*]; eke whan he is in heele [*health*] of body, and wol nat
faste whan other folk faste, withouten cause resonable; eke
whan he slepeth moore than nedeth, or whan he comth by
910 thilke enchesoun [*on that account*] to late to chirche, or to
othere werkes of charite; eke whan he useth his wyf, withouten
sovereyn [*supreme*] desir of engendrure [*procreation*] to the
honour of God, or for the entente to yelde to his wyf the dette
of his body; eke whan he wol nat visite the sike [*sick*] and the
prisoner, if he may; eke if he love wyf or child, or oother
worldly thyng, moore than resoun requireth; eke if he flatere
[*flatters*] or blandise [*fawns*] moore than hym oghte for any
necessitee; eke if he amenuse or withdrawe the almesse of
the povre; eke if he apparailleth [*prepares*] his mete moore
920 deliciously [*luxuriously*] than nede is, or ete it to hastily by
likerousnesse [*through gluttony*]; eke if he tale vanytees at
chirche or at Goddes service, or that he be a talker of ydel
wordes of folye or of vileynye [*evil*], for he shal yelden [*render*]
acountes of it at the day of doom; eke whan he biheteth or
assureth to do thynges that he may nat perfourne; eke whan
that he by lightnesse or folie mysseyeth or scorneth his neighebor; eke whan he hath any wikked suspecioun of thyng ther
he ne woot of it no soothfastnesse: thise thynges, and mo
[*more*] withoute nombre, been synnes, as seith Seint Augustyn.

899–900 Which many a man perhaps does not think of as sins.
913 Or with the intention of paying to his wife.
918–19 Also if he reduces or withholds the alms of the poor.
921–2 Also if he talks about foolish things at church.
924–7 When he promises or gives assurance that he will do things which
  he cannot perform; also when through thoughtlessness or folly he
  slanders or scorns his neighbour.
927–8 Wicked suspicion of something about which he has no certain
  knowledge.

930　Now shal men understonde that, al be it so that [*although*] noon erthely man may eschue alle venial synnes, yet may he refreyne hym [*curb himself*] by the brennynge [*burning*] love that he hath to oure Lord Jhesu Crist, and by preyeres and confessioun and othere goode werkes, so that it shal but litel greve. For, as seith Seint Augustyn, 'If a man love God in swich manere that al that evere he dooth is in the love of God, and for the love of God, verraily, for he brenneth [*because he burns*] in the love of God, looke, how muche that a drope of water that falleth in a fourneys ful of fyr anoyeth or greveth,
940　so muche anoyeth a venial synne unto a man that is perfit in the love of Jhesu Crist.' Men may also refreyne venial synne by receyvynge worthily of the precious body of Jhesu Crist; by receyvynge eek of hooly water; by almesdede [*almsgiving*]; by general confessioun of *Confiteor* at masse and at complyn [*compline*]; and by blessynge of bisshopes and of preestes, and by oothere goode werkes.'

EXPLICIT SECUNDA PARS PENITENTIE

Sequitur de septem peccatis mortalibus et eorum dependenciis, circumstanciis, et speciebus.

Now is it bihovely [*necessary*] thyng to telle whiche been the sevene deedly synnes, this is to seyn, chieftaynes [*chieftains*] of synnes. Alle they renne in o lees, but in diverse maneres.
950　Now been they cleped chieftaynes, for as muche as they been chief and spryng [*source*] of alle othere synnes. Of the roote of this sevene synnes, thanne, is Pride, the general roote of alle harmes. For of this roote spryngen certein braunches, as Ire [*Wrath*], Envye, Accidie or Slewthe [*Sloth*], Avarice or Coveitise [*Covetousness*] (to commune understondynge), Glotonye, and Lecherye. And everich [*every one*] of thise chief synnes hath his [*its*] braunches and his twigges, as shal be declared in hire chapitres folwynge.

De Superbia.

And thogh so be that no man kan outrely telle [*fully count*]
960　the nombre of the twigges and of the harmes that cometh of Pride, yet wol I shewe a partie of hem, as ye shul understonde.

934–5 It shall do but little harm.
938–41 Behold, to the extent that a drop of water falling into a fiery furnace is harmful or troublesome, to the same extent is a venial sin harmful to a man who is perfect in the love of Jesus Christ.
949 They all run on one leash, but in different ways.
951–3 At the root of these seven sins, then, is Pride, the general root of all evils.
958 In the chapters on them that follow.

Ther is Inobedience, Avauntynge, Ypocrisie, Despit, Arrogance, Inpudence, Swellynge of Herte, Insolence, Elacioun, Inpacience, Strif, Contumacie, Presumpcioun, Irreverence, Pertinacie, Veyne Glorie, and many another twig that I kan nat declare. Inobedient is he that disobeyeth for despit to the comandementz of God, and to his sovereyns [*superiors*], and to his goostly [*spiritual*] fader. Avauntour [*boaster*] is he that bosteth of the harm or of the bountee [*good*] that he 970 hath doon. Ypocrite is he that hideth to shewe hym swich as he is, and sheweth hym swich as he noght is. Despitous [*scornful*] is he that hath desdeyn of his neighebor, that is to seyn, of his evene-Cristene [*fellow Christian*], or hath despit to doon that hym oghte to do. Arrogant is he that thynketh that he hath thilke bountees [*good qualities*] in hym that he hath noght, or weneth that he sholde have hem by his desertes, or elles he demeth that he be that he nys nat. Inpudent is he that for his pride hath no shame of his synnes. Swellynge of herte is whan a man rejoyseth hym of harm that he hath doon. 980 Insolent is he that despiseth in his juggement alle othere folk, as to regard of his value, and of his konnyng, and of his spekyng, and of his beryng. Elacioun [*elation*] is whan he ne may neither suffre to have maister ne felawe. Inpacient is he that wol nat been ytaught ne undernome [*reproved*] of his vice, and by strif werreieth trouthe wityngly, and deffendeth his folye. Contumax [*contumacious*] is he that thurgh his indignacioun is agayns everich [*every*] auctoritee or power of hem that been his sovereyns. Presumpcioun is whan a man undertaketh an emprise [*enterprise*] that hym oghte nat do, 990 or elles that he may nat do; and this is called Surquidrie [*arrogance*]. Irreverence is whan men do nat honour there as hem oghte to doon, and waiten [*expect*] to be reverenced. Pertinacie is whan man deffendeth his folie, and trusteth to muchel to his owene wit. Veyneglorie is for to have pompe and delit in his temporeel hynesse, and glorifie hym [*exult*] in this worldly estaat. Janglynge is whan a man speketh to

962–5 Disobedience, Boasting, Hypocrisy, Scorn, Arrogance, Impudence, Swelling of Heart . . . Pertinacity, Vainglory.
970–1 Who hides from sight what he really is, and pretends to be what he is not.
973–4 Or scorns to do what he ought to do.
976–7 Or believes that he deserves to have them, or else imagines that he is something he is not.
981–2 By comparison with his own worth and intelligence, speech and bearing.
982–3 He cannot bear to have a master or an equal.
985 And violently attacks truth with full knowledge of what he is doing.
994–5 Is to parade and delight in one's temporal dignity.
996–8 Babbling is to talk too much before other people, and clack like a mill, and speak heedlessly.

muche biforn folk, and clappeth as a mille, and taketh no keep what he seith.

And yet is ther a privee spece [*secret kind*] of Pride, that
1000 waiteth first to be salewed er he wole salewe, al be he lasse worth than that oother is, peraventure; and eek he waiteth or desireth to sitte, or elles to goon above hym in the wey, or kisse pax, or been encensed, or goon to offryng biforn his neighebor, and swiche semblable thynges, agayns his duetee, peraventure, but that he hath his herte and his entente [*mind*] in swich a proud desir to be magnified and honoured biforn the peple.

Now been ther two maneres [*kinds*] of Pride: that oon [*one*] of hem is withinne the herte of man, and that oother is
1010 withoute [*outside*]. Of whiche, soothly, thise forseyde thynges, and mo than I have seyd, apertenen [*pertain*] to Pride that is in the herte of man; and that othere speces of Pride been withoute. But natheles that oon of thise speces of Pride is signe of that oother, right as the gaye leefsel atte taverne is signe of the wyn that is in the celer [*cellar*]. And this is in manye thynges: as in speche and contenaunce [*behaviour*], and in outrageous array [*display*] of clothyng. For certes, if ther ne hadde be no synne in clothyng, Crist wolde nat so soone have noted and spoken of the clothyng of thilke [*that*]
1020 riche man in the gospel. And, as seith Seint Gregorie, that 'precious clothyng is cowpable for the derthe of it, and for his [*its*] softenesse, and for his strangenesse and degisynesse [*elaborateness*], and for the superfluitee, or for the inordinat scantnesse [*scantiness*] of it.' Allas! may man nat seen, as in oure dayes, the synful costlewe [*costly*] array of clothynge, and namely in to muche superfluite, or elles in to desordinat [*inordinate*] scantnesse?

As to the first synne, that is in superfluitee of clothynge, which that maketh it so deere [*dear*], to harm of the peple;
1030 nat oonly the cost of embrowdynge, the degise endentynge or barrynge, owndynge, palynge, wyndynge or bendynge, and semblable [*similar*] wast of clooth in vanitee; but ther is also costlewe furrynge [*fur trimming*] in hir gownes, so muche

999–1004 That expects to be greeted first before he will offer a greeting, although he is perhaps of less account than the other is; and also he expects or desires to be seated higher at the table, or else to go before the other in a procession, or to be the first to kiss the pax or be censed, or to make an offering before his neighbour, and that sort of thing, against his duty.

1014–15 Just as the leafy arbour in front of a tavern.

1021 Costly clothing is to blame for the dearth of clothing.

1030–1 Not only the cost of embroidery, the elaborate indenting or adorning with bars, wavy patterns, upright stripes, curved or slanting lines.

1033–5 So much punching with chisels to make holes, so much cutting with shears.

pownsonynge of chisels to maken holes, so muche daggynge of
sheres; forth-with [also] the superfluitee in lengthe of the
forseide gownes, trailynge in the dong [dung] and in the mire,
on horse and eek on foote, as wel [both] of man as of womman,
that al thilke trailyng is verraily as in effect wasted, consumed,
thredbare, and roten with donge, rather than it is yeven to the
1040 povre [poor], to greet damage [harm] of the forseyde povre folk.
And that in sondry wise [ways]; this is to seyn that the moore
that clooth is wasted, the moore moot [must] it coste to the
peple for the scarsnesse [scarcity]. And forther over, if so
be that they wolde yeven swich pownsoned [punched] and
dagged [tagged] clothyng to the povre folk, it is nat convenient
to were for hire estaat, ne suffisant to beete [supply] hire
necessitee [needs], to kepe hem fro the distemperance [incle-
mency] of the firmament. Upon that oother side, to speken
of the horrible disordinat scantnesse of clothyng, as been
1050 thise kutted sloppes, or haynselyns, that thurgh hire short-
nesse ne covere nat the shameful membres of man, to wikked
entente. Allas! somme of hem shewen the boce [protuberance]
of hir shap, and the horrible swollen membres, that semeth lik
the maladie of hirnia [hernia], in the wrappynge of hir hoses;
and eek the buttokes of hem faren as it were the hyndre part
of a she-ape in the fulle of the moone. And mooreover, the
wrecched swollen membres that they shewe thurgh disgisynge,
in departynge of hire hoses in whit and reed, semeth that half
hir shameful privee membres weren flayne. And if so be
1060 that they departen hire hoses in othere colours, as is white and
blak, or whit and blew, or blak and reed, and so forth, thanne
semeth it, as by variaunce [difference] of colour, that half the
partie of hire privee membres were corrupt by the fir of seint
Antony, or by cancre [cancer], or by oother swich meschaunce
[affliction]. Of the hyndre part of hir buttokes, it is ful
horrible for to see. For certes, in that partie of hir body ther
as [where] they purgen hir stynkynge ordure, that foule partie
shewe they to the peple prowdly in despit [defiance] of honestitee [decency], which honestitee that Jhesu Crist and his freendes
1070 observede to shewen in hir lyve. Now, as of the outrageous
array [dress] of wommen, God woot that though the visages

1038 So that all the cloth which is trailing is, in effect, wasted.
1045–6 It is not suitable for them to wear in their station of life.
1049–52 Such as these curtailed garments, or short jackets . . . and for
a wicked purpose.
1055–6 Also their buttocks look like the hind quarters of a she-ape when
the moon is full.
1057–9 The wretched swollen members that they show through their
newfangled costume, with their hoses divided into white and red,
make it seem as if half their shameful privy parts have been flayed.
1063–4 fir of seint Antony, St Anthony's fire, i.e. erysipelas.
1070 Were wont to show in their lives.

of somme of hem seme ful chaast and debonaire [*meek*], yet
notifie they in hire array of atyr likerousnesse and pride. I
sey nat that honestitee [*neatness*] in clothynge of man or
womman is uncovenable [*unfitting*], but certes the superfluitee
or disordinat scantitee of clothynge is reprevable [*reprehensible*].   Also the synne of aornement [*adornment*] or of apparaille [*embellishment*] is in thynges that apertenen to ridynge,
as in to manye delicat [*dainty*] horses that been hoolden for
1080 delit [*kept for pleasure*], that been so faire, fatte, and costlewe
[*costly*]; and also in many a vicious knave that is sustened
[*supported*] by cause of hem; and in to curious harneys, as in
sadeles, in crouperes [*cruppers*] peytrels [*breast-pieces*], and
bridles covered with precious clothyng, and riche barres and
plates of gold and of silver.   For which God seith by Zakarie
[*Zechariah*] the prophete, 'I wol confounde the rideres of
swiche horses.'   This folk taken litel reward [*regard*] of the
ridynge of Goddes sone of hevene, and of his harneys whan
he rood upon the asse, and ne hadde noon oother harneys
1090 but the povre clothes of his disciples; ne we ne rede nat [*nor
do we read*] that evere he rood on oother beest.   I speke this
for the synne of superfluitee, and nat for resonable honestitee,
whan reson it requireth.   And forther over, certes, pride is
greetly notified in holdynge [*maintaining*] of greet meynee
[*retinue*], whan they be of litel profit or of right no profit; and
namely whan that meynee is felonous and damageous to the
peple by hardynesse of heigh lordshipe or by wey of offices.
For certes, swiche lordes sellen thanne hir lordshipe to the
devel of helle, whanne they sustenen [*uphold*] the wikkednesse
1100 of hir meynee.   Or elles, whan this folk of lowe degree, as
thilke that holden hostelries [*keep inns*], sustenen the thefte of
hire hostilers [*servants*], and that is in many manere of deceites.
Thilke manere of folk been the flyes that folwen the hony, or
elles the houndes that folwen the careyne [*carrion*].   Swich
forseyde folk stranglen [*strangle*] spiritually hir lordshipes;
for which thus seith David the prophete: 'Wikked deeth moote
come upon thilke lordshipes, and God yeve that they moote
descenden into helle al doun; for in hire houses been iniquitees
and shrewednesses [*wickednesses*], and nat God of hevene.'
1110 And certes, but if they doon amendement, right as God yaf
his benysoun [*blessing*] to [Laban] by the service of Jacob, and
to [Pharao] by the service of Joseph, right so God wol yeve his

---

1072–3 Yet by the manner of their dress they proclaim their licentious-
ness and pride.
1096–7 Especially when that retinue is mischievous and harmful to the
people because of the insolence of high rank or office.
1106–8 May wicked death come upon such people in authority, and
God grant they may sink deep down into hell.
1110 Unless they mend their ways.

malisoun [*curse*] to swiche lordshipes as sustenen the wikkednesse of hir servauntz, but they come to amendement.   Pride
of the table appeereth eek ful ofte; for certes, riche men been
cleped [*invited*] to festes, and povre folk been put awey and
rebuked.   Also in excesse of diverse metes and drynkes, and
namely [*especially*] swich manere bake-metes and dissh-metes,
brennynge of wilde fir and peynted and castelled with papir,
1120 and semblable wast, so that it is abusioun for to thynke.   And
eek in to greet preciousnesse of vessel and curiositee [*elaborateness*] of mynstralcie, by whiche a man is stired the moore
to delices of luxurie [*delights of lechery*], if so be that he sette
his herte the lasse upon oure Lord Jhesu Crist, certeyn it is a
synne; and certeinly the delices myghte been so grete in this
caas that man myghte lightly [*easily*] falle by hem into deedly
synne.   The especes that sourden of Pride, soothly whan they
sourden of malice ymagined, avised, and forncast, or elles of
usage, been deedly synnes, it is no doute.   And whan they
1130 sourden by freletee unavysed, and sodeynly withdrawen ayeyn,
al been they grevouse synnes, I gesse that they ne been nat
deedly.   Now myghte men axe wherof that Pride sourdeth
and spryngeth, and I seye, somtyme it spryngeth of the goodes
[*good things*] of nature, and somtyme of the goodes of fortune,
and somtyme of the goodes of grace.   Certes, the goodes of
nature stonden outher [*consist either*] in goodes of body or in
goodes of soule.   Certes, goodes of body been heele [*health*]
of body, strengthe, delivernesse [*dexterity*], beautee, gentrice
[*noble birth*], franchise [*freedom*].   Goodes of nature of the
1140 soule been good wit, sharp understondynge, subtil engyn [*skill*],
vertu natureel, good memorie.   Goodes of fortune been
richesse [*wealth*], hyghe degrees of lordshipes, preisynges
[*praises*] of the peple.   Goodes of grace been science [*knowledge*], power to suffre spiritueel travaille [*hardship*], benignitee
[*kindliness*], vertuous contemplacioun, withstondynge of
temptacioun, and semblable [*similar*] thynges.   Of whiche
forseyde goodes, certes it is a ful greet folye a man to priden
hym in any of hem alle.   Now as for to speken of goodes of
nature, God woot that somtyme we han hem in [*by*] nature as
1150 muche to oure damage as to oure profit.   As for to speken of
heele of body, certes it passeth ful lightly, and eek it is ful

1118–20 Such kinds as baked meats and pies in dishes, surrounded by
   the flames of burning spirit and painted and castellated with paper,
   and similar extravagances, so that it is shameful to think of.
1127–9 The kinds of sin that spring from Pride, truly, when they arise
   from malice aforethought, deliberate and premeditated, or else from
   habit, are deadly sins, there is no doubt.
1129–32 And when they arise from unpremeditated frailty, and suddenly disappear again, I do not think they are deadly sins, grave
   though they may be.
1132–3 Now men may ask from what Pride springs and arises.
1147–8 It is a very great folly in a man to pride himself on any of them.

ofte enchesoun [*cause*] of the siknesse of oure soule. For, God woot, the flessh is a ful greet enemy to the soule; and therfore, the moore that the body is hool [*healthy*], the moore be we in peril to falle [*of falling*]. Eke for to pride hym in his strengthe of body, it is an heigh folye. For certes, the flessh coveiteth agayn the spirit; and ay the moore strong that the flessh is, the sorier may the soule be. And over al this, strengthe of body and worldly hardynesse causeth ful ofte
1160 many a man to peril and meschaunce. Eek for to pride hym of his gentrie [*nobility*] is ful greet folie; for ofte tyme the gentrie of the body binymeth [*takes away*] the gentrie of the soule; and eek we ben all of o fader and of o mooder; and alle we been of o nature, roten and corrupt, bothe riche and povre. For sothe, o manere gentrie is for to preise, that apparailleth mannes corage with vertues and moralitees, and maketh hym Cristes child. For truste wel that over what man that synne hath maistrie, he is a verray cherl to synne.
Now been ther generale signes of gentillesse, as eschewynge
1170 [*avoidance*] of vice and ribaudye [*ribaldry*] and servage of synne [*thraldom to sin*], in word, in werk, and contenaunce [*demeanour*]; and usynge vertu, curteisye, and clennesse [*purity*], and to be liberal, that is to seyn, large by mesure; for thilke that passeth mesure is folie and synne. Another is to remembre hym of bountee, that he of oother folk hath receyved. Another is to be benigne [*kind*] to his goode subgetis; wherfore seith Senek, 'Ther is no thing moore covenable [*fitting*] to a man of heigh estaat than debonairetee [*gentleness*] and pitee. And therfore thise flyes that men clepen bees, whan they maken hir
1180 kyng, they chesen [*choose*] oon that hath no prikke wherwith he may stynge.' Another is, a man to have a noble herte and a diligent, to attayne to heighe vertuouse thynges. Now certes, a man to pride hym in the goodes of grace [*benefits of fortune*] is eek an outrageous folie; for thilke yifte [*that gift*] of grace that sholde have turned hym to goodnesse and to medicine [*healing*], turneth hym to venym [*poison*] and to confusioun, as seith Seint Gregorie. Certes also, whoso prideth hym in the goodes of fortune, he is a ful greet fool; for somtyme is a man a greet lord by the morwe, that is a

1156-7 The flesh is envious of the spirit.
1159-60 Worldly boldness often brings many a man to peril and mis-fortune.
1165-6 In truth, only one kind of nobility is to be praised—that which adorns man's spirit with virtue and morality.
1167-8 For rest assured that any man over whom sin has mastery is the very slave of sin.
1172-4 And the practice of virtue ... that is to say, generous in modera-tion; for liberality which exceeds reasonable bounds is folly and sin.
1174-5 Another (sign of nobility) is for a man to remember the goodness.
1189-90 A great lord in the morning who is a wretched captive before night falls.

1190 caytyf and a wrecche er it be nyght; and somtyme the richesse
of a man is cause of his deth; somtyme the delices [*pleasures*]
of a man ben cause of the grevous maladye thurgh which he
dyeth.   Certes, the commendacioun of the peple is somtyme
ful fals and ful brotel for to triste; this day they preyse,
tomorwe they blame.   God woot, desir to have commendacioun eek of the peple hath caused deeth to many a bisy
[*active*] man.

Remedium contra peccatum
Superbie.

Now sith that so is that ye han understonde what is Pride,
and whiche [*what*] been the speces of it, and whennes Pride
1200 sourdeth and spryngeth, now shul ye understonde which is the
remedie agayns the synne of Pride; and that is humylitee, or
mekenesse.   That is a vertu thurgh which a man hath verray
knoweleche of hymself, and holdeth of hymself no pris ne
deyntee, as in regard of his desertes, considerynge evere his
freletee.   Now been ther three maneres of humylitee; as
humylitee in herte; another humylitee is in his mouth; the
thridde in his werkes.   The humilitee in herte is in foure
maneres.   That oon is whan a man holdeth hymself as
noght [*nothing*] worth biforn [*in the sight of*] God of hevene.
1210 Another is whan he ne despiseth noon oother man.   The
thridde is whan he rekketh [*cares*] nat, though men holde
hym noght worth.   The ferthe is whan he nys nat sory of his
humiliacioun.   Also the humilitee of mouth is in foure
thynges: in attempree [*temperate*] speche, and in humblesse
[*humbleness*] of speche, and whan he biknoweth [*acknowledges*]
with his owene mouth that he is swich as hym thynketh that
he is in his herte.   Another is whan he preiseth the bountee
[*goodness*] of another man, and nothyng therof amenuseth.
Humilitee eek in werkes is in foure maneres.   The firste is
1220 whan he putteth othere men biforn hym [*himself*].   The
seconde is to chese the loweste place over al.   The thridde is
gladly to assente to good conseil [*counsel*].   The ferthe is to
stonde gladly to the award of his sovereyns, or of hym that
is in hyer degree.   Certein, this is a greet werk of humylitee.

Sequitur de Invidia.

After Pride wol I speken of the foule synne of Envye,
which that is, as by [*according to*] the word of the philosophre,

---

1194 A very false and brittle thing to trust.
1203-5 And does not set a high value on himself and his deserts, but
   always remembers his frailty.
1212-13 The fourth is when he does not grieve over his humiliation.
1218 And in no way detracts from it.
1222-3 The fourth is willingly to abide by the decision.

'sorwe of oother mannes prosperitee'; and after the word of
Seint Augustyn, it is 'sorwe of oother mennes wele [*well-being*],
and joye of othere mennes harm.' This foule synne is platly
1230 [*flatly*] agayns the Hooly Goost. Al be it so that every synne
is agayns the Hooly Goost, yet nathelees, for as muche as
bountee aperteneth proprely to the Hooly Goost, and Envye
comth proprely of malice, therfore it is proprely agayn the
bountee of the Hooly Goost. Now hath malice two speces
[*kinds*]; that is to seyn, hardnesse of herte in wikkednesse, or
elles the flessh of man is so blynd that he considereth nat that
he is in synne, or rekketh nat that he is in synne, which is the
hardnesse of the devel. That oother spece of malice is whan
a man werreyeth [*attacks*] trouthe, whan he woot that it is
1240 trouthe; and eek whan he werreyeth the grace that God hath
yeve [*given*] to his neighebor; and al this is by Envye. Certes,
thanne is Envye the worst synne that is. For soothly, alle
othere synnes been somtyme oonly agayns o [*one*] special
vertu; but certes, Envye is agayns alle vertues and agayns alle
goodnesses. For it is sory of alle the bountees of his neighebor, and in this manere it is divers [*different*] from alle othere
synnes. For wel unnethe is ther any synne that it ne hath
som delit in itself, save oonly Envye, that evere hath in itself
angwissh and sorwe. The speces of Envye been thise. Ther
1250 is first sorwe of oother mannes goodnesse and of his prosperitee; and prosperitee is kyndely [*natural*] matere of joye;
thanne is Envye a synne agayns kynde [*nature*]. The seconde
spece of Envye is joye of oother mannes harm; and that is
proprely [*appropriately*] lyk to the devel, that evere rejoyseth
hym of [*rejoices in*] mannes harm. Of thise two speces comth
bakbityng; and this synne of bakbityng or detraccion hath
certeine speces, as thus. Som man preiseth his neighebor by
[*with*] a wikked entente; for he maketh alwey a wikked knotte
atte laste ende. Alwey he maketh a 'but' atte laste ende,
1260 that is digne [*worthy*] of moore blame, than worth is al the
preisynge. The seconde spece is that if a man be good, and
dooth or seith a thing to [*with*] good entente, the bakbitere
wol turne al thilke goodnesse up-so-doun [*upside-down*] to
his shrewed [*wicked*] entente. The thridde is to amenuse the
bountee of his neighebor. The fourthe spece of bakbityng
is this, that if men speke goodnesse of a man, thanne wol the
bakbitere seyn, 'parfey, swich a man is yet bet than he'; in

1231–2 Nevertheless, inasmuch as goodness pertains especially to the
   Holy Ghost.
1247–9 For there is hardly any sin that does not take some pleasure in
   itself, except Envy alone, that finds in itself nothing but anguish and
   sorrow.
1258–9 A wicked knot at the end of what he says.
1264–5 To detract from the goodness of one's neighbour.
1267 Upon my word, such and such a man is even better than he.

dispreisynge of hym that men preise.   The fifte spece is this,
for to consente gladly and herkne [*harken*] gladly to the
1270 harm that men speke of oother folk.   This synne is ful greet,
and ay encreesseth after the wikked entente of the bakbitere.
After bakbityng cometh gruchchyng [*grumbling*] or mur-
muracioun [*murmuring*]; and somtyme it spryngeth of inpacience agayns God, and somtyme agayns man.   Agayn
God it is, whan a man gruccheth agayn the peyne of helle,
or agayns poverte, or los of catel [*possessions*], or agayn
reyn or tempest; or elles gruccheth that shrewes [*wicked
persons*] han prosperitee, or elles for that goode men han
adversitee.   And alle thise thynges sholde man suffre paciently
1280 for they comen by the rightful juggement and ordinaunce of
God.   Somtyme comth grucching of avarice; as Judas
grucched agayns the Magdaleyne, whan she enoynted the
heved [*head*] of oure Lord Jhesu Crist with hir precious
oynement.   This manere murmure is swich as whan man
gruccheth of goodnesse that hymself dooth, or that oother
folk doon of hir owene catel.   Somtyme comth murmure of
Pride; as whan Simon the Pharisee gruchched agayn the
Magdaleyne, whan she approched to Jhesu Crist, and weep
[*wept*] at his feet for hire synnes.   And somtyme grucchyng
1290 sourdeth of [*arises from*] Envye; whan men discovereth a
mannes harm that was pryvee, or bereth hym on hond thyng
that is fals.   Murmure eek is ofte amonges servauntz that
grucchen whan hir sovereyns [*masters*] bidden hem doon
leveful [*lawful*] thynges; and forasmuche as they dar nat
openly withseye [*gainsay*] the comaundementz of hir sovereyns,
yet wol they seyn harm, and grucche, and murmure prively
[*secretly*] for verray despit [*sheer spite*]; whiche wordes men
clepen the develes *Pater noster*, though so be that the devel
ne hadde nevere *Pater noster*, but that lewed folk yeven it
1300 swich a name.   Somtyme it comth of Ire or prive hate, that
norisseth rancour in herte, as afterward I shal declare.   Thanne
cometh eek bitternesse of herte, thurgh which bitternesse
every good dede of his neighebor semeth to hym bitter and
unsavory.   Thanne cometh discord, that unbyndeth alle
manere of freendshipe.   Thanne comth scornynge of his
neighebor, al do he never so weel.   Thanne comth accusynge,
as whan man seketh occasioun to anoyen [*harm*] his neighebor,

1271 And always increases with the wicked intention of the backbiter.
1284-6 This kind of murmuring is like that of the man who complains
of the good that he himself does, or that other men do with their
possessions.
1290-2 When someone reveals a thing harmful to a man that was kept
secret before, or makes a false accusation against him.
1298-1300 For though the devil never had a *Paternoster*, yet ignorant
people give it such a name.
1306 However well-doing he may be.

which that is lyk the craft of the devel, that waiteth [*watches*]
bothe nyght and day to accusen us alle. Thanne comth
1310 malignitee, thurgh which a man anoyeth his neighebor prively,
if he may; and if he noght may, algate his wikked wil ne shal
nat wante, as for to brennen [*burn*] his hous pryvely, or empoy-
sone [*poison*] or sleen [*kill*] his beestes, and semblable [*similar*]
thynges.

Remedium contra peccatum Invidie.

Now wol I speke of remedie agayns this foule synne of
Envye. First is the love of God principal, and lovyng of his
neighebor as hymself; for soothly, that oon [*the one*] ne may
nat been withoute that oother. And truste wel that in the
name of thy neighebor thou shalt understonde the name of
1320 thy brother; for certes alle we have o [*one*] fader flesshly,
and o mooder, that is to seyn, Adam and Eve; and eek o fader
espiritueel, and that is God of hevene. Thy neighebor
artow holden [*bound*] for to love, and wilne [*wish*] hym alle
goodnesse; and therfore seith God, 'Love thy neighebor as
thyselve,' that is to seyn, to salvacioun [*to the saving*] bothe of
lyf and of soule. And mooreover thou shalt love hym in
word, and in benigne amonestynge and chastisynge, and
conforten hym in his anoyes [*troubles*], and preye for hym with
al thyn herte. And in dede thou shalt love hym in swich
1330 wise that thou shalt doon to hym in charitee as thou woldest
that it were doon to thyn owene persone. And therfore
thou ne shalt doon hym no damage in wikked word, ne harm
in his body, ne in his catel [*goods*], ne in his soule, by entissyng
of wikked ensample. Thou shalt nat desiren his wyf, ne
none of his thynges. Understoond eek that in the name of
neighebor is comprehended his enemy. Certes, man shal
loven his enemy, by the comandement of God; and soothly
thy freend shaltow love in God. I seye, thyn enemy shaltow
love for Goddes sake, by his comandement. For if it were
1340 reson [*right*] that man sholde haten his enemy, for sothe God
nolde nat [*would not*] receyven us to his love that been his
enemys. Agayns [*in return for*] three manere of wronges that
his enemy dooth to hym, he shal doon three thynges, as thus.
Agayns hate and rancour of herte, he shal love hym in herte.
Agayns chidyng and wikkede wordes, he shal preye for his
enemy. Agayns the wikked dede of his enemy, he shal doon
hym bountee [*good*]. For Crist seith: 'Loveth youre enemys,
and preyeth for hem that speke yow harm, and eek for hem

1311–12 Nevertheless his wicked desire is not wanting.
1318–20 You must take the word 'neighbour' to mean your 'brother.'
1327 By kindly admonishing and chastisement.
1333–4 By the enticement of wicked example.
1343 A man shall do three things, as follows.

that yow chacen and pursewen, and dooth bountee to hem
1350 that yow haten.' Loo, thus comaundeth us oure Lord
Jhesu Crist to do to oure enemys. For soothly, nature
dryveth us to loven oure freendes, and parfey, oure enemys
han moore nede to love than oure freendes; and they that
moore nede have, certes to hem shal men doon goodnesse;
and certes, in thilke dede have we remembraunce of the love
of Jhesu Crist that deyde for his enemys. And in as muche
as thilke love is the moore grevous [*painful*] to perfourne
[*achieve*], so muche is the moore gret [*great*] the merite; and
therfore the lovynge of oure enemy hath confounded the
1360 venym of the devel. For right as the devel is disconfited by
humylitee, right so is he wounded to the deeth by love of oure
enemy. Certes, thanne is love the medicine that casteth out
the venym of Envye fro mannes herte. The speces of this
paas shullen be moore largely declared in hir chapitres folwynge.

Sequitur de Ira.

After Envye wol I discryven [*describe*] the synne of Ire.
For soothly, whoso hath envye upon his neighebor, anon he
wole comunly fynde hym a matere of wratthe, in word or in
dede, agayns hym to whom he hath envye. And as wel comth
1370 Ire of Pride, as of Envye; for soothly, he that is proud or
envyous is lightly [*easily*] wrooth.
This synne of Ire, after the discryvyng of Seint Augustyn,
is wikked wil [*desire*] to been avenged by word or by dede.
Ire, after the philosophre, is the fervent blood of man yquyked
[*quickened*] in his herte, thurgh which he wole harm to hym
that he hateth. For certes, the herte of man, by eschawfynge
[*heating*] and moevynge of his blood, wexeth so trouble that
he is out of alle juggement of resoun. But ye shal understonde
that Ire is in two maneres; that oon of hem is good, and that
1380 oother is wikked. The goode Ire is by jalousie of goodnesse,
thurgh which a man is wrooth with wikkednesse and agayns
wikkednesse; and therfore seith a wys man that Ire is bet
[*better*] than pley [*jesting*]. This Ire is with debonairetee, and
it is wrooth withouten bitternesse; nat wrooth agayns the

1352-3 And, to be sure, our enemies have more need of love than our
  friends.
1355-6 And certainly, by doing so we keep in remembrance the love
  of Jesus Christ.
1363-5 The different kinds (of love) referred to in this section will be
  explained more fully in the following chapters.
1367-8 Will generally soon find an occasion for wrath.
1369-70 And Anger comes from Pride as well as from Envy.
1372 According to the description of St Augustine.
1375 As a result of which he wishes harm.
1377-8 Becomes so troubled that he is incapable of rational judgment.
1383 This Anger is characterized by gentleness.

man, but wrooth with the mysdede of the man, as seith the prophete David, 'Irascimini et nolite peccare.' Now understondeth that wikked Ire is in two maneres; that is to seyn, sodeyn Ire or hastif [hasty] Ire, withouten avisement [counsel] and consentynge of resoun. The menyng and the sens of
1390 this is, that the resoun of a man ne consente nat to thilke sodeyn Ire; and thanne is it venial. Another Ire is ful wikked, that comth of felonie of herte avysed and cast biforn, with wikked wil to do vengeance, and therto his resoun consenteth; and soothly this is deedly synne. This Ire is so displesant [displeasing] to God that it troubleth his hous, and chaceth the Hooly Goost out of mannes soule, and wasteth and destroyeth the liknesse of God, that is to seyn, the vertu that is in mannes soule, and put in hym the liknesse of the devel, and bynymeth [steals] the man fro God, that is his rightful
1400 lord. This Ire is a ful greet plesaunce [pleasure] to the devel; for it is the develes fourneys [furnace], that is eschawfed [heated] with the fir of helle. For certes, right so as fir is moore mighty to destroyen erthely thynges than any oother element, right so is Ire is myghty to destroyen alle spiritueel thynges. Looke how that fir of smale gleedes [embers], that been almost dede under asshen [ashes], wollen quike [come alive] agayn whan they been touched with brymstoon; right so Ire wol everemo [always] quyken agayn, whan it is touched by the pride that is covered in mannes herte. For certes, fir ne may
1410 nat comen out of no thyng, but if [unless] it were first in the same thyng natureelly, as fir is drawen out of flyntes with steel. And right so as pride is ofte tyme matere [cause] of Ire, right so is rancour norice [nurse] and kepere of Ire. Ther is a maner [kind of] tree, as seith Seint Ysidre [Isidore] that whan men maken fir of thilke tree, and covere the coles of it with asshen, soothly the fir of it wol lasten al a yeer or moore. And right so fareth it of [it goes with] rancour; whan it is ones conceyved in the hertes of som men, certein, it wol lasten peraventure [perhaps] from oon Estre day unto another Estre
1420 [Easter] day, and moore. But certes, thilke man is ful fer fro the mercy of God al thilke [that] while.

In this forseyde develes fourneys ther forgen three shrewes: Pride, that ay bloweth and encreesseth the fir by chidynge and wikked wordes; thanne stant [stands] Envye, and holdeth the hoote iren upon the herte of man with a peire of longe toonges [tongs] of long rancour; and thanne stant the synne of Contumelie, or strif and cheeste, and batereth and forgeth by vileyns reprevynges. Certes, this cursed synne anoyeth

1392 Which comes from wickedness of heart that is deliberate and premeditated.
1422 Three scoundrels are busy forging.
1427-8 Strife and contention, and batters and forges by means of wicked reproaches.

[*is harmful*] bothe to the man hymself and eek to his neighebor.
1430 For soothly, almoost al the harm that any man dooth to his
neighebor comth of wratthe. For certes, outrageous wratthe
dooth al that evere the devel hym comaundeth; for he ne
spareth neither Crist ne his sweete Mooder. And in his outrageous anger and ire, allas! allas! ful many oon at that
tyme feeleth in his herte ful wikkedly, bothe of Crist and eek
of alle his halwes [*saints*]. Is nat this a cursed vice? Yis,
certes. Allas! it bynymeth [*takes away*] from man his wit and
his resoun, and al his debonaire [*gentle*] lif espiritueel [*spiritual*]
that sholde kepen [*protect*] his soule. Certes, it bynymeth eek
1440 Goddes due lordshipe, and that is mannes soule, and the love
of his neighebores. It stryveth eek alday [*always*] agayn
trouthe. It reveth hym [*robs him of*] the quiete of his herte,
and subverteth his soule.

Of Ire comen thise stynkynge engendrures [*offspring*]:
First, hate, that is oold [*ancient*] wratthe; discord, thurgh
which a man forsaketh his olde freend that he hath loved ful
longe; and thanne cometh werre, and every manere of wrong
that man dooth to his neighebor, in body or in catel [*possessions*]. Of this cursed synne of Ire cometh eek man-
1450 slaughtre. And understonde wel that homycide, that is
manslaughtre, is in diverse wise. Som manere [*one kind*] of
homycide is spiritueel, and som [*another*] is bodily. Spiritueel
manslaughtre is in sixe thynges. First by hate, as seith
Seint John: 'He that hateth his brother is an homycide.'
Homycide is eek by bakbitynge, of whiche bakbiteres seith
Salomon that 'they han two swerdes with whiche they sleen
hire neighebores.' For soothly, as wikke is to bynyme his
good name as his lyf. Homycide is eek in yevynge of wikked
conseil by fraude; as for to yeven conseil to areysen wrongful
1460 custumes and taillages. Of whiche seith Salomon: 'Leon
rorynge and bere hongry been like to the cruel lordshipes,'
in withholdynge or abreggynge of the shepe (or the hyre), or
of the wages of servauntz, or elles in usure, or in withdrawynge
of the almesse of povre folk. For which the wise man seith,
'Fedeth hym that almoost dyeth for honger'; for soothly,
but if [*unless*] thow feede hym, thou sleest hym; and alle thise
been deedly synnes. Bodily manslaughtre is, whan thow
sleest [*kill*] him with thy tonge in oother manere; as whan thou
comandest to sleen a man, or elles yevest hym conseil to sleen
1470 a man. Manslaughtre in dede is in foure maneres. That oon

1458–60 Homicide also consists in giving wicked and fraudulent counsel,
such as giving counsel to levy wrongful customs duties and taxes.
1460–4 'A roaring lion and a hungry bear are like cruel lords,' that is,
in withholding or whittling down the reward (or hire) or wages of
servants, or else in usury, or in keeping back the alms due to poor
people.
1468–9 As when you command a man to be killed.

is by lawe, right as a justice [*judge*] dampneth [*condemns*] hym that is coupable [*guilty*] to the deeth.   But lat the justice be war that he do it rightfully, and that he do it nat for delit to spille blood, but for kepynge of rightwisnesse [*righteousness*]. Another homycide is that is doon for necessitee, as whan o man sleeth another in his defendaunt [*self-defence*], and that he ne may noon ootherwise escape from his owene deeth. But certeinly if he may escape withouten slaughtre of his adversarie, and sleeth hym, he dooth synne and he shal bere 1480 penance as for deedly synne.   Eek if a man, by caas or aven- ture, shete an arwe, or caste a stoon, with which he sleeth a man, he is homycide.   Eek if a womman by necligence over- lyeth hire child in hir slepyng, it is homycide and deedly synne.   Eek whan man destourbeth [*hinders*] concepcioun of a child, and maketh a womman outher [*either*] bareyne by drynkynge venenouse [*poisonous*] herbes thurgh which she may nat conceyve, or sleeth a child by drynkes wilfully, or elles putteth certeine material thynges in hire secree places [*privy parts*] to slee the child, or elles dooth unkyndely [*unnatural*] synne, by which man or womman shedeth [*discharges*] hire nature [*seed*] in manere or in place ther as a child may nat be conceived, or elles if a woman have conceyved, and hurt hirself and sleeth the child, yet [*still*] is it homycide.   What seye we eek of wommen that mordren [*murder*] hir children for drede of worldly shame?   Certes, an horrible homicide. Homycide is eek if a man approcheth to a womman by desir of lecherie, thurgh which the child is perissed [*destroyed*], or elles smyteth a womman wityngly [*deliberately*], thurgh which she leseth [*loses*] hir child.   Alle thise been homycides and 1500 horrible deedly synnes.   Yet comen ther of Ire manye mo [*more*] synnes, as wel in word as in thoght and in dede; as he that arretteth upon [*accuses*] God, or blameth God of thyng of which he is hymself gilty, or despiseth God and alle his halwes [*saints*], as doon thise cursede hasardours [*gamblers*] in diverse contrees.   This cursed synne doon they, whan they feelen in hir herte ful wikkedly of God and of his halwes. Also whan they treten unreverently the sacrement of the auter [*altar*], thilke synne is so greet that unnethe [*hardly*] may it been releessed [*forgiven*], but that the mercy of God passeth 1510 [*surpasses*] alle his werkes; it is so greet, and he so benigne. Thanne comth of Ire attry angre [*venomous rage*].   Whan a man is sharply amonested in his shrifte to forleten his synne, thanne wol he be angry, and answeren hokerly [*scornfully*] and angrily, and deffenden or excusen his synne by unstede-

1480-1 Also if a man, by chance or accident, shoots an arrow.
1482-3 Lies upon her child in her sleep.
1511-12 When a man is sharply admonested in his confession to abandon his sin.

fastnesse [*inconstancy*] of his flessh; or elles he dide it for
to holde [*keep*] compaignye with his felawes; or elles, he seith,
the feend enticed hym; or elles he dide it for his youthe; or
elles his compleccioun is so corageous that he may nat forbere;
or elles it is his destinee, as he seith, unto [*up to*] a certein age;
1520 or elles, he seith, it cometh hym of gentillesse [*nobility*] of his
auncestres; and semblable [*similar*] thynges. Alle thise
manere of folk so wrappen hem in hir synnes that they ne wol
nat delivere hemself. For soothly, no wight [*person*] that
excuseth hym wilfully of his synne may nat been delivered of
his synne, til that he mekely biknoweth [*acknowledges*] his
synne. After this, thanne cometh sweryng, that is expres
[*expressly*] agayn the comandement of God; and this bifalleth
ofte of anger and of Ire. God seith: 'Thow shalt nat take the
name of thy Lord God in veyn or in ydel.' Also oure Lord
1530 Jhesu Crist seith, by the word of Seint Mathew, 'Ne wol ye nat
swere in alle manere [*at all*]; neither by hevene, for it is
Goddes trone; ne by erthe, for it is the bench of his feet; ne
by Jerusalem, for it is the citee of a greet kyng; ne by thyn
heed [*head*], for thou mayst nat make an heer [*one hair*] whit
ne blak. But seyeth by youre word "ye, ye," and "nay, nay";
and what that is moore, it is of yvel,'—thus seith Crist. For
Cristes sake, ne swereth nat so synfully in dismembrynge of
Crist by soule, herte, bones, and body. For certes, it semeth
that ye thynke that the cursede Jewes ne dismembred nat
1540 ynough the preciouse persone of Crist, but ye dismembre hym
moore. And if so be that the lawe compelle yow to swere,
thanne rule yow after the lawe of God in youre sweryng, as
seith Jeremye [*Jeremiah*], *quarto capitulo*: 'Thou shalt kepe
three condicions: thou shalt swere in trouthe, in doom
[*judgment*], and in rightwisnesse.' This is to seyn, thou
shalt swere sooth [*truthfully*]; for every lesynge [*lie*] is agayns
Crist. For Crist is verray trouthe. And thynk wel this, that
every greet swerere, nat compelled lawefully to swere, the
wounde [*plague*] shal nat departe from his hous whil he useth
1550 swich unleveful sweryng. Thou shalt sweren eek in doom,
whan thou art constreyned by thy domesman [*judge*] to
witnessen the trouthe. Eek thow shalt nat swere for envye,
ne for favour, ne for meede [*bribe*], but for rightwisnesse, for
declaracioun of it, to the worshipe of God and helpyng of
thyne evene-Cristene [*fellow Christian*]. And therfore every
man that taketh Goddes name in ydel [*vain*], or falsly swereth
with his mouth, or elles taketh on hym [*himself*] the name of
Crist, to be called a Cristen man, and lyveth agayns Cristes

1517–18 Or else he is so high-spirited by nature that he cannot restrain
    himself.
1536 Anything more than that is evil in origin. (See Matt. v. 37.)
1549–50 While he makes a practice of such unlawful swearing.
1553–4 In order to make a declaration to the worship of God.

lyvynge and his techynge, alle they taken Goddes name in
1560 ydel. Looke [*see*] eek what seint Peter seith, *Actuum, quarto,
Non est aliud nomen sub celo, etc., 'Ther nys noon oother
name,' seith Seint Peter, 'under hevene yeven to men, in which
they mowe be saved'; that is to seyn, but the name of Jhesu
Crist. Take kep [*heed*] eek how precious is the name of
Crist, as seith Seint Paul, *ad Philipenses, secundo, In nomine
Jhesu, etc., 'that in the name of Jhesu every knee of hevenely
creatures, or erthely, or of helle sholde bowe'; for it is so
heigh and so worshipful that the cursede feend in helle sholde
tremblen to heeren it ynempned [*named*]. Thanne semeth it
1570 that men that sweren so horribly by his blessed name, that
they despise it moore booldely than dide the cursede Jewes,
or elles the devel, that trembleth whan he heereth his name.

Now certes, sith that sweryng, but if [*unless*] it be lawefully
doon, is so heighly defended [*strictly forbidden*], muche worse
is forsweryng falsly, and yet nedelees [*needlessly*].

What seye we eek of hem that deliten in sweryng, and
holden it a gentrie [*sign of good birth*] or a manly dede to swere
grete othes? And what of hem that of verray [*sheer*] usage
[*habit*] ne cesse nat to swere grete othes, al be the cause
1580 [*occasion*] nat worth a straw? Certes, this is horrible synne.
Swerynge sodeynly withoute avysement [*consideration*] is eek
a synne. But lat us go now to thilke horrible sweryng of
adjuracioun and conjuracioun, as doon thise false enchauntours or nigromanciens in bacyns ful of water, or in a bright
swerd, in a cercle, or in a fir, or in a shulderboon of a sheep.
I kan nat seye but that they doon cursedly [*wickedly*] and
dampnably agayns Crist and al the feith of hooly chirche.

What seye we of hem that bileeven on divynailes [*in divination*], as by flight or by noyse of briddes, or of beestes, or by sort
1590 [*lots*], by nigromancie [*necromancy*], by dremes, by chirkynge
of dores [*creaking of doors*], or crakkynge [*cracking*] of houses,
by gnawynge of rattes, and swich manere wrecchednesse
[*paltriness*]? Certes, al this thyng is deffended [*forbidden*] by
God and by hooly chirche. For which they been acursed, til
they come to amendement [*amends*], that on swich filthe
[*rubbish*] setten hire bileeve [*belief*]. Charmes for woundes or
maladie of men or of beestes, if they taken any effect, it may
be peraventure that God suffreth [*allows*] it, for folk sholden
yeve the moore feith and reverence to his name.

1600   Now wol I speken of lesynges [*lying*], which generally is
fals signyficaunce of word, in entente to deceyven his evene-
Cristene. Som lesynge is of which ther comth noon avantage
to no wight; and som lesynge turneth to the ese [*convenience*]

1562–3 Whereby they may be saved.
1583–5 Adjuration and conjuration (of spirits), as done by false sorcerers
   or necromancers over basins of water, or on a bright sword, or inside
   a magic circle, or over a fire, or on the shoulder-bone of a sheep.

and profit of o man, and to disese [*inconvenience*] and damage
of another man.   Another lesynge is for to saven his lyf or his
catel.   Another lesynge comth of delit for to lye, in which
delit they wol forge a long tale, and peynten it with alle
circumstaunces, where al the ground [*foundation*] of the tale
is fals.   Som lesynge comth, for he wole sustene his word;
1610 and som lesynge comth of reccheleesnesse withouten avisement; and semblable thynges.

Lat us now touche the vice of flaterynge, which ne comth nat
gladly [*willingly*] but for drede or for coveitise [*covetousness*].
Flaterye is generally wrongful preisynge [*praise*].   Flatereres
been the develes norices [*nurses*], that norissen his children
with milk of losengerie [*flattery*].   For sothe, Salomon seith
that 'flaterie is wors than detraccioun.'   For somtyme detraccion maketh an hauteyn [*haughty*] man be the moore humble,
for he dredeth detraccion; but certes flaterye, that maketh a
1620 man to enhauncen his herte and his contenaunce.   Flatereres
been the develes enchauntours; for they make a man to wene of
hymself be lyk that he nys nat lyk.   They been lyk to Judas
that bitraysen [*betray*] a man to sellen hym to his enemy, that
is to the devel.   Flatereres been the develes chapelleyns, that
syngen evere *Placebo*.   I rekene flaterie in [*among*] the vices
of Ire; for ofte tyme, if o man be wrooth with another, thanne
wole he flatere som wight to sustene [*support*] hym in his
querele.

Speke we now of swich cursynge as comth of irous [*angry*]
1630 herte.   Malisoun generally may be seyd every maner power of
harm.   Swich cursynge bireveth [*tears*] man fro the regne
[*kingdom*] of God, as seith Seint Paul.   And ofte tyme swich
cursynge wrongfully retorneth agayn to hym that curseth, as
a bryd that retorneth agayn to his [*its*] owene nest.   And over
[*above*] alle thyng men oghten eschewe [*avoid*] to cursen hire
children, and yeven to the devel hire engendrure [*offspring*],
as ferforth as in hem is.   Certes, it is greet peril and greet
synne.

Lat us thanne speken of chidynge [*scolding*] and reproche,
1640 whiche been ful grete woundes in mannes herte, for they
unsowen [*unsew*] the semes [*seams*] of freendshipe in mannes
herte.   For certes, unnethes [*hardly*] may a man pleynly
[*fully*] been accorded [*reconciled*] with hym that hath hym
openly revyled and repreved and disclaundred [*slandered*].
This is a ful grisly [*horrible*] synne, as Crist seith in the gospel.

1619-20 But flattery, indeed, makes a man puffed up in his heart and
in his bearing.
1621-2 They make a man think he is like that which he is not like.
1625 *syngen . . . Placebo.* See III. 2075.
1630-1 Cursing generally may be said to have every kind of power to
do harm.
1637 So far as in them lies.

And taak kep [*heed*] now, that he that repreveth his neighebor, outher he repreveth hym by som harm of peyne that he hath on his body, as 'mesel,' 'croked harlot,' or by som synne that he dooth. Now if he repreve hym by harm of peyne, thanne
1650 turneth the repreve to Jhesu Crist, for peyne is sent by the rightwys sonde [*visitation*] of God, and by his suffrance, be it meselrie [*leprosy*], or maheym [*maiming*], or maladie. And if he repreve hym uncharitably of synne, as 'thou holour' [*adulterer*], 'thou dronkelewe [*drunken*] harlot,' and so forth, thanne aperteneth [*is suited*] that to the rejoysynge of the devel, that evere hath joye that men doon synne. And certes, chidynge may nat come but out of a vileyns [*wicked*] herte. For after [*according to*] the habundance [*fullness*] of the herte speketh the mouth ful ofte. And ye shul under-
1660 stonde that looke, by any wey, whan any man shal chastise another, that he be war from chidynge or reprevynge. For trewely, but he be war, he may ful lightly quyken the fir of angre and of wratthe, which that he sholde quenche, and peraventure sleeth hym, which that he myghte chastise with benignitee. For as seith Salomon, 'The amyable tonge is the tree of lyf,' that is to seyn, of lyf espiritueel; and soothly, a deslavee [*foul*] tonge sleeth the spirites [*spirit*] of hym that repreveth and eek of hym that is repreved. Loo, what seith Seint Augustyn: 'Ther is nothyng so lyk the develes child as
1670 he that ofte chideth.' Seint Paul seith eek, 'The servant of God bihoveth [*ought*] nat to chide.' And how that chidynge be a vileyns thyng bitwixe alle manere folk, yet is it certes moost uncovenable bitwixe a man and his wyf; for there is nevere reste [*peace*]. And therfore seith Salomon, 'An hous that is uncovered and droppynge [*leaky*], and a chidynge wyf, been lyke.' A man that is in a droppynge hous in manye places, though he eschewe [*avoid*] the droppynge in o place, it droppeth on hym in another place. So fareth it by [*it goes with*] a chydynge wyf; but she chide hym in o place, she wol
1680 chide hym in another. And therfore, 'bettre is a morsel of breed with joye than an hous ful of delices [*delights*] with chidynge,' seith Salomon. Seint Paul seith: 'O ye wommen, be ye subgetes to youre housbondes as bihoveth in God, and ye men loveth youre wyves.' *Ad Colossenses, tertio.*

1647-9 Either he reproaches him for some painful injury to his body, calling him 'leper' or 'crooked rascal,' or for some sin he has committed.
1659-65 If you would understand what is meant by that, let every man who chastises another beware of chiding or reproaching. For truly, unless a man beware of doing this, he may very easily kindle the fire . . . and perhaps slay him whom he might have chastised in a kindly way.
1671-3 And however wicked chiding may be between all kinds of people, yet it is certainly most unseemly between a man and his wife.
1682-3 'Wives, submit yourselves unto your own husbands, as it is fit in the Lord.' (Col. iii. 18.)

Afterward speke we of scornynge, which is a wikked synne, and namely whan he scorneth a man for his goode werkes. For certes, swiche scorneres faren [*behave*] lyk this foule tode [*toad*], that may nat endure to smelle the soote savour [*sweet smell*] of the vyne whanne it florissheth.   Thise scorneres been 1690 partyng felawes [*sharing partners*] with the devel; for they han joye whan the devel wynneth, and sorwe whan he leseth [*loses*].   They been adversaries of Jhesu Crist, for they haten that he loveth, that is to seyn, salvacioun of soule.

Speke we now of wikked conseil; for he that wikked conseil yeveth is a traytour.   For he deceyveth hym that trusteth in hym, *ut Achitofel ad Absolonem*.   But nathelees, yet is his wikked conseil first agayn hymself.   For, as seith the wise man, 'Every fals lyvynge [*evil liver*] hath this propertee [*peculiarity*] in hymself, that he that wole anoye [*harm*] 1700 another man, he anoyeth first hymself.'   And men shul understonde that man shal nat taken his conseil of fals folk, ne of angry folk, or grevous [*mischievous*] folk, ne of folk that loven specially to muchel hir owene profit, ne to muche worldly folk, namely in conseilynge of soules.

Now comth the synne of hem that sowen and maken discord amonges folk, which is a synne that Crist hateth outrely [*utterly*].   And no wonder is; for he deyde [*died*] for to make concord [*harmony*].   And moore shame do they to Crist, than dide they that hym crucifiede; for God loveth 1710 bettre that freendshipe be amonges folk, than he dide his owene body, the which that he yaf for unitee.   Therfore been they likned to the devel, that evere is aboute to maken [*busy making*] discord.

Now comth the synne of double tonge; swiche as speken faire [*civilly*] byforn folk, and wikkedly bihynde; or elles they maken semblant as though they speeke of good entencioun, or elles in game and pley, and yet they speke of wikked entente.

Now comth biwreying [*betrayal*] of conseil, thurgh which a 1720 man is defamed; certes, unnethe may be restoore the damage.

Now comth manace [*threat*], that is an open folye; for he that ofte manaceth, he threteth moore than he may perfourne [*perform*] ful ofte tyme.

Now cometh ydel wordes, that is withouten profit of [*to*] hym that speketh tho [*those*] wordes, and eek of hym that herkneth tho wordes.   Or elles ydel wordes been tho that been nedelees [*unnecessary*], or withouten entente of natureel

1696 As Achitophel to Absalom (2 Sam. xvii. 1).
1702-4 Nor from folk who love their own profit far too much, nor from folk who are too worldly, especially when it is counsel affecting the soul.
1715-17 Or else they make a show of speaking with good intent.
1720 Assuredly, he can hardly make good the damage.

profit. And al be it that ydel wordes been somtyme venial synne, yet sholde men douten [*fear*] hem, for we shul yeve
1730 rekenynge of hem bifore God.

Now comth janglynge [*idle talk*], that may nat been withoute synne. And, as seith Salomon, 'It is a sygne of apert [*manifest*] folye.' And therfore a philosophre seyde, whan men axed [*asked*] hym how that men sholde plese the peple, and he answerde, 'Do manye goode werkes, and spek fewe jangles [*idle words*].'

After this comth the synne of japeres [*jesters*], that been the develes apes; for they maken folk to laughe at hire japerie [*buffoonery*] as folk doon at the gawdes [*antics*] of an ape.
1740 Swiche japeres deffendeth [*forbids*] Seint Paul. Looke how that vertuouse wordes and hooly conforten hem that travaillen in the service of Crist, right so conforten the vileyns [*wicked*] wordes and knakkes [*tricks*] of japeris hem that travaillen in the service of the devel. Thise been the synnes that comen of the tonge, that comen of Ire and of othere synnes mo [*besides*].

Sequitur remedium contra peccatum Ire.

The remedie agayns Ire is a vertu that men clepen Mansuetude [*meekness*], that is Debonairetee [*gentleness*]; and eek another vertu, that men callen Pacience or Suffrance [*long-
1750 suffering*].

Debonairetee withdraweth [*restrains*] and refreyneth [*curbs*] the stirynges and the moevynges [*motions*] of mannes corage [*impetuosity*] in his herte, in swich manere that they ne skippe [*leap*] nat out by angre ne by ire [*wrath*]. Suffrance suffreth swetely alle the anoyaunces and the wronges that men doon to man outward [*outwardly*]. Seint Jerome seith thus of debonairetee, that 'it dooth noon harm to no wight ne seith; ne for noon harm that men doon or seyn, he ne eschawfeth nat agayns his resoun.' This vertu somtyme comth of [*by*]
1760 nature; for, as seith the philosophre, 'A man is a quyk [*intelligent*] thyng, by nature debonaire and tretable [*amenable*] to goodnesse; but whan debonairetee is enformed of [*informed by*] grace, thanne is it the moore worth.'

Pacience, that is another remedie agayns Ire, is a vertu that suffreth swetely every mannes goodnesse, and is nat wrooth for noon harm that is doon to hym. The philosophre seith that pacience is thilke [*that*] vertu that suffreth debonairely [*meekly*] alle the outrages of adversitee and every wikked word. This vertu maketh a man lyk to God, and maketh hym

1757-9 It does and says no harm to anyone; nor for any harm that men do or say will it get heated against reason.

1770 Goddes owene deere child, as seith Crist. This vertu dis-
confiteth [discomfits] thyn enemy. And therfore seith the
wise man, 'If thow wolt venquysse thyn enemy, lerne to
suffre [endure].' And thou shalt understonde that man
suffreth foure manere of grevances [kinds of hardship] in
outward thynges, agayns the whiche foure he moot [must]
have foure manere of paciences.

The first grevance is of wikkede wordes. Thilke suffrede
Jhesu Crist withouten grucchyng [complaining], ful paciently,
whan the Jewes despised and repreved [reproached] hym ful
1780 ofte. Suffre thou therfore paciently; for the wise man seith, 'If
thou stryve with a fool, though the fool be wrooth or though
he laughe, algate [in any case] thou shalt have no reste [peace].'
That oother grevance outward is to have damage of thy catel
[property]. Theragayns suffred Crist ful paciently, whan he
was despoyled of al that he hadde in this lyf, and that nas but
his clothes. The thridde grevance is a man to have harm in
his body. That suffred Crist ful paciently in al his passioun.
The fourthe grevance is in outrageous labour in werkes.
Wherfore I seye that folk that maken hir servantz to travaillen
1790 to grevously, or out of tyme [season], as on haly [holy] dayes,
soothly they do greet synne. Heer-agayns [against this]
suffred Crist ful paciently and taughte us pacience, whan he
baar [bore] upon his blissed shulder the croys upon which he
sholde suffren despitous [cruel] deeth. Heere may men lerne
to be pacient; for certes noght oonly Cristen men been pacient,
for love of Jhesu Crist, and for gerdoun [reward] of the blisful
lyf that is perdurable [everlasting], but certes, the olde payens
[pagans] that nevere were Cristene, commendeden and useden
the vertu of pacience.

1800 A philosophre upon [once upon] a tyme, that wolde have
beten his disciple for his grete trespas, for which he was greetly
amoeved [perturbed], and broghte a yerde to scoure with the child;
and whan this child saugh the yerde, he seyde to his maister,
'What thenke ye do?' 'I wol bete thee,' quod the maister,
'for thy correccioun.' 'For sothe,' quod the child, 'ye
oghten first correcte youreself, that han lost al youre pacience
for the gilt [offence] of a child.' 'For sothe,' quod the maister
al wepynge, 'thow seyst sooth. Have thow the yerde, my
deere sone, and correcte me for myn inpacience.' Of pacience
1810 comth obedience, thurgh which a man is obedient to Crist and
to alle hem to whiche he oghte to been obedient in Crist. And
understond wel that obedience is perfit [perfect], whan that
a man dooth gladly and hastily [quickly], with good herte
entierly [wholly], al that he sholde do. Obedience generally is

1785-6 And that was nothing but his clothes.
1788 The fourth hardship is to be made to work excessively hard.
1802 Brought a rod to scourge the child with.

to perfourne the doctrine of God and of his sovereyns, to whiche hym oghte to ben obeisaunt in alle rightwisnesse.

Sequitur de Accidia.

After the synne of Envye and of Ire, now wol I speken of the synne of Accidie [*Sloth*]. For Envye blyndeth the herte of a man, and Ire troubleth a man, and Accidie maketh hym
1820 hevy, thoghtful, and wraw. Envye and Ire maken bitternesse in herte, which bitternesse is mooder of Accidie, and bynymeth [*takes from*] hym the love of alle goodnesse. Thanne is Accidie the angwissh of troubled herte; and Seint Augustyn seith, 'It is anoy of goodnesse and joye of harm.' Certes, this is a dampnable synne; for it dooth wrong to Jhesu Crist, in as muche as it bynymeth the service that men oghte doon to Crist with alle diligence, as seith Salomon. But Accidie dooth no swich diligence. He dooth alle thyng with anoy, and with wrawnesse, slaknesse, and excusacioun, and with
1830 ydelnesse, and unlust; for which the book seith, 'Acursed be he that dooth the service of God necligently.' Thanne is Accidie enemy to everich estaat [*every condition*] of man; for certes, the estaat of man is in [*of*] three maneres [*kinds*]. Outher it is th'estaat of innocence, as was th'estaat of Adam biforn that he fil [*fell*] into synne; in which estaat he was holden to wirche as in heriynge and adowrynge of God. Another estaat is the estaat of synful men, in which estaat men been holden to laboure in preiynge to God for amende-ment of hire synnes, and that he wole graunte hem to arysen
1840 out of hir synnes. Another estaat is th'estaat of grace; in which estaat he is holden to werkes of penitence. And certes, to alle thise thynges is Accidie enemy and contrarie, for he loveth no bisynesse [*activity*] at al. Now certes, this foule synne, Accidie, is eek a ful greet enemy to the liflode [*livelihood*] of the body; for it ne hath no purveaunce [*provision*] agayn temporeel necessitee; for it forsleweth and forsluggeth and destroyeth alle goodes temporeles by reccheleesnesse.

The fourthe thyng is that Accidie is lyk hem that been in the peyne of helle, by cause of hir slouthe and of hire hevynesse
1850 [*indolence*]; for they that been dampned been so bounde that

1815-16 To carry out the instructions of God and of one's superiors, to whom a man should in all justice be obedient.
1820 Heavy, moody, and fretful.
1824 It saddens goodness and gladdens evil.
1827-30 But Sloth makes no such effort. He does everything with annoyance, with peevishness, slackness, and excuses, and with idleness and unwillingness.
1835-6 In which condition he was obliged to work, as in praising and adoring God.
1846-7 For it wastes and spoils and destroys temporal goods by care-lessness.

they ne may neither wel do ne wel thynke. Of Accidie comth first, that a man is anoyed [*troubled*] and encombred [*hindered*] for to doon any goodnesse, and maketh that God hath abhomynacion of swich Accidie, as seith Seint John.

Now comth Slouthe, that wol nat suffre noon hardnesse [*hardship*] ne no penaunce. For soothly, Slouthe is so tendre and so delicaat, as seith Salomon, that he wol nat suffre noon hardnesse ne penaunce, and therfore he shendeth [*ruins*] al that he dooth. Agayns this roten-herted synne of Accidie and Slouthe sholde men exercise hemself to doon goode werkes, and manly and vertuously cacchen corage wel to doon, thynkynge that oure Lord Jhesu Crist quiteth [*repays*] every good dede, be it never so lite [*little*]. Usage [*habit*] of labour is a greet thyng, for it maketh, as seith Seint Bernard, the laborer to have stronge armes and harde synwes; and slouthe maketh hem feble and tendre. Thanne comth drede to bigynne to werke [*do*] anye goode werkes. For certes, he that is enclyned to synne, nym thynketh [*it seems to him*] it is so greet an emprise [*enterprise*] for to undertake to doon werkes of goodnesse, and casteth [*considers*] in his herte that the circumstaunces of goodnesse been so grevouse and so chargeaunt [*heavy*] for to suffre, that he dar nat undertake to do werkes of goodnesse, as seith Seint Gregorie.

Now comth wanhope [*despair*], that is despeir of the mercy of God, that comth somtyme of to muche outrageous [*violent*] sorwe, and somtyme of to muche drede [*fear*], ymaginynge that he hath doon so muche synne that it wol nat availlen hym, though he wolde repenten hym and forsake synne; thurgh which despeir or drede he abaundoneth al his herte to every maner synne, as seith Seint Augustin. Which dampnable synne, if that it continue unto his [*its*] ende, it is cleped synnyng in the Hooly Goost. This horrible synne is so perilous that he that is despeired, ther nys no felonye ne no synne that he douteth for to do; as shewed [*shown*] wel by Judas. Certes, aboven alle synnes thanne is this synne moost displesant [*displeasing*] to Crist, and moost adversarie [*hostile*]. Soothly, he that despeireth hym is lyk the coward champioun recreant, that seith 'creant' withoute nede. Allas! allas! nedeles [*needlessly*] is he recreant and nedelees despeired. Certes, the mercy of God is evere redy to the penitent, and is aboven alle his werkes. Allas! kan a man nat bithynke hym on [*remem-*

1860-2 Men should practise doing good works, and in a manly and virtuous fashion acquire the inclination to do well.

1881-2 It is called sinning against the Holy Ghost.

1882-4 This horrible sin is so dangerous that he who is filled with despair knows no crime or sin he fears to commit.

1887-8 He that despairs is like the cowardly and recreant champion, who cries for mercy without need.

1890-1 And is greater than all His works.

ber] the gospel of Seint Luc, 15, where as Crist seith that 'as wel shal ther be joye in hevene upon a synful man that dooth penitence, as upon nynty and nyne rightful men that neden no penitence.' Looke forther, in the same gospel, the joye and the feeste [*festivity*] of the goode man that hadde lost his sone, whan his sone with repentaunce was retourned to his fader. Kan they nat remembren hem eek that, as seith Seint Luc, 23, how that the theef that was hanged bisyde Jhesu

1900 Crist, seyde: 'Lord, remembre of me, whan thow comest into thy regne [*kingdom*]?' 'For sothe,' seyde Crist, 'I seye to thee, to-day shaltow been with me in paradys.' Certes, ther is noon so horrible synne of man that it ne may in his lyf be destroyed by penitence, thurgh vertu of the passion and of the deeth of Crist. Allas! what nedeth man thanne to been despeired, sith that his mercy so redy is and large [*generous*]? Axe [*ask*] and have. Thanne cometh sompnolence, that is, sloggy [*sluggish*] slombrynge, which maketh a man be hevy and dul in body and in soule; and this synne comth of Slouthe.

1910 And certes, the tyme that, by wey of resoun, men sholde nat slepe, that is by the morwe, but if [*unless*] ther were cause resonable. For soothly, the morwe tyde is moost covenable [*fitting for*] a man to seye his preyeres, and for to thynken on God, and for to honoure God, and to yeven almesse [*alms*] to the povre that first cometh in the name of Crist. Lo, what seith Salomon: 'Whoso wolde by the morwe awaken and seke me, he shal fynde.' Thanne cometh necligence, or reccheleesnesse [*carelessness*], that rekketh of no thyng. And how that ignoraunce be mooder of alle harm, certes, necli-

1920 gence is the norice. Necligence ne dooth no fors [*does not bother*], whan he shal doon a thyng, wheither he do it weel or baddely.

Of [*concerning*] the remedie of thise two synnes, as seith the wise man, that 'he that dredeth God, he spareth nat to doon that him oghte doon.' And he that loveth God, he wol doon diligence [*do his utmost*] to plese God by his werkes, and abaundone [*devote*] hymself, with al his myght, wel for to doon [*to well-doing*]. Thanne comth ydelnesse, that is the yate of alle harmes. An ydel man is lyk to a place that hath

1930 no walles; the develes may entre on every syde, or sheten at hym at discovert, by temptacion on every syde. This

1892-5 Where Christ says there shall be as much joy in heaven over one sinful man that repents as over ninety and nine righteous men that need no repentance. (Luke xv. 7.)
1902-3 There is no sin of man so horrible.
1910-11 The time when, in all reason, a man should not sleep is in the morning.
1918-20 And just as ignorance is the mother of all evil, so certainly is negligence the nurse.
1930-1 Or shoot at him when he is unprotected, by tempting him on all sides.

ydelnesse is the thurrok [*sink*] of alle wikked and vileyns [*evil*]
thoghtes, and of alle jangles [*disputes*], trufles [*trifles*], and of
alle ordure [*filth*].   Certes, the hevene is yeven to hem that wol
labouren, and nat to ydel folk.   Eek David seith that 'they
ne been nat in the labour of men, ne they shul nat been
whipped with men,' that is to seyn, in purgatorie.   Certes,
thanne semeth it, they shul be tormented with the devel in
helle, but if they doon penitence.

1940   Thanne comth the synne that men clepen *tarditas*, as whan
a man is to laterede [*slow*] or tariynge [*tardy*], er he wole turne
to God; and certes, that is a greet folie.   He is lyk to hym
that falleth in the dych, and wol nat arise.   And this vice
comth of a fals hope, that he thynketh that he shal lyve longe;
but that hope faileth ful ofte.

Thanne comth lachesse [*laziness*]; that is he, that whan he
biginneth any good werk, anon he shal forleten it and stynten;
as doon they that han any wight to governe, and ne taken of
hym namoore kep, anon as they fynden any contrarie or
1950 any anoy.   Thise been the newe sheepherdes that leten hir
sheep wityngly [*knowingly*] go renne [*run*] to the wolf that is
in the breres [*briars*], or do no fors of hir owene governaunce.
Of this comth poverte and destruccioun, bothe of spiritueel
and temporeel thynges.   Thanne comth a manere cooldnesse,
that freseth [*freezes*] al the herte of a man.   Thanne comth
undevocioun [*lack of devotion*], thurgh which a man is so
blent [*blinded*], as seith Seint Bernard, and hath swich langour
in soule that he may neither rede ne singe in hooly chirche, ne
heere ne thynke of no devocioun, ne travaille with his handes
1960 in no good werk, that it nys hym unsavory and al apalled.
Thanne wexeth he slough and slombry, and soone wol be
wrooth, and soone is enclyned to hate and to envye.   Thanne
comth the synne of worldly sorwe, swich as is cleped *tristicia*,
that sleeth man, as seith Seint Paul.   For certes, swich sorwe
werketh to the deeth of the soule and of the body also; for
therof comth that a man is anoyed [*tired*] of his owene lif.
Wherfore swich sorwe shorteth [*shortens*] ful ofte the lif of
man, er that his tyme be come by wey of kynde [*nature*].

Remedium contra peccatum Accidie.

Agayns this horrible synne of Accidie, and the branches of
1970 the same, ther is a vertu that is called *fortitudo* or strengthe,

1935-7 Also David says that those who do not work with men shall
    not be whipped with men.
1947-50 Straightway stops and gives it up; as do they who have some
    person to take charge of, and who pay no more attention to him as
    soon as they meet with any opposition or trouble.
1952 Or do not bother to take charge of themselves.
1960 Without its being distasteful and stale to him.
1961 Then he grows slothful and sleepy.

that is an affeccioun [*state of mind*] thurgh which a man despiseth anoyouse [*harmful*] thinges. This vertu is so myghty and so vigerous that it dar [*dare*] withstonde myghtily and wisely kepen [*protect*] hymself fro perils that been wikked, and wrastle agayn [*against*] the assautes [*assaults*] of the devel. For it enhaunceth [*lifts up*] and enforceth [*strengthens*] the soule, right as Accidie abateth [*lowers*] it and maketh it fieble [*feeble*]. For this *fortitudo* may endure by long suffraunce the travailles that been covenable.

1980 This vertu hath manye speces; and the first is cleped magnanimitee, that is to seyn, greet corage. For certes, ther bihoveth greet corage agains Accidie, lest that it ne swolwe the soule by the synne of sorwe, or destroye it by wanhope [*despair*]. This vertu maketh folk to undertake harde thynges and grevouse [*painful*] thynges, by hir owene wil, wisely and resonably. And for as muchel as the devel fighteth agayns a man moore by queyntise [*cunning*] and by sleighte [*trickery*] than by strengthe, therfore men shal withstonden hym by wit and by resoun and by discrecioun. Thanne arn [*are*] ther the 1990 vertues of feith and hope in God and in his seintes, to acheve and acomplice the goode werkes in the whiche he purposeth fermely to continue. Thanne comth seuretee [*assurance*] or sikernesse [*self-confidence*] and that is whan a man ne douteth no travaille in tyme comynge of the goode werkes that a man hath bigonne. Thanne comth magnificence [*magnanimity*], that is to seyn, whan a man dooth and perfourneth [*performs*] grete werkes of goodnesse; and that is the ende why that [*for which*] men sholde do goode werkes, for in the acomplissynge of grete goode werkes lith [*lies*] the grete gerdoun [*reward*]. 2000 Thanne is ther constaunce [*constancy*], that is, stablenesse of corage [*spirit*]; and this sholde been in herte by stedefast feith, and in mouth, and in berynge [*bearing*], and in chiere [*countenance*], and in dede. Eke ther been mo speciale remedies against Accidie in diverse werkes, and in consideracioun of the peynes of helle and of the joyes of hevene, and in the trust of the grace of the Holy Goost, that wole yeve hym myght to perfourne his goode entente.

Sequitur de Avaricia.

After Accidie wol I speke of Avarice and of Coveitise [*covetousness*], of which synne seith Seint Paul that 'the root 2010 of alle harmes is Coveitise.' *Ad Thimotheum Sexto.* For

1978–9 May endure by long-suffering such hardships as are fitting.
1981–3 For certainly great courage is needed against Sloth, lest it swallow the soul.
1993–5 When a man does not fear any future hardship connected with the good works he has begun.
2003–4 Also there are other special remedies against Sloth, consisting in various works.

soothly, whan the herte of a man is confounded [*perturbed*]
in itself and troubled, and that the soule hath lost the confort
of God, thanne seketh he an ydel solas [*empty solace*] of
worldly thynges.

Avarice, after [*according to*] the descripcioun of Seint
Augustyn, is a likerousnesse [*greediness*] in herte to have
erthely thynges. Som oother folk seyn that Avarice is for to
purchacen [*acquire*] manye erthely thynges, and no thyng
yeve to hem that han nede. And understoond that Avarice
2020 ne stant nat oonly in lond ne catel, but somtyme in science and
in glorie, and in every manere of outrageous thyng is Avarice
and Coveitise. And the difference bitwixe Avarice and
Coveitise is this: Coveitise is for to coveite swiche thynges
as thou hast nat; and Avarice is for to withholde and kepe
swiche thynges as thou hast, withoute rightful nede. Soothly,
this Avarice is a synne that is ful dampnable; for al hooly
writ curseth it, and speketh agayns that vice; for it dooth
wrong to Jhesu Crist. For it bireveth [*takes from*] hym the
love that men to hym owen, and turneth it bakward agayns
2030 alle resoun, and maketh that the avaricious man hath moore
hope in his catel than in Jhesu Crist, and dooth moore obser-
vance in kepynge of his tresor than he dooth to the service of
Jhesu Crist. And therfore seith Seint Paul *ad Ephesios,
quinto*, that an avaricious man is in the thraldom of ydolatrie.

What difference is bitwixe an ydolastre [*idolater*] and an
avaricious man, but that an ydolastre, per aventure [*perhaps*],
ne hath but o mawmet [*idol*] or two, and the avaricious man
hath manye? For certes, every floryn in his cofre is his
mawmet. And certes, the synne of mawmettrie [*idolatry*] is
2040 the firste thyng that God deffended [*prohibited*] in the ten
comaundementz, as bereth witnesse in *Exodi capitulo vicesimo*.
'Thou shalt have no false goddes bifore me, ne thou shalt
make to thee no grave thyng.' Thus is an avaricious man,
that loveth his tresor biforn God, an ydolastre, thurgh this
cursed synne of avarice. Of Coveitise comen thise harde
lordshipes, thurgh whiche men been distreyned [*oppressed*]
by taylages [*taxes*], custumes [*customs duties*], and cariages,
moore than hire duetee or resoun is. And eek taken they
of hire bonde-men amercimentz [*fines*], whiche myghten moore
2050 resonably ben cleped extorcions than amercimentz. Of

2019–22 And understand that Avarice relates not only to land and
possessions but sometimes to knowledge and glory, and that in every
kind of excessive thing (i.e. excessive desire for worldly things)
Avarice and Covetousness are present.
2031–2 And pays more attention to the keeping of his treasure.
2034 Is in the bondage of idolatry.
2042–3 'Thou shalt not make unto thee any graven image.' (Exod. xx. 4.)
2047–8 *cariages*, a service of carrying, or a payment in lieu of it, owed
by a tenant to his lord; *moore . . . is*, more than is due from them or
reasonable.

whiche amercimentz and raunsonynge of boonde-men somme
lordes stywardes seyn that it is rightful, for as muche as a cherl
hath no temporeel thyng that it ne is his lordes, as they seyn.
But certes, thise lordshipes doon wrong that bireven hire
bonde-folk thynges that they nevere yave hem. *Augustinus,
de Civitate, libro nono.* Sooth is that the condicioun of
thraldom and the firste cause of thraldom is for synne.
Genesis, nono.

2060   Thus may ye seen that the gilt [*sin*] disserveth [*deserves*]
thraldom, but nat nature.   Wherfore thise lordes ne sholde
nat muche glorifien hem in [*exult in*] hir lordshipes, sith that
by natureel condicion they been nat lordes over thralles, but
that thraldom comth first by the desert of synne.   And further
over [*furthermore*], ther as [*whereas*] the lawe seith that temporeel goodes of boonde-folk been the goodes of hir lordshipes [*lords*], ye, that is for to understonde, the goodes of
the emperour, to deffenden hem in hir right, but nat for to
robben hem ne reven hem.   And therfore seith Seneca, 'Thy
prudence sholde lyve benignely [*kindly*] with thy thralles.'
2070 Thilke [*those*] that thou clepest [*call*] thy thralles been Goddes
peple; for humble folk been Cristes freendes; they been
contubernyal [*intimate*] with the Lord.

   Thynk eek that of swich seed as cherles spryngen, of swich
seed spryngen lordes.   As wel may the cherl be saved as the
lord.   The same deeth that taketh the cherl, swich deeth taketh
the lord.   Wherfore I rede, do right so with thy cherl, as
thou woldest that thy lord dide with thee, if thou were in his
plit.   Every synful man is a cherl to synne.   I rede thee,
certes, that thou, lord, werke [*act*] in swich wise with thy
2080 cherles that they rather love thee than drede.   I woot wel ther
is degree [*rank*] above degree, as reson is; and skile [*reasonable*]
is that men do hir devoir [*duty*] ther as it is due; but certes,
extorcions and despit [*contemptuous treatment*] of youre
underlynges is dampnable.

   And forther over, understoond wel that thise conquerours
or tirauntz maken ful ofte thralles of hem that been born of
as roial blood as been they that hem conqueren.   This name
of thraldom was nevere erst kowth, til that Noe seyde that his
sone Canaan sholde be thral to his bretheren for his synne.
2090 What seye we thanne of hem that pilen [*pillage*] and doon
extorcions to hooly chirche? Certes, the swerd that men
yeven first to a knyght, whan he is newe [*newly*] dubbed,

<hr>

2051 *raunsonynge,* ransoming, i.e. oppressing with exactions.
2062–3 And since thraldom first comes as the penalty of sin.
2066–8 That is to be understood thus: they are the goods of the emperor,
     who may defend his title to them, but not rob or take them away.
2076–8 I advise you to treat your churl exactly as you would like your
     lord to treat you, if you were in his place.
2088 Was never known until Noah.

signifieth that he sholde deffenden hooly chirche, and nat
robben it ne pilen it; and whoso dooth is traitour to Crist.
And, as seith Seint Augustyn, 'they been the develes wolves
that stranglen the sheep of Jhesu Crist'; and doon worse than
wolves. For soothly, whan the wolf hath ful his wombe
[*belly*], he stynteth [*ceases*] to strangle sheep. But soothly,
the pilours [*pillagers*] and destroyours of the godes of hooly
2100 chirche ne do nat so, for they ne stynte nevere to pile. Now
as I have seyd, sith so is that synne was first cause of thraldom,
thanne is it thus, that thilke [*at the*] tyme that al this world was
in synne, thanne was al this world in thraldom and subjeccioun.
But certes, sith the time of grace cam, God ordeyned that
som folk sholde be moore heigh [*higher*] in estaat and in
degree, and som folk moore lough [*lower*], and that everich
[*each*] sholde be served in his estaat [*class*] and in his degree
[*rank*]. And therfore in somme contrees, ther [*where*] they
byen [*buy*] thralles, whan they han turned [*converted*] hem to
2110 the feith, they maken hire thralles free out of thraldom.
And therfore, certes, the lord oweth to his man that [*what*]
the man oweth to his lord. The Pope calleth hymself servant
of the servantz of God; but for as muche as the estaat of
hooly chirche ne myghte nat han be, ne the commune profit
myghte nat han be kept, ne pees and rest in erthe, but if
[*unless*] God hadde ordeyned that som men hadde hyer degree
and som men lower, therfore was sovereyntee ordeyned, to
kepe and mayntene and deffenden hire underlynges or hire
subgetz in resoun, as ferforth as it lith in hire power, and nat
2120 to destroyen hem ne confounde [*ruin*]. Wherfore I seye that
thilke lordes that been lyk wolves, that devouren the posses-
siouns or the catel [*property*] of povre folk wrongfully, withouten mercy or mesure [*moderation*], they shul receyven, by
the same mesure that they han mesured to povre folk, the
mercy of Jhesu Crist, but if it be amended. Now comth
deceite bitwixe marchaunt and marchant. And thow shalt
understonde that marchandise [*trading*] is in manye maneres;
that oon is bodily, and that oother is goostly [*spiritual*]; that
oon is honest and leveful [*lawful*], and that oother is deshonest
2130 and unleveful. Of thilke bodily marchandise that is leveful
and honest is this: that, there as God hath ordeyned that a
regne [*kingdom*] or a contree is suffisaunt to hymself [*itself*],
thanne is it honest and leveful that of habundaunce of this
contree, that men helpe another contree that is moore nedy.

2113–15 Inasmuch as the dignity of Holy Church might not have been
    established, nor the common profit safeguarded, nor yet peace and
    quiet on earth.
2119 Within reason, as far as lies in their power.
2123–5 They shall receive, in the same measure as they have meted out
    mercy to the poor, the mercy of Jesus Christ, unless they mend their
    ways.

And therfore ther moote [*must*] been marchantz to bryngen fro that o contree to that oother hire marchandises. That oother marchandise, that men haunten [*practise*] with fraude and trecherie and deceite, with lesynges [*lies*] and false othes, is cursed and dampnable. Espiritueel marchandise is proprely
2140 symonye, that is, ententif [*eager*] desir to byen thyng espiritueel, that is, thyng that aperteneth [*belongs*] to the seintuarie [*sanctuary*] of God and to cure [*spiritual charge*] of the soule. This desir, if so be that a man do his diligence [*utmost*] to parfournen it, al be it that his desir ne take noon effect, yet is it to hym a deedly synne; and if he be ordred, he is irregu-leer. Certes symonye is cleped of [*after*] Simon Magus, that wolde han boght for [*with*] temporeel catel [*goods*] the yifte that God hadde yeven, by the Hooly Goost, to Seint Peter and to the apostles. And therfore understoond that bothe
2150 he that selleth and he that beyeth thynges espirituels been cleped symonyals [*simoniacs*], be it by catel, be it by procurynge, or by flesshly preyere of his freendes, flesshly freendes, or espiritueel freendes. Flesshly in two maneres; as by kynrede [*kindred*], or othere freendes. Soothly, if they praye for hym that is nat worthy and able, it is symonye, if he take the benefice; and if he be worthy and able, ther nys noon. That oother manere is whan men or wommen preyen for folk to avauncen hem, oonly for wikked flesshly affeccioun that they han unto the persone; and that is foul symonye. But certes,
2160 in service, for which men yeven thynges espirituels unto hir servantz, it moot been understonde that the service moot been honest, and elles nat; and eek that it be withouten bargaynynge, and that the persone be able [*deserving*]. For, as seith Seint Damasie, 'Alle the synnes of the world, at regard of this synne, arn as thyng of noght.' For it is the gretteste synne that may be, after the synne of Lucifer and Antecrist. For by this synne God forleseth [*loses*] the chirche and the soule that he boghte [*redeemed*] with his precious blood, by hem that yeven chirches to hem that been nat digne [*worthy*]. For they putten
2170 in theves that stelen the soules of Jhesu Crist and destroyen his patrimoyne [*patrimony*]. By swiche undigne preestes and curates han lewed [*ignorant*] men the lasse reverence of the sacramentz of hooly chirche; and swiche yeveres of chirches putten out the children of Crist, and putten into the chirche the

2145–6 If he is ordained, he violates the rules of his order.

2151 Whether it is done with goods, or by procurement.

2157–8 When men or women solicit someone's advancement.

2159–62 But certainly, it is to be understood that a service for which men give spiritual rewards to their servants must be honourable, or else they should not do so.

2164–5 All the sins of the world, by comparison with this sin, are a mere nothing.

develes owene sone. They sellen the soules that lambes
sholde kepen to the wolf that strangleth hem. And therfore
shul they nevere han part [*share*] of the pasture of lambes,
that is the blisse of hevene. Now comth hasardrie with his
apurtenaunces, as tables and rafles, of which comth deceite,
2180 false othes, chidynges [*reproaches*], and alle ravynes [*thefts*],
blasphemynge and reneiynge [*denying*] of God, and hate of
his neighebores, wast of goodes, mysspendynge of tyme, and
somtyme manslaughtre. Certes, hasardours ne mowe nat
been withouten greet synne whiles they haunte that craft. Of
Avarice comen eek lesynges [*lies*], thefte, fals witnesse, and
false othes. And ye shul understonde that thise been grete
synnes, and expres agayn the comaundementz of God, as I
have seyd. Fals witnesse is in word and eek in dede. In
word, as for to bireve [*take away*] thy neighebores goode
2190 name by thy fals witnessyng, or bireven hym his catel or his
heritage by thy fals witnessyng, whan thou for ire [*anger*], or
for meede [*bribe*], or for envye, berest fals witnesse, or accusest
hym or excusest hym by thy fals witnesse, or elles excusest
thyself falsly. Ware yow, questemongeres and notaries!
Certes, for fals witnessyng was Susanna in ful gret sorwe and
peyne, and many another mo [*besides*]. The synne of thefte
is eek expres agayns Goddes heeste [*commandment*], and that
in two maneres, corporeel [*corporal*] or spiritueel. Corporeel,
as for to take thy neighebores catel [*goods*] agayn his wyl, be
2200 it by force or by sleighte, be it by met or by mesure; by
stelyng eek of false enditementz upon hym, and in borwynge
of thy neighebores catel, in entente nevere to payen it
agayn, and semblable [*suchlike*] thynges. Espiritueel thefte is
sacrilege, that is to seyn, hurtynge of hooly thynges, or of
thynges sacred to Crist, in two maneres: by reson of the hooly
place, as chirches or chirche-hawes [*churchyards*], for which
every vileyns [*wicked*] synne that men doon in swiche places
may be cleped sacrilege, or every violence in the semblable
places; also, they that withdrawen falsly the rightes that longen
2210 [*belong*] to hooly chirche. And pleynly and generally, sacrilege is to reven [*take away*] hooly thyng fro hooly place, or
unhooly thyng out of hooly place, or hooly thing out of
unhooly place.

2175-6 Those (shepherds) who should watch over souls like lambs sell
   them to the wolf that strangles them.
2178-9 Now comes gambling with its appurtenances, such as backgammon and raffles.
2183-4 Certainly, gamblers cannot possibly be without great sin as
   long as they ply that trade.
2194 Beware, you jurymen and notaries.
2199-2200 Whether by force or trickery, or by false measure.
2200-1 By stealing upon him with false indictments.

Relevacio contra peccatum Avaricie.

Now shul ye understonde that the releevynge [*remedy*] of Avarice is misericorde [*mercy*], and pitee largely [*generously*] taken. And men myghten axe why that misericorde and pitee is releevynge of Avarice. Certes, the avaricious man sheweth no pitee ne misericorde to the nedeful [*needy*] man, for he deliteth hym in the kepynge of his tresor, and nat in the

2220 rescowynge ne releevynge of his evene-Cristen [*fellow Christian*]. And therfore speke I first of misericorde. Thanne is misericorde, as seith the philosophre, a vertu by which the corage [*heart*] of a man is stired by the mysese [*trouble*] of hym that is mysesed [*troubled*]. Upon which misericorde folweth pitee in parfournynge of charitable werkes of misericorde. And certes, thise thynges moeven a man to the misericorde of [*compassion for*] Jhesu Crist, that he yaf hymself for oure gilt, and suffred deeth for misericorde, and forgaf us oure originale synnes, and therby relessed us fro the peynes

2230 of helle, and amenused [*lessened*] the peynes of purgatorie by penitence, and yeveth grace wel to do, and atte laste the blisse of hevene. The speces of misericorde been, as for to lene and for to yeve, and to foryeven and relesse, and for to han pitee in herte and compassioun of the meschief [*misfortune*] of his evene-Cristene, and eek to chastise, there as [*where*] nede is. Another manere of remedie agayns avarice is resonable largesse [*liberality*]; but soothly, heere bihoveth the consideracioun of the grace of Jhesu Crist, and of his temporeel goodes, and eek of the goodes perdurables [*everlasting*], that Crist yaf

2240 to us; and to han remembrance of the deeth that he shal receyve, he noot [*knows not*] whanne, where, ne how; and eek that he shal forgon al that he hath, save oonly that he hath despended [*spent*] in goode werkes.

But for as muche as som folk been unmesurable [*immoderate*], men oghten eschue fool-largesse [*avoid foolish generosity*], that men clepen wast. Certes, he that is fool-large ne yeveth nat his catel [*goods*], but he leseth [*loses*] his catel. Soothly, what thyng that he yeveth for veyne glorie, as to mynstrals and to folk, for to beren his renoun in the world, he hath synne

2250 therof, and noon almesse. Certes, he leseth foule [*shamefully*] his good, that ne seketh with the yifte of his good nothyng but synne. He is lyk to an hors that seketh rather to drynken

---

2231-2 And gives us the grace to do well, and in the end the bliss of heaven.
2232-3 The kinds of mercy are to lend and give, and to forgive and release (from debt or obligation).
2237-8 Here, truly, a man needs to consider the grace of Jesus Christ.
2247-50 Truly, anything he gives for vainglory, such as to minstrels and other people, in order to spread his renown in the world, means that he is committing a sin, not doing a good deed.

drovy [*dirty*] or trouble [*troubled*] water than for to drynken water of the clere welle. And for as muchel as they yeven ther as they sholde nat yeven, to hem aperteneth [*belongs*] thilke malisoun [*curse*] that Crist shal yeven at the day of doom [*judgment*] to hem that shullen been dampned.

Sequitur de Gulâ.

After Avarice comth Glotonye, which is expres eek agayn [*against*] the comandement of God. Glotonye is unmesurable 2260 [*immoderate*] appetit to ete or to drynke, or elles to doon [*minister*] ynogh to the unmesurable appetit and desordeynee [*inordinate*] coveitise [*craving*] of eten or to drynke. This synne corrumped [*corrupted*] al this world, as is wel shewed in the synne of Adam and of Eve. Looke eek what seith Seint Paul of Glotonye: 'Manye,' seith Saint Paul, 'goon, of whiche I have ofte seyd to yow, and now I seye it wepynge, that been the enemys of the croys of Crist; of whiche the ende is deeth, and of whiche hire wombe [*whose belly*] is hire god, and hire glorie in confusioun of hem that so savouren erthely 2270 thynges.' He that is usaunt [*addicted*] to this synne of glotonye, he ne may no synne withstonde. He moot [*must*] been in servage of [*thraldom to*] alle vices, for it is the develes hoord [*treasure-house*] ther he hideth hym and resteth. This synne hath manye speces. The firste is dronkenesse, that is the horrible sepulture [*tomb*] of mannes resoun; and therfore, whan a man is dronken, he hath lost his resoun; and this is deedly synne. But soothly, whan that a man is nat wont [*used*] to strong drynke, and peraventure ne knoweth nat the strengthe of the drynke, or hath feblesse in his heed, or hath 2280 travailed, thurgh which he drynketh the moore, al [*although*] be he sodeynly caught with [*snared by*] drynke, it is no deedly synne, but venyal. The seconde spece of glotonye is that the spirit of a man wexeth al trouble [*disturbed*], for dronkenesse bireveth hym the discrecioun of his wit. The thridde spece of glotonye is whan a man devoureth his mete [*food*], and hath no rightful manere of etynge. The fourthe is whan, thurgh the grete habundaunce of his mete, the humours in his body been distempred. The fifthe is foryetelnesse [*forgetfulness*] by to muchel drynkynge; for which somtyme a man foryeteth er the 2290 morwe [*morning*] what he dide at even, or on the nyght biforn.

In oother manere been distinct the speces of Glotonye, after [*according to*] Seint Gregorie. The firste is for to ete biforn tyme to ete. The seconde is whan a man get hym to delicaat

2269–70 And who glory in the shame of those that thus relish earthly things. (Cf. Phil. iii. 19.)
2279–80 Or has a weak head, or has been working hard.
2292–4 The first is to eat before it is time for eating. The second is when a man gets for himself too delicate food or drink.

mete or drynke. The thridde is whan men taken to muche
over [*beyond*] mesure. The fourthe is curiositee, with greet
entente to maken and apparaillen his mete. The fifthe is for
to eten to gredily. Thise been the fyve fyngres of the develes
hand, by whiche he draweth folk to synne.

Remedium contra peccatum Gule.

Agayns Glotonye is the remedie abstinence, as seith Galien
2300 [*Galen*]; but that holde I nat meritorie [*meritorious*], if he do
it oonly for the heele [*health*] of his body. Seint Augustyn
wole that abstinence be doon for vertu and with pacience.
'Abstinence,' he seith, 'is litel worth, but if [*unless*] a man have
good wil therto, and but it be enforced by pacience and by
charitee, and that men doon it for Godes sake, and in hope
to have the blisse of hevene.'
   The felawes [*companions*] of abstinence been attemperaunce,
that holdeth the meene [*mean*] in alle thynges; eek shame, that
eschueth alle deshonestee; suffisance, that seketh no riche
2310 metes ne drynkes, ne dooth no fors of to outrageous apparail-
ynge of mete; mesure [*moderation*] also, that restreyneth by
resoun the deslavee [*inordinate*] appetit of etynge; sobrenesse
also, that restreyneth the outrage [*excess*] of drynke; sparynge
also, that restreyneth the delicaat ese to sitte longe at his mete
and softely, wherfore some folk stonden of hir owene wyl to
eten at the lasse leyser [*less leisure*].

Sequitur de Luxuria.

After Glotonye thanne comth Lecherie, for thise two synnes
been so ny cosyns that ofte tyme they wol nat departe [*separate*]. God woot, this synne is ful displesaunt thyng to God;
2320 for he seyde hymself, 'Do no lecherie.' And therfore he putte
grete peynes [*penalties*] agayns this synne in the olde lawe.
If womman thral were taken in this synne, she sholde be beten
with staves to the deeth; and if she were a gentil womman, she
sholde be slayn with stones; and if she were a bisshoppes
doghter, she sholde been brent [*burnt*], by Goddes comandement. Further over, by [*for*] the synne of lecherie God
dreynte [*drowned*] al the world at the diluge. And after that

2295-6 The fourth is fastidiousness, with great attention to making
   and preparing one's food.
2308-11 Shame, that avoids all unseemliness; contentment, that seeks
   no rich foods or drinks, and cares nothing for the extravagant preparation of food.
2313-15 Frugality also, that curbs the delicious delight of sitting long
   and luxuriously at table.
2321 *olde lawe*, i.e. Mosaic dispensation.

he brente fyve citees with thonder-leyt [*lightning*], and sank
hem into helle.

2330   Now lat us speke thanne of thilke stynkynge synne of
Lecherie that men clepe avowtrie [*adultery*] of wedded folk,
that is to seyn, if that oon of hem be wedded, or elles bothe.
Seint John seith that avowtiers shullen been in helle, in a
stank [*pool*] brennynge of fyr and of brymston; in fyr, for hire
lecherye; in brymston, for the stynk of hire ordure [*filth*].
Certes, the brekynge of this sacrement is an horrible thyng.
It was maked of [*made by*] God hymself in paradys, and
confermed by Jhesu Crist, as witnesseth Seint Mathew in the
gospel: 'A man shal lete [*leave*] fader and mooder, and taken
2340   hym [*betake himself*] to his wif, and they shullen be two in o
[*one*] flessh.' This sacrement bitokneth [*betokens*] the knyt-
tynge togidre of Crist and of hooly chirche. And nat oonly
that God forbad avowtrie in dede, but eek he comanded that
thou sholdest nat coveite thy neighebores wyf. 'In this
heeste [*commandment*],' seith Seint Augustyn, 'is forboden alle
manere coveitise [*craving*] to doon lecherie.' Lo, what seith
Seint Mathew in the gospel, that 'whoso seeth a womman to
coveitise of his lust, he hath doon lecherie with hire in his
herte.' Heere may ye seen that nat oonly the dede [*doing*] of
2350   this synne is forboden, but eek the desir to doon that synne.
This cursed synne anoyeth grevousliche [*harms grievously*] hem
that it haunten [*practise*]. And first to hire soule, for he
obligeth it to synne and to peyne of deeth that is perdurable
[*everlasting*]. Unto the body anoyeth it grevously also, for it
dreyeth hym, and wasteth him, and shent hym, and of his
blood he maketh sacrifice to the feend of helle. It wasteth
eek his catel [*property*] and his substaunce. And certes, if
it be a foul thyng a man to waste his catel on wommen, yet is
it a fouler thyng whan that, for swich ordure, wommen dis-
2360   penden [*spend*] upon men hir catel and substaunce. This
synne, as seith the prophete, bireveth [*takes away from*] man
and womman hir goode fame and al hire honour; and it is
ful plesaunt to the devel, for therby wynneth he the mooste
partie [*greatest part*] of this world. And right as a marchant
deliteth hym moost in chaffare [*business*] that he hath moost
avantage of, right so deliteth the fend in this ordure.

    This is that oother [*the second*] hand of the devel with fyve
fyngres to cacche [*draw*] the peple to his vileynye [*wickedness*].
The firste fynger is the fool lookynge [*foolish gazing*] of the
2370   fool womman and of the fool man, that sleeth, right as the
basilicok [*basilisk*] sleeth folk by the venym of his sighte; for
the coveitise of eyen [*lust of the eyes*] folweth the coveitise of
the herte. The seconde fynger is the vileyns [*vile*] touchynge

2347–8 Whoever looks at a woman to lust after her. (Matt. v. 28.)
2354–5 For it dries up a man, and wastes and shames him.

in wikkede manere. And therfore seith Salomon that 'whoso
toucheth and handleth a womman, he fareth lyk hym that
handleth the scorpioun that styngeth and sodeynly sleeth
thurgh his envenymynge [*poison*]'; as whoso toucheth warm
pych [*pitch*], it shent [*defiles*] his fyngres. The thridde is
foule wordes, that fareth [*act*] lyk fyr, that right anon brenneth
2380 [*burns*] the herte. The fourthe fynger is the kissynge; and
trewely he were a greet fool that wolde kisse the mouth of a
brennynge oven or of a fourneys [*furnace*]. And moore fooles
been they that kissen in vileynye [*wickedness*], for that mouth
is the mouth of helle; and namely thise olde dotardes holours,
yet wol they kisse, though they may nat do, and smatre hem.
Certes, they been lyk to houndes; for an hound, whan he
comth by the roser [*rose-bush*] or by othere [bushes], though
he may nat pisse, yet wole he heve [*lift*] up his leg and make a
contenaunce [*pretence*] to pisse. And for that many man
2390 weneth [*believes*] that he may nat synne, for no likerousnesse
[*lechery*] that he dooth with his wyf, certes, that opinion is
fals. God woot, a man may sleen hymself with his owene
knyf, and make hymselven dronken of his owene tonne [*cask*].
Certes, be it wyf, be it child, or any worldly thyng that he
loveth biforn God, it is his mawmet [*idol*], and he is an ydolastre [*idolater*]. Man sholde loven hys wyf by discrecioun,
paciently and atemprely [*temperately*]; and thanne is she as
though it were his suster. The fifthe fynger of the develes
hand is the stynkynge dede of Leccherie. Certes, the fyve
2400 fyngres of Glotonie the feend put [*puts*] in the wombe [*belly*]
of a man, and with his fyve fingres of Lecherie he gripeth
hym by the reynes [*loins*], for to throwen hym into the fourneys
of helle, ther as they shul han the fyr and the wormes that
evere shul lasten, and wepynge and wailynge, sharp hunger and
thurst, and grymnesse of develes, that shullen al totrede
[*trample on*] hem withouten respit and withouten ende.
Of [*from*] Leccherie, as I seyde, sourden [*spring*] diverse speces,
as fornicacioun, that is bitwixe man and womman that been
nat maried; and this is deedly synne, and agayns nature. Al
2410 that is enemy and destruccioun to nature is agayns nature.
Parfay [*truly*], the resoun of a man telleth eek hym wel that it
is deedly synne, for as muche as God forbad leccherie. And
Seint Paul yeveth hem the regne that nys dewe to no wight
but to hem that doon deedly synne. Another synne of
Leccherie is to bireve [*deprive*] a mayden of hir maydenhede;
for he that so dooth, certes, he casteth a mayden out of the
hyeste degree that is in this present lif, and bireveth hire thilke

---

2384–5 And especially those old doting fornicators who, impotent
though they are, will still steal a kiss and dabble in dirt.
2413–14 St Paul gives them the kingdom which is due to none but those
who commit deadly sin. (Cf. Gal. v. 21.)

precious fruyt that the book clepeth the hundred fruyt.   I ne
kan seye it noon ootherweyes [*in no other way*] in Englissh,
2420 but in Latyn it highte [*is called*] *Centesimus fructus*.   Certes,
he that so dooth is cause of manye damages and vileynyes
[*shameful wrongs*], mo than any man kan rekene [*reckon*];
right as he somtyme is cause of alle damages that beestes don
in the feeld, that breketh [*breaks*] the hegge or the closure
[*enclosure*], thurgh which he destroyeth that [*what*] may nat
been restoored [*made good*].   For certes, namoore may
maydenhede be restoored than an arm that is smyten fro the
body may retourne agayn to wexe.   She may have mercy,
this woot I wel, if she do penitence; but nevere shal it be that
2430 she nas corrupt.   And al be it so that I have spoken somwhat
of avowtrie, it is good to shewen mo perils that longen to
avowtrie, for to eschue that foule synne.   Avowtrie in Latyn
is for to seyn, approchynge of oother mannes bed, thurgh
which tho that whilom [*once*] weren o flessh abawndone hir
bodyes to othere persones.   Of this synne, as seith the wise
man, folwen manye harmes.   First, brekynge of feith; and
certes, in feith is the keye of Cristendom [*Christianity*].   And
whan that feith is broken and lorn [*lost*], soothly Cristendom
stant veyn [*stands barren*] and withouten fruyt.   This synne
2440 is eek a thefte; for thefte generally is for to reve a wight
[*deprive a person of*] his thyng agayns his wille.   Certes, this
is the fouleste thefte that may be, whan a womman steleth hir
body from hir housbonde, and yeveth it to hire holour [*lecher*]
to defoulen [*defile*] hire; and steleth hir soule fro Crist, and
yeveth it to the devel.   This is a fouler thefte than for to breke
[*break into*] a chirche and stele the chalice; for thise avowtiers
breken the temple of God spiritually, and stelen the vessel of
grace, that is the body and the soule, for which Crist shal
destroyen hem, as seith Seint Paul.   Soothly, of this thefte
2450 douted [*feared*] gretly Joseph, whan that his lordes wyf preyed
hym of vileynye, whan he seyde, 'Lo, my lady, how my lord
hath take to me under my warde al that he hath in this world,
ne no thyng of his thynges is out of my power, but oonly ye,
that been his wyf.   And how sholde I thanne do this wikkednesse, and synne so horribly agayns God and agayns my lord?
God it forbeede!'   Allas! al to litel is swich trouthe [*fidelity*]
now yfounde.   The thridde harm is the filthe thurgh which
they breken the comandement of God, and defoulen the
auctour [*author*] of matrimoyne, that is Crist.   For certes,

2418 *hundred fruyt*, i.e. fruit brought forth a hundredfold.   (Cf. Matt.
xiii. 8.)
2428 Can return to it and grow again.
2429–30 But she shall never change the fact that she has been defiled.
2432–3 Adultery in Latin means.
2450–2 Joseph, when his lord's wife asked him to do evil . . . my lord
has entrusted to my safe-keeping all he has in this world.

2460 in so muche as the sacrement of mariage is so noble and so
digne [*worthy*], so muche is it gretter synne for to breken it;
for God made mariage in paradys, in the estaat of innocence,
to multiplye mankynde to the service of God. And therfore
is the brekynge therof the moore grevous; of which brekynge
comen false heires ofte tyme, that wrongfully ocupien folkes
heritages. And therfore wol Crist putte hem out of the regne
of hevene, that is heritage to goode folk. Of this brekynge
comth eek ofte tyme that folk unwar [*unawares*] wedden or
synnen with hire owene kynrede, and namely thilke harlotes
2470 that haunten bordels of thise fool wommen, that mowe be
likned to a commune gong [*public lavatory*], where as men
purgen hire ordure. What seye we eek of putours [*pimps*]
that lyven by the horrible synne of putrie [*prostitution*], and
constreyne wommen to yelden hem a certeyn rente of hire
bodily puterie, ye, somtyme of his owene wyf or his child, as
doon thise bawdes? Certes, thise been cursede synnes.
Understoond eek that Avowtrie is set gladly [*aptly*] in the ten
comandementz bitwixe thefte and manslaughtre; for it is the
gretteste thefte that may be, for it is thefte of body and of
2480 soule. And it is lyk to homycide, for it kerveth atwo [*cuts
in two*] and breketh atwo hem that first were maked o flessh.
And therfore, by the olde lawe of God, they sholde be slayn.
But nathelees, by the lawe of Jhesu Crist, that is lawe of pitee,
whan he seyde to the womman that was founden in avowtrie,
and sholde han been slayn with stones, after the wyl of the
Jewes, as was hir lawe, 'Go,' quod Jhesu Crist, 'and have
namoore wyl [*desire*] to synne,' or, 'wille namoore to do
synne.' Soothly the vengeaunce of Avowtrie is awarded
to the peynes of helle, but if [*unless*] so be that it be des-
2490 tourbed [*prevented*] by penitence. Yet been ther mo speces
[*more kinds*] of this cursed synne; as whan that oon of hem
is religious, or elles bothe; or of folk that been entred into
ordre, as subdekne, or dekne, or preest, or hospitaliers.
And evere the hyer that he is in ordre, the gretter is the
synne. The thynges that gretly agreggen [*aggravate*] hire
synne is the brekynge of hire avow [*vow*] of chastitee, whan
they receyved the ordre. And forther over, sooth is that
hooly ordre is chief of al the tresorie [*treasury*] of God, and his
especial signe and mark of chastitee, to shewe that they been
2500 joyned to chastitee, which that is the moost precious lyf that
is. And thise ordred folk been specially titled [*dedicated*]

2469-70 And especially those scoundrels that frequent the brothels of
foolish women.
2473-5 And compel women to make them a certain payment from the
proceeds of their prostitution.
2488-9 Vengeance on adultery is handed over to the pains of hell.
2492-3 Or when the people concerned are members of a religious
order, such as a subdeacon ... or (knights) hospitallers.

to God, and of the special meignee [*household*] of God, for
which, whan they doon deedly synne, they been the special
traytours of God and of his peple; for they lyven of [*live off*]
the peple, to preye for the peple, and while they ben suche
traitours, here preyer avayleth nat to the peple.   Preestes been
aungels, as by the dignitee of hir mysterye; but for sothe,
Seint Paul seith that Sathanas transformeth hym in [*himself
into*] an aungel of light.   Soothly, the preest that haunteth
2510 [*practises*] deedly synne, he may be likned to the aungel of
derknesse transformed in the aungel of light.   He semeth
aungel of light, but for sothe he is aungel of derknesse.
Swiche preestes been the sones of Helie [*Eli*], as sheweth [*is
shown*] in the Book of Kynges, that they weren the sones of
Belial, that is, the devel.   Belial is to seyn [*means*], 'withouten
juge'; and so faren they; hem thynketh [*it seems to them*] they
been free, and han no juge, namoore than hath a free bole
that taketh which cow that hym liketh in the town.   So faren
[*behave*] they by [*with*] wommen.   For right as a free bole is
2520 ynough for al a toun, right so is a wikked preest corrupcioun
ynough for al a parisshe, or for al a contree [*a whole district*].
Thise preestes, as seith the book, ne konne nat the mysterie of
preesthod to the peple, ne God ne knowe they nat.   They ne
helde hem nat apayd [*were not satisfied*], as seith the book, of
soden [*with boiled*] flessh that was to hem offred, but they tooke
by force the flessh that is rawe.   Certes, so [*just so*] thise
shrewes [*wicked persons*] ne holden hem nat apayed of roosted
flessh and sode flessh, with which the peple feden hem in greet
reverence, but they wole have raw flessh of folkes wyves and
2530 hir doghtres.   And certes, thise wommen that consenten to
hire harlotrie [*evil conduct*] doon greet wrong to Crist, and to
hooly chirche, and alle halwes [*saints*], and to alle soules; for
they bireven alle thise hym that sholde worshipe Crist and
hooly chirche, and preye for Cristene soules.   And therfore
han swiche preestes, and hire lemmanes [*concubines*] eek that
consenten to hir leccherie, the malisoun [*curse*] of al the court
Cristien, til they come to amendement.   The thridde spece
of avowtrie is somtyme bitwixe a man and his wyf, and
that is whan they take no reward in hire assemblynge but
2540 oonly to hire flesshly delit, as seith Seint Jerome, and ne
rekken of [*care for*] nothyng but that they been assembled

2507 Because of the dignity of their office.
2517–18 Any more than a parish bull (i.e. one communally owned)
    that takes any cow in the town it fancies.
2522–3 These priests, as the Bible says, do not understand the ministry
    of priesthood to the people.
2532–3 For they take from all these him (i.e. the priest) who should
    worship Christ.
2537 Until they mend their ways.
2539–40 When they have no regard in their union for anything but their
    fleshly delight.

[*united*]; by cause that they been maried, al is good ynough, as thynketh to hem. But in swich folk hath the devel power, as seyde the aungel Raphael to Thobie [*Tobias*], for in hire assemblynge they putten Jhesu Crist out of hire herte, and yeven hemself to alle ordure [*filth*]. The fourthe spece is the assemblee of hem that been of hire kynrede, or of hem that been of oon affynytee, or elles with hem with whiche hir fadres or hir kynrede han deled in the synne
2550 of lecherie. This synne maketh hem lyk to houndes, that taken no kep [*heed*] to kynrede. And certes, parentele [*kinship*] is in two maneres, outher goostly [*spiritual*] or flesshly; goostly, as for to deelen with his godsibbes [*god-parents*]. For right so as he that engendreth a child is his flesshly fader, right so is his godfader his fader espiritueel. For which a womman may in no lasse [*less*] synne assemblen with hire godsib than with hire owene flesshly brother. The fifthe spece is thilke abhomynable [*unnatural*] synne, of which that no man unnethe [*scarcely*] oghte speke ne write; nathelees
2560 it is openly reherced [*set down*] in holy writ. This cursednesse [*wickedness*] doon men and wommen in diverse entente and in diverse manere; but though that hooly writ speke of horrible synne, certes hooly writ may nat been defouled, namoore than the sonne that shyneth on the mixne [*dunghill*]. Another synne aperteneth to leccherie, that comth in slepynge, and this synne cometh ofte to hem that been maydenes [*virgins*], and eek to hem that been corrupt; and this synne men clepen polucioun [*self-pollution*], that comth in foure maneres. Somtyme of langwissynge [*sickness*] of body, for
2570 the humours been to [*too*] ranke and to habundaunt in the body of man; somtyme of infermetee, for the fieblesse of the vertu retentif, as phisik maketh mencion; somtyme for surfeet of mete and drynke; and somtyme of vileyns [*wicked*] thoghtes that been enclosed in mannes mynde whan he gooth to slepe, which may nat been withoute synne; for which men moste kepen hem wisely, or elles may men synnen ful grevously.

Remedium contra peccatum luxurie.

Now comth the remedie agayns Leccherie, and that is generally chastitee and continence, that restreyneth alle the desordeynee moevynges [*unregulated impulses*] that comen of
2580 flesshly talentes [*desires*]. And evere the gretter merite shal

2546–50 The fourth kind is the union of those who are kindred, or related by marriage, or else of those with one of whom the father or kinsman of the other has had lecherous dealings.
2561–2 For various reasons and in various ways.
2571–2 Because of the feebleness of the retentive faculty, as physicians tell us.
2575–6 For which reasons men must take prudent care of themselves.

he han, that moost [*most*] restreyneth the wikkede eschawfynges
[*inflammation*] of the ardour of this synne. And this is in
two maneres, that is to seyn, chastitee in mariage, and chastitee
of widwehod. Now shaltow understonde that matrimoyne
is leefful assemblynge [*lawful union*] of man and of womman
that receyven by vertu of the sacrement the boond thurgh
which they may nat be departed [*parted*] in al hir lyf, that is to
seyn, whil that they lyven bothe. This, as seith the book, is
a ful greet sacrement. God maked it, as I have seyd, in
2590 paradys, and wolde hymself be born in mariage. And for to
halwen [*hallow*] mariage he was at a weddynge, where as he
turned water into wyn; which was the firste miracle that he
wroghte in erthe [*on earth*] biforn his disciples. Trewe effect
of mariage clenseth fornicacioun and replenysseth hooly
chirche of [*with*] good lynage [*lineage*]; for that is the ende of
mariage; and it chaungeth deedly synne into venial synne
bitwixe hem that been ywedded, and maketh the hertes al
oon [*one*] of hem that been ywedded, as wel as the bodies.
This is verray [*true*] mariage, that was establissed by God,
2600 er that synne bigan, whan natureel lawe was in his right poynt
[*its rightful place*] in paradys; and it was ordeyned that o man
sholde have but o womman, and o womman but o man, as
seith Seint Augustyn, by [*for*] manye resouns.

   First, for mariage is figured bitwixe Crist and holy chirche.
And that oother is for a man is heved of a womman; algate, by
ordinaunce it sholde be so. For if a womman hadde mo men
than oon, thanne sholde she have moo hevedes than oon, and
that were an horrible thyng biforn God; and eek a womman
ne myghte nat plese to [*too*] many folk at oones [*once*]. And
2610 also ther ne sholde nevere be pees ne reste [*quiet*] amonges
hem; for everich wolde axen his owene thyng. And forther
over, no man ne sholde knowe his owene engendrure [*progeny*],
ne who sholde have his heritage; and the womman sholde
been the lasse biloved fro [*from*] the tyme that she were
conjoynt [*joined*] to many men.

   Now comth how that a man sholde bere hym with his wif,
and namely [*especially*] in two thynges, that is to seyn, in
suffraunce [*patience*] and reverence, as shewed Crist whan he
made first womman. For he ne made hire nat of the heved
2620 [*from the head*] of Adam, for she sholde nat clayme to [*too*]
greet lordshipe. For ther as the womman hath the maistrie
[*mastery*], she maketh to muche desray [*confusion*]. Ther

2593-4 The true result of marriage is that it cleanses fornication.
2604-6 First, because marriage symbolizes the union of Christ and
   Holy Church. Secondly, because a man is the head of a woman; at
   any rate, he should be so by God's law.
2611 For each one would make his own demands.
2616 Now comes the matter of how a man should behave towards his
   wife.

neden none ensamples of this; the experience of day by day oghte suffise. Also, certes, God ne made nat womman of the foot of Adam, for she ne sholde nat been holden [*held*] to lowe; for she kan nat paciently suffre. But God made womman of the ryb of Adam, for womman sholde be felawe [*companion*] unto man. Man sholde bere hym to his wyf in feith, in trouthe, and in love, as seith Seint Paul, that a man 2630 sholde loven his wyf as Crist loved hooly chirche, that loved it so wel that he deyde [*died*] for it. So sholde a man for his wyf, if it were nede.

Now how that a womman sholde be subget [*subject*] to hire housbonde, that telleth Seint Peter. First, in obedience. And eek, as seith the decree, a womman that is wyf, as longe as she is a wyf, she hath noon auctoritee to swere ne to bere witnesse withoute leve [*permission*] of hir housbonde, that is hire lord; algate [*at any rate*], he sholde be so by resoun. She sholde eek serven hym in alle honestee [*virtue*], and been 2640 attempree [*discreet*] of hire array. I woot wel that they sholde setten hire entente [*mind*] to plesen hir housbondes, but nat by hire queyntise [*elegance*] of array. Seint Jerome seith that 'wyves that been apparailled in silk and in precious purpre [*purple*] ne mowe nat clothen hem in Jhesu Crist.' Loke what seith Seint John eek in thys matere? Seint Gregorie eek seith that 'no wight seketh precious array but oonly for veyne glorie, to been honoured the moore biforn the peple.' It is a greet folye, a womman to have a fair array outward and in hirself be foul inward. A wyf sholde eek be mesurable 2650 [*modest*] in lookynge and in berynge and in lawghynge [*laughing*], and discreet in alle hire wordes and hire dedes. And aboven alle worldly thyng she sholde loven hire housbonde with al hire herte, and to hym be trewe of hir body. So sholde an housbonde eek be to his wyf. For sith that al the body is the housbondes, so sholde hire herte been, or elles ther is bitwixe hem two, as in that, no parfit mariage. Thanne shal men understonde that for three thynges a man and his wyf flesshly mowen assemble. The firste is in entente of engendrure of children to the service of God; 2660 for certes that is the cause final of matrimoyne. Another cause is to yelden everich of hem to oother the dette of hire bodies; for neither of hem hath power of his owene body. The thridde is for to eschewe [*shun*] leccherye and vileynye [*wickedness*]. The ferthe is for sothe deedly synne. As to the firste, it is meritorie [*meritorious*]; the seconde also,

2655-6 Or else, in that respect, there is no perfect marriage between the two of them.
2657-9 For three reasons a man and his wife may come together in fleshly union. The first is with the intention of begetting children.
2660-3 The second reason is that each shall pay to the other the debt of his body; for neither has power over his own body.

for, as seith the decree, that she hath merite of chastitee that
yeldeth to hire housbonde the dette of hir body, ye, though it
be agayn hir likynge and the lust [*desire*] of hire herte. The
thridde manere is venyal synne; and, trewely, scarsly may ther
2670 any of thise be withoute venial synne, for [*because of*] the
corrupcion and for the delit. The fourthe manere is for to
understonde, as if they assemble oonly for amorous love and
for noon of the foreseyde causes, but for to accomplice
[*fulfil*] thilke brennynge delit, they rekke nevere how ofte.
Soothly it is deedly synne; and yet, with sorwe, somme folk
wol peynen hem moore to doon than to hire appetit suffiseth.
    The seconde manere of chastitee is for to been a clene
wydewe, and eschue the embracynges of man, and desiren the
embracynge of Jhesu Crist. Thise been tho that han been
2680 wyves and han forgoon [*given up*] hire housbondes, and eek
wommen that han doon leccherie and been releeved [*restored*]
by penitence. And certes, if that a wyf koude kepen hire al
chaast by licence [*permission*] of hir housbonde, so that she
yeve nevere noon occasion that she agilte, it were to hire a
greet merite. Thise manere wommen that observen chastitee
moste [*must*] be clene in herte as wel as in body and in thought,
and mesurable [*modest*] in clothynge and in contenaunce; and
been abstinent in etynge and drynkynge, in spekynge, and in
dede [*doing*]. They been the vessel or the boyste [*box*] of the
2690 blissed Magdelene, that fulfilleth [*fills*] hooly chirche of [*with*]
good odour. The thridde manere of chastitee is virginitee,
and it bihoveth [*is necessary*] that she be hooly in herte and
clene of body. Thanne is she spouse to Jhesu Crist, and she
is the lyf of angeles. She is the preisynge [*glory*] of this world,
and she is as thise martirs in egalitee; she hath in hire that
tonge may nat telle ne herte thynke. Virginitee baar [*bore*]
oure Lord Jhesu Crist, and virgine was hymselve.
    Another remedie agayns Leccherie is specially to with-
drawen swiche thynges as yeve occasion to thilke vileynye, as
2700 ese [*idleness*], etynge, and drynkynge. For certes, whan the
pot boyleth strongly, the beste remedie is to withdrawe the
fyr. Slepynge longe in greet quiete is eek a greet norice to
Leccherie.
    Another remedie agayns Leccherie is that a man or a
womman eschue the compaignye of hem by whiche he douteth
[*fears*] to be tempted; for al be it so that [*although*] the dede be
withstonden, yet is ther greet temptacioun. Soothly, a whit

2671–6 The fourth way is to be understood as a union merely for
    amorous love . . . and yet—bad luck to them!—some people will try
    to do what is more than enough to satisfy their appetite.
2683–4 As long as she never gave him cause to sin.
2693–4 And hers is the life of the angels.
2695 And she is on an equality with the martyrs.
2707–9 Truly, a white wall will not burn when a candle is stuck against
    it, yet the wall is blackened by the flame.

wal, although it ne brenne noght fully by stikynge of a candele,
yet is the wal blak of the leyt.   Ful ofte tyme I rede that no
2710 man truste in his owene perfeccioun, but [unless] he be stronger
than Sampson, and hoolier than David, and wiser than
Salomon.

Now after that I have declared yow, as I kan, the sevene
deedly synnes, and somme of hire braunches and hire remedies,
soothly, if I koude, I wolde telle yow the ten comandementz.
But so heigh a doctrine I lete [leave] to divines.   Nathelees,
I hope to God, they been touched in this tretice, everich
[every one] of hem alle.

SEQUITUR SECUNDA PARS PENITENCIE

Now for as muche as the seconde partie of Penitence stant
2720 [consists] in Confessioun of mouth, as I bigan in the firste
chapitre, I seye, Seint Augustyn seith: 'Synne is every word
and every dede, and al that men coveiten [covet], agayn the
lawe of Jhesu Crist; and this is for to synne in herte, in mouth,
and in dede, by thy fyve wittes [senses], that been sighte,
herynge, smellynge, tastynge or savourynge, and feelynge.'
Now is it good to understonde the circumstances that agreggen muchel [aggravate greatly] every synne.   Thou shalt
considere what thow art that doost the synne, wheither thou
be male or femele, yong or oold, gentil or thral, free or
2730 servant, hool or syk, wedded or sengle, ordred or unordred,
wys or fool, clerk or seculeer; if she be of thy kynrede, bodily
or goostly, or noon; if any of thy kynrede have synned with
hire, or noon; and manye mo [more] thinges.

Another circumstaunce is this: wheither it be doon in
fornicacioun or in avowtrie or noon; incest or noon; mayden
or noon; in manere of homicide or noon; horrible grete
synnes or smale; and how longe thou hast continued in synne.
The thridde circumstaunce is the place ther [where] thou hast
do synne; wheither in oother mennes hous or in thyn owene;
2740 in feeld or in chirche or in chirchehawe; in chirche dedicaat
or noon.   For if the chirche be halwed [hallowed], and man or
womman spille his kynde [seed] inwith that place, by wey of
synne or by wikked temptacioun, the chirche is entredited
[interdicted] til it be reconsiled by the bysshop.   And the
preest sholde be enterdited that dide swich a vileynye [wicked

2713-14 Now that I have described to you, as best I can, the seven
deadly sins.
2729-31 Nobly born or in bondage, free or in servitude, healthy or
sick, wedded or single, belonging to a religious order or not, wise or
foolish, cleric or secular.
2731-2 Whether she is of thy kindred, bodily or spiritually, or not.
2735-6 With a virgin, or not.
2740-1 In church or churchyard; in a dedicated church or not.

thing]; to terme of al his lif he sholde namoore synge masse, and if he dide, he sholde doon deedly synne at every time that he so songe [*sang*] masse. The fourthe circumstaunce is by whiche mediatours, or by whiche messagers, as for entice-
2750 ment, or for consentement to bere compaignye with felawe-shipe; for many a wrecche, for to bere compaignye, wol go to the devel of helle. Wherfore they that eggen [*incite*] or con-senten to the synne been parteners of the synne, and of the dampnacioun of the synnere.

The fifthe circumstaunce is how manye tymes that he hath synned, if it be in his mynde, and how ofte that he hath falle. For he that ofte falleth in synne, he despiseth the mercy of God, and encreesseth hys synne, and is unkynde [*ungrateful*] to Crist; and he wexeth the moore fieble to withstonde synne,
2760 and synneth the moore lightly [*easily*], and the latter ariseth, and is the moore eschew for to shryven hym, and namely [*especially*], to hym that is his confessour. For which that folk, whan they falle agayn in hir olde folies, outher they forleten [*abandon*] hir olde confessours al outrely [*completely*], or elles they departen [*divide*] hir shrift [*confession*] in diverse places; but soothly, swich departed shrift deserveth no mercy of God of his synnes. The sixte circumstaunce is why that a man synneth, as by which temptacioun; and if hymself procure thilke temptacioun, or by the excitynge of oother folk;
2770 or if he synne with a womman by force, or by hire owene assent; or if the womman, maugree hir hed, hath been afforced, or noon. This shal she telle: for coveitise, or for poverte, and if it was hire procurynge, or noon; and swich manere harneys. The seventhe circumstaunce is in what manere he hath doon his synne, or how that she hath suffred that folk han doon to hire. And the same shal the man telle pleynly with alle circumstaunces; and wheither he hath synned with comune bordel [*brothel*] wommen, or noon; or doon his synne in hooly tymes, or noon; in fastyng tymes, or noon; or biforn his
2780 shrifte, or after his latter shrifte; and hath peraventure [*per-haps*] broken therfore his penance enjoyned; by whos help and whos conseil; by sorcerie or craft [*cunning*]; al moste be toold.

2748-51 The fourth circumstance to be considered is by what go-betweens or messengers the enticing and consenting to fleshly fellow-ship were contrived.
2760-1 And is the slower to rise (from sin), and the more unwilling to go to confession.
2762-3 For which reason, when people fall again.
2767-9 Why a man sins, and by what temptation; and whether that temptation is of his own seeking, or the result of incitement by others.
2771-3 Or whether the woman has been forced against her will, or not. And this is what *she* must tell: whether it was done out of greed . . . and all such things of this kind.
2775-6 Or how she has come to allow what men have done to her.
2780 Or later, after confession.

Alle thise thynges, after that they been grete or smale, engreg-
gen the conscience of man. And eek the preest, that is thy
juge, may the bettre been avysed of his juggement in yevynge
of thy penaunce, and that is after thy contricioun. For understond wel that after tyme that a man hath defouled his
baptesme by synne, if he wole come to salvacioun, ther is noon
other wey but by penitence and shrifte and satisfaccioun; and
2790 namely by the two, if ther be a confessour to which he may
shriven hym, and the thridde, if he have lyf to parfournen it.

Thanne shal man looke and considere that if he wole maken
a trewe and a profitable confessioun, ther moste be foure
condiciouns. First, it moot been in sorweful bitternesse of
herte, as seyde the kyng Ezechias to God: 'I wol remembre me
[recollect] alle the yeres of my lif in bitternesse of myn herte.'
This condicioun of bitternesse hath fyve signes. The firste is
that confessioun moste be shamefast, nat for to covere ne
hyden his synne, for he hath agilt [offended] his God and
2800 defouled his soule. And herof seith Seint Augustyn: 'The
herte travailleth [suffers] for shame of his synne'; and for
he hath greet shamefastnesse [sense of shame], he is digne
[worthy] to have greet mercy of God. Swich was the confessioun of the publican that wolde nat heven [lift] up his
eyen to hevene, for he hadde offended God of hevene; for
which shamefastnesse he hadde anon [at once] the mercy of
God. And therof seith Seint Augustyn that swich shamefast
folk been next [nearest to] foryevenesse and remissioun.
Another signe is humylitee in confessioun; of which seith
2810 Seint Peter, 'Humbleth yow under the myght of God.' The
hond of God is myghty in confessioun, for therby God
foryeveth thee thy synnes, for he allone hath the power. And
this humylitee shal been in herte, and in signe outward; for
right as he hath humylitee to God in his herte, right so sholde
he humble his body outward [outwardly] to the preest, that
sit [sits] in Goddes place. For which in no manere, sith that
Crist is sovereyn, and the preest meene [intermediary] and
mediatour bitwixe Crist and the synnere, and the synnere is
the laste by wey of resoun, thanne sholde nat the synnere sitte
2820 as heighe as his confessour, but knele biforn hym or at his
feet, but if [unless] maladie destourbe [prevent] it. For he shal

2783-6 All these things, according as to whether they are great or small,
burden the conscience of a man. And also the priest, who is your
judge, may be the better advised in judging what penance to impose
on you, after you have shown contrition.
2787-8 After a man has defiled his baptism by sin.
2789-91 And especially by the (former) two . . . and by the third, if he
should live long enough to make it.
2798-9 Confession must be made in shame, and not to cover or hide
a man's sin.
2816-20 Wherefore, on no account, since Christ is sovereign . . . should
the sinner sit as high as his confessor.

nat taken kep [*heed*] who sit there, but in whos place that he
sitteth.   A man that hath trespased to a lord, and comth for
to axe [*ask*] mercy and maken his accord [*peace*], and set him
[*sits himself*] doun anon by the lord, men wolde holden hym
outrageous [*presumptuous*], and nat worthy so soone for to
have remissioun ne mercy.   The thridde signe is how that thy
shrift sholde be ful of teeris, if man may, and if man may nat
wepe with his bodily eyen, lat hym wepe in herte.   Swich was
2830 the confession of Seint Peter, for after that he hadde forsake
Jhesu Crist, he wente out and weep [*wept*] ful bitterly.   The
fourthe signe is that he ne lette nat for shame to shewen his
confessioun.   Swich was the confessioun of the Magdalene,
that ne spared, for no shame of hem that weren atte feeste,
for to go to oure Lord Jhesu Crist and biknowe to hym hire
synne.   The fifthe signe is that a man or a womman be
obeisant [*obedient*] to receyven the penaunce that hym is
enjoyned for his synnes, for certes, Jhesu Crist, for the giltes
[*sins*] of o man, was obedient to the deeth.
2840   The seconde condicion of verray [*true*] confession is that it
be hastily [*quickly*] doon.   For certes, if a man hadde a
deedly wounde, evere the lenger that he taried to warisshe
[*cure*] hymself, the moore wolde it corrupte and haste [*hasten*]
hym to his deeth; and eek the wounde wolde be the wors for
to heele [*heal*].   And right so fareth synne that longe tyme is
in a man unshewed [*unconfessed*].   Certes, a man oghte
hastily shewen his synnes for manye causes; as for drede of
deeth, that cometh ofte sodeynly, and no certeyn what tyme
it shal be, ne in what place; and eek the drecchynge [*prolonging*]
2850 of o [*one*] synne draweth in another; and eek the lenger that he
tarieth, the ferther he is fro Crist.   And if he abide to his laste
day, scarsly may he shryven hym or remembre hym of his
synnes or repenten hym, for [*because of*] the grevous maladie
of his deeth.   And for as muche as he ne hath nat in his lyf
herkned [*listened to*] Jhesu Crist whanne he hath spoken, he
shal crie to Jhesu Crist at his laste day, and scarsly wol he
[*He*] herkne hym.   And understond that this condicioun
moste han foure thynges.   Thi shrift moste be purveyed
bifore and avysed; for wikked haste dooth no profit; and that
2860 a man konne shryve hym of his synnes, be it of pride, or of
envye, and so forth with the speces [*kinds*] and circumstances;
and that he have comprehended in hys mynde the nombre and

2832-3 That he should not be prevented by shame from making his
   confession.
2834-6 Who did not refrain, for any shame she felt in the presence of
   those who were at the feast, from going to our Lord and confessing
   her sin to Him.
2839 *o man*, one man, i.e. Adam.
2858-60 Your confession must be thought over beforehand and carefully considered . . . and (such consideration is necessary) so that a
   man may be able to confess his sins.

the greetnesse of his synnes, and how longe that he hath leyn
[*lain*] in synne; and eek that he be contrit of [*for*] his synnes,
and in stidefast purpos, by the grace of God, nevere eft [*again*]
to falle in synne; and eek that he drede and countrewaite
hymself, that he fle the occasiouns of synne to whiche he is
enclyned. Also thou shalt shryve thee of alle thy synnes to o
man, and nat a parcel [*part*] to o man and a parcel to another;
2870 that is to understonde, in entente to departe [*divide*] thy
confessioun, as for shame or drede; for it nys but stranglynge
of thy soule. For certes Jhesu Crist is entierly al good; in
hym nys noon imperfeccioun; and therfore outher he for-
:yeveth al parfitly or elles never a deel. I seye nat that if thow be
assigned to the penitauncer for certein synne, that thow art
bounde to shewen hym al the remenaunt [*rest*] of thy synnes,
of whiche thow hast be shryven of thy curaat [*parish priest*],
but if it like to thee of thyn humylitee; this is no departynge
of shrift. Ne I seye nat, ther as I speke of divisioun of
2880 confessioun, that if thou have licence for to shryve thee to a
discreet and an honest preest, where thee liketh [*wherever you
please*], and by licence of thy curaat, that thow ne mayst wel
shryve thee to him of alle thy synnes. But lat no blotte be
bihynde; lat no synne been untoold, as fer as thow hast
remembraunce. And whan thou shalt be shryven to thy
curaat, telle hym eek alle the synnes that thow hast doon syn
[*since*] thou were last yshryven; this is no wikked entente
[*intention*] of divisioun of shrifte.
  Also the verray [*true*] shrifte axeth certeine condiciouns.
2890 First, that thow shryve thee by thy free wil, noght constreyned,
ne for shame of folk, ne for maladie, ne swiche thynges. For
it is resoun that he that trespaseth by his free wyl, that by
his free wyl he confesse his trespas; and that noon oother man
telle his synne but he hymself; ne he shal nat nayte ne denye
his synne, ne wratthe hym agayn the preest for his amonestynge
to lete synne. The seconde condicioun is that thy shrift be
laweful, that is to seyn, that thow that shryvest thee, and eek
the preest that hereth thy confessioun, been verraily in the
feith of hooly chirche; and that a man ne be nat despeired
2900 [*in despair*] of the mercy of Jhesu Crist, as Caym [*Cain*] or
Judas. And eek a man moot [*must*] accusen hymself of his
owene trespas, and nat another; but he shal blame and wyten

2866–7 And also so that he may fear and keep watch over himself.
2871–2 For this is nothing less than strangling your soul.
2873–4 And therefore He forgives everything either fully or not at all.
2875 *penitauncer*, confessor who imposes penance.
2878 Unless in your humility it pleases you to do so.
2879–83 Nor do I say, in so far as I am speaking of the division of con-
    fession . . . that you would not do well to confess all your sins to him.
2883–4 But let no blot remain.
2894–6 Nor shall he withhold or deny his sin, nor get angry with the
    priest for his admonition to give up sinning.

[*reproach*] hymself and his owene malice of [*for*] his synne, and noon oother.   But nathelees, if that another man be occasioun or enticere [*instigator*] of his synne, or the estaat of a persone be swich thurgh which his synne is agregged [*aggravated*], or elles that he may nat pleynly shryven hym but [*unless*] he telle the persone with which [*whom*] he hath synned, thanne may he telle it, so that his entente ne be nat to bakbite [*back-*
2910 *bite*] the persone, but oonly to declaren his confessioun.

Thou ne shalt nat eek make no lesynges [*lies*] in thy confessioun, for humylitee, peraventure, to seyn that thou hast doon synnes of whiche thow were nevere gilty.   For Seint Augustyn seith, 'If thou, by cause of thyn humylitee, makest lesynges on thyself, though thow ne were nat in synne biforn, yet artow thanne in synne thurgh thy lesynges.'   Thou most eek shewe thy synne by thyn owene propre mouth, but thow be woxe dowmb, and nat by no lettre; for thow that hast doon the synne, thou shalt have the shame therfore [*of it*].   Thow
2920 shalt nat eek peynte [*colour*] thy confessioun by faire subtile wordes, to covere the moore thy synne; for thanne bigilestow [*you deceive*] thyself, and nat the preest.   Thow most tellen it platly [*plainly*], be it nevere so foul ne so horrible.   Thow shalt eek shryve thee to a preest that is discreet to conseille thee; and eek thou shalt nat shryve thee for veyne glorie, ne for ypocrisye, ne for no cause but oonly for the doute [*fear*] of Jhesu Crist and the heele [*health*] of thy soule.   Thow shalt nat eek renne [*run*] to the preest sodeynly to tellen hym lightly thy synne, as whoso telleth a jape or a tale, but
2930 avysely [*advisedly*] and with greet devocioun.   And generally, shryve thee ofte.   If thou ofte falle, ofte thou arise [*may arise*] by confessioun.   And though thou shryve thee ofter [*more often*] than ones of synne of which thou hast be shryven, it is the moore [*greater*] merite.   And, as seith Seint Augustyn, thow shalt have the moore lightly relessyng [*forgiveness*] and grace of God, bothe of synne and of peyne.   And certes, oones a yeere atte leeste wey it is laweful for to been housled; for certes, oones a yeere alle thynges renovellen [*are renewed*].

Now have I toold yow of verray Confessioun, that is the
2940 seconde partie of Penitence.

EXPLICIT SECUNDA PARS PENITENCIE

ET SEQUITUR TERCIA PARS EIUSDEM

The thridde partie of Penitence is Satisfaccioun, and that stant [*consists*] moost generally in almesse [*alms*] and in bodily peyne.   Now been ther thre manere of almesse: contricion

2912–13 Saying, perhaps from humility, that you have committed sins.
2917–18 Unless you have become dumb.
2929 Like someone telling a jest or story.
2937 Once a year at least (i.e. at Easter) it is lawful to receive communion.

of herte, where a man offreth hymself to God; another is to
han pitee of defaute [*on the faults*] of his neighebores; and the
thridde is in yevynge of good conseil and comfort, goostly
[*spiritual*] and bodily, where men han nede, and namely [*especially*] in sustenaunce of mannes foode. And tak kep [*heed*]
that a man hath nede of thise thinges generally: he hath nede
2950 of foode, he hath nede of clothyng and herberwe [*shelter*], he
hath nede of charitable conseil and visitynge in prisone and in
maladie, and sepulture [*interment*] of his dede body. And if
thow mayst nat visite the nedeful with thy persone [*in person*],
visite hym by thy message and by thy yiftes. Thise been
general almesses or werkes of charitee of hem that han
temporeel richesses or discrecioun in conseilynge. Of thise
werkes shaltow heren [*hear*] at the day of doom.

    Thise almesses shaltow doon of [*give from*] thyne owene
propre thynges, and hastily [*promptly*] and prively [*secretly*],
2960 if thow mayst. But nathelees, if thow mayst nat doon it
prively, thow shalt nat forbere to doon almesse though men
seen it, so that it be nat doon for thank [*thanks*] of the world,
but oonly for thank of Jhesu Crist. For, as witnesseth Seint
Mathew, *capitulo quinto*, 'A citee may nat been hyd that is
set on a montayne, ne men lighte nat a lanterne and put it
under a busshel, but men sette it on a candle-stikke to yeve
light to the men in the hous. Right so shal youre light
lighten [*shine*] bifore men, that they may seen youre goode
werkes, and glorifie youre fader that is in hevene.'
2970   Now as to speken of bodily peyne, it stant in preyeres, in
wakynges [*vigils*] in fastynges, in vertuouse techynges of
orisouns. And ye shul understonde that orisouns or preyeres
is for to seyn a pitous wyl of herte, that redresseth it in God
and expresseth it by word outward, to remoeven harmes and
to han [*obtain*] thynges espiritueel and durable, and somtyme
temporele thynges; of whiche orisouns, certes, in the orison
of the *Pater noster* hath Jhesu Crist enclosed moost thynges.
Certes, it is privyleged of thre thynges in his dignytee, for
which it is moore digne than any oother preyere; for that
2980 Jhesu Crist hymself maked it; and it is short, for it sholde be
koud [*learnt*] the moore lightly, and for to withholden [*keep*]
it the moore esily in herte, and helpen hymself the ofter with
the orisoun; and for a man sholde be the lasse wery to seyen
[*of saying*] it, and for a man may nat excusen hym to lerne
[*from learning*] it, it is so short and so esy; and for it compre-
hendeth in it self alle goode preyeres. The exposicioun of

2965 Neither do men light a lantern. (Matt. v. 15.)
2971–2 In the virtuous teaching of prayers.
2972–3 You shall understand that by orisons or prayers is meant a
    piteous desire of the heart, that addresses itself to God.
2978–80 Certainly, it is privileged in three things: in its excellence, which
    is outstanding because Jesu Christ himself made it.

this hooly preyere, that is so excellent and digne, I bitake [entrust] to thise maistres of theologie, save [except that] thus muchel wol I seyn; that whan thow prayest that God sholde
2990 foryeve thee thy giltes [sins] as thou foryevest hem that agilten to [sin against] thee, be ful wel war that thow ne be nat out of charitee. This hooly orison amenuseth [lessens] eek venyal synne, and therfore it aperteneth [pertains] specially to penitence.

This preyere moste be trewely seyd, and in verray feith, and that men preye to God ordinatly [methodically] and discreetly and devoutly; and alwey a man shal putten his wyl to be subget to the wille of God. This orisoun moste eek been seyd with greet humblesse [humility] and ful pure; honestly [decently],
3000 and nat to the anoyaunce of any man or womman. It moste eek been continued [supplemented] with the werkes of charitee. It avayleth eek agayn the vices of the soule; for, as seith Seint Jerome, 'By fastynge been saved the vices of the flessh, and by preyere the vices of the soule.'

After this, thou shalt understonde that bodily peyne stant in wakynge [watching]; for Jhesu Crist seith, 'Waketh and preyeth, that ye ne entre in wikked temptacioun.' Ye shul understanden also that fastynge stant in thre thynges: in forberynge of [abstinence from] bodily mete and drynke, and
3010 in forberynge of worldly jolitee [amusement], and in forberynge of deedly synne; this is to seyn, that a man shal kepen hym fro deedly synne with al his myght.

And thou shalt understanden eek that God ordeyned fastynge, and to fastynge appertenen foure thinges: largenesse [generosity] to povre folk; gladnesse of herte espiritueel, nat to been angry ne anoyed, ne grucche [grumble] for he fasteth; and also resonable houre for to ete [eating]; ete by mesure [in moderation]; that is for to seyn, a man shal nat ete in untyme [out of season], ne sitte the lenger at his table to ete for
3020 he fasteth.

Thanne shaltow understonde that bodily peyne stant in disciplyne or techynge, by word, or by writynge, or in ensample; also in werynge of heyres, or of stamyn, or of haubergeons on hire naked flessh, for Cristes sake, and swiche manere penances. But war thee wel [take good care] that swiche manere penaunces on thy flessh ne make nat thyn herte bitter or angry or anoyed of thyself; for bettre is to caste awey thyn heyre, than for to caste awey the swetenesse of Jhesu Crist. And therfore seith Seint Paul, 'Clothe yow, as

2991-2 Take good care that you are not out of love (with your fellow Christians).
3015-16 Spiritual gladness of heart . . . nor sit longer eating at his table because he is fasting.
3023-4 Also in the wearing of hair-shirts, or shirts of coarse cloth, or of coats of mail on their naked flesh.

3030 they that been chosen of God, in herte of misericorde [*compassion*], debonairetee [*gentleness*], suffraunce [*patience*], and swich manere of clothynge'; of [*with*] whiche Jhesu Crist is moore apayed [*pleased*] than of heyres, or haubergeouns, or hauberkes.

Thanne is discipline eek in knokkynge [*beating*] of thy brest, in scourgynge with yerdes [*rods*], in knelynges, in tribulacions, in suffrynge paciently wronges that been doon to thee, and eek in pacient suffraunce of maladies, or lesynge [*loss*] of worldly catel [*goods*], or of wyf, or of child, or othere
3040 freendes.

Thanne shaltow understonde whiche thynges destourben penaunce; and this is in foure maneres, that is, drede, shame, hope, and wanhope [*despair*], that is, desperacion. And for to speke first of drede; for which he weneth that he may suffre no penaunce; ther-agayns [*against it*] is remedie for to thynke that bodily penaunce is but short and litel at regard of [*by comparison with*] the peyne of helle, that is so crueel and so long that it lasteth withouten ende.

Now again the shame that a man hath to shryven hym, and
3050 namely thise ypocrites that wolden been holden [*held*] so parfite [*perfect*] that they han no nede to shryven hem; agayns that shame sholde a man thynke that, by wey of resoun, that he that hath nat been shamed to doon foule things, certes hym oghte [*he ought*] nat been ashamed to do faire thynges, and that is confessiouns. A man sholde eek thynke that God seeth and woot alle his thoghtes and alle his werkes; to hym may no thyng been hyd ne covered. Men sholden eek remembren hem of the shame that is to come at the day of doom to hem that been nat penitent and shryven in this present
3060 lyf. For alle the creatures in hevene, in erthe, and in helle shullen seen apertly [*openly*] al that they hyden in this world.

Now for to speken of the hope of hem that been necligent and slowe to shryven hem, that stant in [*consists of*] two maneres [*kinds*]. That oon is that he hopeth for to lyve longe and for to purchacen muche richesse for his delit, and thanne he wol shryven hym; and, as he seith, hym semeth thanne tymely [*early*] ynough to come to shrifte. Another is of surquidrie [*over-confidence*] that he hath in Cristes mercy. Agayns the firste vice, he shal thynke that oure lif is in no
3070 sikernesse, and eek that alle the richesses in this world ben in aventure [*jeopardy*], and passen as a shadwe on the wal; and, as seith seint Gregorie, that it aperteneth to the grete rightwisnesse of God that nevere shal the peyne stynte [*cease*]

3044-5 Because of which a man believes he cannot endure penance.
3051-3 In opposition to that shame a man should think that, in all reason, a person who has not been ashamed.
3064-5 To live long and acquire great wealth for his delight.

of hem that nevere wolde withdrawen hem fro synne, hir thankes [of their own will], but ay continue in synne; for thilke perpetueel wil to do synne shul they han perpetueel peyne.

Wanhope is in two maneres: the firste wanhope is in the mercy of Crist; that oother is that they thynken that they ne 3080 myghte nat longe persevere in goodnesse.   The firste wanhope comth of that he demeth that he hath synned so greetly and so ofte, and so longe leyn [lain] in synne, that he shal nat be saved.   Certes, agayns that cursed wanhope sholde he thynke that the passion of Jhesu Crist is moore strong for to unbynde than synne is strong for to bynde.   Agayns the seconde wanhope he shal thynke that as ofte as he falleth he may arise agayn by penitence.   And though he never so longe have leyn in synne, the mercy of Crist is alwey redy to receiven hym to mercy.   Agayns the wanhope that he demeth that he 3090 sholde nat longe persevere in goodnesse, he shal thynke that the feblesse of the devel may nothyng doon, but if men wol suffren [allow] hym; and eek he shal han strengthe of the help of God, and of al hooly chirche, and of the proteccioun of aungels, if hym list [he wishes].

Thanne shal men understonde what is the fruyt of penaunce; and, after [according to] the word of Jhesu Crist, it is the endelees blisse of hevene, ther [where] joye hath no contrarioustee [opposition] of wo ne grevaunce; ther alle harmes been passed of this present lyf; ther as is the sikernesse fro the 3100 peyne of helle; ther as is the blisful compaignye that rejoysen hem everemo, everich of [each in] otheres joye; ther as the body of man, that whilom was foul and derk, is moore cleer [bright] than the sonne; ther as the body, that whilom was syk, freele [frail], and fieble, and mortal, is inmortal, and so strong and so hool [healthy] that ther may no thyng apeyren [impair] it; ther as ne is neither hunger, thurst, ne coold, but every soule replenyssed [replenished] with the sighte of the parfit knowynge of God.   This blisful regne [kingdom] may men purchace [gain] by poverte espiritueel, and the glorie by 3110 lowenesse [lowliness], the plentee of joye by hunger and thurst, and the reste by travaille, and the lyf by deeth and mortificacion of synne.

HEERE TAKETH THE MAKERE OF THIS BOOK HIS LEVE

Now preye I to hem alle that herkne [listen to] this litel tretys or rede, that if ther be any thyng in it that liketh [pleases] hem, that therof they thanken oure Lord Jhesu Crist, of whom procedeth al wit [wisdom] and al goodnesse.   And if ther be

3080-1 The first kind of despair comes from his supposing.
3098-9 Where all the evils of this present life are past.

any thyng that displese hem, I preye hem also that they arrette it to the defaute of myn unkonnynge, and nat to my wyl, that wolde ful fayn [*very gladly*] have seyd bettre if 3120 I hadde had konnynge. For oure book seith, 'Al that is writen is writen for oure doctrine [*instruction*],' and that is myn entente. Wherfore I biseke [*beseech*] yow mekely, for the mercy of God, that ye preye for me that Crist have mercy on me and foryeve me my giltes [*sins*]; and namely [*especially*] of my translacions and enditynges [*compositions*] of worldly vanitees, the whiche I revoke in my retracciouns: as is the book of Troilus; the book also of Fame; the book of the .xxv. Ladies; the book of the Duchesse; the book of Seint Valentynes day of the Parlement of Briddes [*Birds*]; the tales of 3130 Caunterbury, thilke that sownen into synne; the book of the Leoun; and many another book, if they were in my remembrance, and many a song and many a leccherous lay; that Crist for his grete mercy foryeve me the synne. But of the translacion of Boece de Consolacione, and othere bookes of legendes of seintes, and omelies, and moralitee, and devocioun, that thanke I oure Lord Jhesu Crist and his blisful Mooder, and alle the seintes of hevene, bisekynge hem that they from hennes forth unto my lyves ende sende me grace to biwayle my giltes, and to studie to [*for*] the salvacioun of my soule, and 3140 graunte me grace of verray [*true*] penitence, confessioun and satisfaccioun to doon in this present lyf, thurgh the benigne grace of hym that is kyng of kynges and preest over alle preestes, that boghte [*redeemed*] us with the precious blood of his herte; so that I may been oon of hem at the day of doom that shulle be saved. *Qui cum patre et Spiritu Sancto vivit et regnat Deus per omnia secula. Amen.*

HEERE IS ENDED THE BOOK OF THE TALES OF CAUNTERBURY, COMPILED BY GEFFREY CHAUCER, OF WHOS SOULE JHESU CRIST HAVE MERCY. AMEN

3117–18 I also pray them to put it down to my lack of skill.
3120–1 Cf. Rom. xv. 4 and II Tim. iii. 16.
3126 Which I repudiate in this retraction of mine.
3127–30 *the book of the .xxv. Ladies*, i.e. the *Legend of Good Women*; *the tales of Caunterbury ... synne*, those of the *Canterbury Tales* which show a sinful tendency.
3130–1 The *book of the Leoun* is now lost.
3134–5 *Boece de Consolacione*, i.e. Chaucer's translation of *De Consolatione Philosophiae* by Boethius; *omelies ... devocioun*, homilies, and moral and devotional works.
3140–1 To make confession and satisfaction in this present life.

APPENDICES

I. NOTE ON PRONUNCIATION

(Line references are to the *General Prologue*)

SHORT VOWELS

a   as in German *Mann*, French *patte*:   Wh*a*n th*a*t 1, M*a*rch 2.

e (stressed)   as in *men*:   *e*very 3, v*e*rtu 4, t*e*ndre 7.

e (unstressed)   as in *about*:   shour*e*s 1, soot*e* 1, perc*e*d 2.

i, y   as in *bit*:   w*i*th 1, *i*nspired 6, kn*y*ght 42.

o   as in *bog*:   cr*o*ppes 7, h*o*lpen 18, *o*n 19.

u (sometimes written *o*)   as in *full*:   y*o*nge s*o*nne 7, b*u*t 35.

LONG VOWELS

a, aa   as in *father*:   sm*a*le 9, m*a*ken 9, c*aa*s 323.

e, ee, ie (close)   as in German *lehnen*, French *été*:   sw*ee*te 5, sl*e*pen 10, coverch*ie*fs 453.

e, ee (open)   as in French *père*:   w*e*re 26, *e*sed 29, nathel*ee*s 35.

i, y   as in *see*:   insp*i*red 6, *y*e 10, sh*i*res 15.

o, oo (close)   as in German *Sohn*, French *beau*:   s*oo*te 1, r*oo*te 2, w*o*lden 27.

o, oo (open)   as in *saw*:   *o*pen 10, g*oo*n 12, sp*o*ken 31.

ou, ow, o(gh)   as in *moon*:   sh*ou*res 1, dr*o*ghte 2, f*ow*eles 9.

u   as in French *tu*:   vert*u* 4, nat*u*re 11, avent*u*re 25.

DIPHTHONGS

ai, ay, ei, ey   approximately a combination of *a* and *i*:   v*ey*ne 3, d*ay* 19, w*ey* 34.

au, aw   as in *house*:   str*au*nge 13, C*au*nterbury 16, fel*aw*eshipe 32.

eu, ew   as in *few*:   n*ew*e 176, kn*ew* 240, tr*ew*e 531.

oi, oy   as in *boy*:   c*oy* 119, L*oy* 120.

CONSONANTS

Unfamiliar sounds and spellings include:

ch, cch   as in *church*:   *ch*ivalrie 45, re*cch*elees 179.

g, gg   as in *bridge*:   cora*g*es 11, ju*gg*ement 818.

gh (after a front vowel)   as in German *ich*:   ny*gh*t 10, kny*gh*t 42.

gh (after a back vowel)   as in Scots *loch*:   dro*gh*te 2.

h   is silent in French loan-words like *honoured* 50, and weakly pronounced in native words like *he, his, her*(*e*), *hem*.

609

r as trilled *r* in Scots: Apr*i*ll 1, shou*r*es 1, d*r*oghte 2.

sh, ssh as in *shall*: pari*ssh*e 491.

wh as in Scots *white*: *wh*ich 4, *wh*an 30.

Note: Both consonants should be pronounced in words like *kn*ew 240, *wr*ite 96, ha*lv*e 8, yo*ng*e 7; double consonants should be distinguished from single consonants, e.g. *sonne* (pronounced *sun-ne*) 7 and *sone* (pronounced *su-ne*) 336.

II. NOTE ON GRAMMAR

The following brief note includes some of Chaucer's grammatical forms which may cause difficulty to a modern reader.

1. *Nouns.*

(i) Some nouns have no ending in the genitive singular: *his lady grace*, 'his lady's grace'; *hir doghter name*, 'her daughter's name'; *by my fader kyn*, 'by my father's kin.'

(ii) A few nouns have no ending in the plural: *hors*, 'horses'; *yeer* (beside *yeres*), 'years.'

(iii) A few nouns form their plural in –(e)n: *eyen*, 'eyes'; *sustren*, 'sisters'; *toon*, 'toes.'

2. *Adjectives.*

(i) The plural ends in –e: *olde bokes*, 'old books'; *swiche men*, 'such men.'

(ii) The singular of the weak form of adjectives (used after demonstratives and in the vocative) also ends in –e: *the yonge sonne*, 'the young sun'; *O goode God.*

3. *Pronouns.*

(i) *Second Person.* The singular pronouns *thou, thee* are used in familiar talk, in addressing an inferior, or in a prayer to God; the plural pronouns *ye, you* are used in addressing a superior. *Ye* (nominative) is kept distinct from *you* (accusative and dative).

(ii) *Third Person.*
  (a) The possessive singular feminine is *hir(e), her(e)*, 'her.'
  (b) The possessive singular neuter is *his*, 'its' (nominative *it, hit*).
  (c) The plural forms are *they*; *hir(e), her(e)*, 'their'; *hem*, 'them.'

4. *Relative.*

(i) *That* is the commonest form, and is used for persons as well as things.

(ii) *Which(e)* is also used, frequently preceded by *the* or followed by *that*: *the Erl of Panyk, which that hadde tho Wedded his suster*, 'the Earl of Panyk, who had then married his sister.'

5. *Verbs.*

(i) The present indicative second and third person singular endings are –*(e)st*, –*(e)th*. Contracted forms ending in –*t* are sometimes found in the third person : *bit*, 'bids'; *rist*, 'rises'; *rit*, 'rides'; *sit*, 'sits.'

(ii) The present indicative plural ending is –*(e)n*: *they wende*, 'they go'; *Thanne longen folk*, 'then people long.'

(iii) The imperative plural ends in –*(e)th* or –*e*. A polite imperative is sometimes used, preceded by *as*: *as beth of bettre cheere*, 'please be more cheerful.'

(iv) The past participle often retains the old prefix *y*–: *ybore(n)*, 'born'; *ykept*, 'kept.'

(v) Reflexive and impersonal verbs are both commoner in Chaucer's English than in modern English: *noght avaunte thee*, 'don't boast'; *deliteth hym*, 'he delights'; *me were levere*, 'I would rather'; *hym oghte*, 'he ought.'

(vi) *gan* is often used with an infinitive to form the simple past tense: *oon of hem gan callen to his knave*, 'one of them called out to his servant.'

III. NOTE ON VERSIFICATION

During the past four hundred years there have been several shifts of opinion about the nature of Chaucer's versification. From the sixteenth to the eighteenth centuries his verse was generally considered to be rhythmical, but not metrically regular. There was some dissent, but most readers would have agreed with Dryden that Chaucer's verse had 'the rude Sweetness of a *Scotch* Tune . . . which is natural and pleasing, though not perfect' (Preface to *Fables Ancient and Modern*, 1700). After the publication in 1775 of Tyrwhitt's *Essay on the Language and Versification of Chaucer* (vol. iv of his edition of the *Canterbury Tales*), the opinion gained ground that Chaucer had made extensive metrical use of inflectional –*e*, and that if this is pronounced where it should be the apparent irregularities of his verse largely disappear. Opinion hardened into dogma during the second half of the nineteenth century with the appearance of F. J. Child's *Observations on the Language of Chaucer* (1861–3) and of a series of editions of the *Canterbury Tales* based on a normalized Ellesmere text (headed by Skeat's great Oxford Chaucer in 1894). But since then the publication of Manly and Rickert's text of the *Canterbury Tales* (1940) has encouraged the belief that the late nineteenth-century editors went too far in the direction of metrical regularity, basing their theories on 'an artificial text made regular by all the devices at the disposal of the scholar' (Manly and Rickert, ii. 40–1). J. G. Southworth, in his *Verses of Cadence* (1954), flatly denies that Chaucer pronounced final –*e* either within the verse or at the end of it, and maintains that he wrote in freely rhythmical verse rather than in iambic foot-units.

These two different ways of reading (and hearing) Chaucer's verse are perhaps not as completely irreconcilable as they seem to be at first glance. A great many of Chaucer's verses can be read quite naturally with an

iambic movement if final –e is normally pronounced within the line, but
elided before an initial vowel or a weak h, and slurred at the end of such
words as *youre, hire, whiche, were*:

> A Clérk ther wás of Óxenfórd alsó,
> That únto lógyk háddë lóng(e) ygó. . . .
> Sównyng(e) in móral vértu wás his spéche,
> And gládly wóld(e) he lérn(e) and gládly téche.

Further, it has to be remembered that Chaucer is always varying the
regular iambic-decasyllabic pattern, as the rhythms of natural speech
dictate. For example, at the beginning of the third verse above the
iambic is replaced by a trochaic movement. If we read Chaucer's verse
with natural stressing and with due regard for the elision or slurring of
final –e, we find that he gives us a strongly rhythmical movement of infinite
variety, but one which is disciplined by the basic pattern of iambic verse.

Note: Readers who are unfamiliar with the sound and movement of
Chaucer's verse will find it useful to study H. Kökeritz, *A Guide to
Chaucer's Pronunciation* (New York, 1962), and to listen to Nevill Coghill
and H. Kökeritz reading passages from the *Canterbury Tales* on gramo-
phone records (Columbia DX 1572 and Lexington 5505). Another
Chaucer record is that of Robert Ross reading the *Pardoner's Prologue*
and *Tale* and the *Nun's Priest's Tale* (Caedmon TC 1008).